P9-CEN-512

The Effectiveness
of a Prison and
Parole System

The Effectiveness of a Prison and Parole System

DANIEL GLASER

UNIVERSITY OF ILLINOIS

★ ★ ★

THE BOBBS-MERRILL COMPANY, INC.

A SUBSIDIARY OF HOWARD W. SAMS & CO., INC.

PUBLISHERS · INDIANAPOLIS · NEW YORK · KANSAS CITY

Foreword

Several times in the past few years, Prison Director James V. Bennett has brought to my attention the study of federal correctional practices financed by the Ford Foundation and conducted by Dr. Daniel Glaser of the University of Illinois. I have come to have a great deal of interest in this project. It represents a major step forward in American corrections—the application of the analytical techniques of social science to the study of one of the largest and most advanced correctional systems in the world.

We in the federal government already have benefited in many ways from the findings and recommendations emerging from the study. With the publication of Dr. Glaser's book other correctional systems as well as scholars in the developing science of criminology and corrections can share in this invaluable stockpile of data and philosophy.

ROBERT F. KENNEDY
*Attorney General
of the United States*

Based upon the University of Illinois–Ford Foundation
Research Program in the Federal Correction System

Director: Daniel Glaser

RESEARCH ASSISTANTS
(in order of length of service)

George A. Pownall

Roger J. Fisher

Charles W. Dean

Bruce K. Eckland

Ernest Works

David A. Ward

John R. Stratton

Richard John

Glenn Hutchinson

William Nardini

Martin L. Dosick

Marcia Armstrong

Joseph Godwin

Kent Rice

Dale F. Lytton

Roland B. Westerlund

RESEARCH ADVISORY BOARD

Dr. Francis B. Sayre, Chairman

Representing the U. S. Bureau of Prisons

James V. Bennett, Director

Frank Loveland, Assistant Director, Retired

H. G. Moeller, Assistant Director

John J. Galvin, Assistant Director

Dr. Benjamin Frank, Chief of Research, Retired

Representing the U. S. Board of Parole

Richard A. Chappell, Chairman

George J. Reed, Member, former Chairman

Representing U. S. Courts

Judge William J. Campbell

Louis J. Sharp, Chief of Probation Services,
Administrative Office of U. S. Courts

Ben S. Meeker, Chief U. S. Probation Officer,
Northern District of Illinois

Representing State Correctional Services

Richard A. McGee, Administrator
California Youth and Adult Correction Agency

Russell G. Oswald, Chairman, New York Board of Parole

Representing Academic Interests

Dr. Lloyd E. Ohlin, Sociology and Social Work, Columbia University

Dr. Phillip Monypenny, Political Science, University of Illinois

Dr. Charles H. Bowman, Law, University of Illinois

vii

Preface

Both academic and popular treatises on correctional practices tend to be long on theory and impressionistic conclusions and short on solid information. Corrections officials must share some of the blame for this because they have not always been eager to subject their programs to study by outsiders. Then, too, resources for research in our field have traditionally been limited.

Dr. Glaser's book is based on extensive observation, large numbers of interviews, and study of numerous case records. Five of his assistants spent a full year in each of five different institutions of the Federal Prison Service and a second year in several U. S. Probation and Parole offices. The interview schedules, questionnaires, and case reports utilized in his research extended to some thousands of Federal prisoners and ex-prisoners.

Dr. Glaser himself consulted personally and by correspondence at frequent intervals over a five-year period with personnel in our central office and institutions. His own personal experience in correctional work was helpful to him in planning his research and evaluating results.

It is a pleasure to see a book with such extensive factual grounding added to the literature of criminology and corrections. This is not to imply that we agree with or endorse every finding or recommendation in the book—nor that we took pleasure in those items relative to our shortcomings. Nevertheless we see this project as a successful testing out of the values of a lively partnership between the social scientist and the correctional practitioner.

Such reservations as we may have concerning Dr. Glaser's conclusions and recommendations represent no reflection on his scholarship. In the instances I have in mind, he is careful to indicate that his findings are tentative and his proposals experimental.

On the basis of my special concerns, we would like to have seen the book organized a bit differently in certain respects. The relationship of particular correctional programs and methods of recidivism would have been more persuasive had it been set forth concisely in one place. As it is, much of this material must be culled out of chapters covering different programs.

I was quite interested in the material in Part I on the subject of recidivism, including figures presented indicating a recidivism rate of only about one-third among releasees from Federal prisons. Dr. Glaser's review of recidivism studies and analysis of the issues involved represent major contributions to correctional science.

For many years we have emphasized the need to attract, retain, and provide extensive training for line personnel in our correctional institutions. Considering the amount of time officers in living quarters and on work details spend with prisoners, it seemed obvious to us that the ability and attitudes of these personnel were a major factor in determining the nature of the prison experience of most offenders. We are much encouraged to find in Dr. Glaser's report ample justification for our intuition in this area. Beyond this his findings point up rather clearly the qualities to be encouraged in officers not only through recruitment standards and training but through administrative policies which affect the specific approaches they make in day-to-day work with prisoners.

Another objective we have long stressed has been the individualized handling of institutional behavior incidents with provision of follow-up counseling to encourage improved adjustment. Although he was initially skeptical, Dr. Glaser's investigation appears to have convinced him of the value of this approach as contrasted with more hard and fast application of particular penalties for particular institutional offenses.

But my purpose here is not one of critical review but of introduction. In other times and places our dialogue with Dr. Glaser concerning policies and methods can continue. As the book reveals, such conversations have been frequent and useful over these past several years while the study was underway and the report being completed.

During this period numerous experimental projects have been undertaken, many of which were related to preliminary findings of this study. Our Service has significantly improved its prisoner statistics program, expanded its research potential, and otherwise profited from the observations of Dr. Glaser. As his data and findings are analyzed further advantage is to be taken of them.

We have looked forward eagerly to the publication of Dr. Glaser's book, though we also were reluctant to see this stimulating and instructive project come to a close. We expect to derive much value from the book as a training reference, as a suggestive guide in program development, as a major resource in planning on-going statistical and research activities.

I wish to use this opportunity to express my respect and gratitude to the people and organizations making this project possible. To list each would be impractical because literally hundreds of people made contributions along the way. But certainly much credit is due to Dr. Francis Sayre, the prime initiator of the study, to the Ford Foundation for its generous grant, to the

University of Illinois, to members of the advisory committee for the project, and especially to Dr. Glaser, the scientist and artist without whom all of the supportive resources would have counted for nothing.

JAMES V. BENNETT, *Director*
Bureau of Prisons
U. S. Department of Justice
Washington, D. C.

ACKNOWLEDGMENTS

The history of this volume, reported in chapter 1, suggests the wide range of our indebtedness. Our undertaking began with proposals by Dr. Francis B. Sayre, former Assistant U. S. Secretary of State, and by officials of the U. S. Bureau of Prisons, under the leadership of Director James V. Bennett. Funds for this project were provided through the generosity of the Ford Foundation. Assistance in research operations was received from numerous employees of the federal prisons, from members and staff of the U. S. Board of Parole, from officers of the U. S. Probation Service, and from thousands of federal prisoners and parolees. An Advisory Board, representing federal and state correctional agencies and several academic disciplines, contributed useful counsel. To all of these, the author is most grateful.

Any listing of individual names for special expressions of appreciation could be interminable. Nevertheless, a few men contributed so extensively to whatever may be considered this project's achievements that failure to give them personal credit would be an injustice. Mr. Frank Loveland, the Bureau's Assistant Director for Classification and Treatment when the project began, directed federal prison planning and assistance for this research, and consulted regularly with us even after his retirement in 1961. These functions he shared from the outset with Mr. H. G. Moeller (his deputy at first, and then his successor), and with Dr. Benjamin Frank (the Bureau's Supervisor of Education when the project began, then its Chief of Research, and after his retirement in 1962, our neighbor as Professor at Southern Illinois University). Dr. Frank was succeeded at the Bureau by Mr. John Galvin, its first Assistant Director for Research and Development, who earlier had been a major stimulus to us as warden of federal prisons at Ashland, Kentucky, and El Reno, Oklahoma. Innumerable other federal prison personnel also aided the research operations and sharpened the focus of our observation and analysis. Especially significant in the latter function was Warden T. Wade Markley of the U. S. Penitentiary at Terre Haute, Indiana.

In the U. S. Probation Offices, where we based our studies of released federal prisoners, we also have many debts. The Chief of Probation in the Administrative Office of U. S. Courts, Mr. Louis Sharp, and the Chief U. S. Probation Officer in Chicago, Mr. Ben Meeker, were repeatedly helpful, from the beginning of the project to its end. Many others aided in specific research activities of briefer duration.

The research assistants on this project, from those employed part time and for only a few months, to the few employed full time for several years, contributed both to our research methods and to analysis of the results. Here we are especially indebted to George Pownall and Roger Fisher, not only because they were with the project more than twice as long as any of the others, but because of the large extent to which their suggestions guided us. Many students and student wives did clerical work for the project, at various times, usually performing above the minimum requirements of their jobs.

Professors Clarence Schrag of the University of Washington and Robert Mc-Ginnis of Cornell University provided helpful comments on parts of the final draft. Professors Lloyd Ohlin and Richard Cloward of the New York School of Social Work of Columbia University and Professor Richard McCleery of Antioch College gave valuable counsel in the initial planning of the project.

Last but not least, the author wishes to give credit to the contributions of his most effective literary critic, his wife, Pearl B. Glaser, and to thank her and his daughters for tolerating the extensive neglect and inconvenience which this project brought them. For the deficiencies of this report, the author alone assumes responsibility.

DANIEL GLASER
Urbana, Illinois
June 1964

Contents

Part I
THE KNOWLEDGE NEEDED FOR
A SCIENCE OF CORRECTION

★　★　★

CHAPTER 1

Introduction: A Problem and a Project

Over two million Americans become prisoners each year in jails, police stations, institutions for juvenile delinquents, and prisons. We know that 99 per cent are released, most of them within a year, but no one knows how many are confined again or how soon the average rearrest occurs. What is more important, no one has adequate evidence as to what can be done to reduce the probability that those released will commit crime again.

There are about a quarter of a million inmates in the prisons administered by state and federal governments in the United States. These prisoners generally were convicted of the most serious offenses. Nine-tenths also had a crime or juvenile delinquency record before the law-breaking which led to their current incarceration. Indeed, about half previously served at least one other term in such a prison. Around 115,000 are released from these institutions each year, but they are replaced by an even larger number of new prisoners.[1]

The adult male prisoners in these federal and state prisons will be the principal concern of this volume. They are men whose prior failures suggest poor prospects for the future. Yet, many are known to pursue legitimate and successful lives after prison. How can the frequency of such success be increased? This is the question we seek to answer.) Answer

The number of persons received by all agencies dealing with criminals is mounting. This growth is partly explained by the rise in our birth rate during the 1940's. The fecundity that has crowded American colleges in the 1960's also crowds American prisons with young adults. What is their future? The answer is especially ominous because greater use of probation

---

[1] Population, admission, and release figures for state and federally operated prisons are from U. S. Bureau of Prisons, "Prisoners in State and Federal Institutions 1961," *National Prisoner Statistics,* no. 30 (August 1962). Figures on the prior criminal records of prisoners are compiled by only a few prison systems, and each tabulates them somewhat differently, so that the figures are not comparable. The statement that nine out of ten have some prior crime or delinquency record and half have a prior prison record is based upon California Department of Corrections, *California Prisoners 1958 and 1959,* Table 20A, p. 47. It is probable that California's greater use of probation instead of prison for less advanced offenders gives its prison inmates a higher frequency of prior criminality than prisoners in most other states. However, other states are approaching California in the extent to which probation is used. For fuller discussion of these shortcomings in available statistics see James A. McCafferty, "Can We Find Standard Statistical Definition of Recidivism?" *Proceedings, American Correctional Association* (1958), pp. 190-206.

and other alternatives to imprisonment means that the average new prisoner now has a more extensive record of prior criminality than the average prisoner of former years.

There have been many responses to this problem. New prisons, costing ten to fifteen thousand dollars for each inmate, are regularly constructed. New psychological, psychiatric, and other treatment facilities are added to prison services, so that the annual cost of operating a prison system now reaches two thousand dollars per inmate—more than twice this amount at some specialized institutions. Unfortunately, there is no convincing evidence that this investment reduces what criminologists call "recidivism," the offender's return to crime. However, since there is little knowledge on overall rates of return to crime, how can we know at all precisely the effects on recidivism of specific prison and parole practices?

PATHS TO MORE ADEQUATE KNOWLEDGE

The most readily visible alumni of a prison are the men who are returned because they commit new crimes. Since released offenders who reform generally strive to hide their criminal past, their reformation usually is unknown to correctional officials. The consequent confrontation primarily with failures, and ignorance of the outcome of effort to change criminals, may partially explain the widespread dissatisfaction with correctional efforts.

Criticisms of prisons and parole, as well as recommendations for change, have come from correctional officials, ex-prisoners, journalists, and others, including professors in various fields. The American Correctional Association (formerly American Prison Association) has held an annual Congress of Correction for more than ninety years. Local and regional organizations also have frequent meetings; one of these, the Pennsylvania Prison Society, has been active since 1787. Indeed, there has been such a plethora of cerebration on corrections, both in the United States and abroad, that it is unlikely that any new writing today will result in recommendations not conceived by someone previously. Instead, the major path to new knowledge is through research, which may marshal more adequate evidence than has been previously available for assessing the validity of recommendations.

Two types of scientific effort are essential in research on criminal correction. One type can be called *correlational* and the other *experimental*. Both are necessary, and each one can help the other.[2]

Correlational research collects and organizes information on current or past features of the world around us without altering that which is studied. This is illustrated in correctional study by surveys of staff opinions, by

[2] These two types of research and their interrelation are similar in medicine, education, psychology, and many other fields of knowledge. See Lee J. Cronbach, "The Two Disciplines of Scientific Psychology," *Am. Psychologist, 12,* no. 11 (Nov. 1957), 671-84.

tabulations of inmate characteristics, or by systematic observations of parolee performance. The purpose of correlational research is the determination of existing relationships. The research reported here is primarily correlational, focused on relationships between correctional policies and subsequent criminality.

Although correlational research may indicate that recidivism is lower with one correctional practice than with another, there are several reasons why such findings can only provide a beginning for scientific direction of correctional policy. In the first place, it is often difficult to determine whether the apparent success or failure of a correctional program results from the program itself, or from the selection of offenders to which it is administered (and the consequent uncontrolled influence of related variables). Obviously one would expect better postrelease behavior from first offenders than from hardened criminals. Secondly, correctional situations which seem to differ only in the presence or absence of a particular practice may actually differ in other overlooked respects which may account for their varied effectiveness. Thirdly, one may infer from research on existing practices that some new policy would be effective, but such an inference cannot be verified unless the new policy is tried and the results carefully measured.

In corrections, as in medicine, all the foregoing problems in developing more effective practice are most adequately solved by controlled experiments. Experimental research is concerned with creating *new* conditions designed so that only what one is studying can account for the results. In corrections this can sometimes be achieved by randomly dividing a group of offenders into a treatment and a control group. If a particular correctional service is provided only for the treatment group, comparison of recidivism rates for the two groups may indicate the impact of this service.

For a variety of administrative reasons, scientifically adequate experimental research has been infrequent in corrections. Better evaluation and analysis of existing practices often is desired by policy makers to justify the costs and risks of experimentation. Some types of experiments, however, involve no risk, are not costly, and would more conclusively evaluate current or proposed practices than is possible with correlational research. Nevertheless, in any rocket of correctional progress, the controlled experiment is likely to be a second stage which can be fired only by a first stage of powerful correlational research. Most effort thus far has been devoted to getting the first stage "off the ground," but signs of the second stage already are visible. The progress of both will be described here.

THE CORRECTIONAL RESEARCH MOVEMENT

A classical sociological observation, especially identified with the late Professor W. F. Ogburn, is that most major inventions are made almost simultaneously and independently by several separate investigators. Thus the automobile, the airplane, the radio, and other devices were developed in the same period in the United States, Germany, France, England, and elsewhere. Ogburn contended that each idea appears only when there exists an appropriate "cultural base" of necessary prior knowledge or point of view, and the same or similar ideas will develop independently wherever this cultural base is shared.[3]

A new cultural base apparently was reached by the midpoint of the twentieth century, for a new form of correctional research developed independently in several parts of the world. This cultural base emerged as the culmination of a series of slow changes readily traced back for two centuries and conveniently summarized as a sequence of three "R's" in the handling of criminals: Revenge, Restraint, and Reformation. In this sequence, however, the new mingles with the old, instead of completely replacing earlier patterns.

Primary interest in revenge against criminals, by capital punishment for felonies and by corporal punishment for misdemeanors, was reduced markedly during the late eighteenth and early nineteenth centuries, although interest in revenge has never completely disappeared. With the rise of democratic governments and a new accent on liberty, imprisonment gradually became the dominant penalty for crime. Prisons promised protection to society by incapacitating criminals, satisfied those who thirsted for revenge by denying the blessings of liberty to offenders, and satisfied nineteenth-century religious interest in reforming criminals by including programs presumed to serve this purpose. The latter object is implied in the derivation of the word "penitentiary" from "penitence."

In the twentieth century it became increasingly apparent that prisons met public demands efficiently only in restraining criminals: few prisoners escape, and almost all of these are recaptured quickly. Although restraint incapacitates criminals, the restraint is temporary, since the average prison commitment is for less than two years. More use of probation instead of prison, and more willingness to parole early, reflect progressive reduction of interest in revenge and increased concern with the noncriminal potential in offenders. This concern with changing offenders was the main component for the cultural base which had to exist before there could be widespread research on the effectiveness of correctional programs.

The second component in this new cultural base was an increased recognition, in legislative circles and in the general public, that there is no con-

---

[3] W. F. Ogburn, *Social Change* (New York, Viking, 1922). That this discovery of independent multiple development in all types of invention and discovery is itself a multiple discovery has been pointed out by a leading American sociologist, Robert K. Merton. In a lecture at the University of Illinois in February 1962, Merton cited well over a dozen predecessors of Ogburn in this field, including Macauley, Comte, and Marx.

clusive evidence that modern ways of handling criminals reduce return to crime any more than older ways. This realization, together with an increase in crime and in the cost of recommended treatment of criminals after World War II, completed the prerequisite for a striking mid-century event: the nearly simultaneous emergence of a new pattern in correctional research, independently, at scattered points throughout the world.

Three attributes sharply differentiate this new correctional research from most prior criminological study. The first is that the research programs were requested by government officials, rather than by the university men who conduct the research. The second is that this research has not been designed primarily to test theories of crime causation and contribute to the academic debates on that topic, but to evaluate correctional practices (although this may also contribute to the testing of causation theories). A consequence of these two features is a third attribute, that of a much greater and more interested audience of correctional administrators than criminological research generally attracted heretofore.

One illustration of this independently developing new pattern was the British Parliament's provision for government-sponsored research to evaluate correctional programs, which was included in the Criminal Justice Act of 1948. After some delay its first project produced in 1956 an influential work, *Prediction Methods in Relation to Borstal Training,* by Hermann Mannheim and Leslie T. Wilkins. This resulted in establishment of the Home Office Research Unit under Wilkins and in a flurry of research, such as the seventy-nine projects within Britain listed in the parliamentary "White Paper" of 1959 entitled *Penal Practice in a Changing Society.*

In 1957 the Budget Committee of the California legislature was also taking initiative in establishing correctional research. Faced with demands for more and more millions of dollars to provide treatment staff and facilities for the criminals in California's burgeoning population, this Committee insisted that some of the correctional appropriation be spent to determine if the "treatment" was "curing" its patients. Research divisions, staffed with Ph.D.'s in psychology and sociology, were established in both the Department of Corrections and the Youth Authority. For some years the number of personnel and the annual expenditure for correctional evaluation research in California, by both foundation-financed projects and state-financed enterprises, probably totaled more than all that of the rest of the country combined. Today, however, the research movement is manifest in many locations.

BIRTH OF A PROJECT

Simultaneously with the beginnings of the California and British programs, the enterprise reported in this book was conceived in the United States Bureau of Prisons. Its initiation can be credited to Dr. Francis B. Sayre, retired U. S. Assistant Secretary of State and leading architect of

Philippine independence. Before entering two decades of prominent diplomatic service, Dr. Sayre was a professor of law at Harvard and a temporary Commissioner of Corrections in Massachusetts. During the mid-1950's he explored with Director James V. Bennett and Assistant Director Frank Loveland, of the U. S. Bureau of Prisons, the possibility of procuring foundation support for research and demonstration on measures to reduce the extent to which released prisoners return to crime.

In 1958, after a decision that the research be conducted by a university or other agency not engaged in correctional administration, this project began with a Ford Foundation grant to the University of Illinois for a study, to be directed by the author, on "measures to increase the effectiveness of the federal correctional system." Funds for the project totaling $264,500 were supplied by the Foundation and were expended over a five-and-one-half-year period. Although the research was centered in federal correctional agencies, the project founders retained their original interest in all American correctional programs.

A distinctive feature of the research administration was the Advisory Board, representing federal and state correctional and judicial agencies and relevant academic fields, whose names are listed on the frontispiece. Dr. Sayre served as public representative on the Board, and was elected its chairman. We have worked in close communication with the British and California researchers, and with others as they have entered this field. This was consistent with the conception of our project as a temporary primer, to promote evaluation research as a routine function of correctional agencies everywhere.

The initiators of this project intensely desired that their enterprise have practical consequences. They expressed the hope that the outcome of this project would not be "just a book." That is why the project's activities and this book, as well as prior project publications (listed in Appendix F), do not deal merely with project research. They have all involved endeavors to promote continuous correctional research by government agencies, including the experimental application of new correctional measures suggested by prior research. A gratifying aspect of the present writing is that it can also report on many beginnings in such government action. This project has tried to be both a part and a propellant of the research movement in corrections.

SPECIFIC OBJECTIVES AND OPERATIONS

The original prospectus for this project described "the broad objectives of the proposed research program" as:

1. to determine specifically the failure rates of different types of offenders released from prisons;

2. to determine the factors involved in their reversion or nonreversion to crime, with particular emphasis on their behavior and experience within the first years following release;

3. to determine, insofar as possible, what practicable measures and programs are best suited to reduce recidivism.

From pursuit of these objectives, nine separate research enterprises developed, described briefly as follows:

1. *Analysis of the Statistical Relationships Between Crime, Age, and Employment*

The project's first study may seem tangential to its other undertakings, but it was intended as a test of an assumption underlying much other inquiry. This assumption is simply that variations in economic opportunity have a major influence upon the rate at which adult males commit crime.

Although previous investigations had failed to indicate marked and consistent relationships between crime and unemployment, it was hypothesized in this study that such failure was a consequence of opposite types of relationship existing for persons in different age ranges. There was reason to suspect that crime by juveniles increases somewhat during periods of full employment for adults, because there is less supervision of children at those times (due to the larger proportion of mothers working outside the home, greater use of commercial recreation facilities, and other increases in the separation of parental and children's activities). On the other hand, there was reason to believe that juvenile crimes tend to decrease somewhat with unemployment, because unemployment fosters more cohesive relationships between parents and children. However, it was expected that crime by adults old enough to be economically independent of their parents would increase sharply with unemployment and decrease sharply with full employment. If these two opposite patterns exist, they might have been hidden in previous research which disregarded age of offenders and compared employment rates only to trends in total crimes reported to police; any decrease in offenses committed by adults would be offset in such total crime figures by an increase in crimes by juveniles, and vice versa. Despite deficiencies in available statistics, we found strong evidence for the hypothesized relationships.[4]

[4] Daniel Glaser and Kent Rice, "Crime, Age and Employment," *Am. Sociological Rev., 24,* no. 5 (Oct. 1959), 679-86; Edwin H. Sutherland and Donald R. Cressey, *Principles of Criminology,* 6th ed. (Philadelphia, Lippincott, 1960), pp. 192-93. The University of Chicago economist Belton M. Fleisher has reported to us in correspondence a reanalysis of some of the national data used in this study. Using complex mathematical procedures to make corrections for long-run trends in the variables studied, he confirms our primary finding of a positive relationship between crime and unemployment. He concludes that this relationship is marked only for property crimes, rather than for crimes against persons. He finds some positive relationship between property crimes and unemployment for all age groups which he considers.

2. *Statistical Analysis of Recidivism from Prison Records on Released Offenders*

This undertaking was expected to demonstrate efficient procedures with which correctional agencies might appraise their work by the recidivism rates of the prisoners they release. Such activity would be comparable to bookkeeping and quality control in industry. However, this operation required a degree of coordination among government agencies which is not quickly achieved. Chapter 2 describes some problems and some progress in routinization of this type of government accounting for correctional activity.

In the fall of 1958 the project assigned one full-time research employee for one year to each of five federal prisons. The institutions selected for study were the maximum-security penitentiary at Leavenworth, Kansas; the intermediate penitentiary at Terre Haute, Indiana; the correctional institution at Milan, Michigan; the reformatory at Chillicothe, Ohio; and the special youth institution at Ashland, Kentucky. These were chosen partly because of their proximity to the University of Illinois, and partly because each represented one of the major types of prison into which the more than thirty institutions of the federal system are classified.

In the autumn of 1959 the project's work in the prisons was terminated in order to place one researcher for a year in each of four U. S. Probation Offices, located in Cleveland, Chicago, Detroit, and St. Louis. These offices, which are attached to U. S. District Courts, supervise parolees and conditional releasees from federal prisons, in addition to their presentence and probation supervision work for the courts.

3. *Comparison of Returned Violators with "Successful" Releasees*

This required two almost independent studies. The violators were seen in the five prisons described above, from which they previously had been paroled and to which they had been returned for new offenses or serious parole rule violations. The procedures for interviewing such men had to be made final rather quickly when it was discovered that there might be difficulty in finding available, during the one year of operations in these prisons, the target of three hundred such cases. Only when our staff was in the probation offices could they interview nonviolators, for comparison with the returned violators. These "success" cases were primarily men under postrelease supervision for over a year (some for over five years), who had a record of at least one felony offense prior to that for which they were last imprisoned. Although this sample target was finally reduced to 250 cases, achieving it required that we interview every federal releasee with the specified "success" characteristics not only in the four federal judicial districts in which the project's full-time staff was based but, later, in eight adjacent federal judicial districts. Details of the sample and procedures in this study are set forth in Appendix D.

4. *Prison Panel Study*

This was the project's largest undertaking. About 1200 interviews were conducted to study the impact of imprisonment by comparing responses of inmates at different stages in their prison experience. Newly admitted inmates at each prison were interviewed during their first week of confinement; half of these were interviewed during their fourth month in prison; and all were again interviewed when they had been confined for about six months (except for the few no longer at these prisons then). Other inmates, mostly serving terms of two years or longer, were interviewed during the middle of their prison term. Finally, a large group of inmates was interviewed shortly before their release from prison. Details of the samples and procedures used in this study are presented in Appendix B.

5. *Postrelease Panel Study*

This consisted of interviews with all men released to four months or more of parole or conditional release supervision at the four probation offices where our staff was stationed. An effort was made to interview each releasee during his first week of freedom and once a month thereafter. As anticipated, such scheduling was not as easy in the postrelease situation as in prison, since the subjects could not as readily take time off from work and other obligations in the community in order to be interviewed. Nevertheless, almost two hundred cases received this unique type of study. Details on the sample and the procedure employed in this study are elaborated in Appendix C.

6. *National Survey of Financial Assistance to Released Prisoners*

Sponsorship and assistance were received from the John Howard Association in sending a questionnaire in 1960 to correctional officials throughout the United States, Britain, and Canada. Information was collected on the extent to which money can be earned during confinement by inmates at all state and federal prisons, on the compulsory savings requirements for these inmates, on gratuities of cash, clothing, and transportation issued to them at release, and on loans which are available to them from state agencies and from private philanthropic associations.[5]

[5] Daniel Glaser, "Research on Economic Assistance for Released Prisoners," *Proceedings, American Correctional Association* (1960), pp. 363-80; Daniel Glaser, Eugene S. Zemans, and Charles W. Dean, *Money Against Crime: A Survey of Economic Assistance to Released Prisoners* (Chicago, The John Howard Association, 1961).

7. *Prison Panel Supplemental Study*

This also employed a written questionnaire but was administered in 1961-62 to inmates at eight federal and six state prisons. Details of this enterprise are presented in Appendix E. Both this and the preceding study provided some perspectives on the extent to which our findings from the federal correctional system could be generalized to state systems.

8. *Time-Activity Study*

In the fall of 1961, a sample of thirty-one federal probation officers, representing urban, suburban, and rural areas from all regions of the United States, logged their daily activity for three weeks to provide the data for this research. This program was administered from the office of Mr. Albert Wahl, Chief Probation Officer for the U. S. District Court in San Francisco, and Chairman of the Committee on Professional Standards of the Federal Probation Officers Association. I drafted directions for the study, in consultation with officers of the Association and the Administrative Office of U. S. Courts. The data were tabulated by the Statistical Section of the Administrative Office, under the supervision of Mr. Ronald Beattie, and the tabulation sheets were then sent to me. Mr. Wahl and I then prepared a special report on this study for the U. S. Probation Service.[6] The study was an impressive example of cooperation by many independent agencies.

9. *Survey of Federal Parole Supervision*

In this study, developed by George A. Pownall of our staff, questionnaires were completed and returned by over 96 per cent of the 501 U. S. Probation Officers actively employed for four months or more as of June 1962. They indicated their principles and their practices in assisting parolees and in parole rule enforcement. They also reported on their training, experience, community ties, professional identification, interpretation of crime, and sense of autonomy in their work.

In addition to these nine major research operations, several lesser investigations were also conducted. For example, in the five prisons, we studied some aspects of the administration of correspondence courses to inmates, the prison disciplinary practices, and the systems for recording staff impressions of inmate work performance. Findings from all of these efforts will be reported and discussed wherever they are relevant to our systematic assessment of prisons and parole.

[6] Albert Wahl and Daniel Glaser, "A Pilot Time Study of the Federal Probation Officer's Job," *Federal Probation 27,* 3 (Sept. 1963), 20-25.

CHAPTER 2

How Many Prisoners Return?

THE LEGEND THAT TWO-THIRDS
RETURN TO PRISON

Diatribes against correctional practices frequently ascribe a specific high recidivism rate to American prisons. For example, one of our country's most distinguished journalists of crime, John Bartlow Martin, confidently asserts: ". . . it is true that between 60 per cent and 70 per cent of the men who leave prison come back for new crimes."[1] Martin's certainty probably is inspired by the fact that similar generalizations are uttered occasionally by police chiefs, judges, wardens, and professors of criminology. He could also hear the same conclusions from inmate "politicians" in prison office jobs, or from inmate contributors to prison publications, who assume the role of spokesman for the society of convicts in transmitting complaints to journalists, sociologists, and other outsiders. They eagerly grasp statistics which justify their complaints. For example, an inmate magazine article comments: "We must ask if our present penal systems have accomplished . . . [their] purpose. One would hardly think so when we consider that our rate of recidivism is approximately 65 per cent. . . ."[2]

Where does this figure come from? Released prisoners in the United States have not been regularly traced to determine the extent to which they return to prison. As we shall show, the findings of those studies which have attempted to follow releases do not justify this confidence in a two-thirds return figure.

It appears likely that this estimate of postrelease imprisonment stems from knowledge of the prior prison records of men in certain penitentiaries. This sort of reasoning is made explicit in the following publication by an ex-inmate:

In January of this year, in the prison where I served thirteen years of a life sentence, 20 per cent of the inmates had done a single previous jolt in that or another penitentiary, 16 per cent were three-time losers and 37 per cent had four or more prison commitments on their records. Only 27 per cent of the inmate body were first-timers, and of this group 6 per cent were twenty-one

[1] John Bartlow Martin, *Break Down the Walls* (New York, Ballantine Books, 1954), pp. 233-34.
[2] Ross Crider, "Progressive Amelioration of Punishment," U. S. Penitentiary, Leavenworth, Kansas, *The New Era, 15,* no. 2 (1961), 54.

years of age or under and therefore hadn't yet had a fair chance to demonstrate their capacity for long-haul jousting with the law.

If these figures are typical of prisons throughout the land—and all available evidence says that the national record is actually even worse—then it's apparent that we taxpayers are pitching a great deal of money down an extremely deep rathole. If more than two-thirds of the inmates discharged from the nation's penal institutions are destined to pick up the pistol, the jimmy or the forger's pen again, then it's quite clear that prisons are thundering failures at the business of protecting society by reforming the criminal.[3]

Such predictions of future failures from the frequency of past failures of men in prison are misleading. Their most blatant error is neglect of the fact that offenders with prior imprisonment generally get longer sentences, and are much less readily paroled, than first imprisonment cases. Therefore, these "two- and three-time losers" accumulate in prison, so that they become higher as a percentage of men *in* the prison at any given time, than as a percentage of men *received* or *released* by the prison in a given period. For example, in California prisons during 1960, 33 per cent of the men received had previously been imprisoned, but of the men imprisoned as of December 31st, 1960, 48 per cent had served a previous prison term.[4]

A second source of error underlying this two-thirds return to prison estimate is generalization about an entire prison system from the few institutions in which offenders with prior imprisonment are unusually concentrated. Correctional systems operating more than one place of confinement usually separate inmates according to the extent of their previous incarceration, in addition to separating by age, length of sentence, and other considerations. In California, for example, on June 30, 1961, over half the state's prisoners had not previously served a prison term, but this proportion at different institutions varied from a low of 14 per cent at Folsom to a high of 82 per cent at Deuel.[5] In the quotation from an ex-prisoner that we used to illustrate the chain of reasoning leading to a two-thirds return conclusion, a prison was described in which only 27 per cent of the inmates had not served previous prison terms. Since about half the inmates of most prison *systems* have not previously served sentences in prison, this ex-prisoner's institution must have been part of a system which also included one or more prisons with well over half serving their first prison term.

A third reason has been advanced by Sol Rubin for questioning estimates of a reimprisonment rate such as this two-thirds figure. This reason, as he

[3] Hal Hollister, "I Say Prisons Are a Failure," *The Saturday Evening Post, 234,* no. 34 (August 26, 1961), 13.

[4] California Department of Corrections, *California Prisoners 1960.* Table 9A, p. 22 and Table 20A, p. 42.

[5] California Department of Corrections, *Characteristics of Resident Population of California State Prisons by Institution, June 30, 1962,* Research Div., Adm. Statistics Section. P. 2a and p. 2c.

puts it, is that "the rate is impossible." In this contention, Rubin cites figures showing that the number confined in state and federal prisons in the United States is less than two and one-half times the number which the prisons release per year. Rubin then assumes, in his argument, that the average newly sentenced prisoner who is committed for his second or subsequent prison term is confined on his new term for at least four years. If two-thirds of the men released each year were returned to prison for an average period of four years, the number of men confined at any one time on their second or subsequent prison term would alone be over two and one-half times the total number of prisoners released per year.[6]

Data are not readily available on the validity of Rubin's four-year reimprisonment assumption. Nevertheless, a *National Prisoner Statistics* report in preparation by the U. S. Bureau of Prisons in 1963 indicated that as of December 31, 1960, for 149,617 inmates of the state prisons that compiled prior criminal record information, 51.2 per cent had no prior commitment. When one considers Rubin's argument in conjunction with the fact that about half the men confined in American prison systems are serving their first term in prison, one has strong logical grounds for dismissing the "two-thirds return to prison" speculation. But if this figure is spurious, what is the actual reimprisonment rate?

INDICATIONS THAT ABOUT TWO-THIRDS DO NOT RETURN

The only conclusive way to find out how many men released from prison are imprisoned again is to follow for a number of years all those released in a given period, in order to count the number who get back into prison. These prisoners of a given period would be what the statisticians call a "cohort"; and this would be a "cohort follow-up study." It would be extremely expensive, and it could raise questions of civil rights, if it meant hiring detectives to follow everyone about. However, every newly confined prisoner now has his fingerprints sent by the prison administration to the Federal Bureau of Investigation. Therefore, examination of a released prisoner's F.B.I. fingerprint file a few years after his release permits one to determine quickly whether he has been reimprisoned.

The prison dispatches inmate fingerprints to the F.B.I. for custodial and police purposes, to permit identification of escapees from prison, and to provide evidence of a prior prison record when released prisoners have further conflict with the law. However, were the F.B.I. fingerprint files of

[6] Sol Rubin, "Recidivism and Recidivism Statistics," *National Probation and Parole Assoc. J., 4,* no. 3 (July 1958), 236. Rubin is also assuming here that those who return to prison do so soon enough to be able to serve several four-year (or longer) terms before death.

all men released from prison in a given year to be checked a number of years later for evidence of reimprisonment, we would know precisely the proportion that are returned to prison. We would then not have to speculate as to whether this figure is two-thirds, one-third, or four-fifths. It is a striking illustration of the non-coordination of police and prison components in government efforts to cope with crime that this sort of checking has seldom been attempted, although it is a relatively minor clerical task. As a consequence, prisons must operate like businesses without bookkeeping, in blissful ignorance of the extent of their profit or loss.

Actually, for a period of about five years, terminating in 1950, the F.B.I. regularly supplied follow-up information to all prisons. During this period, whenever a new arrest report was received by the F.B.I. on a man whose fingerprint file indicated previous imprisonment, a copy of the entire fingerprint record was sent to the last prison in which the man had been confined. This was a golden opportunity for prisons to learn how effective they had been with their prior inmates. It also would have been possible for them to compare, from their records, the characteristics and the prison programs of men with and without a further criminal record in the postrelease years.

It is believed that there were only two instances, which will be described, where the follow-up information provided to prisons by the F.B.I. during 1945-50 was systematically used by prisons for compiling statistics on their effectiveness. The cultural base for correctional research had apparently not yet been achieved. Instead, in most prisons, almost all F.B.I. fingerprint reports received on prisoners already discharged were either filed and forgotten, or just thrown away. Is it any wonder that, when the Korean conflict created manpower and financial difficulties in provision of government services, this is one service that was discontinued?

U. S. Bureau of Prisons Research

As far as we have been able to learn, only one systematic check on the records of released prisoners from an entire prison system was conducted with fingerprint records furnished by the F.B.I. This was done by the U. S. Bureau of Prisons in the summer of 1949. It covered 2747 prisoners released from federal prisons during August and November 1943, and January and March 1944. The findings of this study, circulated within the Bureau of Prisons, showed that 32.6 per cent of federal prisoners released five years earlier were "sentenced to new terms of imprisonment" or returned to prison as parole violators. However, this includes 8.6 per cent reported to have received new sentences of only one year or less. Such "imprisonment" probably was in a jail (or equivalent institution for misdemeanants) rather than in a prison, since prison sentences usually are required by law to be for terms of over one year. (Indeed, some of these 8.6 per cent may have had terms of only a few days in jail.) Therefore, we can conclude that only *about one-fourth of the men released from federal prisons in 1943 and 1944 were returned to prison during the next five years.*

As might be expected, there was some variation in this postrelease reimprisonment rate for different federal prisons. The following are the rates of reimprisonment (on a new sentence of over a year or on parole violation) for the eleven federal prisons which released over a hundred men in the four months of 1943 and 1944 for which five years of postrelease record were checked:

	Per cent reimprisoned
Ashland (Kentucky) Correctional Institution	9.5
Lewisburg (Pennsylvania) Penitentiary	15.0
Danbury (Connecticut) Correctional Institution	15.8
Petersburg (Virginia) Reformatory	18.3
Atlanta (Georgia) Penitentiary	23.5
U. S. Prisons Medical Center (Springfield, Mo.)	23.7
McNeil Island (Washington) Penitentiary	26.4
Chillicothe (Ohio) Reformatory	27.2
El Reno (Oklahoma) Reformatory	27.5
Leavenworth (Kansas) Penitentiary	30.9
Terre Haute (Indiana) Penitentiary	32.1

During this period the institutions with the lowest percentages of reimprisonment were characterized by high proportions of southern rural offenders, many of them for "moonshine"—untaxed liquor—manufacture (Ashland, Petersburg, and Atlanta), or high proportions of white-collar offenders (such as income-tax violators) and Selective Service Law offenders (Danbury and Lewisburg).

Two federal institutions with a predominantly juvenile population were excluded from the above listing because they released less than one hundred inmates during the four months of 1943-44 which the survey covered. It is of interest that their releasees were more often reimprisoned in the subsequent five years than those of any other institution in the federal system. Their reimprisonment figures were as follows:

Englewood (Colorado) Youth Institution (66 releasees)	41.5 per cent
National Training School (Washington, D. C.) (91 releasees)	44.0 per cent

On the basis of our project's study of statistical relationships between crime, age, and employment (see page 9), one would expect relatively high crime rates for juveniles and low crime rates for adults during the wartime and postwar prosperity of the Bureau's 1943-49 postrelease checking period. Since federal prisoners are predominantly adult males, the reimprisonment rate of only about 25 per cent was probably lower than one might find in other periods. In addition to the full-employment situation to which these men were released, many were able to enter wartime military service, despite a criminal record that would bar them from the military in peacetime. The Illinois Selective Service Felon Study has shown that wartime military service offered a particularly favorable situation for the rehabilitation of a released prisoner.[7] Furthermore, the federal prisoners in this period included a high proportion of Selective Service Law violators, who are not typically criminals at other times. Recidivism rates for institutions for juveniles also can be expected to exceed rates for the adult prisons because probation and other alternatives to confinement are used more liberally for juveniles than for adults. Hence, only the worst risks among juveniles are committed to institutions, whereas prisons for adults receive more diverse risks. A second reason for expecting higher reimprisonment rates for juveniles is simply the consistent statistical evidence that the earlier the age at which an individual is first committed for criminal behavior, the more likely he is to continue in that behavior.[8]

Minnesota Reformatory Statistics

The only systematic use of F.B.I. follow-up records for compiling statistics on prison effectiveness, other than that by the U. S. Bureau of Prisons, was made by the Minnesota Reformatory at St. Cloud. The postrelease F.B.I. records through June 30, 1950, on the 345 men whom this institution released between July 1, 1944 and June 30, 1945, were checked by several members of the institution staff. They also checked state parole and police records. They found that 21 per cent of these released inmates had received new felony convictions in the five-year follow-up period, 2 per cent had been returned as parole rule violators without new sentences but were suspected of committing felonies, and 15 per cent had been returned to prison for other types of parole violation. This makes a total of *38 per cent returned to prison during the follow-up period.*[9] It should be noted that these were reformatory inmates, ranging in age from 20 through 29, rather than a cross-section of the inmates of the Minnesota prison system.

The Glueck Study

In one of the most distinguished American criminological research undertakings, a cohort of 510 inmates released from the Massachusetts Reforma-

[7] Hans W. Mattick, "Parolees in the Army During World War II," *Federal Probation, 24,* no. 3 (Sept. 1960), 49-55.

[8] For some of this evidence see chapter 3, and also Thorsten Sellin, "Recidivism and Maturation," *National Probation and Parole Assoc. J., 4,* no. 3 (July 1958), 241-50.

[9] S. B. Zuckerman, A. J. Barron, and H. B. Whittier, "A Follow-Up Study of Minnesota State Reformatory Inmates," *J. Crim. Law, Criminology and Police Science, 43,* no. 5 (Jan.–Feb. 1953), 622-36.

tory in 1921 and 1922 were traced in the free community every five years over a fifteen-year postrelease period. This outstanding effort, directed by Sheldon and Eleanor Glueck, is famous for its judgment, at the end of the first five years, that almost 80 per cent were not rehabilitated. However, the Gluecks conclude:

. . . . 135 (32.3 per cent) of the 418 men whose behavior over the entire fifteen-year period can be adequately described persisted in serious criminality throughout the three follow-up periods; . . . 21 men (5 per cent) though they had abandoned criminalism during either the first or second five year span, relapsed into criminal ways during the third, and then again became non-criminals.[10]

The number confined in prisons and reformatories during the first five-year follow-up period is reported as 133, which is 26 per cent of the original sample of 510 parolees. In the second five years out 105 were in prison, and in the third five years ninety-nine, but the Gluecks' discussion indicates that the same men are frequently involved in the prison figures for two or more of these periods, and they do not publish a single figure on the total number of their original 510 who were at any time in a prison or reformatory in the fifteen years.[11] Their reimprisonment figure for the first five years out, in the early 1920's, is lower than the cited reimprisonment figure for a five-year follow-up of Minnesota Reformatory releasees twenty years later, in the 1940's.

1956 Federal Prison Releasees

As indicated on page 10, our project began its statistical analysis of records of released offenders by drawing every tenth case from a list of adult males released from federal prisons during 1956. This yielded a sample of over one thousand. After F.B.I. fingerprint report sheets had been procured by the Bureau of Prisons in 1959 for 194 of these cases, a shortage of clerical assistance and pressure of other work in the F.B.I. prevented their supplying more of this special service to the Bureau of Prisons. Therefore we employed the following alternative checking procedure, which might usefully be copied by any state correctional agency desiring some follow-up of its releasees even without current fingerprint reports.

During the summer of 1960, the cases in our sample for whom current F.B.I. reports had not been received were, first of all, checked in the U. S. Bureau of Prisons and Board of Parole files in Washington for records of reimprisonment in federal institutions, either for violation of parole or of

[10] Sheldon and Eleanor T. Glueck, *Criminal Careers in Retrospect* (New York, The Commonwealth Fund, 1943), p. 121.

[11] *Ibid*, pp. 116-18, 348.

conditional release or under new federal sentences. (A state correctional system would first check a list of releasees of a past year in its own system's central files.) A list of the men who had no record of new federal imprisonment was sent by the Bureau of Prisons to the prisons from which they had been released and in which the complete institutional files of these men were kept. If, after the 1956 release, one of these men had been confined in a nonfederal prison, his file probably would contain a request from the new place of confinement for the behavior record and case analysis of the man during his federal confinement. (Most prisons today send such requests to every recidivist's institution of last confinement.) If no subsequent imprisonment had been recorded in the institution of last release, the Bureau of Prisons wrote to the U. S. Probation Office of the judicial district to which the man had been expected to go in 1956, asking whether this man had had any further difficulties with the law. (In a state system, such inquiry would be addressed to the local parole officer.) Generally, the probation office checked with local police in completing its reply to such a letter.

By the above process, of 1015 cases constituting a random sample of adult male prisoners released from federal prisons in 1956, a total of about 31 per cent were found to have been reimprisoned:

26.6 per cent on new felony sentences;
1.7 per cent as parole or conditional release violators, when suspected of new felonies;
2.8 per cent as parole violators with no felonies alleged.

An additional 3.9 per cent received nonprison sentences for felony-like offenses (e.g., petty larceny, carrying concealed weapons). Including the latter, we arrived at what we call a total *"failure rate" of 35 per cent*. This consists of everyone returned to prison or convicted of a felony-type offense. The remaining 65 per cent were classified as "successes." They included:

52.2 per cent who had no further criminal record whatsoever;
2.4 per cent with one or more nonfelony arrests, but no convictions;
4.8 per cent with one or more arrests on felony charges, but no convictions;
4.5 per cent with one or more misdemeanor convictions, but no arrests on felony charges;
1.1 per cent with one or more misdemeanor convictions, and one or more arrests on felony charges, but no felony convictions.

It is clear that the last of the "success" categories above may include some marginal failures, while the nonfelony parole violators in the "failure" group may include some marginal successes. A line was drawn at what seemed to be the most reasonable boundary point, which would keep to a minimum the number of errors from classification of every case as either a "success" or a "failure." It is notable that few cases fell into the marginal categories.

Wisconsin and California Research

Parole supervision records provide a relatively simple source of post-release criminality data for those prison systems which release almost all of their inmates by parole. This should yield complete reimprisonment information for the period of supervision, although its value is limited by variation in the duration of supervision. However, Wisconsin and California, which in recent years have released eighty to ninety per cent of their inmates by parole or conditional release, use state fingerprint files to determine criminal records after the period of supervision. This probably provides nearly complete information on postrelease imprisonment, even though, like our follow-up of the 1956 releasees, it may miss some reimprisonment outside of the state after the termination of parole or conditional release supervision.

Wisconsin's two-year follow-up found that, of all inmates paroled from 1952 to 1956, only 13.7 per cent were convicted of a new offense, but an additional 22.1 per cent were declared in violation of parole or conditional release, making a total of 35.8 per cent eligible for reimprisonment. However, only 31.3 per cent actually were returned to Wisconsin institutions.[12]

California, where the period of parole supervision almost invariably is at least three years, reported a follow-up through January 1, 1953, of parolees released from 1946 through 1949. They found 20.2 per cent imprisoned for a new felony and 23.3 per cent returned to prison for parole violations without felony conviction in this period. The latter figure includes 7.3 per cent who were suspected by their parole supervisors of having committed new felonies. An additional 5.5 per cent were declared violators but not returned to prison.[13] The extensive use of probation in California, as compared with many other states, would tend to send fewer of the best risks to prison, and could make the California prisoners have exceptionally high prospects of recidivism. Also, California has one of the highest crime rates, in relation to population, of any major state.

More recent California tabulations of postrelease imprisonment data, for 1950-61, do not provide details on the basis for reimprisonment but involve a longer follow-up period. In 1951, 75 per cent of California male prisoners released were paroled. Of those paroled, 34.5 per cent had been

[12] Wisconsin State Dept. of Public Welfare, Bureau of Research and Statistics, *Failure Rates of Prisoners Paroled from Wisconsin Adult Correctional Institutions* (Dec. 11, 1958).

[13] California Director of Corrections and Adult Authority, *California Male Prisoners Released on Parole 1946-1949* (1953) pp. 12-14.

returned to prison within three years after parole. This percentage rose only to 36.5 per cent by the sixth year after parole, to 36.7 per cent by the 9th year after parole, and to 37.0 per cent at the end of the 11th year after parole. *Apparently, a three year follow-up provides about 90 per cent of the probable future returns to prison data.*[14]

New York State Follow-Ups

New York State, which paroles about three-fourths of those whom it releases from prison, publishes follow-ups of its parolees which cover only the duration of the parole supervision period or five years, whichever is shorter. Their parole supervision periods vary in length from less than three months to a lifetime. In 1956 their median parole supervision period was about two and one-half years; and of those paroled in that year, 44 per cent were reimprisoned before the end of their supervision period or before December 31, 1960, whichever was earlier. However, in this follow-up period only 7 per cent were convicted of new felonies; most of the remaining 37 per cent returned to prison were either charged with "general violation of parole" (perhaps when suspected of felonies) or declared parole violators after being convicted of misdemeanors.[15]

Youth Correction Act Statistics

The Federal Youth Correction Act, which went into effect in 1954, provides judges with an unusual kind of optional sentence for persons who are under the age of twenty-two at the time of conviction for a federal offense. Those sentenced to prison under this Act may be paroled after sixty days, must be paroled within four years, and are under federal supervision for six years after the beginning of their sentence (unless given a special discharge somewhat earlier). Therefore, a postrelease follow-up for at least two years, and generally for longer, is available on such cases from the files of the U. S. Board of Parole, which receives regular reports on each parolee from the local Federal Probation Offices.

Because of this availability of follow-up information, in the summer of 1960 we made a compilation of the postrelease criminal record of all male Federal Youth Correction Act offenders paroled through June 30, 1958. This covered 969 cases, of whom 49 per cent were found to have been returned to prison. This 49 per cent consists of:

19.1 per cent who received new felony sentences;

10.2 per cent who were returned as parole violators after allegedly committing new felonies for which they were not sentenced;

---

[14] California Department of Corrections, *Number of Men Paroled and Cumulative Percentage of Parolees Returned to Prison Each Year After Parole, 1950-1961,* Research Div., Admin. Statistics Section (Sept. 6, 1962).

[15] State of New York, *31st Annual Report of the Division of Parole,* Legislative Document 1961, no. 106, pp. 158-67.

4.2 per cent returned after receiving nonprison sentences for felony-like offenses;

15.5 per cent returned as parole violators without being suspected of a new felony.

The U. S. Board of Parole, in handling Youth Act cases, has frequently designated return to prison as "return for further treatment," viewing it more as a therapeutic than a punitive action, so that some of those returned may be reparoled in a relatively short time. This approach may be taken with any parolee, but it is particularly applicable to the Youth Correction Act cases, as Youth Act sentences stipulate long government supervision and permit much flexibility with parole. The U. S. Board of Parole conducted a long-term follow-up of the first 322 cases completing full sentences under this Act. They concluded that 58.1 per cent of these had been successfully released. However, they found that only 38.5 per cent were immediately successful, while 19.6 per cent were "belatedly successful," in that they first were paroled and were returned, but later were reparoled successfully. One-third of these reimprisoned youth cases were returned for behavior not involving new crime.[16] It should be stressed that the cases in this Parole Board study were not typical federal offenders, since, first of all, they were youth cases, and, secondly, they were the first cases to receive this Youth Correction Act sentence, when it was an option infrequently employed by federal judges.

Washington State Data

Washington State, because it paroles 99 per cent of its prisoners, has more complete data than any other state for statistical evaluation of its correctional programs. Although it has lagged behind several of the other states, such as California and Wisconsin, in the exploitation of this research opportunity, it has evaluated and reported postrelease record statistics as of December 31, 1959, for the 1731 prisoners who were paroled from July 1957 through June 1959. In this one-half to two-and-one-half-year follow-up there was no further penal action for 62 per cent of the parolees, 13 per cent were convicted of new felonies, 7 per cent were returned to prison as technical violators, and 18 per cent were wanted at the end of this period as absconders from parole supervision.[17]

Pennsylvania Records

The correctional system in Pennsylvania is distinguished by having not one, but two, excellent statistical agencies. From the standpoint of evalu-

[16] The "immediate" and "belated" success figures are from tables prepared by James Neagles, Staff Director, U. S. Board of Parole. The one-third felony figure is from our project's codification and tabulation of case data supplied by Mr. Neagles from this U. S. Board of Parole Study.

[17] State of Washington, Department of Institutions and Board of Prison Terms and Paroles, *Adult Parolee Study* (1960).

ating correctional operations, this division is unfortunate. The statisticians of the Bureau of Correction tabulate information on the prison record, and those of the Board of Parole tabulate the postrelease record, but the latter data are limited to the 70 per cent released by parole. The Pennsylvania Board of Parole has compiled, since 1947, a five-year follow-up of those whom it paroles. This indicated that 51 per cent of the parolees had been satisfactorily discharged from parole by expiration of sentence within five years of release (the average parole supervision period for this group being about two years and four months). Another 16 per cent were still on parole at the end of five years, 31 per cent were returned to prison, and 2 per cent had died on parole.[18]

Hypotheses of Recidivism

The evidence presented here from the various follow-up studies is summarized in Table 2.1. The contrast of entries on the various lines of that table certainly highlights our lack of uniform information on the postprison consequences of efforts to rehabilitate men in prison. Nevertheless, if there is to be cumulative growth of a science of penology, we must attempt to express what seem, at present, to be the generalizations that our data make most tenable. Setting them forth in formal fashion should make it easier for future research to address itself to testing these generalizations, so as to lead either to their further confirmation or to their modification or replacement. For this purpose, the following statement is presented as the principal hypothesis for further testing suggested from the material summarized thus far in this chapter:

A1. In the first two to five years after their release, only about a third of all the men released from an entire prison system are returned to prison.

The variation above or below one-third apparently may range as much as ten or fifteen percentage points. Highly limited evidence suggests the supplementary hypothesis:

A2. The proportion of releasees returned to prison tends to be higher:
   a. where probation is used extensively, so that only the worst risks go to prison (although this use of probation may make the long-run recidivism of all felons lower);
   b. where parole is used extensively, so that many poor-risk parolees are released on a trial basis;
   c. where a large proportion of parolees are returned to prison when they have violated parole regulations but have not been charged with or convicted of new felonies;

[18] Pennsylvania Board of Parole, *Five Year Studies of Parolees* (Harrisburg, the Board, 1963). Average parole period of those on parole less than five years provided by communication from William L. Jacks, April 17, 1963.

TABLE 2.1   Summary of Follow-Up Studies of Inmates Released from U.S. Prisons
Part 1, Total Systems

Prison system	Year of release	Duration of follow-up	Releases covered	Researchers	Sources of follow-up information	Per cent returned to prison	Per cent convicted or accused of new felony
Federal	1943–44	Approx. 5 yrs.	All releases (25% parolees)	U.S. Bureau of Prisons	F.B.I. fingerprint record	24	(not tabulated)
California	1946–49	3 yrs.	The 88% who were paroled	Calif. Bd. of Corrections (Beattie)	State parole and criminal identification records	44	28
Wisconsin	1952–56	2 yrs.	The approx. 85% who were paroled or conditionally released	Wisc. Dept. of Public Welfare (Mannering)	State parole and criminal identification records	31	14 (convicted)
New York	1956	Parole period or up to 5 yrs.	The 76% who were paroled	N.Y. Board of Parole (Stanton)	State parole records	44	7 (convicted)
Federal	1956	Approx. 4 yrs.	Every 10th adult male releasee (31% parolees)	U. of Ill. (Glaser)	Some F.B.I. fingerprint records; prison and probation office tracing	31	28
Washington	1957–59	½ to 2½ yrs.	99% of all releases	Wash. Dept. of Institutions (Babst, Suver, Kusano, Little)	State parole records	20 (another 18% in "wanted" status)	13
Pennsylvania	1947–57	Parole period: Aver. 2⅜ yrs. Max. 5 yrs.	The approx. 70% who were paroled.	Pa. Board of Parole (Jacks)	State parole records	31	17

TABLE 2.1 Summary of Follow-Up Studies of Inmates Released from U.S. Prisons
Part 2, Youthful Offenders Only

Youth prisons	Year of release	Duration of follow-up	Releases covered	Researchers	Sources of follow-up information	Per cent returned to prison	Per cent convicted or accused of new felony
Massachusetts Reformatory	1921	5 yrs. post-parole (8–10 yrs. post-release)	The 83% that could be traced (all parolees) of 510 total cases	Sheldon and Eleanor T. Glueck	Field inquiries; state and local records	31.5 (of those traced); 26.1 (of total)	36.1 during parole (of total); 43.8 post-parole (of those traced)
Minnesota Reformatory	1944 –45	Approx. 5 yrs.	All releases (53% parolees)	Zuckerman, Barron, and Whittier	F.B.I. fingerprint and state parole records	38	23
Federal Youth Correction Act Cases	1955 –58	Parole period (2–4 yrs.)	Those committed 1954–55 (all parolees)	U. S. Board of Parole (Neagles)	Federal parole records	58	36 (includes some serious misdemeanors)
Federal Youth Correction Act Cases	1955 –58	Parole period (2–4 yrs.)	All released 1955–58 (all parolees)	U. of Ill. (Glaser)	Federal parole records	49	34

d. where there is a high overall crime rate in the communities to which prisoners are released, so that there is high prospect of the releasee coming from and going to highly criminogenic circumstances.

Analysis of other factors in the variation of these rates, such as the higher rates for youth, will be deferred to the next chapter.

Clearly, the second of the two formal propositions above is based on limited evidence. Before describing the type of research program by which these hypotheses could be tested more rigorously, it is appropriate to clarify some terminological confusion which arises from the problem of interpreting postrelease behavior which can send a man back to prison only if he is on parole. How should these infractions be distinguished from clearly felonious postrelease conduct?

LESSER INFRACTIONS AND THE INTERPRETATION OF PAROLE OUTCOME

Men usually are confined in a prison only for the commission of felonies, and for sentences of more than a year. Most frequently, prison incarceration is for grand larceny, auto larceny, burglary, forgery, robbery, murder, or narcotics or sex offenses; less frequently it may be for any of a variety of other serious crimes, from counterfeiting to kidnapping. Offenses considered less serious than these are called misdemeanors, and persons confined for them are placed in jails or in other institutions for misdemeanants (state farms, houses of correction, workhouses, etc.) rather than in state or federal prisons. Misdemeanor confinement normally ranges in duration from a few days to several months, but does not exceed one year. Most frequently misdemeanor confinement is for drunkenness, disorderly conduct, vagrancy, petty larceny, gambling, or nonsupport of dependents. Although court action does not clearly differentiate felonies from misdemeanors, on the whole, felonies are acts regarded as much more disturbing to society than misdemeanors.

When men who are sent to prison for felonies commit no crime after release, they clearly appear to be complete successes from the standpoint of reducing return to prison. If they commit no new felonies but are committed to jail for misdemeanors, can they not generally be considered as at least partial successes? As the data which we shall present in ensuing chapters will make evident, many prisoners have had long preoccupation with felonious pursuits, have had little successful experience at legitimate activities, and are extremely handicapped economically and socially when they seek a conventional way of life on release. In such cases, a postrelease record of occasional drunkenness or arrest only on suspicion, until noncriminality is clearly established, would indicate major progress towards a conventional life.

Unfortunately, statistics on the postrelease behavior of prisoners frequently are summarized without making any distinction between new serious felony convictions and misdemeanor sentences, or even between felony sentences and misdemeanor arrests that are followed by release with charges dismissed. In most of the studies already cited, which reported one-fourth to one-third reimprisoned, the statistic presented as the major finding was that about fifty per cent of released prisoners had further difficulty with the law.[19] Although the first five-year follow-up in the Glueck study asserted that 80 per cent were not rehabilitated, less than half were alleged to have committed felony or felony-like offenses in this period, and only about a fourth were placed in prison or in a reformatory.[20]

Our project has focused on the extent of reimprisonment and on the extent of alleged felony commitment by released prisoners, because the public establishes prisons primarily to protect itself from felons rather than to cope with lesser misbehavior. If prison or parole experience changes a man from a heinous malefactor to a hallowed saint, that is excellent, but if it merely changes him from a felon to a nonfelon, its primary objective has still been achieved.

Today prisoners increasingly are released by parole. This is a release before the sentence is over, on condition that these men obey certain rules of proper conduct, and generally also on condition that the men have approved postrelease jobs and home arrangements. The purpose of parole is to protect the public, first, by releasing a prisoner only to the circumstances which are the best available for maximizing his chances of achieving a noncriminal life, and secondly, by permitting return of the parolee to prison for all or part of the balance of his sentence if he fails to comply with the rules of parole behavior believed conducive to the prevention of felonies.

The extent to which parolees are returned to prison without being sus-

[19] The 1949 follow-up of 1943-44 releases from federal prisons found that 47.1 per cent had some further criminal record entry, although for 14.5 per cent this was a record of arrest not followed by any confinement, and for 8.6 per cent it was confinement for less than a year. The Minnesota Reformatory follow-up concluded that 52.8 per cent had some further police record or suspicion of criminality, including misdemeanors and nonfelonious parole rule infractions (Zuckerman, Barron, and Whittier, *op. cit.*). Similarly, California found that 49.0 per cent of its 1946-49 parolees had committed or been suspected of some sort of law violation by 1953 (California Director of Corrections and Adult Authority, *op. cit.*). Our follow-up of 1956 federal releasees revealed that 47.8 per cent had some further criminal record, including 2.4 per cent receiving a nonfelony arrest or warrant but no reported conviction, 4.8 per cent receiving a felony arrest or warrant but no conviction, 5.6 per cent receiving misdemeanor convictions only, 4.4 per cent imprisoned for parole violation without being convicted of a felony, 3.9 per cent convicted of a felony-like offense but receiving a nonprison sentence, and 26.6 per cent receiving new prison sentences.

[20] Sheldon and Eleanor T. Glueck, *500 Criminal Careers* (New York, Knopf, 1930), pp. 167-68, 189-90; *idem., Criminal Careers in Retrospect,* p. 348.

pected of committing another felony is a function of two factors. First, the philosophy of the parole authority determines how readily reimprisonment is imposed for "technical" violations (for example, for leaving the assigned district, for associating with ex-criminals, for not diligently seeking work, or for drinking to excess). Secondly, the nature of parole supervision determines the extent to which rule violations are discovered and acted upon. This can be illustrated by two extremes encountered in the twelve federal judicial districts where our staff interviewed successful releasees. Where the parole officer merely accepts the parolee's oral or written monthly report, without further inquiry or without even an extensive interview with the parolee, the officer knows about the parolee's infractions only when a police report of an arrest is received. Conversely, where the officer makes frequent and unexpected visits to the parolee's residence and place of employment, where unemployed parolees are required to check in at the parole supervision office early each morning to prove that they are awake and looking for work, and where rules against drinking, extra-marital cohabitation, or traveling outside the county are strictly enforced, many "technical" violations are reported which otherwise would never be known.

It is the prevailing opinion in corrections that the public is best protected from crimes by released prisoners by: (1) sentencing and parole policies which enable most prisoners to leave prison by parole rather than by outright discharge; (2) an optimum amount of surveillance of parolees, rather than none at all or a gross excess (as well as more positive supervision functions, of course, such as counseling and assistance); (3) some revocation of parole for nonfelonious behavior. However, the more these three policies are adopted, the greater will be the proportion of released prisoners returned to prison for nonfelonious behavior. Therefore, parole agencies injure themselves by their practice of designating all return of parolees to prison by a single term, such as "violation" (or, in New York, "delinquency"). Perhaps this is one reason why parole officials often seem reluctant to report their violation rates.

It seems desirable to differentiate clearly between return of parolees to prison for felonies and return for nonfelonies. This would be facilitated by labeling each of these actions with a clearly different term. For example, one could have a rate of "Return for New Felonies" and a rate of "Return for Felony Prevention." This would make explicit to the public the two very distinct reasons for revoking parole. The figure on "Return for Felony Prevention" could not as readily be used by critics to oppose parole as is possible now, when the two figures are combined into a single overall violation rate. Indeed, omnibus terms like "violation" for these different types of action should be abandoned.

The designation "Return for Felony Prevention" might help make explicit to parole supervision officers what supervision is for. It might thereby discourage arbitrary rule enforcement irrelevant to felony prevention while reminding them of their safeguarding function with respect to felonies. The phrase "return for further treatment" has been employed by parole boards to distinguish some reimprisonment action with parolees, but this may connote more distinctive treatment than is actually available, and it is not clearly used to differentiate all actions where no felony was proven or alleged.

"Return for New Felonies" and "Return for Felony Prevention" clarify thinking about parole outcomes when conceived as polar opposites. Yet, as with "felony" versus "misdemeanor," each polar category includes borderline cases for which classification on one side or the other must be arbitrary. "Return for New Felonies" may well be based not only on ex-prisoners receiving new felony sentences but also on those parolees officially returned to prison for rule violations whom the parole supervision office has strong reason to suspect of felony. Frequently our overcrowded courts utilize the prospect that a man will be reimprisoned as a parole violator on an old sentence to justify avoiding the time and cost of trying him for a new felony. This often is accomplished by dropping felony charges if a parolee pleads guilty to a misdemeanor. It is possible that some parolees who are innocent of felonies are returned to prison by these procedures. However, the error from including such cases in the count of parolees returned for new felonies is likely to be less than the error of understating the amount of felony activity on parole if only cases with new felony convictions are counted. It will be noted that all postrelease offense tabulations presented thus far in this chapter included more felony information than the new felony conviction data, whenever more was available.

To be comprehensive, of course, statistics should be tabulated on both returned and wanted status. Ultimate categories could therefore be "Returned or Wanted for New Felony" and "Returned or Wanted for Felony Prevention." While this count also will include some parolees who ultimately may be proven innocent of felonies, this error is likely to be less than the error of not counting parolees wanted for felonies in reporting rates of parolee involvement in felonies.

Since the primary function of prison and parole is to protect the public from felonies, then to evaluate the effectiveness of these services, parole revocation information alone cannot substitute for long-run postrelease felony information. For example, one can learn the consequence of greater or lesser use of parole only by comparing the long-run felony rates of releasees from prison systems which have different parole policies. One could also compare sentencing policies in this way. This would require that for standard types of offender (classified by age, offense, and criminal record, at least), one determine the per cent of all released prisoners (both parolees and dischargees) who commit new felonies in a given number of years following conviction. This even permits comparison of different policies with respect to length or conditions of parole supervision, and it could permit comparison of the records of those sentenced to probation with the records of those sentenced to prison. One could thus evaluate a total sentencing and parole policy, as one unit, for specific types of criminals.[21]

The diversity of topics dealt with in this book testifies to the fact that much information other than postrelease felony rates is essential for evaluation of all aspects of correctional policy. Nevertheless, for practical significance and scientific adequacy in all these types of inquiry, the foundation is postrelease felony information. Only when such information becomes more readily and completely available can criminal correction become a science in the sense that medicine is a science. It must rigorously demonstrate the effectiveness of its treatment for some types of criminal, as well as explain the treatment in terms of testable principles.

RECORD-KEEPING AND SCIENTIFIC CRIMINAL CORRECTION

The research findings which have been summarized thus far in this chapter indicate that prisons and parole, as procedures for dealing with felons, are far from complete failures, although they also are far from "sure cures." Apparently no more than a third of the men released from prison acquire a record of further felonies, even where half have some further difficulty with the law. Clearly, there is much variation in the behavior that follows correctional experience. The problem of this project, and of the entire research movement in corrections, is to determine what factors most affect this variation in postrelease behavior. The first step in solving this problem is to improve our knowledge of postrelease felony rates for different types of offenders, under alternative correctional programs.

A crude method of procuring the postrelease criminal record was described in reporting this project's study of 1956 releasees from federal prisons. An alternative method, utilizing state parole supervision files and state criminal identification records, was employed by Wisconsin and California to procure a postrelease record on their parolees. However, after the expiration of the parole supervision period, such information is limited to criminality within the state, and it is inadequate at all times for prison systems which release a large proportion of their inmates without parole.

The first part of this chapter referred to a 1945-1950 service of the F.B.I. in sending complete fingerprint report sheets to each prison where any

21 See also Lloyd E. Ohlin and Frank J. Remington, "Sentencing Structure: Its Effect Upon Systems for the Administration of Criminal Justice," *Law and Contemporary Problems, 23,* no. 3 (Summer 1958), 495-507.

newly fingerprinted person had previously been confined. It was pointed out that, except for the 1949 federal study and the Minnesota Reformatory study, the prisons did not utilize this material to compile postrelease felony rates. Their failure to take advantage of this opportunity reflects the fact that the research movement in corrections became strong only around 1958-61, almost a decade after this F.B.I. service ceased. It may also reflect the non-coordination of correctional efforts; the postrelease reports from the F.B.I. were handled by prison identification and clerical personnel and did not routinely come to the attention of treatment specialists or top administrators.

The time now is ripe for renewal of this federal postrelease reporting service, but in a manner which assures that it will not be wasted. Several alternative arrangements are possible. A minimum program would be simply for the F.B.I. to renew this service to states and to the U. S. Bureau of Prisons when the service is requested specifically for penological research and a research office is designated to receive the reports. For budgeting purposes, the maximum-sized sample for which reports on postrelease criminality would be provided could be specified, perhaps varying according to the population of the jurisdiction requesting this service. These limits could be modified on the basis of subsequent experience.

A second type of federal program might provide for an office within the Department of Justice to compile statistics on the felony-reduction effectiveness of all state and federal penal systems. This would assure comparability of information for the different states and the federal system, which is not likely to be achieved in compilations by the separate states. Indeed, the variation of investment in correctional services today by states of diverse economic wealth makes it unlikely that all states would compile statistics on their correctional effectiveness if left to their own resources. A federal recidivism statistics compilation would be an extension of the service now provided by the Department of Justice in its Uniform Crime Reports and National Prisoner Statistics publications, and would be comparable to statistical services provided by other government agencies, such as the Bureau of Labor Statistics and the Children's Bureau.

Information contained in the F.B.I. fingerprint reports of criminal record permit a national agency to make separate compilations for ex-prisoners according to last offense, prior offenses, prior incarceration, age, or race. Thus it could compare the effectiveness of different correctional systems not only as wholes, but also for specific types of offender. It is possible that correctional actions make little difference in post-release criminality for certain types of offender but considerable difference for other types, or that one system is more effective for certain types and another for other types. More important, as the number of records for such "criminal career statistics" accumulate to an appreciable total, it would be possible to classify them not just by type of offender, but by the duration of prison confinement and by whether release was through parole or through outright discharge. Such comparative statistics on the postrelease criminality of similar types of offender who were given different kinds of correctional treatment would help to provide guidelines for judges and parole boards, who must decide on an optimum length of confinement and mode of release. Indeed, as was indicated in the preceding section, an ultimate extension of this type of study would include long-run checks on the recidivism of all persons sentenced for felonies in each jurisdiction, including probationers, to evaluate the effectiveness of probation as a sentencing alternative in conjunction with prisons and parole, for specific types of offender.

Only through research in individual prisons or parole agencies can postrelease criminality information be correlated with more details of the personal background of offenders, such as their education, psychological test results, marriage, or employment history. Only through the correctional agencies also can the recidivism information be correlated with details of correctional experience, such as the prison work record of offenders, their social relationships in prison, or their type of parole home and job placement. Indeed, only with parole supervision records can one discern those parole revocations without felony convictions in which strong evidence of felonies was present. Furthermore, only state or federal prison or parole agencies can undertake controlled experiments with specific types of treatment program; such experiments, however, can be interpreted adequately only if these agencies procure the postrelease felony records of their treatment and control groups. Therefore, the minimum program suggested of supplying F.B.I. postrelease criminality records to state and federal penal research agencies would still be desirable even if the federal government also adopted the more ambitious second program of making a national compilation of recidivism statistics.

The two types of operation described here would involve an annual cost ranging from tens of thousands to hundreds of thousands of dollars, depending on how ambitiously they were pursued. This is a very small cost for some fundamental accounting to determine the effectiveness of the half-billion-dollar annual investment for prison and parole services in the United States, as well as the additional investment in police, court, and jail services to send felons to prison. Proportionately slight reductions in this national burden achieved by learning the relative effectiveness of alternative judicial or correctional policies would more than offset the monetary cost of the proposed accounting operations for procuring such information. In addition, reducing the human costs of crime would be even more significant than reducing its monetary cost.

When the assessment of correctional operations in terms of their consequences for postrelease criminality becomes routine, knowledge, hence savings also, is likely to be cumulative. Research in isolated small-scale studies, such as those cited in this chapter, does not seem to get beyond the level of determining gross rates of overall effectiveness; but with routine collection of recidivism information by the federal government, coordinated with the work of permanent research staffs in correctional systems on the state and federal level, one can go beyond answering first questions, on gross recidivism, and advance to questions on the success and failure of particular correctional strategies with specific types of offenders.

A future snowballing of statistical knowledge on the effectiveness of crime control measures may someday be traced back to a modest beginning in 1962, when the F.B.I. Uniform Crime Reporting Office undertook a pilot study on the feasibility of compiling criminal career statistics on a small sample of federal parolees and probationers.[22] The F.B.I.'s information on the criminal record of felons after their release from probation, prison, or parole, and their experience and resources for handling these records, make them the agency best equipped to ascertain the long-run felony recidivism rates which follow alternative judicial and correctional action for particular types of offender.

The F.B.I.'s famed thoroughness, and its periodic consultation with users of its services, have made the information on crime incidence in its Uniform Crime Reports progress steadily in quality and quantity. The persons directing the pilot study in 1962 were familiar with my 1957 publications on utilization of fingerprint information for recidivism statistics,[23] and have received from the dean of American criminal statisticians, Ronald H. Beattie (now of the Administrative Office of U. S. Courts), memoranda outlining possibilities of using such new F.B.I. statistics for the guidance of the federal judiciary.[24]

Future experience alone can determine the optimum uses of F.B.I. recidivism statistics in the guidance of legislation to control crime and in the evaluation of judicial, penal, and parole policies. Certainly, maximum benefits will come not from omnibus evaluation of an overall program or a broad policy for all criminals but from specific evidence as to which practices reduce recidivism most for which types of offender. Almost all of the evaluation of prison and parole programs set forth in this volume can cer-

[22] Reported by Jerome J. Daunt, Chief, Uniform Crime Reporting, Federal Bureau of Investigation, at the Annual Meeting, Research and Statistics Committee, American Correctional Association, Sept. 18, 1962, in *Proceedings, American Correctional Association,* 1962, pp. 92-94.

[23] Daniel Glaser, "Criminal Career Statistics," in *Proceedings, American Correctional Association* (1957), pp. 103-06; Glaser, "Released Offender Statistics: A Proposal for a New National Program," *Am. J. Correction* (March–April 1957), 15-17, 25.

[24] It has been a pleasure to share with the Uniform Crime Reporting Office an earlier draft of this chapter, in the hope that by the time of this book's publication this new F.B.I. service will be much closer to routine operation.

tainly be improved when long-run recidivism information is marshaled for this evaluation task. In crime control, paralleling experience in medicine, progress will be especially rapid when knowledge of post-treatment behavior is applied to evaluating carefully controlled experiments with alternative judicial or correctional treatment.

CHAPTER 3

Preprison Influences on Recidivism

The preceding chapter dealt with rates of reimprisonment for all released prisoners. The rest of this book deals with sources of variation in these rates, especially with the extent to which they may be influenced by prison and parole experiences. Before investigating such influences, however, it is appropriate to determine how recidivism may be affected by those preprison attributes of offenders which cannot be changed by correctional programs. Prominent among these attributes are age, offense, prior criminal record, and presumed biological endowments, such as race and intelligence. If such attributes of offenders strongly influence recidivism, they suggest variations in commitment to crime with which correctional programs must cope and which must be taken into account in appraising the effectiveness of these programs.

AGE AND RECIDIVISM

A firmly established finding in criminological research is that of a predominantly inverse relationship between age and recidivism. One can generalize with much confidence for any large cross-section of offenders:

B1. The older a man is when released from prison, the less likely he is to return to crime.

TABLE 3.1   Postrelease Failure Rate of Federal Prisoners
in Relation to Age at Release

Age at release	18–19	20–21	22–23	24–25	26–30	31–35	36–40	41–49	50 and over
Failure rate	51%	46%	42%	38%	36%	30%	28%	25%	29%
Number of cases	53	90	90	88	256	150	106	124	58

Table 3.1 relates age at release from prison to a total postprison "failure rate" for our sample of federal offenders released in 1956. This failure rate, which is 35 per cent for the sample as a whole, combines returns to prison for parole violations, returns to prison because of new sentences, and nonprison sentences for felony-like offenses.

36

Table 3.1 indicates that the failure rate declines somewhat for each successive age group, from a peak of 51 per cent for those eighteen or nineteen years old at release to a low of 25 per cent for those in their forties when released.[1] Similar findings of predominantly declining recidivism with increasing age have been reported by studies conducted in many countries, and over a long period of time.[2] There also is evidence that as age at release increases, the probability increases that any further criminality will be a misdemeanor rather than a felony.[3] This, and the leveling off of the failure rate in the older age ranges, reflects the development in older age periods of some highly persistent criminal activity associated with alcoholism and senility. It should be noted that the upper age range in this tabulation is too low for differential life expectancy to be an appreciable factor in the "success" rate on this three-year follow-up.

A stronger relationship than that between age at release and recidivism usually has been found between recidivism and age of first officially recorded criminality.[4] For prisoners at any age, it generally is the case that:

B2. The younger a prisoner was when first arrested, convicted, or confined for any crime, the more likely he is to continue in crime.

Table 3.2 demonstrates this for our sample of 1956 federal prison releasees.[5] The postrelease failure rate for each age of first arrest declines steadily from a high of 49 per cent failures for those of age fourteen or less when first arrested to a low of only 11 per cent failures for those aged thirty-five or over when first arrested. In Table 18.2 of chapter 18 we cross-

[1] Point-biserial coefficient of correlation between age at release and success is 0.17. A point-biserial correlation this high in a sample of this size and dispersion would occur by chance alone much less than once in a thousand times.

[2] Detailed statistics on age and recidivism for several countries, covering a long period of time, and dealing with both age at release and age at each conviction, are provided in Thorsten Sellin, "Recidivism and Maturation," *National Probation and Parole Assoc. J., 4,* no. 3 (July 1958), 241-250. Another thorough summary and analysis of world research on this subject is found in Barbara Wooton, *Social Science and Social Pathology* (New York, Macmillan, 1959), chapter 5. Her discussion points out some deficiencies in evidence for conclusions that the earlier "delinquency" begins, the more likely it is to continue as lifetime criminality. However, the evidence she summarizes is highly consistent in supporting our conclusion that the recidivism rate of those released from prison at any age is greater, the earlier their *official* criminal record began.

[3] For one confirmation see: California Director of Corrections and Adult Authority, *California Male Prisoners Released on Parole 1946-49,* pp. 23, 46 (tables 7 and 31). These tables provide postrelease felony and misdemeanor information separately, for first paroles and for reparoles, by year of birth.

[4] Sellin, *op. cit.*

[5] Point-biserial coefficient of correlation between age of first arrest and success is 0.23. A point-biserial correlation this high in a sample of this size and dispersion would occur by chance alone very much less than once in a thousand times.

tabulate age at release with age at first arrest, revealing that violation rates still decline with increasing age at first arrest for each age-at-release category taken separately.

TABLE 3.2   Postrelease Failure Rate of Federal Prisoners
in Relation to Age at First Arrest

Age at first arrest	14 and under	15–16	17–18	19–20	21–23	24–27	28–34	35 and older
Failure rate	49%	42%	41%	35%	27%	27%	23%	11%
Number of cases	159	145	170	145	159	112	70	55

Interpretation of this predominantly inverse relationship between age and recidivism usually equates crime with immaturity, as in the following statement:

Crime is essentially the solution of personal problems at a childish level of conduct either because basic attitudes have never developed beyond that level or because there has been regression to childish attitudes as a result of frustration. It is natural for a young child to lie, to strike others, to intrude, to be indecent (if judged by adult standards) and to take the belongings of others. . . . But some children are not properly trained; they do not abandon their early attitudes. . . . Some proceed directly into juvenile delinquency; others . . . give way in later life when they are faced with that particular stress or temptation to which their early training, or lack of it, has left them vulnerable. Generally speaking, the older one grows the less this vulnerability and it is not surprising that crime is predominantly a weakness of the young.[6]

Further analysis, however, suggests a more complex interpretation of the relationships between early introduction to criminality and later recidivism. The more complex interpretation has more specific correctional implications than are indicated by the foregoing identification of crime with infantile behavior.

It should be stressed that criminals are not necessarily less mature than noncriminals in biological development, or even in attributes of social development, such as facility in social interaction with their peers. What seems to be a distinguishing feature of most criminal careers is a deviation from the usual sequence of cultural conditioning through which members of all societies normally progress in moving from childhood to adulthood. This is a sequence of changes from high dependence on others and few responsibilities in childhood to higher independence and more responsibilities in adulthood. The earlier this sequence is interrupted, the more difficult its restoration seems to be.

[6] W. F. Roper, as quoted in Wooton, *op. cit.*, p. 161.

In those countries that have the greatest industrialization and urbanization, such as the United States, young people go through a long period of transition, or adolescence, between child and adult roles. Contrastingly, in the so-called "underdeveloped countries," this transition is briefer because full-time responsibility for unskilled types of adult labor, or apprenticeship in the skilled trades, begins in the early teens. This also was the case in the United States of the nineteenth century. However, in industrialized countries today, particularly in the United States, the education of youth and their dependence on adults generally extends for four to eight years beyond puberty, and adult regulation of behavior in this period is much less rigorous than it was formerly.

Starting in the teen-age period, young people in the United States and in other highly urbanized and industrialized societies are especially likely to spend most of their waking hours in a purely adolescent social world. Isolation of this age group promotes the development of "adolescent subcultures," which may have standards of behavior, sources of personal gratification, and even styles of speech different from those of the adult world. However, by promoting self-reliance and developing social skills, much of this adolescent social life has the function that Merton calls "anticipatory socialization," or preparation for future roles.[7] Of course, when adolescent social pressures preoccupy a youth with activities and values inconsistent with conventional adult roles, extreme commitment to an adolescent subculture may impede his preparation for self-sufficiency in a law-abiding adult life.[8]

Home, school, and church endeavor to direct adolescent activities into patterns that serve as preparation for conventional adult life. Alienation from these influences often promotes varieties of adolescent subculture which interrupt or even directly oppose such preparation. It has been observed that adolescents who experience failure or conflict in school, neglect or hostility from parents, and frustration in efforts to acquire employment are especially inclined to join together in promoting delinquent varieties of adolescent subculture. These delinquent subcultures promote high valuation of crime, fighting, drug use, or other alternatives to the conventional pursuits and associations in which these youth have failed, and commitment

[7] Robert K. Merton, *Social Theory and Social Structure*, rev. ed. (Glencoe, Ill., Free Press, 1957), pp. 265-68.

[8] For fuller discussion of the functions and dysfunctions of adolescence as preparation for adulthood, see: James S. Coleman, *Adolescent Subcultures* (Glencoe, Ill., Free Press, 1961); Ruth Benedict, "Continuities and Discontinuities in Cultural Conditioning," *Psychiatry, 1* (May 1938), 161-67; Kingsley Davis, "Adolescence and the Social Structure," *Annals Am. Academy of Political and Social Science, 236* (1944), 9-16; Kingsley Davis, "Sociology of Parent-Youth Conflict," *Am. Sociological Rev., 5* (August 1940), 523-35; Ralph W. England, "A Theory of Middle Class Delinquency," *J. Crim. Law, Criminology and Police Science, 50* (Mar.–Apr. 1960), 535-40.

to such alternative behavior retards preparation for conventional adult life.[9]

The influence of delinquent subcultures in promoting youth crime is strongly suggested by the fact that eighty to ninety per cent of offenses referred to juvenile courts involve two or more juveniles as associates in the offense. Similarly, the proportion of inmates having co-defendants or "rap-partners" in their offense also is regularly higher in youth prisons and reformatories than in penitentiaries for adult offenders, being about three-fourths in the former institutions and half or less in the latter. (It also is higher among urban than among rural offenders.) Youth crime seems to be predominantly a phenomenon of urban adolescents giving each other social support in the promotion of delinquent subcultures. Each involvement in crime, and each experience of arrest and correctional confinement, may increase a youth's alienation from home and school at the same time that it enhances his prestige and self-esteem in delinquent social circles. This would explain the inverse relationship between ages of first arrest or conviction and recidivism.

The foregoing implies that crime is fostered by the failure of the home to achieve adequately the conventionalizing influences which it is expected to have upon the transition from childhood to adulthood. Such an interpretation is supported by the finding that, despite the frequent inadequacy of parents of criminals as anticriminal influences:

B3. The earlier an offender of any age left home, the more likely he is to continue in crime.

As Table 3.3 indicates, this pattern of higher failure rate with earlier departure from home predominated in our sample of 1956 federal releasees, although it was not as consistent as the relationships of age of release and age at first arrest to failure rates.[10]

TABLE 3.3   Postrelease Failure Rate of Federal Prisoners in Relation to Age of First Leaving Home or Foster Home for Six Months or More

Age of first leaving home	14 and under	15	16	17	18	19	20–21	22–25	26 and over	No info.
Failure rate	50%	40%	41%	39%	36%	26%	25%	36%	22%	25%
Number of cases	122	53	88	178	139	84	120	83	41	107

[9] Prominent in the literature on the development of delinquent subcultures are: Richard A. Cloward and Lloyd E. Ohlin, *Delinquency and Opportunity* (Glencoe, Ill., Free Press, 1960); Albert K. Cohen, *Delinquent Boys* (Glencoe, Ill., Free Press, 1955); Clifford Shaw and Henry D. McKay, *Juvenile Delinquency and Urban Areas* (Chicago, University of Chicago Press, 1942).

[10] Point-biserial correlation coefficient between age at first leaving home and postrelease success was 0.13. A point-biserial correlation this high in a sample of this size and dispersion would occur by chance alone less than once in a thousand times.

Some years ago I demonstrated that violation or nonviolation of parole by young Illinois felons could be predicted more accurately by knowledge of when they first left home for six months or more (or by any of several other objective facts) than by the prognoses made by psychiatrists or sociologists from their case studies of these parolees.[11]

The finding that the later a person is first involved in crime, the less likely he is to continue in crime, presumably reflects the fact that the later he is first involved in crime, the further the home and other agencies have been able to progress in preparing him for conventional adult roles. It also suggests that his identification with conventional persons is more firmly rooted and thus can compete more successfully with any criminalizing influences which he may experience in the pursuit of crime or in prison.

The analogy between crime and infancy, cited earlier as an explanation for the inverse relationships between age and recidivism, carries only the correctional implication that training programs should be provided for youthful criminals. The evidence that youth involved in crime are alienated from conventional adults and have internalized delinquent subcultures, as an explanation for these inverse relationships, has a somewhat different correctional implication. It suggests that even more important than the training programs is alteration of the social relationships of these offenders, in and out of prison, so as to alter the types of persons they aspire to become.

The implications of juvenile and youth crime for lifelong recidivism appear particularly ominous in view of current population trends. It is anticipated that between 1960 and 1970, when the total population of the United States increases by about 19 per cent, the population in the age range fifteen through nineteen will increase by about 44 per cent, and the population in the age range twenty through twenty-four will increase by 53 per cent. At the same time, the median number of years of schooling completed by the United States population will increase from 10.8 to 12 years.[12] This means that there will be larger numbers of youth and a longer period in which they can become diverted from the prevailing training requirements for conventional adult life, so that more may be attracted by delinquent subcultures. The fact that our population is increasingly becoming more urban further augments the prospect for an increase in the extent of youth crime.

OFFENSE AND RECIDIVISM

In discussing crime and its correction it generally is convenient to refer to all types of felony offenses, and to the prisoners who have committed them, as though the offenses were identical. This may sometimes acquire

[11] Daniel Glaser, "The Efficacy of Alternative Approaches to Parole Prediction," *Am. Sociological Rev., 20,* no. 3 (June 1955), 283-87.

[12] Phillip M. Hauser, *Population Perspectives* (New Brunswick, N. J., Rutgers University Press, 1960), pp. 41, 45.

a *post hoc* justification by the fact that, to a large extent, correctional agencies treat persons who commit all types of felonies very similarly, regardless of differences in the nature of their offenses. All felons are placed in institutions and released under the same parole procedures. All grounds for confinement in prison lead to the same ultimate status, that of ex-convict.

Apart from this uniformity in consequences, over ninety per cent of the felony crimes reported to the police have another major characteristic in common: they are economic offenses, that is, efforts to procure someone else's money or property. Nevertheless, there are vast differences in the types of behavior that may serve as illegal means to economic ends. One offender may "borrow" or rent a car with no intention of returning it, while another procures the victim's goods by waving a gun and threatening to shoot; one offender misrepresents his purposes so that his victims voluntarily, even eagerly, relinquish their money, while another procures money by forging a signature or by altering records. Of course, the most common technique in economic offenses is to remove the victim's goods by stealth, when no one is watching. The crimes that have no readily evident economic objective are also diverse in behavior, ranging from homicidal assault to indulgence in narcotics, and from felonious avoidance of military service to indecent sexual liberties.

One barrier to classification of criminals by offense is the frequency with which they mix their offenses. Most drug addicts in prison both purchased narcotics illegally and paid for them with stolen money. Often autos are stolen for use in the commission of burglaries or robberies, or youths flee across country in a stolen car and commit other crimes to meet their needs during the trip. Nevertheless, most criminals are committed to prison for only one type of offense, and others can be classified by that offense which the law has treated most seriously. It is especially important to consider separately those offenses that are differentiated in the social relationships by which they are promoted, in the self-conceptions they inspire, in the risk of apprehension they involve, and in the sentence and parole decisions they are likely to evoke.

Table 3.4 presents the relationship of offense to failure rate for three samples of federal offenders and for California parolees. The 1956 federal releasees (also used for the preceding tables in this chapter) and the Federal Youth Correction Act cases were described in chapter 2. The sample called "long-termers" consists of all federal male prisoners released during the fiscal year 1957-58 on sentences of five years or more, for the offense categories indicated in Table 3.4. (These offenses covered about three-fifths of all federal releasees with such sentences.) Postrelease information was available in parole supervision files for these cases because federal prisoners with sentences of this length are either paroled for as much as two-thirds of their sentence or are released by "mandatory release" (formerly called

Table 3.4 Postrelease Failure Rate of Federal and California Prisoners in Relation to Offense

Primary offense on last sentence	1956 FEDERAL RELEASES				ALL FEDERAL YOUTH CORR. ACT RELEASEES, 1955–58		FEDERAL "LONG-TERMERS" RELEASED 1957–58		ALL CALIFORNIA PAROLEES, 1959	
	Failure rate	Median age		No. of cases	Failure rate	No. of cases	Failure rate	No. of cases	Reimprisonment in two years	No. of cases
		At first arrest	At release							
Auto theft	47%	17.2	25.6	341	55%	656	55%	143	52%	185
Other theft or burglary	38%	20.8	30.3	141	43%	77	46%	72	42%	1412
Forgery or counterfeiting	35%	20.6	34.3	68	45%	64	44%	70	42%	1116
Narcotics offenses	30%	20.5	30.7	132	—	—	28%	281	40%	825
"Moonshine" (illicit liquor transactions)	29%	21.3	38.4	106	—	—	—	—	—	—
Robbery or kidnapping	28%	21.2	29.8	32	35%	37	30%	125	38%	829
Nonrobbery assault (including homicide and rape)	18%	22.2	28.5	40	—	—	—	—	24%	288
Income tax fraud or embezzlement	16%	31.8	43.5	25	—	—	—	—	—	—
All other offenses	22%	21.6	30.4	130	23%	135	—	—	31%	543
Total cases	35%	20.6	29.6	1015	49%	969	—	—	39%	5198

43

"conditional release") and supervised as though on parole for the time deducted from the sentence for good behavior in prison, less 180 days. The median postrelease supervision period for these long-termers was 17.2 months.

It should be noted that 53 per cent of the returns of parolees to prison in California did not involve conviction for new felonies and that the follow-up period was only two years.[13]

The several samples in Table 3.4 all support the same broad conclusion:

B4. Felony offenses fall into three broad rankings of recidivism, as follows:
    a. The most recidivistic category consists of economic offenses not involving violence (larceny, burglary, auto theft, and forgery), and the most recidivistic single type of felony is auto theft.
    b. Consistently intermediate in recidivism rate are several common but diverse types of crime, such as narcotics offenses, robbery, and kidnapping.
    c. The lowest recidivism occurs with those offenses most associated with unusual circumstances in the offender's life rather than with offenses pursued as vocations; notable here are murder, rape, and embezzlement.

Auto Theft

Stealing cars is primarily an offense of young persons. The high failure rate with this type of thief reflects the inverse relationship between age and recidivism, already discussed. As Table 3.4 shows, these are the youngest federal offenders in terms of both age at release and age at first arrest. Federal auto thieves are mostly tried for interstate transportation of stolen autos (Dyer Act violations), so that, on the whole, they are probably more mobile persons than auto thieves in state prisons. This also is evident in their relatively high rates of escape from prison and absconding from parole. Over ninety per cent of stolen autos are recovered, although only about a fourth of the thefts are cleared by arrest, slightly fewer lead to persons being charged, and only 23 per cent of persons charged are found guilty.[14] This high rate of recovery of stolen autos but not of the thieves confirms impressions that this crime generally is committed to provide immediate

[13] California Department of Corrections, *Number and Percent of Men Returned to California Prison With a New Commitment During 24 Months After Parole Date* (Research Division, Admin., Statistics Section, March 1, 1962).

[14] Federal Bureau of Investigation, *Crime in the United States,* Uniform Crime Reports—1962 (Washington, D. C., 1963), pp. 87, 89. On auto theft see also Erwin Schepses, "Boys Who Steal Cars," *Federal Probation, 25,* no. 1 (March 1961), 56-62; William W. Wattenberg and James Balistrieri, "Automobile Theft: a 'Favored Group Delinquency,'" *Am. J. Sociology, 57* (May 1952), 575-79; Irwin A. Berg, "A Comparative Study of Car Thieves," *J. Crim. Law, Criminology and Police Science, 24,* no. 6 (Mar.–April 1944), 392-96.

transportation rather than as a criminal vocation. However, the relatively low rate of apprehension and conviction suggests that most auto thieves have considerable experience in using stolen vehicles without police interference, and thus may readily be tempted to gamble on another theft. For example, one of our returned violator cases boasted that he had stolen over two hundred cars and had been caught only five times.

Forgery

Forgers generally are older than most prisoners, as indicated in our 1956 sample by a median age at release of 34.3 years. However, a distinctive characteristic of forgers is the large proportion who are chronic alcoholics. They commonly have a misdemeanor record in conjunction with drinking which begins at a much earlier age than their forgery, though frequently early forgery is paid off and settled out of court by their families. This misdemeanor record accounts for their having a median age at first arrest fourteen years lower than their median age at release. Data are not available on rates of apprehension in forgery, but the nature of the offense means that the risk involved seldom is immediate: the falsity of a check generally is discovered only some days after it is cashed. Forgery also differs from most other offenses in being more often committed alone, and by individuals who do not seem to identify themselves with other criminals.[15]

Larceny and Burglary

As the high recidivism rate for larceny and burglary suggests, these crimes are often pursued as regular occupations. Specialists in such larceny as shoplifting, theft from parked autos, theft from mail boxes, and pickpocketing are commonly encountered among professional felons. Burglary also is plied as a regular trade for long periods. Many narcotic addicts support their habit by larceny. The proportion of burglary and larceny offenses cleared by arrest and conviction is low. Also, larceny often is prosecuted only as a petty-larceny misdemeanor when the amount taken is small, even when the offender's prior criminal record permits his prosecution for the felony of grand larceny, regardless of the amount stolen. Furthermore, involvement in burglary and larceny promotes personal relationships that

[15] See Edwin M. Lemert, "The Behavior of the Systematic Check Forger," *Social Problems, 6* (Fall 1958), 141-49; E. M. Lemert, "An Isolation and Closure Theory of Naïve Check Forgery," *J. Crim. Law, Criminology and Police Science, 44,* no. 3 (Sept.–Oct. 1953), 296-307; Irwin A. Berg, "A Comparative Study of Forgery," *J. Applied Psychology, 28,* no. 3, (June 1944), 232-38. See also the description of alcoholic forgers in Norman S. Hayner, "Characteristics of Five Offender Types," *Am. Sociological Rev., 26,* no. 1 (Feb. 1961), 96-102.

encourage crime. Familiar in life histories of criminals are accounts of the influence of dealers in stolen property ("fences") in promoting crime, as well as the influence of some lawyers or corrupt officials from whom the thief may procure assistance in reducing penalties. (Usually, this reduction is achieved by pleading guilty to a lesser charge while indicating that the prosecutor will find prosecution on a more serious charge highly time-consuming and perhaps uncertain.) Finally, considerable association among thieves is reported, not only as accomplices, but also in various taverns and other "hangouts" where they recognize each other as thieves and thus give a social support to their crimes.[16]

Narcotics Offenses

Some theorists on the subject of drug addiction assume that virtually no one ceases a drug habit once he has become addicted. Table 3.4 indicates that an appreciable proportion of men released from prison for narcotics offenses have no further difficulty with the law. Unfortunately, the available records do not permit us to tabulate postrelease data separately for drug traffickers who were addicts and for those who were not.

Drug usage was associated with middle age until after World War II, but there is evidence that most new drug addicts since 1945 became addicted before the age of 25.[17] If addicts never stopped using drugs, however, there

[16] The classic work here is E. H. Sutherland, *The Professional Thief* (Chicago, University of Chicago Press, 1937). See also David W. Maurer, *Whiz Mob: A Correlation of the Technical Argot of Pickpockets With Their Behavior Pattern* (Gainesville, Fla., American Dialect Society, 1955); Alfred T. Nelson, *Car Clouting* (Springfield, Ill., C. C. Thomas, 1959); Gerald D. Robin, "Patterns of Department Store Shoplifting," *Crime and Delinquency, 9,* no. 2 (April 1963), 163-72. My references to the associations of thieves are derived also from many long conversations with Chicago burglars and "boosters" in Illinois prisons.

[17] See statistics in James V. Lowry, "Hospital Treatment of the Narcotic Addict," *Federal Probation, 20,* no. 4 (Dec. 1956), 42-51; California Bur. of Criminal Statistics, *Narcotic Arrests and Their Dispositions in California, 1960* (Sacramento, 1961), p. 19. Principal works on drug addiction include: David W. Maurer and Victor Vogel, *Narcotics and Narcotics Addiction* (Springfield, Ill., Thomas, 1954); David P. Ausubel, *Drug Addiction* (New York, Random House, 1960); Alfred R. Lindesmith, *Opiate Addiction* (Bloomington, Ind., Principia Press, 1947). None of the above treats adequately the relationship of narcotics usage in the United States today to a life in crime. Also, none deals with stimulation to drug usage from the addict's conception of himself and his colleagues as living a life superior to that of most other people ("squares") by virtue of his distinctive experiences, a conception which is promoted by the addict social world. This is well described in Harold Finestone, "Cats, Kicks and Color," *Social Problems, 5* (July 1957), 3-13, and in Marsh B. Ray, "The Cycle of Abstinence and Relapse Among Heroin Addicts," *Social Problems, 9,* no. 2 (Fall 1961), 132-40.

would now be in the United States either: (1) a majority of addicts over 30 years of age, (2) a multiplication by several fold since 1955 in the rate of early-age introduction to drug usage, or (3) a more than 50 per cent rate of death before the age of 30 among addicts. While available statistics are imperfect, they strongly suggest that none of these alternatives has occurred. Therefore, one must assume that a substantial proportion of those who became involved in narcotic offenses in the 1945–55 period have ended this activity, as is suggested by the information in Table 3.4. Long-run programs for statistical research by the Sociology Section of the U. S. Public Health Service Addiction Research Center at Lexington, Kentucky, may provide more precise knowledge of rates of return to drug usage and may relate these rates to age, length of confinement, and other variables. Their preliminary data, in 1962, suggested that rates of return to drug usage are high when an addict returns to a community where addiction is concentrated, such as slum areas of our largest cities, but are not nearly as high if he settles elsewhere.

In our long-termer sample, those convicted for marijuana offenses were separated from other narcotics-law violators. Fifty-two marijuana cases had only 17 per cent failure rate, and only 10 per cent incurred new prison sentences. The other narcotics cases had a 30 per cent violation rate, with 14 per cent convicted of new felonies. Much state legislation on narcotics does not distinguish between marijuana and heroin or other narcotics offenses, on the assumption that involvement in marijuana necessarily leads to involvement in more addictive drugs. This seems to be a questionable assumption. In general, more diverse treatment of narcotics offenders than present laws permit, dealing with each according to his individual characteristics, is suggested by most of this project's findings on these cases.

Illicit Liquor Transactions

The "moonshiners," a distinctive type of federal prisoner, are almost entirely from Southern rural areas, although a few are Southern migrants in Northern cities who met unemployment by this resource from their cultural heritage. Our interviews in the Federal Probation Offices in Kentucky and on rural field trips with the staff of these offices revealed the extent to which this is a crime of cultural conflict. In the areas where this offense is concentrated, the techniques have been passed down from generation to generation, with little change for more than a century. Indeed, the "stills" usually are family enterprises. Although most of the imprisoned moonshiners studied in this project were of lower-economic-class background and many had a prior misdemeanor record, some had no other misconduct and were well accepted in community social life. Penalties in moonshine offenses often are mild at first, and recidivism may be kept at a moderate level in part by shifting the risk of apprehension to other members of the family when one member becomes vulnerable to more severe penalties.

Robbery

Robbery probably has an intermediate recidivism rate because much of it is committed by persons who are not habitual criminals but who seek money with a gun when they feel themselves in desperate financial straits. Of course, there also are professional armed robbers, including a number of specialists in bank robbery who receive federal prison sentences. These are not as numerous among releasees as in the total prison population because their sentences are extremely long. Most federal robberies are armed robberies, frequently in the daytime, and the attention they receive from the police may deter their repetition. Unarmed night robberies by slum gangs, such as the "rolling" of drunks, more often lead to state imprisonment, are less readily solved by police action, and have entrenched support in delinquent subcultures; these features may contribute to greater recidivism rates for robbers in state correctional systems. For robbery in the United States as a whole, police report 40 per cent cleared by arrest.[18]

Assault and Other Offenses

The lowest recidivism rates indicated in Table 3.4 are for offenses which are least often criminal vocations. Assaultive acts, such as homicide and rape, occur in situations of unusual emotion and seem to be greatly deterred by confinement. Embezzlement or income-tax fraud are offenses of older persons in business or professional occupations who had to succeed in noncriminal careers before they could reach the positions where they committed these crimes. Therefore, they are better equipped than most released prisoners in the abilities, personal ties, and motivation needed to achieve a noncriminal life. The "other offenses" category, for California parolees, has a rather high violation rate because about a third of its cases are persons serving sentences for escape from a correctional facility; these had a 67 per cent parole violation rate—even higher than that of California auto thieves.

The tabulations in Table 3.4 show the relative rank, from a recidivism risk standpoint, of the most common types of offense leading to confinement in prison in the United States. This relative rank is shown to be highly uniform in the diverse samples studied, despite somewhat different indexes of recidivism in the federal and the California cases. Some further differentiation of offenses would be useful, particularly with respect to sex offenders in state prisons, but such a refinement of this analysis must wait until more adequate postrelease information is available, on larger samples of cases,

18 Federal Bureau of Investigation, *op. cit.*, p. 87.

through the programs suggested in chapter 2. The data presented here suffice to indicate much of the variation in commitment to crime that is encountered among American prisoners.

PRIOR CRIMINAL RECORD AND RECIDIVISM

The most obvious index of the extent of commitment to crime is, of course, the number of previous offenses that a prisoner is known to have perpetrated. As indicated in the preceding section, only a fraction of the total felonies committed are officially recorded, since criminals are arrested in only about a fourth of all major crimes, and over a third of the arrests that "clear" these offenses in police records are not followed by convictions. Nevertheless, one can classify released prisoners only by the prior offenses that appear in their official record and assume that the frequency of these officially recorded prior offenses is roughly proportional to the total volume of their prior criminality. All the evidence tends to support the obvious conclusion:

B5. The extent of the offender's prior criminal record and the likelihood of his becoming a recidivist are directly correlated.

There are many ways of classifying a record of prior offenses. Some of these alternatives are indicated in Table 3.5. The variation in such modes of classification makes it difficult to compare data from different tabulations. Somewhat diverse ways of categorizing this record occur even with the two samples of federal releasees analyzed in Table 3.5. This is because the 1956 cases were classified into categories developed by project staff using narrative information in prison case study reports, while the Youth Correction Act cases were tabulated by utilizing cards on which they already had been classified by the Bureau of Prisons.

Table 3.5 indicates that no matter how one counts the volume of prior felony involvement, the failure rate tends to increase as the magnitude of prior criminality increases. However, the effects of prior criminality and of age seem to counteract each other. After a certain point, an increase in prior sentences, which is directly related to recidivism, also means an increase in age, which is inversely related to recidivism. This may explain the tendency of recidivism rates to stop increasing appreciably with additional prior felony convictions after the first two or three, although there is a sharp increase from none to one prior conviction.

An alternative to classifying prior criminality by the number of felony convictions or penal confinements is to assess prior sentences in terms of their presumed seriousness. As can be seen in Table 3.5, the most unfavorable prognosis is not for the institution usually regarded as most serious, the penitentiary. The greatest recidivism occurs with those prison inmates who previously were committed to a juvenile training school and have not previously been in a reformatory or penitentiary. This probably is a con-

TABLE 3.5   Postrelease Failure Rates of Federal Prisoners in Relation to Various Classifications of Prior Criminal Record

Classification of prior criminal record	10% SAMPLE, 1956 FEDERAL RELEASEES		FEDERAL YOUTH CORRECTION ACT RELEASEES, 1955–58	
	Failure rate	No. of cases	Failure rate	No. of cases
Number of prior sentences for felony-type offenses:				
None	25%	425	—	—
One	37%	221	—	—
Two	44%	153	—	—
Three	47%	96	—	—
Four or more	46%	120	—	—
Number of prior penal institution commitments (nonmilitary):				
None	—	—	42%	519
One	—	—	51%	287
Two	—	—	64%	153
Three or more	—	—	68%	63
Most serious prior penal institution commitment (nonmilitary):				
None	24%	334	42%	519
Jail (or equivalent institution)	30%	203	48%	166
Training school (or other institution for juveniles only)	55%	84	65%	210
Reformatory	41%	46	57%	44
Penitentiary	43%	348	47%	30
Most serious record of those with no prior penal institution record:				
No prior criminal record at all	15%	124	—	—
Arrests or fines only	25%	135	—	—
Probation only (without jail sentence)	35%	75	—	—

sequence of the inverse effects of age of first arrest and first leaving home, already discussed. Commitment to juvenile training schools generally occurs at fifteen to seventeen years of age, and those sent to these institutions usually have a serious prior arrest, supervision, and detention record in their communities.

Table 3.5 also indicates definitely less recidivism when there is no prior criminal record whatsoever, as against having a prior record of arrests, fines, or probation. This also is confirmed in state tabulations. In addition, California statistics indicate that prisoners with three or more prior sentences for misdemeanors, without previous felony sentences, have as unfavorable a prognosis with respect to either parole violation or new felony conviction as those with two or more prior prison commitments.[19]

RECIDIVISM IN RELATIONSHIP TO OTHER VARIABLES

Attributes such as nature of offense, prior criminality, and age, which are related to recidivism, provide an index of the quality of the raw material with which a correctional program must labor to promote noncriminal post-release lives. Many other characteristics of offenders are relevant for this purpose, such as their education or work experience, but since these can be altered by correctional programs, it is more appropriate to discuss them when reporting on these programs later in this volume. However, many other variables besides offense, prior criminality, and age cannot be changed by the prison. Those attributes presumed to be especially immune to alteration are traits that are considered part of one's biological endowment, such as race, intelligence, and bodily structure.

Race

In every tabulation that we have made of the failure rates of federal prisoners, and in every tabulation that we have encountered of recidivism of state prisoners, little difference was found between the recidivism rates of Negroes and whites. Our sample of 1956 federal releasees included 732 white inmates whose failure rate was 34.7 per cent, 269 Negro inmates whose failure rate was 35.3 per cent, and fourteen inmates classified in other racial categories (Indian or Oriental) of whom six were failures. Our Youth Correction Act sample included 810 whites with a failure rate of 50.6 per cent, 147 Negroes with a failure rate of 52.4 per cent, and eleven classified in other racial groups with a 36 per cent failure rate. In the California study we have cited, 3741 whites had a 51.5 per cent violation rate, 1071 Negroes had a 50.5 per cent violation rate, and 710 Mexicans had a 49.6 per cent violation rate. None of these differences, in any of the studies, is statistically significant. The only appreciable difference found to be related to race was the California category of "other races," presumably mostly Orientals, in which 148 cases had a 30.4 per cent violation rate.[20] Probably cultural differences and the close community and family mutual aid in Oriental minorities account for both their low recidivism rate and their low overall crime rates. However, the economic or other factors responsible for differences between Negroes and whites in overall crime rates

[19] California Director of Corrections and Adult Authority, *California Male Prisoners Released on Parole 1946-49,* p. 21.
[20] *Loc. cit.*

do not seem to have an unequal effect upon postrelease recidivism rates of Negro and white prisoners.

Intelligence

Intelligence is another variable usually presumed to be a function of biological inheritance, although every measurement of intelligence seems to be affected somewhat by nonhereditary differences in learning experience and in motivation to perform well. All efforts to correlate intelligence and parole violation or recidivism rates have indicated a rather small relationship only, usually not involving a consistent pattern. This was evident with our 1956 federal releasees, for whom the lowest failure rate among ten-point ranges in I.Q. was 29 per cent, which was found in both the 80 through 89 and the 110 through 119 range. The intervening range, 90 through 99, had the highest failure rate, 40 per cent. All of the other ten-point ranges in I.Q. were within two or three percentage units of the sample's overall rate of 35 per cent. In the California 1946-49 analysis parole-violation rates varied from a low of 44.4 per cent for the brightest parolees, classified "superior," to a high of 52.1 per cent for the next to the lowest intelligence category, "borderline"; the "bright normal," "average," "dull normal" and "defective" categories differed by less than one per cent from the sample average of 50.6 per cent.[21]

Body Build

Not much information is available on the relationship of other presumed biological factors to recidivism. In a parole-prediction analysis some years ago, Vold found that height and weight had no appreciable relationship to parole violation.[22] In our 1956 releasees, both the 8 per cent with slight physical handicaps and the 3 per cent with major disabilities (severely restricting employability) had a 31 per cent failure rate, as against 35 per cent for the rest of the sample. Elaborate research has been conducted on the relationship between delinquency and body build, leading to the conclusion that delinquents are husky (mesomorphic) somewhat more frequently than nondelinquents, the latter being more often thin (ectomorphic) or paunchy (endomorphic).[23] Such research, however, has yet to show that it is not simply demonstrating the social selection of husky youth by

[21] *Ibid.*, p. 25.

[22] George B. Vold, *Prediction Methods and Parole* (Hanover, N. H., The Sociological Press, 1931).

[23] Sheldon and Eleanor T. Glueck, *Physique and Delinquency* (New York, Harpers, 1956); William D. Sheldon, Emil M. Hartl, and Eugene McDermott, *Varieties of Delinquent Youth* (New York, Harpers, 1949); E. H. Sutherland, "Critique of Sheldon's *Varieties of Delinquent Youth*," *Am. Sociological Rev., 16* (Feb. 1951), 10-13.

delinquent gangs in high delinquency areas. Furthermore, research on released prisoners, rather than on delinquents, would be necessary to show any relevance of body build to recidivism reduction.

An assumption of this book is that the treatment of criminals can be based on scientific knowledge only if the effects of correctional action are systematically investigated. This chapter has discussed a further prerequisite to such science—namely, that those factors which affect recidivism independently of correctional action should be investigated. It has been shown that especially important among these factors are age, type of offense, and previous criminality. Some interrelationships of these variables with each other are reported in chapters 13 and 18, and they are interrelated throughout this book with aspects of prison and postrelease experience.

CHAPTER 4

Variations in Postrelease
"Success" and "Failure"

To permit brief generalizations, it is convenient to classify released prisoners as either "successes" or "failures" with reference to their reformation. Such classification makes the statistical statements and tables in this book less complex than they otherwise would be. Nevertheless, the practice of merely dichotomizing postrelease performance hides a tremendous amount of variation. Each case is unique in some respect, and the most intriguing details will be overlooked if one presses too hard for simple conclusions.

Those who have lived in both the criminal and the conventional social worlds may walk a zig-zag path between the two, although many eventually make a clear turn into one or the other of these worlds. In hopes of adding a more clearly human picture to our statistics in the preceding and the following chapters, it seems appropriate at this point to describe some specific cases illustrative of the many variations in postrelease "success" and "failure." These cases are drawn from our "Intensive Study of Matched Samples of Violators and Nonviolators."

The *successes* to be described here were men whom we interviewed when they had been on federal parole or mandatory release for over a year (in 1960 and 1961). The *failures* were men whom we interviewed in federal prisons in 1958 and 1959, where they had been returned for a previous parole or mandatory release violation. (See Appendix D for further details on the sample and on the research procedure.)

Each success case was classified as having made either a *clear reformation* or a *marginal reformation*. Persistence in the pursuit of legitimate occupations and avoidance of clearly delinquent or criminal associates were taken as indexes of clear reformation. The marginal reformation category comprised all cases who were not declared violators despite failure to meet these two criteria of clear reformation. Each failure case was classified as a *marginal failure* if he committed no postrelease felonies and a *clear recidivism case* if he had returned to felonious behavior. Variation within these four broad categories, each of which has been subdivided from a different standpoint, is described in this chapter. These subdivisions, and the fictitious names assigned to actual cases which are presented to illustrate them, are as follows:

"Success" Cases
  Clear Reformation
    a. Late reformation after criminal career (Lawrence, Louis, Lester, Leonard, Lee)
    b. Early reformation after criminal career (Ernie, Elwood, Eddie)
    c. Crime-facilitated reformation (Frank, Felix)
    d. Reformation after crime interval (Ira, Ichabod)
    e. Reformation after only one felony (Oliver, Oscar)
    f. Crime-interrupted noncriminal career (Ivan, Irwin)
  Marginal Reformation
    a. Economic retreatism (Everett, Ezra)
    b. Juvenile retreatism (Jerry, Jimmy)
    c. Addictive retreatism (Albert, Arthur, Angus)
    d. Crime-contacting noncriminality (Clifford, Clarence)
    e. Nonimprisoned criminality (Nick, Norman)

"Failure" Cases
  Marginal Failure
    a. Defective-communication cases (Dennis, Dave, Don)
    b. Other nonfelony violations (Tom, Dick, Harry)
  Clear Recidivism
    a. Deferred recidivism (Dudley, Douglas, Duncan)
    b. Immediate recidivism (Ralph, Robert)

CLEAR REFORMATION CASES

The releasees who appeared clearly to have become noncriminal in behavior and associates were differentiated according to the extent of their prior criminality. Those who had three or more felony convictions at different times, counting that on which they last were released, or who had depended primarily on crime for a livelihood for five or more years, were designated as having had *criminal careers.* Those with only two such felony convictions, or with one conviction but evidence of having also been involved in a felony at another time, but with less than five years' dependence primarily on crime, were referred to as having had *crime intervals.* Finally, those who appeared to have committed but one felony, which resulted in their one prison sentence, were called *one-crime* cases.

The criminal-career cases were further divided into *late-reformation* cases, where their last release from prison was at the age of thirty or more, and *early-reformation* cases, where their last release from prison occurred before their thirtieth birthday. Independently of this, one separate group of criminal-career cases was noted whose change from crime was *facilitated by crime.* Also considered separately are one-felony and crime-interval cases for whom a year or more of clear self-sufficiency in a noncriminal occupation, without disorderly or criminal associates, preceded the federal imprisonment from which they were successfully released. In these cases, the postrelease behavior was seen not so much as reformation as a renewal of precriminal behavior that had been *interrupted* by crime.

Late Reformation After Criminal Career

These are the cases that justify the maxim that no human being should ever be regarded as hopelessly criminal. Today all are law-abiding and orderly, yet a decade or less earlier most were condemned as psychopaths. They include men who were considered the most criminal and intractable prisoners in the entire federal system. Such was the record of Case S-122, who shall be called "Lawrence."

Lawrence had an almost continuous history of criminality from his commitment to a state training school when thirteen years old to his release at age thirty-one on his fourth prison sentence. His crime generally was auto theft, at first for transportation, but, at his last two convictions, as part of a ring which was forging ownership papers and selling the automobiles. On the three previous imprisonments he violated parole or conditional release, each time by a new felony, but this time he has been out of prison over seven years and has given no indication of further criminality. After his last release he held his first job for five years, starting as a stock clerk and ending as head of the shipping department. When sale of the firm with which he was employed was followed by the new management's requirement that all employees be bonded, he quit from fear that his criminal record would prevent his being accepted by a bonding company.

Impatient after some months of unemployment, Lawrence took a job as an insurance salesman, despite a bonding requirement. While in prison the last time he had completed high school and had taken correspondence courses in salesmanship and practical psychology. He hoped to utilize this training now, if only to earn a few weeks' income before the company processed his bond. He was indeed rejected by the bonding firm, but this was three months later. By that time his new employers were so pleased with his work that they allowed him to post a cash bond, part of which they lent him. After a year as a salesman he opened his own insurance brokerage, employing several salesmen. When we interviewed him and his probation officer a year later, his business was reported to be secure and prosperous. Although two marriages on previous paroles ended in divorce, his current marriage, despite a rocky beginning, has lasted five years. He has his own home and there is every reason to believe that he will continue indefinitely as a stable and conventional member of his community.

"Louis," Case S-837, was introduced to crime at the age of eleven when he was placed with a foster family who earned their living by bootlegging. A few years later, when prohibition was repealed, he and his foster brothers entered the bank-robbery business. After a few months he split with them, but continued robbing banks and other establishments alone or with other partners. For five years he was on the F.B.I.'s "Most Wanted" list. He also was addicted to narcotics. Most of this time he lived with a female addict and moved from city to city, spending his money lavishly on night clubs, narcotics, and gambling.

Today Louis has been out of prison almost seven years, after sixteen years in prison. He now is so respected in the small community where he lives that he has been asked to run for elective office. He refused because of fear that such public attention might lead to publicity about his criminal background. He has had regular employment at a skilled trade learned in prison, and lives on a small farmstead from which he procures most of his family's food. He is an excellent husband and a devoted father to children whom his wife brought from a previous marriage. He seemed nervous during the interview and explained that this was because he has tried not to think of his earlier criminal life.

"Lester," Case S-517, started his criminal record with six months' probation for larceny, when fourteen years old. He subsequently completed another probation term, a reformatory sentence, and was twenty-five years old and in the fifth year of a state penitentiary term when he escaped. The next six months were filled with bank robberies. On two occasions he and his associates disarmed and kidnapped law-enforcement officers who tried to stop them. He was captured after gunfire exchange with F.B.I. men, then served twenty-two years in federal confinement, ten of them in Alcatraz. He next was released to the state prison from which he had escaped more than two decades earlier, and was immediately given thirty days' solitary confinement on bread, water, and occasional peanut butter, to demonstrate to others the state's attitude on escaping. Eight months later he was paroled under joint federal and state supervision.

In his three years of freedom, Lester has progressed from poorly paid and temporary employment as a hamburger cook, to employment as a new-car salesman, working on commission only. He has become the top salesman with his company. Lester, now around fifty years old, makes such a favorable impression that it is difficult to picture him as the dangerous criminal he was in his twenties. His major complaint concerns the unethical sales technique of some of his colleagues, and he has been seeking employment in another field.

"Leonard," Case S-534, ran away from home when thirteen years old. The first entry in his F.B.I. fingerprint file is arrest for vagrancy, far from home, just before his sixteenth birthday. Half a year later, still a migrant during the 1930's, he received a prison sentence for burglary. He escaped, was soon recaptured and was given additional sentences for escape and assault. He had falsified his name, age, and life history, so his parents could not be informed of his criminality. Three years later, when paroled to a city in the state where he was incarcerated, he absconded to the home of his parents, in another region of the United States. Three months after this he robbed a bank, for which he was arrested a week later, but not before he had shot one state policeman and kidnapped another.

Leonard was paroled in 1954 after seventeen years of federal confinement, half at Alcatraz and half at Leavenworth. He was unemployed for several months, but finally obtained a job as a carpenter's helper. When the construction season ended, he was employed in a steel mill until a retired policeman working on plant security recognized him as a notorious criminal of twenty years earlier, and he was discharged. He obtained other jobs, however, primarily as a shipfitter. In his free time he started construction of his own home, doing all work himself, and he moved into it in 1956. Our research staff member interviewed him there in 1961, and was most impressed by the craftsmanship of the home and the cordiality of his host.

"Lee," Case S-109, was a professional robber for ten years. His correctional experience began with a state-training-school commitment at age thirteen and included his voluntary recommitment there after maladjustment in a foster home. He subsequently acquired a reformatory sentence, a prison sentence, and several jail terms before he began his federal imprisonment when he was twenty-six years old. When he was released to Chicago after fifteen years' confinement, he was so disturbed by the downtown noises that he was afraid to seek employment, and expressed to his federal probation officer a desire to return to the prison. The officer took him to a relatively quiet neighborhood, where he procured a room overlooking a park. Fortunately, he had a few hundred dollars in prison savings, and it was suggested that he start with leisurely trips into the city, when he felt more confidence. Two weeks later he found temporary employment at unskilled work in a printing company. In a few months he procured work as a maintenance machinist, a task which he had performed well in prison industry. He remained at this job over four years, then moved to similar employment under better pay and working conditions elsewhere. About two years after his release from prison he married a divorced woman with several children, and they have had an additional child. He now is purchasing a home in the suburbs and seems securely established and contented in a conventional life.

The cases of Lawrence, Louis, Lester, Leonard, and Lee could be supplemented by many others from our files, equally illustrative of a pattern of clearly conventional life for many years after a fairly long period of criminality and a long incarceration. Most of these individuals had difficulties in procuring employment at first, but were assisted in this initial period by savings from prison earnings and by helpful relationships with their federal probation officers. Their ultimate success reflected useful work skills, education, or habits of diligence and perseverance, which most of them achieved for the first time in their lives in the course of a long prison term.

Early Reformation After Criminal Career

Most of the men in the category described and illustrated in the preceding section were past thirty years old at their last release from prison. As the statistics of chapter 3 indicate, they were at an age where a decline in recidivism could be expected. However, many of our cases who established a clearly conventional life after an appreciable criminal career were less than thirty at the time of their last release.

"Ernie," Case S-981, violated five state-training-school and state-reformatory paroles between the age of thirteen and his commitment as a Federal Youth Correction Act offender at age twenty. His parole on this federal sentence occurred after thirty months of confinement, during which he had a poor prison record at first, and participated in an attempted riot. He states that when he was released he expected to have as much difficulty on this parole as on the previous ones which he violated, but when he saw that the federal probation officer was going to help him, he decided to make more of an effort to complete parole than he had previously.

During Ernie's first six months out, he had conflicts with older brothers with whom he first resided, his employment was unstable, and he received a short jail term for driving without a license. However, at last report Ernie, who now was not living with relatives, had been employed for nearly two years as steadily as weather permitted on outside construction work, had saved money, and was deliberately avoiding his former associates. Ernie's probation officer was confident that we were now dealing with an ex-criminal.

"Elwood," Case S-148, first was arrested for theft when ten years old. He was given probation for car theft when thirteen and was sent to the state training school a few months later for violating probation by stealing another car. He was paroled from the training school when fourteen years old. For the next two years his official criminal record was limited to disorderly conduct, reckless driving fines, and illegal possession of a pistol, but when sixteen he was given a Federal Youth Correction Act sentence for interstate transportation of a stolen auto. His prison record was not always good, but he progressed well in clerical work and was paroled when nineteen.

Elwood started his postrelease record with a resumption of drinking and reckless driving which led to a $200 fine and almost led to his return as a violator. However, at this point he was permitted to enroll in a court-reporting school at a metropolis several hundred miles away from the town in which all of his delinquency had occurred. He now lived in a YMCA and worked there part time while going to school. He later procured stenographic and court-reporting employment. Elwood has had no further difficulty in two years away from home. He has mastered an occupation for which there seems to be a steady demand, and he is now engaged and saving money for married life.

"Eddie," Case S-652, began his police record at age eleven by running away from home, and for the next eight years he was repeatedly in difficulty for running away, burglary, vandalism, car theft, and other offenses. During this period he received one state and one federal training-school commitment, and was finally sentenced to prison under the Federal Youth Correction Act for interstate transportation of stolen cars. Eddie seems to be an expert on the ignition switches of various autos. He explained to our interviewer how each variety of auto can be started by shorting the switch without also keeping the motor running. He said that he could not count the number of cars he has stolen for parties at drive-in movies, or for other escapades. Eddie also reminisced on committing many burglaries.

Eddie was paroled after thirty-two months of imprisonment, when twenty-one years old. During four of his first eight months out, he had fifteen to twenty-two contacts per month with his probation officer and six to eight contacts in each of the other four months, as contrasted with the usual one to four contacts per month expected of most parolees. This frequency, when Eddie was unemployed, was primarily at the insistence of his unusually strict, but concerned, probation officer. The probation officer made several score contacts with other persons on Eddie's behalf, and these efforts got Eddie four jobs, but he did not last long on any of them; either he quit in a few days or he was fired after a few weeks for being idle on the job. During the latter part of his first year out he was idle for several months when he was diagnosed as having tuberculosis, but this diagnosis was reversed a few months later after further tests.

In his second year on parole, Eddie worked two to four months at each job he received. His job termination always was due to completion of available work or his leaving to take a better job, rather than a discharge for unsatisfactory performance. At the time of our interview, during Eddie's third year on parole, his major accomplishment, in his own eyes and in those of the probation officer, was the fact that he had held one job for almost a year. He had also been saving regularly. After almost three and one-half years of supervision, he was discharged from his sentence.

Crime-Facilitated Reformation

A few releasees who now seem to be living clearly noncriminal lives, usually after long careers in crime, did not have nearly as severe a struggle as that of most ex-prisoners because their crimes provided resources for easily shifting to noncriminal success.

Perhaps the most striking of this group is "Frank," Case S-612, who at the age of fifty was publicized in national magazine articles as "the million dollar fence" and "the best friend a thief ever had." His twenty years in the stolen goods business had been interrupted by two years in a state prison, but apart from this, he survived numerous arrests and raids without receiving another conviction until a federal sentence in 1954. Following his mandatory release in 1959, Frank purchased a large trailer camp, in a state other than that in which his crime had been pursued. His lawyers successfully negotiated the withdrawal of new warrants initiated against him in his home state. As far as officials have been able to determine, he now is leading a noncriminal life, busily developing his trailer park into a showplace and actively participating in local civic and fraternal organizations.

Another case of this rare type is "Felix," S-308, convicted after a long career of labor-racketeering. He went from prison to a well-paid job with a construction firm arranged through union friends, and he had extensive assets left even after paying fines and income-tax debts at the time of his conviction. He now is barred from unions and has been watched closely by the F.B.I., but as far as can be determined he is not engaging in illegal activities or associating with clearly criminal persons.

Reformation After Crime Interval

Although cases of success in a noncriminal life after long criminal careers are most intriguing, the statistics presented in the preceding chapter validate the common assumption that there is a larger proportion of successes among those released after brief criminal experience than among those released following long criminality. Among the most frequent sources of encouragement to parole supervision officials are the cases of postrelease noncriminality in youth who have had an intensive, though brief, crime experience, but who seem to change rather quickly and dramatically to a conventional way of life.

"Ira," Case S-511, had appeared in juvenile court for running away and for traffic offenses, but his first felony arrest, for forging and passing postal money orders, did not occur until he was eighteen. When Ira was placed on probation for this crime, he made a very poor adjustment; he did not seek regular employment, led a wild and disorderly life, and was in continuous conflict with his parents and probation officer. They were especially disheartened when, a few months after his probation began, Ira was arrested for interstate transportation of a stolen automobile and sent to prison with a Federal Youth Correction Act sentence.

Ira had an excellent record in all phases of prison activity, including work, study, and conduct. He was paroled after fourteen months' confinement. His parole record has been a sharp contrast to his probation behavior, although both parole and probation were under the supervision of the same U. S. Probation Officer. Ira claims that he "grew up" when "on his own" in prison. It was in prison that he seems to have first started to work for long-range self-sufficiency, rather than depending on parental support. He has worked regularly since release, and the jobs and pay that he has been able to command have steadily improved. His attitude towards his parents and his probation officer seemed to change radically when he was in prison, and since release he has been fully cooperative with them. The officer now proudly points Ira out as one of the best "success" cases under his supervision.

"Ichabod," Case S-514, was a rather transient individual but did not incur any serious difficulty with the law until he was nineteen years old. At that time he received a state prison sentence for an auto theft which he and some other youths committed while hitchhiking across the country. He was paroled in fifteen months but was not closely supervised, and he continued his transient pattern by joining a traveling magazine-sales crew. Again he and some friends stole a car, and this time he received a Federal Youth Correction Act sentence, on which he was confined for twenty months. Ichabod had spent much of his earlier life in orphanages, and he told a prison psychologist that he followed delinquent activities and got into trouble in order to be placed in an institution, as he was happier in institutions than anywhere else. In the federal prison he worked well as a hospital orderly, but he never persisted in the educational programs in which he enrolled.

Ichabod was twenty-three years old when paroled. In keeping with his prison record, and because he had no family to offer him a home and job assistance, employment was procured for him by the prison Employment Placement Officer as an orderly in a hospital. He worked there about fifteen months, and during the latter part of this period he courted a young woman from a town sixty miles away whom he had met when she was a paraplegic polio patient where he worked. He then procured employment at a hospital closer to her home and in a few months married this woman, despite being counselled by the probation officer to defer such a marriage until he was in a better position to handle the responsibilities it involved. Shortly after his marriage he started to seek factory work because of its higher pay rates, and after unsteady employment at first, he progressed markedly in pay and job security. He seems to have procured a new lease on life from the marriage, as well as from good relationships with relatives by marriage and with blood relatives whom he discovered only when his marriage was publicized in local newspapers. He now is a much more self-sufficient person, in sharp contrast to the dependent individual who earlier sought refuge from responsibilities in institutions.

Reformation After Only One Felony

Prominent among one-crime "success" cases is the reformation of individuals who may have led disorderly lives, but whose only clearly felonious action was followed by a severe prison sentence. This is a familiar pattern in murder and rape cases. In most prison systems such offenders are among those with the lowest parole-violation rate. A post-prison change to a stable and conventional life also occurs in many men who were never felons until they made one impulsive effort to solve their financial dilemmas by crime.

"Oliver," Case S-302, was confined thirteen years before his parole on a twenty-one-year sentence imposed when he was in the Army and killed another soldier in a scuffle growing out of a gambling quarrel. In civilian life Oliver had once served a misdemeanor term for violence in a similar quarrel, but he did not change his way of life radically until the long imprisonment following his clearly felonious action in the Army. Since release he has been extremely conscious of the need to avoid association with people he calls "troublemakers," for fear of being returned to prison for the many years remaining on his sentence. He has worked steadily, has been close to his parents and active in church, and has developed a social and recreational life in circles where he is not likely to encounter violence.

"Oscar," Case S-538, had no prior felony convictions when imprisoned but did have a thirteen-year record of arrests, fines, and jail terms for intoxication, drunken driving, and similar misdemeanors. These were especially intense after he dropped out of school at age sixteen to work continuously as a dock laborer. However, this pattern terminated when at the age of twenty-four he received a fifteen-year sentence for robbing a bank with three associates. He completed high school in prison, had an excellent behavior record, and was paroled after five and one-half years. His crime had been conceived in a bar, and apparently its consequences had much to do with his being highly restrained in his drinking since release. He has worked steadily as a truck driver for over two years on parole, and has had no further difficulties with the law.

Crime-Interrupted Noncriminal Career

When an offender has definitely established himself in a noncriminal life before his crime, one conviction generally seems sufficient to discourage further adventures in criminality. However, only a minority of prisoners have a record of clear success in a noncriminal life before their crime, partly because such men have the best prospects for receiving probation rather than prison sentences.

"Ivan," Case S-573, came from a relatively poor family, but by dint of his own strong ambition and family encouragement he worked his way through law school. Within a year of his admission to the bar he changed from a law-clerk position to his own law practice, operating in office space rented from a large law firm. He married a woman who seemed to equal or exceed him in social-climbing aspirations. They lived lavishly, and thus acquired large debts. Ivan, as a lawyer, became trustee of several thousand dollars paid for claims against the federal government. When he "borrowed" from these funds beyond his capacity to repay, he was sent to federal prison for embezzlement.

Ivan was a model prisoner and contributed the benefits of his education to fellow inmates by serving as an instructor in the prison school. On release he was employed at analysis and correspondence work by a large corporation and quickly advanced to a position of considerable importance there. He has been assured that if, upon completion of his parole, he procures readmission to the bar, he will be welcomed into the legal staff of this corporation.

Ivan was divorced by his wife while he was in prison, but he remarried her after release. He then left her when he could not discourage her excessive spending, but they have once again reunited. Since she is reported to have become more moderate in her expectations, and he now seems able to resolve their crises without jeopardizing his future, it does not seem likely that he will have further difficulty with the law.

Another example of this pattern, in a prisoner with a less distinguished profession, is provided by "Irwin," Case S-508. Irwin left school at seventeen to work in the printing trade. He progressed well in learning this trade, and three years later he and another youth opened their own printing business. The business did not prosper. When Irwin could not earn enough money to meet expenses of his wife's pregnancy, he and his partner printed their own money. The government, to discourage competition in this printing specialty, soon placed Irwin and partner in federal prisons.

Irwin was paroled in less than two years, and rejoined his wife and the son born during his incarceration. After a few months of diverse employment, he received a job as a printer again. When interviewed by us two years later he had been advanced to a foreman position, had paid his preprison debts, and was saving money toward purchase of a home.

MARGINAL REFORMATION CASES

These releasees, who were classified as only marginally pursuing a non-criminal life, exhibited one of two broad patterns. The first can be called *retreatism,* following Merton's use of this term,[1] in that they pursued neither noncriminal nor criminal goals vigorously, by either legitimate or illegitimate means. The second broad pattern was that of maintaining *contacts in the criminal world* while acquiring a livelihood by noncriminal—or at least, nonfelonious—enterprises.

Economic Retreatism

These are men who seem to have given up all striving for what would generally be considered even a modest economic self-sufficiency. They seem content with a bare subsistence, as long as it is provided with little or no effort or uncertainty for them. It is as though they continued to live the dependent life of an institution inmate when outside the institution.

When last released from prison, in 1955, shortly before his fiftieth birthday, "Everett," Case S-544, had no appreciable work experience outside of that acquired during five prison commitments for robbery over a period of more than thirty years. Yet when interviewed by us in 1960, Everett had been free for over five years, far longer than at any time since his childhood, and he seems to have been law-abiding, despite occasional drunkenness. His source of income in these years of freedom alternated between car-washing, unemployment compensation, and working as a porter in businesses or buildings in slum areas. His last and longest job, at which he was still employed when interviewed, was as barbershop porter for room and board plus $7.50 per week. This economic security at a low level seems to express Everett's retreat from the risks of both the conventional and the criminal worlds. His place of work, in back of which he also sleeps and eats, is like the institutions to which he had grown accustomed, for it encompasses almost the totality of his activity. Yet here Everett has freedom to wander off on Sundays or in free hours; this freedom was sufficiently important to him to motivate his preserving it by not reverting to crime.

"Ezra," Case S-655, is a younger type of economic retreatist. He was twenty-six years old when we interviewed him, in 1960. His parents were divorced when he was twelve, and after that he lived mainly with his father. He never has worked extensively, nor committed crime extensively. His offenses were all petty thefts, at fairly wide intervals of time. They led to probation when

[1] Robert K. Merton, *Social Theory and Social Structure,* rev. ed. (Glencoe, Ill., Free Press, 1957), chapter 4.

he was sixteen, then to two jail terms of ten days, and culminated with a Federal Youth Correction Act sentence when he was twenty-one, for theft of money from a letter in a rural mailbox.

Ezra was not quite twenty-three when paroled to live with his father. He had no job at release and has had little success in finding jobs since, or in holding those which the probation officer has arranged for him. About a month after his release he married a fourteen-year-old girl. In nearly four years that they had been married at the time of our interview, they had lived together for a total of eight months. A child was born to them about a year after their marriage, and his wife was expectant at the time of our interview.

Ezra seems to be a dreamer. At the prison it was noted that he told fantastic tales. An employer said he discharged Ezra because he was always telling stories about himself which could not possibly be true. Ezra has been referred to psychiatrists both in prison and on parole, but no treatment was indicated. He is pleasant in manner and takes the initiative to talk to many people, including the judges and members of the probation office staff, all of whom he frequently has phoned at night.

Ezra continually provided for his family by purchases on credit beyond his capacity to repay. He then would have to go to a finance company to consolidate his debts to stores and eventually would need another company to consolidate his debts to finance companies. During his third year on parole he got a house free of rent by agreeing to do repair work on it, but was evicted before long as he never got around to doing this work. When all his furniture was reclaimed by a finance company, he managed to rent a furnished apartment. When the probation officer had him list all his debts and work out a budget, it turned out afterwards that creditors whom he had forgotten to list were pressing him.

When Ezra thought that he could get work in another city, he was transferred briefly to another judicial district with a much larger probation staff, but he soon returned to his original district. His officer here is unusually strict in surveillance and in the requirement that parolees not working report to his office each morning but Ezra says that when he was under the larger office he missed the interest and attention he received from his old probation officer.

Ezra seems to have been in no crime whatsoever, during nearly four years on parole. There was just enough improvement in his work and spending habits from year to year to encourage the probation office to keep trying hard to help him, rather than return him to prison as a violator. Yet Ezra can hardly be considered a clear success despite his final discharge from parole after our interview. This is well summarized in what the probation officer said to him when introducing him to our interviewer: "You used to be the most contemptible, lying, disrespectful, undependable, deceitful, lazy fellow we ever had, but you're not quite so bad any more." The officer added that this was all "water under the bridge," and that they were proud of him now. Ezra agreed with all of this, and he continually interrupted the interview to boast that the office was proud of him now.

Most of the "Economic Retreatism" cases among our "successes" and in our Postrelease Panel Study were older men with various ailments who finally gave up crime and accepted a low level of support by children, old-maid sisters or other relatives, or by welfare payments. One such individual maintained a myth that this was merely a temporary status by always talking of the large corporation where he applied for work almost a year earlier, although he had no qualifications for working there. The corporation personnel had politely advised him that they would write when they needed him, and he always thereafter described his employment condition as waiting for this large corporation to call him, seeming to gain status from the prestige of the corporation with which he identified himself. This might be called the "Major Hoople" variant of the economic retreatist.

Juvenile Retreatism

A second type of marginal "success" are cases who are, as the criminologist Joseph D. Lohman used to say, "young beyond their years." They are youth who, even after adolescence, maintain association predominantly with juveniles and do not seem realistically oriented to achieving adult independence. However, they may manage to avoid serious difficulty with the law for long periods. "Jerry," Case S-563, illustrates this pattern.

Jerry was eighteen when arrested with other youth for interstate transport of a stolen car, and for breaking into a veteran's club, where they took only a few bottles of whiskey. When he was paroled after a year's good behavior in prison, the firm that had agreed to employ him went bankrupt. Jerry then lived with his parents, as he always had, and procured employment as a guitar player in local taverns and clubs. This paid only about ten dollars a night, and the working nights were often few and far between. When not working as an entertainer he practiced with his guitar in the company of the juveniles who most admired his art.

Jerry twice was arrested for questionable activity with thirteen- to sixteen-year-old girls. Once he was released, and another time a statutory rape charge was reduced to contributing to delinquency of a minor, for which he served a month in jail. Parole was not revoked in the latter instance, partly on the evidence that he had been more seduced than seducing. After interviewing Jerry, two members of our staff went to the club where he was entertaining. One of the staff members reports:

We observed an extremely youthful group of males and females between the ages of fourteen and eighteen or nineteen at this bar. The parolee was playing his guitar along with two other guitar players and a drummer, who was also doing the vocal. The dancing was wild and the beat fast. The T-shirts and jeans were dirty and the sideburns long. Although most of the customers were drinking beer, many were drinking Cokes and Pepsis. During intermissions the juke box would blare, and the parolee would join his fifteen-year-old girlfriend, a blond with a luscious figure. And prevailing over the entire scene was a sense of the naturalness of this surrounding to the individuals who were involved in it.

Perhaps Jerry was en route to international fame as an entertainer of adolescents, but this seems most unlikely. At any rate, some time after our interview we learned that his parole was revoked after further complaints were filed for his contributing to the delinquency of a juvenile girl.

"Jimmy," Case S-310, was twenty-four when interviewed for this project, and had been on parole almost two years. He is described by our interviewer as "having an unbelievably enormous amount of hair, combed in a 'hoodish' manner, with a shirt deeply open in front, and no undershirt." "Swinging" was the most favorable adjective in Jimmy's vocabulary; he used it to describe his probation officer, his girl friend, his brother, and himself. Within a week of his parole from a federal reformatory Jimmy married a teen-age girl without discussing this first with his U. S. Probation Officer. The probation officer's investigation and Jimmy's admissions indicate that, following a fight on their honeymoon, he and his bride were both separately picking up members of the opposite sex in neighborhood taverns. Jimmy claims he married this girl only because he promised to do so if she wrote to him when he was in prison, which she did, so he paid a debt of honor. Allegedly she was a streetwalker, and he too was interested in others. They were divorced after around nine months of marriage, most of which were spent living apart, generally with their separate parents. When the probation officer was informed of the divorce he counseled Jimmy on being more cautious regarding another marriage, only to be informed by Jimmy that he had been remarried since the day after the divorce, this time to a sixteen-year-old graduate of the state reformatory for girls.

Jimmy's second marriage was almost as turbulent as the first, with frequent returns to the parents, but it had persisted for about a year at the time of our last report. Jimmy was usually employed, and was most proud of his seventh job in less than two years, where he apparently was doing well as a junior office helper, a sort of glorified office boy and mimeograph operator. Previously he had worked only at factory-machine tending. Possibly Jimmy will avoid further entanglements with the law, but his continued association with juveniles, including many who are clearly delinquent, suggests that he still only is marginally successful in an adult noncriminal life.

Addictive Retreatism

The retreatism concept, for analysis of criminal behavior patterns, is chiefly concerned with drug addicts or alcoholics. If a parolee or mandatory releasee returned to clearly felonious drug usage, he could not be considered even marginally reformed. However, a few men who formerly were felonious drug addicts compromised between their desire for drugs and their desire to avoid the costs and risks of heroin usage by maintaining a heavy dosage of some legal drug. Actually, cases of this type which we encountered displayed this pattern only temporarily and eventually manifested either clear success or marginal failure.

"Albert," Case S-610, has a criminal record that began when he received probation for burglary at the age of twelve and continued with little interruption for about forty years, during which he received nine different probation, jail, or prison terms. He started narcotics usage when twenty-three years old, he reports, when he received drugs through contraband channels in a penitentiary. When released he regularly supported addiction by a combination of petty thievery and check forgery. He is an intelligent and articulate individual who has advanced his education well into the college level through study in federal prisons.

At the time of our interview, Albert had been free for two and one-half years. He had no regular employment for three months after release, but managed to support himself by a combination of welfare assistance and odd jobs. During his initial period of unemployment, and during his first job as helper in a restaurant, the probation officer and an F.B.I. agent checked his room several times, and each time saw several empty bottles of paregoric, a common medicine containing a mild opiate. Several persons were interested in helping him, but were concerned with what seemed to be his sickly condition, which the officer presumed was from paregoric.

When Albert had been out of prison for about six months he became interested in a woman, and then seemed to terminate drug usage. The probation officer got a job for him with a manufacturing concern, at which Albert progressed in a few months from unskilled laborer to machinist, a trade he had learned in prison. Subsequently he developed a painful ailment, requiring hospitalization on several occasions, and indications of some type of drug usage again became evident, but Albert denied that he used narcotics. His employer complained to the probation officer that Albert had become so lethargic he could not be employed much longer. The officer advised Albert to commit himself to Lexington, if addicted, and warned of the prospect of parole violation for narcotics usage. Albert again denied drug usage, but after this there were only favorable reports on his work and other behavior. This was eight months before our interview, and his postrelease record from then on best fits our category of late reformation after a criminal career.

"Arthur," Case S-918, first said he was not well enough for an interview, but when our interviewer mentioned that he could pay a small amount for his trouble, Arthur eagerly cooperated on condition that the interviewer first buy him a large bottle of a particular type of cough syrup. Arthur visibly recuperated from his apparent illness as he gulped most of the bottle during several hours of conversation in the interviewer's car. When he revealed that he had been consuming a pint of codeine cough syrup a day, it seemed probable that his illness had consisted of mild withdrawal symptoms.

Arthur's criminal and narcotics record spanned over twenty-five years. He was handicapped by loss of his left forearm and supported himself mainly by peddling pencils. He was nominally employed at a restaurant of a relative, but only called there for free food. He was provided with a free room in a slum building by another relative, who was the absentee owner. He claimed to have sometimes made as much as fifteen dollars a day selling pencils, mostly by going into taverns at night where drunks gave him as much as a dollar for a single pencil. Nevertheless, it was difficult to sell these long in one neighborhood, and unless he traveled widely he often did not even earn the three dollars per day needed for his cough syrup. However, he periodically supplemented this income by procuring nylon hose from a shoplifter and selling them to prostitutes.

Arthur also had difficulty buying enough cough syrup in his home community, for he sought only one type, and most druggists knew him and would not sell it to him. Therefore, he made regular trips to other cities, sold pencils there, and purchased a supply of the cough syrup. On these trips he traveled by hitchhiking or freight-riding. He would sleep in skid-row missions at his destination. The probation officer suspected that Arthur was involved in crime, and a few months after our interview we learned that Arthur was returned to prison as a violator after he was caught out of the judicial district without permission, and was suspected of violating many other supervision rules.

Persistent and extreme alcoholism was a rarity in releasees who succeeded in remaining under federal supervision for more than a year without being declared violators. "Angus," Case S-119, was one of these exceptions.

Angus served a state reformatory term for auto theft during the 1930's, then had no serious difficulty with the law until he was in the Army overseas during World War II. Just after returning from combat, while in a cafe and drinking, Angus was shot in the mouth by the accidental discharge of a French policeman's gun. Angus immediately drew his gun and shot two gendarmes, killing one. His original life sentence was reduced several times, and he finally was paroled after eleven years in prison.

Angus had fifty dollars in cash when he left the prison, but he drank all of this up on the 400-mile bus trip to his mother's home. She had over $2,000 for him from the prison earnings which he sent home. He bought a car for $500 and drank up the rest in a three- or four-month period, then sold his car and drank up the proceeds. He had no job when released, but a contractor had a few days of manual work for him to do, and he has persisted in working only a few days a month, at odd jobs. He claims that he cannot get a better job because people ask him what he has been doing for the past ten years, and he cannot tell them that he has been in prison.

Now in his mid-forties, Angus is supported mainly by his mother, on a very indigent level. He uses what money he can pick up at his odd jobs to engage in drinking. Like most addictive releasees, Angus combines the addictive and economic retreatism patterns. He has, for some time, talked of going to work for an uncle who has a farm in the South, but apparently he will not make such a decision until more desperate than he has been thus far.

Crime-Contacting Noncriminals

Another type of marginal reformation is found in individuals who appear to have legitimate occupations, but still have extensive contacts with underworld figures. Because of their continued association with known criminals they could be considered in technical violation of parole rules barring such contacts, and these contacts also cause them to be suspected of further crime. However, they seem to confine their economic endeavors to non-criminal activity. This type is well illustrated by "Clifford," our Case S-528.

Clifford spent a year in a state training school for auto larceny when sixteen years old. He then was in the C.C.C. and the Army, and had no serious difficulty with the law until he was twenty-six, when he was fined and placed on probation for possession of lottery slips. This was followed in about a year by a prison term for an armed robbery in which he was an employee of one syndicate which was using violence to steal slot machines owned by another syndicate. About three years after his parole on the robbery sentence he received a federal sentence for interstate transportation of a prostitute. Clifford had been employed as a door-to-door salesman at this time, and he claims he was not working for a prostitution syndicate in this offense, but just doing a single prostitute a favor, which she returned by her services. However, he admits that he was then employed part time in syndicate gambling operations, at night, while working as a brush salesman in the daytime.

When paroled, Clifford was reemployed by the brush company, and he soon supplemented this by also selling men's suits, which he purchased wholesale and altered himself to fit each customer. The latter business did so well that he borrowed money from a brother and from his parole adviser to procure a larger clothing stock, so that he could devote himself entirely to the clothing sales. He seems to be doing well at this business, has purchased a home for himself and his family, making the purchase, incidentally, through a prominent criminal bondsman. He sells suits to many of the leading noncriminal persons in several small cities, but it is also well known that he sells extensively to many figures in the criminal world, most of whom he has known for many years. He has been arrested on suspicion several times, but always was cleared, and even passed a lie-detector test three times.

Our interviewer and the probation officer concurred in the impression that a significant factor in the post-release legitimacy of Clifford's business is not only that he is prospering at it, but that he is proud of the extent to which he has gained recognition for this success from both his criminal and his noncriminal contacts. The criminals are reported to show much envy at Clifford's ability to prosper legitimately, which reinforces Clifford's pride in this ability.

When we checked on Clifford's record in January 1962, a year and a half after our interview, which was shortly before his parole termination, the probation officer wrote: "Since his case terminated he has occasionally contacted this office just to visit. His name comes up continually, in both federal and local police organizations. I cannot say that he served his parole without incident, but for all intents and purposes he did not commit any violations that would necessitate his being considered for violation."

"Clarence," Case S-541, is another example of a crime-contacting noncriminal. He had a few arrests and one acquittal but no felony conviction until he was thirty-seven years old, when he received his federal prison sentence for sale of narcotics. Despite this lack of convictions, he admits having had much prior contact with criminals. This was unavoidable, as Clarence is part of a closely knit family, various members of which were long known for operation of businesses such as speakeasies, saloons, and bail bonding. He generally was employed in these family enterprises.

Upon his parole after four years' confinement, Clarence worked only in businesses of friends or family. He finally became a partner with two brothers in a firm which supplies hot lunches to factory workers on all shifts. This business keeps Clarence busy twelve to twenty hours a day. It is clearly profitable, so Clarence is not believed to be involved in further criminality. However, the recurrent suspicions aroused by his associations lead one to classify him as a marginal rather than a clear success in noncriminal life.

Nonimprisoned Criminals

These men are clearly marginal from a reformation standpoint, since they supported themselves by crime while under parole supervision. However, as far as can be determined, their crimes were restricted to offenses not prosecuted extensively, and when prosecuted, resulting more often in fines and short jail terms than in new prison sentences. What is involved in most of these cases is illegal-service crime rather than predatory crime.

Predatory crime consists of all offenses in which there is clearly someone who considers himself a victim of the criminal. These crimes include most felonies, such as burglary, larceny, robbery, and rape. In illegal-service crimes, however, the person with whom the criminal is involved thinks of himself as a customer rather than a victim. Examples of illegal-service crimes include the provision of illegal gambling facilities, prostitution, and the sale of moonshine (untaxed liquor), narcotics, and stolen goods. In common speech the illegal-service crimes are often called "the rackets," although this term has a somewhat more ambiguous reference.

Illegal-service crimes exist because there are customers for them. They are relatively safe, as compared with predatory crimes, partly because customers do not report offenses to the police as victims would. They may gain added safety where the operators can corrupt the police.

As long as a service is both widely demanded and illegal, it offers business opportunities inaccessible to legitimate businessmen. It also creates the only labor market in which a prior conviction may be a favorable employment reference rather than a handicap, as a prior conviction suggests willingness to operate outside the law. Actually, because of their less severe public condemnation and penalty, involvement in the illegal-service rackets might be thought of as representing a small degree of reformation in a releasee who formerly was a predatory criminal. However, the leaders of large racket organizations, though seldom imprisoned, have been exposed by journalists, crime commissions, and congressional committees as among the most ruthless and predatory of all offenders, and the most costly to the public.

"Nick," Case S-113, was past sixty-four when released from Leavenworth in 1957. While his total confinement in his two separate prison commitments was less than seven years, his last legitimate employment was in 1928. He claims to have supported himself entirely by gambling and to a lesser extent by narcotics sales, for which he was last confined. He now expresses great remorse over his "flyer" in narcotics, and while on parole he served as an undercover agent for the police narcotics squad. This was stopped at the request of the probation office. His other income apparently all came from gambling. A quotation in the probation officer's log reads: "Gambling seems to be a way of life for him, and efforts to change him have not proved feasible." Actually, he reported only twenty-five to fifty dollars per month income from this, and he was supported by the daughter with whom he lived and by a woman friend with whom he apparently visited daily.

"Norman," Case S-324, had a record of probation, a training-school term, and a federal sentence, all for thefts in the large truck-loading yards near which he has resided most of his life. On parole he had no job for four months, worked irregularly for $1.25 an hour for a few months, and was idle for eight months. He then got a service-station job at $100 per week, but told our interviewer: "The people here in the probation office were on my back for not working, so I took the job even though I really was not seeking it myself." He apparently had no regret when he was discharged from this job in a few months, for he said that even with this job he had always made most of his income from gambling and from helping friends dispose of stolen goods.

MARGINAL FAILURES

This is the broad category of all persons returned to prison for mandatory-release violation who were not alleged to have committed any felony during their release. The most striking characteristic of this group is that they come disproportionately from certain federal parole supervision districts and are conspicuously absent in others.

The geographical unit for the administration of federal parole and mandatory release supervision is the federal judicial district. This is because supervision is performed by U. S. Probation Officers, who are employees of the U. S. District Courts. In addition to this parole supervison function, these officers perform probation services, that is, preparation of presentence investigations and advisory reports for the judge, and supervision of federal probationers. The officers are appointed by the courts, in which, incidentally, the judges have lifetime appointments.

From the standpoint of the administration of the law, there are unquestionable advantages of lifetime tenure in the judge's position, and there are sound economic and other arguments for federal parole supervision by the probation officers. However, these arrangements make for variations in supervision practice from one district to the next.

One presumed source of variation in supervision practice is the diversity of standards which judges employ in the selection of their probation officers. Qualifications of these officers increasingly include social work and other relevant academic training and experience. Nevertheless, in some courts the probation officers are former policemen, secretaries, court clerks, teachers, lawyers, or of diverse other vocational backgrounds.

There is reason to believe that an even more important influence on supervision practice than the education or experience of the officers is the judges' conception of probation. This varies from granting probation reluctantly, and expecting supervision to be punitive, to granting it liberally and expecting supervision to stress assistance and guidance. Perhaps in large courts the Chief Probation Officer determines this approach somewhat independently of any particular judges. At any rate, it seems reasonable to assume that the procedures which become routine in probation supervision will be extended by the officers to parole and mandatory-release supervision. Furthermore, a study by Piven has shown dramatically that the standards expected in a specific agency have much more to do with the way parole and probation officers interpret and perform their job than does their prior education or experience. Social-work-trained officers in a police-oriented supervision agency become police oriented (emphasizing rule enforcement, surveillance, etc.); police or other non-social-work-trained officers in a social-work-oriented office become more social-work oriented (permissive, psychotherapeutic, etc.).[2]

A number of influences make for uniformity in federal probation office work, and these partially counteract the sources of disparity. Most notable here is the work of the Administrative Office of U. S. Courts, which suggests standards for personnel selection, issues uniform regulations, and conducts a service-wide training program for U. S. Probation Officers. Also influential are the communications of the U. S. Board of Parole to the separate offices, especially in response to requests by these offices for warrants, discharge, or other board action in specific cases. Indeed, considering the administrative autonomy of each separate court, it is remarkable that standards and practices are not more diverse than they are. Nevertheless, considerable variation was observed in the supervision practices of the twelve federal judicial districts in which we interviewed "successful" releasees; our violator sample came from the same twelve districts, plus three others (see Appendix D).

[2] Herman Piven, "Professionalism and Organizational Structure" (Unpublished Doctor of Social Work thesis, Columbia University, 1961).

The marginal-failure cases may be divided into two categories: defective-communication cases and other nonfelony violation cases. It is especially in the defective-communication cases that differences in parole-supervision practice become evident. Most of the remaining nonfelony failure cases exhibited some sort of retreatist behavior, like that of the marginal successes.

Defective-Communication Cases

In these cases, in my judgment, either no violation occurred or the violation was of a type that would not ordinarily lead to revocation of federal parole. This judgment is based upon examination of official records, interviews with the violator, and, in some cases, interviews with the probation officer. A violation warrant is issued by the U. S. Board of Parole on the basis of a form called "Referral for Consideration of Alleged Violation," in which the probation officer reports the relevant facts and recommends issuance or nonissuance of a warrant. In the cases discussed here, my interpretation of the violation is not based on disagreement regarding the facts, although inconsistencies between various accounts of these facts sometimes are indicated. My comments reflect instead an observation of divergence in supervision policy from one case to the next within our sample, particularly with reference to referring nonfelony matters to the Board and recommending issuance of a warrant. These cases are not presented to challenge any of these policies, but to provide illustration of the variety of behavior which is lumped together in overall statistics on violations or successes.

Three distinctive characteristics of the violations involving defective communication might be noted. First, they were significantly more frequent in certain judicial districts from which our sample comes than in other districts. Secondly, a disproportionate number involve youth residing in rural areas. Thirdly, a high proportion were illiterate or mentally retarded.

"Dennis," Case V-497, left school at the age of fourteen when in the fifth grade. His I.Q. on the Revised Beta Examination, for illiterates, is 72. One factor in his school retardation may have been that he was reared in a very isolated rural area, the farm of his parents being three miles from the nearest road. From the age of seventeen on he lived with his older brother in a large city whenever he could work there, and returned to the farm whenever he could not work in the city. The farm and this city were in different states, though less than 150 miles apart. On his first arrest, when he was twenty years old, he was committed to prison under the Federal Youth Correction Act; his offense apparently was the acceptance of a ride from the city to his home area with three friends, who apparently took the initiative in their procurement of transportation by stealing an automobile.

Dennis was paroled in less than a year to live on a farm about thirty miles from his parents and to work in a coal mine. In three months the mine closed up, and after a sojourn with his parents he received permission to go to his brother's home to seek work in the city. He found a job there and about four months later received permission from the city U. S. Probation Officer to marry a widow, seven years his senior, whom he met on the job. A week later he was injured in an accident at his job, and he claims he received permission to return with his wife to the home of his parents. Not long afterwards he procured a farm job a few miles from the home of his parents, and he was working and living there with his wife when he was arrested as a violator.

The probation office "Referral for Consideration of Alleged Violation" requested that the U. S. Board of Parole issue a warrant in Dennis' case because of his "loss of contact, failure to submit monthly reports, and leaving district without permission." It states that reports for one month were not received and those for the next month, mailed to him by the probation office, were returned with the entry "moved—left no address." The warrant referral also mentions that the officer was told in the community of Dennis' parents home that Dennis had gone to another state.

Dennis claims to have given his report for mailing to the farmer for whom he works; there is no rural delivery in this relatively untraversable area, mail being picked up only in the village. The probation officer could not visit Dennis' parents unless he were willing to walk several miles from the road, and Dennis claims that a substitute for his regular probation officer inquired about him in the village and received some misinformation. Dennis says that his parents and employer later confirmed that he had never left the area. Regardless of the veracity of these several accounts of the violation, revocation appears to have been a much more rigid reaction than would occur in this type of circumstance in most judicial districts. In this case geographical isolation and the illiteracy of the subject added to communication difficulty.

"Dave," Case V-407, was reared mostly in rural areas. His parents were divorced when he was four. He stayed with his mother and his stepfather in the Middle West until he was seventeen, when he ran away to his father in California. He did not find a warm reception there and was living on his own in California when he had his first difficulties with the law. He asserts that he first wrote checks that were covered by his pay check, but that these "bounced" because his employer went bankrupt. At any rate, he then wrote clearly bad checks. He received a Federal Youth Correction Act sentence for carrying forged checks interstate when he returned to his mother's home.

Dave's mother died while he was incarcerated, and he was paroled without a job to a large city where a younger sister lived. Within a week he found employment as a handy man and kitchen steward in a country club. This provided room and board, in addition to $150 per month, until the club closed for the winter. Dave managed to stay employed fairly continuously for two and a half years on parole, generally working at country clubs, where he procured room and board, and sometimes working at a restaurant. His return as a violator was for not submitting three monthly reports, changing job and residence without permission, and associating with another parolee where he was employed. Dave claims he submitted the reports, and that he thought he only had to avoid association with the other parolee after work. The prison file includes a carbon of a letter from the probation office to the parole board, indicating that there might have been a mix-up regarding the reports.

"Don," Case V-458, is an illiterate youth, of rural background. When he was ten his father died. His mother did not remarry, but the home she maintained for her seven children was very impoverished. They often lived with various relatives in rural shacks, with the older males in the household frequently drunk. In Don's original offense he apparently rode with a cousin in a stolen car, for which he was given probation while his cousin went to prison. When, without permission, Don left the state in search of work, his probation was revoked and he was given a Federal Youth Correction Act sentence. He was confined for almost two years, during which great efforts were made to raise his educational level before it was concluded that he had reached his limit when he mastered third grade.

Don was supposed to be employed by a cousin on release, but the cousin did not reply to a letter about the job. When the probation officer went to check on this job, the cousin's wife told the officer to leave. This job never was available, and the officer had Don stay at a mission for homeless men rather than live in the rural community with his relatives. Nevertheless, Don repeatedly departed to visit his mother and other relatives. Several unskilled jobs were procured for him, but he was unable to keep any for long. On one occasion he visited relatives in another state without permission, to seek work there.

It is understandable that Don's probation officer became rather distraught with him, and Don also was hostile towards the officer. Don does not communicate well in any case, for which he is a frequent butt of jokes, and he has particular difficulty in expressing himself when angry. After he was seen in association with other ex-convicts among his relatives, he was returned as a violator. It was clear that Don needed an unusually protective environment for highly satisfactory adjustment, and the prison is functioning as a mental institution in his case. Efforts to facilitate and encourage his achievement of a noncriminal and self-sufficient life away from his relatives seem likely to continue to be futile, since his relatives provide his most reliable source of affection and respect, as well as economic assistance. With them, however, there also seemed to be some prospect of his joining relatives in the commission of further crime.

Other Nonfelony Violations

Most violations not involving felonies resulted from some variety of the retreatist behavior noted in marginal success cases: drinking, persisting in a juvenile social life, or not seeking work. In many cases, however, these violations were associated with inability to procure employment, despite sincere efforts. A large proportion of these infractions also involved illicit sexual pursuits of the newly released prisoners. The actual violation in all of these cases was a noncriminal violation of rules, especially absconding. Generally, absconding only made the offenders' economic problems worse, and several turned themselves in to the police when utterly destitute, homeless, and hungry. A few examples will illustrate this potpourri.

"Tom," Case V-042, came to this country from Canada when nineteen and thereafter had a continual series of arrests in the United States, culminating in his third prison commitment in 1937, on a twenty-year federal sentence for counterfeiting. He was mandatorily released in 1949 and worked in an automobile plant for three years until a defense contract led to the discharge of all who could not prove their citizenship. After several months, during which he was able to find only temporary employment, he was assisted by a nephew in opening a small store for the sale of costume jewelry. This prospered through the Christmas season, but he had to sell out in February and was then unemployed until August. He claims that at this time he asked permission to transfer to another city to seek employment and was told that he could not do so unless he already had a job arranged there. This appears to have been a misunderstanding on his part, since the customary procedure in most federal supervision is to authorize short trips to seek work, but not to transfer a man to supervision by another district office until a satisfactory job and residence are procured in the new area. At any rate, after over five years of nonviolation, Tom absconded. Two years later, when he was approaching sixty years of age, he was returned to federal prison on a warrant for mandatory-release violation.

"Dick," Case V-498, is the oldest of six children of a poor rural family who were orphaned when he was thirteen, and were placed in foster homes. He had stopped attending school when he was twelve and in the third grade. When he was fourteen he was sent to a state training school for bicycle theft. Two years after release from there he received a Federal Youth Correction Act sentence for auto theft. When paroled he procured a job as a cook, but was soon demoted to dishwasher. Meanwhile he maintained an avid interest in guitar playing, and when a girl pressed him for marriage on the grounds that she was pregnant, he fled to Las Vegas to seek work as an entertainer. Two weeks later he returned and turned himself in to his probation officer, who had him jailed, as a warrant already had been issued. Medical tests which the officer asked the girl to take proved that she was not pregnant, and in a few weeks the officer was able to arrange withdrawal of the warrant and Dick's reemployment at his old job. About four months later, however, he again departed across country to become an entertainer, this time taking two girls and another would-be guitarist. They were arrested following an auto accident on the first day of the trip, and Dick was returned to prison as a parole violator.

"Harry," Case V-456, was the oldest of five children deserted by their mother when he was seven. When he was fifteen his father died, and he then ran away from three foster homes and an orphanage, until placed for a year in the Boys' Republic in Michigan. A few months after placement from there to a farm family, he was involved in a car theft for which he was sent briefly to a state industrial school. On his eighteenth birthday he joined the Army, but a year later he went AWOL and stole an automobile, for which he received his Federal Youth Correction Act sentence.

Harry was paroled after nearly three years in prison, where at first he made a poor adjustment. A job arranged for him by the probation officer proved unavailable for three weeks, during which he incurred some indebtedness, and he finally went to work for only $42 per week. However, shortly thereafter he acquired $1,300 that was left in trust for him from his father's life insurance policy. He kept his job, but proceeded to spend several hundred dollars for clothes and $740 for a used car. It proved to be a "lemon," and he spent more money to trade it for a motorcycle and another used car. Within three months these were both used as down payment for another used car, for which he also signed a note for $69 per month payments, from his salary of less than $200 per month. Within three months he had gone through his legacy, was in debt, and was involved in a complicated relationship with a woman from which he wished to withdraw. With sixty dollars left from a pay check he boarded a bus and three days later, in a remote part of the country, penniless and feverish with a cold, he turned himself in to a small-town police department.

CLEAR RECIDIVISTS

Those returned violators who committed new felonies on parole or mandatory release are divided into two major types. The first consists of those who, when first released, clearly endeavored to pursue a noncriminal life and only later reverted to crime. The residual consists of those who appeared to have had no intention of avoiding crime upon release and promptly initiated felonies.

Deferred Recidivism

The median time between release and violation, for the 308 returned violators whom we interviewed and investigated, was 3.6 months. However, 19 per cent of these men who violated did not do so until more than a year after their release, and 5½ per cent had been free more than two years before they violated. Obviously, the latter cases could have been included in our "success" category had we interviewed them in the free community shortly before their violation. Indeed, of the 250 "successful" releasees we interviewed in 1960 and 1961 who had been out of prison for over a year, 23 had been returned to prison according to a check of the records in January 1962, and so could no longer be considered successes.

The foregoing makes abundantly clear the lack of a sharp line between reformation and recidivism. Our Postrelease Panel Study and our analysis of the previolation behavior of our failure cases indicate conclusively that at least 95 per cent of released prisoners at first endeavor to "go straight." However, these statistics in chapter 2 confirm that about a third eventually revert to felonies. These contrasting figures reflect the fact that releasees vary greatly in the extent of economic, social, and other frustration which they encounter in seeking a noncriminal life, and they also vary greatly in the extent to which they cope with these frustrations by behavior that is both rational and noncriminal. The following cases illustrate some of this variation as it is reflected in the extent to which returned violators deferred criminality.

The life of "Dudley," Case V-499, provides an extreme illustration of the habit of reacting to problems by irrational flight. As in some of the marginal-failure cases already described, frequently this flight does not involve the commission of felonies, although cars may be stolen when flight is difficult. The consequences of flight generally also increase the intensity of economic and other problems that provoke felonies.

Dudley came from a home of continuous bickering in which his parents twice were divorced and twice remarried. He was placed in a private boys' school when eleven, but was expelled when they could not control him. He was sent to a state training school when thirteen, for incorrigibility. Dudley was paroled from this school four times in the next five years, always violating parole by leaving home, and the violations always were reported to the parole officer by his mother. Dudley's federal offense was a car theft while hitchhiking far from home on his last state training school parole.

Dudley got along very well on his federal parole, working regularly a twelve-hour day at a grocery store. He had become engaged by correspondence while in prison to a girl whom he had known for many years. She lived in another judicial district, in the same state, but he obtained permission from the probation officer to visit her every other weekend. One weekday the girl called him when she was upset over a quarrel with her mother. Dudley left immediately, and joined the quarrel that evening. He says he missed the bus back to his home and he believed that his mother probably had already reported his flight, so that he would be returned to prison as a violator. He hitchhiked to the home of a friend from the training school, and after three days there they both hitchhiked across the country. Eventually they were arrested with another stolen car.

In Dudley's case the probation officer filed a report with the Parole Board recommending that no warrant be issued pending further investigation. He remarked that this was merely a repetition of Dudley's previous flight behavior, on which he generally did not commit felonies. Dudley, on the other hand, had misperceived the consequences of his initial flight to his girl's home, and in many other respects operated with an inadequate view of reality, which presumably reflected his chaotic upbringing.

"Douglas," Case V-207, was sentenced to federal prison for desertion and other violations of military law growing out of a group's drunken escapade on his second army enlistment, which followed a wartime enlistment in which he earned two Purple Heart decorations and was honorably discharged as a First Lieutenant. Douglas was an only child whose parents separated when he was three. By the time he entered prison when he was thirty-three there were no relatives to write to him, and none to whom he could turn on release. On his first day out of prison he chanced to meet a girl whom he had known in high school, and he told the probation officer that in order to impress her and her friends that he was doing well he took them all out for dinner and entertainment. This used up most of the $125 of prison industry earnings he had saved for release, and when his job-searching was fruitless he soon had to move from the YMCA hotel to a skid-row flophouse.

Douglas obtained intermittent day-labor jobs through employment agencies specializing in the provision of unskilled manpower, which take a large commission and rotate jobs among applicants to keep the available applicants numerous. Because at better jobs employees usually are not paid until they have been employed a week or more, men with insufficient funds to provide them with food until payday often are forced to persist in low-paid labor for the sake of the daily cash income. The probation officer's log of parole supervision contacts with Douglas is full of references to the irregularity and inadequacy of his employment. This culminates, six months after his release, with a note that Douglas called saying "I am on the bottom and want you to have a warrant issued." The probation officer tried to give Douglas some reassurance and asked him to come to the office. He reported there a week later, "ill, drunk, filthy and in tears," asking again to be returned to federal facilities, but after counsel from the probation officer he seemed willing to try again. Arrangements for emergency assistance were made with the Salvation Army, where he was given five dollars, which he used for flophouse accommodations.

The probation office did not hear from Douglas again for six weeks, when they were notified of his arrest. Police and probation office records verify that Douglas went into a large department store, picked up a shirt, walked over to the store detective, and told him he was going to steal it. The store officials tried to persuade him to leave, but he told them he would steal other articles until they had him arrested, so they called the police. After serving five months in county jail on a larceny charge, he was returned to a federal penitentiary as a parole violator. He relates that he had been unemployed for several weeks, had no money for food, rent, or carfare to employment agencies, and he decided to return to the federal penitentiary. He hoped to earn some money from prison industry while confined, and then to be released at the end of his sentence, without parole supervision, so that he would be free to travel wherever jobs might be more plentiful. This postrelease plan, of course, could readily lead to a recurrence of his previous desperate straits.

"Duncan," Case V-073, was about forty when mandatorily released after thirteen years' confinement on a bank-robbery charge. This was his second conviction for armed robbery, and he apparently had been a professional criminal from an early age on, with twenty-two different aliases noted in his criminal record. He had $866 in savings from prison earnings at release, and he had a prearranged home with a married sister. He managed to procure moderately regular work, at a good salary, through the boilermakers' union, with other work irregularly as a waiter and as a tuck pointer. Before a year had passed after his release, he had a regular job as a stoker mechanic for $135 per week, he was living in his own apartment, and he had a car. Not long afterwards, however, the probation office was notified of Duncan's arrest, with two other men, for a $62,000 bank robbery in a city several hundred miles from his place of residence.

Duncan relates that an old friend from his robbery days looked him up because he had spotted this bank as a good robbery possibility. Duncan says that he persuaded himself that he would engage in just this one offense, then open a restaurant with his share of the loot. The perpetually mythical nature of a criminal's thinking that he will take only one more gamble on crime, of course, makes it likely that most felons get caught eventually. Duncan will now have to live to be a rather elderly man before he again will be free to risk committing "one more" crime.

Immediate Recidivism

Although the number of convicts who leave the prison gates with a firm resolution to commit more crimes is much smaller than generally is presumed, a few have made this decision before they leave or make such a decision soon after their departure. This is suggested by the fact that, of the 308 returned violators who were interviewed and investigated for this project, 6 per cent (19 cases) committed the act for which they were returned to prison within a week of their release and 17 per cent (53 cases) during their first month out of prison. There doubtless are other violators in our sample who also committed new felonies this early but were not caught until a later infraction, and have not admitted earlier offenses; however, for most violators such early crimes seem unlikely, as there is clear evidence of regular employment or job search at first, and of a living standard within their known resources. It should be remembered also that the above proportions apply only to the sample of returned violators. Less than one-fourth of all federal parolees and mandatory releasees are returned to prison as violators, and chapter 2 indicates that only about a third of all federal releasees are returned to prison on any basis.

"Ralph," Case V-026, is a professional burglar and proud of it. He was thirty-three years old when mandatorily released from prison on his fifth felony conviction, and he reports that he committed a burglary that night. He committed another three days later, but that same night he was investigated by the police when he drove into a gas station and appeared drunk. He was found to have over forty dollars in coins and over three hundred cartons of cigarettes in his car, in addition to burglar tools. While free on bond following this arrest, he was caught in a gambling raid and found with identifiable stolen property. For this he served a two-year state prison term before being returned to federal prison for mandatory release violation.

Ralph told us that he concentrates on small burglaries and returns regularly to one city where he has numerous contacts for disposing of stolen goods. He also values contacts with criminal lawyers there, who can make the prosecutor's task so difficult that he can bargain for a light penalty in exchange for pleading guilty. He is a constant student of burglar alarms and continuously "cases" places for burglary possibilities, just as some insurance salesmen habitually "size up" as a potential customer every person whom they meet. He tries not to burglarize an establishment until some months elapse after he has "cased" it, so as to reduce the prospect of his presence there being recalled. When his funds permit, he spaces his burglaries a week or two apart.

Ralph is of superior intelligence and won a county spelling bee before he dropped out of school in the ninth grade. He was reared by grandparents following the divorce of his parents and illness of his mother. In prison he has served as an effective schoolteacher. It seems obvious that, had he persisted in a noncriminal occupation, by this time he would be earning as much or more than he does by burglary, and much more securely. He had a wife and three children, but she divorced him and remarried during one of his earlier imprisonments, and he no longer has any contact with them. During two interviews in prison following his quick return from mandatory release, he seemed committed to continuing his criminal career. He boasted that prior to his federal sentence he had supported himself by burglary for twenty-two months, and he hopes to have such luck again. He is careful to avoid areas where a burglary would give him a very long sentence. Whether he ever will fall into our category of "late reformation after criminal career" will long remain uncertain.

"Robert," Case V-413, was reared by indulgent grandparents following the divorce of his parents when he was four. He was involved in theft and alleged rape charges when twelve, received probation for burglary when fourteen, in the same year was committed to a state training school for auto theft, and received a federal sentence for interstate transport of a stolen auto when sixteen. He has had very little work experience, and most of his association outside of prison has been with delinquent gang members. In prison he sought easy and unconstructive jobs as cell-house or dormitory orderly, and devoted himself to practicing the guitar and weight lifting. He was nineteen when released, but he had an appreciable criminal career behind him already and he still identified himself with the juvenile delinquent group of his preprison days.

Robert says that when in prison he tried without success to arrange a post-release job in a foundry where his stepfather worked, and that he and a cousin looked for work on one day, shortly after his release, by making the rounds of all construction companies in their town. They did not look again. He admits that his first interest on release was in sexual and alcoholic satisfaction, and he went on an orgy with a group of his old cronies. His grandparents supplied him with some spending money, but during his first night out, and frequently thereafter, he and his friends supplemented this by committing strong-arm robberies, generally "rolling" drunks. During his second week out, on a trip to a large city, he was initiated into heroin usage, and he also procured a gun. However, he was not caught on a felony until three months after his release, when he was arrested in a burglary and an auto theft.

"Richard," Case V-254, was reared in a slum community by a paternal aunt and had little contact with his parents, who separated when he was an infant.

He dropped out of school when sixteen and had very little legitimate employment thereafter. He started to use marijuana in his teens and soon graduated to heroin. He married a woman who was also an addict, and he then lived from her prostitution and from the sale of heroin, for which he received his first federal imprisonment when twenty-two years old.

Richard says that he planned not to contact his wife on release, as he feared it would lead to drug usage, and he expected to have a job at cleaning and pressing, a trade he learned in prison. On his first day out, however, he learned that the job was no longer available. That night he had some marijuana at a friend's house, and before the night was out he looked up his wife. The next day, he says, when lying in bed watching her injecting herself with heroin, he decided to try it again. He then resumed his preprison way of life, but was not caught until five months later, when he and his wife were observed making a purchase of heroin. For this he was returned to prison with a new five-year sentence.

THE RELATIVE FREQUENCY OF POSTRELEASE BEHAVIOR PATTERNS

The careers of men are so infinitely diverse that we have to classify them into categories and types in order to comprehend patterns and relationships in their diversity. It should be remembered, when we do this, that the categories often have arbitrary boundaries, which create many borderline cases. Also, when types are based on several somewhat independent characteristics, an individual may be like one type in one respect and like another in some other respect. Thus, some of our releasees who were unemployed extensively were difficult to classify as "clear reformation" rather than "economic retreatism," since one could not be certain how persistently they had sought work. Similarly, two or even all three of the retreatism patterns —economic, addictive, and juvenile—sometimes were manifested in a single case.

Perhaps a greater barrier to classification than the diversity of human behavior is its instability. People who behave in one way at any given time are likely to behave differently later. This is especially evident in the lives of those who have been involved in criminality. Almost all criminals have pursued noncriminal occupations at one time or another, and almost all will resume such pursuits at some time in the future. This is repeatedly indicated by our statistics and by our case studies. The classifications assigned to men in the compilation presented in this chapter were, in the success cases, those which seemed to fit them at the time they were interviewed by our staff; the classifications assigned the returned violators, who were interviewed in prison, were the patterns which seemed to describe their behavior at the time they were under the parole or mandatory-release supervision which they violated. If we had interviewed the success cases later, especially the "marginal" successes, doubtless some would be classified differently. This is evident from the fact that our follow-up in January 1962, on the 250 men interviewed in 1960 and 1961, revealed that in the post-interview interval twenty-three had violated. These included only 6 per cent of the clear-reformation cases, but 25 per cent of the marginal-reformation cases. It is also probable that some of the marginal-success cases had become "clear" successes during this period.

In addition to bearing the foregoing considerations in mind when assessing the relative frequency of the postrelease behavior patterns distinguished here, it should be noted that our sample of "success" cases is not a representative sample of non-recidivating federal releasees. As indicated in Appendix D, this sample was deliberately biased in two respects. First of all, by selecting only men under supervision for one year or more, it was limited to less than half of men released from federal prisons; to have over a year of postrelease supervision they had to be parolees with sentences of more than eighteen months or mandatory releasees with sentences of somewhat over five years (with a few exceptions of unusual early release dispensation). Secondly, the sample was deliberately selected to include men with as much or more prior criminality as the violators already interviewed; starting early in 1960, no one was added to this sample who did not have a record of felony behavior prior to the offense for which he was then successfully released. Therefore, the one-crime cases among federal successful releasees are grossly underrepresented in our sample.

A total of 250 successful releasees were interviewed, constituting over 90 per cent of men under federal supervision, in the areas of seven midwest states listed in Appendix D, who fit the selection specifications stated in the preceding paragraph. Of these 250 cases:

210, or 84 per cent, were classified as *clear reformation* cases, as follows:
Eighty, or 32 per cent of all the 250 successful releasees, were classified as *late reformation after criminal career;*
Thirty-seven, or 15 per cent, classified as *early reformation after criminal career;*
Three, or 1 per cent, classified as *crime-facilitated reformation;*
Forty-eight, or 19 per cent, classified as *reformation after crime interval;*
Twenty-six, or 10 per cent, classified as *reformation after only one felony;*
Sixteen, or 6 per cent, classified as *crime-interrupted noncriminal career.*

In addition, in these 250 successful releasees:

Forty, or 16 per cent, were classified as *marginal reformation* cases, as follows:
Twelve classified as *economic retreatism;*
Nine classified as *juvenile retreatism;*
Four classified as *addictive retreatism;*
Thirteen classified as *crime-contacting noncriminals;*
Two classified as *nonimprisoned criminals.*

The Returned Violator sample is believed to be fairly representative of all midwest returned federal-parole violators. As indicated in Appendix D, the 308 cases in this sample consisted of every returned violator in four federal prisons who had been returned from one of fifteen federal judicial districts (in nine states) after parole or mandatory release from one of these four prisons, or from one other prison (Ashland) to which parole violators are not returned. Of these returned violators:

Ninety-three, or 30 per cent, were classified as *marginal failure cases,* including:
Nine, or 3 per cent, classified as *defective communication;*
Eighty-four, or 27 per cent, classified as *other nonfelony violations.*

In addition:

215, or 70 per cent, were classified as *clear recidivism* cases, including:
178, or 58 per cent, classified as *deferred recidivism;*
Thirty-seven, or 12 per cent, classified as *immediate recidivism.*

It should be noted that the above frequency distribution has very little relationship to the number of illustrative cases presented for each category. When the number of cases in each category in the 250 "successes" and 308 violators was counted, the low frequency of some types that impressed us during the data collection came as a surprise to us. It is my belief that this is illustrative of a common source of error in generalization from case study impressions. Cases are best remembered when they are outstanding illustrations of a type that one finds interesting to distinguish, and perhaps to argue with, to illustrate a point. After they are cited often, or are merely thought about much, one may acquire a grossly exaggerated impresson of their frequency in the total population studied. This is an especially serious matter when major policy decisions are made on the basis of impressions from remembered cases, without relevant statistical information.

What becomes increasingly clear from all of the case studies and statistics on criminal careers presented thus far, or to be cited later, is that almost all criminals follow a zig-zag path. They go from noncrime to crime and to noncrime again. Sometimes this sequence is repeated many times, but sometimes they clearly go to crime only once; sometimes these shifts are for long duration or even permanent, and sometimes they are short lived.

What influences affect these rates of variation? Most important, to what extent can they be altered by government action, in prison or on parole? The rest of this book is concerned with the answers that the latter questions can now receive, and with the methods by which these answers may be improved.

Part II
THE EFFECTS OF IMPRISONMENT

★ ★ ★

CHAPTER 5

Relationships Among Inmates

In concluding our interviews with 250 "successful" releasees, we asked the broad question: "When would you say you changed most permanently from being interested in committing crime?" Four per cent said that they changed before sentencing, 13 per cent placed the change at the time of sentencing or between sentencing and imprisonment, 52 per cent said that they changed during imprisonment, and 16 per cent said that they changed after release. In addition, 10 per cent denied that they had ever changed, most of these claiming either innocence or only unwitting involvement in their offense, and 4 per cent did not know when they changed.

The findings that 52 per cent dated their reformation during imprisonment and 13 per cent from the time of first confronting the prospect of imprisonment, have an implication in common with that of the statistics in chapter 2, which indicated that most released prisoners are not reimprisoned. These diverse data all suggest that much reformation of criminals does occur with imprisonment, even though prisons certainly have deficiencies and may make some of their inmates more criminal. The problems with which Part II will grapple are those of determining the effects of prison experience on various types of offenders.

The literature on the prison inmate's social world, from Clemmer's pioneer *Prison Community* to later works such as Sykes' *Society of Captives,*[1] suggests that the major influence on a prisoner during his confinement comes from other inmates. Nevertheless, this literature evokes an inconsistent and unstable image of these inmate-inmate relationships: on the one hand, inmates are portrayed as predominantly cohesive, with a strong code of loyalty to other inmates; on the other hand, they are portrayed as having a jungle-like existence in which the stronger prey on the weaker and no one trusts anyone. Inmate social types, such as the "right guy," the "politician," the "merchant," the "rat," the "punk," the "outlaw," and the "gorilla,"

---

[1] Donald Clemmer, *The Prison Community* (New York, Rinehart, 1958; re-issue of original 1940 ed.); Gresham M. Sykes, *The Society of Captives* (Princeton, N. J., Princeton University Press, 1958); Richard A. Cloward et al., *Theoretical Studies in Social Organization of the Prison,* Pamphlet 15 (New York, Social Science Research Council, 1960); Donald R. Cressey, ed., *The Prison: Studies in Institutional Organization and Change* (New York, Holt, Rinehart & Winston, 1961).

have been distinguished by Sykes, Schrag, and others[2] as extreme, and often opposite, types of adaptation to this prison social world.

Thus, the relevant literature and common experience in prisons suggest that the extent and nature of inmate relationships with other inmates vary considerably. As a first step in assessing their importance it would appear crucial to know the pattern of their variation. A number of the questions in our prison interviews and questionnaires were concerned with providing rough measurements on some dimensions of these inter-inmate relationships.

FRIENDSHIP VERSUS ISOLATION

In Clemmer's research in a state penitentiary in the early 1930's, overall impressions from a series of questions on inmate-inmate relationships were used to classify prisoners into four categories:

(1) The *"Complete Clique Man"* is described as one of a group of three or more men who are very close friends, share each other's luxuries and secrets, and accept punishment for each other. Eighteen per cent of the inmates were reported to be in such primary groups.

(2) The *"Group Man"* is one who is friendly with a small group of inmates, but does not subject himself as completely as the "clique man" to the wishes and acts of the group-as-a-whole, nor so completely shares confidences and restricts his association with one group. Thirty-six per cent of the inmates were classified by Clemmer as "group men."

(3) The *"Semi-solitary Man"* was described as one who is civil with other inmates, but never becomes really intimate with them. Thirty-four per cent of the prisoners were placed in this category.

(4) The *"Complete Solitary Man"* designated only three and one-half per cent of the men. As the name suggests, these were men who kept completely to themselves and shared nothing with other inmates.

Nine per cent of the inmates whom Clemmer attempted to fit into his four rubrics gave responses too questionable or unsatisfactory to permit him to classify them. Combining his first two categories as "grouped men" and the last two as "ungrouped," Clemmer found that serious offenders and long-termers were more often grouped than were trivial offenders and short-termers, and that men who were married or had siblings at home were less likely to be "grouped" than were their opposites.[3] We infer from this that the family can significantly compete with prison groups in attracting an inmate's loyalties; one may presume, therefore, that they compete as well in influencing an inmate's moral values and personal goals.

During each of our Prison Panel Study interviews we presented the inmate

[2] Sykes, *op. cit.,* chapter 5; Clarence Schrag, "Some Foundations for a Theory of Correction," chapter 8 in Cressey, *op. cit.;* Daniel Glaser and John R. Stratton, "Measuring Inmate Change in Prison," chapter 10 in Cressey, *op. cit.*

[3] Clemmer, *op. cit.,* chapter 8.

with a card containing four statements (in systematically varied sequence), and asked him: "Which of these tells best what you try to do with the other inmates?" Twenty per cent of the prisoners endorsed the statement, *"Try to stay to myself as much as possible."* Seventeen per cent asserted that they *"Try to know many inmates, but not be very friendly with any of them."* The most preferred statement, chosen by 38 per cent, was *"Try to make a few inmate friends,"* but 24 per cent chose instead the statement *"Try to make as many friends as I can among the other inmates."*

Our inquiry was not identical with Clemmer's, but his "Complete Solitary Man" and his "Semi-solitary Man" seem similar, respectively, to our respondents who preferred the statements "Try to stay to myself as much as possible" and "Try to know many inmates, but not be very friendly with any of them." Clemmer referred to these types collectively as the "ungrouped" inmates, and 37 per cent were classified in his study, as well as in ours, into this category of low intimacy of interaction. In both studies also, an additional group of approximately the same proportion limited themselves to a few inmate friends. In general, our findings repeat those of Clemmer—that inmates are far from an integrated social body; for most inmates, strong ties with other inmates either seemed absent entirely, or were limited to a few other inmates only.

While only one per cent of our subjects refused to accept any of our four statements, many seemed to have some uncertainty in making a choice. When, in response to our inquiry, the interviewees selected the statement that best described how they try to live with other inmates, we asked them "Why?" Their uncertainty, perhaps a deficiency of the question, seems to be both revealed and explained in Table 5.1 by the fact that they found similar justifications applicable to different statements.

As Table 5.1 reveals, those who asserted that they try to stay to themselves as much as possible most frequently commented that inmate friends "get you in trouble" or "take advantage of you." This is consistent with the slogan, "Do your own time," which is widely supported by both the inmates and the staff, the implications of which are discussed in chapter 7, "Isolation Promotion and Custody Grading."

Most inmates seemed to be ambivalent towards other inmates. Mixed feelings were conveyed by both the statement "Try to know many inmates, but not be very friendly with any of them," and the statement "Try to have a few inmate friends." Appropriately, inmates selecting either of these two statements gave somewhat similar justifications. As with the more complete isolates, their most frequent main reason for this preference was that inmate friends "get you in trouble," but they differed from the isolates in that their second reason was a desire for sociability. This was indicated by such expressions as "you need friends to talk to in here" and "friends help you do time easily." Interest in mutual aid, almost exclusively a second reason rather than a first one, was expressed in terms of friends being necessary for protection from other inmates, as well as friends being valued for material aid, such as sharing commissary items when one runs out of money. It was clear that for most inmates, social life with other inmates creates continuous uncertainty.

TABLE 5.1   Friendship with Other Inmates vs. Isolation: Preferences and Reasons (Prison Panel Study)

| | PREFERENCES ON HOW TO LIVE WITH OTHER INMATES | | | |
| | ISOLATION | GUARDED FRIENDSHIP | | FRIENDSHIP |
	(1) Try to stay to myself as much as possible.	*(2) Try to know many inmates but not be friendly with any.*	*(3) Try to make a few inmate friends.*	*(4) Try to make as many friends as I can among inmates.*
Statement chosen, all cases (1137 interviews; 11 no preference)	20%	17%	38%	24%
First reason given for choosing the statement: (Percentages add vertically to 100%)				
1. Sociability desired	—	12%	27%	58%
2. Mutual aid desired	—	1%	4%	2%
3. Just prefer being alone	30%	3%	3%	—
4. Inmate friends bring trouble	59%	41%	35%	—
5. Any inmate not a friend may cause trouble	—	4%	1%	26%
6. Ambivalence: combination of No. 4 with No. 1 or No. 2	3%	23%	20%	2%
7. Other	8%	17%	11%	12%

Most of those who asserted that they try to make as many friends as they can among other inmates indicated a psychological need for sociability in prison, with such explanations as "you can't stand it in here unless you have people to talk to." Mutual aid was common as a second justification. However, a manifestation of fear that any inmate not a friend would be likely to make trouble for them was also associated with interest in making many friends.

The uncertainty of inmates in choosing among our four statements, indicated by the overlap of their justifications for different choices, also was shown in the reliability test. When sixty inmates in a midterm panel were reinterviewed by a different researcher about three months after the original interview, 39 per cent picked a statement from among these four different from that which they had indicated on the original interview. However, less than 4 per cent changed from the maximum isolation to the maximum friendship statement, or vice versa; most of them shifted to adjacent statements on the four-item scale, and the two "guarded friendship" statements in the middle were involved in over nine-tenths of the shifts. This suggests that the four statements are of value primarily for distinguishing three types of prisoners: the men extremely eager for friendship with other inmates, the men most concerned with isolating themselves from other inmates, and the men intermediate between these extremes. This rough three-step scale also is suggested in Table 5.1 by the fact that similar reasons tend to be given for the items most adjacent on the four-statement scale, especially for the two middle statements. Finally, the scale proves useful because of the correlates which we find it to have.

Age and Inmate Relationships

Table 5.2 indicates that preference between friendship and isolation in dealing with other inmates is very much a function of age. The younger

TABLE 5.2   Friendship with Other Inmates vs. Isolation: Relationship to Age (Prison Panel Study)

		PREFERENCES ON HOW TO LIVE WITH OTHER INMATES			
		ISOLATION	GUARDED FRIENDSHIP		FRIENDSHIP
	Number of interviews	*(1) Try to stay to myself as much as possible.*	*(2) Try to know many inmates, but not be friendly with any.*	*(3) Try to make a few inmate friends.*	*(4) Try to make as many friends as I can among inmates.*
Age at admission:					
Under 21	323	11%	17%	32%	38%
21 through 30	414	24%	16%	41%	18%
Over 30	400	24%	19%	38%	18%

inmates are much more concerned with making many friends among other inmates than are the older ones.[4]

Of the inmate attributes which we investigated, none differentiated friendship- from isolation-oriented inmates as much as did age at admission. Race was of no significance; Negroes and whites had virtually identical proportions committed to each of our four statements. Length of sentence had little relationship to friendship versus isolation after one removed those with Federal Youth Correction Act or Federal Juvenile Delinquency Act

[4] A distribution as different as Table 5.2 is from the same proportions of the four responses for each age group could occur by chance, with this size sample, much less than once in a thousand times (Chi Square is 64.7, with 6 degrees of freedom). For the under-21 age group taken separately, a difference as large as that between the proportion preferring the "isolation" response and the proportion preferring the "friendship" response could occur by chance, in this size sample, less than once in a hundred times. Note that rows in Table 2 add to one or two per cent less than 100 per cent due to omission of cases in which the subjects claimed none of our statements applied to them. Goodman-Kruskall Lambda for this table is only .08, that is, 8 per cent improvement in predicting age, given response, over predicting age by the modal age category alone. Of course, this reflects in part the fact that there are only three age categories, hence high initial predictability.

commitments, who had the youth pattern indicated in Table 5.2. Prior confinement had a slight relationship to friendship versus isolation preferences, with prior confinement making for more frequent interest in isolation from other inmates. In our sample, as in Clemmer's, married inmates were somewhat more frequently inclined to isolation from other prisoners than were single inmates; this difference was not clear in the first-week interviews, but was definite in the midterm and near-release panel data.

Table 5.3 illuminates the foregoing by comparing inmates at different prisons with respect to change in their isolation versus friendship interest

TABLE 5.3   Friendship with Other Inmates: Change with Time in Prison
(Prison Panel Study)

| | | | PREFERENCES ON HOW TO LIVE WITH OTHER INMATES | | | |
| | | | ISOLATION | GUARDED FRIENDSHIP | | FRIENDSHIP |
Institution	Stage of confinement at interview	No. of Cases	(1) Try to stay to myself as much as possible.	(2) Try to know many inmates but not be friendly with any.	(3) Try to make a few inmate friends.	(4) Try to make as many friends as I can among inmates.
Leavenworth	First week	60[b]	25%	17%	40%[d]	15%[e]
(maximum-	Fourth month	30	23%	10%	53%	13%
security	Sixth month	43	23%	9%	61%	7%
penitentiary)	Near release	49	29%	16%	43%	12%
Terre Haute	First week	50[a]	24%	18%	36%	20%
(medium-	Fourth month	17	18%	6%	65%	12%
security	Sixth month	36	17%	19%	50%	14%
penitentiary)	Near release	48	19%	23%	44%	15%
Milan	First week	60	18%	23%	32%	25%
(adult	Fourth month	24	38%	17%	33%	13%
correctional	Sixth month	41	42%	15%	29%	15%
institution)	Near release	50[a]	26%	20%	26%	26%
Chillicothe	First week	60	18%	17%	32%	33%
(youth	Fourth month	30	23%	13%	50%	13%
reformatory)	Sixth month	52	23%	8%	56%	14%
	Near release	50	22%	22%	36%	20%
Ashland	First week	53[b]	11%	9%	28%	49%
(youth	Fourth month	17	None	18%	12%	71%
correctional	Sixth month	34	12%	18%	15%	56%
institution)	Midterm	53	9%	26%	15%	49%
	Near release	51[c]	2%	16%	45%	33%
All institutions	First week	283	19%	17%	34%	28%
	Fourth month	118	22%	13%	44%	21%
	Sixth month	206	24%	13%	44%	19%
	Near release	248	19%	20%	39%	22%

[a] One case refused to choose alternative.

[b] Two cases refused to choose alternative.

[c] Three cases refused to choose alternative.

[d] Italic indicates highest entry on each line.

[e] Percentages are based on total number of cases but may sometimes total less than 100 because some cases were noncommittal, usually in the first-week interviews.

with time served. The midterm panel interviews are excluded from this comparison at every institution except Ashland, because only at Ashland was the midterm panel similar to the other panels in type of sentence and other inmate attributes, and only at Ashland did most of the midterm panel subjects have less time served on their sentence when interviewed than did those of the near-release panel.

Length of Imprisonment and Relationships

Table 5.3 indicates that orientation to friendship with other inmates generally changes in a U-shaped curve during imprisonment, being different in the middle than at the beginning or near the end of the prison term. However, there is much disparity among institutions. At Leavenworth, the maximum-security penitentiary, where the inmates are predominantly older and with more prior imprisonment than at the other institutions, there is less fluctuation in orientation to friendship with other inmates than elsewhere. Here, about a quarter say that they try to stay to themselves as much as possible, and about half say that they try to make only a few inmate friends. However, the latter proportion is somewhat lower at the beginning and near the end of the prison term than in the middle. At Terre Haute, the medium-security penitentiary, the pattern is similar to that at Leavenworth but with more fluctuation in the U-shaped curves, particularly the inverted U-curve showing more willingness to have a few inmate friends after a brief period of socialization in the inmate community. The U-shapes also are more pronounced at the Chillicothe Reformatory, with less initial limiting of association than prevails in the penitentiaries.[5]

The U-shaped curves in these three institutions are consistent with those found by Wheeler at the Washington State Reformatory in measuring inmate conformity to inmate (as opposed to staff) moral codes. Wheeler found inmates most likely to endorse staff positions on moral issues at the beginning and at the end of imprisonment. His questions involved hypothetical situations in the prison, such as whether the subjects would hide another inmate's contraband when the other inmate's cell was likely to be searched, and whether they would allow themselves to be unjustly sentenced rather than tell on inmates actually responsible for serious infrac-

[5] The U-shaped curve was found on the most preferred of the four statements (column with the most italics) at every institution. For each of the institutions taken separately, on this most preferred statement, a deviation from equal proportions in every stage of confinement as large as that found could occur by chance, with subsamples of this size, once in five to ten times at Terre Haute and Leavenworth, and once in ten to twenty times at Milan, Chillicothe, and Ashland (by Chi Square test). Knowledge of response would improve one's prediction of time in prison by 11 per cent in Ashland, 9 per cent in Chillicothe, 7 per cent in Milan, 5 per cent in Terre Haute and 2 per cent in Leavenworth (by Goodman-Kruskall Lambda test).

tions. In order to maximize frankness of inmate response, Wheeler employed questionnaires on which the inmates were not asked to identify themselves, and he was identified with the University of Washington rather than with the prison. He concludes from his data that, at the beginning or the end of their term, most inmates are predominantly influenced by noncriminal outside affiliations (relatives, friends, employers, etc.) whom they have just left or whom they look forward to rejoining; these outsiders are the "reference groups" whose behavior norms become those of the inmates. During the intervening period in the prison, however, the subjects were most involved in the inmate social world. It was presumed that the increasing extent to which other inmates became the subjects' reference groups accounted for their preference for inmate rather than staff ethical values in the middle of their term. Wheeler's interpretation of these findings is supported by his also finding, as we did, a U-shaped pattern of maximum aloofness between inmates at the beginning and at the end of the prison term. This pattern was also found in the Washington State Penitentiary by Garabedian, with indications—from a very small near-release sample—that the U-shaped pattern is confined to the "Right Guy" and "Square John" social types among prisoners, with no such upswing in those whom he called the "Outlaw" and "Politician" types.[6]

Prison Heterogeneity and Inmate Relationships

At the Milan and Ashland prisons our findings were the most deviant from those of the other institutions. At Milan there is the largest shift of inmates to seeking isolation from other inmates, starting early in imprisonment, although diminishing somewhat near release. The median age at Milan, 32.6 years, is almost as high as at Leavenworth, but the sentences for most of the inmates involved in the comparisons of Table 5.3 were much more diverse. A third of the Milan inmates interviewed for Table 5.3 had sentences of under a year, and about half were under eighteen months, as compared to less than 5 per cent under eighteen months at Leavenworth. These Milan short-termers were mostly petty offenders from the Detroit area, including many white-collar criminals without much prior prison experience. However, in the Milan institution as a whole, about half of the inmates had sentences of over three years, most of these on narcotic offenses, for which parole is prohibited. This diversity in prospects for

[6] Stanton H. Wheeler, "Social Organization and Inmate Values in Correctional Communities," *Proceedings, American Correctional Association* (1959), pp. 189-98; Stanton H. Wheeler, "Socialization in Correctional Communities," *Am. Sociological Rev., 26,* no. 5 (Oct. 1961), 697-712; Peter G. Garabedian, *Western Penitentiary: A Study in Social Organization* (Ph.D. thesis, University of Washington, Seattle, 1959); Garabedian, "Social Roles and the Process of Socialization in the Prison Community," *Social Problems, 11,* no. 2 (Fall 1963), 139-52.

release among the inmates at this prison, as well as more dissimilarity in age and in social and cultural background than at the other institutions, would seem to account for the high variation in response to our question at Milan. The diversity probably is a major factor in the rapid increase there in the proportion of inmates who seek to isolate themselves from other inmates and become what Clemmer called "Complete Solitary Men."

The Ashland inmates were unique for the predominance of an interest in maximizing friendship with other inmates in much of the time covered, as well as for the large range of their swings in a U-shaped pattern during the course of their imprisonment. These inmates have a small range in age, most of them have not had prior imprisonment, and a majority are sentenced for interstate transportation of stolen automobiles. This offense suggests involvement not so much with crime as a profession as with a youth society and youth culture that has expectations conflicting with those of the adult world. These interstate auto thefts typically begin as a flight, in response to actual or expected social pressures or restrictions by the adult world. Two or more youths commonly support each other in the resolution to take flight. This reliance on peers seems to be maintained in the prison, diminishing only at the approach of the release date. Indeed, Ashland is the only one of the five institutions in which interest in making as many inmate friends as possible increased after the first week in prison.

One should note the relevance of Table 5.3 to published theoretical analyses of prison life. Most important, perhaps, is the variation from one prison to the next, which suggests that there is need for much qualification of prevailing generalizations on prisons as a whole. Four of the five prisons seem to contradict the implication of Sykes and Messinger that prison populations reduce "the pains of imprisonment" by moving "in the direction of solidarity."[7] Only the Ashland population clearly moved in the direction of increased inter-inmate friendship from the first week on, and inmates in all five prisons appear to have increasingly isolated themselves from each other near release. Possibly progressive alienation of inmates from staff, particularly in the authoritarian prison where Skyes centered his study, was misinterpreted as evidence of movement of inmates towards solidarity. Our data suggest that they may move mainly towards isolation from other inmates as they become isolated from staff (see chapter 6).

Population features at the separate prisons which may account for some of the variation in inmate solidarity, particularly the divisiveness at Milan, have already been indicated. Our impression is that the federal-prison feature most influential in reducing solidarity of inmates is the highly developed body of individual incentives such as pay, meritorious good time, industrial good time, and, especially, the system of custody grading. Clow-

---

[7] Gresham M. Sykes and Sheldon L. Messinger, "The Inmate Social System," in Cloward, et al., op. cit., p. 16.

ard well summarizes the social effects of such a system of granting inmates more freedom within the prison if they conform to behavior expectations. As he puts it:

(1) Individuals who are motivated to seek higher custody status are under pressure to become isolated because of the prevailing definition of conformity. Upward-oriented individuals are motivated to avoid entangling alliances with their fellows lest they jeopardize the chances of achieving a high position. (2) Those who have achieved higher status become all the more wary of entangling alliances in order to avoid being downgraded in custody. In short, one function of these systems of stratification is to sort inmates into various geographically and socially distinct strata; this reduces interaction and splits the strength of inmate organization.[8]

Other influences that may strongly compete with inmate solidarity in reducing the pains of imprisonment are positive relationships of inmates with staff and with noncriminal persons outside the prison, which are discussed in later chapters.

The following statements are set forth as tentative conclusions of this section of our data:

C1. Prisoners, as a whole, are more oriented to maintain voluntary isolation from other prisoners than to achieve solidarity with other prisoners.

C2. Voluntary isolation of prisoners from each other is correlated directly with age of the prisoners; at low ages, the inverse of the first proposition above may occur.

C3. Voluntary isolation of prisoners from each other is correlated with the amount of prior correctional confinement that they have experienced.

C4. Voluntary isolation of prisoners from each other is correlated directly with the degree of heterogeneity of prisoners in an institution. This heterogeneity may be measured in terms of: (a) race, (b) length of sentence, (c) social class, or (d) prior correctional confinement.

C5. Voluntary isolation of prisoners from each other varies in a U-shaped curve, being high at the beginning of confinement, decreasing towards the middle, and increasing near release.
   a. The amplitude of this curve varies inversely with age or prior confinement of the prisoners.
   b. The shape of this curve will be modified somewhat by the linear relationships with age, heterogeneity, and other variables indicated in the previous propositions.

Some practical implications of the foregoing propositions, from the standpoint of prison management, are elaborated in chapter 7.

ADVICE EXCHANGED BY INMATES

One dimension of inmate relationships is the type of advice that inmates exchange with each other. Inmates at three stages of sentence (first week,

---

[8] Cloward, *et al., op. cit.,* pp. 23-24, *fn.*

fourth month, and midterm) were asked the following questions: "What is the most valuable advice you ever got from another inmate? When and where did you get it?" and "What is the most valuable advice you ever gave to another inmate? When and where did you give it?"

Sixty-two per cent of these interviewees specified a particular type of valuable advice which they had *received from* other inmates, and 38 per cent stated that they had never received any valuable advice or had rejected inmates as a source of information. Sixty per cent indicated a specific type of valuable advice they had *given to* another inmate, and 40 per cent stated that they did not believe in giving inmates advice.

Table 5.4 indicates that the advice inmates valued most is on prison adjustment, such as getting along with staff and avoiding troubles from other inmates ("do your own time"). Before they are long in prison they also

TABLE 5.4 "Most Valuable" Advice Exchanged Among Inmates
(Prison Panel Study)

| Types of advice | Direction of advice | ENTRANCE PANEL | | Midterm panel |
		First-week interviews	Fourth-month interviews	
(1) Limit interaction with other inmates ("Do your own time," "Mind your own business," refuse favors, avoid certain types of inmates, etc.).	Received	29%	34%	22%
	Given	22%	13%	16%
(2) Conform to staff expectations (obey rules, keep in good with officials, control yourself to make parole, talk out of fights, etc.).	Received	28%	22%	30%
	Given	27%	43%	39%
(3) Going straight on the outside (control vices, etc.) or supportive remarks.	Received	23%	24%	18%
	Given	32%	29%	24%
(4) Learn a trade, study, etc. while incarcerated.	Received	9%	7%	18%
	Given	8%	6%	13%
(5) Advice on committing crime successfully.	Received	—	2%	1%
	Given	—	—	—
(6) Advice not classified above.	Received	10%	13%	12%
	Given	11%	9%	9%
Number of responses (Base for above percentages)	Received	174	56	193
	Given	160	53	199
Number of nonresponses (rejects inmates as a source of advice or doesn't believe in giving advice to inmates).	Received	109	63	88
	Given	123	66	82
Nonresponses as per cent of total interviews.	Received	39%	53%	31%
	Given	43%	55%	29%

are giving other inmates what they regard as valuable leads on getting along with the staff. This is support for our Proposition C8, below, on the extreme concern of inmates with adjustment to prison, as well as for Proposition C1, on orientation to isolation from other prisoners. The midterm panel was more concerned than others with learning a trade, but since this sample had longer sentences than the others, on the average, they had more prospect for such learning in prison.

At the termination of our interviews with the 250 successful releasees (mentioned in the opening paragraph of this chapter), we followed up our inquiry as to when they changed from interest in crime with a question on how this change came about. Although 122 said that they changed during imprisonment, only eleven credited other inmates as a major influence in this change. Of these eleven, four mentioned older inmates who recounted all the years they had wasted in prison and advised younger ones against risking return, two mentioned aid and encouragement in vocational and academic study, one mentioned his distrust and dislike of prisoners as deterring him from crime, and four were indefinite as to the nature of the reformative influence that other inmates had provided. In general, reference to other inmates as a rehabilitation influence was strikingly infrequent. This contrasts with their references to staff, cited in chapter 6.

Rehabilitation presumably requires that the criminal identify with non-criminals. In social-psychological terms, it is the prisoner's reference groups that influence his behavior on release, and the reference groups of rehabilitated criminals apparently do not correspond to their inmate membership groups when confined. Possibly this accounts for the research results, cited in chapter 8, indicating no recidivism reduction from the early use of group counseling in California prisons.

Table 5.5 indicates, as was expected, that nearly all valued advice given or received by the prisoners was exchanged on their current commitment, although the newly received inmates still stressed advice exchanged in prior commitments. Less learning was ascribed to the jail than we expected, and time served did not differentiate advice givers from advice recipients as clearly as we thought it might. Conforming to our expectations, these inquiries did provide marked support for another proposition:

C6. The flow of inter-inmate advice is predominantly from older to younger inmates.

Some practical implications of this finding for prison policies on the separation of inmates of different age are discussed in chapter 7, on "Isolation Promotion and Custody Grading."

INMATE PERCEPTION OF VARIATION IN INTER-INMATE RELATIONS IN DIFFERENT PARTS OF THE PRISON

One aspect of inmate-inmate relationships is the effect of job assignments on the development of harmony or conflict between inmates. The following two pairs of questions were administered in interviews with inmates at three stages of their prison term (first week, fourth month, and midterm):

TABLE 5.5   Places Where Inmates Most Frequently Exchanged Most Valuable Advice, and Relative Age and Time Served of Those to Whom Advice Was Given (Prison Panel Study)

	Direction of advice	ENTRANCE PANEL		Midterm panel
		First week	Fourth month	
Place where advice was given				
On this commitment, at this institution	Received	41%	95%	81%
	Given	51%	96%	94%
Prior state or federal commitment	Received	32%	2%	7%
	Given	27%	4%	2%
In jail	Received	16%	4%	3%
	Given	23%	—	1%
Other institution, on this commitment	Received	1%	—	9%
	Given	—	—	4%
Relative age of inmate to whom advice was given				
Older		15%	19%	22%
Younger		59%	53%	60%
About same or doesn't know		26%	28%	19%
Relative amount of time served by inmate to whom advice was given (compared to giver)				
More time		31%	42%	36%
Less time		41%	36%	44%
About same or doesn't know		28%	23%	21%
Number of responses (Base of above percentages)	Received	173	56	193
	Given	154	52	198
Number of nonresponses (none, don't know, can't remember, etc.)	Received	110	63	88
	Given	129	67	83
Nonresponses as per cent of total interviews	Received	39%	53%	31%
	Given	46%	56%	30%

"At what assignment in this institution do you think you could get along best with other inmates? Why?"; and "At what assignment in this prison do you think you would have the most trouble with other inmates? What kind of trouble?"

Sixty-one per cent of our sample indicated a specific assignment as the one in which they would get along best with other inmates. The remaining 39 per cent stated that they would get along well on any assignment, or they did not know enough about the institution to say where they would get along best. Only 44 per cent of our subjects indicated a specific assignment as the one in which they would most expect trouble with other inmates, the remaining 56 per cent rejecting the suggestion that they might have trouble with other inmates anywhere, or stating that they did not know where they might have trouble. On the question of where they would get along best, such nonperception cases were only a slightly larger proportion of inmates just entering prison than of those interviewed at a later stage of their sentence. However, on the question of where they would have most trouble with other inmates, the proportion who gave a "don't know" type of response dropped from 64 per cent in the newly received prisoners to 55 per cent when these men were interviewed during their fourth month, and to 48 per cent in the midterm group. Apparently men come to perceive new "trouble spots" in the prison more definitely than they learn new perceptions of assignments as places where they would get along best.

As indicated in Table 5.6, half of the inmates who perceived a trouble spot designated the culinary-service assignments (particularly dining room) as the place where they would have most trouble with other inmates. Rea-

TABLE 5.6   Inmate Perception of Where They Would Get Along Best and
Where They Would Have Most Trouble with Other Inmates
(Prison Panel Study)

	(1) Where get along best	(2) Where have most trouble	Ratio of 2 to 1
Type of response:			
Indicated a perception of a particular assignment as fitting the question	61%	44%	0.7[c]
"Don't know," "Makes no difference," etc.	39%	56%	1.4[c]
Type of assignment indicated (as percentages of total indicating a particular assignment as fitting the question)[d]:			
Culinary service	6%	51%	8.4[c]
Laundry	1%	8%	8.0[c]
Skilled trade	22%	2%	0.1[c]
Industries	16%	10%	0.7[a]
Farm	12%	5%	0.4[b]
Orderly or janitor	9%	6%	0.7
Heavy manual labor details	9%	7%	0.7
Clerical	7%	2%	0.2[c]
Others not readily classifiable	19%	10%	0.5[b]
(683 Interviews: first week 283, fourth month, 119, and midterm 281)			

Deviation from equal proportions as great as these, for this size sample, would occur by chance alone:
[a] less than once in twenty times;
[b] less than once in one hundred times;
[c] less than once in a thousand times.
[d] Tests in the lower section of the table, on type of assignment, are by comparison of Bernoulli populations, per B. W. Lindgren, *Statistical Theory*. New York, Macmillan, 1962, pp. 337-38. Similar results were obtained with an arcsin transformation, per Helen M. Walker and Joseph Lev, *Statistical Inference*. New York, Holt, 1953, pp. 423-24. A Chi Square test for independence, applied to this table, yields Chi Square 16,456, 8 df, p<.001.

sons for this were evident in the comments of those who were articulate when asked "What kind of trouble?" A first group of complaints seems to stem from the fact that the culinary assignments have a large number of inmates, all of whom cannot be closely supervised. As one inmate put it: "There are a lot of dirty jobs there nobody wants to do so you have trouble with guys goofing off. I'd have to hit some of them on the side of the head to keep from having to do their share of the work." Others said they would always have to tell the officer to keep from getting blamed for what others didn't do, and this would get them in trouble with the inmates. When an inmate is serving food, or is presumed to be in a position to sneak extra delicacies, he is likely to offend many inmates who will pressure him for favors he cannot satisfy. As one inmate put it, "If your friends come through your serving line, they'll want more than they're supposed to get."

Another reason for inmate conflict in culinary assignments may be that a disproportionate concentration of contentious or unstable inmates tend to remain there, while others are moved to assignments that require more patience, skill, or sense of responsibility, or involve more escape risk. Finally, inmates frequently view culinary work as undesirable in itself, perhaps because it is predominantly a feminine concern outside the prison, and because it is used as punishment in the military services. As one put it, "I wouldn't like the work and I'd try to take it out on anyone around me." In a personal letter commenting on my early reports on this segment of our research, former Bureau of Prisons Assistant Director Frank Loveland writes:

There has been a long history of the culinary service as a place of assignment. It requires, or at least uses, a large number of inmates—certainly more than like that type of work. A number of suggestions have been made over the years as to the solution of the problem. Some wardens have taken the view that all new inmates should be assigned there initially and "earn" their way to a preferred position. I have never believed in this view, since it runs contrary to the principle that a person should be placed where he can be benefited, and placed as soon as possible before he loses interest. In general, the kitchen and dining room have been assigned inmates who were not up to the standards of ability of those assigned to industries and the shops. This has been generally true, except for inmates specifically assigned to culinary service for vocational training (as bakers, butchers, cooks, etc.).

In recent years there has been an attempt to lower the number of inmates employed in the culinary departments and to increase the number of training assignments there in order to reduce the unpopularity of the assignment.

The laundry ranked next to the culinary services in the ratio with which it was designated as a trouble spot rather than a place where inmates would get along well. Like the dining room, the laundry involves a fairly large number of inmates working together, is not very selective, and places some inmates in a position where they will be pressured to give special favors to others in the handling of clothing. (Perhaps as a reaction against the regimentation of their situation, some inmates become fantastically concerned with procuring subtle variations in tailoring or pressing of what are presumed to be uniform items of inmate clothing.) Prior work experience and postrelease employment prospects in laundries are more frequent among Negro than among white inmates. This leads to a high concentration of

Negroes assigned to the prison laundry; consequently, some white inmates explained their expectation of trouble at a laundry assignment in terms of their admitted race prejudice.

Table 5.6 also shows that inmates who perceived of some assignment as that at which they would get along *best* with other inmates most often designated a place involving a skilled trade, such as the institution machine shop or plumbing shop, or an automobile or airplane mechanics' training school. These assignments tend to have fewer and more highly selected inmates than the culinary services, have less turnover of inmate personnel, and offer a career training program which provides most of the inmates there with a strong common interest. The high evaluation of these assignments by inmates placed there also motivates them to avoid difficulties with other inmates so as to prevent their being moved elsewhere in the prison. On the other hand, removal from a dining-room detail is less likely to be perceived as a loss. It is notable that the skilled-trade assignments were designated as those in which the inmate would get along best with other inmates ten times as often as they were designated as the assignments where they would have most trouble with other inmates (considering only the responses of subjects who distinguished between assignments from these standpoints). Conversely, the culinary and laundry assignments were designated as trouble spots eight times as often as they were designated as places where the subject thought he would get along best with other inmates. As a preferred assignment, culinary service frequently included designation of a small skilled-trade unit, such as the butchers' or bakers' vocational training program.

The second most frequent choice of those who indicated a preference among assignments was prison industries. Industry provides incentives in the form of pay and extra days off the sentence for good behavior. This may account for the fact that the largest percentage of inmates selecting industries favorably were in the midterm panel, which had predominantly longer sentences than the other samples. However, the most common reason given by the appreciable number who anticipated trouble with others in industry was that they were made nervous by the noise, dirt, and heat. The lack of close supervision in some industry units may occasionally result in abuses responsible for miscellaneous complaints on industry, such as a few statements that other inmates in industry "give you an unfair share of the work," that there was homosexual propositioning there, and that inmates favored by the staff ran the others.

The farm was the third most frequent selection as a place where the inmate would get along best. Its low selection by the midterm panel may be due to the escape risk inhibiting placement of long-term men on the farm except when their release date is near; this may mean that these inmates were less likely than others to consider the farm as a possibility when indicating their preference. For the others, of course, the farm probably was attractive because of the freedom it provides. Some youthful inmates of rural background said they like the farm mainly because they like the country boys there, while some city youths indicated they would have trouble on the farm because they "don't get along with country boys."

After the subjects indicated the assignment on which they thought they would get along best, they were asked "Why?" Twenty-six per cent answered with statements which dealt with liking the work involved or desiring to learn the work. Twenty-one per cent indicated that they got along best where the men know and like their work. Twenty per cent expressed the inmate value of "doing your own time," since these answers stressed the limited interaction with others or limited responsibility for other inmates at the preferred assignment. Sixteen per cent made specific reference to the type of inmates assigned to the preferred job, such as that their interests were similar to those of the subject or that they were not troublemakers. Other types of explanation totaled 17 per cent, of which the most frequent was reference by 5 per cent to the teamwork and mutual aid of the inmates at the preferred work place.

Our data in this section can be summarized by the following pair of related clusters of hypotheses:

C7a. Inmates will get along best with other inmates at jobs where they find: (1) a small number of other inmates; (2) low contact with the rest of the inmate population; (3) a trade training program; (4) limited access to contraband services or supplies; (5) careful selection of assignees.

Or, stated conversely:

C7b. Inmates are most likely to have trouble with other inmates at jobs with: (1) a high concentration of men rejected for assignment elsewhere; (2) a large number of prisoners assigned; (3) much contact with the rest of the inmate population; (4) access to services or supplies highly valued by most prisoners.

We did not have sufficient information to explore interrelations among these components—for example, the extent to which specific favorable features offset the unfavorable. If not all the unfavorable features can be eliminated, it would seem wise to try, at least, to have presumable compensating favorable features at those assignments where the unfavorable cannot be avoided. Thus prison industry assignments are often hot, noisy, and otherwise unpleasant, but offer pay, good-time, and trade training as compensatory advantages.

Our data in this section especially suggest the shortsightedness of using a few assignments as places for concentrating men with frequent disciplinary difficulty. The Terre Haute prison reported a marked reduction in behavior problems when a labor detail of this type was abolished and its assignees distributed throughout the institution. Similarly, much improvement in the behavior of many inmates occurred there when a period of good behavior at the current assignment was abolished as a prerequisite for placement in the preferred skilled-trade, industrial, and farm assignments. The *Institution Regulations* issued for Terre Haute in 1963 assert, with respect to prison industries assignments, ". . . the needs of the individual shall be paramount and the presence of disciplinary reports (recent or remote) will not preclude consideration." As Warden Markley expressed it, all inmate supervision staff should share the task of trying to improve some difficult inmates instead of overburdening some and sparing the others.

The requirement that inmates exhibit good behavior during a waiting period at distasteful assignments before being eligible to move elsewhere results in prolonged concentration of disgruntled individuals at these assignments. The atmosphere for all inmates starting their prison experience at these jobs promotes in them an exaggerated perception of the extent to which others are hostile. They may develop aggressive habits in adapting to these situations, thus getting into difficulties which prolong their stay there. These social environments also encourage prisoners to evaluate their own worth mainly in terms of their toughness and aggressiveness. Because of such consequences, the good-behavior waiting period rules may have the opposite of their intended effect of promoting good behavior.

INTERESTS INFLUENCING INMATE AFFILIATIONS

Another card which we presented to our interview subjects was headed "How I try to live with the other inmates," and contained five statements formulated from narrative material in pretest interviews, representing possible interests influencing affiliation with other inmates. After the five statements were read, the inmate was asked to indicate which ones described how he tried to live with other inmates. An average of 2.9 of the statements were endorsed by each inmate. Their endorsements were recorded and tabulated by us in the sequence in which they were mentioned, thus providing a rough index of the relative importance which the inmates attached to the several statements with which they agreed. The statements, and the frequency of their endorsement on all 1137 interviews, are indicated in Table 5.7.

Statement *e,* "Try to keep away from certain kinds of inmates," was the most frequently endorsed of all the statements. It was chosen most often not only in all interviews taken collectively, but also in each prison, in each of the separate panels, in each interview with the entrance panel, and both as first choice and in total selections. This is further strong support for our Proposition C1: "Prisoners as a whole are more oriented to maintain isola-

TABLE 5.7 How Inmates "Try to Live with Other Inmates"
(Prison Panel Study)

	Per cent rating this statement the most applicable (first selections)	Per cent rating this statement as applicable (total selections)
a. Try to be with inmates with whom I have a lot to talk about, to make the time pass quickly.	22	60
b. Try to be with inmates that I can learn something from.	20	61
c. Try to be "in touch" with inmates who can help me make out better here.	3	25
d. Try to have a few inmate friends on whom I can depend.	20	62
e. Try to keep away from certain kinds of inmates.	32	82
None of these statements endorsed:	3	3
Total	100	

tion from other prisoners than to achieve solidarity with other prisoners."
The least endorsed statement was c, "Try to be 'in touch' with inmates who
can help me make out better here." The latter statement was phrased "try
to be 'in good' with important inmates here" on the first-week, fourth-
month, and midterm interviews, but we changed it because inmates frequently resented the implication that other inmates were important. The
change in wording did not alter its low frequency.

When each inmate concluded his endorsements of statements from this
card, he was quizzed on various aspects of each of his choices. The inmates
who had expressed agreement with statement a ("Try to be with inmates
with whom I have a lot to talk about, to make the time pass quickly") were
asked: "Now think of an inmate who is an example of someone that you
have a lot in common with, so that you have much to talk about. Don't
tell me his name, but keep him in your mind. What do you most often talk
about with him?" Of 586 responses to this inquiry, 63 per cent were classified by us as involving some type of *small talk* (such topics as sports, women,
hobbies, and acquaintances). Sixteen per cent of the responses were classified as *noncriminal plans for the future* (such as going into business, or
plans in regard to their families). Eight per cent designated *academic subjects* (such as science, mechanics, news, and religion). Only 5 per cent
indicated as their principal topic some aspects of *prison life* (such as work
assignments, rules, inmates, or staff). Only 3 per cent designated *conviction, parole, or legal matters,* and only 3 per cent said they talked most
often about *crime.* There was little difference between stage-of-sentence
groups in regard to topics of conversation, although topics classified by us
as noncriminal plans for the future were somewhat more often reported by
inmates in the near-release panel, while in the first-week interview inmates
more often reported discussing conviction, parole, legal matters, or crime.

Inmates who had selected statement *b,* "Try to be with inmates that I can learn something from," were asked to think of an example of such an inmate and were then asked: "What kind of things do you try to learn from him?" Topics classified by us as *nonvocational education* and *business or trade* together comprised 59 per cent of the 588 inmate responses to this question, while *learning about crime* comprised only 3 per cent of the responses. There was only a slight increase, near release, in references to this learning of business or trade information, but an increase of from 3 to 16 per cent in references to learning helpful character traits (responsibility, religiosity, etc.) from another inmate. The learning of modes of adjustment to prison life was reported as the best advice from another inmate by 33 per cent in the first week in prison, and by only 8 per cent near release.[9]

Respondents who endorsed statement *c,* "Try to be 'in good' with important inmates" (or "in touch with inmates who can help men make out better here"), were asked to think of such an inmate and were then asked: "Why does it help to be 'in good' (or 'in touch') with this inmate?" Of 168 cases, 32 per cent gave reasons which could be classified as the desire to learn something from this inmate, generally to learn how to stay out of trouble in the prison. Thus it overlapped their endorsement of statement *b.* Twenty-one per cent asserted that achieving relationships with important inmates *provides material rewards or advantages.* This usually was reported as contraband items or services, ranging from better clothing issue to nutmeg stolen from the kitchen, which was taken with water as a presumed intoxicant. Thirteen per cent specified that these contacts gave them some form of *access to staff,* 9 per cent indicated *access to official records,* and 25 per cent gave other reasons not classifiable in the foregoing. Notable in this "other" group of responses was frequent mention by Ashland inmates that "officers judge you by the company you keep, so you make out better if you're seen with someone whom the officers respect." Apparently this was an effective indoctrination by the staff. Some inmates mentioned instead that their associates determined their prestige with other inmates, and frequently they indicated that they wanted to be on good terms with inmates who would make trouble for them if they were not on good terms.

Inmates who had selected statement *d,* "Try to have a few inmate friends on whom I can depend," were asked: "What would be a good example of a situation where you would want an inmate friend to be dependable?" Table 5.8 reveals several differences between beginning and end of imprisonment in regard to the situations in which inmates perceive it desirable to have a dependable friend. *Protection* and *prison adjustment advice* both were more often designated by new inmates than inmates terminating their sentences. This suggests the initial fears and anxieties of prisoners, par-

---

[9] Differences in proportions as great as those described above could occur by chance alone, in samples of this size, less than once in a hundred times.

TABLE 5.8   Matters for Which Inmates Depend upon Another Inmate, as Reported by Those Inmates Who State They Try to Have a Few Inmate Friends on Whom They Can Depend (Prison Panel Study)

	First-week interviews	Near-release interviews	All other interviews	All interviews
Material aid (share or loan goods)	21%[a]	*44%*[a,c]	39%	35%
Psychological support (listen to troubles, advice, etc.)	13%[a]	28%[a]	21%	20%
Protection (self or property)	27%[a]	10%[a]	18%	19%
Work (help perform duties, etc.)	7%	7%	7%	7%
Prison adjustment advice	*13%*[b]	5%[b]	4%	6%
Connections (assignments, contraband, information, etc.)	*4%*	1%	2%	3%
Other matters	*15%*[a]	4%[a]	9%	10%
Number of respondents	167	135	354	656

[a] Differences as large as those indicated between first-week and near-release prisoners could occur by chance alone, with samples of this size, less than once in a hundred times.

[b] Could occur by chance less than once in twenty times.

[c] Italic indicates highest percentage on a line.

ticularly first-timers, entering what they apparently perceive as a jungle-like surrounding. In this connection it should be remembered that many of these inmates probably had experienced days or weeks of disorganized existence in county or city jails just prior to entering the federal institutions; it generally is agreed that operations of "kangaroo courts," sex deviants, and other sources of inmate pressures are much less impeded in jails than in well-run prisons, and jail experience is likely to influence an inmate's early prison behavior.

The increase, near release, in inmate dependence on other inmates for *material aid* and for matters of *psychological support* (e.g., "someone I can tell my troubles to who won't tell it all over the compound") suggests the progressive integration of inmates into informal social relationships through which they can reduce the discomforts of their situation. However, the responses indicated in the discussion of friendship versus isolation earlier in this chapter suggest that, in most cases, such mutual aid is achieved in the federal prisons by having a few inmate friends, rather than by identification with a total inmate social unit. With tested inmate friends, fears and suspicions can be replaced by reciprocal social support to relieve tensions aroused by other inmates, and there can be a sharing of goods and services. These data seem to identify networks of inmate-inmate relationships which may form numerous separate or perhaps loosely linked informal social structures within the prison community, rather than a tightly integrated total inmate social system. New prisoners apparently are integrated into these structures only gradually.

The most frequent remark recorded in our "other" category, on things for which an inmate friend should be depended upon, was to be able to depend upon an inmate leaving the prison to contact persons on the outside. These reports were especially high in the first-week and near-release interviews. This is consistent with the notion of a U-curve in reference to outsiders. It also suggests the sense of isolation of prisoners, particularly of the many to whom writing is not a familiar means of transacting affairs or whose interest is to communicate with persons not on their prison-approved list of correspondents.

The 82 per cent of our interviewees selecting statement *e,* "Try to keep away from certain kinds of inmates," were asked "to think of an inmate who is an example of someone to keep away from." If they said they had someone in mind, they were asked: "What is your main reason for trying to keep away from him?" Nearly half of the respondents gave a reason which indicated the other inmate to be a *troublemaker,* such as one who likes to fight, "gets you into trouble with officers," or breaks rules. The most criminal inmates were seen as a threat by 15 per cent in the first week, but by only 5 per cent in all other interviews.[10] Troublemakers were perceived as a threat somewhat more frequently after the first week. This suggests that as prisoners are integrated into informal inmate social relationships, they shift from perceiving other inmates as a threat according to their presumed personal attributes, and judge them instead by their current behavior, as either "troublemakers" or dependable friends. When they get to know an individual inmate personally, his criminality is less important than his behavior in the prison. This phenomenon of persons having a status based upon their ascribed qualities when they first encounter one another, but having their status become increasingly dependent upon achievement or performance as acquaintance continues, is familiar in many social situations.[11]

After discerning the inmate's reason for trying to keep away from certain prisoners, each respondent who had selected statement *e* was asked: "Do you have any trouble keeping away from him?" At every stage of sentence only 8 per cent admitted such difficulty. Then the respondents were asked: "How do you handle it?" Again there were no significant differences among stage-of-sentence samples; 77 per cent asserted that they handled situations of undesirable inmate pressures by techniques which we classified as avoiding or ignoring them, while 20 per cent asserted that they coped with such situations by what we classified as rebuff, threat, or violence.

Our five statements, each of which was to be either endorsed or rejected, were unreliable in that, when reinterviewed, inmates changed the number

[10] A difference in proportions as great as this could occur by chance alone, in samples of this size, less than once in a hundred times.

[11] Cf. Talcott Parsons, *The Social System* (Glencoe, Ill., Free Press, 1950), pp. 58-67.

of statements they endorsed. For the 60 midterm-panel cases reinterviewed by a different staff member as a reliability test, the general tendency was to endorse fewer statements on their reinterview than on their original interview. (However, some of our staff generally elicited more endorsements than other staff members, apparently through some interviewing mannerisms which encouraged longer responses.) Only 20 per cent of these inmates endorsed the same number of statements on each interview. However, 85 per cent of them endorsed on both interviews all statements they had endorsed on that interview in which their least number of endorsements occurred. The remaining 15 per cent of the inmates endorsed most—but not all—of the same statements on both interviews.

In spite of the limitation indicated by the foregoing, it is believed that the responses presented in this section are of interest as a portrayal of the types of concern that inmates have in their dealings with other inmates, and of some shifts in these concerns in the course of imprisonment. In general, they confirm the overall impression that in the inmate world there is a diversity of interests and a wariness of other inmates. The dominant concern with keeping away from certain kinds of inmates was strong confirmation for our Proposition C1—that prisoners, as a whole, are more oriented to maintain isolation from each other than to achieve solidarity with other prisoners. The topics of concern in conversation and in learning from other inmates, and the reasons for avoiding other inmates suggest:

C8. A predominant interest of prison inmates is to adjust to the expectations of their keepers in order to stay "out of trouble" while confined.

C9. Most prison inmates maintain strong noncriminal interests, including vocational aspirations of a legitimate nature.

If these propositions are valid, and we have had many types of evidence that they are, they indicate that much rehabilitation assistance to inmates is possible even in that deplored institution, the prison. However, evidence of a potential does not mean that the potential is realized in all or most cases. Determining the circumstances under which assistance is maximized is, of course, the ultimate concern of all our research, and can be the basis for much more research.

INMATE INTERESTS AND PERCEPTIONS OF THE INTERESTS OF OTHER INMATES

Diverse responses of inmates to our early exploratory inquiries on their concerns and interests in prison were summarized by us in nine statements, which are presented in Table 5.9. These numbered sentences, arranged in systematically varied sequences, were placed on cards headed "What an Inmate Might Try to Get or Do in Prison, and Why." Each interview sub-

TABLE 5.9   Per Cent of Inmates Selecting Each Statement as One of Their Three Major Interests in Prison, Compared with the Per Cent Who Select the Statement as One of the Three Major Interests of Other Inmates, at Various Stages of Prison Term (Prison Panel Study)

Statement	To whom applied	PER CENT AT EACH STAGE OF PRISON TERM		
		First week	Sixth month	Near release
1. Try to get the most comforts possible in prison, get the most pleasant assignment, and do the easiest time possible.	Self	10	10	12
	Others	11	19	19
2. Try to show the other inmates they can't give you a hard time or push you around.	Self	1	1	1
	Others	2	7	9
3. Try to keep from getting segregation or other kind of punishment.	Self	7	12	11
	Others	9	14	13
4. Try to learn a trade or get more school credit to help you get a better job on the outside.	Self	26	22	21
	Others	24	15	12
5. Try to improve abilities or knowledge for some reason other than getting a job, such as improving in some sport, study, or hobby.	Self	8	9	12
	Others	8	7	10
6. Try to learn or figure out a way to keep from getting caught at crime and make more money at it.	Self	1	—	1
	Others	2	9	11
7. Try to get a pay job to make some money while in prison.	Self	16	13	11
	Others	16	19	18
8. Try to be more conscientious about religious duties or think out your religion better.	Self	12	12	12
	Others	11	3	3
9. Try to improve yourself psychologically by getting counseling or by study; try to understand yourself better.	Self	19	20	19
	Others	18	7	6
Total responses (maximum of 3 per respondent; each figure represents 100% in terms of the percentages above it, for either self or others).	Self	841	600	675
	Others	789	553	654
Total responses of "none of these," "don't know," "none others," etc. as percentage of total possible responses (at 3 per respondent for self and for others).	Self	0.9%	2.9%	9.3%
	Others	7.1%	10.5%	12.1%
Total respondents		283	306	248

ject was given the card and the statements were read over with him, after which he was asked a series of questions, starting with: "Which says best what you are most interested in doing here? . . . Which is second? . . . Which is third?" Subsequent questions included: "Which sentence on this card says best what most other inmates are interested in? . . . Which is second? . . . Which is third?" Responses to the inquiries on their own current interests and on the interests of other inmates, are summarized in Table 5.9.

Even granting the probable tendency of inmates to try to describe themselves favorably, it is of interest that, considering all interviews collectively, learning a trade or in other ways preparing for a better job opportunity outside of prison was the first interest of most inmates at every prison studied. It was most frequent among the nine interests covered on our card both as first choice and when totaling first, second, and third choices, as in Table 5.9. This is consistent with Proposition C9 set forth in the preceding section and with the findings in every comparable inquiry on other components of our project, which suggest that the predominant concern of most federal offenders is with their economic problems.

The initial high interest in trade and related studies declined somewhat during the course of imprisonment at all of the institutions studied, but especially at Terre Haute and Milan. Only at Ashland, where this interest always was higher than at other institutions, was it still clearly more frequent than other interests in the near-release interviews.

The second most frequently designated interest was trying to improve oneself psychologically, or to understand oneself better. Most inmates at every institution included this, as well as learning a trade or other occupational preparation, in their first three choices. There is no very clear pattern of institutional differentiation or of change over time on this item, although of some interest is its sharp increase in the middle of the inmate's term at Ashland, the institution with the most extensive counseling program, and its subsequent decline there. Another frequently indicated self-improvement interest was in religion. It will be noted in Table 5.10 that those with least prior confinement are most likely to be concerned with learning a trade and with religion, while those with most prior confinement emphasize psychological self-improvement. This suggests the possibility that inmates with most prior confinement have tended to give up trade training and religious self-improvement because these demand what are to them more definitely specifiable types of effort than does the psychological. "Changing oneself psychologically" is a glib phrase. It may connote a magic transformation which appeals to wishful thinking, and may, in fact, be an index of a sense of hopelessness, a barrier to the effort which psychotherapy requires.

Our major concern with the material in Tables 5.9 and 5.10 was to compare the inmate's perception of interests of other inmates with designations of his own interests. Such comparison, as might be expected, yields the sharpest contrasts on items related to conventional conceptions of self-improvement.

The extent to which the subjects identified an interest in themselves more frequently than in other inmates was greatest on Item 8 (religious interests), followed by Item 9 (improving oneself psychologically) and Item 4 (trade training). Among the officially derogated interests, the difference between

TABLE 5.10   Most Serious Prior Sentence as Related to Per Cent Including Three
of the Statements in Table 5.9 in the First Three of Nine Possible Interests
of Themselves and of Other Inmates

Statement (abbreviated from Table 5.9)	To whom applied	Most serious prior sentence	PER CENT AT EACH STAGE OF PRISON TERM		
			First week	Sixth month	Near release
4. Learn a trade or get more school credits, for better job on the outside.	Self	None or fines	84	70	58
		Jail or probation	78	64	57
		Prison[a]	68	59	62
	Others	None or fines	44	50	22
		Jail or probation	41	40	32
		Prison[a]	38	41	28
8. Become more conscientious about religion.	Self	None or fines	42	58	42
		Jail or probation	36	35	32
		Prison[a]	30	20	28
	Others	None or fines	12	12	7
		Jail or probation	9	9	8
		Prison[a]	9	4	6
9. Improve self psychologically.	Self	None or fines	44	55	50
		Jail or probation	55	59	51
		Prison[a]	59	61	54
	Others	None or fines	4	22	23
		Jail or probation	12	17	15
		Prison[a]	17	18	10

[a] "Prison" here includes reformatories and training schools, as well as penitentiaries and other institutions primarily for felons.

frequency of perceiving the interest in themselves and frequency of perceiving it in other inmates was greatest on Item 6 (learning crime), followed by Item 2 (on showing other inmates that they cannot push one around), and Item 1 (on maximizing comforts in prison).[12] On most of these items, especially in the first week, contrast between perception of self and perception of others was greatest at the youth institutions, Ashland and Chillicothe, and least in the penitentiaries, particularly Leavenworth.

Differences between perceptions of self and perceptions of others as expressed in the percentages in Table 5.9 increased from the first week to near release, on most items, everywhere except at Ashland. At Ashland

[12] For the 5 prisons taken separately, difference between the perception of interests of self and those of others in Table 5.9 are in the same direction on Items 1, 2, 4, 5, 6, 8 and 9 more frequently than could occur by chance alone in this number of independent samples once in a thousand times (by Sign Test). Item 3, avoiding punishment, has a predominance of "other" over "self" that could occur by chance alone about once in fifty times. Only Item 7, on procuring a pay job, does not have a directionality of self-other differences in appreciable excess of chance expectation.

the percentages for self and other converged on every item except 5, and on that item the difference remained constant. However, at Milan there was a markedly increasing contrast in the inmates' perceptions of their own interests and their perceptions of the interests of other inmates, notably on Item 6, on interest in crime. These trends have a remarkable similarity to the changes in inter-inmate communication at these two institutions, summarized in Table 5.3. Ashland, where interests perceived in self and others converged, was the institution with the most marked increase of inmate interest in maximizing friendship with other inmates, while Milan, where they diverged most, was most distinguished for the progressive concern of its inmates in isolating themselves from other inmates.

The fact that inmates more often report having anticriminal interests than they report perceiving that other inmates have these interests, and the converse for procriminal interests, could simply be interpreted as their trying to present themselves favorably to our interviewers. While this may be a major explanation for the contrast, evidence of much sincerity in their responses is indicated by: (1) the extent to which some interests they ascribe to themselves are not virtues; (2) the shifts over time in these responses; and (3) the differences among groups of different prior record, already discussed in preceding paragraphs.

In interpreting further the contrast between the inmate's perception of his own interests and his perception of the interests of other inmates, it may be well to recall that our panel projects were inspired by the pioneer correctional panel research completed by Richard Cloward in a postwar military prison (and by oral reports on the Ohlin and Cloward panel study in juvenile institutions, which was under way when our project began). Cloward introduced the term "pluralistic ignorance" to interpret his finding that, when most of the military-prison inmates were conforming to staff urgings by applying for restoration to military service, they all believed that few or none of the other inmates were applying for restoration; the alternative to restoration, at the end of the prison term, was dishonorable discharge from military service. Apparently, inmate misperception occurred because the inmate social world was dominated by the longest-confined inmates, who disparaged official recommendations, so that other inmates found it easiest to manifest agreement with the opinion leaders publicly, even when privately they were conforming to staff recommendations. As Cloward puts it:

Because conforming prisoners feel constrained to pay lip-service to deviant norms, their visibility to conformists is obscured. The consequence of this is the fact that each conformist comes to believe that he is the only one who holds sentiments which support socially acceptable values. In other words, it is this condition of ignorance of the attitudes of others which, above all else, explains the fact in prison life (perhaps in many other situations) that small numbers of relatively cohesive deviant groups successfully control the larger aggregate of individuals.[13]

Actually, Cloward's conclusion could be deduced with the rigor of a syllogism. Let us take as a major premise that inmates opposed to staff values exceed inmates accepting staff values in the inclination to aggress verbally or physically against those who publicly disagree with them. (This is an unavoidable premise, of course, if staff values include nonaggression). Let us take a minor premise that thoughts which would elicit aggression against the speaker are not likely to be expressed. If one accepts these two premises, it follows deductively that in a population comprising both inmates who oppose and inmates who support staff values, those who are staff-opposing will publicly express their values more than will those who are staff-supporting. This leads to our proposition:

C10. Prisoners perceive other prisoners as having less commitment to staff-supported values than is, in fact, the case.

There is evidence from all components of our study, including the observation of postrelease behavior, that most inmates are considerably concerned with trying to "go straight" (our Proposition C9). It seems evident that both they and sociologists are pluralistically ignorant of the distribution of this interest in their group. Sociological ignorance, I suspect, comes from a similar process; academic students of prison-inmate life are disproportionately in contact with "front office politicians," who are the most articulate spokesmen of antistaff values. Expressed in current social-psychological terminology, one might say that both inmates and others commonly err in assuming that the inmate's membership group in the prison represents his primary reference group, especially in his orientation to life after release. However, Part III of this report, on the postrelease experiences of prisoners, indicates the extent to which the prison social world becomes the only one in which some inmates are successful in their endeavors, because of their disappointment in other pursuits immediately after release.

One factor accounting for part of the distribution in our tabulation of reported interests of other inmates is the frequency with which prisoners were reluctant to give their impressions of the interests of other inmates. What Table 5.9 summarizes as nonresponses in the interviews conducted during the inmates' first week in prison were mostly inmate protestations of ignorance because they were so new to the prison. However, nonresponses from inmates interviewed at a later stage of imprisonment increas-

---

[13] From termination of his summary, pp. 80-91, in the edited transcript of a Children's Bureau conference published as: Helen L. Witmer and Ruth Kotinsky, eds., *New Perspectives for Research on Juvenile Delinquency* (U. S. Children's Bur. Publication No. 356, 1956). See also Stanton H. Wheeler, "Role Conflict in Correctional Communities," chapter 6 in Cressey, *op. cit.*

ingly grew out of their expression of the staff and inmate-supported norm
of "doing your own time"—not being involved with the problems of other
inmates—as well as the inmate anti-informing norm. This inmate attitude
is discussed in the first part of chapter 7. The virtual absence of nonresponses at Chillicothe and Ashland is believed to result from a combination
of less-prisonized subjects with more persistently probing interviewers.

As might have been expected in a task of picking the first three from a
list of nine widely shared inmate interests, midterm-panel inmates frequently
made different selections when reinterviewed by another researcher as a
reliability check on the original interviews. Changes could occur readily if
several of the interests appear almost equal in importance to the inmates.
Also, of course, having a large number from which to pick increases the
possibility of inconsistency. The subjects' selections of their first five interests would have yielded more stable percentages than selections of their
first three, but this gain in reliability would have been at the cost of a loss
in the measure of relative intensity provided by selecting only three. Sixty
reinterviewed midterm-panel inmates repeated only two-thirds of the selections of their own interests and half of the selections of the interests of other
inmates when they were reinterviewed by another researcher about three
months later. Over a fourth of the nonrepetitions involved Item 9, on
improving oneself psychologically, and the next most unreliable item was
Item 8, on religion. The contrast in self and other selections, however, was
repeated on the reinterviews.

SUMMARY

Of the inmates studied, about a quarter reported trying to make as many
inmate friends as possible and three-fourths reported some concern with
maintaining isolation from other inmates, although most of these reported
trying to make a few inmate friends. This impression that most inmates
continuously are wary of other inmates was conveyed repeatedly, by responses to diverse questions. Interest in isolation from other inmates
increased with age, young inmates being predominantly concerned with
making a maximum number of inmate friends. Most inmates seemed to
change in these interests in the course of their imprisonment, especially
those at the youth prisons. Shifts in inmate attitude on these matters were
found generally to follow a U-shaped curve, with more concern with isolation at the beginning and at the end of confinement. Where the inmates in
an institution were most diverse in race and sentence, there was the sharpest
shift to their seeking to avoid friendship with other inmates.

It was found that the flow of advice valued by inmates tends to be predominantly from older to younger inmates, much more than from those
with more imprisonment to those with less. Chapter 7 proposes this

could be utilized effectively if there were less reluctance to mix offenders of diverse ages, provided in such mixtures a limited number of younger prisoners were mixed into institutions for older prisoners of lesser experience in correctional institutions.

Inmates were shown very markedly to perceive the culinary and laundry assignments as those in which they would have the most trouble with other inmates, and to perceive skilled trade assignments as characterized by the most accord. Reasons for these differences were indicated. It was suggested that rehabilitative goals for all would be furthered if one could avoid concentrations of "troublemakers" in certain assignments, and that rigid good-behavior-period requirements as prerequisite to transfer of inmates to more desired assignments may, in practice, deter good behavior.

Our findings from several different types of inquiry indicated that inmates have a predominant interest in adjusting to the demands of the institution and that they have strong noncriminal aspirations. However, evidence and deductive reasoning supported the notion that inmates and others generally overestimate the extent of inmate opposition to staff-supported standards, because inmates who oppose these standards are most articulate. It is probable that in some prisons, or sections of prisons, inmate leaders who identify with staff and promote conventional moral values are so clearly dominant that the conventional values are the most commonly articulated and non-conforming values are not extensively expressed. Such a situation has been described in some exceptional prison units for highly selected inmates.[14]

An objective of the strategies described in chapters 7, 8, 9, and 10 is to increase the situations where there is such concord between staff and inmate values. However, inmate-inmate relationships may so often be affected by inmate-staff relationships that it is appropriate to deal with the latter before discussing practical suggestions on manipulation of the total social world of the prison.

---

[14] For a description of this type of situation in a prison camp, see: Oscar Grusky, "Organizational Goals and the Behavior of Informal Leaders," *Am. J. Sociology, 65,* no. 1 (July 1959), 59-67. A study which compared six juvenile training schools of contrasting types concluded, on inmate (client) leadership, ". . . in the more custodial institutions the leaders have more negative perspectives than do the other clients, while in the treatment-orientated organizations the leaders have more positive perspectives than do the other boys." Robert D. Vinter, Morris Janowitz, *et al., The Comparative Study of Juvenile Correctional Institutions: A Research Report* (Ann Arbor, University of Michigan School of Social Work, Dec. 1961), p. 654.

CHAPTER 6

Inmate-Staff Relationships

THE TRADITIONAL GAP AND ITS MANY CROSSINGS

Prison administrators often find that abstract theoretical analyses by sociologists of prison social organization present an excessively melodramatic view of relationships between prison staff and inmates. However, to perceive principles that explain the varieties of human behavior in a complex organization often requires that we start with overstatements. Only then may we see how these abstractions must be qualified to fit the facts more perfectly.

One of the more brilliant analyses was provided by Erving Goffman. In speaking collectively of mental hospitals, prisons, and similar institutions he says:

> . . . . there is a basic split between a large class of individuals who live in and who have restricted contact with the world outside the walls, conveniently called inmates, and the small class that supervises them, conveniently called staff, who often operate on an 8-hour day and are socially integrated into the outside world. Each group tends to conceive of members of the other in terms of narrow hostile stereotypes, staff often seeing inmates as bitter, secretive, and un-trustworthy, while inmates often see staff as condescending, high-handed and mean. Staff tends to feel superior and righteous; inmates tend, in some ways at least, to feel inferior, weak, blameworthy and guilty. Social mobility between the two strata is grossly restricted; social distance is typically great and often prescribed; even talk across the boundaries may be conducted in a special tone of voice. The restrictions on contact presumably help to maintain the antagonistic stereotypes. In any case, two different social and cultural worlds develop, tending to jog along beside each other, with points of official contact but little mutual penetration.[1]

Similarly, with respect to prisons viewed as a type of closed social unit, Lloyd E. Ohlin says:

> The chief characteristic of this prison social system is the caste-like division between those who rule and those who are ruled. The atmosphere of the prison in varying degrees is strictly authoritarian. The essential character of the relationship between the administrative staff and the inmates is one of conflict.

[1] Erving Goffman, "Characteristics of Total Institutions," *Symposium on Preventive and Social Psychiatry* (Washington, D. C., Walter Reed Army Institute of Research, 1957), pp. 46-67. This article was restated by Goffman in chapters 1 and 2 of D. R. Cressey, ed., *The Prison* (New York, Holt, Rinehart and Winston, 1961); and in Goffman, *Asylums* (New York, Doubleday, 1961).

There is a gulf of fear and distrust in most prison systems separating the authorities on the one hand from the inmate body on the other.

But, he adds:

This gulf is bridged in many ways and at many points, for otherwise the system could not function.[2]

Our observations, and the literature on prison social relationships, suggest three main ways in which communication between inmates and staff is regulated. The first is by inmate pressure, the second by informal staff-inmate contacts, and the third by formal arrangement.

Inmate Pressure

Describing inmate-staff social relationships in a prison when the administration was highly authoritarian in its approach to inmates, McCleery says:

. . . inmate society developed a power hierarchy as sharply defined and immobile as that of the administration. The survival of that inmate hierarchy . . . depended on a basic rule of the inmate code: *Never talk to a screw.*

The absence of published regulations and the lack of a formal orientation program, . . . the shocking unfamiliarity of the prison situation, and the demands that regimentation imposed, all combined to make the newly admitted inmate completely dependent on the experienced prisoner. In a unique sense, his knowledge was power. He could share on his own conditions his knowledge of the limits of official tolerance. . . . The conditions of . . . inclusion in the inmate community were acceptance of a subordinate role in the community and adoption of its attitudes and values. Its values began with rejection of contact with officials and culminated in rejection of allegiance to society as a whole. . . .

By constant emphasis on the idea of the *rat,* and the use of isolation as a sanction, inmate society retained its maximal valuation of power and still restricted the most obvious recourse to power—the appeal to official sanctions by individuals in their own interest. . . .

Leadership in the inmate society involved the ability to explain, predict, or control to some degree a situation in which others were uncertain or helpless. Other inmates gained protection and security by attaching themselves to the leaders and rendering them the petty tributes that conveyed status. This type of dominance depended on access to informal communications, whereas in a society in which information is a free good, leadership normally depends on the functions that one performs in meeting the needs and problems of the group. . . . The problems of the prison society were not those of food, shelter or management, but of uncertainty and ego threat in an environment of arbitrary power. Hence, leadership there meant having contacts with the "grapevine" and with official sources. Whether the leaders actually manipulated power

[2] Lloyd E. Ohlin, *Sociology and the Field of Corrections,* New York, Russell Sage Foundation, 1956, p. 14.

or simply manipulated belief, they . . . were given license to talk with officials that was never extended to men of unproven dependability.[3]

What we see in the authoritarian prison is inmate pressure operating, although never with perfect success, to confine extensive inmate communication with staff to a few inmates variously called "big shots," "front-office men," or "politicians." As Cloward puts it: "The politician is a figure of power, commanding a superior position because he manipulates the transmission of information between official and inmate systems. . . . He obtains access to the control of information by conniving . . . , or by obtaining employment in a location that is strategic because information is available."[4] Cloward contends that this arrangement is advantageous to custodial interests in a prison not undergoing change, because this inmate elite has a vested interest in the *status quo*. Any major disorder or work failure at assignments where the inmate leaders are located is likely to lead to alterations in assignment of inmates and in staff-inmate relationships there. Such changes may alter the relative position of these leaders compared to other inmates, with respect to access to information, freedom of movement, or access to contraband. Thus the "old cons" keep the others "in line" to "keep down the heat" and so protect their jobs and rackets.

This perception, which Cloward calls "the conservative ideology of the inmate elite," also underlies the Hartung and Floch explanation for the 1952-53 prison riots. They see these riots mainly as consequences of reform tactics which deprived the inmate leaders of their advantages or power without providing compensating behavior incentives or safeguards. While doubtless not complete, this is one of the few explanations that accounted for the riots in terms of conditions more demonstrable in the institutions involved than in riotless prisons. Many other alleged riot causes, such as overcrowding, lack of treatment services, poorly trained staff, politics, unsanitary conditions, and poor physical facilities, were more characteristic of the relatively riot-free prisons of the Southeast and South Central states than of the more riot-ridden Northeast and North Central States.[5]

Inmate-Staff Contacts

The second major influence on inmate-staff communication arises from the work situation and often acts in opposition to the influence of inmate pressures. Officials supervise inmates at work and at recreation. In the

---

[3] Richard McCleery, "Communication Patterns as Bases of Power," in Richard A. Cloward *et al., Theoretical Studies in Social Organization of the Prison,* pamphlet 15 (New York, Social Science Research Council, 1960), pp. 57-59. See also McCleery, "The Governmental Process and Social Control," in Cressey, *op. cit.,* chapter 3.

[4] Richard Cloward, "Social Control in the Prison," in Cloward *et al., op. cit.,* p. 34.

[5] Frank E. Hartung and Maurice Floch, "A Social-Psychological Analysis of Prison Riots: An Hypothesis," *J. Crim. Law, Criminology and Police Science, 47* (May–June 1956), 51-57.

traditional authoritarian institution, staff regulations place considerable stress on the maintenance of social distance between staff and inmates. For example, in state prisons which I knew well, officer-training programs emphasized the untrustworthiness of all inmates and their potential for assault; occasionally officers were suspended or otherwise penalized for fraternization with inmates; and one of the most tabooed actions was for a member of the staff to address an inmate as "Mister." Nevertheless, considerable staff-inmate communication on a personal level does develop even in the most authoritarian institution. It seems most frequent where the inmate serves as an official's personal clerk or servant, where the official is dependent upon the inmate's skill or responsibility, or where an assignment is small and isolated. Thus, the requirements of essential prison administration and maintenance tasks foster some personal ties between inmates and staff despite official policy opposing these. Sykes distinguishes three major sources of personal bonds that break down authoritarian relationships between staff and inmates: friendships from long and regular intimate face-to-face contact, reciprocal favors, and inmate performance of administrative tasks for staff.[6]

It follows from the above analysis that where the requirements of assigned tasks are the only significant source of informal staff-inmate communication, inmate leaders have their greatest influence upon the lives of the other inmates. Inmates given assignments permitting unusual communication with staff tend disproportionately to be inmates with seniority in the prison, for inmates have to be known before they can be trusted or trained adequately. However, the men confined the longest in prison are disproportionately those with the most extensive criminal record. Consequently, efforts to restrict inmate-staff communication, which often are intended to reduce the possibilities of inmates corrupting staff, may simply increase the extent to which the most criminal prisoners can corrupt the rest of the inmate population.

The foregoing suggests that inmate-inmate relationships would be radically altered if staff-inmate communication were greatly expanded, so that staff contacts would no longer be a rare commodity which gives its possessors unusual advantages in inmate society. McCleery's distinctive contribution to penological literature is his account of the alteration of relationships in a prison following change from an authoritarian administration to one by men relatively inexperienced in prisons, who introduced into the prison the freer atmosphere of the schools, industry, and boys' camps which they previously had administered. Following this change, McCleery reports:

. . . new activities and relationships in the treatment and production units created new communities of interest in the inmate body with functional leader-

6 Gresham M. Sykes, "The Corruption of Authority and Rehabilitation," *Social Forces, 34* (March 1956), 257-62.

ship of their own. Especially where cooperative supervision by officials was involved, the concept of the *rat* in the old culture and its sanctions against contact with officials had collapsed.[7]

It is my impression that the practices that McCleery saw as a "liberal revolution" in an authoritarian prison had long previously been firmly established in most federal prisons. Further measures for reducing restrictions on inmates and increasing informal relationships of inmates with both staff and outsiders were introduced during the year that our interviewers were in the five institutions. Notable among measures to reduce rigid staff policing of inmates, and antedating our project, was abolition of the practice of moving the inmates to the dining room in formal lines or groupings. Instead, in a "continuous feeding" program, inmates moved freely to and from the dining room on their own during meal hours and sat at small tables for four. This practice was established in one federal prison after another. At Terre Haute, following earlier use at other federal institutions, an "open door hour" was also established, during which all treatment staff offices were manned, and were open to any inmate wishing to see staff without an appointment. The routine censorship of inmate mail was abolished in several federal youth institutions in 1958, in Terre Haute in 1960, and throughout most of the federal prisons by 1962.

Numerous other innovations to facilitate inmate-staff communication occurred in federal prisons throughout the four-year life of our project. Some of these changes are described in detail in the chapters of this book to which they are relevant, especially in chapters 7 through 10. The climate of change was well portrayed by Myrl E. Alexander, then Assistant Director of the Bureau of Prisons, in a staff-training speech in June 1960 shortly after he had visited Leavenworth:

Where once long lines of men marched down the corridors in the Big House, I saw men walking to the dining hall, two and three together, just as you and I will walk when we go to lunch today. . . . This in the United States Penitentiary at Leavenworth! One of the older lieutenants mentioned that it's difficult to describe the change that has taken place. Men who have been in for 10 to 15 years, who followed the "code" and who, if you spoke to them, would give you a monosyllabic answer because they didn't want to be seen talking to officers, now walk up and say, "Good morning, Lieutenant. Good morning, Mr. Jones. How are things going?"[8]

[7] McCleery, *op. cit.,* p. 72. As one would expect from the Hartung-Floch theory, this change was not without some disturbing reactions. McCleery points out that when the "old cons" no longer had the power to keep the "young toughs" in line, and the old prison staff tried to regain their former influence, conflicts erupted.

[8] Myrl E. Alexander, "Corrections Looks Ahead," *The Progress Report* (U. S. Bureau of Prisons), *8,* no. 3 (July–Sept. 1960), 5-6. Mr. Alexander now directs Southern Illinois University's distinctive Institute for Training and Research in Corrections and Delinquency.

Formal Arrangements

In addition to these diverse patterns of informal relationship, various formal arrangements have been deliberately created for conducting communication between staff and inmates. Probably the most universal of these is the classification casework interview, in which a staff member gets information from the inmate on which to base a report to guide other officials. The inmate may also take the initiative of requesting an interview in order to convey desires or to get information or advice. A related formal arrangement for staff-inmate communications is the Classification Committee. In the course of our research there was considerable Bureau of Prisons discussion of and experimentation with the size and membership of these committees and the frequency and duration of their contact with the inmates.

A newer development in formal arrangements for communication between inmates and staff is group counseling or therapy, discussed in chapter 8. Although generally considered desirable, this still is scarce because the casework staff, while formally assigned a counseling responsibility, is too limited in size and too involved in writing reports and handling individual inmate requests to provide extensive group counseling. In the California, District of Columbia, and some federal prisons, group counseling by staff members not specializing in casework services is organized on a large scale. A few special programs have been initiated in several federal prisons to facilitate increased staff-inmate communication. These programs include the special educational counseling project described in chapter 12, and the "Cottage Life Intervention Program" described in chapter 9.

Still another formal arrangement for bridging the gap between staff and inmates is the Inmate Advisory Council. Its primary function seems to be to organize inmate recreation and amusement activities and to communicate inmate tastes and preferences to staff. Some responsibility for the regulation of inmate behavior may also be given these inmate bodies, and here they serve as a means of communicating staff demands to inmates. They will be dealt with further in chapters 9 and 10.

Changes in prison operations and policies usually are made on a piecemeal basis, so that the new is mingled with the old. In a century of relatively rapid change, all prisons are bound to have, along with their latest innovations, some heritages from an antecedent condition. This mixture is especially prevalent where staff promotions depend heavily on seniority. However, it was apparent in the federal system that prisons can change, especially if new policies are integrated into line operations by active in-service training programs and by the continuous leadership of progressive penal administrators. Before considering the possibilities for change in inmate-staff relationships, it is appropriate to examine the dimensions of these relationships, and their correlates.

INMATE REPORTS ON THEIR STAFF PREFERENCES
AND PREJUDICES

In the sixth-month and near-release interviews of our Prison Panel Study, we asked the inmates the following series of questions:

I'd like you now to think of the member of the prison staff that you like best—don't tell me his name, but keep him in mind. It can be anyone from the warden down to the unit officer, an industries officer, or anyone else who is employed here. Do you have in mind the prison employee whom you like best (or dislike least)? Can you tell me your main reason for liking him (or disliking him less than others)? What other reasons do you have for liking him?

Can you tell me what job he does here?

Have you ever gone to him to talk about any of your problems, or to get help from him? If yes: What kind of problems? Was he much help? When? If no: Why not?

Is there any other prison employee whom you feel is interested in helping you? If yes: Who? If no: Which is second most interested in helping you?

Have you actually gone to him to talk about any of your problems, or to get help from him? If yes: What kind of problems? Was he much help? When? If no: Why not?

Now I'd like you to think of the member of the prison staff whom you dislike most (or like least, if dislikes none). Do you have him in mind? What is your main reason for disliking him? What other reasons do you have for disliking him?

Can you tell me what job he does here?

Variations Among Prisons

In response to the above questions, in all of our interviews taken collectively, 24 per cent of the inmates claimed that they could think of no officer whom they liked better than any other officer, and 43 per cent claimed that there was no specific officer whom they disliked more than others. There were no appreciable differences on these responses between the sixth-month and the near-release interviews at any of the five prisons where the interviewing was done. However, as Table 6.1 shows, there were large differences between prisons in this lack of specific preference or prejudice; it was relatively absent in the two youth institutions, Chillicothe and Ashland.[9] Part of this variation may be a consequence of differences

[9] The percentages at the two youth institutions (Ashland and Chillicothe) differ from the percentages at the other three institutions, both for liking and for disliking specific officers, to an extent that could occur by chance alone, with samples of this size and dispersion, much less than once in a hundred times.

TABLE 6.1   Responses to Request that Inmates Think of the Specific Officer Whom
They Like Best and the Specific Officer Whom They Dislike Most
(Prison Panel Study, sixth-month and near-release interviews)

Type of response	PER CENT AT EACH PRISON				
	Leavenworth	Terre Haute	Milan	Chillicothe	Ashland
On liking:					
Likes a specific officer best	68	67	56	92	96
Indifferent, knows none, dislikes none least	32	33	44	8	4
On disliking:					
Dislikes a specific officer most	38	46	37	80	80
Indifferent, knows none, dislikes none most	48	46	10	12	17
Dislikes none	14	7	53	8	3
Number of cases	92	84	91	102	80

between interviewers, in the extent to which they pressed the inmates to commit themselves to a preference or prejudice regarding a specific staff member. However, the interviewers recorded verbatim notes of the responses, and it is clear from these that the inmates at Leavenworth, Milan, and Terre Haute were much more often noncommittal from the outset than were inmates at Chillicothe and Ashland. Typical noncommittal responses to the question which asked them to think of the staff member that they liked best are the following:

I have nothing against these people, but I try to avoid them all I can. I don't speak to them unless they speak to me. I won't shoot bull with them because it causes hard feelings with the other inmates. (Leavenworth)

No, they're all the same. You do your work and they won't bother you. It's like the army. You do what you're told and you get along with everybody. They're all the same, I've worked under a lot of them. (Leavenworth)

I've come in very little contact with any of them. I go my way and they go theirs. (Leavenworth)

No one. I respect all of them equally because they are doing a job. I have little contact with any of them except my immediate boss. (Milan)

They're all the same. You got time and they got a job. I just try to do what they say. (Chillicothe)

In response to the question on staff member most disliked, some of the nonspecific responses were without strong feeling, such as:

They're all trying to help me the best they can. This place is like the army: if you stay out of trouble and out of their way they don't even know you're around. (Chillicothe)

However, most of the nonspecific answers seemed to express a generalized hostility, with such gratuitous remarks as:

They're all the same, all will say their hands are tied. (Milan)

They all act the same way. None of them are any good. They all treat you like little kids. (Chillicothe)

I don't have anything to do with them. They can't do anything for you, and if they can hurt you, they will. (Leavenworth)

I'm impartial to all of them. It's just like the Gestapo. You go before the court and they find you guilty. I don't know them and I don't want to know them. (Leavenworth)

It is believed that the high response on both liking and disliking specific officers at Chillicothe and Ashland mainly reflects more widespread staff-inmate interaction there than at Leavenworth, to cite the other extreme. The narrative content of the responses suggests that even those inmates who reported favorably on a specific officer at Leavenworth were likely to be isolated from and hostile toward most other officers, as in the following:

Except for Mr. X [with whom subject works], I am impartial to all of them. I come in very little contact with any of them and avoid them whenever possible. I go my way and they go theirs.

I have had no trouble with any of them, but I favor the ones I work for because I know them better. Mr. Y is broad-minded and tolerant. I don't think he has shot [submitted a disciplinary report on] anyone.

Differences between the sixth-month and the near-release interviews do not seem large enough to be very significant on these questions regarding inmate preferences and prejudices with respect to staff, and we shall treat both sets of interviews together in the remaining tabulations.

McCleery's interpretation of the effects of authoritarian versus liberal administration on inmate pressures seems to be supported by the data we have presented here. Leavenworth inmates averaged more prior prison experience than did those in the other institutions studied. During most of our interviewing, Leavenworth and Milan were under the direction of wardens who were to retire within a year, and many federal prison innovations, such as those described by Myrl Alexander, had not yet been introduced in these two prisons. For this reason, as well as because of the type of inmate sent there, Leavenworth clearly was the most authoritarian of the five prisons. Here we found the most frequent evidence of an inmate code and inmate pressures against communicating with officers except as necessary in work situations. These influences seem to explain why, in Table 6.1, there is a moderately high percentage of inmates at Leavenworth who like a specific officer better than others, at the same time that there are few who dislike one officer more than others; the spread between percentage specifically liking and percentage specifically disliking is greatest at Leavenworth, with a high amount of indifference expressed on the dislike question. This is what one would expect if the inmate were predominantly isolated from most officers at Leavenworth, if nevertheless there were a few staff members with whom each inmate had to communicate, if the staff were generally stereotyped by the inmates as hostile, and if the inmates usually found the few staff members with whom they communicated to be much better than expected.

Other material to be presented suggests that the isolation from officers indicated at Milan partly reflects ethnic sensitivities; most of the inmates there were Negro. While prejudice might be suspected in the predominantly white staff, our impression was that most inmates simply were not accustomed to communicating easily with whites, a consequence of segregation in their neighborhoods and schools.

The youth institutions had by far the least regimented and least authoritarian administration, and here we find the most personalized and intense feelings toward staff, both in likes and dislikes. It is unfortunate that we could not study a single institution before and after administrative changes, as McCleery did, so that we might know more adequately the extent to which the differences in staff-inmate relationships may be a function of inmate age alone, independently of administrative policy. However, on the basis of our data and his, and on the basis of the theory developed in the first part of this chapter from the observations of other analysts of prison experience, it seems appropriate to state, at least tentatively:

D1. Inmate pressure on other inmates to avoid communication with officers varies directly with the extent to which there is an impersonal and authoritarian orientation of staff to inmates.

Corrupt Activity Among Inmates

We did not attempt to obtain systematic information on corrupt influences of inmate on inmate by direct questioning in the course of our interviews. Like that of everyone else who has written about it, our knowledge on this subject is impressionistic. Much that touched on aspects of corruption was part of the commentary in response to our questions, some of which is quoted in this report from time to time. A small amount of corrupt inmate activity was directly observed by our staff, but most of their impressions were from casual conversations with inmates. In much of such conversations, the inmates undoubtedly were conveying exaggerated hearsay, sometimes mingled with facts and sometimes not. At any rate, our impression from these sources is that we encountered more evidence of corrupt operations by inmates presuming to have "inside dope" and staff "contacts" the more we moved from Ashland and Chillicothe through the scale of author-itarianism to Milan, Terre Haute, and Leavenworth.

The observed or reported corrupt activity by inmates with presumed unusual access to information varied from creating a sense of obligation in less informed inmates, in exchange for advice on how to get prison jobs or other desiderata from staff, to actual acceptance of commissary goods or other compensation for allegedly changing official records or "arranging" desired assignments. The "arrangement" sometimes meant an inmate clerk suggesting the name of an inmate for a job to his staff "boss," and some-times it just meant guessing the assignment the man could get anyhow, especially if he followed the inmate clerk's advice in requesting it. From their office positions, the clerks often did know prevailing policies and prac-tices well and could predict official actions fairly accurately. If the man got the job desired, the "arranger" would claim credit; if he did not get the job, the "arranger" would have an explanation for this failure and would promote another "arrangement." In one case, we were told of a "well-heeled" new inmate who was convinced of the legitimacy of an arranger's claims by being shown what were purported to be copies of the new inmate's prison records; actually, these were imitation records, prepared by a clerk with access to standard forms, rather than copies of any originals.

Another trait that we observed repeatedly in such "inside dopester" inmates, generally front-office clerks or inmate newspaper staff, was their eagerness to enlighten the outsider regarding their expert knowledge of the deficiencies of the prison administration and the alleged poor character of its staff. This usually was told in a paranoid fashion, as though key officials were all conspiring against the inmates. However, it was essential for our researchers, especially at the federal adult penitentiaries, to be good listen-ers, and to have the support of these inmate politicians rather than their antagonism, in order to gain the cooperation of our other interview subjects.

On the basis of the foregoing impressions, and of the logic of the "eco-nomic model" of supply and demand which fits this situation, it seems safe to assert:

D2. The value in the inmate community of any inmate's presumed unusual access to staff, or to prison files and records, varies directly with restriction of personal communication or friendship between staff and inmates.

As suggested earlier, this poses a dilemma for prison management. Re-striction of communication between staff and inmates maintains the formal authority of the staff and is presumed to reduce the possibility of their being corrupted by inmates. However, it increases the possibility of inmates cor-rupting other inmates. I suspect that authoritarian staff policies may not actually reduce the incorruptibility of staff, because: (1) staff always has to rely on some inmate clerks, technicians, and other assistants; (2) by virtue of their advantageous position for communication and friendship, these are the inmates most likely to achieve any corrupting of staff; (3) authoritarian policy promotes confidence-game orientations of these inmates to other inmates, since it enhances the apparent value of the position of these inmates in inmate society; (4) these confidence-game orientations thereby become more habitual behavior of such inmates, making them more likely to use them in dealing with staff as well as with inmates, and perhaps with outsiders also, before and after their release from prison.

Inmate-Staff Isolation

It is noteworthy that the foregoing material on institutional differences in inmate-staff isolation closely parallels that reported in chapter 5 on inter-inmate friendship versus isolation. The increasing isolation of inmates from other inmates at Milan, as shown in Table 5.3 of chapter 5, appears to be a generalized pattern of avoiding others which also extends to the inmate relationships with officers. This supports the contention in chapter 5 that inmate isolation from officers in the authoritarian prison was misinterpreted by Sykes and Messinger as a movement toward inmate solidarity; rather, it appears to be a general isolation of prisoners from each other and from staff. Contrastingly, the emphasis on seeking inmate friendships in the youth institutions, especially Ashland, seems to be part of a relatively easy socializing atmosphere there which is expressed in inmate relationships both to staff and to other inmates. All this suggests that, despite some cohesion of small groups of inmates when in conflict with staff, on the whole:

D3. Voluntary isolation of inmates from each other varies directly with their isolation from officers.

This implies that staff attitudes toward inmates are the most independent variables and that if they are changed, there will be a change not only in inmate attitudes to staff but in inmate attitudes to each other.

The ratio of inmates to staff could conceivably be an additional factor explaining differences in staff-inmate relationships among the five prisons. During our interviewing, the following figures were reported:

Leavenworth:	population 2500,	staff 390,	ratio 1 staff to 6.4 inmates
Terre Haute:	population 1325,	staff 245,	ratio 1 staff to 5.4 inmates
Milan:	population 650,	staff 146,	ratio 1 staff to 4.5 inmates
Chillicothe:	population 1325,	staff 280,	ratio 1 staff to 4.7 inmates
Ashland:	population 510,	staff 160,	ratio 1 staff to 3.2 inmates

Ashland, with twice as many staff in relation to inmates as Leavenworth, provided statistically twice as much opportunity for staff-inmate contact. However, the tenor of inmate responses indicated that the major difference between Leavenworth and Ashland inmate orientations to others reflected the prison subculture of aloofness and "doing your own time," independently of staff-inmate ratios. This view is supported also by the fact that Milan inmates were characterized by much more isolation from staff and from each other than were inmates at Terre Haute or Chillicothe, although Milan had a smaller inmate-to-staff ratio than either of these two prisons.

I have thus far adduced that the inmate subcultural emphasis on isolation is a function of inmate age, prior penal experience, and heterogeneity, as well as an inmate adaptation to official policies opposing staff communication to inmates other than on an impersonal level. Of these variables, only staff policies may be a function of inmate-to-staff ratios—both ratios for the prison as a whole and for separate staff posts within a prison. However, staff policies are not completely determined by these ratios.

Personality Attributes of Staff

We recorded verbatim the reasons inmates gave for liking or disliking a specific staff member best. These reasons were classified into the categories indicated in Table 6.2. Support for Proposition D3, on the parallel between inmate-inmate and staff-inmate relationships, is suggested by the

TABLE 6.2   Reasons Given for Liking or Disliking a Specific Staff Member
(Prison Panel Study, sixth-month and near-release interviews)

	PER CENT AT EACH PRISON				
	Leavenworth	Terre Haute	Milan	Chillicothe	Ashland
Reasons for liking:					
Accommodating (grants requests, does favors, flexible)	17	18	20	17	23 [a]
Friendly (acts like an equal, socializes, jokes)	19	20	20	20	*38*
Fair (predictable, dependable, know where you stand)	27	*45*	33	40	26
Personal traits not cited above, or nonspecific, as "real man," "nice guy," etc.	*36*	18	28	22	13
Reasons for disliking:					
Alleged acts (refusal of help, harmful actions, plays favorites)	20	*28*	26	16	16
Hostile manner (acts superior, yells at you, harasses)	60	38	47	*78*	75
Race prejudice	3	13	*21*	2	2
Personal traits not cited above: "weak man," "stupid," etc.	17	*21*	6	3	8
Number indicating a specific staff member:					
Liked most	63	56	51	94	77
Disliked most	35	39	34	82	64
(Bases for above percentages)					
Remainder claiming no staff member:					
Liked most	29	28	40	8	3
Disliked most	57	45	57	20	16

[a]   Italic indicates highest percentage on a line.

fact that only at Ashland were friendliness and socializing the main reasons for liking one officer more than the others; as Table 5.3 in chapter 5 indicated, Ashland also was the institution where inmates were most concerned with maximizing inter-inmate friendship. Terre Haute and Chillicothe, which have the most "intractable" youthful prisoners, stood out from the others for the frequency with which their inmates emphasized fairness and predictability of behavior as reasons for liking officers.[10] It is of interest that remarks emphasizing permissiveness nowhere exceeded friendliness and fairness as reasons for liking a particular staff member best.

Table 6.2 also shows that at every one of the five prisons studied, the most frequently cited type of reason for disliking an officer was his manner of expressing himself toward inmates, rather than specific things he did. This is one of many kinds of evidence suggesting the importance to the offenders of their self-esteem, and the difficulty of influencing them in a desired fashion if one fails to take into account their need to defend whatever favorable conception they may have of themselves, or to achieve a still more favorable self-conception. McCorkle and Korn have pointed out that the prisoner, having been rejected by society, finds that one of the most effective ways of living with this condition is to "reject his rejectors."[11] The best defense of the ego against its attackers appears to be to counter-attack by directing hostility and disparagement against the attackers. A necessary condition, if not alone sufficient, for a staff member's favorable influence upon a prisoner appears to be the capacity to treat the prisoner pleasantly. Such an attitude conveys to the prisoner the notion that he is accepted as a person even when his attitudes or actions are opposed. There is ample evidence that control can be achieved by staff without a hostile or superior attitude, and that positive leadership and influence is difficult to achieve without at least a minimum of friendliness and respect.

The previously cited greater concern with race prejudice at Milan is indicated in Table 6.2.[12] However, it is noteworthy that, despite the fact that two-thirds of our sample there were Negroes and our interviewer was a Negro, race prejudice was not nearly the principal complaint about disliked staff members.

[10] The Ashland difference from other institutions in emphasis on friendliness and equality as the reason for liking officers, and the Chillicothe and Terre Haute differences from other institutions in emphasis on fairness and predictability, are greater than could occur by chance alone, with samples of this size and dispersion, once in a hundred times.

[11] Lloyd W. McCorkle and Richard R. Korn, "Resocialization Within Walls," *Annals Am. Academy of Political and Social Science, 293* (May 1954), 88-98.

[12] The difference between the percentage citing race prejudice as the reason for disliking an officer at Milan and the percentage citing race prejudice at the other institutions is greater than could occur by chance alone, in samples of this size and dispersion, once in a hundred times.

It is, of course, conceivable that the rehabilitation goals of a prison could be perverted by staff members if they made their popularity with inmates too primary an influence on their policies. This is suggested when the staff of an institution boasts of its treatment achievements mainly in terms of the recreation and fun which the inmates enjoy. Such a staff emphasis may successfully adjust an inmate to imprisonment, and it may result in low escape rates under minimum custody conditions; however, it is hard to believe that making prison pleasant suffices to create anti-criminal values, prepare a man for legitimate economic self-sufficiency, or otherwise adjust the inmate to the circumstances he is likely to encounter after prison. The latter objectives may require a prison that is not liked as much by inmates, at least in the short run, as a more pleasure-oriented prison might conceivably be liked, but it still would require a staff that, on the whole, would be liked by the inmates. A variety of social-psychological research confirms the proposition that people most often acquire someone else's attitudes if they like him, and less often if they dislike him. If the staff is to compete successfully with the criminal associates of an inmate and inspire anti-criminal values, being liked certainly is a major staff asset, although not a guarantee of success.

If we are correct in assuming that being somewhat liked by inmates assists staff in influencing inmates, then the materials in Table 6.2 may be summarized as:

D4. Staff influence on inmates varies directly with staff manifestation to inmates of the same types of personal behavior that cause a man to be liked in nonprison relationships.

    a. Inmates are most influenced by staff who act towards them in a friendly and considerate—rather than hostile—tone and manner.

    b. Inmates are most influenced by staff who treat them with fairness and predictability.

It will be suggested shortly that, to some extent, the manifestation of these attributes is a function of the staff member's position and duties, independently of his personality. At the same time, these obviously are personality qualities also, and an individual staff member may be able to modify unfavorable qualities by personal effort.

Functions of Staff

After asking the inmates about the officer they liked best, and about the officer they disliked most, we asked them to tell us the position held by this officer (not his name, although this often was volunteered). In Table 6.3 the officers are grouped into functional categories. In all of the prisons except Ashland the best-liked officer was most often a work supervisor. At Ashland custodial officers were somewhat more often the best liked, but

TABLE 6.3   The Positions of Staff Members Selected as Liked or Disliked Most (Prison Panel Study, sixth-month and near-release interviews)

Categories of staff position (with examples of staff included in each category)	PER CENT AT EACH PRISON									
	LEAVEN-WORTH		TERRE HAUTE		MILAN		CHILLICOTHE		ASHLAND	
	Like	Dislike	Like	Dislike	Like	Dislike	Like	Dislike	Like	Dislike
Senior officials (Warden; Asst. Warden; Captain; Lieutenant)	11	24	11	15	18	37	10	7	6	5
Custodial officers (cell, unit, or gate officer)	23	41	34	51	14	17	28	60	52	75
Work supervisors (foreman; shop or detail officer; steward)	48	9	45	18	45	29	51	20	32	13
Educators (teacher; vocational training instructor)	8	3	2	3	—	—	9	1	3	5
Chaplains	5	—	2	—	12	—	1	—	3	—
Clinical (doctor, psychologist, psychiatrist)	—	—	4	—	4	—	1	—	3	—
Caseworkers (all called "parole officer" in federal prisons)	2	12	2	8	6	14	1	1	1	—
Other (record clerk; clothing room, placement, or recreation officer)	3	12	2	5	2	3	—	11	—	3
Number of cases	63	35	56	39	51	34	94	82	77	64

they also were even more frequently the most disliked, so that the work supervisor could be considered the most predominantly liked category of officer at every prison. Custodial officers predominated in the most-disliked designations everywhere except Milan, and if we combine them with the senior officers, who were predominantly custodial in function, it is clear that this is the most-disliked category everywhere. Also, custodial officers can be said to have the greatest total impact everywhere, except at Milan, if we measure impact as the sum of most liked and most disliked selections. This suggests the significance of their job in terms of potential for favorable or unfavorable influence.

The remaining staff distinguished in Table 6.3, often called "treatment personnel," had the distinction of being least frequently the most disliked, but their relatively low frequency of selection for either the liked or disliked designation suggests that they have less influence than other staff on the prison experience of most inmates. Of course, if they, nevertheless, change the abilities of inmates markedly, they could still most affect the inmate's postrelease experience. The parole officers or caseworkers were more often designated the most disliked than the most liked staff members, but like the teachers, chaplains, and clinical staff, their overall selection as either most liked or disliked was not great.

Our findings of a predominance of dislike for the caseworker, and of liking for the work supervisor, parallel the pattern of social perception esteem scores which we procured for these staff categories by questionnaire, notably at Ashland. These are summarized in Appendix E. A long series of correctional institution "impact" studies, conducted at Ohio State University under the direction of Professor Walter Reckless, had similar conclusions. In 1947, Edward J. Galway, interviewing 247 men just before their release from the U. S. Reformatory at Chillicothe, Ohio, asked which officer knew them best. Fifty per cent of the designations were of staff in assignments having primarily a work supervision relationship to inmates (industry, farm, maintenance, etc.), 39 per cent were in custody, 5 per cent were caseworkers, 3 per cent were teachers, 2 per cent were medical staff, and 1 per cent were chaplains. Similar inquiries by David Bright in 1950, at the Ohio Penitentiary, found that custodial and work-supervision personnel were the staff whom inmates most often credited with helping them. Another study of Chillicothe releases in 1953, by Mark R. Moran, also yielded findings on staff similar to those reported by Galway.[13]

Table 6.4 indicates that the reasons for liking or disliking an official vary with his position. For custodial officers, what seems to have been a trait

TABLE 6.4 Reasons for Liking and Disliking Staff Members, by Staff Position of Person Designated Most Liked or Most Disliked
(Prison Panel Study, sixth-month and near-release interviews)

	Warden, assoc. warden, capt., or lieutenant	Custodial officer	Work supervisor	Treatment staff[a]
Reasons for liking:				
Permissive (grants requests, does favors, flexible)	31%	14%	17%	30%
Friendly (acts like an equal, socializes, jokes)	14%	32%	20%	23%
Fair (predictable, know where you stand)	39%	37%	39%	9%
Personal traits not cited above or nonspecific, as "real man," "nice guy," etc.	16%	17%	24%	37%
Number most liked (100%)	36	106	·152	43
Reasons for disliking:				
Alleged acts (refusal of help, harmful actions, plays favorites)	23%	13%	16%	63%
Hostile Manner (acts superior, yells at you, harasses)	51%	74%	66%	21%
Race prejudice	17%	5%	5%	5%
Personal traits not cited above: weak man, stupid, etc.	9%	8%	13%	10%
Number most disliked (100%)	35	136	44	19

[a] Teachers, chaplains, physicians, psychologists, caseworkers, etc.

[13] Walter C. Reckless, "The Impact of Correctional Programmes on Inmates," *British Journal of Delinquency, 6,* no. 2 (Sept. 1955), 138-47.

of fairness and predictability was the major influence upon inmate preference or prejudice, with manner of expression, whether friendly or hostile,
next in importance.[14] The same influences operated in inmate evaluation
of work supervisors, but with less frequent emphasis on friendliness or
hostility of manner. Perhaps these mannerisms are most important in
determining reactions of inmates and staff to each other when their interaction is relatively on an impersonal basis, as happens more in custodial
than in work supervision relationships. When staff develop variety and
depth in their relationships to an inmate through more personal interaction
with him over a longer time, one would expect more of their primary influence to be a result of their basic personalities and their shared experience
with him; influence by their more immediately observable personal mannerisms, such as friendliness or hostility, is likely to be secondary.

The senior officers were evaluated more exclusively by their fairness and
by the extent to which they were sympathetic to requests. This probably
reflects their role as arbiters in disciplinary matters and as decision-makers
in requests for change in assignment or for special privileges. In this connection, it is of interest that associate wardens, who handle those matters
more than others, were chosen as most disliked more than twice as often
as they were chosen most liked, while the other senior officers were chosen
as most liked more than twice as often as they were chosen most disliked.[15]

The treatment staff are predominantly disliked on the basis of their negative response to requests. They differ from the other disliked categories of
staff in much less frequently being accused of hostile mannerisms.[16]

A questionnaire administered by graduate students of the University of
Wisconsin School of Social Work, and based on responses from 300 inmates randomly selected from the Wisconsin State Prison, had the interesting
finding that inmate contact with institution social workers is very much a
function of the inmate's educational attainment. Twenty per cent of the
Wisconsin inmates who had gone beyond the eighth grade reported six or
more contacts with social workers, as compared with only 12 per cent for

[14] The manner of expression, friendly as a basis for liking and hostile as a basis
for disliking, was emphasized more frequently for custodial officers than for other
staff to an extent that could occur by chance alone, with samples of this size and
dispersion, less than once in a hundred times.

[15] The differences in ratios of most liked to most disliked selection, between assistant wardens and other senior staff, and also the emphasis on permissiveness as a basis
for liking senior or treatment staff more frequently than for liking custodial officers
or work supervisors, could occur by chance alone, with samples of this size and dispersion, less than once in a hundred times.

[16] Alleged acts as reasons for disliking were emphasized more frequently and
hostile manners were emphasized less frequently for treatment staff than for other
staff, to an extent that could occur by chance alone, with samples of this size and
dispersion, less than once in a hundred times.

those whose educational attainment was eighth grade or less. Included in the latter group were those with less than five years of schooling, of whom none reported six or more contacts with the social workers. This suggests that the higher educational level of institution caseworkers, compared with most of the remainder of the prison staff, may impair the caseworker's ability to communicate with inmates who are of low education. Also, inmates with less education may be more ill at ease in the formal interview situation where casework contacts occur, and may therefore less frequently initiate such contact. Forty-seven per cent of the Wisconsin inmates thought their social workers were helpful, while 53 per cent thought they were of no help or were uncertain as to whether they were of any help.[17]

As stated previously, the distinctive feature of responses on the treatment staff from inmates of five federal prisons was the infrequency with which treatment staff were mentioned as either the most liked or the most disliked. This suggests that these personnel have less total impact on inmates than might be expected from the emphasis on treatment as the main function of these modern prisons. All of this suggests the need for a major reassessment and alteration of the way in which the classification and casework job is performed in the prison, for which some suggestions are presented in chapters 8, 9, and 10.

What seem to be involved in the reasons for likes and dislikes are differences in the tasks that persons in these several positions are expected to perform. The treatment staff is less called upon to give orders to inmates or to initiate disciplinary action, so they are less frequently evaluated for their fairness than persons in other major staff categories.[18] On the other hand, the associate wardens and the treatment staff are most often the persons to whom special requests are directed, so their response to these greatly affects the reactions they arouse in the inmate population. Custodial officers are very frequently the most liked, in addition to being more often than others the most disliked staff members. This suggests that inmate reaction to them is not as much a function of their staff position as may be the case with inmate reaction to the treatment personnel and the work-supervision employees. Rather, these data suggest that, despite the demands of their position, many custodial officials and some other staff members could greatly alter the type of reaction they arouse.

Nevertheless, the contrasts between inmate relations with work supervisors and with custodial staff indicated in Tables 6.3 and 6.4 suggest one persistent theme on staff function as determinant of social attitude. This is

[17] *Prison Inmate Attitudes Toward Social Services,* Research Bulletin C-5 (Madison, Wisconsin Dept. of Public Welfare, January 1962).

[18] Fairness and predictability, as reasons for liking, were emphasized more for nontreatment than for treatment staff to an extent that could occur by chance alone, for this sample, less than once in a hundred times.

a principle evident in many of McCleery's observations, but rooted as well in much other old and new behavioral science theory. It has been expressed in the latter literature with a variety of labels, such as primary versus secondary group relationships, particularistic diffuse versus universalistic specific orientations, and community (*Gemeinschaft*) versus societal (*Gesellschaft*) living. This principle can be formulated in several ways for the prison situation, and I shall suggest two alternative forms. Focusing on particularistic diffuse, primary, or community relationships, one can assert:

D5a. The more comprehensive and nonritualized the duties of any employee become in dealing with inmates, the more he is inclined to treat them on the basis of their personal attributes as individuals rather than on the basis of attitudes toward inmates as a class or social status, and the more inmates are inclined to reciprocate this treatment.

This proposition readily accounts for the extent to which work supervisors are liked. The work supervisor not only is responsible for maintaining custody and order, but he also is concerned with training, with directing the division of labor, with making individual work reports, and with innumerable other duties involving him in daily personal relationships with a relatively small number of inmates. It is believed that the proposition also applies to many other situations on which our data do not provide detailed information.

The difference between what sociologists call a diffuse and a specific relationship may have much to do with differences between the many custodial officers who are most liked and those who are most disliked. For example, as shown in the discussion of social perception measures in Appendix E, inmates in close custody at Ashland were found to rate their unit officers more favorably than did inmates in other parts of the prison. This may be because the officer-inmate relationship in close-custody units is diffused in continuous contact, involves relatively few inmates per officer, and encompasses the inmates' leisure as well as their work (at least, their housekeeping work). Thus an officer in a close-custody unit can develop a more personal relationship with the inmates than can be achieved as readily by officers with many inmates, or by officers who deal with inmates only in a specific type of situation and activity. This diffuseness of the relationship apparently more than offsets the presumed greater custodial orientation of officers in the close-custody unit compared with officers elsewhere at Ashland.

The second formulation is the converse of the first:

D5b. The more ritualistic and routinized the duties of an employee become in dealing with inmates, the more he is inclined to become authoritarian and punitive toward them (regardless of official policies and directives), and the more he is inclined to rationalize punitiveness by stereotyped unfavorable conceptions of inmates, which they are inclined to reciprocate.

It is believed that this accounts for the frequent dislike for custodial officers indicated in Table 6.3, and it may also be a factor in the inmate dislike for some of the less accessible caseworkers. The phenomena involved here have been rather vividly described by McCleery in analyzing a particular prison situation:

There was a direct relation between gratuitous authoritarianism and certain characteristics of the requirements of a position. The repeated performance of routine tasks seems to pass imperceptibly into ritual behavior, and the ritual performance, in turn seems to assume a symbolic meaning. Any challenge or interruption to narrowly defined routines was met with bitter resentment and a sense of sacrilege. The rituals of security seemed to stand as a substitute for the effective practice of security. . . . Although the guard force was in close and constant contact with inmates, the narrow and routine definition of their duties seemed to prevent their seeing inmates as individuals and responding to them as humans. Other officials whose duties were less rigidly defined were less inclined to stereotype the inmate and more able to react to individual differences, even though they were farther removed from daily contact with the men. . . .

Where the work was routine, menial and undifferentiated, the authoritarian behavior of supervisors was much like that of the guards. Where the work was differentiated and complex, where supervision was more individual, the general patterns of attitude and behavior of the supervisor were more liberal. . . . In a very general way, authoritarianism seemed to increase . . . as an individual was removed from the main stream of communication.[19]

The principles involved in these two propositions have been confirmed in a variety of other group situations in social-psychological research. The next chapter considers their practical implications.

Nature of Problems Taken to Staff

Inmate responses to our questions on what problems they took to the staff member they liked best, as indicators of institutional differences in staff-inmate communication, were consistent with the findings on the proportion designating any staff member as liked more than others. As Table 6.5 shows, not only did inmates of the penitentiaries and the Milan prison frequently deny liking any staff member better than others, but a major proportion of those who admitted liking one officer better than others still

[19] Richard McCleery, "Conflict and Accommodation in a Penal Institution," paper presented at Annual Meeting, American Political Science Association, Sept. 1958.

TABLE 6.5   Problems Taken to Staff Members Liked Best
(Prison Panel Study, sixth-month and near-release interviews)

Problems	PER CENT AT EACH PRISON				
	Leavenworth	Terre Haute	Milan	Chillicothe	Ashland
Denies taking any problem to staff member liked best	53	55	47	44	38
Prison comfort: job or quarters change, etc.	62	40	33	34	27
Relationships to inmates or to staff	10	—	26	19	4
Parole preparation or post-release job	7	16	—	11	29
Other outside problems: family, property, etc.	10	24	30	30	29
Other	10	20	11	6	11
Number liking a specific staff member best (base of percentages on first line above)	63	56	51	94	77
Number taking problems to staff member liked best (base of percentages below the first line)	29	25	27	53	48

denied taking any problems to this officer.[20] When asked why they did not, they either denied having a problem, claimed they could take care of their own problems, or asserted that the officer could not help them. Of the problems taken to the most-liked officer in the penitentiary, the most frequently stressed concerned prison comfort, while in the youth institutions there was more stress on matters outside the prison.[21] The shorter sentences, less prior imprisonment, and more frequent release by parole in the youth institution and in the short-term component of the Milan population, as compared with the penitentiary population, all help to explain their more frequent concern with problems outside of prison life. The contrast in inmate concerns between the long-term and the short-term prisons also indicates the difference in "prisonization"—or mental adjustment to a life of confinement—in these institutions.

About 90 per cent of those who reported taking problems to the staff whom they liked best said that this led to their being helped with their

[20] The difference between the two youth prisons, Ashland and Chillicothe, and the other prisons in the percentage who claimed to like no specific staff member better than others was greater than could occur by chance alone, with samples of this size and dispersion, once in a hundred times. The difference between these two youth institutions and the other prisons in the number who denied taking any problems to the officer they liked best, as a percentage of only those who indicated that they liked a specific officer best, was greater than could occur by chance alone, with samples of this size and dispersion, once in twenty times.

[21] Differences between the two youth prisons, Ashland and Chillicothe, and the other prisons, as great as those found for frequency with which problems taken to officers liked best were matters of prison comfort, or were matters of parole arrangement or other outside problems, would occur by chance alone, with samples of this size and dispersion, less than once in twenty times.

problem. Over half of these reported that the officer gave them some specific assistance, such as making some special arrangement or sending an appropriate letter. Most of the remainder reported receiving some psychological assurance, ranging from an adequate explanation to "talking it out" and having their "mind put at ease." All except one of the 10 per cent who reported that they were not helped by this staff member gave a nonhostile response, such as "he tried but he couldn't do anything" or "it wasn't his fault."

Staff-inmate relationships were not a topic of direct inquiry in the first interview forms developed for our Prison Panel Study because this seemed too sensitive an area to probe. We were just overcoming initial suspicions of lower staff members that we were trying to evaluate their work for the Bureau of Prisons, and inmate suspicions that we were trying to get information about them for the staff, so we were reluctant to start asking inmates about staff. We lost this concern only when we had been in the prisons more than eight months, and our remaining interviews consisted only of our last contact with the entrance panel and our interviews with the near-release panel. Had we started inquiries on orientation to staff earlier we would have sampled more cases and more change over time in prison, and we also might have been able to revise our questions on the basis of more experience with them. In the Prison Panel Supplement Study, of course, we devoted much more attention to inmate perceptions of each other and of staff, employing the social perception measures described in Appendix E and also cited here.

THE PERSONAL INFLUENCE OF STAFF MEMBERS

In the highly general questions with which our 250 successful releasee interviews were concluded, after asking the postrelease "successes" when they changed from crime, we asked how this change came about and who, if anyone, was instrumental in it. Of the 131 who reported that they changed during imprisonment, sixty-five, or about half, credited a staff member with being influential in their reformation. Only eleven, or 8 per cent, credited the influence of fellow inmates as a factor in their change. The others who reported that their shift from criminal interests occurred in prison credited their own maturation, the deterrent effects of imprisonment, or the influence of persons outside the prison who wrote or visited them. These influences are discussed in chapter 10.

The prison staff cited by the sixty-five successful releasees as contributing to their rehabilitation were distributed among prison positions, in relation to these inmates, as follows:

35 cases, or 54   per cent: Work supervisors
 9 cases, or 14   per cent: Chaplains

2 cases, or	3	per cent:	Volunteer auxiliary religious workers (staff members in other positions: one taught Bible class and one worked with Alcoholics Anonymous).
4 cases, or	6	per cent:	Quarters officers
6 cases, or	9	per cent:	Senior officials (3 wardens and 3 lieutenants)
3 cases, or	4½	per cent:	Caseworkers (parole officers)
3 cases, or	4½	per cent:	Psychologists (2) and psychiatrist

In addition, mentioned by only one case each, were the positions of vocational teacher, employment placement officer, and athletic officer. Seven inmates credited "the guards" or "the officers" in general, in some cases elaborating on their predominant character, without citing a specific officer. The above compilation counts twice seven cases who mentioned two specific staff members; five of these duplications involved work supervisors and two involved chaplains.

The predominance of work supervisors in these citations, of course, reinforces the conclusions of preceding sections on the favorable influence of work supervisors. Of the thirty-five work supervisors, fourteen were in prison industries, five were in maintenance trades (electric, plumbing, and auto mechanics), four were in culinary services, and three were in medical services, with the remainder distributed in a variety of other positions.

Only three men mentioned the vocational training contribution of these work supervisors. One officer was said to be "able to make plumbing interesting, so it didn't seem like work." One former prisoner, successful as a baker since release, ascribed his present cake-baking skill to the prison, and showed our interviewer snapshots of special-occasion cakes he had made in prison. A medical technician emphasized that the prison hospital staff were never too busy to answer his questions and show him things when he learned his trade in prison.

It is striking that about 90 per cent of the remarks by the successful releasees on the rehabilitative influence of their work supervisors do not mention vocational teaching by these men; instead, they stress only their personal relationship to the work supervisor. Frequently a paternal relationship seems to have existed. For example, S-106, speaking of the Chief Engineer at Leavenworth's powerhouse, says:

He was a nice old man and retired after I left. When I left he shook hands with me and said: "You big son-of-a-bitch, if you come back to this place I'll kill you, much as I like you. You don't belong in this place." Tears were in his eyes.

Another releasee mentioned that he felt proud and obligated on overhearing his boss in the prison bet that he wouldn't be in trouble with the law again. S-558 told our interviewer:

I guess the man I worked for at the woolen mill (Terre Haute) helped me more than anyone. He was like a father to me. He gave me advice and was on my back all the time, but in a nice way. He tried to keep me out of trouble and help me. He picked me up and took me to the bus when I left. He was the key to my change.

Most of the influence of the work supervisors seems simply to have resulted from close personal contact with the inmates with whom they worked. Several inmates mentioned the fact that they worked right next to their supervisor, often for several years, and they therefore had many long talks. S-554, who had a poor record at Ashland and improved after transfer to Chillicothe, said:

At Ashland I got all tied up, so I settled down and tried to help myself at Chillicothe. I talked to my boss at the chair factory quite a bit and he encouraged me and gave me a different outlook. He taught me to think.

Similarly, S-519 credited his work supervisor in Chillicothe's Electric Shop with "straightening him out," saying:

He treated you like everyone else. He went home every night, but he didn't seem to hold anything against you. He'd talk about your problems. He was friendly. He always seemed to want to help and do things that he could for you.

I have the impression that the inmates who have had a long history of failure, rejection, and ego-deflation were especially appreciative of attention, encouragement, and compliments from staff. The work supervisors were in a unique position to influence inmates by a personal relationship, but many other staff also had this opportunity. S-540 had two training-school and two reformatory commitments, all for felonies, before his eleven-year federal imprisonment, from which he was released in 1949. When we interviewed him, his twenty-five years of continuous criminality or imprisonment had been followed by twelve highly conventional years, in the last nine of which he was steadily employed as an X-ray technician. He says:

My change occurred at Leavenworth, primarily because of the respect I had for one man there—the warden. He was highly qualified. When I got to work in the kitchen, and finally in the officer's mess, he talked to me all the time. He was very friendly all the time I worked there. He was impartial to you in treating inmates. He was fair. He treated all the same. There were no big shots around him. . . . You had to earn favors under him. Once he brought me my jacket [prison case file] down to me and he said to me: "Out of such a small amount of adventure and pleasure, look how much sorrow you have." And we talked about my case and this one thing seemed to direct me to my realization of mistakes.

S-122, the "Lawrence" whose case was the first to be summarized in chapter 4, speaks of a psychiatrist whom he knew in Atlanta:

I had given up any hope of making parole because of my long sentence, but he encouraged me and became a friend to such a degree that I saw some hope and began to work for it, and this psychiatrist recommended me for parole and I was fortunate enough to be granted it. He was only a young fellow, about 26, I happened to see him when I was in the hospital with an inflammation of a heart muscle. It was not that he was a psychiatrist, but that he was a person that helped me. If he was just a hack [derogatory name for custodial officer] he would have helped me just as much. I wrote to him for a long time after I got out, and he wrote to me.

Several of the successful releasees who had prior experience in some of the more backward state prisons mentioned a contrast between federal and state prison officers. S-528 ("Clifford," the "crime-contacting noncriminal" in chapter 4) stressed that the federal officers were not like the ones he had at the state reformatory "who were just there to make a buck, and would do anything for an inmate to get money." The federal officers, he said, "were understanding, they had a job to do, so I could respect them." As S-552 put it, the federal officers "treat you like a man, not like an animal." S-815's summation was:

Them people were wonderful to me. They had a lot to do with my thinking. They were *just* in everything they done. I even went back in '56 to visit them. My boss, Mr. L., he had influence on a lot of people. When I come home he came and took me to his house for breakfast, then to the train. He used to be a guard at Alcatraz, but I never heard a man say one bad thing about that man. Now don't get me wrong, he was the law, but he was so good and so just, everybody liked him.

What seems to be common to all of these testimonials is that the officers whom these men credited as having been rehabilitative influences gave the inmates self-respect. This did not mean that the officers were unusually lenient, lax, or permissive; it meant only that they treated the men with a personal interest and without pretension or condescension. The officers were friendly in a way that inspired confidence and respect rather than contempt; they were frank, fair, and considerate.

It is impressive how often the inmate's regard and respect for the officer was cemented by the officer's maintaining the same attitude and availability to the inmate outside of prison as in. The small voluntary gestures of some officers—taking a man to the train or bus, giving him breakfast, or corresponding with him—seemed to confirm that the officer was not false in his gestures of interest and respect in the prison. These incidents are particularly interesting to me because I have known state prisons where any of these acts by an officer could lead to suspension or termination of his prison employment. In some state prisons there is often an especially rigid prohibition of employee familiarity with released prisoners, which stems from certain custodial bogeymen. Officials enforcing such a restriction harp on a few isolated incidents in past decades, in which some untrained staff, appointed through political patronage, were induced by released prisoners or inmate relatives to smuggle things in or out of the prison. These fears continue to influence policy even when the prison force no longer is affected by the course of politics, its pay is comparable to the best, and its morale is relatively high.

The federal experience suggests that prison security is aided not so much by nonfraternization rules as by the staff's inculcation with the goals of the prison service, with moral responsibility, and with sufficient sophistication regarding criminal machinations to prevent their being "conned" too readily. California prisons have even found it worthwhile to have their employees bring successful ex-prisoners back to the prison to counsel prisoners nearing release, and this also has been done in some federal prisons. Moreover, the custodial security record in federal prisons, and in California, measured in terms of serious riots or smuggling, probably is better than that of the states with rigid nonfraternization rules.

It is especially striking that, of the successful releasees who credited a specific staff member with being a major influence in their reformation, one-sixth cited the prison chaplains and religious workers, although these employees constitute only a fraction of one per cent of the total prison staff. Catholic and Protestant denominations were about equally mentioned in these citations.

S-957 already had served two prison and several jail and military stockade sentences for repeated armed robbery, auto theft, and drunkenness when he started nine years of confinement at Leavenworth in 1949. However, he has led an exemplary life in over three years on parole. He had not bothered with religion much previously but, he said, in prison the chaplain would come out in the yard and play checkers with him, so they became friendly. He then took religious instruction, and became converted in prison. He now is highly devout, and attributes his change to his religious faith. He became quite emotional when talking of the chaplain. He says he decided in prison that when a man like the chaplain could give up life on the outside to come inside a place like Leavenworth, to try to help the kind of men they have there, there must be something to religion, and he would accept it.

S-110 served a federal prison sentence for killing another soldier in a fight while he was in the Army. Prior to this he had served three jail terms, two for larceny, and he had led a disorderly life. However, when we interviewed him he had completed over five years of stable and responsible life on parole. Asked the reasons for his change, he said:

I used to have a quick temper. This got me into fights and into the trouble I had in the Army that got me to Terre Haute. At Terre Haute, though, I learned to control this temper. I converted to Catholic in prison and I had a very close relationship to the priest. He was largely responsible for me learning to control my temper. I also got some help from some of the different officers and guards who talked to me a lot. One officer in quarters was especially helpful.

This man's prison classification report quotes the quarters' officer as saying "I have seen this man grow from a cynical youth to a mature man." It may be of interest that this releasee was a Negro from a very poor family, reared under oppressive conditions, and the staff he mentioned were almost entirely white.

I have the impression that these staff reformative influences on criminals involve a change in the offender's perception of his relationship to others in our society. These men, previously treated as though members of an untouchable caste, were accepted in prison as a matter of course, in long periods of daily contact, by persons who were secure and content in a respected social status. Gradually this seems to have given the offenders the habit of identifying themselves with persons in these legitimate and conventional statuses, rather than thinking of themselves as in a distinct criminal group rejected by the noncriminal world.

One can formalize the main implications of these testimonials in two simple propositions:

D6. The prison employee who has the greatest reformative influence on an offender is the one who is able to demonstrate sincere and sustained concern for and confidence in the offender's rehabilitation.

D7. The prison employee's concern is most effectively manifested by gestures of interest and acts of assistance for the offender which exceed the minimal requirements of the employee's job in the prison.

The testimonials that were cited suggest that prison staff could easily achieve a much greater influence on a larger proportion of inmates than they now affect if the prison employees focused their attention on the two principles set forth above. Of course, our data in later chapters also suggest that stable conversion of criminals to noncriminals often requires that the prison's favorable changes in the criminal's self-conception be reinforced, first by the anticipation of real possibilities for noncriminal success and acceptance after release, and secondly by events following release. There always is the possibility that a reformative change in an offender may be interrupted or even reversed by later rejections or disappointments. Nevertheless, each favorable experience seems to enhance an offender's ability to overcome whatever obstacles he may later encounter.

SUMMARY

In opening this chapter I indicated three ways by which communication between inmates and staff is regulated. The first two operate informally, and in opposition to each other: they consist of, first, inmate pressure on other inmates not to communicate with staff, and, secondly, inmate-staff contact at work and in other personal confrontation situations in the prison which promote communication. Data on variation in inmate-staff contact were presented in this chapter. Chapters 7 through 10 deal with the third major influence affecting staff-inmate communication: formal programs prescribing role relationships, such as counseling, disciplinary procedures, and the use of inmate advisory councils.

Impressionistic data by our staff and by other intimate observers of the prison community were cited as the best available data to support the proposition that inmate corruption is a function of the isolation of inmates from staff. With this isolation, those inmates having real or alleged unusual access to knowledge about the prison or influence on the status of other inmates in prison may exploit this position to an extent that tends to decrease as staff becomes more accessible to inmates. In this situation of isolation from officers and corruption by other inmates, the tendency of inmates to isolate themselves from other inmates, observed in the preceding chapter, seems to increase. It was noted in comparisons between prisons that the extent to which inmates were willing to say that they could think of one officer that they liked better than others varied directly with the extent of their pursuit of friendship with other inmates at that prison.

In general, friendliness of manner and fairness of treatment were the most common reasons for preferring one officer to others, and the opposite attributes were the most common reasons for disliking an officer more than others. At all prisons, the work supervisors were the most liked of all officers.

That the prison caseworkers have relatively little impact on inmates was suggested by their being infrequently selected as either the most liked or the most disliked, but they were more often given the latter distinction. Custodial officers were the most frequent among officers whom the inmates most disliked, but they also were highly frequent in the most liked designations. In terms of total selections, as either most liked or most disliked, the custodial officers were highest, and may therefore be thought of as having the greatest impact on inmates. It is rather interesting that wardens were selected as most liked six times as often as disliked, but associate wardens were selected as most disliked more than twice as often as most liked. Despite a relatively small number of selections of these senior officers for either choice, this disparity was well beyond chance variation.

As indicated in the previous chapter, about half of the successful releasees whom we interviewed said that their change from criminal interests occurred while they were in prison. About half of these—or one-quarter of all the successful releasees—credited one or more prison staff members as being major influences in this change. In turn, half of the latter group—or about one-eighth of all the successful releasees—cited a particular work supervisor as a major reformative influence. Next in frequency of prison staff cited in this connection were the chaplains and their auxiliary religious workers, although these are a minute proportion of total prison employees.

The testimonials of the successful releasees regarding the staff who helped them were consistent with the reasons tabulated from the Prison Panel Study for liking one staff member more than others: friendliness and fairness were stressed, rather than permissiveness or leniency. But above all, these testimonials indicated the significance of the personal interest and encouragement which these officers gave these inmates. Also notable was the frequency with which small postrelease gestures were cited by these men, such as the officer's taking them to the train or writing to them, as evidence that the officer's interest was sincere, and extended beyond his duty hours in the prison.

It is believed that the apparent extent of inmate dislike for caseworkers and associate wardens is a consequence of the specialization of these officers in handling requests and complaints from inmates, and the associate wardens' handling of disciplinary action. Both the associate wardens and the caseworkers, but especially the latter, have counseling and diagnosis responsibilities in dealing with inmates. These might be more effective were they to have greater rapport with the inmates. Possibly some changes from individual to group methods of promoting discipline and changes in the circumstances under which caseworkers interview inmates would alter their relationship with inmates and enhance their counseling and diagnostic effectiveness. Prospects for such changes are presented in chapters 7, 8, 9, and 10.

CHAPTER 7

Isolation Promotion and Custody Grading

In the two preceding chapters, research findings were presented on inmate-inmate and on inmate-staff relationships. A problem in inferring the practical implications of the findings in these two chapters is that a change in either relationship tends to alter the other. Therefore, it is appropriate to encompass them both in discussing strategies by which management endeavors to manipulate interpersonal influences within a prison for the achievement of inmate rehabilitation.

Seven broad forms of strategy will be discussed, in four chapters. These strategies are: (1) isolation promotion; (2) custody grading; (3) disciplinary action; (4) counseling; (5) expanding prison casework relationships; (6) inmate group responsibility; (7) integration of inmates in prison management. Some of these strategies focus mainly on altering inmate-inmate relationships and some on staff actions toward inmates, but all can greatly affect the social climate of the entire prison community. Some of these strategies have long been used, and others are newly proposed, but none are completely untried.

The concern of chapters 7 through 10 is to formulate the important issues regarding the seven strategies enumerated above. Opinions differ on those issues, partly because knowledge on the effectiveness of these strategies and of their alternatives is incomplete. The relevant evidence and argument for each viewpoint will be summarized, drawing on our research and on other data, with no problem dodged because available evidence on it is inconclusive. Since correctional decisions must every day be made on the basis of the best evidence available, a tentative position will be taken here on each major issue connected with these strategies. However, further research and experiment which may more adequately test the validity of each position will be reported or proposed.

ISOLATION PROMOTION

Promoting the isolation of inmates from each other has been a primary concern in architectural design of prisons, as well as in their management, throughout the history of penology. A number of the earliest European correctional institutions copied the separate-cell principle from monasteries.

149

Several used buildings originally designed for solitary contemplation by members of monastic orders. However, in the workhouses of the sixteenth through eighteenth centuries, group confinement predominated. Later, solitary confinement became the dominant theme of the Pennsylvania prison system, which spread through Europe and much of the United States in the nineteenth century. Even the Auburn system, which was the most influential in American prison construction, stressed solitary confinement at night, as well as silence rules, lock step, and other procedures to prevent communication during the day when inmates were congregated.[1]

Psychological devices for promotion of inmate isolation have also featured staff programs for the initial indoctrination of new inmates in the typical custodially oriented prison. Exhortation to self-isolation is epitomized by the slogan "Do your own time," which receives both staff and inmate support. Indeed, for inmates in the early months of imprisonment "Do your own time" was the most frequent answer to our question as to the most valuable advice they had received from another inmate. (Details on this inquiry were presented in chapter 5.) It connotes exclusiveness and autonomy, including neither burdening other inmates with tales of personal woe, nor being concerned with their affairs, nor asking their help.

Isolating inmates from other inmates has always been justified in penological writings primarily as a device for impeding the spread of criminal ideas among prisoners. Ostensibly it also fosters custodial control, since large-scale contraband enterprises in prison, as well as riots, require collusion among inmates. Furthermore, isolation may reduce violence between inmates, for hostility and aggression often are generated in inter-inmate argument, obligation, and rivalry. In chapter 6, analyses by McCleery, Cloward and others were cited which suggest that inmate leaders join staff in promoting the "Do your own time" principle among other inmates because this keeps most inmates ignorant and uninfluential with respect to prison life, thus enhancing the value of the leaders' prison knowledge and influence.

These various sources of isolation promotion apparently are effective, for chapter 5 revealed that inmates do try to isolate themselves from other inmates, to a predominant extent, in most of the prisons studied. Inmate justifications for their avoidance of friendship with other inmates indicated that their major concern was fear of troublemaking by other prisoners. Desire for isolation from other inmates was relatively absent only among the most youthful prisoners whom we studied.

In addition to serving custodial interests, promoting isolation of inmates from other inmates may be justified as permitting staff and outside treatment

[1] The most thorough discussion available on the evolution of prison design and its relation to penal philosophy is the U. S. Bureau of Prisons, *Handbook of Correctional Institution Design and Construction* (Washington, U. S. Dept. of Justice, 1949), especially chapters 1 through 4.

influences on inmates to compete more successfully with peer influences in prison. Also, isolation permits the inmate to focus on his long-range problems and interests instead of being preoccupied with the immediate expectations of those around him. This viewpoint, as applied particularly to the youth offender, is well expressed by Dr. Cecil R. Chamberlin of the Menninger Clinic, formerly psychiatrist at the Ashland federal prison:

Lack of privacy not only increases homosexual pressures; the chance to be alone is also important for another reason. The developing, growing, changing adolescent needs time and a place to think and reorganize his concepts, and the occasional chance for privacy is important in this process. It is true that most of the time he needs help from others, but once in a while he must withdraw and reflect upon what is happening to him. If the opportunity is not readily available, he may resort to "the old way" of satisfying his needs and behave unacceptably with the result that he is sent to a segregation cell where his need for privacy is then satisfied.[2]

In contrast to this physical facilitation of privacy, the prison's psychological isolation promotion, as expressed in the "Do your own time" slogan, can have implications of "Do not be your brother's keeper." Indeed, it may promote the lack of conscience commonly ascribed to the psychopath. This was illustrated in one inmate's justification for not reporting or otherwise interfering when he knew that a methane alcohol duplicating fluid, which other inmates planned to drink, might blind or kill them; the aloof inmate was proud that he "Did his own time."

Identification with one's fellow man, and empathy, generally are regarded as the natural basis for human morality. From this standpoint, the "Do your own time" precept of the so-called "inmate code" is antirehabilitative. Yet rehabilitation presumably requires replacement of the inmate's identification of himself with other offenders by his identification of himself with persons who are not criminal. This suggests that the rehabilitation of inmates might be furthered by prison staff through the replacement of interinmate by inmate-staff communication, to promote inmate identification with staff and thereby to promote acceptance of staff values. The preceding chapters indicated that inmate communication with staff does not necessarily replace communication between inmates; inmate-staff and inmate-inmate communication frequently increase or decrease together. This chapter, and chapters 8, 9, and 10, describe strategies for manipulating this communication so as to augment inmate rehabilitation.

The Custody-Treatment Dilemma

Efforts to increase inmate-staff communication pose what some sociologists imply is a custody-treatment dilemma in the operation of correctional

[2] C. R. Chamberlin, "Some Problems of Youthful Offenders," *The Progress Report* (U. S. Bureau of Prisons), *8*, no. 4 (Oct.–Dec. 1960), 4.

institutions. On the one hand, it is alleged that requiring staff to enforce custodial restrictions impairs the possibility of their developing personal relationships with inmates which could have a rehabilitative influence. On the other hand, it is contended that a permissive atmosphere, which facilitates inmate-staff communication, also can promote procriminal communication between inmates.

These dilemmas are avoided in many progressive prisons by a variety of housing and work-assignment practices to prevent the most criminal inmates from congregating without supervision. The most common method of pursuing these objectives is to separate from each other those inmates thought to be the greatest custodial or treatment malinfluence. All prison systems, and most separate prisons, have cell houses in which inmates whose behavior is considered uncertain or likely to be disturbing are locked in their cells whenever close supervision is not available. At the same time, these prisons also operate dormitories and buildings with unlocked separate rooms for inmates selected as custodially safe and not bad influences on other inmates. These housing variations will be discussed further in considering the strategy of custody grading.

Another staff program directed to reconciling treatment communication interest with custody isolation interest consists of rewarding inmates for their discrimination in choice of friends. This is illustrated by staff promulgation of the notion that the behavior of an inmate's friends influences his chances of procuring desirable assignments, favorable recommendations to the parole board, or other rewards in the prison. The dangers of creating a concentration of inmates of bad reputation at particular assignments were discussed in chapter 5. The practice of promoting inmate discrimination of better or worse inmate associates must continuously be reviewed to see that it does not lead to excessive rejection of some inmates and their acquisition of a reputation as "bad" beyond all redemption. Where the latter development is extensive and persistent, the negative aspects of this practice for some may outweigh whatever rehabilitation merits it has for others.

The Terre Haute Experience

A striking illustration of undesired consequences following the concentration of inmate "troublemakers" in a single unit, and dramatic relief of this situation by separating these inmates, occurred during the course of our research in the Terre Haute Federal Penitentiary, where Muslim inmates had been a continual source of trouble.

The Muslims are a religious sect among American Negroes. They claim to be a branch of Islam, but their present organization and philosophy among American Negroes is unique. The most distinctive feature of this movement, from the standpoint of prison administration, is its militant racism. In reaction to anti-Negro prejudice among whites, the Muslims claim racial superiority for the colored people of the world and work toward the complete separation and autonomy of colored persons. This movement appeals particularly to those Negroes who have suffered unusual frustration, and, therefore, American prisons have been a principal area for the movement's promulgation. The most spirited Muslims among the prisoners make a point of not cooperating with any white man in any situation where they can avoid cooperation.[3]

In late 1959 and early in 1960, at Terre Haute, there always were several of the Muslim leadership in the segregation cells, which are used for disciplinary purposes, and in the administrative segregation cells, which are special maximum-custody cells for intractable inmates. The Muslims were disproportionately represented on an unskilled labor crew of inmate "troublemakers," which was used mainly for clean-up or miscellaneous other unpleasant tasks but generally did very little work. Also, officers placed the Muslims under close surveillance; they would stop these prisoners and "frisk" them for contraband, or search their cells, more often than was their practice with most inmates. In addition, it was the impression of some staff that conduct rules, such as those on possession of contraband, were more strictly applied to the Muslim inmates than to others. There seemed to be a powerful determination of staff to keep this group "in line" completely, in order to prevent them from spreading their rebellious beliefs to other Negro inmates.

In early 1960 the new warden, T. Wade Markley, made a series of quick and drastic changes in this reaction to the so-called "Muslim problem." The special labor detail was completely abolished, and inmates assigned to it were scattered throughout the prison. Rigidly enforced "waiting periods," during which inmates were required to have perfect behavior records, were eliminated as requirements for admission to the more constructive trade-training assignments and the paid jobs in prison. Finally, against considerable opposition by some of the custodial staff, the warden stopped the practice of singling Muslims out for specially strict surveillance or overly rigid interpretation of the rules.

By 1961, when the new practices had been enforced for over a year and there also had been a change in a number of key custodial positions as well as a more effective staff training program, the Muslim problem had virtually disappeared at Terre Haute. It no longer was a problem even in 1963, when the prison had taken in Muslim leaders deliberately transferred to

---

[3] For accounts of the Muslim movement in the United States see: C. Eric Lincoln, *The Black Muslims in America* (Boston, Beacon Press, 1961); E. U. Essien-Udom, *Black Nationalism: A Search for Identity* (Chicago, University of Chicago Press, 1962); Donald Clemmer and John M. Wilson, "The Muslim in Prison," *Proceedings, American Correctional Association* (1960), pp. 147-55.

federal prisons because of their intractability in District of Columbia prisons. The inmates in this sect were no longer conspicuous in the disciplinary units. It was, indeed, evident that many converts to this sect had returned to their prior religious practices. Sect leaders of the District of Columbia group, although still dedicated to the Muslim religion, became enthusiastic participants in prison vocational training programs in agriculture; to their surprise, they were immediately scattered in prison farm assignments when they said that they wanted to learn farming in order to develop a separate country for their people. The main change in their behavior seemed to result from their being involved in constructive programs, in farming, industry, or elsewhere. This offered them challenge and hope, as well as socialization with inmates other than those identified with this sect. In this fashion, a voluntary isolation of the members of this group from each other developed through their acquisition of more satisfying relations with others, including staff, and Muslim opposition to prison rehabilitation programs was eliminated.

ARCHITECTURAL FACTORS IN ISOLATION PROMOTION

Certainly one major determinant of inmate isolation from other inmates is the physical arrangement of prison housing units. Our data on self-isolation of older inmates, and pursuit of close friendships by younger inmates, are relevant here. They suggest that dormitories, honor units, and other inmate housing which facilitate inter-inmate socialization do not promote the spread of criminal attitudes as much among older inmates as among younger ones. This conclusion contradicts prevailing practice in prison and training-school architecture, where dormitories predominate in juvenile and youth institutions, with no privacy possible for an inmate, and are decreasingly used as the average age of institution population increases. Dormitories would appear to be least conducive to inmate influences opposed to correctional goals in institutions such as Milan, where the age and diversity of the inmate population greatly restrict interaction with other inmates; dormitories would appear to be most conducive to an independent inmate subculture in youth institutions such as Ashland.

Single rooms or cells seem preferable to dormitories as housing for all inmates, to permit privacy and to reduce the competition of inmate influences with other influences (staff, correspondents, studies, etc.). Presumably inmate criminogenic influences are most effective during the unprogrammed parts of the inmate's day, when he has free time, as opposed to the periods of organized work, study, or recreation activity. Accordingly, effective strategy would appear to be to maximize privacy during periods when activities are not directed by the organized institution program.

Prisons vary greatly in the extent to which inmates are allowed to leave and enter rooms or cells freely to visit each other, when not in programmed activities, or to use dayrooms or other group facilities. This variation may be a function of construction and of custodial as well as treatment considerations. In the typical large inside cellblock of most state prisons, unrestricted freedom of movement to and from all cells generally is out of the question from a custodial viewpoint, in addition to its antirehabilitative significance in preventing privacy. Treatment interests in facilitating certain inter-inmate communication and impeding other inmate contacts suggest the need for compartmentalization of large residential structures into smaller units, with considerable freedom of interaction within units.

Compartmentalization probably has been most developed in the newer California prisons, which include separate dining halls and recreation facilities for each major residential unit. In such structures, placing inmates in different units separates them more completely than usually can be done in a single prison without extreme restriction of freedom.

Our data in chapter 5 indicated that youthful offenders, especially the more hardened ones at Chillicothe, saw most inmates as particularly concerned with keeping from being pushed around by other inmates. This is consistent with our impressions from Chillicothe's graduates contacted at other prisons, and from asking Chillicothe inmates about facial bruises or lost teeth. Certainly, the need for a façade of "toughness" does not foster the attitude needed for stability in adult roles. This is an argument for compartmentalization of large prisons, especially those for youth, and for facilitation of privacy in unprogrammed periods. Fortunately, the large number of federal prisons, and the small size of many, permit much transfer of inmates to other institutions as a means of breaking up criminogenic groups.

Procurement of quiet and privacy, when desired, may become more difficult for an inmate in a small unit because of the greater intimacy of the group there and their mutual involvement in group programs. Possibly the staff can facilitate privacy when inmates desire it by an effort to keep unstructured activities of two or more inmates in dayrooms or other public areas. Perhaps an ideal solution involves single-room housing for inmates, away from dayroom area, with a means by which inmates can lock their rooms, even though custodians also have master keys for opening and locking any rooms, and the custodians also can view and audit inmate activity without opening the door. This has been instituted in prison construction at the Federal Correctional Institution at Seagoville, Texas, at the California Men's Colony at Los Padres, near San Luis Obispo, and in part of California's Soledad prison. In these prisons, inmates are issued keys with which they can lock their separate cells or rooms. These institutions all have a surprisingly large variety of penitentiary-type inmates.

The California "isolation promotion" cells, for which the inmates carry their own keys, are designed in a rather interesting manner for single occupancy. These designs, officials advised me, were deliberately intended to make it difficult for a later administration to house more than one inmate in the cell, as an alternative to constructing additional housing units, if the prisons become overcrowded. The cells in the "North Facility" at Soledad are square, with the prisoner's cot fitting only against the wall which has a window (plumbing and the door prevent use of the other sides for the cot). Therefore, replacing the single cot by a double-deck cot would mean blocking the window.

The California Men's Colony cells have vertically zig-zagged walls on one side of each cell, designed to place the two levels of a double-deck bed in different cells; one cell has only the upper deck and the adjacent cell has only the lower deck. With this "over-and-under" design there is insufficient floor space left to place a second cot in any cell. Such cells also are used as an isolation promotion device at the Reception Center for new prisoners at Chino, where the newly received inmates, of course, are not given their own keys. This "over-and-under" design permits construction of four single cells in the floor space normally used for three, so it has economy appeal as well as isolation promotion advantages, but it is not as economical as would be the abandonment of privacy facilitation by construction of cells housing two or more inmates, or by dormitory construction.[4]

The foregoing analysis of isolation promotion policies may be summarized in a few simple propositions:

E1, Promoting the isolation of inmates from each other fosters rehabilitation where the techniques for promoting isolation consist of:
   a. Providing physical arrangements of inmate housing which facilitate an inmate's achievement of privacy when he desires it;
   b. Separating inmates considered criminogenic influences on each other;
   c. Encouraging staff-desired patterns of inmate discrimination in choice of prisoner associates.
E2. Promoting the isolation of inmates from each other impedes rehabilitation where the technique employed is to promote the "Do your own time" ideology of the prison subculture, which includes the subcultural theme of indifference to the welfare of other inmates.

Techniques for achieving the objectives of the first of these propositions were described. With respect to the second proposition, it should be

[4] California and U. S. Bureau of Prisons architects have had divergent evaluations of this over-and-under cell design. Federal objections were on aesthetic grounds, and also involved some questioning of California's economy and space justifications for this design. However, California, after initial experience with these cells at Chino, has built all 1600 cells of the new Men's Colony structures in this over-and-under design, using a steel zig-zag wall between cells, and solid masonry end walls. California officials expressed great satisfaction with this design when I visited in 1961. See: U. S. Bureau of Prisons, *Recent Prison Construction, 1950-60,* Washington: U. S. Dept. of Justice, 1960, p. 16.

stressed that the "Do your own time" ideology may serve custodial ends, for it discourages antiadministration collusion among inmates. However, as indicated in chapter 6, this ideology may not, in the long run, serve custodial aims because: (1) it may impede cooperation with staff in the service of both custodial and treatment objectives; (2) by reducing inmate-staff communications it enhances opportunities for the exploitation of inmates by those inmates who are most "prison-wise," who thereby subvert staff control of inmate activity; (3) the "Do your own time" ideology may be antirehabilitative simply through its impeding other presumably rehabilitative staff strategists, such as individual and group counseling, group responsibility, and integration of inmates in prison management, which will be discussed later.

AGE AS A CRITERION IN SEPARATING PRISONERS

In the early workhouses of Europe, which preceded the nineteenth-century development of specialized prisons, offenders of all ages were often locked in the same halls. However, separate institutions gradually were established for younger offenders, because they were presumed to be more innocent, less responsible for their offenses, or more salvageable than the fully mature criminals.

Throughout the history of penal treatment, it has usually been possible to procure more public support for rehabilitative facilities and nonpunitive programs for youthful offenders than for adults. Indeed, this may be the only incontrovertible argument for having a juvenile or youth correctional system administratively independent of a government's correctional system for adult offenders; legislatures usually are more willing to appropriate funds for youth correctional facilities when their demands are submitted as a budget separate from the overall correctional budget. Many people dedicated to penal reform still become emotionally exercised on finding young and old offenders mixed, regardless of the type of offender or the situation in which the ages intermingle.

Actually, as was shown in chapter 3, a prisoner's age and his prospects of continuing in crime are inversely related. The younger prisoners are more likely to revert to crime when released than are the older prisoners. This was interpreted in chapter 3 as a consequence of youthful offenders failing to make the conventional transition from childhood to adult roles in our society, especially if their conflict with the adult world begins early. The major process emphasized as promoting this failure to become conventional adults was the tendency for adolescents to mingle predominantly in their own social world, having limited communication with adults, so that the adolescent society develops much of its own culture. Adolescents who have failed in school, job, and other channels to conventional adult success are likely to reinforce each other in supporting the anticonventional and procriminal norms that we identify with delinquent subcultures.

This tendency of youthful offenders to band together and form their own social world was shown again in chapter 5, which indicated that socialization, rather than isolation, in dealing with other inmates was predominant only among younger prisoners. Chapter 5 also presented evidence that the predominant flow of advice among prisoners is from older prisoners to the younger ones.

In view of this greater prospect of further crime among younger prisoners than among older ones, and the tendency for advice to flow from older to younger inmates, one may well question the wisdom of rigorously separating younger from older offenders in prison. Perhaps the tendency for advice to flow from older to younger inmates might usefully be exploited in the placement of prisoners of different ages. Such applications need not violate that first rule of inmate classification practice—that younger offenders should not be placed with those older offenders who are more confirmed in criminality. Conceivably, older first offenders, or other older inmates not professionally oriented to crime and not highly institutionalized, may be an extremely useful influence in the rehabilitation of younger inmates. We have been advised of several experiments in such age mixtures with small numbers of prisoners which seemed to work very well at those federal prisons known as "correctional institutions." Youths persistently in difficulty with other inmates in a reformatory, and resistant to training programs, have reversed in both of these respects when placed with the predominantly older and not highly criminally oriented inmates of these correctional institutions. However, this requires that not too many youths be assigned to one place.

Fears of homosexual exploitation of youth might be warranted were they to be placed with old penitentiary inmates who have been repeatedly confined since early youth. However, Kinsey noted that "in a short-time prison the majority of the men do not accept homosexual contacts."[5] He adds:

Since younger boys have not acquired all of the social traditions and taboos on sex, they are more impressionable, more liable to react *de novo* to any and every situation that they meet. If these adolescent years are spent in an institution where there is little or no opportunity for the boy to develop his individuality, where there is essentially no privacy at any time in the day, and where all his companions are other males, his sexual life is very likely to become permanently stamped with the institutional pattern. Long-time confinement for a younger male is much more significant than a similar period of confinement for an older adult.[6]

Kinsey seems to imply here, and in the fuller discussion of his study, that there is least likelihood of homosexuality developing in prison among men who have made a heterosexual adjustment on the outside, such as would be most frequent among short-term older inmates with little or no prior

[5] Alfred C. Kinsey, Wardell B. Pomeroy and Clyde E. Martin, *Sexual Behavior in the Human Male* (Philadelphia and London, W. B. Saunders Co., 1948), p. 210.
[6] *Ibid.*, p. 224.

confinement. Inmates institutionalized at an early age, with little opportunity for normal heterosexual experience on the outside, would seem most
likely to become involved in homosexuality in prison. From this standpoint, a young prisoner might encounter more serious homosexual pressures
in his normal commitment to a youth institution than he would encounter
in a correctional institution with more mixed population, provided the
older inmates are not advanced in criminality and have relatively short
sentences.

Of course, the possibilities of such age-group mixing are limited by the
relative number of prisoners available in different age and criminal-record
categories. It probably only is practical in the transfer of some selected
youth to those correctional institutions with older inmates which happen to
have training programs appropriate for youth. The isolated experiments
of this sort described to us by some federal officials involved youth transferred because they were having difficulty in avoiding peer-group pressures
or conflict in youth institutions.

The youth most appropriate for transfer to short-term correctional institutions with older inmates probably are those with some period of good
work record in their past. There may, however, be other reasons for
confidence that certain youth can work diligently towards long-range self-
improvement goals if they can disentangle themselves from their relationships and reputation among their peers. Those who show some deference
to older persons also are likely to be most amenable to such interinstitution
transfer.

The prospect of older offenders beneficially influencing younger ones
probably is much less with transfer of a few selected older inmates to youth
institutions than with transfer of a few younger inmates to short-term
institutions for older inmates. This follows from our data on the tendency
of older inmates to isolate themselves from other prisoners and the tendency
of younger prisoners to try to maximize friendships. Psychologically, the
older inmates may also influence such transferred younger prisoners by
serving as father figures. However, an old but inexperienced inmate in a
youth institution may well be victimized by the more aggressive youth, and
he then would be especially likely to isolate himself from the others.

Since more inmates are likely to be available for these suggested types
of transfer than it will seem prudent to transfer, a major research contribution to our validated knowledge on transfer policy is easily feasible. This
would be achieved by designating as eligible for transfer twice as many as
one decides should be transferred (without notifying the inmates of this
designation). If purely random methods then are employed to select from
the eligibles a group to be transferred and a control group not to be transferred, subsequent comparison of the two groups, in terms of both prison
and postrelease adjustment, would quickly indicate the treatment significance of the transfer policy.

CUSTODY GRADING

One of the oldest approaches to making a rational scheme out of prison management is the classification of prisoners into ranks or grades by some explicit principle. Notable historically was the nineteenth-century "mark system," in Ireland, Australia, and the Elmira Reformatory of New York. Under this system each inmate earned a given number of points or "marks" by each day of good work and good behavior, and he lost marks by misbehavior. Whenever he accumulated a specified number of marks he was entitled to a larger degree of freedom and privilege in the prison, culminating in parole when he had earned a sufficient number of marks.[7] Various more or less analogous systems developed in other countries, such as the *Stufe* (or "step") system in Germany, and a similar system has been used in U. S. Army penal institutions. They all involved the inmate's "earning" less close surveillance and more "comforts" in confinement, by his good conduct. However, the grading now is based mostly on the judgments of key staff regarding each prisoner's behavior prospects, instead of on a mechanical point system. Also, escape risk is a major limiting consideration in this grading.

United States prisons have now evolved several independent broad grading systems. A source of some confusion is that the same terms may be applied both to physical structures and to inmates, although the terms, of course, have somewhat different definitions in each context. With respect to physical structure, capsule descriptions are provided by Tappan, as follows:

The maximum-security prison is . . . characteristically surrounded by a masonry wall 18 to 25 feet high. . . . Some of the more recently constructed maximum-security institutions have been built with two surrounding wire mesh fences, topped by barbed wire (cyclone fences), or with perimeter-enclosing buildings. . . . Maximum-security prisons have traditionally been built with "inside" cell blocks, constructed back to back, with corridors running between these and the outside shell of the cell house. . . .

Institutions of medium security reproduce the basic pattern of the maximum-security prison for the most part. Ordinarily a cyclone fence, 12 to 14 feet high, topped by barbed wire, is used rather than a wall, and there are fewer guard towers. "Outside" cell construction with an inner corridor is characteristic. . . .

Minimum-security institutions are operated without armed guard posts, though they sometimes have a fenced enclosure, particularly where they are located in or near populous urban areas. Dormitories are commonly used for a greater part of the population.[8]

[7] Paul W. Tappan, *Crime, Justice and Corrections* (New York, McGraw-Hill, 1960), pp. 711-14; Albert Morris, *Criminology* (New York, Longmans, Green, 1934), pp. 370-74.

[8] Tappan, *op. cit.,* pp. 636-38, 642.

Actually, prisons are classified as maximum, medium, or minimum only by their predominant construction; most maximum- or medium-custody prisons have some minimum-custody farm units outside their enclosures, and most medium- and minimum-custody prisons have some maximum-security cells for inmates temporarily requiring the most secure custody.

With respect to the classification of prisoners, federal practice distinguishes the following four categories:

1. Maximum custody implies the inmate is living in the most secure housing facility available and will be eligible for assignments and activities within the housing facilities under constant supervision.

2. Close custody implies that the inmate may be assigned to regular housing facilities and be eligible for all regular assignments and activities under normal supervision, but not for in-and-out or outside work details.

3. Medium custody implies the inmate may be assigned to the least secure housing units within the institution and that he is eligible for in-and-out or outside work details under constant officer supervision.

4. Minimum custody implies that the inmate is eligible for the least secure housing facilities, including honor camps and farms, and has minimum or two-hour interval supervision on work assignments.[9]

Superimposed on these two types of American custodial differentiation is a third system of "honor" stratification, a finer gradation in the extent of officer surveillance of inmates. This variation occurs within predominantly maximum-, medium-, or minimum-custody structures. Indeed, in federal prisons close- and medium-custody inmates often live together in an honor unit within a medium-custody prison enclosure, although only the medium-custody inmate works outside the enclosure. Honor units may vary in the extent to which officers are present, in the hours during which the dormitory or open-room buildings have their outer doors locked, in the "lights out" time, and in many other subtle shadings of prison restriction. In some federal prisons we encountered half a dozen or more gradations of freedom among various inmate housing units, the differences being matters of as little as half an hour in the "lights out" schedule or in the extent of staff supervision. "Honor," "semi-honor," "medium out" and various *ad hoc* labels designate differentiations within medium-custody classifications.

These many housing alternatives serve staff as a supply of incentives, or of penalties, for encouraging inmate conformity to staff-prescribed behavior standards. They also are a means of restricting the communication potential of presumed antirehabilitative or custodially dangerous inmates; not only may these inmates be retained in close custody, but as brought out by inmate responses reported in chapter 5, the incentive of movement to more attractive custody levels leads prisoners to avoid "troublemakers."

[9] U. S. Bureau of Prisons, *Manual of Policies and Procedures,* part 5, section 2, chapter 4 (May 1960 draft).

Custody Grading and Rehabilitation

Some journalistic accounts of prison honor units of a minimum-custody level seem to imply that the inmates who prove trustworthy in these units are the most reformed. However, it is well known in penal administration that many confirmed criminals adjust well in prison and can be trusted there without supervision. The overall statistical relationship between the custody classification of federal prisoners and their postrelease success, procurable for two of our samples of released federal adult male prisoners, is indicated in Table 7.1. As in previous tabulations, success for the 1956 releasees is defined as no return to prison (on a new sentence or as a parole violator) and no nonprison sentence for a felony-like offense. For the inmates committed under the Federal Youth Correction Act in fiscal year 1954, for whom the U. S. Parole Board collected more than the usual amount of recorded information on prison experience, "success" is defined as nonviolation of the first parole. For these cases we have information on custody change, as well as on last custody grade.

It will be seen from Table 7.1 that there is some statistical correlation between custody level and success, but it is not extremely high. Minimum-custody inmates definitely had higher success rates than those in close custody, although the relationship of medium custody to the other categories was not so clear-cut. The youthful prisoners whose custody was reduced during confinement, and to a lesser extent those who advanced toward honor housing units, were more often successful than those who failed to progress in the custody-grading system.

The relationships between custody level and postrelease success were not sufficiently pronounced to warrant reliance on an inmate's custody grade as a major index of his rehabilitation. More important here, the statistics leave us with the problem of assessing the extent to which the differences in success rate reflect selection of the most rehabilitated inmates for reduced custody and the extent to which rehabilitation itself results from the incentives to conforming behavior provided by the custody-grading system. Ideally, answers to these questions should be sought by controlled experiment involving postrelease follow-ups of similar prisoners assigned to institutions identical in all respects except for their custody-grading system. Since such experimentation is not feasible, one must rely on a less adequate evaluation by inferences from some of our correlational research findings.

Use of Time Among Custody Grades

As part of our interviews in the Prison Panel Study, we asked inmates in five federal prisons to recount for us their activity in the preceding day, from the time they awoke to the time they retired. We also asked whether they talked to inmates or staff in each period, and what they talked about.

TABLE 7.1 Per Cent of Federal Inmates in Various Custody Categories Who Were "Successful" After Release

Sample and custody classification	Per cent successful	No. of cases
1956 Federal Releasees		
Custody grade indicated in last classification progress report: ***a		
Close	55	274
Medium	63	287
"Medium out"	77	43
Minimum	70	367
Not indicated	84	44
Federal Youth Correction Act offenders committed in fiscal year 1954		
Custody grade at release: **b		
Close	31	61
Medium	29	87
Minimum	47	166
No information	25	8
Custody-grade change during confinement: *c		
Increased	25	12
No change	28	82
Reduced	44	220
No information	25	8
Progress to more relaxed supervision (honor) housing: d		
No	34	127
Yes	42	187
No information	38	8

Differences as large as these would occur by chance, in samples of this size:
*less than once in 20 times   *** less than once in 1,000 times
** less than once in 50 times   (by Chi Square test)
Goodman-Kruskall Gamma Coefficient of Association:
a —0.24; b —0.29; c —0.34; d —0.18.
These calculations exclude "no information" cases.

While these matters could not be recalled by the inmates with exact precision, some of our interviewers became quite skilled at reconstructing the previous day with the inmate, knowing in advance the times of major events in the prison. There was no reason to believe that accuracy would vary in a particular direction according to the type of housing the inmate had. Therefore, it is interesting to compare average reported time utilization for inmates living under different housing conditions.

Table 7.2 contrasts the activities of men who were in single rooms, crowded dormitories, and uncrowded dormitories. Crowdedness here is defined arbitrarily as under 70 square feet per man. Excluded are cells with two or more inmates. It will be seen that the differences in activity associated with these types of housing vary considerably from one institution

TABLE 7.2   Average Hours per Day at Various Activities by Type of Housing Unit, Weekdays Only
(Prison Panel Study; all but first-week interviews)

Institution and housing[a]		ACTIVITY						No. of cases
	Work	Just talk with inmates	Play	Read	Eat	Sleep	
LEAVENWORTH								
A. Single cell	6.7	1.0	1.6	2.6	2.6	8.8	42
B. Crowded dormitory	6.7	0.6	2.9	1.9	2.5	8.6	36
C. Uncrowded dormitory	6.0	0.8	3.6	1.1	1.8	9.3	8
TERRE HAUTE								
A. Single cell	5.0	0.5	3.8	1.6	2.6	9.2	61
B. Crowded dormitory	5.5	0.8	3.7	1.3	2.5	9.1	66
C. Uncrowded dormitory	5.0	0.6	3.6	2.4	3.0	9.1	5
MILAN								
A. Single cell	6.3	0.4	2.3	2.4	2.3	8.8	24
B. Crowded dormitory	5.0	0.5	3.2	1.7	1.9	9.2	94
C. Uncrowded dormitory	5.0	0.6	3.6	1.8	2.0	8.8	24
CHILLICOTHE								
A. Single cell	4.0	0.8	2.8	2.3	2.6	9.3	18
B. Crowded dormitory	6.0	0.9	2.0	1.5	2.4	9.4	30
C. Uncrowded dormitory	5.6	0.7	3.1	1.1	2.4	9.2	87
ASHLAND								
A. Single cell	5.8	1.5	3.0	0.8	2.3	8.9	26
B. Crowded dormitory	6.6	0.9	2.9	0.7	2.3	9.0	31
C. Uncrowded dormitory	6.5	1.3	2.5	1.4	2.2	8.9	60
ALL INSTITUTIONS								
A. Single cell	5.6	0.8	2.8	1.9	2.5	9.0	171
B. Crowded dormitory	5.9	0.7	3.1	1.5	2.2	9.1	257
C. Uncrowded dormitory	5.8	0.8	3.0	1.3	2.2	9.0	184

[a] *Housing Code:* A. Man alone in cell;   B. Crowded dormitory: under 70 square feet per man;   C. Uncrowded dormitory: 70 or more square feet per man.

to the next; every conclusion which one may make from the "All Institutions" section is contradicted by at least one of the sections which represents a single institution. This inconsistency in the results suggests that other factors must affect inmate activity more than it is affected by the attributes of residence dealt with in Table 7.2. Ideal research on the effects of housing would require random assignment of two or more samples of inmates with a given program to different types of housing. Nevertheless, some trends in Table 7.2 are of interest.

The most consistent of the imperfect relationships evident in Table 7.2 is that of more reading in single cells, as compared with dormitories, and also that men in single cells spent more time eating than did men in dormitories. One would expect a single cell to be conducive to reading, of course, and we presume it also is associated with more time at eating because eating represents an escape from the isolation of the cell. We expected less play in the cells than in the dormitories, but this occurs only at Leavenworth and Milan, where those in the cells happen to put in more hours at work than do those in the dormitories. Incidentally, the "sleep" tabulation in our tables is a midnight-to-midnight total which includes daytime naps in addition to sleeping at night. It might be mentioned also that in 1960-62 the Terre Haute work hours were increased to about eight through more than doubling inmates permitted to work outside the prison, eliminating general service labor crew assignments, and keeping many work assignments less heavily manned than previously.

We also compared detailed play activities in various institutions and types of housing, but found differences only in the three institutions for adults (Leavenworth, Terre Haute, and Milan). There the inmates in cells spent less time in listening to radio or watching television and more time at physical culture and at art than inmates in dormitories.

At Chillicothe Reformatory our researcher noted the specific dormitory designation on his interview forms in order to procure square feet data later. This permitted us to analyze the relationship of inmate activity not only as first planned, to the physical attributes of the housing, but also to the custody grading system's progressive reduction of surveillance. This also provides an illustration of extreme development in an honor stratification system in inmate housing.

There were six dormitory structures through which inmates were transferred at Chillicothe as their behavior warranted. At the time of our research an inmate remained at least thirty days in one unit before being eligible for transfer to a more favorably graded unit. Relevant policies and physical conditions at the time of our interviews, in 1959, are described below, with the dormitories arranged in order of increasing honorific status in the custody grading system:

F-DORMITORY: This is a three-story structure, each floor consisting of a 6500-square-foot room with 88 to 100 steel cots on either side of a small central recreation area and officer's glass-walled office. There is a small separate locker for each man by his cot, and welded to the cot, beneath the spring, is a small drawer for which the inmate receives a key lock and may purchase a combination lock. Each floor has a washroom and television set. This is the first dormitory in which inmates are placed when they are permitted to advance out of the cellhouses (which also are graded). Men in this dormitory are required to be in their beds from 10 P.M. to 6:50 A.M. (8 hours, 50 minutes). An officer always is present on each floor.

A-DORMITORY: This is physically like F-Dormitory except that it has only two floors. Inmates are moved here when their behavior earns them movement out of F-Dormitory in the direction of more "honor" and lower custody. Men in this dormitory are required to be in their beds from 10 P.M. to 6:30 A.M. (8 hours, 30 minutes). An officer always is present on each floor, but one leaves occasionally when also supervising B-Dormitory.

C-DORMITORY: Physically identical with A-Dormitory, and scheduled and staffed like A-Dormitory, this unit is one step higher on the "honor" scale, so inmates may move here from A-Dormitory.

D-DORMITORY: Physically this is not the kind of structure usually connoted by the term "dormitory," since inmate housing consists of 150 separate one-man rooms, the doors of which are never locked. Each room has 50 square feet of floor space. The men in this unit are to be in their rooms from 10 P.M. to 6:30 A.M. on Sunday through Thursday nights (8 hours, 30 minutes), and from 11 P.M. to 7:30 A.M. on Friday and Saturday nights. This is the highest-grade dormitory to which men can be advanced who are classified for "medium custody," so those who, at release, will be wanted by another law-enforcement agency on a serious charge are not likely to be moved beyond this unit regardless of how well they behave. It is a semi-honor unit in that, although an officer is always at the door, the men are not as continuously under his surveillance as in lower-grade dormitories.

B-DORMITORY: This also houses men in separate rooms, the doors of which are never locked. There are 123 rooms, each of 50 square feet. Men are to be in their rooms from 10 P.M. to 6:15 A.M. on Sunday through Thursday nights (8 hours, 15 minutes), but on weekends they may be out of their rooms until 11 P.M. Men in this dormitory include those classified in a special category not standard in federal prisons, called "Medium Out" custody, who are medium-custody inmates but work outside the prison fence, always under the surveillance of an officer. It is an honor unit in that at times, when most of the men are out at work, it may be supervised only by an officer of adjacent A-Dormitory, who mostly locks and unlocks the B-Dormitory entrance to let men in and out.

G-DORMITORY: This unit is a true "honor" unit in that officers are not routinely present there at any time, although it is checked at night, when there is a count, and rooms are periodically inspected to observe housekeeping. This dormitory provides a separate room for each inmate, 75 square feet in area, with the doors never locked. It has bed capacity for only 51 inmates, but this includes a few new transfers there who sleep in a large room until a single-room vacancy occurs. All men quartered here are classified "minimum custody," and the outside door to this dormitory is never locked. Men in this unit can go to the dining room at any time in which meals are being served, rather than in a limited period, as is the case with the other housing units even under continuous feeding. The men are expected to be in their own rooms no later than 11 P.M. Sunday through Thursday night, and they arise at 6:45 A.M. (7 hours, 45 minutes). On Friday and Saturday night, and on some holidays, they need not retire to their rooms until midnight. It also is noteworthy that they may have the light on in their room at any time. The elected inmate advisory council member there has an office and has some authority in coordinating housekeeping and in selecting television programs.

The behavior distinguishing inmates interviewed from each of these dormitories at Chillicothe is summarized in Table 7.3. Here, for the first time in the application of our daily activity data to analysis of the effects of hous-

TABLE 7.3 Average Utilization of the Day by Prisoners in Dormitories of Different Custody Grading, at Chillicothe Federal Reformatory, for Weekdays Only (Prison Panel Study; all except first-week interviews)

	F-DORM 1st Dorm	A-DORM 2nd Dorm	C-DORM 3rd Dorm	D-DORM Semi-Hon.	B-DORM Honor	G-DORM Top Honor
TYPE OF ACTIVITY:						
Work	5.6 hrs.	5.9 hrs.	6.2 hrs.	6.9 hrs.	5.0 hrs.	4.3 hrs.
"Just talk" with inmates	0.5 hrs.	0.5 hrs.	0.7 hrs.	0.3 hrs.	1.1 hrs.	0.6 hrs.
Play	3.0 hrs.	2.7 hrs.	2.1 hrs.	1.9 hrs.	3.7 hrs.	4.6 hrs.
Read	0.8 hrs.	1.4 hrs.	1.2 hrs.	1.2 hrs.	1.2 hrs.	0.2 hrs.
Write	0.6 hrs.	0.5 hrs.	0.5 hrs.	0.4 hrs.	0.5 hrs.	0.5 hrs.
Eat	2.2 hrs.	2.3 hrs.	2.2 hrs.	2.6 hrs.	2.3 hrs.	2.9 hrs.
Sleep	9.4 hrs.	8.9 hrs.	9.5 hrs.	8.9 hrs.	9.0 hrs.	9.5 hrs.
Other	1.8 hrs.	1.7 hrs.	1.4 hrs.	1.3 hrs.	1.0 hrs.	0.7 hrs.
PER CENT OF PLAY AT	All Play	All Play	All Play	All Play	All Play	All Play
VARIOUS TYPES OF PLAY:	3.0 hrs.	2.7 hrs.	2.1 hrs.	1.9 hrs.	3.7 hrs.	4.6 hrs.
Cards	7%	4%	11%	8%	24%	20%
Radio and TV	28%	46%	58%	50%	41%	60%
Weight lifting, boxing, wrestling	18%	8%	—	—	6%	10%
Other sports	19%	15%	11%	17%	12%	10%
Art	5%	12%	—	—	—	—
Checkers, chess, etc.	5%	8%	—	—	—	—
Yard, unspecified	18%	8%	21%	17%	12%	—
Other	—	—	—	8%	6%	—
TALK TOPICS FREQUENCY:						
Sentences	1%	2%	1%	—	1%	—
Paroles	2%	4%	7%	4%	11%	15%
Work assignment	24%	25%	17%	27%	23%	17%
Studies	3%	5%	9%	7%	4%	—
Play and hobby activities	16%	9%	5%	4%	16%	15%
Punishment	1%	1%	2%	—	—	2%
Food and comfort	5%	4%	4%	7%	7%	4%
Correspondence and visits	1%	2%	—	—	—	—
About inmate acts and traits	5%	5%	5%	2%	4%	4%
About staff acts and traits	3%	1%	3%	2%	3%	6%
Other prison-life topics	—	1%	1%	1%	2%	2%
Total prison-life topics	62%	56%	54%	53%	70%	64%
Sports	8%	10%	3%	6%	5%	5%
Work or trade on past jobs	—	—	3%	2%	—	—
Work or business plans	1%	3%	6%	4%	2%	—
Fun we used to have	2%	1%	2%	1%	—	—
Crime	1%	—	—	3%	—	1%
Women, sex, dirty jokes	5%	6%	4%	9%	—	—
Family and home	1%	4%	3%	3%	—	—
Mechanics and science	1%	1%	2%	3%	1%	—
Religion	—	1%	—	—	—	—
News, politics, war	—	2%	6%	2%	2%	—
Weather and small talk	18%	16%	18%	14%	14%	30%
All other talk	2%	1%	1%	2%	4%	—
Total non-prison topics	38%	44%	46%	47%	30%	36%
Number of cases, by interview: Fourth month	18	4	—	—	—	—
Sixth month	10	13	9	3	—	—
Midterm	9	3	2	5	6	2
Near release	7	3	9	3	7	4
All interviews	44	23	20	11	13	6

ing, marked and interesting relationships were indicated, despite a relatively small number of cases for some units. It will be noted that work increased and play decreased as one moved up the grading system, until the honor units. Here a sharp reversal of trend occurred, with work decreasing and play increasing. Also, the type of play changed, to consist more of card-playing in both honor dormitories. A similar curve was found in the talk topics distribution, in that prison-life topics continually decrease as one progresses up the custody-grading hierarchy until the honor units, at which point there suddenly is peak concern with prison-life matters.

The foregoing suggests an increasing orientation to self-improvement and preparation for postrelease life in the beginning stages of the custody-grading system, but a replacement of this in the honors units by what Clemmer seemed to have in mind by the term "prisonization." In the honor units, although nearer to release, the men seem more concerned simply with maximizing their pleasure in prison. Like the proverbial mice when the cat is away, the inmates in groups completely free of the surveillance of officers seemed to follow the behavior dictated by their most pleasure-oriented members. We heard repeated inmate reports of large-scale gambling in G-Dormitory while our research was under way. Organized cliques of inmates set up the games, posted lookouts for officers, recruited participants with high commissary resources to wager, and promoted election of the inmate council representatives most tolerant of this activity. Other residents of the dormitory, mostly the rural ones, according to our informants, opposed these game operators, but collaborated in smuggling coffee into the dormitory for late television-watching parties and other diversions.

Although the number of cases covered in Table 7.3 is small, the pattern is consistent enough on markedly different items to warrant considerable confidence. One should note especially that the behavior trends continue to be away from the honors-unit pattern even in C and D dormitories, where the proportion of inmates near release is increasing; therefore, the high proportion near release does not seem sufficient to account for the change of behavior in the honor units.

We also procured completely independent and large-scale information with which to check on this picture of the constructive and unconstructive behavior in honor and nonhonor units at Chillicothe. We made an analysis of 1136 correspondence-course records at that institution, primarily to investigate certain aspects of course administration not connected with the study of the effects of housing. However, the housing unit of the student was entered in these records, permitting an analysis which is summarized in the following paragraph from a report submitted to the Bureau of Prisons in August 1959:

At Chillicothe, 26 per cent of enrollments occur when inmates are quartered in the Admission and Orientation unit, but only 13 per cent of course completions occur there. Only 6 per cent of both completions and enrollments occur in the cellhouses. F-Dormitory, the first unit to which inmates move when promoted from the cellhouses, has 19 per cent of both enrollments and completions, and A-Dormitory has 21 per cent of enrollments and 23 per cent of completions. The next higher units in the honorific hierarchy, C and D-Dormitories, have, respectively, 12 and 10 per cent of enrollments and 19 and 14 per cent of completions. When we get to highest honor ranking, we find only 5 per cent of enrollments and 6 per cent of completions in B-Dormitory, which houses about 9 per cent of the inmate population, and absolutely no participation in correspondence courses by the 4 per cent of the inmate population in the most honored unit, the inmate-run G-Dormitory.

The fact that honor dormitories had more prisoners nearing their date of release than did other housing units undoubtedly accounts, in part, for their low rate of participation in education. Our data on education as well as on other activity suggest that there is a general relaxation of behavior expectations from inmates as they approach return to the free community. Prison personnel often talk of once diligent inmates "coasting" as their parole date approaches. This was illustrated even more dramatically in two state penitentiary prerelease units in which our Prison Panel Supplement questionnaire was administered. One was a parole camp at "Full" state with minimal work program, and the other, at "Slow" state, had no work program at all. An opposite trend near release, to closer approximation of the responsibility, industry, and self-discipline needed for achievement of security in a legitimate way of life in the free community, would seem preferable to an easing of work and an expansion of mere time-killing diversions near release. This is most successfully achieved by the new federal prison Prerelease Guidance Centers, described in chapter 16, where men still legally prisoners may begin employment at their postrelease jobs some months before they actually start parole.

Honor Units and Rehabilitation

The conclusion on the effects of housing policy which the foregoing, and other data, repeatedly suggest is that the "honor" units may often contribute more to the comfort of both the inmates and staff than to the reformation of the inmates. One would expect extreme honor programs to be corrupted most frequently by youthful prisoners; with these inmates, group pressures for conformity to the most delinquent behavior suggested are likely to be greatest, and are most readily enforced by violence if there is no surveillance. Our data suggest that one cannot equate staff permissiveness with rehabilitative treatment; where staff permissiveness includes nonsurveillance, it may simply create a power vacuum which the more prisonized components of the inmate population will fill. Inmate surveillance replaces staff surveillance, and inmate life may become less permissive in terms of the freedom available to choose between alternate modes of behavior. Certainly reduction of formal surveillance is appropriate in the development of inmate responsibility, but the complete elimination of inmate-staff contact in quarters arbitrarily impedes informal surveillance by staff and blocks the development of reformative personal relationships between staff and inmates.

The arguments for permissiveness from the standpoint of intense milieu psychotherapy do not apply to the reformatory honors dormitory. The permissive group-psychotherapeutic institutions have about a one-to-one staff-inmate ratio. They favor continuous staff observation of inmate interaction in order to learn from it, and also, to some extent, to manipulate it. The honors-dormitory situation in the reformatory, on the other hand, permits a prolonged and complete daily escape from staff observation and from staff communication and manipulation. The opportunity to manipulate inmates then may fall more exclusively than ever into the hands of those inmates in the dormitory most opposed to staff-promoted values. As our Proposition C10 in chapter 5 and Cloward's "pluralistic ignorance" observations imply, the behavior most visible to inmates as representing the expectations of other inmates will be the behavior of the most delinquent components of the inmate population.

Possibly what is confounded in the nonsurveillance "honor" conception is the difference between permissiveness in the psychotherapeutic sense of a situation encouraging the spontaneous expression of impulses, and freedom in its most sophisticated political sense, as a condition where there is widespread individual responsibility rather than dependence on authoritarian direction. It is freedom in the latter sense that is involved in what is described later in this chapter as the strategy of group responsibility, which may be highly rehabilitative. This type of freedom need not mean absence from staff observation, but more emphasis on the staff as assisting and coaching rather than as driving the men in their work.

I encountered in some federal prisons other objections by some senior officials to as fine a stratification of housing units by behavior requirements as that in Chillicothe and in certain other federal prisons. These men argued that having many units through which individuals must progress tends to create in some of the low-rated housing units concentrations of inmates who create an antirehabilitative climate that impedes the progress of other inmates. These units are a sort of "bottleneck" to movement through the many strata. The opposite approach in custody grading involves what has been called "balance," or the distribution of many types of inmates in housing and work units, so that there is nowhere a concentration of inmates reinforcing each other in antirehabilitative attitudes who might dominate the situation.

Although the limitations of our data on the effects of custody grading make our conclusions on it more tentative and hypothetical than most of our other research findings, further test of the custody-grading conclusions may be facilitated by stating them formally, as follows:

E3. Custody-grading systems foster rehabilitation by providing effective incentives to self-improvement activity, and to inmate discrimination in choice of associates, but they impede rehabilitation:

    a. if the rewards for conformity to prison regulations include such reduction of inmate-staff contacts in quarters as to facilitate domination by inmate elements there who seek hedonistic escape from the effort of rehabilitation;

    b. if they provide freedom without effectively imposing responsibility;

    c. if one of their consequences is such concentration of antirehabilitative inmates in certain units that they dominate other inmates there and seriously impede their reformation, particularly in a unit through which most inmates are expected to pass in their progression up a custody-graded hierarchy of units.

A check on the consequences of custodial grading systems should be a routine part of prison-records analysis. It should compare the records of men during the months preceding their entrance into an honor unit with their records thereafter. For these comparisons, a variety of objective indexes of rehabilitative progress might well be tabulated, including educational advancement, work ratings, letter writing, and other variables. Patterns of change in performance with change in housing, using several independent performance indexes, would be most convincing. However, evaluating men in different housing according to their official infraction record would be rather pointless if the honor units permit and promote the commission of infractions without staff knowledge.

CHAPTER 8

Disciplinary Action and Counseling

The term "discipline" has a variety of connotations in prison. This chapter is concerned with its more negative aspects, which may be defined as all actions taken by a prison administration to stop and deter any inmate behavior which the administration considers intolerable. "Counseling" implies the giving of advice or the stimulation of thinking. This chapter deals with both individual and group counseling of prison inmates by staff, but is limited primarily to disciplinary actions applied to individual prisoners, rather than to groups of prisoners. Counseling may or may not be related to discipline, depending on the manner and purpose with which each is pursued.

DISCIPLINARY ACTION

Discipline, as the arrest and deterrence of intolerable inmate behavior, is a feature of prison staff activity to which our study was not extended very thoroughly and systematically. To my knowledge, prison discipline, in this sense, also has not received extensive objective research by anyone else. Nevertheless, the prison staff's concern with discipline and their policies with regard to it may have far-reaching effects on their relationships to inmates and, hence, on other prison programs. Furthermore, discipline involves issues on which much staff disagreement and uncertainty is readily discoverable. Therefore, a discussion of the research issues relevant to the evaluation of discipline, and of the knowledge available on these issues, is appropriate in a chapter on the rehabilitative use of prison social relationships.

The immediate concern in discipline is with procuring conformity of inmates to the behavior required of them for smooth functioning of the institution, but the *Manual of Correctional Standards* of the American Correctional Association asserts further:

Discipline . . . looks beyond the limits of the inmate's term of confinement. It must seek to insure carry-over value by inculcating standards which the inmate will maintain after release. It is not merely the person's ability to conform to institutional rules and regulations but his ability and desire to conform to accepted standards for individual and community life in free society. Discipline must . . . develop in the inmate personal responsibility to that social community to which he will return.[1]

Like so much other professional literature in corrections, this asserts an objective without considering how one might go about determining the extent to which the objective is achieved. Nevertheless, it points up the fact that prison administrators justify discipline as a character rehabilitation measure, in addition to justifying it as an essential for efficiency in the operation of a prison.

The Uniform Penalty vs. Individual Case Approach

One of the first issues that arise in connection with disciplinary policy is whether penalties for a particular type of infraction should be fairly uniform or should be determined by the characteristics of the inmate who commits the infraction. A major theme of modern criminal and correctional law is that confinement should vary according to the attributes of the offender: probation, the indeterminate sentence, judicial discretion in sentencing, and parole serve as alternative, complementary, or supplementary devices for achieving such variation. In applying these devices in the spirit of the so-called "new penology," the nature of a man's offense is only one of many pieces of information considered in attempting to achieve an understanding of the offender as a person.

Despite this trend in the law to stress the offender rather than the offense, it is widely contended that within the closed and limited social world of the prison, effectively motivating all inmates to conformity with institution rules requires that similar penalties be imposed on all who commit similar rule infractions. This position has been stated by Korn and McCorkle as follows:

. . . When inmates fail to conform, it is necessary for discipline to operate in its negative aspect as an inhibitor of deviations introduced by inmates. The disciplinary court is responsible for the disposition of reports of conduct infractions made against inmates by officials. The actions of the court are crucial to the disciplinary usages of the institution and its procedures reflect the soundness of other operations. Efforts to "individualize" these procedures and to relate them to individual treatment programs may have the unanticipated consequence of weakening the social structure of the institution. The eyes of all inmates and custodial officers are on the disciplinary court, and loose, vague, contradictory, and inconsistent dispositions of charges preclude a stable atmosphere of inmate expectations around the definition and limits of orderly behavior.

Furthermore, unless the correctional officers have confidence in the court, they may apply their own informal punishments or rely on powerful inmates to assist in the maintenance of order. Both officers and inmates need to know

[1] American Correctional Association, *Manual of Correctional Standards* (New York, The Association, 1959), p. 232.

that the same offense will result in the same punishment without regard for the status of the inmate charged. Only when these expectations have been confirmed and the uniformities in punishment clearly defined can due regard be given by the disciplinary court to the peculiarities of individual cases.[2]

One of the striking things about federal prison disciplinary practice is what appears to be a contradiction of the Korn and McCorkle injunctions. Penalties for rule infractions in federal prisons are not closely dependent upon the infraction; they are indeterminate, that is, not fixed at the time of the disciplinary hearing. However, we observed considerable variation among federal prisons, and changes within single institutions, in the extent of this independence and indeterminateness.

The disciplinary agency in a federal prison is called the "adjustment committee." It formerly was called the "disciplinary court," and this designation sometimes recurs in prison parlance but is frowned upon by senior staff. The committee usually is presided over by the associate warden for custody and has two additional members, one being either the associate warden for treatment or the chief of classification and parole, and the other being the senior custodial captain or lieutenant. A prison psychiatrist or other medical officer may be asked to participate as an adviser in some cases.

When the adjustment committee believes that an inmate's conduct warrants placing him in a segregation cell, he is sent there not for a given number of days but for a period during which officers representing the adjustment committee talk to him several times each day, he is routinely checked by a physician, and, in some federal prisons, the chaplain visits him daily. These visitors are consulted by the members of the adjustment committee, who release the man from segregation when they believe that his "attitude" warrants his release.

Prevailing Punishment Practice

My impression in checking cases in disciplinary units of many prisons is that the duration of disciplinary segregation is much briefer in federal prisons than in most state prisons; the median period in federal prisons seems to be two or three days. Also, although many state prisons serve a restricted diet to men in disciplinary confinement and deny them reading and writing matter, in federal prisons men in segregation now receive the regular inmate food (but without seconds), they may have a Bible, and they may write and send letters, but may not receive them. Like other prisons, however, the federal prisons also have a few completely stripped and closed "isolation" cells for any inmates extremely noisy, abusive, or suicidal in the regular

[2] Richard R. Korn and Lloyd W. McCorkle, *Criminology and Penology* (New York, Holt, 1959), pp. 476-77.

open cells normally used for disciplinary segregation. These isolation cells usually are empty.

If an inmate, when not being dealt with for a specific rule infraction, is considered seriously disturbed, assaultive, homicidal, or suicidal, or seems to be in extreme fear of assault from other inmates, he may be placed in a nondisciplinary maximum-custody unit. These exist in almost all prisons, regardless of the predominant custody level of their construction. Such units, occasionally called "administrative segregation" in federal prisons, resemble the regular disciplinary section of a prison in that the men are kept almost continuously confined in cells, even having their meals brought to them. Unlike the men in disciplinary segregation, men administratively placed in a maximum-security unit have their personal possessions in the cells and may receive study material and some types of art and game material. Within such maximum-custody units there sometimes are variations in the extent to which the inmates are restricted to their cells, but usually they are taken from the cells only on an individual basis, always accompanied by a custodial officer. Inmates believed to require a long term of such maximum custody are transferred to the federal prison designed primarily for maximum custody (formerly Alcatraz, and now the federal prison at Marion, Illinois), where they can eat, work, and play in small groups, within closed sections of the prison.

A number of lesser penalties are used more frequently than segregation in most federal disciplinary practice. The inmate may be restricted to quarters temporarily without being transferred to the segregation unit, he may be barred from a particular activity temporarily, he may be warned, and/or he may be asked to apologize to an injured party. In addition, the "good time" deducted from a prisoner's sentence for his conforming behavior during confinement and also meritorious service pay and meritorious service good time (discussed in chapter 11) are withheld if he misbehaves. Very serious misconduct may even result in revocation of previously granted good time. (Withheld or revoked good time may also be returned for exemplary conduct.) In general, time off for good behavior is much less automatic and secure in federal prisons than in many state prisons (indeed, no inmate receives more than 180 days of good time unconditionally; any time off above this figure is granted on a conditional basis, under the same terms as parole, and all may be canceled for postrelease misbehavior and have to be served again). Finally, where an infraction in prison constitutes a clear felony, especially an assault to kill or to do great bodily harm, the prisoner is taken into the federal court in whose district the prison lies, where he may receive a new sentence for his commission of a felony on a federal reservation. All the foregoing, in federal prisons, are parts of what probably is the most diversified and flexible system of incentives and deterrents in any American correctional system.

The variety of institutional disciplinary actions taken in the Terre Haute federal penitentiary in a 15-month period in 1958-59 are indicated in Table 8.1. Although in this period the average number of disciplinary actions was about 100 per month for about 1300 prisoners, by 1962 it had declined to about 65 per month for over 1400 inmates. There was also a decline in the use of segregation and isolation for discipline in the latter years, even though the prison's population growth was mainly from its receiving more of the most intractable young federal offenders.

Staff Views on Discipline

While discipline was an aspect of prison operations which we could not include as a major focus of our research, David A. Ward, our staff member at Terre Haute, was encouraged in his personal interest in studying discipline there. The data in Table 8.1 are from his study.[3] However, his inquiry was limited by the project's other demands on his time, particularly by the need to move him out of this prison to a federal probation office at the end of about a year.

It is indicative of the diversity and change in disciplinary philosophy of federal staff that in interviews with thirty-three officers believed to be a fairly representative sample of the Terre Haute employees, Ward found that 62 per cent favored the determination of penalties according to the individual case, 27 per cent favored standard penalties for standard infractions, and 11 per cent were ambivalent, favoring a combination of the two approaches.

Of course, the standard-penalty and the individual-case methods of fixing penalties often are combined. First of all, one can have standard penalties for some infractions and flexible penalties for others. Secondly, as Table 8.1 brings out, even with the individual-case approach there is some tendency for penalties to vary in severity with the offense. Some increased emphasis on imposition of restraint as a disciplinary measure, with increase in the threat to order involved in an infraction, would inevitably occur even with a case rather than an offense focus in penalty determination. This is because the infraction is one index of how dangerous an individual is to the prison community, and a major consideration in all disciplinary action is to protect the community, in addition to trying to change the offender. However, those federal staff who objected to the case method in Ward's poll probably were expressing thinking habits first acquired before their entry into the federal prison service; they express the deep-rooted classical tradition of criminal law, that of "making the punishment fit the crime." It is the impression of the warden that considerable shift of staff opinion occurred during the two years subsequent to Ward's

[3] David A. Ward, *Prison Rule Enforcement and Changing Organizational Goals* (Ph.D. Dissertation, University of Illinois, 1960).

TABLE 8.1 Inmate Rule Infractions and Their Dispositions
(Terre Haute Federal Penitentiary, June 1958 through September 1959)

Infractions	DISPOSITIONS (ADD TO 100% HORIZONTALLY)					Total infractions (add to 100% vertically)
	Segregation	Restriction of privileges and loss of good time	Warnings and suspended sentences	Other[a]	No action or referral to psychiatrist	
Insolence, refusing to work, and refusing to obey direct orders	59% (267)	18% (83)	12% (54)	7% (33)	3% (13)	31% (450)
Fighting	75% (139)	10% (19)	10% (19)	0% 0	5% (9)	13% (186)
Contraband	32% (118)	36% (132)	25% (90)	5% (17)	2% (9)	25% (366)
Group disturbances	89% (58)	6% (4)	3% (2)	2% (1)	0% (0)	4% (65)
Sex infractions, racial provocation, attempted escape, assaulting an officer	90% (55)	3% (2)	3% (2)	2% (1)	2% (1)	4% (61)
Improper movement: out of work area without permission, etc.	19% (18)	46% (44)	27% (26)	7% (7)	1% (1)	7% (96)
Destruction of property	52% (25)	15% (7)	19% (9)	8% (4)	6% (3)	3% (48)
Violation of safety or sanitary regulations	10% (8)	41% (32)	26% (20)	19% (15)	4% (3)	5% (78)
Other (gambling, poor work report, miscellaneous)	4% (4)	27% (27)	7% (6)	59% (59)	3% (3)	7% (99)
Infraction cases	48% (692)	24% (350)	16% (228)	9% (137)	3% (42)	100% (1449)

[a] Required to apologize; change in job, unit, activity, or custody; miscellaneous.
Where several of the above categories of disposition were applied in a single case, it was classified by the most serious, ranking seriousness from left to right.

177

poll, when the prison's penalties were increasingly made to fit the offender, and at the same time, inmate rule infractions decreased.

Related to the question of whether penalties should be determined by the offense or by the offender is the question of how specifically rules and infractions can be defined, and how rigorously they should be followed. This usually is put in terms of the officer's "going by the book" versus depending upon his own judgment in determining what constitutes an infraction and how it should be handled. In Ward's survey at Terre Haute he asked: "When supervising inmates, do you think that the situations and problems that arise in the performance of this duty should be dealt with according to the 'book' (defined as the institution rules and post orders), or should the officer use his own judgment?" Fifty-eight per cent of the officers favored using "judgment," and 38 per cent preferred "going by the book," with the remainder preferring some combination of the two. None of the seven lieutenants in his sample favored "going by the book" exclusively. This is consistent with official policy which prescribes issuance of a minimum of rules, and reliance on "the rule of reason."

ALLEGED IMPERSONAL DISCIPLINE VERSUS DISCIPLINE AS COUNSELING

My primary concern here is to consider the relationship of disciplinary policies to inmate-staff relationships. This is an area in which conflicting hypotheses may reasonably be formulated. For example, one point of view can be summarized by:

X. Disciplinary penalties which are by the offense rather than by the offender, and interpreted "by the book" rather than flexibly, create shared expectations in staff and inmates as to what penalty is mandatory; therefore, the person guilty of the offense knows the penalty is prescribed by agencies beyond the control of the officers confronted with his offense, so he does not become hostile toward the staff because of it.

This implies that when the offender commits an infraction he knows what penalty to expect if he is caught, and he feels that the staff is obliged to impose this penalty on him should they catch him, regardless of how friendly they may feel toward him. Actually, such shared expectations could also occur with penalties which varied "by the offender," but under explicit rules, such as one penalty on the first infraction, and increasing penalties specified for those with given numbers or frequencies of prior infractions.

If hypothesis X were valid, it would follow that administrative regulations fixing penalties for each infraction would minimize strain in such inmate-staff relationships that contribute toward rehabilitation, as those described in the last part of chapter 6; the officers directly involved in the discipline would not be considered responsible for the penalties. In terms of a current sociological idiom, hypothesis X favors "universalistic" rather than "particularistic" action in rule violations.

Some years ago I presented what I thought was a fairly strong argument for the X type of hypothesis.[4] It has been concurred in by many state correctional officials with whom I have discussed it, and also by some inmates. Examples of its success in reducing specific types of infraction have been cited. For example, at one state institution for "young and improvable" offenders, a penalty of seven days of isolation always was imposed on every inmate involved in a fight, unless he not only did not start it, but made every possible effort to retreat from it and not fight back, or where there were other very clearly extenuating factors. More severe penalties were imposed for anyone clearly established as the initiator of the fight, and for anyone using any kind of weapons in the fight. In this situation it was evident that most new inmates with a history of ready fighting got into fights only once or twice, then learned to avoid them. Inmates remarked that they developed a capacity to walk away from provocations in prison to which they previously would have habitually reacted by immediate fighting. In terms of psychological learning theory, old habits seemed to be extinguished by this punishment, and by the rewards of "extra privileges" and favorable assignments for conforming behavior.

Despite this type of support for hypothesis $X,$ the arguments of federal officials and readily available observations in federal prison, notably Terre Haute in 1961-63, provide a strong case for quite opposite hypotheses, such as the following:

F1. Objectionable behavior by men in prison is so diverse that no set of rules will encompass it all without being so long and complex as to be difficult to apply, or so arbitrary as to arouse resentment by dealing similarly with highly diverse acts; therefore, strain in inmate-staff relationships is minimized by a policy of flexible rules interpreted to fit each case, taking into account primarily the probable effect of each penalty on the future behavior of the offender.

F2. The administration of disciplinary penalties is most effective if it simultaneously:

    a. minimizes alienation of the rule-violating inmate from staff;

    b. maximizes his alienation from inmate supporters of his infraction;

    c. promotes in him a clear regret over having committed the infraction; but

    d. provides him with a perception of clearly available opportunities to pursue a course of behavior which will restore him to good standing in the prison and give him a more favorable self-conception than he had as a rule violator.

[4] Daniel Glaser, "How Institution Discipline Can Best Serve Correctional Purposes," *Am. J. Correction, 17,* no. 2 (March–April 1955), 3-6, 22.

It is particularly evident in federal experience that incapacitating penalties such as solitary confinement in idleness rapidly lose effectiveness as they are prolonged. The first one to three days of such an experience seem to have much more impact than any subsequent days. Even the first day or few days seem useful only in influencing the inmate's communication to staff—but not to infraction-supporting inmates—during this period and removing him from all diverting stimuli. For most infractions serious enough to warrant the staff's segregating the rule violator, a few hours of segregation, or an overnight stay in the case of infractions occurring in the evening, permit the staff to complete their investigation of the infraction and of the offender's attitude. In their talks with the inmate during this period, they usually are able to evoke in him a willingness to cooperate in a program in which his prison activities may be somewhat restricted, but he is able to earn back at least as satisfactory a prison status as he previously had. The few cases where this type of response is not elicited are likely to be transferred to a closer-custody institution or to be held for some time in a maximum-custody unit.

When prison staff perform both counseling and disciplinary functions, it is difficult for the latter not to affect the former. The impersonal view of punishment by those punished, implied in hypothesis X, seems to exist, if at all, only when a person is punished by nature rather than by another human. For this reason, a deliberate effort to integrate discipline with counseling is appropriate. Psychological learning theory also opposes hypothesis X in that habits are best extinguished if they are not merely punished, but if alternative behavior is rewarded while the old habits are not rewarded.[5]

Proposition F2 requires a degree of imagination from staff administering discipline which is in sharp contrast to the simple thinking that treats every infraction merely by ordering a given number of days in solitary confinement. The specific rule approach of hypothesis X leads to the passing of new rules whenever new types of inmate behavior disturb staff, until more rules exist than are likely to be rigorously enforced and many rules survive when the circumstances which prompted them are long gone. It is under these circumstances that the remarks made by Austin H. MacCormick in 1926 become applicable:

Discipline today is largely mental lock-step. It emphasizes adherence to rules. It teaches men to walk chalk-lines which they will not find outside. It is satis-

[5] For psychological analyses of punishment, see: B. F. Skinner, *Science and Human Behavior* (New York, Macmillan, 1953), ch. 12; Ernest R. Hilgard, *Theories of Learning*, 2nd ed. (New York, Appleton-Century-Crofts, 1956), pp. 109-13, 274-78; Hilgard, *Introduction to Psychology*, 3rd ed. (New York, Harcourt, Brace, and World, 1962), pp. 327-31; Gregory D. Kimble, *Principles of General Psychology*, (New York, Ronald, 1956), pp. 272-74.

fied with good conduct—good surface conduct—and does little to strengthen character.[6]

The fixed-rule and fixed-penalty approach is one that confronts each new inmate behavior irregularity by looking purely for new ways to instill fear.

The flexible-rule and constructive-penalty approach, set forth in Propositions F1 and F2, is more concerned with giving the deviant inmate new hope than with giving him new fears. Under the flexible approach a minimum number of broad rules can, if administered by a well-trained staff, generally be "sold" to most inmates as necessary to maintain order in the institution. Of course, the enforcement of any rule should not depend on its being approved by the inmates. Nevertheless, it follows from any conception of rehabilitation as a change in a man's inner values that discipline rehabilitates inmates most in the long run of their lifetimes, and probably most improves their behavior in prison as well, if the rules became internalized as their personal moral opinions. If rules are accepted only as part of the restrictions of the immediate environment to which one must learn to adjust in order to avoid penalties, there is no interest in following them when the environment changes, or whenever the risk of being caught and punished is considered negligible.

It is obvious that Propositions F1 and F2 depend upon the existence of a prison staff of high calibre. Flexible handling of disciplinary infractions requires keen judgment by staff and an ability to suppress hostile impulses and prejudices. An impressive feature of the best federal prison discipline I have seen (not found at all federal prisons) is the imperturbability of the staff after a major individual infraction, such as an escape. Instead of the hysterical tightening of the whole institution for some days and the establishment of new restrictions on everyone which would occur in most prisons, the best federal prison officers quietly and efficiently execute an appropriate "escape plan." The plan varies with the place of the escape and the time before it is discovered, but usually one officer notifies police officials and F.B.I., another prepares extra photographs and fingerprints for these agencies, another calls aside likely informants for interrogation as to the course and probable destination of the escapee, and others make appropriate patrols of the institution grounds and surroundings. There are few escapes per year, almost all are "walkaways" from outside jobs, and the escapees generally are caught in a day or two. Often most of the prison is unaware of the escape until they learn of it through news media, usually after the escapee is captured. Escapes are reviewed locally and in Washington, and sometimes at the national meetings of federal wardens that are held every few years. However, remedies which would have prevented a particular

[6] Austin H. MacCormick, " 'Send Them Up'—to What?" *Survey Graphic, 8,* no. 6 (March 1926), 601.

escape but would grossly limit prison programs and impair inmate-staff relationships are invariably rejected.

Essentially, one might say that Propositions F1 and F2 call for a government of men, not laws, in the prison, which might seem against the American governmental tradition. However, it is appropriate to deviate partially from this tradition in a prison which achieves its primary goal, that of rehabilitating offenders, through relationships between staff and inmates. With good staff it is possible to achieve a consensus among most staff and inmates as to what handling of infractions is fair and constructive, even when the handling is as flexible as F1 and F2 suggest. Of course, any American prison staff still has some limits to its behavior set by law, both statutory law and administrative regulation. The issue is how much latitude these laws and regulations should allow staff.

Commenting on the foregoing in a personal communication to me, former Assistant Director Frank Loveland writes:

The present handling of disciplinary matters, as you found them, has evolved over a period of 30 years. In 1930, the "Deputy Warden" handled discipline. This responsibility was placed on a committee to avoid the possible tyrannical action of one person, but particularly, to bring to bear the knowledge and information of several staff members. The committee was not to have a set of rules but was to consider the behavior and the individual involved. We recognized that we could not on the one hand urge courts to individualize treatment and then when the inmate made a misstep in prison, "make the punishment fit the crime." I am sure that during the earlier years of the Bureau's existence a survey would have shown that most officers believed in a set of rules accompanied by a rigid set of punishments. But discipline has been continually discussed in conferences of Wardens, Associate Wardens, Captains, and in training courses for officers.

At one time isolation carried with it the traditional bread and water diet. That was modified to an unappetizing diet. And that in turn was modified to the regular diet without dessert. Isolation is no longer thought of as a "cure all" for disciplinary infractions and is used much less than in former years. Emphasis was given to prevention of the causes of disciplinary problems. One approach to this has been an analysis of the record of disciplinary infractions by the disciplinary (now "adjustment") committees.

The ideal of a "government by laws, not men" developed in a period of rebellion against the abuses of tyranny. Prison staff have the power to be tyrannical, and where they lack the qualification and training to use this power wisely, a government by rigid laws may be most appropriate. In other words, the very specific regulation of discipline by rules suggested in hypothesis X might be preferable in a prison with staff incapable of handling their authority with the wisdom which Propositions F1 and F2 demand. Indeed, in a prison operating under a punitive tradition, with poorly selected, sadistic, or relatively untrained or improperly trained staff, introduction of the flexible disciplinary policy suggested by Proposition F1 might be disastrous. However, in a prison with staff such as prevail in federal and in some of the best state prison systems, flexible disciplinary policy may enhance prison order and also augment the rehabilitative influence of inmate-staff relationships.

The most rigorous research to compare custodial with treatment-oriented correctional institutions has been conducted in juvenile training schools by a large University of Michigan staff, under the direction of Vinter and Janowitz. The segment of this research especially relevant to disciplinary techniques was done by David Street. His questionnaire findings indicate that the inmates at the treatment-oriented institutions were friendlier to both staff and to other inmates than the inmates at custodially oriented institutions, and were more positively oriented to the institution and its objectives. He concludes:

Custodial staff members often seem to become involved in an interesting self-fulfilling prophecy: because they define inmate association and activities as potentially negative and disruptive to the stability of the organization, they suppress them as much as they can; and when they do so, they make it probable that what association and activities do occur will in fact be negative. In contrast, staff of the treatment organizations find a different prophecy fulfilled: less frequently attaching tremendous importance to the threats to institutional stability and containment offered by the development of relationships among the inmates, they find that such threats usually do not come to fruition. . . .

All correctional organizations exercise considerable control over their inmate members, but while the custodial organizations emphasize the use of formal and severe sanctions directed at ordering and containing the inmates, the treatment institutions stress relatively greater use of informal, personal, and mild sanctions and greater numbers of incentives directed more often at behaviors perceived as relevant to inmate change. In the context of this discussion, it is apparent that the implementation of a treatment program in a previously custodial environment constitutes a shift not to less control, but rather a change to *different types of control* exercised on the bases of different criteria.[7]

The most adequate test of the foregoing assertions would consist of experimentation by prisons in the gradual alteration of their disciplinary policies. This should be accompanied by the compilation of statistics both on prison behavior and on the postrelease criminality of rule violators, before and after the disciplinary change. This change can be undertaken

[7] David Street, *Inmate Social Organization in Custodial and Treatment Settings,* Working Paper No. 9, Center for Social Organization Studies (Department of Sociology, University of Chicago, April 1963), pp. 33-35. See also: Robert D. Vinter, Morris Janowitz, *et al., The Comparative Study of Juvenile Correctional Institutions: A Research Report* (Ann Arbor, University of Michigan School of Social Work, December 1961).

piecemeal by cautious administrators, with respect to only a few types of infraction at a time.

My hunch is that the approach expressed in Propositions F1 and F2 is most advantageous over a rigid-rule policy in dealing with major infractions, which traditionally receive automatic and severe penalties. Nuisance infractions, involving little serious threat to prison order, such as those from careless habits in putting away equipment or clothing, or doing work wrongly, might be administered under the fixed rules of hypothesis X without seriously violating the objectives of Proposition F2. This assumes that the fixed penalties imposed would not be such as to seriously alienate the offender from staff if imposed uniformly, and that the infractions are not such as are likely to receive appreciable inmate support.

In conclusion, it should be stressed that order in a prison is a collective event rather than the behavior of any few individuals. It reflects the overall patterns of relationship between staff and inmates, as well as intra-staff and intra-inmate relationships. Therefore, all topics in chapters 5 through 10 have a close relationship to discipline in prison.

As indicated earlier, the disciplinary committee in federal prisons, formerly called the "court," has been redesignated the Adjustment Committee. In order to change further the image of this committee in the minds of inmates and staff, the penitentiary at Terre Haute in 1962 made it a subcommittee of the institution's classification committee. Its membership and functions were made to overlap that of the reclassification subcommittee. Therefore, in consultation with the inmate involved and his caseworker, it can make changes in an inmate's program, or refer to the main classification committee recommendations for the inmate's transfer to another prison. The adjustment committee was "to direct its actions towards securing acceptable social adjustments both during and after confinement." Stress was placed on changing programs to try to achieve this function rather than punishment.

SPECIAL INDIVIDUAL AND GROUP COUNSELING PROGRAMS IN PRISONS

The Manual of Correctional Standards of the American Correctional Association asserts:

. . . Counselling, as the term is coming to be used in working with offenders, encompasses the personal and group relationships undertaken by staff with voluntary participation by inmates or parolees. It has as its goals either the immediate solution to a specific personal problem, or a long-range effort to develop increased self-understanding and maturity within the offender. . . .

Counselling, casework and clinical services are to be seen as a continuous part of the total correctional program . . . in the institutional system, from reception through parole and discharge.[8]

There were two main reasons why counseling in prison was not a major focus of investigation by our project. First, the counseling that occurs in federal prisons, as in most other correctional institutions, is highly diffused throughout inmate-staff relationships rather than concentrated primarily at a particular time, done by specific personnel whose counseling work could be studied separately.

In federal prisons, counseling is considered one of the caseworker's major responsibilities. In practice, time pressures for preparation of his reports and correspondence, on which other officials rely, often makes the report-writing take precedence over counseling. Teachers, work supervisors, custodial staff, and all others dealing with inmates are also expected to do a certain amount of counseling whenever the need and opportunity arise. In federal prisons, as in most other prisons, inmates may send a note to any staff member requesting an interview, but many are reluctant to undertake this deliberate message writing. Indeed, in prison argot, such a request is called a "cop out," the same label used for the admission of an offense to police or to the court, which suggests that prisoners seeking interviews may be suspected of being informers. Nevertheless, such interview requests are often numerous, and frequently inmates must wait long before an interview can be scheduled by the staff member whom they wish to see. An interesting development in several federal prisons in the course of our research was an "open door" period, generally during the noon hour, when caseworkers and some staff remained available in their offices for a visit by any inmate not in maximum custody, without an appointment or formal request.

In line with the diffusion of counseling in federal prisons, it should be noted that the emphasis in chapter 6 was on the rehabilitative effect of what could be called "counseling relationships" throughout the prison. The view of discipline now developing in federal prisons, as discussed in the preceding section of this chapter, makes the disciplinary process an aspect of correctional counseling. Purely counseling functions were assigned to some federal prison staff only after our project was far advanced, as part of experimental research projects growing out of the commitment of the Bureau of Prisons to develop its own permanent research operations. These counseling positions are in the special education experiment at Englewood, in the Cottage Life Intervention Program of the National Training School, and in the prerelease training centers, which are described in other chapters of this book.

The second reason for not studying counseling separately was that simultaneously with our project there developed three other research programs,

---

[8] American Correctional Association, *op. cit.,* pp. 298, 303.

each larger in manpower, funds and duration than our project, and several smaller programs, all of which were devoted primarily to evaluating counseling programs in prison. These projects, concentrated in California, deal with special programs exclusively concerned with counseling in which extra personnel or new tasks for old personnel were introduced. The three large projects are: the PICO (Pilot Intensive Counseling) project of the California Youth Authority; the California Study of Correctional Effectiveness at the University of California at Los Angeles; the IT (Intensive Treatment) project of the California Department of Corrections. In addition, several smaller counseling research programs are being conducted by these California agencies and by others. It will be appropriate here only to discuss some of the issues which are being studied in these projects, some other issues which might well be studied, and some of the preliminary findings these projects have yielded.

The Pilot Intensive Counseling Organization

The Pilot Intensive Counseling Organization, or "PICO," started in 1955 with inmates committed as Youth Authority wards to the Deuel Vocational Institution, an adult prison operated by the Department of Corrections. About 1600 youth had been involved in this experiment by 1961, and the project is continuing. At admission the youth were classified by clinical judgment as either amenable or nonamenable to treatment by individual counseling. (These two categories were almost equal in number during the first two years of the program, after which about two-thirds were classified amenable and one-third nonamenable.) Then, independently of this classification, half of all of the cases were randomly selected as control groups and placed in units with no special counseling staff, while half entered treatment units for which individual psychotherapy was provided by social caseworkers with a caseload of approximately twenty-five per therapist.

Postrelease results of the PICO experiment, available at this writing for 856 cases released for more than thirty months, show dramatically less return to prison for the individually counseled amenable cases than for the amenable cases in the control group. However, cases classified at admission as not amenable for this treatment reacted quite differently; there was a somewhat higher failure rate for those not amenable who were in the intensive counseling program than for those not amenable who were placed in the control units.

As of thirty-three months after release, those amenable cases who received intensive counseling averaged two and three-fourths months less time back in prison than those amenable cases who were in the control group. Conservatively estimating the cost of reimprisonment as $150 per month, this amounts to an average saving of about $412 per case. Since the average duration of counseling was nine months and each therapist maintained a twenty-five-man caseload, each therapist completed treatment on about thirty-three cases per year. This would make the average therapist responsible for a savings of $13,500 if he treated only the amenable cases, which is considerably over his salary. Furthermore, this is the savings on reimprisonment after only thirty-three months following release of treated and nontreated cases, but evidence from cases released up to five years now indicates that the savings from less reimprisonment of treated than of nontreated amenable cases keep mounting up for many years. In addition, the public saves police, court and jail costs when a man is not returned to prison, plus the more important saving to society of fewer crimes committed by those treated, and less subsequent anguish to the offenders and to those who love them. The large sample studied, which has yielded a consistent pattern of findings for over five years of experiment, makes this one of the most conclusive findings achieved in this type of penal research.

It should be recalled that the savings just described were demonstrated only for half of the cases studied, those who were classified initially as amenable to treatment; a slight loss, rather than a savings, resulted from counseling with the cases classified as nonamenable. It should also be noted that this experiment was confined to older youth offenders, with a median age of about twenty. Findings might be quite different with other age groups. Subsequent phases of the PICO project research involve specifying as objectively as possible the attributes which differentiate those who are amenable to this individual counseling treatment from those who are not, so that even greater profit from counseling may be discernible in the future by sharper differentiation of those most likely to benefit from it.[9]

Group Counseling and the California Study of Correctional Effectiveness

The California Department of Corrections has invested a tremendous amount of time and effort in promoting improved inmate-staff communication within its institutions. Long before they had much research, "group counseling" was introduced in the adult institutions. This involves the line custodial staff and work supervisors, as well as teachers and other specialists, in regular meetings with small groups of inmates, to guide the inmates in discussion of inmate problems.[10] In the major prisons and in Sacramento,

[9] Stuart Adams, "Interaction Between Individual Interview Therapy and Treatment Amenability in Older Youth Authority Wards," in California Board of Corrections Monograph No. 2, *Inquiries Concerning Kinds of Treatment for Kinds of Delinquents* (Sacramento, 1961), pp. 27-44. Republished in Norman Johnston *et al.*, *The Sociology of Punishment and Correction* (New York, Wiley, 1962), pp. 213-24.

[10] See Norman Fenton, *An Introduction to Group Counselling in State Correctional Service* (New York, American Correctional Association, 1958).

full-time nonresearch staff now are employed solely in coordinating these efforts.

The evaluation of such intra-institution communication has lagged far behind the actual communication efforts. There seems to be no doubt that the opportunity to "ventilate" feelings in these programs has, on the whole, improved relationships between staff and inmates, as well as helped inmates to get along with each other in the institution. I am sure that this has been a major factor in the virtual absence of riots in this large correctional system, a calm which is especially striking because of my impression that there is more overcrowding and inmate idleness in California prisons than I have observed in prisons of some other states and in federal prisons. Whether improved communication in the institutions also reduces the extent to which inmates return to crime upon release is another matter, and my main concern here is the extensive California research dealing with this question.

In 1958 the California Study of Correctional Effectiveness was established in the School of Social Welfare of the University of California at Los Angeles, financed by grants from the National Institutes of Health. Its first two years were under the direction of Dr. Joseph W. Eaton, a sociologist. During the 1958-60 period this project's staff made an extensive study of the history of correctional reform in California, observed group counseling practice, interviewed correctional staff at many levels of authority, and prepared a long questionnaire on staff perception and evaluation of group counseling and on other correctional issues. The questionnaire was completed by 3654 employees in California Department of Corrections prisons and offices.

The foregoing studies were summarized by Eaton in 1960 in a long mimeographed report entitled "A Case History of Scientific Newism: Group Treatment in the California Department of Corrections."[11] This report portrayed group counseling in California prisons as a social movement, indicating staff organization for and against it, and distinguishing the stages in its acceptance, according to concepts from sociological theory on social movements.

According to Eaton's questionnaire responses, 35 per cent of California's Department of Corrections employees in 1959 were leading an inmate counseling group or had previously led such a group. This 35 per cent consisted of 27 per cent of the line correctional officers, 55 per cent of the custody administrators, 57 per cent of the educators and researchers, 74 per cent of the chaplains, and 86 per cent of the mental health personnel. About half of the employees endorsed the opinion that group counseling brings about

<hr/>

[11] Published later as: Joseph W. Eaton, *Stone Walls Not a Prison Make* (Springfield, Ill., C. C. Thomas, 1962).

personality changes in offenders and reduces prison rule infractions; only about a quarter thought it reduces recidivism; and 9 per cent thought it had no proven effects. Indeed, when asked to pick one out of four specified correctional activities which makes the greatest impact on an offender's reformation, 51 per cent of the employees picked "advice and help from the parole officer," 27 per cent picked "punishment and surveillance aspects of parole," only 9 per cent picked group counseling, and 6 per cent picked psychotherapy.

Partial explanation for the extent of California staff participation in group counseling may be provided by the finding that about a third of the staff believe this participation helps an employee's chances of promotion. The participation of about half the California prisoners in these counseling groups may also be explained, in part, by its contributing to their chances for an earlier parole; at any rate, 48 per cent of staff thought that this participation helped inmates obtain an early parole. These factors, of course, need not prevent the program's promoting inmate tractability and even reformation; promotion and parole certainly were not the only motives in staff and inmate participation in group counseling.

In 1960 the U.C.L.A. research project was shifted to the university's School of Public Health.[12] A striking feature of this second phase in the U.C.L.A. research is a controlled experiment at the new California Men's Colony Los Padres unit, at San Luis Obispo. This prison is compartmentalized into four identical quadrants, each holding 400 men and each operated almost independently of the other. The researchers supervised random distribution of the prisoners received to open three of the quadrants in 1961-62; this was to maximize similarity of inmates in each quadrant. Under the experimental design, one quadrant receives no special counseling program, one has the regular type of California group counseling, and one has what is called a "therapeutic community" program. In the latter program, men live and work together in groups of about eighty, with morning counseling meetings of the entire group for about one hour daily, plus afternoon meetings of ten- or fifteen-man groups for another hour daily. Trained psychotherapeutic personnel plus regular staff participate in these meetings. The U.C.L.A. research staff is observing the experiment and will evaluate the results by a postrelease follow-up. In addition, the U.C.L.A. researchers have administered another questionnaire to all state correctional staff and are conducting other special studies in California prisons.[13]

[12] Dr. Daniel M. Wilner, a social psychologist, was overall supervisor. Dr. Gene G. Kassebaum became project director and Dr. David A. Ward associate director (both are sociologists, and Ward was employed on our 1958-60 field staff).

[13] See: Gene G. Kassebaum, David A. Ward and Daniel M. Wilner, *Group Treatment By Correctional Personnel: A Survey of the California Department of Corrections*, California Board of Corrections Monograph No. 3 (Sacramento, 1963).

Intensive Treatment Program

The Intensive Treatment, or IT program of the California Department of Corrections involves "therapeutic communities" of about eighty inmates who work and live in single dormitory units at Chino and San Quentin prisons. They hold one large and one small group counseling meeting per day, like those described in the Los Padres experiment. Parole officers visit these sessions on a regular schedule to initiate in the institution some of the contacts expected to continue after the inmate's release. Psychotherapists lead the groups, and special research operations are under way to follow up these cases, to try to determine the effectiveness of this treatment for various types of offender.

Other California Research

Other experimental research is well advanced on evaluation of the use of a full psychiatric team, consisting of psychiatrist, psychologist, and social worker, for California Youth Authority institutions. Preliminary results indicate that these teams are of significant value for that one-sixth of the inmates who are considered most in need of such treatment. Elaborate further research is in progress to develop tests or interview procedures for reliably distinguishing those juveniles whom such expensive treatment is most likely to benefit from those on whom it is likely to be wasted.

In sitting in on seven group sessions in three California institutions, I was impressed by the tremendous variation of staff leadership activity in the inmate discussions. Conversations with staff revealed diversity of opinion as to their most appropriate role. One psychologist held that the leader should discourage inmates from talking about anything but their immediate problems of living together in the prison; at his unit the concern of the inmates was that those in one end of a dormitory tended not to talk much to the newly received inmates at the other end. Other psychologists, by questions, led the inmates to analyze their own and each other's personality and to discuss their relationship to parents and siblings. Still other leaders, particularly two of the custodial staff, gave hardly any direction to the inmate discussion, which sounded like ordinary conversations of inmates in prisons; the most delinquent seemed to be the most articulate here, the youth extolling past "kicks" from drugs, drinking, and girls, while the penitentiary inmates bemoaned persecution of ex-cons by the police. The less staff-directed groups seemed to focus most on the future, but with the least conventionally oriented inmates defining the situation to be expected after prison, and apparently rationalizing reversion to a criminal or disorderly way of life. Here the meetings formalize, and make staff an audience to, types of conversation that otherwise occur anyhow among inmates. It seems to me that future experiments with group-treatment programs in prison should evaluate variations in the extent and nature of the direction given these groups, which may be much more important than the factors now being studied, such as size, frequency, and staffing of group meetings.

Research findings on the treatment of inmates as groups in California thus far are more limited and somewhat less encouraging than the PICO data on individual therapy. Initial explorations indicate no significant relationship between participation in group counseling and parole outcome, although there is a suggestion that participation in one group with only one leader, for more than a year, is associated with parole success. This is being investigated further. Conclusions on California's experience with group treatment should be deferred, since the most elaborate experiments and analysis procedures in the history of penal research have been initiated to evaluate these programs.[14]

[14] Department of Corrections, *Research Annual Review 1963* (Sacramento, Dec. 1962), pp. 29-36.

CHAPTER 9

Expansion of Prison Casework Relationships

A history of changes in the federal prisons during the course of our project will illustrate the complex interrelationship between correlational and experimental aspects of correctional research. These changes, initiated in a few federal institutions, affect the role of the prison caseworker and his relationship to other staff and to inmates.

THE CORRELATIONAL RESEARCH FINDINGS AND THEIR INTERPRETATION

It will be recalled that in our findings on inmate-staff relationships, reported in chapter 6 and in Appendix E, a sharp contrast was repeatedly indicated between the relatively great impact of some work supervisors on inmates and the lesser influence of caseworkers. Work supervisors acquired more inmate esteem than any other staff and were most often cited by successful releasees as a major reformative influence. On the other hand, there were very few inmates on whom the caseworkers seemed to have any impact—favorable or unfavorable—comparable in intensity to that of other staff. Custodial officers were cited frequently, but diversely, by inmates; some were the most liked staff, and the prison personnel considered most reformative by successful inmates, while others were the most disliked prison employees.

In interpreting these findings, I suggested that the work supervisor's continuous and close contact with inmates in cooperative tasks placed him in the best position to develop personal relationships with the inmates. The fact that the education and social-class background of inmates generally is closer to that of the work supervisors than to that of the caseworkers also gives the work supervisors an advantage; most caseworkers have a master's degree, but work supervisors usually have little or no college education. Furthermore, each work supervisor normally is employed all day with a small number of inmates, but the caseworker deals with several hundred inmates, averaging only a few contacts per year with each. Therefore, the work supervisor usually is the staff member who can follow most extensively the injunction to "demonstrate sincere and sustained concern and confidence in the offender's rehabilitation" (Proposition D6, of chapter 6).

Traditionally the institution caseworkers, known in federal prisons as "parole officers," select their cases by a randomizing procedure based on the last digit of the inmate's institution registry number. Thus, in an institution with five parole officers, one officer would take all inmates whose number ended with "zero" or "one," another those ending in "2" or "3," and so forth. Each caseworker retains the same cases from their admission to the institution until their departure, except for shifts in caseload required by staff vacancies or other difficulties. Therefore, one caseworker prepares the initial admission classification report for a given inmate, handles other casework services which this inmate may require, and prepares all subsequent progress reports or special reports for the inmate's reclassification, transfer, or parole hearings, and for several other types of case action. The number of inmates per caseworker varies from a low of about a hundred at federal youth institutions to around three hundred at federal maximum-security penitentiaries. The national average, in institutions for adult males on December 31, 1961, was 196 prisoners per caseworker in federal prisons and 314 prisoners per caseworker in state prisons.[1]

The main arguments for this prevailing system of case assignment have been: first, it maximizes the caseworker's knowledge of the individual case; secondly, it is efficient, since changing caseworkers means that the new caseworker must familiarize himself with the file and with the men already known to the first caseworker; thirdly, by maximizing a caseworker's contact with an individual inmate, it increases the possibility of a therapeutic relationship developing between the caseworker and the inmate.

One of the major deficiencies of the prevailing system of casework operation is that, by randomizing his caseload through the last number assignment system, the caseworker in a large prison inadvertently reduces his chances of knowing the social environment in which his clients live. By scattering his caseload throughout the prison population, the caseworker minimizes the probability of his also knowing the cellmates or dormitory colleagues, coworkers, recreational partners, or other close inmate friends or associates of any specific client. By having the caseload distributed over all assignments, the caseworker in the large institution reduces to an absolute minimum his ability to learn the special competencies, personal styles, or individual standards of the work supervisors and unit officers who submit reports on his clients. Also, when the caseload is scattered, it clearly becomes more difficult for the caseworker to see his client's customary behavior in the institution, away from the casework interview.

An additional deficiency in the quality of casework operations which we observed was that some caseworkers seemed to conceive of their work as

[1] Calculated from "Personnel in State and Federal Institutions, 1961," *National Prisoner Statistics, no. 31* (Washington, U. S. Bureau of Prisons, March 1963), Table 1.

evaluated primarily by the skill and sophistication which their reports displayed, rather than by their actual knowledge about inmates or influences on inmates. This condition could result from the circumstances of the caseworker's contact with his superiors, in the classification committee. If this deficiency is rooted in staff procedures, it can develop unwittingly, despite the best intentions of caseworkers, and it can deter the caseworker from leaving his office extensively and systematically for observation of inmate life in the rest of the prison.

In the traditional classification meetings of a large prison, a committee of several senior officials hear ten to thirty cases at a session, with each case summarized by its caseworker. Copies of the casework report usually are provided for all committee members, and the complete institution file also is on hand. Especially at initial classification of new inmates, each caseworker reports on fewer cases than the total on whom the committee must decide, and committee members have had little contact with most of the inmates whom they consider. In this situation, the caseworker's written reports provide senior officials with about the only basis for evaluating his work for the committee. They can judge the validity of these reports only by their styles and by their consistency with the other contents of the inmate's file. Therefore, the caseworker's efforts at "interviewing the file" and "polishing the report," as they sometimes express it, may be more important in the impression he creates than his efforts to know each inmate's prison conduct and experience as perfectly as possible. When this condition prevails it greatly reduces the practical value of "observation in prison" as a basis for diagnostic and prognostic knowledge of prisoners, although classification and parole policy assumes that much is learned about a man when he is imprisoned.

THE PROJECT PROPOSALS FOR EXPERIMENTAL RESEARCH ON THE CASEWORKER'S ROLE

In this project's reports to the Bureau of Prisons and the Advisory Board, as early as 1959 but culminating in an April 1961 report on the entire Prison Panel Study ("Measuring Inmate Experience in Prison"), several major changes were proposed in the caseworker's role and procedure. The primary arguments for these changes were that the caseworker's influence would be much greater, for more inmates, if one could:

(1) Make the caseworker's influence depend on work, play, school, and quarters relationships with inmates more than on office relationships;
(2) Make the caseworker's information about each inmate, and his influence on each inmate, be a function not merely of his contact with the inmate,

but of his contacts with the inmate's associates in daily prison life, including both other inmates and staff.

A series of specific measures were proposed to achieve those two objectives. The proposals were partly inspired by experimental alterations of the caseworker's job reported in juvenile institutions, but were mostly developed independently of these reports on juvenile experience.[2]

Dispersion of Caseworkers and Group Loads

It was suggested that each caseworker be assigned to handle all inmates in certain parts of the prison. For example, all inmates in the prison industry installation would be served by one caseworker, all those employed in an administrative building would be served by one caseworker, all those on the farm would be served by one caseworker, and so forth. The units per caseworker would have to be decided uniquely at each prison so as to create an equitable division of the total workload there. Some flexibility in such a plan was considered feasible without interfering with the basic principle of group case loads: for example, the caseload could be based on residence units instead of work units, or on some combination of these.

By having the entire population in a work or quarters unit as his caseload, each caseworker would know the other inmates and staff workers in the immediate environment of each of his clients, and he could observe them at work, residence, or play more readily. Indeed, part of the proposed change in case assignment procedure was that the caseworkers should be given offices in the major units comprising their workload, such as a large prison factory or a farm dormitory. They would conduct their interviews there and keep locked files and a dictation machine there, but still maintain a desk and clerical services, preferably not performed by inmates, at the main classification and parole office. Ideally, they should never have an inmate clerk mediating between them and the inmates in their work unit office.

These caseload and office location arrangements, it was suggested, would enable the caseworker to observe the behavior of his clients much more adequately, and to understand their problems in the institution. This would enable him to anticipate problems the inmates are likely to have outside the

---

[2] I believe that measures for altering casework jobs, like those discussed in this chapter, had been initiated only in hospitals and juvenile correctional institutions, and not in adult prisons as far as I know, not because the measures are less suited to adult prisons, but because hospitals and institutions for juveniles have always been more receptive to innovation than have adult prisons. These measures are described and evaluated, as applied in a girl's training school, in: Lloyd E. Ohlin, "The Reduction of Role Conflict in Institutional Staff," *Children, 5* (March–April 1958), 65-69; A. G. Novick, "Classification and Treatment: Altering Delinquent Values via an Administrative Change, *National Probation and Parole Assoc. J., 4* (Jan. 1958), 34-42.

prison, and to make more appropriate recommendations in his progress reports for reclassification or parole hearings. Also, by being more readily available, the caseworker probably could give better service to the inmate requiring special help or other assistance.

It seemed evident that by having a more personal acquaintance with his clients and their friends, the caseworker could gain their confidence to a greater extent. This would increase the prospect of his influencing inmates through his own personal relationship to them. It would also facilitate any group counseling the caseworker might undertake and various other forms of manipulation of inmate relationships in the prison. For example, the caseworker might persuade some inmates to help others in specific tasks, in studies, or in getting along with others; this usually is good for both the helpers and the helped. On some work units, it also would be significant that the caseworker would learn the problems which inmates encounter in mastering specific tasks, and would know the pressures at key jobs in a production process; this should permit the caseworker to be more effective in helping inmates adjust to their job situation.

Under this staff dispersion and group caseload system, when two or more caseworkers have had the same inmate in their caseload at different times as a result of the inmate's transfer within the institution, the caseworkers would be encouraged to consult with each other before submitting any recommendations on the inmate. The fact that each had known the same inmate in a different situation and perhaps had a different type of experience with him should enhance their collective ability to appraise him. This contrasts with the present situation in which only one caseworker knows the inmate and has not had much contact with him outside the office interview situation.

In addition to the foregoing, a major argument for the staff dispersion and group caseload proposals was that they would increase communications between treatment staff, such as caseworkers, psychologists, and teachers, and line work supervisory, custodial, and other staff. It was suggested that this would reduce tendencies for the several staff components to have conflicting points of view. Some evidence of these conflicts, especially between treatment and custodial staffs, was encountered by our researchers in all prisons studied, despite the distinctive staff training programs of the federal prisons. Systematic interviews with custodial officers at Terre Haute in 1958-59 suggested that they were inadequately directed regarding treatment objectives and policies and that there prevailed among them a sense of being insufficiently consulted by treatment staff regarding individual inmates.[3]

The proposed alterations in the caseworker's mode of operation, by promoting more communication between custodial and treatment staff regarding

[3] David A. Ward, *Prison Rule Enforcement and Changing Organizational Goals* (Ph.D. dissertation, University of Illinois, 1960), chapter 7.

common problems, might do more to reduce differences between these staff components than any number of official training sessions, only because the communication between treatment and custodial staff would become more frequent but especially because it would deal with the rehabilitation of specific inmates rather than with abstractions. Differences in social-class background and level of education probably impede treatment staff somewhat in achieving rapport with both inmates and other prison staff; the proposed changes in caseworker relationships, by facilitating communication across traditional intra-staff lines, should enhance the ability of the treatment personnel to influence the other prison staff.

It should be pointed out that in discussions between staff components, the custody staff frequently influences the treatment staff more than vice versa, thus causing the treatment staff to give more concern to the maintenance of order, achievement of production, and prevention of escapes, and less to the rehabilitation of the individual offender, than might be expected from formal statements on the caseworker's duties. Such influence of custody on the goals which treatment staff serves seems to occur in most prisons, to a greater or lesser extent, through the warden's initiative. This is inevitable if we are correct in assuming, first, that no prison can operate without concern for custody and for production, and secondly, that the caseworker's concern with these goals must be acquired on the prison job, rather than in college.

Management View of Rehabilitation vs. Security

Studies by Ohlin and associates in parole and probation offices suggest that the relative emphasis given by staff to the detection and restriction of rule-violating behavior, as against the promotion of conforming behavior or therapeutic experience, is much more a function of agency leadership than of prior training of staff. They indicate that staff who remain in these agencies tend to adopt the particular agency's solution to conflicts between these correctional interests.[4] I am convinced from personal observations that these conclusions also apply to prisons. This means that the prison management's expectations also are the main influence upon the extent of attention to inmate rehabilitation of all prison staff, regardless of the staff member's training or his verbalizations, for the management determines what staff actions are encouraged and rewarded. If I am correct in this, then management's requirement that caseworkers and custodial staff share

[4] Lloyd E. Ohlin, Herman Piven, and Donnell M. Pappenfort, "Major Dilemmas of the Social Worker in Probation and Parole," *National Probation and Parole Assoc. J.,* 2 (July 1956), 211-25; Herman Piven, *Professionalism and Organizational Structure: Training and Agency Variables in Relation to Practitioner Orientation* (D. S. W. thesis, Columbia University, 1961). See further discussion of these studies, and our data relevant to them, in chapter 17.

common responsibilities would give them more identical commitments to custody and to rehabilitation. If I also am correct in believing that custodial security and inmate rehabilitation are not necessarily incompatible, nor need even be inversely correlated, then it is possible for a prison administration to make all staff give increasing weight to the objective of inmate rehabilitation without jeopardizing custodial security. Only with the promotion of rehabilitation objectives by the prison's staff leadership will increased intra-staff communication on lower levels greatly serve these objectives.

This brings us to the problem of administration techniques for motivating the caseworker to achieve all the advantages that might become possible under the proposed reorganization of casework activities. In any organization, all employees have a tendency to work with greatest zeal at those facets of their jobs in which their performance is most visible to their superiors. As indicated in the preceding section, the most visible part of the caseworker's performance is the way in which he writes his reports. Unfortunately, senior prison officials cannot assess the actual validity of the caseworker's assertions about his clients nearly as well as they can judge whether the report is written as though the caseworker understood his client. As suggested previously, this may create a tendency for caseworkers to give more attention to how their report is written than to how thoroughly they really know their client or how effectively they influence him. Indeed, sometimes a more impressive report can be written with little or no contact with the client than with many hours of intensive communication, especially if the file contains a few cues for psychological speculation.

I indicated earlier the evidence from parole and probation studies which suggest that management leadership greatly influences the manner in which correctional staff members pursue their duties. Under the proposed new arrangements of staff dispersion and group caseloads, the caseworker would be expected to describe in more detail than he generally can at present the nature of an inmate's relationships to other inmates and to his work and unit officers. The reports could also summarize the gist of the caseworker's conversations with other officials, indicating the variety of considerations raised by each and the extent of consensus achieved. This would contrast with the present verbose narrative listing of grades, scores, or numerical ratings which can be more concisely communicated in a tabular form, like a school report card. The reports would change if the administration encourages change and if line staff that know the client have an opportunity to react to the reports. But this prompts a further proposal.

Work Unit Subcommittee

Not only would I expect that line staff under the proposed programs would have more informal discussions with caseworkers, but I suggested that formal devices also be developed for intra-staff communication at lower levels. One such device would be work unit subcommittees of the institution classification committee. These could deal with one or more of the work units served by a particular caseworker and could include some of the work-supervising and custodial officers from these units. They could be presided over by the chief of classification and parole, by one of the captains, or by an assistant warden, at various times.

The proposed classification subcommittees could refer to the main classification committee only decisions recommending requests for action by agencies outside the prison, normally the Bureau of Prisons or the Board of Parole. The subcommittees could recommend work and housing transfers within the prison, with the caseworker or higher official at the subcommittee conducting any consultation necessary with staff at other units. Since the highest institution officials would not have to be involved regularly in the subcommittees, this might reduce the present great demands which the main prison classification committee makes on their time. Both the subcommittees and the main committee, under this proposed arrangement, might find it feasible to meet less frequently or for a shorter duration than do the present committees.

In making the foregoing proposals, it was recommended that they be carried out gradually, because they required extensive adjustments by inmates, custodians, and treatment specialists, many of whom would fear some type of personal loss or cost in the changes. It was suggested that evaluation of the validity of the proposals set forth above required experimentation, which could most readily be undertaken in a single institution of a large prison system. It was also urged that such trial be conducted with a series of research operations before, during, and after the change.

FEDERAL PRISON INNOVATIONS IN CASEWORK

One of the most gratifying developments in the course of this research project has been the observation in the federal prison system of experiments like those proposed in the project reports. However, it should be stressed that these innovations are by no means only what I proposed. The new measures reflect extensive discussion of this project's correlational data, my suggestions on staff dispersion and group caseloads, and numerous other ideas of prison officials, including many ideas that they had long before the initiation of our research in 1958. It seems that the research project was both a product of, and a further stimulus to, a "climate of progress" in the federal prison system.

Most of the experimental research in federal prison casework procedures to which I refer began in 1961-62, and many dedicated federal prison employees contributed to the planning and execution of these new measures.[5] Four experiments will be described here, all introduced in 1960-62. First and foremost, from the standpoint of project proposals, is the *Treatment Team* as a replacement for the institution classification committee. (This was developed under John J. Galvin, now a Bureau of Prisons Assistant Director, when he was warden of the Federal Reformatory at El Reno, Oklahoma, and reflects some preliminary experimentation with a classification subcommittee system when he was warden of the Federal Youth Correction Institution at Ashland, Kentucky.) The second innovation was the *Intake Screening Program,* experimentally introduced at four federal prisons (the Federal Correctional Institutions at Danbury, Connecticut, and Tallahasee, Florida, and the U. S. Penitentiaries at Lewisburg, Pennsylvania, and Atlanta, Georgia). The third is the *Cottage Life Intervention Program,* begun at the National Training School. The fourth experiment is the creation of a *Casework Aid* position on federal prison staffs, experimentally tried at the Federal Penitentiary at Terre Haute, Indiana, the Federal Reformatory at Chillicothe, and the Federal Youth Correctional Institution at Ashland, Kentucky. For this Casework Aid experiment three other institutions serve as a control group: the Federal Penitentiary at McNeil Island, Washington, the Federal Reformatory at Lompoc, California, and the Federal Youth Correctional Institution at Englewood, Colorado.

It will be noted that each of these four experiments was conducted in a different institution or set of institutions. This was deliberately planned, and is highly recommended for any large prison system. By limiting each institution to a single innovation during an experimental period, it is much easier to evaluate the effect of each new measure than would be possible if several changes were introduced simultaneously in one prison. Ultimately all four of these measures, with slight adaptations for distinctly different types of institution, could be introduced at all prisons. However, each of these four measures is rather complex, and they also could be studied by further experimentation, varying their components at different prisons.

A fifth innovation in federal prisons stimulated by our research and proposals on the caseworker's role is currently planned, but has not yet been introduced and will not be discussed in detail here. This innovation is found in Bureau of Prisons architectural plans for construction of new federal institutions, which provide offices for the caseworkers in the inmate housing buildings. These plans scatter the caseworkers about the prison,

[5] Especially noteworthy was the leadership and initiative of Bureau of Prisons Assistant Director H. G. Moeller and Chief of Research and Statistics Dr. Benjamin Frank, before the latter's retirement in June 1962. The measures also reflect the discussions of these officials with Assistant Director Frank Loveland before his retirement early in 1961. Finally, of course, this experimentation could occur only because of its continuous encouragement by the Bureau's Director James V. Bennett, who was consulted on each major step.

instead of following the traditional pattern of concentrating their offices in one central location. The new offices should be of some influence in reducing the extent to which prison caseworkers operate apart from the rest of the prison staff and have minimal contact with most of the prisoners in their caseload.

The Treatment Team as a Replacement for the Institution Classification Committee

Late in 1960 at the Federal Youth Correctional Institution at Ashland, under Warden Galvin, four classification subcommittees were created, each dealing with the caseload of one of the four caseworkers in the institution's parole and classification staff. The associate warden, the captain, the psychologist and the supervisor of education each assumed chairmanship of one subcommittee. An overlap of two work shifts of the prison staff, between four and four-thirty P.M., was created to permit movement of staff members at all levels to classification subcommittee or other special meetings at this time without leaving any post undermanned.

Under this Ashland program the subcommittees meet four days a week, generally taking only one case per day. At each meeting the work supervisor (detail officer), quarters officer, recreation staff member, and educational adviser of the inmate being considered serve as members of that subcommittee. The chaplains visit as many subcommittees as they can, trying to participate in all that deal with members of their faith. All cases to be considered are scheduled well in advance so that overlap of committee membership on any particular day can be kept to an absolute minimum and generally can be completely avoided.

The main purpose of this subcommittee system at Ashland is to give the caseworkers and senior staff more direct and intimate communication with members of the line staff having continuous daily contact with the inmates. Since an average of only four cases could be reviewed each week at such team meetings, this approach was being used only on selected cases at such times as a comprehensive progress review was in order for them. The procedure was more of an experiment and demonstration than a full-scale operation plan.

The treatment-team procedure was developed in the reformatory at El Reno gradually, following Warden Galvin's transfer there in 1961. It required many months of staff training and preparation. One should note that El Reno, with approximately 1100 inmates, had twice the population of Ashland. Substituting the treatment teams for the classification committee at El Reno required the creation of four new staff positions.

The personnel change at El Reno which involved the most highly ranked officials perhaps was not essential for the treatment-team program. This change combined the two managerial positions that have come to be quite standard in modern American prisons, associate warden for custody and associate warden for treatment, into one new position called "associate warden for inmate management." It was hoped that this would reduce the conception of custody and treatment as two separate functions, with separate staffs. The business manager, who also had associate warden status at El Reno, was assigned supervision of mechanical services (construction and maintenance), traditionally under the associate warden for custody. Apart from this, the new position of associate warden for inmate management involved responsibility for all prison operations previously supervised by the two associate warden positions that were replaced.

The second personnel change at El Reno was to designate one senior custodial officer as "assignment officer," under the new associate warden for inmate management. The assignment officer must keep fully informed of the opportunities for inmate employment in the prison, must maintain inmate waiting lists for those prison assignments in high demand, and must be able to advise the treatment teams on assignment opportunities and on the size of the waiting lists, at all times.

The agencies deciding on assignments and on all other classification matters at El Reno are six treatment teams, one for each caseworker at this institution. Each team is assigned the regular caseload of its caseworker, a caseload selected by the traditional system of taking all cases whose registry number ends with certain digits. However, every treatment team's caseload has gradually been concentrated into a limited number of housing units.

The third new position created at El Reno was that of liaison officer. Three experienced and well-regarded custodial officers were selected for these positions, each serving two treatment teams. Most of the inmates not in the admission or honor dormitories, who are assigned to the two treatment teams of one liaison officer, are housed in a single large dormitory building. The liaison officer spends much of his time there, where he can readily observe these inmates and talk to them. He also interviews the work supervisors and the housing quarters officers of all inmates to be considered at classification hearings by his teams.

The fourth new position at El Reno was the admission and orientation coordinator (hereafter called "A. and O. coordinator," its usual designation in the prison). This officer combines assignment and liaison officer functions for newly received inmates. As is customary in most prisons, the newly received inmates in this institution are at first kept in a separate section of the prison, where they are tested, interviewed, medically examined, familiarized with the prison's programs and facilities, and instructed in prison rules and routines. Unique at El Reno, however, and introduced in conjunction with the treatment team, is a second phase of the admission and orientation period.

In this second phase, the new inmates are given one week at each of two work assignments, of a largely unskilled nature and in different parts of the prison. This permits their behavior at work to be observed by two different work supervisors, in two different social and job situations. The A. and O. coordinator, in consultation with the inmate and with various staff, decides where the new inmate is given his trial work assignments. He later interviews the work supervisors regarding the inmate's behavior on these jobs, directly observes the inmate, and inquires about the impressions the inmate has made on quarters and recreation officers. Finally, the A. and O. coordinator reports all of his findings from these operations to the treatment teams at their initial classification meetings on each new inmate.

After the first nine months, other custodial staff were placed in the assignment, liaison, and A. and O. coordinator posts. This rotation policy spreads the contribution of such experience to many officers.

Each of the six treatment teams at El Reno is headed by a senior staff member, considered a "representative of the prison management." These include the associate warden for inmate management, the director of education, the psychiatrist, the captain, the chief of classification and parole, and the associate warden for business management. The treatment teams meet twice weekly. Three to six of the chairmen also meet weekly as the "chairmen's team." The chairmen's meetings review major actions of the treatment teams, particularly actions that require special authorization from an outside agency, as in the transfer of an inmate to another institution. An audit of treatment-team decisions is made every six weeks to determine the amount of consensus in policy among the teams, and this is discussed at staff and chairmen meetings.

No two teams meet simultaneously. The psychiatrist, in addition to heading a treatment team, assists the other teams. Moreover, a full-time psychologist and part-time psychiatrist and psychologist also serve on teams as "behavior consultants." Each team also includes one of the two institution chaplains, or one of the student chaplains who train for federal prison employment at El Reno. When the teams are making an initial classification, the A. and O. coordinator attends. The assignment officer also tries to attend all initial classification meetings and advises the teams on all assignment possibilities. In addition, each team other than that headed by the captain has a representative of the custodial force besides the liaison, assignment or A. and O. coordinator; most frequently, this is a custodial lieutenant. Finally, each team other than that headed by the director of education includes a vocational instruction supervisor or a teacher from the prison school, who serves as an educational adviser.

Before initial classification and routine review hearings, three to five members of the team interview or investigate each inmate on whom the team must act. Each of these team members prepares a written report for the other members of the team. Those regularly supplying such reports include the caseworker, the educational adviser, and the liaison officer or the A. and O. coordinator. In addition, there may be reports from the chaplain and the psychiatrist or psychologist. The teams routinely hold a review hearing on each inmate ninety days after his initial classification hearing, again when he has served six months, and every six months or less thereafter, plus one prior to any parole hearing. In addition, special review hearings are conducted on requests for change in an inmate's assignment, for custody reduction, for transfer, for special awards, and so forth.

The caseworker's significance in the classification process may seem to be lowered by the treatment-team program, through the relative increase in the importance of other positions. The role and status of the caseworker on the team is well summarized by the following excerpts from a paper prepared on this subject by Assistant Director Galvin:

The caseworker . . . is looked to as the prime source of information concerning the inmate's history, legal status, community ties, and release plans. He is the committee's link with the central file "record," with the Parole Board, the Bureau of Prisons, and interested agencies and persons outside the institution. He continues to be the coordinating agent of classification, although he is relieved of detail. . . .

. . . Distribution of the former responsibilities of the caseworker among team members has made his contribution possibly seem somewhat less vital in the task of individualizing classification work. The caseworker accustomed to having a key role in individualizing the evaluations and decisions of the classification committee is confronted with a challenge by the team system. . . .

Only as his perspective broadens and he appreciates the values inherent in better communication and more extensive staff involvement in individual treatment, can the caseworker overcome such initial resistance as he may have to the sharing of traditional responsibilities and prerogatives. His new role calls for even more careful preparation, for clearer thinking through of diagnostic and treatment concepts, and more skill and vigor in presenting his interpretations and recommendations.

Any superficial loss suffered by the caseworker in the new system is offset by many compensations. He is now in a position to become much better informed concerning various areas of the institution and its program. He has fuller and more accurate information concerning persons in his caseload. He has a much greater opportunity to share his ideas and insights with staff of other departments. Ultimately he has the satisfaction of playing a key role in a program which represents a more vigorous and concerted attack on the problem of chronic criminality than is possible with the more traditional approach.

The caseworker's responsibility is enhanced quite a bit in one sense. Previously he sat on a committee which included his department head and the associate warden in charge of his division. Now four of our parole officers are on teams which do not include either of these supervisors, so that the burden of representing the socio-legal disciplines (i.e., criminology and correctional laws and practices) rests squarely on them. This further adds to the challenge of the caseworker's new role.[6]

The treatment-team system gives the caseworkers much better reports from the work supervisors, through the liaison officers and A. and O. coordinator, than were available previously in most cases. Also, when there is discussion in the meetings of treatment teams, it is likely to deal with differences in the impressions received by several people who personally interviewed and investigated the inmate, rather than merely their disagreements in interpreting the file, although these still occur and merit discussion. Finally, because the meetings discuss only a few cases at each session, those present can remember each case distinctly without relying on hasty scanning of the single complete file.

After some trepidation in the liaison officer roles, during which they were teasingly called "social workers" by their fellow correctional officers, the men in these new positions became the major influence in selling the rest of the custodial force on the virtues of the treatment-team system. Before long the line custodial staff seemed unanimous in considering the new system "the best thing that ever happened" in the prison. They feel it gives them a chance to be heard, and it raises their prestige with the inmates. Previously, inmates often considered the line staff relatively unimportant in affecting their future, and sometimes they played custodial staff against treatment staff in taking complaints to the latter. Now the liaison officer is informed of all institution problems addressed by the inmate to either the casework staff or to custodial personnel and transmits them to the other. It was found that some inmates, on learning of the key role played by the liaison officers, would make special efforts to curry favor with them and to bring their problems or complaints to them. The liaison officers decided to deliberately avoid the possible deflation of the importance of other staff which this inmate practice would create by referring such inmates to the appropriate other officials and declining to transmit problems directly from inmates to other officials. In selected cases, however, the liaison officer may function as special counselor for the inmate, coordinating his efforts with other staff through the medium of the team meeting.

Each treatment team sees only about a sixth of the number of men, per meeting, that were seen by the institution classification committee. Especially at reclassification meetings, most of the classification committee members had not interviewed the inmate, nor even studied the file, in advance of

[6] John J. Galvin, "The Caseworker and Classification Team," U. S. Bureau of Prisons *Progress Report, 10,* no. 2, (April–June 1962), 20-21.

the meeting, as occurs with the treatment teams. Therefore, the treatment-team meetings devote less time to waiting for members to study the file than did classification-committee meetings. As a result, the treatment teams have more meeting time available for discussion among the members present or with inmates who are called into the meetings after the staff discuss their cases.

One of the major tasks of senior institution staff has been to train the treatment teams to develop new habits so as to use their extra time for each inmate more effectively. They need to develop the practice of making explicit and objective the reasons for their conclusions on a particular case, rather than simply asserting one or two evaluational adjectives to character-ize each inmate. They also must be taught to spend more time listening to the inmates, to draw out their reactions to the programs proposed for them. This is necessary if inmates are to be counseled effectively and if their probable reactions are to be taken into account in program planning.

The treatment teams at El Reno were found to vary appreciably in the rigidity or imagination of their decisions. This was a function of their membership, and it occurred despite the efforts of staff training sessions and of the chairmen's team to develop a uniformly high standard. Nevertheless, considerable growth in perspective and judgment has been evident in most of the staff who participate. Under Warden Arnold Pontesso in 1962, the director of industries was being trained to become chairman of a team, and plans were under way to train some assistant heads of departments as team chairmen. This would permit the associate warden for inmate management and the chief of classification and parole to cease heading separate teams, and instead, to visit different teams each week. so as to increase their ability to train all teams to a similar extent. This also would increase the number of staff to which the communication and training functions of the team system are extended.

The treatment-team system has several major advantages, at a large prison like El Reno, over the original staff dispersion system that I proposed. These advantages arise from the selection for liaison officers and A. and O. coordinators of the custodial officers with the best knowledge of the institu-tion, and the greatest capacity for rapport and communication with line staff. This means, first of all, that the treatment teams acquire reports much superior in quality to those they would get, under my proposal or the Ash-land system, from the least articulate line officers. Secondly, as the liaison officer and A. and O. coordinators become expert at assessing and describ-ing an inmate's behavior, they communicate this ability to line staff through the types of questions they ask and by the contents of their reports, which are frequently checked with line staff. Thirdly, it follows that these new positions provide an outstanding way of training staff for higher positions in the prison administration, for they learn all aspects of the prison's interest in an inmate, and deal with more components of staff than they would in their normal assignments. Finally, by rotating the liaison and A. and O. coordinator jobs, the entire level of staff qualification and performance seems to be raised considerably.

In 1963 the treatment-team system was extended to the National Training School and to the Federal Youth Institution at Englewood, Colorado. Whether this system is the most satisfactory for all institutions remains a problem for further experimental research. It seems especially advantageous for large institutions; possibly the Ashland system of classification subcommittees is preferable for small prisons. The evolution of both of these new measures illustrates the contribution of interaction between correctional administrators and researchers in converting abstract ideas from correlational research to measures which are practical in an existing administrative situation.

Although I have referred to the treatment-team innovation as experimental research, it is regrettable that this innovation was developed without extensive procedures for measuring its rehabilitative significance. It can be demonstrated, however, that under this system of staff dispersion there is more communication of inmates with classification staff, and more communication of classification with line staff, than under the usual top-level committee system. It seems reasonable to infer that this communication makes for sounder classification decisions and more rehabilitation impact of staff on inmates. An optimum test of the validity of this inference, however, would require at least before and after measurements of recidivism rates and, ideally, controlled experiments in which the innovation is introduced in only one of two similar institutions, the other serving as a control.

The Intake Screening System

This innovation in federal casework practice is largely without direct relationship to our research in origin, but is part of an independent and complementary effort to utilize the prison caseworker's time and skill more efficiently. For this program a staff position recently established in a few institutions proved to be an important resource. This position is known as the casework supervisor, intermediate between chief of classification and parole and the line caseworkers in the federal prison administrative structure. In the U. S. Penitentiaries at Atlanta and Lewisburg the new position has intake screening as a major responsibility. In the other institutions it is a special part-time function of a senior caseworker, who also carries a limited caseload. After more than a year's trial at a few institutions, the intake screening system was extended in 1963 to all federal prisons for adult offenders.

The casework supervisor in the intake screening system studies the documentary material received by the prison initially on each new inmate and interviews him, if necessary, as a means of making advance judgments as to the types of diagnostic casework the inmate will most urgently require and the types which will not be important in his case.

Two main functions are served by this screening process. First of all, the supervisor can decide that, in many cases, the gathering of certain information is unnecessary. For example, if a thorough presentence report is received, or if the inmate is a recidivist with brief freedom after his last release, the file may already be well provided with information on the offender's earlier work, family, military, correctional, and educational history.

Secondly, the screening process can quickly indicate, in many cases, what type of casework is going to be most useful and feasible for an inmate in the time available, and this will determine what type of diagnostic services are worthwhile for him. For example, if an inmate has an urgent medical problem, it may be appropriate to concentrate on providing medical care quickly and to defer psychological or educational testing and other studies or plans until the probable solution of the medical problem is known. Similarly, if a prisoner has a long time of confinement ahead of him, elaborate diagnostic study and program planning may be appropriate, but if the inmate's sentence is short, release planning and arranging may be the only prison service of much worth. Within both these extremes of sentence, as well as with cases of intermediate or highly indeterminate sentences, it still may be possible in a screening process for the casework supervisor to guide the casework staff to the diagnostic or treatment services most relevant to an offender's unique needs.

An ultimate objective which the intake screening process can facilitate is the development of more functionally specialized types of caseloads for prison caseworkers. For example, one caseworker might be assigned primarily cases requiring intensive counseling, while another might be assigned primarily cases requiring postrelease arrangement services or assistance in straightening out business affairs in the world outside the prison. Their two caseloads need not be of the same size, and the caseworkers could differ greatly in their training, experience, and personality qualifications.

There might be problems of integrating a functional caseload system with a caseload of all inmates assigned to a specific segment of a prison or to a specific treatment team. Some reconciliation of these approaches probably can be worked out if it is considered desirable to extend all these innovations to most prisons. One solution might be to have two or more caseworkers involved in services to certain inmates, each providing a different type of specialized service, with all these caseworkers consulting each other in these cases.

The Cottage Life Intervention Program

This is a program of group counseling in the only juvenile training school in the federal prison system. It is relevant to the concerns of this chapter because it involves the caseworker in new relationships with inmates and with other staff and because it could readily be extended to prisons for adults.

Under the Cottage Life Intervention Program, one of the school's dormitory buildings, called "cottages," was made the special caseload of one caseworker. This cottage holds seventy-five boys, who were divided into three groups of twenty-five, each assigned to one specially selected and trained custodial staff member for individual and group counseling, and for supervision during daily periods of group recreational activity. A psychologist, a social worker with group psychotherapy experience, and group therapy consultants trained and supervised the custodial staff counselors in this all-out effort to maximize institutional influences on the personalities of these boys.

Inmates in this special-treatment cottage were randomly selected from a longitudinal cross-section of the training-school population. In addition, two control groups were also randomly chosen to match the treatment group closely on major variables. One of these control groups consists of seventy-five boys concentrated in a single cottage, and another consists of thirty boys distributed throughout the remaining cottages. To facilitate evaluation of this experiment, intercottage transfer was not permitted for boys in the treatment and control cottages, but inmates in the control group scattered throughout the remainder of the institution were subject to the usual intercottage transfers, on an individual basis.

It is interesting that both the treatment and the control cottages have shown greater achievement than the control group distributed in the remaining training-school population. This achievement was observed both in positive institutional indexes of rehabilitation, such as work performance and progress in education and vocational training, and in negative indexes, such as absence of misconduct reports. The treatment cottage has had a somewhat better record than the control cottage, but the latter's behavior is an interesting example of the so-called "Hawthorne" or "placebo" effect. The mere fact that the control cottage received special attention and its residents were aware of their status as a control group motivated both its inmates and its staff to unusual behavior.

It is possible that nontransfer of inmates among cottages, which characterized both the treatment and the control cottages, is a major treatment variable. Nontransfer would promote the sense of group responsibility discussed in chapter 10. A postrelease comparison of the treatment and the two control groups is planned which will provide a more adequate evaluation of the rehabilitative effect of this program.

As indicated in chapter 8, our project was not designed to analyze and evaluate special counseling programs. The Cottage Life Intervention Program is of interest here because it employs the group caseload system, and especially because of the interesting evaluation design and its early findings.

A special report eventually will be prepared by its directors on the impact of their program.[7]

The "Casework Aid" Position

In 1961 the position of casework aid was created in federal prisons as a means of giving custodial officers firsthand acquaintance with the caseworker's job and as a method of relieving the caseworkers in some tasks for which their special training is not essential. Regular custodial staff were encouraged to volunteer for a temporary term as casework aid. During this period they were transferred to the classification and parole office, and they gradually assumed all casework functions for which they were qualified.

At the end of a period as casework aid, these officers return to their custodial position, but the casework aid experience is viewed by the Bureau of Prisons as augmenting qualifications for promotion within custodial positions. This program should complement the treatment team and other innovations described here in reducing tendencies to isolation within and alienation between casework and custodial staffs.

To evaluate the effect of the casework-aid program on the work of the caseworker, the Bureau of Prisons undertook a series of time and motion studies. The procedures in their studies were modeled on this project's time and motion study of the U. S. probation officer's job. Detailed records of the caseworker's conduct of his job were maintained during periods of one or two weeks each, both before and during the employment of the casework aid, and in both the institutions where casework aids were appointed and in the control institutions without such aids. Time and motion studies also were made on the work done by the aids. The conclusion from these studies was that, in the initial trial years, the casework-aid system did not contribute materially to reducing the work of the caseworker, but it was highly successful in augmenting communication among treatment staff, training staff, and line personnel.

SUMMARY

Our findings on inmate-staff relationships, presented in chapter 6, indicated less influence on inmates by prison caseworkers than by other prison staff. These data, and other observations and inferences on defects of prevailing prison casework, provided a correlational research foundation for several experimental research proposals to alter the performance of case-

[7] See: Robert B. Levinson and Howard L. Kitchener, "The Demonstration Counseling Project," U. S. Bureau of Prisons *Progress Report, 10,* no. 4 (Oct.–Dec. 1962), 5-9; National Training School for Boys, Washington, D. C., *Demonstration Counseling Project, First Annual Report,* Oct. 15, 1961–Oct. 15, 1962.

work tasks. In early reports of this project to the Advisory Board, I argued for innovations which included:

(1) assignment of all inmates in particular work or housing units of a prison as the caseload of a single caseworker, so that he might readily know an inmate's experience in prison through acquaintance with the inmate's social environment;

(2) classification of inmates by subcommittees dealing only with men assigned to a limited segment of the prison, and including as members the line staff in direct contact with the inmates to be classified;

(3) revision of casework reports to make their preparation less time-consuming, their recording of objective information more concise and standardized, and their reporting on the inmate's prison experience more adequately grounded on observations of the inmate's conduct outside of the caseworker's office.

Four experimental programs subsequently were initiated in federal prisons, stimulated in part by this project's findings and the above proposals. The organization of a separate treatment team for each caseworker, to replace the institutional classification committee of large prisons, was the innovation most exclusively relevant to the issues raised by our project reports. Each treatment team is aided by selected custodial personnel in newly created staff positions, who devote themselves almost exclusively to transmitting to the team the impressions each inmate has made on his work supervisors and on custodial and recreational personnel. Some of the many advantages of the team procedures are that they: (1) increase the time which can be devoted to classification study and discussion for each inmate; (2) expand intrastaff communication; (3) facilitate the training of all staff in perceptive observation and reporting of inmate behavior; (4) raise staff morale by making line personnel more aware of their importance to top management; (5) greatly increase the extent to which the caseworker's classification reports reflect knowledge of the inmate's experience in prison.

The second innovation, an intake screening system, assigns to a casework supervisor the task of determining what are likely to be the most valuable diagnostic and treatment services for each case, and perhaps the optimum sequence for such service. This eliminates the waste of specialized staff time in those cases which do not require all of the types of study and testing usually applied routinely to every case. It also lays a groundwork for the development of specialized caseloads in which each man is assigned to a caseworker uniquely competent for his needs.

The third innovation, known as the Cottage Life Intervention Program, was initiated in the National Training School and emphasizes primarily a special group activity program and counseling service. Nevertheless, it is of interest to us here because it also concentrated all inmates assigned a single caseworker into one housing unit, where the caseworker became part of a close-knit staff team. A dual-control-group research design, with one control group concentrated in a single cottage without the special services provided for the experimental cottage, and one control group scattered in the rest of the institution, revealed the so-called "placebo" or "Hawthorne" effect; those inmates and staff in the control cottage, aware that they were the object of special observation, manifested exemplary conduct almost to the same extent as those who received special counseling and casework services, in addition to special observation.

The fourth innovation was the temporary assignment of selected custodial officers as casework aids. This augments intrastaff communication, adds to the qualification of these custodial officers for higher prison administrative positions, and relieves caseworkers of some duties not requiring their special training.

A fifth innovation contributing to the expansion of casework relationship was the introduction in 1962 of a split shift for caseworkers at the Federal Youth Correctional Institution at Englewood, Colorado. Caseworkers work from 12:30 to 9:00 P.M. four nights a week. From 4:15 to 9:00 on these days they visit living quarters, work details, and other sections of the institution. They pay particular attention to the postadmission orientation unit of inmates new to regular assignment in the general population of the institution.

The foregoing proposals and innovations are all consistent with an emerging theme in mental-hospital programs and in research on juvenile correctional institutions.[8] It is also a principle underlying group counseling programs, such as those of the California and District of Columbia prisons. This theme may be formulated as:

G1. The advancement of treatment goals requires centralization of more *authority* in the officials who are spokesmen for treatment interests, but decentralization of treatment *activity,* so as to increase the extent to which all staff in contact with inmates have a strong interest in treatment.

Deficiencies in the quality and standardization of casework records were noted, which have not yet been appreciably reduced in federal prisons. For special projects and innovations such as those described here, however, the prison system increasingly requires that special records be maintained

[8] See, for example: Maxwell Jones, *The Therapeutic Community* (New York, Basic Books, 1953); Morris Schwarz, "What Is a Therapeutic Milieu?" in M. Greenblatt, D. J. Levinson, and R. H. Williams, eds., *The Patient and The Mental Hospital* (Glencoe, Ill., Free Press, 1957), pp. 130-44; Oscar Grusky, *Treatment Goals and Organizational Behavior: A Study of an Experimental Prison Camp* (Ph.D. thesis, University of Michigan, 1957); Robert Vinter and Morris Janowitz, "Effective Institutions for Juvenile Delinquents: A Research Statement," *The Social Service Review, 33* (June 1959), 118-30; Mayer N. Zald, "Organizational Control Structures in Five Correctional Institutions," *Am. J. Sociology, 68,* no. 3 (Nov. 1962), 335-45.

in a sufficiently concise and standardized manner to permit their use for statistical analysis. When such practice becomes more extensive and results indicate which types of record are most useful, it should be possible to incorporate such record-keeping into routine procedures. This will facilitate evaluation of file information for casework and classification decisions, and it will be necessary for progressive expansion of statistical information on what types of treatment are most rehabilitative for particular types of inmate.

CHAPTER 10

Inmate Group Responsibility and Integration of Inmates in Prison Management

This chapter concerns strategies for staff use of inmate groups in the achievement of staff goals. These involve a process known in administration literature as "cooptation," the common strategy of absorbing, as colleagues in an organization, those outside the organization who lead opposition to it, or impede its activities.[1] In a few prison systems, notably Arkansas, this process occurs literally, in the staff's assigning certain prisoners to guard other prisoners. While most prison administrators would abhor this process, assignment of inmate leaders as "barn boss" or "straw boss" is a common technique of prison custodial strategy, either through formal designation or informally, by officers transmitting instructions through these inmate leaders.

INMATE GROUP RESPONSIBILITY AND INTERGROUP COMPETITION

Perhaps the simplest manipulation of inmate relationships for staff purposes is group punishment for the conduct of its individual members. A common illustration of this practice is its use as a custodial device, particularly with honor groups or when groups of inmates are taken on excursions outside the prison grounds. There are many accounts of inmates preventing other inmates from escaping under such circumstances. Even inmate leaders who usually are strongly antistaff often justify cooperation with staff in preventing escapes where violation of trust would jeopardize valued freedoms and pleasures for inmates as a whole.

Another common and successful promotion of inmate group responsibility is the use of rewards to an entire prison housing unit for housekeeping by its individual members. In Terre Haute, when rewards of various extra privileges were introduced for the residence unit which received the highest score on housekeeping inspections, the unit in which the inmates pre-

---

[1] While "cooptation" also is defined more widely as any selection or election to a group, such as a managerial board, the special usage of recent management literature, presented in this chapter, generally is traced to Phillip Selznick, *TVA and the Grass Roots* (Berkeley, University of California Press, 1949). See also: Selznick, *Leadership in Administration* (Evanston, Row, Peterson, 1957).

viously were the least cooperative frequently won the award, and their general behavior was reported to have improved greatly. Competition between units for a limited number of rewards not only adds motivation but can considerably improve relationships between the inmates and their unit officers. This is because it makes each unit's staff cooperate with inmates in common tasks instead of driving inmates in a task which they resist.

Promoting competition among groups of inmates adds to available incentives an inmate's pride in belonging to a group which exceeds other groups. Psychologically this may become a stronger motivation than the specific prison pleasure or material reward offered to a group for achieving a given standard. This motivation may especially attract the most aggressively competitive members of an inmate group and may quickly reveal leadership qualities among the inmates.

Competition among groups can have the major advantage for the prison administration of keeping rewards scarce but not unobtainable. Some authors have observed that most other behavior incentives granted to prisoners, such as statutory good time, lose much of their motivating value because they come to be issued to almost everyone. When intergroup competition is promoted, the number of awards can always be kept fewer than the number of groups competing, or there can be graded awards of differing appeal.

Management of incentives requires that no unit should reach the state where its prospect of winning anything becomes hopeless. Uneven chances can be offset by a variety of awards for different performance attributes. One can also limit the number of awards which a single unit can obtain at any time, or in succession. Skilled prison leadership is distinguished by the ability to keep inmate groups and all their members challenged by a goal in the achievement of which they can take pride. This challenge can involve a goal that provides a rehabilitative experience, such as success in performing a job, in learning, or in a social service.

Group responsibility, to be clearly consistent with correctional objectives, should promote individual responsibility rather than dependence on peers. Competitive rewards may promote individual responsibility if the rewards issued to an entire group are for demonstration separately, by all individuals of a group, of such virtues as workmanship, educational attainment, consideration of fellows, neatness, production, sportsmanship, or dependability. Group rewards are likely to promote these habits much more than individual rewards or penalties, because group rewards direct peer pressures and group loyalties to the motivation of individual effort.[2]

[2] For a brilliant demonstration and analysis of the effects of actual and prospective official policies and programs in mobilizing peer-group influences to determine the interests of high-school students, see: James S. Coleman, *The Adolescent Society* (Glencoe, Ill., Free Press, 1960).

Competition can be conducted among work units, classes, recreational teams, residential units, or any other inmate groups, but preferably among groups having some stability of membership. Chapter 5 suggests that group rewards will be most effective with youth groups, since they show the highest concern for the friendship of other inmates, especially in the middle of their prison terms. However, competition between units has been found to be highly motivating to individual performance even in adult prisons. Judiciously employed group rewards and penalties may be a means of making existing and frequently criminogenic peer-group pressures have an anti-criminogenic consequence.

In using group rewards or group penalties, both with youth and with older inmates, prison management must take continuous care to see that group pressures on certain inmates do not become excessively severe. With group responsibility for skilled or careful work, inmates sometimes use extreme psychological or physical pressures to make the sloppier inmates improve. Such pressures are a staff problem especially when they are directed against an individual inmate who has inherent limitations in his capacity to meet the standards expected of the other members of his group. Also, the effectiveness of any motivation diminishes if the standards are beyond the capabilities of many members; a series of progressively higher standards, as successive challenges, may maximize continuous motivation.

If a group of men is rewarded or penalized according to the way in which they fulfill their individual and group work responsibilities, staff may not have to supervise the men as closely as they would without such group pressures. Group responsibility for the quality of each man's work should reduce inmate tolerance of anyone's shirking work or indulging in horseplay excessively when the supervisor is gone. Nevertheless, staff must still observe the prisoners in order to coordinate group activities where essential, to guard against excess inmate pressure on those not doing their share, to prevent rackets in which some inmates coerce or bribe others to do their work for them, or to note early any rate-setting or "rate-busting" conflicts or conspiracies which can develop.

A major further reason for staff observation even with group responsibility is simply that staff still must be able to evaluate, report on, and make decisions or recommendations for each inmate as an individual. However, informal contact and observation of one or only a few inmates at a time, at irregular periods, is more effective for this purpose than the continuous issuance of orders and impersonal surveillance over many inmates. Motivating inmate groups to compete with each other in their work makes the officer assigned to each group acquire more of the role of a coach, as in athletics, sharing the group's motivation to win; this gives the officer less of the role of a "boss" or overseer, even when his actual task consists of supervising the inmate's work. When the officer identifies with the inmate group and the group begins to accept him as identifying with them, an extremely potent relationship develops. Such relationships are most effective in promoting high morale and inmate assimilation of staff-supported attitudes and values.

Self-direction of inmate work groups may be difficult to elicit with the less tractable inmates, particularly if two or more are together and give each other mutual support in deviance. However, such inmates may greatly change if they can be transferred to units in which their intractability is exceptional.

An important aspect in both individual and group motivation is offering a challenge, so that there is great pride in accomplishment. Frequently work and other activities offer little challenge. The administration must furnish this element; sometimes it is necessary only to be conscious of the challenge which a goal constitutes, and to call this to the inmates' attention. Officials report many examples of so-called intractable inmates responding favorably to the staff approval that follows their meeting a challenge successfully, but this requires a finesse which not all staff develop.

The conclusions of this section can be summarized by the propositions:

H1. Judiciously employed rewards and penalties to inmate groups, for the performances of the individual members of these groups:
  a. mobilize for rehabilitative purposes the peer-group support and pressure that normally is more likely to be criminogenic;
  b. reduce the authoritarian role of staff;
  c. provide prison management with a powerful means of motivating individual inmates.
H2. Intergroup competition for a limited number of rewards usually is a way of increasing the total motivation yielded by whatever supply of rewards to inmates the prison has available.

INTEGRATION OF INMATES IN PRISON MANAGEMENT

One step beyond making a group of inmates responsible for the conduct of their individual members is the integration of inmates into prison management. This has had a fascinating history in American corrections.

On several occasions in the nineteenth century, and conspicuously in the first few decades of the twentieth century, a few daring American prison officials turned correctional institutions almost completely over to self-government by the inmates. Zebulon Brockway claimed, fifty years afterwards, to have organized a system of self-government in the Detroit House of Corrections in the 1860's. In 1895 a movement to organize training schools for delinquents into self-governing "Junior Republics" began, under the leadership of William George, and eventually spread to scattered privately run "Junior Republics" across the country. Thomas M. Osborne, after experience in the George Junior Republic in New York state, extended this system to the New York penitentiary at Auburn in 1914, and later introduced it in Sing Sing and in the Naval Prison at Portsmouth, New Hampshire. Many other prisons made less publicized experiments of this type around the same time.

Under the systems of nearly complete prison government by prisoners, rules for inmates were established by an elected body of inmate representatives, internal surveillance was performed by inmate "police," and inmates who misbehaved were tried and punished by inmate courts. For brief periods these self-government systems were reported to be very successful, especially from a custodial standpoint; for example, Sutherland and Cressey report:

The whole population of the Preston State School was permitted to attend the state fair; the president of the self-government organization, a boy eighteen years of age, assumed the entire responsibility for the return of the group, and not one of the five hundred boys escaped. The previous year, before self-government started, the boys were taken to the state fair with one guard for each eight boys and thirteen boys escaped. Twenty prisoners from Auburn prison constituted an honor camp (with self-government in the prison and in this camp) about eighteen miles from the prison and remained there for three months with only one guard and for one week with no guard at all, though the average term of these prisoners was eleven years, though they had been convicted of serious crimes—burglary, robbery, murder, and manslaughter—and though only one of the twenty had less than a year to serve. Osborne took nine cars of prisoners from Auburn, New York, to a town in New Hampshire to give a play; on the return the cars became separated in the darkness, some of them went astray, and Osborne returned with only two cars; the rest kept straggling in until they had all returned by ten o'clock in the morning.[3]

The success of these systems always was short-lived. It appeared that their survival required continuous dynamic leadership by an outstanding personality, and even such leadership was ultimately ejected. Persons with aspirations for the warden's job, or for other reasons bent on undermining his authority, eventually stirred up newspaper and political reaction to such "mollycoddling" of felons. In several institutions corrupt inmates got control of the self-government and used it for their own purposes. In many instances disciplinary penalties imposed by inmate courts were more severe than those which staff could tolerate. The New Jersey State Reformatory at Rahway, and several other northeastern institutions, abolished self-government by a vote of the inmates after this government had become corrupt.

Professional opinion regarding inmate self-government still is divided in the United States. I once heard a president of the American Correctional

---

[3] E. H. Sutherland and D. R. Cressey, *Principles of Criminology*, 6th ed. (Philadelphia, Lippincott, 1960), pp. 490-91.

Association and head of a state prison assert that inmate councils would be established in his institution over his dead body. One federal warden, highly imaginative and innovating in many other ways, told me that delegation of authority to an inmate council was dereliction of duty by the warden. J. E. Baker, Associate Warden for Treatment at Terre Haute, polled fifty-two state penitentiary wardens on inmate self-government and received forty-four replies. Only seven of the forty-four reported having an inmate council, and they were predominantly favorable in evaluating the councils, but most of the remainder, who had little or no experience with councils, vehemently denounced them.[4] At the Federal Prison Wardens' Conference in Boulder, Colorado, in June 1962, a poll by Director Bennett indicated that only eight of the thirty-two federal prisons had inmate councils.

Where elected inmate advisory councils exist in federal and state prisons in the United States today, they have no appreciable authority. The principal function of these councils seems to be one of communicating inmate preferences with respect to recreational matters: for example, the council often selects the movies to be shown, plans special inmate talent shows, and organizes leagues and tournaments for various types of athletic and other games. Where one radio or television receiver serves a large number of inmates, an elected council frequently decides on the programs, sometimes polling the other inmates. Sometimes they also organize campaigns for blood bank donations and other charity, sanitation, or safety drives. All actions of these councils are subject to veto by the wardens, or by other officials, and inmates may be barred from the council for misbehavior.

From successful experience with group responsibility for housekeeping and other work and study, the possibility of extending the use of inmate councils suggests itself. This does not mean reestablishing the forms of inmate government of the institution attempted under Osborne. A more secure extension of the use of inmate councils is to employ them: (a) as an agency for *two-way* communication, by making them a means of transmitting to other inmates some of the staff expectations regarding inmate behavior, as a condition for a favorable response by staff to the council's communication of inmate recreational or other desires; (b) as a means of promoting the conception of staff and inmates as part of a single organization responsible for operating the prison, hence concerned with common problems, even though inmates are at the lowest level of rank in this organization.

In pursuit of these objectives, starting in 1960, the Terre Haute inmates were told, essentially, that they were part of the prison's operating staff. The elected inmate advisory council was given access to prison financial and

---

[4] J. E. Baker, "Inmate Self-Government," *J. Crim. Law, Criminology, & Police Science, 55,* no. 1 (March 1964), 39-47.

other records relevant to the management problems with which they were concerned. As Warden Markley summarized it:

There is little about an institution and its business that the inmates do not know. If they learn it from their own resources, it is subject to misinterpretation and distortion. Many inmates feel that we have almost unlimited funds but use them to give raises to the personnel, to buy cars for the brass, or for other purposes which divert them from the legitimate purpose of providing for inmate needs. An inmate worker in the storeroom sees refrigerated boxes full of sides of beef or cuts of pork. Having no knowledge of poundage or food requirements, he reports to other inmates that the administration is deliberately feeding the inmates "slop" and that they are not getting the meat which is rightfully theirs. This can be accepted as fact by the entire population. It can be overcome if the facts are communicated to the inmate body, but it must be done fully and openly. It is too late if used to counteract a rumor which has been accepted as fact. We are advising the entire inmate body of our allotments and how we allocate them. We have had some interesting sessions in which we allowed smaller groups such as the inmate council to study our allocations and try to find a source from which additional funds could be made available for food or clothing. They have been unable to find a better solution and usually give up in a short time when the effect of any transfers are pointed out. They have even developed insights into the needs for personnel and of the effect on them of personnel shortages. They also develop some understanding that the unfavorable publicity of their own acts has much to do with the lack of public acceptance which in turn is responsible for much of the limitations of appropriations.

As a result of the understanding developed from these communications, the level of expectation was lowered considerably. Many even express surprise that the food can be so good. Thus we are able to attain a position whereby, to the inmate body, the food is as good as can reasonably be expected under the circumstances, and it has become acceptable. There is a second dividend that is even more important. A toe hold for the development of an acceptance of group responsibility is furnished. They begin to see that if they steal or waste food, or fail to take care of clothing or maliciously damage bedding or equipment, they are hurting only themselves. They cannot control the situation as individuals, but must act as a group. It has prompted spontaneous campaigns to control waste and has actually reduced losses. . . .

An informed council which understands the situation begins to develop a social consciousness. They were concerned about the same problems as the administration and were willing to help but didn't know how to go about it. We have furnished guidance and provided the means where necessary. Most councilmen are trying to set examples, to sell the importance of order and to counsel the other inmates in their units. They are conducting sanitation campaigns and participate in the weekly inspections. Also, they are conducting programs aimed at preventing waste and malicious damage, controlling homosexuality and theft, and against the use of vulgarity and inmate slang.

In addition to setting an example and taking individual actions in the housing units, the council as a whole has sponsored newscasts, issued leaflets and posters, and prepared articles and a series of cartoons for the Terrescope (the prison newspaper). The cartoons are humorous but directed toward improving behavior. The two characters depicted are So Seedy, the typical inmate rationalizer who contaminates himself and others, and Preston Forward, who approaches problems positively and realistically assumes his responsibilities. Of course, Preston Forward is the hero who always wins while So Seedy is made to look ridiculous and the weakness of his position is evident. Another interesting innovation in the council-administration relationship was the development of agenda for the monthly meetings held with various staff members. These agenda include matters the inmates want to discuss with the staff member and those the administration wants to discuss with or get across to the inmates. The agenda are issued prior to the meeting and allow the staff member to consult with others if necessary and the council to discuss and consider items before entering the meeting.[5]

At Terre Haute the idea that inmates are members of the institution staff has also been extended by allowing inmates to enter the regular federal prison employee suggestion award contests. Suggestions by inmates are judged together with the suggestions of prison employees, and the inmates are eligible for the same cash awards. (No trips to Hawaii are included in the prizes!) Members of the inmate advisory council at Terre Haute also are called upon to serve as guides to student and professional visitors to the prison, and at such times they eat with the visitors in the staff dining room. In turn, the inmate advisory council is charged with communicating to inmate groups their responsibility for helping to solve prison management problems—from sanitation, or reducing food waste, to restricting the activities of aggressive prison homosexuals.

At Leavenworth, Warden John C. Taylor claims, there is no single inmate council representative of all inmates in the institution, but there are about forty separate committees, each of which might be thought of as serving a separate council function. When a specific recreational, welfare, or other project is suggested by inmates, a committee of interested inmates is formed and charged with responsibility for developing the project. This divides power, responsibility, and participation more widely than occurs with a single council, and may have advantages in as large and potentially conflict-ridden an inmate population as that of Leavenworth. At Terre Haute, in 1963, the elected council was divided into a number of autonomous committees, each of which had three inmate members and two or three staff members, and was the sole institution committee for both immediate and long-range planning in its field. These committees included an activities committee (on nonathletic recreation and education programs), a sports committee, a care committee (on food, sanitation, laundry, and safety),

[5] T. Wade Markley, *Progress Report, Fiscal Year 1961, U. S. Penitentiary, Terre Haute,* p. 64 and p. 66.

and a resident-institution coordinating committee (on improving inter-inmate and staff-inmate relationships).

My conversations with a number of federal prison wardens indicate that they conceive of the councils as "give me" organizations, acting only to transmit and discuss an agenda of requests from inmates. Several wardens with whom I spoke prior to the 1963 reorganization at Terre Haute were amazed to learn that at that institution the administration gave the council an agenda of requests, rather than leaving the initiative solely to inmates. Since 1963, under the committee system there, the staff and inmate influences are largely fused in joint decisions representing the cooperative thinking of all.

Wardens seem to fear mainly that inmate councils may unify inmates and give unusual power to a few inmate leaders who can dominate the council. They fear that these leaders can create a mass disturbance if they are not satisfied with staff responses to their requests, or that they can use the threat of organizing a mass disturbance as a means of blackmailing the prison management into granting requests. These fears can be allayed by a few simple precautions in the integration of inmates into prison management. First of all, inmates can be divided into several separate advisory committees with no overlapping membership, as at Leavenworth and now at Terre Haute. These might include, for example, a food committee, a sanitation committee, an athletics committee, a nonathletic entertainment committee, a hobby craft committee, a school committee, and so forth. Each committee can then be given only the financial and other background information relevant to its tasks. Secondly, good conduct records are often required for committee membership. Thirdly, staff maturity, and their ability to discuss rather than order, facilitates resolution of differences.

All of the practices described in this chapter are presumed to bolster inmate conceptions of their integration with staff. No one is yet in a position to demonstrate the implications of these practices for recidivism reduction, but their contribution to inmate morale and to inmate cooperation with staff in secure and efficient operation of the prison are readily apparent at some prisons. From the data presented in chapter 6, on the significance of personal relations with staff for rehabilitation, these measures would appear to be rehabilitative. Finally, from the standpoint of criminological theory, integration of inmates in prison management would be rehabilitative, since it promotes the inmates' identification with anticriminal persons.

On the basis of the foregoing, one may assert as a conclusion meriting serious testing:

H3. The cooperation of inmates with staff and inmate identification of themselves with noncriminal persons are enhanced by treating inmates as though they were subordinate members of a single staff, sharing with employees the task of running the prison for the maximum long-run benefit of all. This means:

a. Giving responsible inmate committees such nonpersonal prison financial and administrative information as is relevant to their understanding of those prison management problems in which inmates have an interest and which inmate cooperation can help solve;

b. Charging the committees with conveying this information to other inmates, and facilitating this, in conjunction with

c. Holding inmate groups responsible for behavior contributing to the solution of specific prison-management problems, as a condition for improvements in pleasures or privileges for inmates, particularly benefits to inmates made possible primarily by their improved behavior.

CHAPTER 11

Work for Prisoners

THE ACTIVITIES OF PRISONERS

The use of imprisonment as punishment, rather than merely for detention pending trial, began from an interest in assuring that certain types of offenders would be usefully employed. The so-called "workhouses," generally considered the first prisons, were established in London and Amsterdam in the sixteenth century so that vagrants and "sturdy beggars" might be forced to labor.

Imprisonment did not become the primary punishment for felonies in the Western world until the nineteenth century. In the history of prison practice, the extent to which men have been employed while imprisoned has fluctuated sharply, allegedly varying inversely with the labor supply outside of prison.[1] During the depression of the 1930's, when millions of Americans outside of prison were unemployed, pressure of both business and labor unions resulted in laws prohibiting the employment of prison labor in the production of goods offered for sale. Since then the "state use" system has been the dominant policy in the employment of prisoners in the United States. Under this system, and in its supplementation by the "public works" system, prisoners can labor only at prison maintenance tasks, and in supplying goods and services for other government agencies.[2] Even the latter functions have often been restricted in state prisons, to reduce the possible competition of prisons with private enterprises doing business with state governments. In over two-thirds of United States prison systems no prison goods are sold on the open market; in most of the remainder, farm lobbies have prevented termination of small prison industries manufacturing agricultural tools and supplies, but all other types of manufacture for sale have ceased in the prisons.[3]

As a consequence of these developments, prisons often have trouble keep-

[1] A history of punishment practices with particular stress on the alleged influences of economic forces is provided in: Georg Rusche and Otto Kirchheimer, *Punishment and Social Structure* (New York, Columbia University Press, 1939).

[2] For further details on prison labor practice see: Rusche and Kirchheimer, *op. cit.;* United Nations, Department of Economic and Social Affairs, *Prison Labour* (1955).

[3] "What's New in Prison Industries," United Prison Association of Massachusetts, *Correctional Research,* Bulletin No. 6 (April 1955), 6-7.

ing all inmates occupied. The predominant situation is summarized in the following appraisal:

The public image of state prisons as bee-hives of productive activity, with "cons" working long hours manufacturing auto tags, road signs, brooms, and clothing, is largely erroneous. Even the few so employed seldom work more than six hours a day. The rest are subjected to the demoralizing and wasteful assignment of trying to appear busy at housekeeping tasks, most of which can be completed easily in the first hour or two of the work period. . . .

Among the doctrines of contemporary American correctional thought, state use is regarded as the most promising means of providing full employment for those prisoners who should be assigned to work. . . .

But is our confidence in this system justified? Has its alleged potential yet been realized in any state? Has it provided full employment for those prisoners who should work? Has it ended complaints of competition? Has it produced the expected diversification of prison work experience? Has it resulted in the growth of prison industries organized along modern lines, economically and technologically appropriate to the larger industrial world? A realistic appraisal of existing accomplishments prompts negative answers to all these questions. . . .

The basic weakness of state use is due to its character as a residual category of prison work. It is a retreat to which prison administrators have been driven. Consequently, as a form of prison production more or less acceptable to free interests, state use is so organized as to lose connection with economic realities. Insulated from the free economy and hedged about by restrictions, state use is hard put to respond adaptively to those outside economic and technological changes to which private industries must adjust if they are to survive. Outmoded machinery, inadequate marketing practices, severely curtailed markets and poorly motivated workers are conditions under which few private interests could long exist, but prison industries are obliged to put up with them.[4]

That there is more potentiality in state use than generally is realized becomes apparent when we compare one state with another. For example, Iowa prisons in 1961-62 claimed to have more work than manpower, while Missouri and California penitentiaries had several hundred men unassigned due to lack of work. Also, there is idleness in many foreign prisons which do not have the state use system. Apparently the amount of work available is a function of economic conditions in the state and of government interest and initiative in seeking work for prisoners.

Federal prisons have more industry than most others. One reason for this is that their market consists of all federal government agencies, including the armed forces. This is much broader than the market of state government agencies to which state prison industries must be confined. Secondly, because federal government purchases, especially those of the armed forces, are so much more extensive than federal prison industries could pro-

[4] Ralph W. England, Jr., "New Departures in Prison Labor," *The Prison Journal, 41,* no. 1 (Spring 1961), 21-26.

vide, it has been possible to permit the prison industries to fill a portion of any purchase orders placed on the market by the government for competitive bidding. This has made it necessary for Federal Prison Industries to meet the same rigid quality inspection standards to which private suppliers are subjected. The accounts of Federal Prison Industries, a government corporation, are credited for prison products with the price that the government has to pay for the same type of products purchased from competitive bidding. They must then show a "profit" when charged with the cost of raw materials, the cost of prison industry buildings, the salaries of all prison staff involved in industries (including much vocational training staff), and appropriate portions of other prison operation costs. These requirements have meant that industries in federal prisons must use more modern machinery, and more efficient and skilled inmate labor, than are found in most of the state prison industries referred to in the above quotation.

Actually, less than a fourth of inmates in federal or state prisons are employed in prison industries. This is partly because the maintenance and sanitation of the prisons and the care and feeding of inmates requires the employment of a considerable number of prisoners in kitchens, dining rooms, and laundries, in food, clothing, and supply storage and distribution, in growing food on prison farms, in butchering, dairying, and baking, and as janitors, builders, and repairmen. Many inmates must also be employed for administrative or clerical tasks; while there are risks in some of this use of prisoners, a certain amount of such employment is unavoidable, as funds never suffice for hiring noninmate employees in all administrative or clerical work.

Despite prison industries, prison housekeeping and feeding tasks, and the work of maintaining prison plants, it still is difficult to keep most prisoners employed as much as forty hours a week with an efficiency comparable to that expected in outside employment. Inability to habituate most prisoners to the conditions of nonprison employment is especially acute in state prisons, but it is evident in federal prisons as well. A major factor in employment inefficiency, even where it is possible to expand prison industries, is prison management's custodial problem: the need to guard against escape or disturbance by inmates and to keep the prison running smoothly, with a budget that limits availability of custodial staff at all hours of the inmate's working day.

Both circumstances and considerations of policy affect the custodial problem in restricting the amount of work that inmates can be made to perform. Relevant circumstances include the number of inmates to be handled, the most severe custodial risks among them, the prison's architectural design, and the custodial dangers in the work to be performed. Obviously less danger is involved if a few men are in a closed room shelling peas by hand than if many men are in a large yard chopping up timber. Similarly, there is less risk in allowing carefully selected inmates to move freely from one section of a prison to another when all sections are connected by closed passages (the "telephone pole" design in prison construction), than in allowing a mixed cross-section of newly arrived inmates to move freely between prison buildings that are completely separate and far apart. Notable among policy considerations relevant to this custody problem are: (1) risks of escape or disturbance that prison administrators are willing to tolerate in order to increase inmate activity (actually, these risks may be lessened through measures which improve morale); (2) realism of administrators in assessing risks; and (3) the use of positive moral influences as alternatives to custodial procedures for reducing these risks.

Considerable time that might be devoted to work or to other constructive activities is lost completely when the administration is too mechanical in its custodial precautions. In many state prisons the average inmate is held up four to six times per day, often in a long line, in order to be routinely "frisked" for contraband. Unavoidable, but varying greatly in duration, is the staff's counting of inmates, and cessation of all inmate movement until the count checks. Federal prison experience has shown that it takes prisoners about twice as long to get their meal when they must go to and from the dining hall in lines and eat as a unit, as when they go and leave on their own in a "continuous feeding" arrangement. Similarly, such ordinary tasks as procurement of haircuts, clothing, library books, cigarettes, and sometimes even shaves and showers, are much more time-consuming in most prisons than they would be on the outside. In a majority of prisons, custodial concern and staff budgets require that most of these activities, as well as much athletics and other organized recreation, be performed during the working hours of the "main shift" of the custodial staff, for example, between 8 A.M. and 4 P.M. on weekdays.

Such custodially derived impediments to full employment of inmates are much less present in federal prisons than in most state prisons. One of many reasons for this is that federal prisons, on the average, are smaller than state prisons, and there are so many more prisons within the federal system that each institution can hold a relatively homogeneous prisoner population. Also, federal prisons, especially those built since the late 1930's, are architecturally designed with "telephone pole" or quadrant-enclosing continuous buildings. These permit much more freedom of inmate movement within institution confines, without severe custodial risk, than would be possible in the predominantly older and more poorly designed state prisons. But most important, the federal prisons have a variety of inmate morale-producing programs and behavior incentives, discussed in various parts of this book. Also, they have overcome many of the excessive fears of prison administrators regarding the custodial risks of reduced regimentation of inmate activity. Federal prisoners, for example, are seldom "frisked," and more than in most state prisons, federal inmates move freely within the prison enclosures, rather than in lines. Also, more of this movement occurs in the evening and on weekends, rather than just in a work day. Yet the federal prisons have a better custodial security record than most state prisons.

Our Prison Panel Supplement questionnaire concluded with a section which began as follows:

Think back over what you did here yesterday, from the time you woke up in the morning until you went to bed at night yesterday. Please answer the following as accurately as you can:

I woke up about _____ o'clock.
I went to work about _____ o'clock.
I spent, during the whole day, a total of about _____ hours
at my work assignment.
I spent about _____ hours actually working there.

This inquiry then continued with "I spent about _____ hours in class," "I spent about _____ hours watching television," and so forth. These activities in the nonworking portions of the day are discussed in other chapters. Our inquiries about time of awakening and time of going to work were only intended to start the inmate off at reconstruction of the past day in his memory. In "Busy" State Penitentiary the day prior to our questionnaire distribution was a holiday, and at "Slow" State Penitentiary our questionnaire was administered on a Monday, so in these cases we had to alter the questionnaires and give special oral instruction so that the inmates would report on their last workday, rather than "yesterday."

The responses to these inquiries are summarized in Table 11.1. It will be seen that inmates of federal prisons report more work than do those of any of the state prisons except "Busy" State Penitentiary and "Full" State Prison Camp. At most of the prisons, the group just starting their sentence included many who had not yet received regular work assignments when they completed our questionnaire. That is why their time at work assignments, and their time "actually working," often were especially low. "Actual work" reported by those near release was highest at Leavenworth, a highly industrialized institution with a large proportion of long-term inmates. Next in extent of "actual work" were "Busy" and all of the prison camps. Reformatory work hours were shortest, because more time there was devoted to education and to recreational programs. My impression from working and visiting in state prisons of various parts of the country is that the "Full," "Tight," and "Slow" work schedules are more typical of other state prisons than are the "Busy" work schedule. State prison camps, however, are

TABLE 11.1 Median Hours Reported at Work Assignment, and Actually Working, by Prison and by Stage of Prison Term
(Prison Panel Supplement Study)

PRISON	Stage of prison term[b]	At work assignment	Actually working	No. of cases	PRISON	Stage of prison term[b]	At work assignment	Actually working	No. of cases
		MEDIAN HOURS[a]					MEDIAN HOURS[a]		
Federal Penitentiary:					*Federal Reformatory:*				
Leavenworth					Chillicothe	Start	7.3	5.3	63
Maximum	Start	5.9	3.0	76		End	7.3	5.3	51
Security	End	7.7	6.7	81					
Terre Haute					El Reno	Start	6.1	4.3	63
Medium	Start	6.9	4.8	65		End	7.1	5.0	84
Security	End	7.7	5.9	79					
					State Reformatory:				
State Penitentiary:					"Slow"	Start	5.7	3.1	36
"Busy"	Start	7.6	4.8	67		End	5.2	4.4	70
	End	7.1	6.1	48					
					"Tight"	Start	4.6	3.2	64
"Slow"	Start	0–89%	0–89%	27		End	6.8	4.6	57
	End	6.1	4.6	67					
					Prison Camps:				
"Full"[c]	Start	0–70%	0–66%	69	Allenwood	Start	7.2	6.0	10
Inside	End	7.6	5.1	23	Federal	End	7.1	5.8	55
Outside	End	5.4	4.0	69					
					McNeil Island	Start	6.4	6.1	14
Seagoville Federal					Federal	End	6.9	6.1	31
Correctional	Start	7.3	6.0	53	"Full" State	Start	6.5	4.7	19
Institution	End	7.3	6.0	52		End	7.5	6.3	56

[a] Where median is zero, the percentage reporting zero follows the dash.

[b] "Start" is in first six months, "End" is in last six months; for details see Appendix E.

[c] "Full" State Penitentiary end of sentence cases are divided into two groups: those *inside* the main prison enclosure, and those *outside* at an adjacent prerelease honor camp.

uniquely located to provide an extensive conservation work program in public parks or forests. Outside of these camps, most state prisoners are idle, except in the few southeastern states which employ many prisoners, under armed guards, in the maintenance of rural roads or the operation of large plantations. In most prisons, especially state prisons, there are numerous housekeeping and janitorial assignments at which, in six or eight hours at the job, the inmate is expected to do only an amount of work that would require an hour or two at a normal pace.

The decline of the prison as a production agency in the second quarter of the twentieth century created an idleness which prison treatment programs rarely fill and for which prison industries still are what Ben Frank has called "a hodgepodge of expedient compromises." But should available tasks for prisoners become adequate to occupy the inmates fully, prison work programs would still have problems in coping with deficiencies in the prior work habits of the men confined.

THE WORK EXPERIENCE OF PRISONERS

Since over 90 per cent of major crimes reported in the F.B.I.'s *Uniform Crime Reports* for the United States involve taking someone else's money or property, it is appropriate to say that most crime is either a supplement to or a substitute for work as a means of procuring an income. The employment histories of most prisoners make it evident that their crime generally has been pursued in lieu of work, for their employment has been sparse indeed.

According to the information in the prison classification reports for our 1015-case sample of 1956 adult male federal prison releasees, only a quarter of the federal prisoners were employed during 75 per cent or more of their last two years of civilian life in the free community, 38 per cent were employed 25 to 74 per cent of the time, 27 per cent had worked less than 25 per cent of the time, 6 per cent had never had any legitimate employment, and 4 per cent had been full-time students during 75 or more per cent of their last two years of freedom. When the prison caseworkers prepare reports like those from which we compiled these statistics, they procure each inmate's account of his employment history. Although the caseworkers write some major employers for validating information, it is well known that when employment histories based on inmate reports err, they generally err by exaggerating the amount and calibre of employment, rather than by understatement. Finally, it should be noted that when offenders reach the prisons which can provide some work for them, many have been for so long in jail, where hardly any work is available for them, that deterioration has occurred in whatever work habits they may once have had.

Among those inmates in the above group who had some prior employment, the medium duration of the longest job ever held was 10.4 months. Twenty-four per cent of those who reported some employment had never been employed on one job for more than three months. For 53 per cent of those reporting any employment, the *longest* job held was one in which their labor could be classified as unskilled; 15 per cent were classified by us as semiskilled machine tenders or as apprentices or helpers at skilled trades in which they had less than two years' experience; 10 per cent worked as truck, tractor, or automobile drivers; 8 per cent were in a skilled trade in which they had over two years' experience; 7 per cent were in sales or clerical work; 7 per cent were in professional or executive employment, or employed in their own business or farm. When we tabulated separately the attributes of each man's *last* job, whether or not it was also his *longest* job, the proportions in these various types of employment were almost the same on the last as on the longest jobs.

Information on the longest job ever held and on the last job was also procured by us for 812 inmates of five midwest federal prisons who were interviewed one or more times during 1958-59 for our Prison Panel Study. The median time employed on the longest jobs was 1.1 years, somewhat longer than the 10.4 months median for the cross-section of 1956 federal prison releasees. The distribution of types of prior employment was almost identical for the 1956 released and the 1958-59 confined inmates; for 56 per cent of the 1958-59 group the longest job was at unskilled labor; for 8 per cent it was vehicle driving; 15 per cent had semiskilled work; 10 per cent skilled work; 7 per cent sales or clerical; 4 per cent executive, professional, or entrepreneurial. Again, these percentages were almost the same for their last jobs as for their longest jobs.

Table 11.2 shows that this absence of persistent work experience is much more pronounced among younger than among more mature prisoners. How-

TABLE 11.2   Age at Release and Prior Work Record
(1956 Federal Prison Releasees)

| | | AGE GROUPS (for all cases) | | | | |
	All cases	25 or under	26–30	31–40	41 and over	Negroes only
Employment during last two years of civilian life outside of prison						
Employed 25 per cent of time or less	27%	34%	28%	21%	22%	28%
Employed 26 to 50 per cent of time	19%	16%	21%	24%	13%	19%
Employed 51 to 75 per cent of time	19%	17%	21%	19%	17%	20%
Employed 76 to 100 per cent of time	25%	17%	24%	30%	35%	24%
Student 75 per cent or more of last two years	4%	12%	1%	1%	—	2%
Never employed in last two years	6%	4%	5%	6%	13%	7%
Duration of longest job ever held						
No information, or never employed	12%	14%	10%	9%	18%	11%
Less than 3 months	21%	31%	20%	16%	14%	19%
3 to under 6 months	11%	17%	10%	8%	3%	8%
6 months to under 1 year	17%	20%	20%	18%	8%	19%
1 year to under 2 years	14%	13%	17%	14%	11%	16%
2 years to under 5 years	14%	5%	18%	22%	14%	21%
5 years or more	10%	1%	5%	13%	32%	7%
Total cases (100%)	1015	321	256	256	182	269

ever, a rather sporadic employment record is indicated even for appreciable fractions of older inmates. While no information on longest job was available for almost one-tenth of these cases, this failure to report the longest job usually occurred in accounts which indicated no appreciable employment, and often no long period when not confined; therefore "no information" cases should be considered as probably near the bottom of the scale, if duration of longest job were known.

Although unemployment rates for nonwhite males are more than twice as high as those for white males in the U. S. labor force generally,[5] Table 11.2 indicates that the prior employment record of Negroes released from federal prisons is about the same as that for white releasees. There is evidence that, within any given type of occupation, white and Negro unemployment rates do not differ nearly as much as they do for the entire labor force; overall rates of unemployment are higher for Negroes because they have a large proportion in the low-skill occupations in which every racial group has its highest unemployment rates. Also, Negroes have larger proportions entering the labor force early, rather than continuing in school, and high unemployment rates characterize youth of all races who enter the labor force early.[6] In the prison population, both whites and Negroes are predominantly unskilled, and have dropped out of school early, hence both racial groups are highly similar in the extent of their unemployment.

The practical implication of the information in Table 11.2 can be summarized in the following proposition:

I1. Regular work during imprisonment, for even as little as one year, would be the longest and most continuous employment experience that most prisoners, and especially the younger prisoners, have ever had.

Table 11.3 indicates the close relationship between previous work record and postrelease failure rates for our sample of adult male federal prisoners released during 1956. It will be recalled that failure rates were defined as the percentage reimprisoned, either for a new felony or for parole violation, plus the small percentage convicted of a postrelease felony-like offense who are given a jail or probation term. Steadiness of employment, as indicated by per cent of time employed and by length of time on one job, is shown to be markedly associated with low failure rates. Failure rates varied inversely with per cent of time employed, from 22 per cent failure for those employed 76 to 100 per cent of their last two years of civilian life outside of prison, to 44 per cent failure for those employed less than 25 per cent of the time.

The classification of occupations is one of the most vexing methodological problems in statistical survey analysis. Our solution of this problem here may well not be the optimum one, but it was dictated by the quality of information available and by the relatively limited range of occupational experience which distinguishes prison from nonprison populations. For example, in reporting type of employment, particularly for young prisoners, frequently the prison classification records which we used stated that a man worked as a helper in one of the construction trades, or with an auto

---

[5] *Statistical Abstract of the U. S., 1963,* Table 290, p. 221.

[6] See Table 12.5. Also: Ralph H. Turner, "The Nonwhite Male in the Labor Force," *Am. J. Sociology, 54,* no. 4 (Jan. 1949), 356-62.

TABLE 11.3   Previous Employment and Postrelease Failure Rate
(1956 Federal Prison Releasees)

	Failure rate	Total cases
Employment during last two years of civilian life[a]		
Employed 25 per cent of time or less	44%	275
Employed 26 to 50 per cent of time	38%	190
Employed 51 to 75 per cent of time	36%	188
Employed 76 to 100 per cent of time	22%	256
Student, or never employed in last two years	36%	106
Longest time on one job[b]		
Less than six months	43%	322
Six months to under one year	39%	175
One year to under two years	31%	143
Two years to under five years	25%	145
Five years or more	14%	104
Never employed, or no information on duration	42%	126
Type of job on which longest employed		
Unskilled labor	38%	503
Car, truck or tractor driver	31%	99
Semiskilled or less than two years at skilled	34%	146
Skilled trade two years or more	19%	72
White collar, or business owner	28%	124
Never employed, or no report on type of longest employment	46%	71
Type of job on which last employed		
Unskilled labor	37%	516
Car, truck or tractor driver	33%	78
Semiskilled or less than two years at skilled	35%	142
Skilled trade two years or more	21%	58
White collar or business owner	34%	116
Never employed, or no report on type of last employment	44%	85
Total cases	35%	1015

[a] Point-Biserial Correlation Coefficient 0.175, p <.001.
[b] Point-Biserial Correlation Coefficient .058, p <.001.

mechanic. In order to separate helpers, novices, and apprentices from relatively skilled craftsmen, since level of skill was rarely indicated, we arbitrarily set two years of employment at a skilled trade as the minimum for classification as skilled; those with less than two years in skilled fields were grouped with the semiskilled.

Taking into account the duration-of-employment component built into our definition of "skilled," and the few cases that were "skilled" by this definition, Table 11.3 supports the conclusion:

12. Regularity of prior employment is more closely related than type of work previously performed to the postrelease success of prisoners in avoiding further felonies.

The casual work records of most prisoners, shown in Table 11.2, do not seem merely illustrative of the employment pattern prevalent in the low-status occupational groups from which prisoners disproportionately come; there is variation in employment regularity within these groups, and Table 11.3 indicates that this regularity distinguishes the less persistently criminal from the most recidivistic.

Table 11.2 suggested that employment in prison may usually be the first steady work ever experienced by most prisoners. Perhaps it is not too far-fetched to infer from Table 11.3 that providing an offender with his first regular and rewarding work experience of appreciable duration, even if it is in prison, might be a major step towards promoting in him the work habits and values necessary for a stable noncriminal life. But how can work experience in prison be rewarding?

MOTIVATING INMATES FOR WORK IN PRISON

Because the prison receives a work force of predominantly unskilled men, unaccustomed to the pace and schedule expected in outside employment, many inmates must be trained before they can be given assignments at even semiskilled labor. To motivate inmates to pursue training for skilled jobs and to work at a vigorous pace, most prisons find it desirable to have a system of variable rewards for different tasks. These rewards do not have to be great to be highly attractive in the prison situation.

To increase the qualifications of prisoners for legitimate postrelease employment, to provide the skilled workers needed for prison maintenance and prison industries, and to usefully occupy prisoners so as to maintain their morale, modern prisons devote considerable attention to inmate training and education. Vocational education is especially stressed. In the fiscal year 1961, when there was an average population of 23,378 inmates in federal prisons, Federal Prison Industries, Incorporated, employed a daily average of 4902 inmates, or 21 per cent of the total. In the course of the year there were 12,700 enrollments in federal prison vocational training programs by 12,339 different prisoners. These training programs were not only for industrial skills, but also in such fields as dairying, butchering, cooking, baking, and the construction trades.

Pay and Good-Time Grants

To motivate federal prison inmates to train for industry jobs and to work diligently when they get such jobs, nominal wages are paid to those employed in prison industries. Wages vary from about $10 to $75 per month, the average in 1960 being $31.36. In addition, monthly payments known as

"Meritorious Service Awards" are made to selected inmates on nonindustry jobs. During the fiscal year 1959, 20 per cent of federal prisoners received prison industry wages and 35 per cent received meritorious service awards. Even if only half the inmates are receiving pay at a given time, it can safely be said that almost all who serve much over a year and need prison wages are likely to earn them before release.

In the prison situation, for inmates of poor families who can expect little money from home, even a few dollars a month are tremendously valued for the small luxuries in commissary goods they can procure, such as tobacco, candy, and various small personal items. Also, as will be indicated in later chapters, prison wages may be important as means of saving money for a postrelease start at a legitimate life. Frequently the money permits psychologically significant inmate gifts or allotments to wives or others, thus helping to promote inmate self-respect and to enhance their ties with outside persons.

In our national survey of financial assistance to released prisoners, conducted with the John Howard Association, information on the proportion of prison inmates receiving pay was provided by forty-nine states (all except Arkansas). Twenty states and the District of Columbia reported that ninety to one hundred per cent of their inmates earn money in prison. These include states with above average per-capita revenue, such as Massachusetts, Connecticut, New York, and Minnesota, as well as some of the lower-income states, such as South Carolina and Kentucky. Conversely, six states permit no inmate earnings in prison, and in five states no more than ten per cent of the inmates earn money. While these do not include the wealthiest states, they are states of somewhat diverse per-capita income, including Texas, Alaska, Idaho, Nevada, New Mexico, and North Carolina, as well as Alabama, Mississippi, and Georgia.[7]

What appears to be the only collection of information on rates of payment to inmates in various prison systems is contained in a 1957 survey of prison industries conducted by T. Wade Markley for the Correctional Industries Association. This indicates that in the thirty-three states which supplied information on wages, the rate of payment ranged from a low of 4 cents per day to a high of $1.30 per day, with the average for these states 34 cents per day.[8]

Federal prison inmates assigned to industrial work, farm work, and work which receives meritorious service awards also have two to five days removed from their sentence for each month that they are assigned to these jobs. This incentive of quicker freedom makes these assignments attractive

[7] State income classification is by *Statistical Abstract of the U. S., 1963*, Table 441, p. 329.

[8] T. Wade Markley, *A Current Look at Prison Labor in the United States* (Paper prepared for Correctional Industries Association, 1957), p. 5.

even to those inmates who have sufficient economic resources to forego the small prison wages or meritorious service payments. It should be noted that the industrial, farm, and meritorious service "good time" are in addition to the regular time off for good behavior which is awarded to all inmates. In Markley's 1957 survey of prison industries, only ten out of forty-one states responding reported that they made sentence reduction awards for industrial work, and it was believed that one or two of these ten had confused industrial good time with the regular good time program for all inmates.[9]

Prevailing inmate pay and good-time systems can be criticized from many standpoints. The late G. I. Giardini, long in charge of parole supervision in Pennsylvania, called good time the "placebo of correction." His primary complaint was that good time, in all forms, reduces the range of indeterminacy in a sentence, thus diminishing the power of the parole board to release a man at the optimum time.[10] Regular good time also is defective as an incentive in many prison systems because the procedure for denying good time is so cumbersome that it seldom is denied. In this situation inmates come to regard good time as a right rather than as a special reward, and it thereby loses its motivational value. However, industrial, farm, and meritorious service good-time awards can easily be removed if the quality of an inmate's work and behavior declines, simply by changing the work unit to which he is assigned. In the federal system, withdrawal of any type of good time, and even revocation of that previously earned, is a fairly simple administrative procedure when such action is desired for disciplinary purposes. Nevertheless, in those systems where maximum sentences are high and almost all release from prison is by parole, any form of good time is likely to have little significance in determining a prisoner's release date.

One major criticism of pay, good-time grants, or any special comforts which are given to inmates on some assignments and denied to those on other assignments is that this may interfere with an inmate's motivation to pursue that program which best fits his needs. Farm work often is assigned at penitentiaries to inmates near release to accustom them to harder work and less regimentation than the prison can provide. However, many an inmate seeks farm work for the time off their sentence and more pleasant living and visiting arrangements provided there, even where the prison is not appreciably less regimented than the farm. Indeed, the farm work often interrupts acquisition of a trade in the prison, a trade which the inmate is much more likely to use in postrelease life in the city than his experience at farm work. Also, within the prison, many inmates will seek jobs in prison industry because of the pay and good-time benefits there, even when these

[9] *Ibid.,* p. 6.

[10] G. I. Giardini, "Good Time—Placebo of Correction," *Am. J. Correction, 20,* no. 2 (March–April 1958), 3-5, 25.

jobs offer less useful experience for them than some other prison jobs that have no pay or good time rewards.

Our national survey of financial assistance to released prisoners found that in twenty-four states, the federal prisons, and the District of Columbia, inmates are required to save a specified proportion of their prison earnings, to provide them with funds at release. Frequently, in federal prisons, an inmate's need for funds at release, or to send to his dependents from prison, is cited at classification meetings as the major reason for assigning him to prison industry. Certainly such savings or payments to dependents would have a postrelease utility to many prisoners for whom the optimum vocational training in prison is at an assignment other than the limited number in prison industry. This is one further objection to the restriction of pay only to arbitrary segments of prison work.

The meritorious service awards in the federal system, which are financed by Federal Prison Industries, Incorporated, apply only to nonindustry assignments in the prisons. This increases the number of inmates paid. It also offsets the disturbance of an optimum incentive system which occurs when industry jobs are the only ones for which inmates receive pay or special good time. Prison industry jobs not only are not necessarily more rehabilitative, but they are not necessarily more useful to the state than other jobs in the prisons, such as institution maintenance or inmate feeding, at which prisoners are not reimbursed. The most appropriate programs, from both a rehabilitation standpoint and in terms of fairness, would offer all inmates an opportunity to earn money by diligently pursuing that prison program which best promotes their long-run self-sufficiency in a noncriminal life.

The widespread practice of limiting wages primarily to inmates working in prison industries seems to have had its origin in government bookkeeping and political expediency. In dealing with legislative appropriation and budget committees, it often has been easier to procure wage funds for inmates as an allotment from income which the prisons might acquire through the labor of inmates, and against which they were entitled also to charge industry staff wage and raw material expenses, than to seek an appropriation from tax funds. Nevertheless, our survey's findings that the prisons of twenty-four states and the District of Columbia pay ninety or more per cent of their inmates indicate that obeisance to the political expediency of paying only in industry is not always necessary. However, the amount paid in some of these states is extremely low, frequently one to two dollars per month. Ten dollars per month probably is close to the minimum rate for significant motivation of most inmates, and a range of variation to several times that amount is needed to provide continuous monetary incentives for more diligent and skillful work.

If prison pay is to be a greater incentive to rehabilitative effort in prison, not only should every inmate be able to earn pay, but the pay should not be provided at a uniform rate to all inmates, for that would eliminate monetary advantage in improvement. However, variation in rates of pay should not depend on where an inmate is assigned; higher rates of pay in industry than elsewhere in the prison are as incompatible with an optimum incentive system as having inmate pay exclusively in prison industry. Variables relevant to rehabilitation, on which pay rates might vary at all assignments, include diligence, persistence, improvement in skill, and perhaps vocational or academic courses completed and tests passed.

Other Labor Incentives

Advocacy of more widely distributed and rationally differentiated monetary and time rewards for inmate labor does not imply that these are the only significant incentives. As indicated in chapters 6 and 7, as well as in small-group and industrial sociology studies, the most motivating rewards for effort frequently are gestures of recognition for this effort from coworkers and superiors rather than pay. Many an inmate foregoes opportunities for better paying or more vocationally advantageous jobs in prison because he is happiest with his coworkers or with the staff "boss" at another assignment.

In addition to these monetary and group support or recognition incentives in the prison situation, many work assignments carry unofficial rewards from the advantages they give the occupant in the inmate community's bartering of information, actual or alleged influence, contraband goods, and commissary purchases. Sometimes the dentist's clerk can move an inmate ahead on a waiting list in exchange for a few packages of cigarettes, the kitchen or bakery worker can sneak out food for his friends or for those with something to trade for it, the inmate worker allegedly "close" to a key officer can claim to "put in a good word" for someone, or an inmate clerk can advise others on what he has typed or heard that may be of interest to them. In a prison where this unofficial bartering provides the major opportunities for mitigating the pains of imprisonment, inmate attitudes regarding work approach the extreme which McCorkle and Korn aptly described when they wrote:

The freedom from the necessity of earning a living in prison introduces a striking difference between the requirements of material success within and without the walls. . . . In prison the direct relationship between work done and material value received has largely broken down. . . . Strategic placement and effective informal connections rather than individual productivity are the crucial methods for the attainment of material goods.

As a consumer-producer, the inmate lives and trades in two economic worlds: . . . As a trader in the informal inmate barter system, he is resourceful, ingenious, and usually cooperative: there is a kind of "Better Business Bureau" tradition which is generally effective in encouraging the liquidation of debts. As a wage earner in the prison labor system he is, by contrast, encouraged to be nonproductive, dilatory, and contentious, articulating his work relations with the institution in terms of declarations of rights and grievances. . . .

The fundamental authority in defining the inmate's job obligation is tradition. Inmates are to be required to work only so much as the tradition concerning given jobs requires. Any departure from these traditions—especially those departures in the direction of increased work for the same pay—are violations of the inmates' work rights and justify obstructionism. (In a certain penal institution, for instance, "tradition" had established that one inmate lay out all the salt cellars on the mess tables while a different inmate was required to lay out the pepper.)

Increases in the amount of time or output may only be required under extraordinary circumstances and merit increased pay or special benefits, since these added efforts are "favors" extended by the inmates. The inmates have a right to resent and take reprisals against any of their number who "show the rest up" by doing more than the traditional amount of work. These hostile attitudes toward more energetic inmates effectively condemn them to the deteriorating work patterns enforced by the group. Any inmate who performs more than the usual expectation must prove that he has received a special award—usually food or informal permission to evade some institutional rule. . . .

Once assigned to a job, there are only a limited number of legitimate reasons for which an inmate may be "fired." None of these legitimate reasons includes adherence to the accepted job tradition. Thus an inmate rarely feels that he may rightfully be dismissed for laziness, if he performs only the usual amount of work traditionally required, despite an increase in institutional needs, since the tradition protects him from any definition of himself as lazy. Inmates generally feel that the fact that they are paid less than comparable civilian workers entitles them to produce less.

The total result of the prevalence of these attitudes has been to reduce "imprisonment at hard labor" to a euphemism existing chiefly in the rhetoric of sentencing judges and in the minds of the uninformed public. The inmate social system not only has succeeded in neutralizing the laboriousness of prison labor in fact, but also has more or less succeeded in convincing prison authorities of the futility of expecting any improvement in output. Responding to a multitude of pressures within and without the prison, most institutional work supervisors have adopted patterns of expectations which are largely supportive of the inmate position.[11]

These unofficial influences on the motivation to work diminish markedly only when they cannot compete successfully with legitimate incentives, in

[11] Lloyd W. McCorkle and Richard Korn, "Resocialization Within Walls," *Annals of the Am. Acad. of Political and Social Science, 293* (May 1954), 91-92; reprinted in Korn and McCorkle, *Criminology and Penology* (New York, Holt-Dryden, 1959), pp. 483-84.

terms of supply and demand in the inmate economy. When most prisoners can expect to earn ten to fifty dollars per month by work in prison, when the amount that they earn is a function of their work performance, when they never reach a point at which the prison staff no longer has additional material or psychological rewards with which to challenge them to continued effort, and when the "goodies," influence, or information which the illegitimate barter system can offer an inmate have negligible advantages over that which he can acquire legitimately, the McCorkle and Korn portrayal of the inmate's economy will be almost completely inapplicable. While this alternative to the McCorkle and Korn description has not been fully realized in any prison, it has been approached closely in the best federal prisons.

Our research employee at the Federal Reformatory at Chillicothe, George Pownall, endeavoring to learn something of the prison industry program there, was encouraged by the institution's supervisor of industries to solicit written answers to a few questions from the heads of all industry shops. One of the questions was: "What goals of accomplishment do you, as an individual shop instructor, set for your trainees in the development of trade skills, work habits and attitudes?" The following, adapted from the answer prepared by Joseph A. Madru, foreman in the foundry, reveals the subtle interplay of psychological, monetary, and social incentives that can be developed even in a large, dirty, and unpleasant work situation:

The first two weeks to a month after a young man is assigned to the foundry, we try to get him into condition, physical and mental. This includes the hard work, and the heat from pouring molten metal; he is taught to respect molten iron, but not to fear it, and to be familiar with the routine operation of the work. Pride and accomplishment is instilled within the young man as he builds a mold, pours the mold, and then sees his finished product. It provides an excellent motive.

As a general rule, the young man will progress rapidly and then reach a plateau. Sometimes this leveling-off place is a hard obstacle to overcome. However, they generally manage to continue learning. As the apprentice continues to progress, his work must show more quality and more speed. He is given an extra motive in that as he shows these required qualities, he has earned and receives a higher pay grade.

Inmates in the foundry are on an hourly pay rate: fourth grade pay is twelve cents an hour; third grade pay is eighteen cents an hour; second grade pay is twenty-four cents an hour; and first grade pay is thirty cents an hour. Also, inmates in the foundry, by good work habits and conduct, earn extra good time. It is at the rate of two days each month for the first year that he works in industries. Starting his second year and until the end of his fourth year, he earns extra good days at the rate of four each month. Starting his fifth year in industries, he earns good time at the rate of five days each month.

Needless to say, these incentives are very valuable in giving the young man a desire to show progress in his learning, and in his attitude to get along with people on the job and off the job. His work must show the quality and quantity of a person at the same level of training in an "outside" foundry. The foundry apprentice receives at least 144 hours of classroom training each year that covers subjects related to foundry work. This includes demonstrations, sound films, slides, charts, and the "Foundrymen's Course" through the International Correspondence School. He is given a background in manufacturing processes other than that which he gains in our shop.

When an inmate leaves the institution and goes into an outside foundry, we are sure that he can hold the job as a foundryman that is on the same level as the number of hours and the type of training that he has received at our foundry. If an inmate cannot do the work that is acceptable to the number of hours that he has put in our foundry, then he only receives credit for the number of hours that he can "back up" with his working ability. At no time will an inmate receive more hours of foundry work than he has actually put in.

The young man working in our foundry is encouraged to start work promptly in the morning and continue working till quitting time. We have no coffee breaks, he smokes while he works. He is being prepared to work at production. The foundryman is willing to do any work, technical or hard labor. We do not keep a detail to do our labor; we all pitch in and get the job done. The inmate starts working in the foundry at the orderly job and continues to work his way up the ladder.

In a small assignment the personal relationship of the inmates with each other and with their work supervisor becomes a crucial factor in their motivation. This is suggested by the following, from the answer to Pownall's question submitted by Mr. Earl H. Ebenhack of Chillicothe's industries electrical shop, a small maintenance unit serving the prison industries compound only:

We have a small shop, usually three inmates. As a result there is closer supervision and more individual training can be given each man. Most of them have had long enough sentences that they have stayed in my shop at least a year or more. I think that one of the hardest goals is to get the men to get along with each other and to take instruction from the older men in the shop. Another hard job is teaching these men how to work and do the job as laid out for them. Some of the men have never really had to work, so now they must learn. But after being in the shop for awhile, they seem to realize that these are the requirements necessary to remain in the shop and for promotion. They then make an effort to live up to these requirements. With very few exceptions, I would say most of the men have made a special effort to accomplish these goals. It takes weeks and weeks of working together to make the grade.

The first few weeks the new man goes on every job regardless of how large or how small it may be. In this way he learns his way around the plant, learns the location of the various departments, machines, panels and control equipment. At the same time he is learning something about how to do the work. In other words, he is just a plain helper.

As he becomes more proficient at the work, and conditions warrant, he is promoted to the higher grade of pay, and at the same time assumes greater responsibilities. There is a danger period reached after several weeks of training where the man thinks that he knows all there is to learn. This is a trying period where he either falls by the wayside or finally realizes he doesn't know very much. When this happens he then digs in, studies and works harder, thereby making a good man.

These are the men that continue on with the trade, when they are released, and make a good electrician for some employer. I would say that most of the men fall in this category.

A major problem for classification and parole decisions, and for research, is to capture and objectify some of the knowledge of the individual inmates which a keen work supervisor can acquire in a situation like that which Mr. Ebenhack describes.

RECORDS OF WORK IN PRISON

One of the most serious barriers to assessing the effectiveness of correctional operations is the fact that research must rely on prison and parole office records which were not designed for research purposes. These records are used primarily as a guide in making administrative decisions on individual cases and therefore vary considerably in content and style from one case to the next; they emphasize the problems which staff considered uniquely important in each separate case, and they reflect the somewhat diverse interests of different staff members.

The treatment-team system at El Reno and the classification subcommittees at Ashland, both described in chapter 9, greatly improve the quality of observations on inmates' work behavior in classification reports, for they promote intensive interviewing of the work supervisors by classification staff. However, much variation in the written reports on inmate work occurs despite some effort to standardize the printed forms used for correctional records and to use standard section headings on narrative reports.

This record situation is not nearly as serious a problem for administrative purposes as for research. Some staff members do not need detailed records to assess their cases well and report on them effectively. From an administrative standpoint, the officer's performance may be the best test of the adequacy of his records. However, standardized and complete record forms are also desirable administratively to facilitate continuity when there is a change in the staff member handling a particular case.

For purposes of research to evaluate the effectiveness of a correctional program, it is especially important that all records be complete on every item with which the research is concerned, and that the form of the records be standardized, so that information on one case is comparable to that of another. Other obvious desiderata are that the records be as precise as possible and that they be preserved long enough after the inmate has been released to permit their use in interrelating prison and postrelease information. Unfortunately, none of these conditions is fully met in the research areas with which this project deals, and the deficiencies of records were especially acute with respect to prison work performance.

In our utilization of federal prison records, reliance had to be placed on the narrative case reports prepared in the prisons for classification committee and parole board meetings. These are prepared by the institution caseworkers, from reports submitted by work supervisors.

The narrative reports by caseworkers tend to be rather lengthy and redundant. Factual details, such as what assignments a man had and for how long, are buried in rambling paragraphs instead of being systematically listed. Evaluations of work are not made and recorded in a uniform style. As an aid in research, but also for administrative utility and as a means of reducing the need to rely on inmate clerical assistance in copying and handling confidential case material, I have strongly urged that prisons experiment with records like those which colleges and universities use to summarize an individual's academic career.

Prison case records modeled on scholastic records would consist of one or two master record sheets on each inmate, concisely listing all his major assignments, courses, disciplinary reports, test scores, prior commitments, custodial classifications, and so forth. This would be maintained in one central office, from which inmates would be barred. Whenever copies of these master sheets might be desired, they would be made with one of the several types of copying machines now common in the office equipment field. Narrative reports prepared as a supplement to this record could then be briefer than they are now, providing opinions relevant to the decision at hand, but leaving factual information more concisely and completely available on the master sheet transcripts.

Ratings by Work Supervisors

Prison records on the quality of a prisoner's work—his habits, aptitudes, and attitudes—are especially unsatisfactory. It has long been recognized that an adequate picture of the inmate's behavior and experience in the institution cannot be procured in the interview situation alone. Consequently, caseworkers are urged to consult other members of the prison staff who have personal contact with the inmate. It is evident from chapter 6 that one of the most important sources of information on a prisoner is the staff member with whom most inmates have their closest relationship, their work supervisor.

In order to systematize procurement of information from work super-

visors, many prisons have developed forms on which the supervisors periodically transmit to the caseworkers their impressions of each inmate who
works under them. These are among the least standardized of prison records, varying from institution to institution and sometimes from one assignment to another within institutions. In one prison we found a full-page
"Parole Work Report" on which the officers wrote a sentence or two in
response to sentence-length questions on the inmate whom the report
covered. For example, one of these questions was: "What skills has he
gained or improved since assignment to your crew?" This was commonly
answered with the stereotyped sentence: "He has improved to the point
where he is a qualified operator." Since such reports were prepared by an
inmate clerk for the officer's signature, the officer and his inmate clerk often
simplified their reporting task by the clerk's inserting identical phrases on
reports for almost every inmate, without consulting the officer in advance.
It should be stressed that this great a reliance on inmate clerks was not
typical, but typing and handling of these reports by inmates was common
when long comments were solicited on the reporting form.

The use of an inmate clerk destroys the prospect that the report might
be kept confidential. Under these circumstances, uniform and favorable
phrasing of work reports may be partially intended to prevent resentment
from developing among those inmates who might merit less satisfactory
reports than other inmates. However, this uniformity also destroys the
value of the reports as an aid in decisions by classification committees or
parole boards. Also lost by such uniformity is the possible incentive effect
of more deliberately advising selected inmates of the reports they earn, and
their consequences. Finally, uniform evaluation reports make research
pointless on the objective statistical relationships between prison work behavior and postrelease conduct.

Within the same prison which employed the narrative type of report
described above, we also found most inmate work evaluations on three-
by-eight-inch slips of paper on which a few adjectival rating scales were
checked. Other prisons had variations and combinations of sentence-com-
pletion, adjectival check-list, and completely narrative reports. The check
sheets, of course, reduce the officer's need to rely on inmate clerks. The
adjectives usually are a series like "outstanding, very good, fair, poor," or
"above average, average, below average, unsatisfactory." On the latter
scale, despite the mathematical incongruity, most inmates are evaluated as
"above average." Nevertheless, a few morose officials rate everyone poorly,
and there is sufficient variation in most use of adjective designations to
make their interpretation extremely difficult.

The diversity of interpretation given to scales of adjectival evaluation
is indicated in Table 11.4, which shows variation among prisons within the
federal prison system. It will be seen that at Terre Haute over a third of

TABLE 11.4 Evaluations of Inmate Work Performance by Supervisors in Five Prisons (From Files of Midterm and Near-release Inmates, Prison Panel Study)

Last work evaluation	Leavenworth	Terre Haute	Milan	Chillicothe	Ashland
Excellent, or outstanding	14%	36%	3%	33%	7%
Very good, or above average	40%	45%	64%	22%	65%
Good, or average	45%	15%	30%	43%	25%
Fair, or below average	1%	4%	2%	1%	2%
Poor, or unsatisfactory	none	none	1%	none	2%
Number of cases for whom ratings were available	105	47	101	49	60

the inmates receiving work evaluations were rated excellent, while at Milan only three per cent were given such an evaluation. Over four-fifths of the Terre Haute inmates, and two-thirds of those at Milan and at Ashland, were rated more favorably than "good" or "average," while barely over half received this evaluation at Leavenworth and Chillicothe. But this indicates only the problems of comparing ratings from different institutions. Still greater diversity of evaluation may be encountered among officers and assignments within a single prison.

This diverse reference of adjectival evaluation terms, or of grades, is not unique to the prison situation. It is a familiar problem in personnel evaluation at other large establishments, and regularly confronts academic officials who must appraise grade records of students. The first step in coping with this problem is to know what the grade distribution is and to try to keep its variation within reasonable limits. Wherever large numbers of inmates are evaluated, much control over the significance of grades can be achieved by specifying to staff the approximate percentage who should receive each grade, or by converting grades into percentile ranks. Thus, it is much more meaningful, both for research and for administrative decisions, to know that an inmate's performance ranks in the top 20 per cent of all inmates rated than to be told that he is "above average" or "excellent." Table 11.4 indicates that in a comparison of samplings of work ratings from only five federal prisons the proportion called "excellent" varied from 3 to 36 per cent, and the proportion called "above average" varied from 22 to 65 per cent.

Research on Measurement of Work Behavior

The most significant development toward improvement of records on inmate work activity is emerging from a special research project devoted exclusively to this problem. One of the first projects of the Research and Statistics Office of the Bureau of Prisons, when it was established in 1960, was to contract for such research with Professor Antanas Suziedelis, of the Psychology Department at Catholic University of America. He formerly was a psychologist at the federal reformatory in Chillicothe. The research problem is specified as the measurement of inmate "participation" in the rehabilitative aspects of the work program of federal prisons.

The first step in Suziedelis' study was to have eleven prison psychologists submit short sentences, in simple language, describing aspects of a prisoner's behavior at prison work which might be considered relevant to his rehabilitation. Emphasis was placed on language referring to objective behavior. For example, the statement "Inmate is interested in his work" was considered too general and too dependent upon inference; a somewhat preferable statement was "Inmate has mentioned to his supervisor that he likes his work." They also sought statements applicable to inmates at almost any prison work assignments. Three hundred and twenty-three such statements were collected from the psychologists, of which 158 were found to be nonduplicating and consistent with requirements.

The second step in this research was to procure ratings of these 158 statements from fifty-five federal prison associate wardens, directors of education, and chiefs of classification and parole. They were asked to rate each of the statements numerically, from minus three for statements indicating extreme nonparticipation in rehabilitative work programs to plus three for extreme participation. On the basis of these ratings, items were dropped which had an average score close to zero, or which were rated in opposite directions (positively or negatively) by over ten per cent of these officials.

The third step was to have the remaining statements applied by work supervisors in five federal institutions to a total of sixty-one randomly selected inmates at six types of work assignments. From an analysis of the results, items were eliminated which were not found applicable to at least 90 per cent of the cases or on which over 85 per cent of the cases at an assignment had similar ratings. Since most of the ratings were highly favorable with respect to inmate participation, a number of statements were added which set more difficult standards. These, plus all items not eliminated by the preceding steps, now were tested on a new sample of ninety-five inmates, from five different federal institutions, and all procedures described above, and others, were again applied. The end product was a rating sheet on which work supervisors are asked to answer "Yes" or "No" with respect to whether each of fifty-eight statements describes the work of an inmate at a prison work assignment.

Professor Suziedelis and the Bureau of Prisons then selected a random sample of 425 prisoners sentenced under the Federal Youth Correction Act and 115 other federal prisoners, all confined for over three months. The rating sheet was applied to all of these 540 inmates by their work supervisors. A lengthy questionnaire describing the preprison background of each inmate, his prison assignment, and his prison disciplinary and activity record was completed by the caseworkers. In addition, a form to evaluate postrelease adjustment was prepared, to be completed by a U. S. probation officer on each of these inmates six months after their release.

While waiting for the postrelease data, Professor Suziedelis conducted an analysis of these 425 ratings of program participation by federal youth prisoners which indicates that he has developed a highly meaningful instrument. The ratings have proven unusually reliable, as measured by a work supervisor's consistency in rating a prisoner a second time, and more important, by the extent of agreement when two different work supervisors at one assignment rate the same inmate. The program participation score from this rating sheet differentiates significantly between inmates high or low in custody level, assigned to honor quarters or not, with or without major disciplinary infractions, and according to criminal record, maturity, age at first arrest, preprison work record, and other independent indexes of adjustment.

As a master's thesis project under Professor Suziedelis at Catholic University, J. W. Jones administered to 150 inmates a questionnaire known as the "Work Values Inventory," on which the inmates indicated their reasons for working or not working—for example, material gains, pleasantness of work conditions, prestige, or opportunity for creative effort. It is interesting that inmates who indicated that they liked to work received high program participation scores in the independent ratings by their work supervisors. Those inmates who placed special emphasis on the satisfaction they derived from the work itself as their reason for liking to work were the ones most highly rated on the participation scale.[12]

For the most significant exploration of the meaning of this program participation scale, Professor Suziedelis employed a statistical procedure known as factor analysis. This indicates which groups of statements from the scale seem to be measuring approximately the same thing, in that inmate's rating on one item in the group tended to be predictive of his rating on the other items. Each such group of items is called a factor. In interpreting the results one must study the groups of items that form a factor in order to judge what common trait they all seem to be measuring and to try to label this trait. In the analysis of the ratings of the 425 federal youth prisoners, four factors of some independence from each other emerged, illustrated as follows, for which appropriate labels are suggested:

Factor A: "Good and Hard Work." This group of statements, on which ratings of inmates were highly intercorrelated and rather independent of their ratings on other groups of statements, seems to refer to the extent to

[12] J. W. Jones, "Relationship of Work Value Orientation to Participation in Training Programs of Federal Penal Institutions" (Master's thesis, Catholic University of America, 1962).

which an inmate works diligently and obediently. The following are some of the statements, together with the ratings on them which were scored positively on this factor:

The quality of inmate's work is high. (Rated "True")

Even after being corrected the inmate seems to persist in doing a task his own way. (Rated "False")

Inmate doesn't seem to learn from the mistakes he makes. (Rated "False")

Inmate begins work immediately upon arrival, and continues until told to stop. (Rated "True")

Factor B: "Expressed Interest and Satisfaction In Work." This title seems to describe another group of statements on which the ratings of inmates were highly intercorrelated and independent of their ratings on other statements. They include the following, with the "high" answer indicated:

Inmate asks about the salary scale of his work in the community. (Rated "True")

Inmate asks for reading references relative to the training program. (Rated "True")

Inmate has never mentioned to his supervisor that he likes his work. (Rated "False")

Factor C: "Leadership." These statements, on which ratings were found to be interrelated, cover the assumption of responsibility and initiative by an inmate in regard to the work of other inmates. Among these items, with the "high" answer indicated, were the following:

When a task is assigned to a group of inmates it is usually this inmate who takes charge. (Rated "True")

Supervisor finds himself using this inmate as his "Assistant." (Rated "True")

Inmate shows another inmate how to do something only when specifically instructed to do so. (Rated "False")

Factor D: "Dependency on Supervisor and Conformity." Another group of statements on which ratings varied together seem best described by the above label. These include the following items:

Inmate very often comes to the supervisor to seek help with each new phase of the task. (Rated "True")

Inmate seeks advice with personal problems from the supervisor. (Rated "True")

Inmate rarely, if ever, asks the supervisor for additional work. (Rated "False")

The first check on the predictive significance of these program participation scales was completed in 1963, when reports were available from federal probation officers on the first six months of postrelease behavior of 136 inmates who had been rated on the scale while in prison. The A Scale, "Good and Hard Work," proved highly predictive of whether complaints had been received about the parolee's behavior; 60 per cent of the low A group were reported in some way "troublesome," while only 29 per cent of the high A group were complained about. Factor B, "Expressed Interest and Satisfaction in Work," was highly predictive of the probation officer's judgment on whether the parolee considered his job permanent; 50 per cent of high B inmates considered their job permanent, as against 15 per cent of low B inmates. Both the B scale and a Total Participation Score based on items from all four of the scales were moderately predictive of parole violation at six months; 38 per cent of the low Total Participation Score inmates had violated, as against 22 per cent of the high Total Score inmates.

Research is continuing on the longer-range prediction power of these scales and on their different predictive significance for different types of inmates. Preliminary tabulations suggest that they are of the greatest predictive utility for inmates with the least prior criminal record. It also will be of interest to evaluate how useful such scales are for a running record of an inmate's progress or regress in rehabilitation during confinement, as an adjunct to other information for reaching parole decisions.

One presumes that in skilled trades, such as that of auto mechanic, machinist, or cook, the level of skill which a man attains, and perhaps his speed and his aptitude for further learning, may be important variables somewhat independent of the four factors in "Program Participation" distinguished above. Where standard tests of skill, speed, or aptitude are available, they could well be appended to Suziedelis' scale in a prison work evaluation report. Where they are not available, the work supervisor might well be asked to answer a series of questions in addition to the Suziedelis scale, such as:

1. Indicate the type of work which the inmate is performing (based on standard U. S. Employment Service job titles assigned to all inmate jobs in prison).
2. Would you consider the inmate's *skill* at this type of work similar to that of (check one):
   _____the most skilled 25% of persons employed at this type of work on the outside
   _____the next most skilled 25% employed at this type of work on the outside
   _____the third most skilled 25% employed at this type of work on the outside
   _____the least skilled 25% employed at this type of work on the outside
3. Would you consider this inmate's *speed* at this type of work (check one):
   _____satisfactory for employment at this type of work on the outside
   _____unsatisfactory for employment at this type of work on the outside
4. Do you think the inmate will be able to improve his skill or speed at this work sufficiently to alter any of the above ratings (check all which apply):

_____no

_____yes, with further assignment at this work in prison

_____yes, with employment at this type of work on the outside

One further issue in evaluating work in prison is whether or not the inmates should know the ratings they receive. The Suziedelis scale requires that the work supervisors conceal their ratings from all inmates on the reasonable assumption that the raters would be less objective if their ratings were disclosed. In many personnel evaluation reports in government, business, and industry, supervisors are expected to discuss their ratings with the subject rated as a means of motivating the subject by making him aware of the areas where he is evaluated favorably and the areas where he is thought to have deficiencies. Such a practice would grossly damage the reliability and validity of the Suziedelis rating scale, but rating items like the four in the preceding paragraph might be safely shown to an inmate for educational and motivational purposes. An interesting experiment would be to compare the favorability of these ratings and their rate of improvement where they are shown to the inmates rated and where they are not shown to these inmates, and to compare immediate changes in ratings with two types of switch in policy (from showing to not showing, and from not showing to showing). The findings would permit inference as to the effect of revelation on the ratings.

POSTRELEASE UTILIZATION OF PRISON WORK EXPERIENCE

A really adequate evaluation of the utilization of prison experience in postrelease employment would require a separate large-scale research project, employing job analysis specialists to procure detailed information on each inmate's prison training and postrelease employment. While our project was not staffed in this fashion and available records did not permit anything like optimum precision in job descriptions, several of the research operations in which our project was involved made some exploratory inquiries into postrelease utilization of prison work experience.

On our Postrelease Panel Study, 193 men paroled or conditionally released for four or more months of supervision in 1959 to the U. S. Probation Offices in Chicago, Detroit, Cleveland, and St. Louis were seen by our staff as soon as possible after they left the prison, and up to five times thereafter, at approximately monthly intervals. Detailed questions about postrelease employment were asked at each interview. During the fourth interview, for which the median time after release was 4.1 months, questions regarding use of prison work experience and prison education were asked about each job that the releasee had held for one week or longer.

A total of 140 releasees received the fourth interview. (There were, by then, 53 cases lost by violation, transfer or death, or by their non-cooperation in arranging further interviews.) At the time of the fourth interview, 24 of these 140 releasees had not yet found any postrelease employment (of 15 hours or more in a week) and two had had no work assignment in prison, due to hospitalization. This leaves 114 men who had both work in prison and postrelease jobs.

With each of these 114 men, in that part of the interview which dealt with use of prison work experience, our interviewer began by reviewing a list of all assignments which prison classification reports indicated the man had held in prison. Then, after identifying each postrelease job that the man had held for one week or longer, our interviewer asked, "Is the work you did [or are doing] there in any way like any of the jobs you had at [prison name, or names]?" Frequently the list of prison work assignments was reviewed with the man again. Only 33 men replied in the affirmative to the above question, on one or more of their jobs. This suggests that during about the first four months out of prison, *prison work experience is used in postrelease employment by only about a quarter of those releasees who by then have some postrelease jobs of one week or more and some work in prison.* These releasees held a total of 184 jobs; 47, or *about a quarter of these postrelease jobs, were related to prison work experience.*

For the 47 postrelease jobs in which a relationship with prison work experience was indicated, the prison job which the releasee considered relevant was noted. Fifty-one per cent of these references were to relatively unskilled jobs in the prisons, such as construction labor or unskilled kitchen and dining room work (rather than skilled cook or baker jobs). This high proportion indicates the predominantly unskilled nature of the employment these men procured after prison. However, even at relatively unskilled jobs the familiarity with a job gained in prison was considered an asset. For example, one man had baled scrap in prison, so he sought a job in a junkyard on the basis of his experience with the baling machine in prison. Thirty-one per cent of the references to prison work were to relatively skilled work in the prisons, such as electrician, printer, machinist, cook and baker assignments. The remaining 18 per cent of the references were to "white collar" assignments in the prison, predominantly clerical jobs. The median time that the releasees were assigned to the prison work cited was 12.4 months, and about a quarter spent over two years on these prison assignments.

The next question asked about these prison assignments was whether they involved kinds of work which the prisoner had done before he came to prison. Forty-eight per cent replied that they had not done such work before. For the remaining 52 per cent, the median amount of preprison experience claimed was 3.6 years.

Our final question on the 47 jobs related to prison work experience was:

"What part of the work at [name of prison] has been most helpful on this job on the outside, and in what way was it helpful?" Nine, or about 19 per cent, of the responses were to the effect that the prison work, while related to the outside work, was not particularly helpful. Fifteen per cent said that the prison experience had not been useful for learning new skills but was valuable for maintaining skills acquired before imprisonment. However, 41 per cent said that they were helped in prison by the acquisition of job knowledge and skill that was new to them. Another 16 per cent stressed the physical conditioning from heavy work in prison which prepared them for the heavy labor they did on the outside. The remaining four cases, or 9 per cent, may best be described as crediting the prison with making them at ease in the social position in which their postrelease job placed them: on two hospital orderly jobs, gaining familiarity with medical personnel and patients in the prison hospital was considered beneficial; in the case of one man who was a clerk to a prison engineer, postrelease work in an engineering employment agency was attractive because in prison he "got used to being around engineers;" finally, one man indicated that he would not have accepted the low postrelease social position of janitor if he had not become used to it from being a janitor in the prison!

Combining the above figures for the 47 jobs that had some relationship to prison work with the fact that these were only about one-fourth of the 184 postrelease jobs of the 140 fourth-interview subjects, one can make the tentative generalization that *in about one-tenth of inmate postrelease jobs there are benefits from new learning acquired in prison work, in about three or four per cent of these jobs there are benefits from the preservation of old skills through practice in prison, and in about five or six per cent of the postrelease jobs the prison provided useful physical or psychological conditioning.* In an additional three or four per cent of the cases the prison work was related to the postrelease work, but was not particularly helpful.

It is unfortunate that the releasees available for these Postrelease Panel Study interviews were so few in number. However, a survey like that described here of the postrelease use of prison work and training could be administered by all of the local office staffs of any parole supervision system, in order to cover a larger number of cases. This could be done either routinely or as periodic surveys, on standardized forms for statistical tabulation. Such information would be invaluable as a source of guidance to prison administrators, in maximizing the utility of their work programs. A small version of such a survey was conducted on a sample of federal youth offenders.

Other Postrelease Employment Surveys

Stimulated by 1959 and 1960 preliminary accounts of the economic problems at release reported by the returned violators whom we had interviewed, the Research and Statistics Branch of the Bureau of Prisons, shortly after its establishment, initiated a survey of "The Financial and Employment Resources of Persons Released From Federal Institutions." Reports on the cash in hand and the job prospects at release were procured by the Bureau from all federal prisons for adult offenders, for 1225 consecutive releases over a six-week period in the winter of 1960-61. Of the group as a whole, 701 (57.2 per cent) were reported as having postrelease jobs arranged while they still were in prison. After comparing these jobs with prerelease employment and the prison work experience and training of these inmates, the Bureau's report concludes:

While the evidence is . . . not conclusive, a pattern seems to be present, i.e., that the distribution of occupational levels and type of work of inmates prior to admission is similar to the distribution of the types of work and occupational levels of inmates on release: Those who were salesmen before commitment return to sales jobs when released; those who were agricultural workers return to agricultural work or unskilled labor; those who were skilled workers return to their trades or occupations but with a fairly sizeable proportion who take jobs at lower occupational levels; and those who come in as unskilled workers return to unskilled jobs. All of this suggests the hypothesis that, whatever the underlying factors may be, the intervention of institutional work experience or vocational training has a negligible impact on the level or type of work inmates go to upon release.[13]

In the U. S. Board of Parole's study of the first 322 males committed to prison under the Federal Youth Correction Act, for which our project developed and applied machine tabulation procedures, several judgments by correctional staff were solicited on the offender's utilization of prison experience in his postrelease employment. According to special reports prepared for the study by each youth's prison caseworker, 62 per cent of these youth obtained definite postrelease job offers while in prison, as part of their parole plan, and in the judgment of the caseworkers, 32 per cent of these offers were for jobs which used prison experience.

In the postrelease phase of this U. S. Parole Board study, federal probation officers supervising these youth cases were asked whether each youth's first, second, and third postrelease jobs "used institutional training." Replies were received on the first postrelease jobs of only 230 of the 322 cases, but 86 per cent of these for whom no report was received violated their first parole, presumably before they had any postrelease job. For the 230 reported cases with one or more jobs, only thirty-two, or 14 per cent, were judged to be using institution training on their first postrelease job. Another eight, or a total of 17 per cent, used their prison training on a second or

[13] U. S. Bureau of Prisons, Research and Statistics Branch, *The Financial and Employment Resources of Persons Released From Federal Institutions* (mimeographed report, Jan. 1962), p. 13.

third job, but not on the first job. Those using prison training on one or more jobs had a 55 per cent violation rate on first parole, as compared with 51 per cent for those with employment not using prison training and 86 per cent for those for whom no job was reported.

Prerelease Employment Counseling

A dramatic development, stimulated in part by reports from our research project, promises to augment impressively the specialized staff available to procure information from the postrelease situation for the guidance of federal prisons. This is the establishment of federal prison prerelease centers, described in chapter 16, which were organized late in 1961 in New York, Chicago, and Los Angeles, and in late 1962 were extended also to Detroit. While not primarily intended for research on the postrelease utility of prison programs, their service in this function may be an important by-product of their operation. The staff of each center includes one employment counselor, in addition to other personnel. These employment counselors have prior experience in personnel work, and their main task in the centers is to instruct, counsel, and assist the prereleasees in their search for jobs, and in performing well at the jobs they procure.

The staffing of the prerelease guidance centers with specialists in employment, who rely on information from the prisons in assisting releasees with employment problems, should permit attainment of more sophisticated knowledge on the utility of prison work than was possible in the research described thus far in this chapter. When more experience in the operation of prerelease centers is accumulated, analysis of the employment counselor's records, coordinated with the prison work records of the men released through these centers, should permit major advances in the adaptation of prison training to the job market for released prisoners.

A quite different type of specialized assistance in the evaluation of the postrelease significance of prison work programs is obtained by California correctional officials. In that state there is a system of trade advisory councils and committees, through which the California Department of Corrections and the California Youth Authority have procured the voluntary services of over six hundred management and labor representatives from the outside community. These volunteers serve as consultants on vocational training programs in the prisons and youth institutions. Each council represents an entire industry, such as the garment industry; the committees represent specific trades, such as machinists. As leaders in their occupational fields, the members of these organizations are in an expert position to advise on the relevance of prison training programs to the needs of outside employers, in addition to assisting in the placement of released prisoners

trained in these trades at the prison.[14] Several of these councils and committees have made small surveys of the postrelease employment record of
inmates trained in their particular specialty. More systematic research on
these matters is being organized by the research staffs of the Department
of Corrections and Youth Authority. The public relations value of the
councils and committees in promoting community responsibility for absorbing released prisoners is obvious.

PRISON WORK AND RECIDIVISM

It has been indicated in this chapter thus far: (1) that prisons have
difficulty procuring enough work for all of their inmates, (2) that incentives
are frequently not optimum for motivating inmates to pursue the prison
work that can be most useful to them in their postrelease life, (3) that
records of prison work performance are poor, and (4) that relatively small
proportions of released prisoners find employment which utilizes their
prison training. It follows from this that one should not expect to find a
close relationship between prison work experience and recidivism rates.

In our interviews with returned violators and with "successful" releasees,
when discussing their first and their longest postrelease jobs, we asked if
these jobs had utilized prior training, experience, or study, and if so, whether
this prior preparation has occurred in prison. As indicated in Table 11.5,
about twice as large a proportion of "successes" as of violators reported the
use of prison training on postrelease jobs, but for no group was this proportion more than one-fifth. For about three-fifths of both groups, the first and
the longest postrelease employment was at work in which they reported that
no training was required. The largest differences between these two groups
were in the proportion who had no postrelease jobs, which was highest for
the violators, and in the proportion who had jobs requiring training, which
was highest for the "successes." For those jobs in which prison training was
reported useful, the only notable difference between violators and nonviolators in the type of prison training used was the nonviolator's greater
use of prison industry experience.

When, in terminating our interviews with the "success" cases, we asked
them when and why they changed from interest in pursuing crime, thirty
per cent mentioned their improved work habits or skills as a factor in their
change. A number of these mentioned trades learned in prison as a factor,
especially the secure and skilled "career" trades, such as printing, electrical,
and machinist trades. It was quite clear that the few whose vocational prospects in the noncriminal world had been completely metamorphosed by

[14] Wesley O. Ash and Walter Barkdull, "California's Trade Advisory Councils,"
Am. J. Correction, 23, no. 3 (May-June 1961), 10-14.

TABLE 11.5   Comparison of Returned Violators and "Successes" with Respect to Use of Prison Training on Postrelease Jobs

	FIRST POSTRELEASE JOB LASTING ONE WEEK OR MORE		LONGEST POSTRELEASE JOB	
	Returned violators	*Successes*	*Returned violators*	*Successes*
Unskilled job—no training required	59%	61%[a]	56%	60%
Some training required	21%[a]	34%[a]	24%[a]	36%[a]
No postrelease job of one week or more	20%[a]	5%[a]	21%[a]	5%[a]
Total cases	308	250	308	250
Total postrelease jobs requiring training	64	86	73	89
Men using prison training or experience:				
As per cent of total cases	9%[b]	18%[b]	10%[b]	19%[b]
As per cent of men with jobs requiring training	44%	53%	41%	53%
Major source of prison aid in jobs requiring training:				
Prison vocational training	19%	19%	18%	19%
Prison industry experience	2%	10%	1%	9%
Prison maintenance experience	12%	13%	12%	10%
Prison clerical experience	6%	1%	4%	2%
Prison school training	5%	8%	5%	9%
Other prison training or experience	—	2%	—	3%
Used no prison training or experience	56%	47%	59%	47%

[a] Differences this large or larger could occur by chance alone, in samples of this size, less than once in a thousand times.

[b] Differences this large or larger could occur by chance alone, in samples of this size, less than once in five hundred times.

their acquisition of a rewarding trade in prison were extremely appreciative.

We also endeavored to relate the inmate's work assignment in prison to his postrelease success or failure. This is indicated in Table 11.6 for the 1956 federal releasees. It will be recalled that "failure rates," in our usage, indicate the proportion who were returned to prison, either for a new offense or for parole violation, plus the proportion who received some nonprison penalty for a felony-like offense. Variation in these failure rates for different assignments are not very great. However, it will be noted that the lowest failure rates were associated with semiskilled work, most of which was in prison industries.[15] Semiskilled work assignments had the lowest failure rates also for every category of inmates classified by prior crime, age, or duration of assignment, when we considered these categories separately.

The highest failure rates were in those inmate positions which are conducive to the most influence in the inmate community. These are the prisoners who were personal assistants to officers, as clerks, orderlies, and runners, or were "front office" clerical personnel. Men in these positions who

[15] Differences as large as those between the failure rate of semiskilled work and that for the total sample would occur by chance alone, in samples of this size, less than once in twenty times.

TABLE 11.6   Failure Rates of 1956 Federal Prison Releasees, by Last Prison Work
Assignment Lasting Three Months or More

Last assignment	Failure rate	No. of cases
Food service	39%	178
Typing and bookkeeping	40%	50
Orderly, runner, or officer's clerk	44%	107
Skilled work (other than above)	35%	105
Semiskilled work (other than above)	28%	186
Unskilled work (other than above)	35%	239
Other, or no information	31%	150
Total cases	35%[a]	1015

[a] Differences as great as those between the failure rates for the separate work assignments and that of the total cases would occur by chance alone in samples of this size less than once in fifty times (by Chi Square test.)

had two or more prior felony convictions had a 66 per cent failure rate, as compared with a 45 per cent failure rate for all of the 1956 releasees with such a prior record.[16] Inmates in these positions have unusual contacts with staff and with other inmates. This gives them access to information or special influence which can bring them deference from other inmates. Only in a small proportion of cases do these jobs supply work experience of practical significance for the inmates assigned there. Indeed, the orderly and the personal clerk, runner or messenger jobs generally involve little work of any sort, in relation to the man hours assigned to them. As Table 11.5 indicates, the clerical experience in prison seldom is related to post-release employment.

It is my impression, shared by many others who have studied the prison community, that the clerical jobs tend to attract the inmate politicians, whom Schrag calls "pseudo-social."[17] These are men of extensive criminal experience who "know how to do time" by serving the officials dependably. Simultaneously, they are leaders in the inmate community, so that they are useful as an aid to prison administrators because they know the prison. Indeed, they are the only inmates who can communicate extensively with staff without jeopardizing their identification with the most prisonized inmates. One wonders whether the most criminally oriented inmates are

[16] Differences as large as those between the failure rate for orderly, runner, or officer's clerk and that for the total sample would occur by chance alone, in samples of this size, less than once in twenty times.

[17] Clarence Schrag, "A Preliminary Criminal Typology," *Pacific Sociological Review, 4,* no. 1 (Spring 1961), 11-16; also his summary in Donald R. Cressey, ed., *The Prison* (New York, Holt, Rinehart and Winston, 1961), pp. 346-56. See also: Richard H. McCleery, "The Government Process and Informal Social Control," in Cressey, *op. cit.,* pp. 149-88; Richard A. Cloward, "Social Control in the Prison," in Cloward, Cressey, *et al., Theoretical Studies in Social Organization of the Prison,* Pamphlet 15 (New York, Social Science Research Council, 1960).

attracted to these jobs, or whether the jobs themselves promote crime by encouraging the inmates to be manipulators, and by giving them a conception of themselves as of a leadership or executive elite. The latter influences could give these men, at release, a combination of unusually high aspirations with less than average prison preparation for the types of employment likely to be available to them.

The inadequacy of the data in Table 11.6 for fine analysis of the recidivism reduction effects of prison jobs supports earlier discussion in this chapter on the need for better records of prison work. It also indicates the desirability of using vocational placement specialists to study postrelease jobs in relationship to the prison work.

Table 11.7 indicates that the association between work evaluation in the prison and postrelease failure rates was relatively slight. This may, in part,

TABLE 11.7   Prison Work Evaluation and Recidivism
(1956 Federal Prison Releasees)

Last prison work evaluation cited in casework report	Failure rate[a]	No. of cases	Per cent of total cases
Excellent or outstanding	32%	269	27%
Good, or above average	35%	496	49%
Fair, or average	48%	54	5%
Poor, or unsatisfactory	42%	19	2%
No work evaluation cited	36%	177	17%
Total cases	35%	1015	100%

[a] Chi Square 4.6, 3 df, p <.3 (not significant, by usual standards).

result from the fact that prison work supervisors do not differentiate the quality of inmate work very extensively (as shown also in Table 11.4). In the discrimination that they do report, about three-fourths of the inmates are rated as above average.

The postrelease employment problems of inmates, which will be described in detail in later chapters, indicate the probable utility of any prison program which increases the salable work skills of releasees. The deficient records on prison work performance, and the absence of details on prison assignments in those records preserved long after the inmate is released, reduce one's ability to analyze detailed relationships between specific types of prison training and postrelease success or failure.

The data brought together in this chapter, in conjunction with those presented elsewhere, suggest the conclusions that:

I3. At present the postrelease employment of at least half the men released from prison does not involve a level of skill that requires an appreciable amount of prior training, but for the minority who gain skills in prison at which they can find a postrelease vocation, prison work experience and training is a major rehabilitative influence.

The above should be considered with the findings that: (1) prison work can readily provide the most regular employment experience most prisoners have had; (2) prior work regularity is more closely related to postrelease success or failure than type of work; (3) relationships with work supervisors are the most rehabilitative relationships with staff that prisoners are likely to develop. From this diversity it seems reasonable to conclude:

I4. Not training in vocational skills, but rather, habituation of inmates to regularity in constructive and rewarding employment, and anti-criminal personal influences of work supervisors on inmates, are—at present—the major contributions of work in prison to inmate rehabilitation.

Possibly skills learned in prison are used more at jobs after the immediate postrelease months which our study covered. As automation increases the demand for skilled labor and decreases job opportunities for the unskilled and semiskilled, the vocational-training aspect of prison work is likely to increase in potential rehabilitative significance. The influence of a work supervisor probably will be, if anything, more important if training in skilled work increases in prison, for in teaching, and in inspiring an interest in learning, the work supervisors can have their greatest personal influence. More research certainly is needed on the relationships between prison training and postrelease employment.

In an era of growing financial problems among the states and mounting evidence of the influence of economic factors in adult crime, timidity of state correctional administrators with regard to trying to expand state-use industry in prison and to rationalize work and payment opportunities for prisoners seems less warranted than ever before. Expanding state universities and colleges are an especially large and predominantly untapped market for the products of state-use prison industries. State law frequently permits sale of prison goods to municipal agencies and to other tax-supported bodies, in addition to state agencies, but only a minute proportion of this market is utilized. Private businesses which currently supply these agencies undoubtedly will resist loss of their market to prison manufacture. Also, for many products prison industry will have to raise its standards of efficiency markedly, despite its cheap labor supply, if it is to sell its products to other state agencies at prices competitive with the open market. But these are old problems which have yielded to the efforts of enterprising correctional administrators in many prison industry fields, and doubtless can yield further.

CHAPTER 12

Education in Prison

American prisons, especially those for youthful inmates, have been distinctive for the extent of their investment in educational programs. This dates from the "reformatory movement" of the late nineteenth century, which seems to have been a reaction to the failure of the earlier Pennsylvania and Auburn systems. The older programs emphasized severe discipline and isolation, in order to make men penitent. The new movement fostered efforts to achieve more positive changes in the offenders by education and by vocational training.

The first "reformatory" in the United States was opened at Elmira, New York, in 1876, with William Z. Brockway as superintendent. As reported in chapter 7, it generally is credited with introducing the mark system to American prisons, as well as the indeterminate sentence and parole. Much emphasized at its inception also was the goal of teaching men vocational skills, in addition to raising their general literacy level. The full-time teachers in the reformatory became a new type of prison employee.[1]

Since the opening of Elmira, most of the penal systems in the United States which have more than a single institution for males have designated one of their prisons as a "reformatory." Here they confined their younger felons, and in this institution they generally established a larger school program than existed in most of their other prisons. As work available for prisoners decreased, education programs were expanded in most prisons, both to contribute to inmate rehabilitation and simply to help fill the prisoners' time. This trend considerably reduced the difference between reformatory and penitentiary confinement. However, reformatories and other youth prisons still have the highest ratio of paid teachers to inmates, the penitentiaries more often employing selected inmates as teachers.

DISTINCTIVE FEATURES OF EDUCATION IN PRISON

Statistically, retardation in educational pursuits is highly correlated with progress in delinquent and criminal careers. Although the median schooling completed by the United States population as a whole is past tenth grade, most compilations of the highest grade completed by prison inmates have

[1] Joseph D. Lohman, "Reformatory School," *Encyclopaedia Britannica,* 1960 ed., *19,* pp. 43-44; Blake McKelvey, *American Prisons* (Chicago, University of Chicago Press, 1936), pp. 107-18.

a median in the eighth grade. Tests of educational attainment, in terms of ability to answer passably questions and problems from school work, place the actual knowledge of prison inmates at a median of fifth or sixth grade. From ten to more than thirty per cent of prison inmates are classified as "functional illiterates" by various studies, which usually define this condition as inability to exceed the minimum test scores for fourth grade. One-sixth of our sample of 1956 federal prison releasees had not advanced beyond fourth grade, including one-fourth of the releasees who were forty-one years of age or older. Only one to three per cent of men admitted to prison had completed high school.[2] It is clear that most prisoners would be better prepared for today's job market and for other responsibilities of a noncriminal life if they had more education.

Despite their deficiencies in education, the intelligence of men in prison is not markedly different from that of men out of prison. The average intelligence quotient of prisoners in most compilations is in the upper nineties, and there are many prisoners in every range of intelligence.[3] Improvement in the educational attainment of persons retarded in school is known to be correlated with some increase in their scores on intelligence tests. Therefore, it seems probable that much of the small deficiency in prisoner intelligence scores, by comparison with average scores, is due to school retardation. Furthermore, the smallness of the inmate deficiency in intelligence score compared with their deficiency in schooling suggests that most of their school retardation is due to lack of motivation to perform well in school rather than to intelligence below the level needed to progress at a normal rate. Their lack of past educational effort generally reflects the interruption of their schooling by delinquent and criminal activity and by incarceration. It also reflects the conflict with school authorities which is provoked by delinquent behavior and the failure of the home to effectively motivate a high interest in educational attainment.

Inmates seldom are assigned more than half time to an academic school program in prison, and such assignment commonly is reserved for youthful prisoners with less than eighth-grade attainment. Some vocational training

[2] See: Price Chenault, "Education," in Paul W. Tappan, *Contemporary Correction* (New York, McGraw-Hill, 1951); State of New York Department of Correction, *Educational Achievement Research Project on Male Adolescent Offenders, June 1957– May 1958* (Albany, 1961); U. S. Board of Parole, *Annual Report, 1958* (Washington, D. C., 1959), pp. 44ff.

[3] State of New York Department of Correction, *op. cit.,* p. 33. On our sample of 1956 federal prison releasees, the median I.Q. was 101.2, with 1.5 per cent less than 60 in I.Q., 11 per cent 60 through 69, 13.2 per cent 80 through 89, 21.5 per cent 90 through 99, 24.8 per cent 100 through 109, 18.5 per cent 110 through 119, 8.1 per cent 120 through 129, and 1.5 per cent 130 or higher. Most of these I.Q. ratings were based on a U. S. Public Health Service examination, on which scores are reported to average a few points higher than on most other tests.

programs are full-time assignments; others, perhaps ideally, combine class-room or shop training with a regular job, sometimes on an apprentice basis, in meeting the prison's needs (for example, as butcher, barber, or plumber). Most high-school and college level academic training in prison still is on a part-time basis, in the late afternoon or evenings. Few prison schools offer classroom work on all subjects in a high-school academic curriculum, and none offers more than a handful of courses which could be considered of college level. The latter courses, when available, may be taught in the evening by the extension service of a state university or by a teacher from any college near the prison; occasionally they may be taught by some member of the prison staff or even by an inmate who has an advanced degree.

Courses required for a high-school diploma or a college degree which are not available in the prison school may be procured by prisoners from commercial correspondence schools or from the correspondence instruction offered by many state and private universities. Some prisons purchase sets of correspondence-course material from an outside school, then employ prison school staff to administer the course repeatedly to many inmate students, who complete the assignments in their cells or dormitories. Some prisons have prepared their own correspondence courses for inmates, and some have contracted with established correspondence schools. Such programs are common especially in vocational fields, where a prominent part has long been played by the International Correspondence School. In addition, when inmates register for correspondence courses with outside schools or universities at their own expense, the prison school supervises the examinations.

Only if prison schools are fully staffed with teachers holding state certificates and their programs are approved by the appropriate county or state agencies can the prison itself issue a bona fide diploma. Usually these diplomas do not identify the prison; they may cite a name for the prison school which is unrelated to the name of the prison, or they may contain only the name of the certifying county or state board of education. These practices are common for eighth-grade diplomas. If the prison school is not fully staffed by licensed teachers but instruction is provided by inmates or by correspondence, diplomas generally can be provided through special examination by an outside agency. The General Educational Development tests, widely employed by high-school authorities for the issuance of diplomas to veterans of World War II, have been conducted in many prisons for both veterans and nonveterans. In addition, for prison courses which cannot serve as a basis for issuance of accredited diplomas, many prison schools have their own certificates of course completion, usually identified only by a name for the prison school which does not reveal the school's location in a prison.

The foregoing suggests some features unique to educational administration in prisons: (1) Prison schools teach mainly educationally retarded students who have a history of hostility towards school. (2) Inmate students come and go at all times of the year, rather than at the beginning and end of school terms. (3) The prison situation permits tactics and strategies for motivating student interest and effort which may make it a somewhat advantageous location for making students out of men with the background of most prisoners. (4) However, the prison also creates unusual incentives and opportunities for corruption of the education process. (5) The prison school is expected to justify itself, at least in part, by its effects on recidivism. The last three of these features will be dealt with in this chapter.

INMATE MOTIVATION TO PRISON SCHOOLING

Commitment to prison, in most cases, symbolizes the double failure of the prisoner. For the more than ninety per cent whose crimes were the taking of someone else's money or property, recourse to crime implies some failure in the satisfaction of materialistic desires by legitimate means. Subsequently, commitment to prison indicates failure in crime also.

Presumably failure promotes change in the goals men seek or in the means by which they seek them. From this standpoint, the prison receives its inmates at a time which should be strategic for changing their attitude towards schooling, particularly if they perceive schooling as a means towards success in a legitimate livelihood. Unfortunately, men resist seeing themselves as failures. The often long interval of idleness in jail, between arrest and delivery to prison, is frequently reported by prisoners as a period in which they and their jail mates assist each other in working out a rationalization of their failures, thus salvaging a favorable conception of themselves. Nevertheless, the facts of the prisoner's past failures usually are inescapable when he is in prison, and the prison administration expects him to utilize his time more fully than he did in jail. In this situation education may be "sold" by the prison staff as an opportunity to compensate for past failures. This is a major theme in orientation programs for new inmates, especially at youth prisons. "Don't serve time, let time serve you" is one of many slogans employed to express this approach.

Apart from such rational appeals to their long-run self-interest, inmates can be given a strong short-run incentive to improve their school record if they can be convinced that the duration of their confinement may be appreciably diminished if their grade level increases. Inmates are repeatedly exhorted to show evidence of self-improvement, partly by educational progress in prison, if they wish to improve their chances for parole. In addition to this powerful incentive of freedom, motivation to schooling sometimes is given inmates by establishing academic education prerequisites for attractive work or vocational training assignments in the prison. For example, the attainment of a certain grade level or the passing of specific courses often is necessary for training as machinist, electrician, barber, airplane mechanic, and other especially popular trades. These educational requirements usually arise from license laws or apprenticeship regulations governing these trades in the free community.

In the Federal Correctional Institution at Seagoville, Texas, a "self-help program" has been organized which is conceived as having diverse "phases" of varied significance. Each phase consists of participation in a voluntary education program conducted outside of the inmate's regular work assignment. Involvement in a minimum number of phases is required for various special awards and privileges. The phases are evaluated mainly on the amount of time a program requires of the inmate. For example, the high school, junior high school or elementary school program is considered as two phases, while a single separate course of a demanding nature, such as mathematics, English, any International Correspondence Schools course, or the Great Books course, is counted as one phase. In addition, a half-phase is credited for participation in self-improvement programs which meet less frequently than the foregoing, such as the chapel services, meetings of religious organizations, and religious instruction classes, or for participation in programs which meet frequently but are not considered so relevant to self-improvement, such as the band or the craft shop. An inmate must be involved in a total of three phases of the self-help program in order to be eligible for industrial or meritorious service good time credit.

In 1960 an exceptionally fruitful program was begun at the Southern Michigan Prison at Jackson, to involve inmates and outside persons in a joint effort to improve the prison school program. This program, called "Operation Bootstrap—Rehabilitation Through Education," emphasized communication from the prison to leaders in business, industry, and education, soliciting their assistance in providing speakers, instructional material, and advice for the prison school. The results were especially gratifying in trade-training fields; there were extensive donations of equipment, supplies, and expert guidance for instruction in horticulture, office machine operation, radio-television repair, and automobile manufacture and maintenance. The *Bootstrap* newsletter is sent to over seven hundred participating firms, institutions, and individuals. Probably most prisons could develop similar projects, and indeed, many have done this on a less systematic basis.[4]

Even without these special efforts to motivate school effort, school may be more attractive to a criminal in prison than it was on the outside because the available alternatives to being a student are often less attractive than the prison school. This is in sharp contrast to the alternatives to school attendance which the prisoners knew when not in prison. Finally, in a prison

[4] John H. Hoffman, "Operation Bootstrap," *J. Correctional Education, 14,* no. 2 (April 1962), 18-22.

school the inmate may find himself not more retarded than his classmates and not burdened with a reputation for misconduct, as he often was in schools on the outside.

Prison Panel Study and Education Motivation

As reported in chapter 5, the interviewers in our Prison Panel Study confronted inmates at several stages of their prison term with a card containing nine statements under the heading "What an Inmate Might Try to Get or Do in Prison, and Why." The statements, derived from inmate responses in earlier interviews, covered: (1) getting the most comforts and the most pleasant assignments possible in prison, in order to do the easiest time possible, (2) keeping from being "pushed around" or "given a hard time" by other inmates, (3) avoiding segregation or other prison punishments, (4) learning a trade or getting more school credit, to help get a better job on the outside, (5) improving abilities or knowledge for some reason other than getting a job, such as improving in a sport, study, or hobby, (6) learning how to commit crime more successfully, (7) getting one of the paying jobs in prison, (8) being more conscientious about religion, and (9) trying to improve oneself psychologically.

The fourth item in the foregoing list, interest in schooling and in learning a trade in order to get a job, was the item most often chosen from this list by inmates of five federal prisons as describing their major interests in prison. This item was one of the first three choices of 94 per cent of inmates in their first week of confinement at the youth prison (Ashland, Kentucky), but of only 67 per cent at the maximum-security penitentiary (Leavenworth, Kansas), with three other institutions intermediate between these two extremes. When the same inmates were reinterviewed during their sixth month of confinement and presented with the same card of nine statements, the percentage choosing this schooling and trade-learning as one of their first three interests declined at all institutions, but it remained highest at the youth institution (88 per cent) and lowest at the maximum-security penitentiary (53 per cent); it still was one of the major interests indicated by inmates everywhere. When a cross-section of inmates near release were interviewed and presented with the same list, schooling and trade learning was still one of the first three choices of 82 per cent of inmates at the youth institution and of 59 per cent at the maximum-security penitentiary, but it had declined to a low of 56 per cent at the reformatory (Chillicothe, Ohio), 48 per cent at the medium-security penitentiary (Terre Haute, Indiana), and 38 per cent at the adult correctional institution (Milan, Michigan).

After these inmates were asked what items on this list best described their own interests in prison, they were asked which best described the interests of most other inmates. They responded most frequently that the other inmates were mainly interested in getting the greatest comforts and the most pleasant assignments possible in prison. This is a conclusion which could have included some projection of themselves, but I believe it also reflects what was discussed in chapter 5 as "pluralistic ignorance" in inmate-inmate relationships. At any rate, the interviewees saw interest in schooling for job improvement and interest in procuring one of the paying jobs in the prison as closely tied for second place among the interests of other inmates.

Obviously, these inquiries explored inmate interests in only a crude fashion. Nevertheless, the prisoners' consistent identification of education as their first interest in prison and as the second interest of other inmates indicates that they had been effectively indoctrinated with the idea that educational pursuits are desirable in prison. In prison, as in the nonprison world, learning may be pursued as a means to attain economic or other objectives, in addition to interest in learning for learning's sake.

Some suggestions as to a source of inmate interest in education was revealed when our interviewers, still holding the card with nine statements, asked which of the prison interests indicated there helps most in getting a parole. At every stage of their sentences the prisoners most frequently stated that learning a trade or getting more school credit was the most important of these items for procuring a parole. Avoidance of prison punishments and improving oneself psychologically approximately tied for second. Again, inmates of the youth institution gave greater emphasis than inmates at other prisons to education as a means of achieving parole.

It seems clear from the foregoing that prison officials are eminently successful in their efforts to inspire inmates with the belief that they can "learn their way out of prison" by studying. A major factor in the extremely high stress on education by inmates of the youth prison (Ashland) may have been the unique assignment of an "educational adviser" to each inmate there. Every member of the prison school teaching staff had a case load of advisees. Each prisoner had his educational adviser, to discuss such things as courses, grades, and studying, in addition to his regular prison caseworker, with whom he could discuss questions of assignment, parole plans, and other nonschool problems. Regular conferences were scheduled by the teachers with each advisee, and additional conferences were readily arranged whenever the inmate requested them.

The Prison Panel Study inquiry, with the nine statements presented above, indicated that such decline of interest in academic and trade training as occurred among inmates after their first week in prison was partially replaced by an increase of interest in study and training for various sports and hobbies. Art, music, physical culture, bridge, chess, and many other types of avocational interests are promoted in most prison programs. These preoccupations certainly make inmates more adjusted to their life in prison, and conceivably they could lead to a postrelease use of leisure time that is less conducive to crime than their previous avocations. These activities are clearly antirehabilitative only when the inmates develop unrealistic expectations that they can rely upon their hobby as a primary occupation, as happens with some juvenile retreatists who learn to play a guitar or other musical instrument in prison.

Prison Panel Study and Educational Experience

While prisoners, on the whole, seem moved to want schooling in prison, what do they think of the schooling after they get it? In the six-month and near-release interviews in our Prison Panel Study, some exploratory inquiries were made on inmate experience in education programs. Of the 449 inmates seen in these two sets of interviews, 292, or 65 per cent, had been enrolled in one or more courses in the prison school. Those inmates who reported such enrollment were asked a series of questions on their reaction to the last course that they had taken.

When asked if the last course they took was difficult, three-fourths said that it was not. When they were asked why it was not difficult, the most frequent answer, by one-third, was that the material taught had not been new to them, it was something they had learned before. This situation is a consequence of students being assigned to the grade indicated by their score on an achievement test, in which they are likely at first to score several grades below the grade that they last attended outside of prison. For such students, the teaching is a review operation, but they are placed with students to whom the course content is new. It appears that the prison school has the same kind of problems that outside schools have in keeping the gifted student challenged rather than bored, but the prison school has this problem with ungifted as well as with gifted students. This points up the desirability of small classes in prison schools, to permit much individual attention, so that those students who are capable of rapidly raising their educational attainment score may legitimately be promoted rapidly.

The 292 inmates who had been enrolled in one or more courses also were asked, with respect to their last course, "Do you think you learned as much in this course as you would be expected to learn in a similar course outside of prison?" The answer to this question was not sought as a means of actually comparing the adequacy of prison and outside courses, since an inmate's opinion on this comparative adequacy would not be an expert judgment. Rather, the question was designed to procure another index of inmate motivation to attend school in prison. Actually, 58 per cent said they learned as much in prison as they would on the outside, with 9 per cent insisting that they did not know and the remaining third of the prisoners saying that they learned less in prison than they would on the outside.

When those who said they learned less in prison than on the outside were asked why they learned less, 44 per cent deplored the quality of prison teachers or equipment. However, this percentage varied from a low of only 14 per cent at Ashland to 71 per cent at Chillicothe and 50 per cent at Leavenworth and Milan. Both Ashland and Chillicothe prison schools are characterized by staff rather than inmate teachers, and Chillicothe has somewhat older and more criminal youth, but the distinctive feature of Ashland is the education adviser system described in the preceding section of this chapter. When we questioned inmates further regarding their complaints about the teaching, we received anecdotes and allegations which supplemented other reports indicating problems of corruptibility of the education process in prison.

THE CORRUPTIBILITY OF PRISON EDUCATION

In prison—as in the world at large—the fact that evidence of educational attainment is rewarded often motivates students to be more concerned with acquiring a record of educational attainment than with learning. This motivation, plus aspects of educational administration in prisons that are particularly amenable to corruption, create a constant danger that education according to prison records will not correspond with education attained in fact. Two aspects of prison educational programs create unique administrative problems. These are the use of inmates as teachers and the accrediting of correspondence study in prison.

The Inmate as Teacher

A major problem in the administration of education programs in most American prisons has been the need to rely on inmates as teachers. In youth prisons in the federal and progressively more of the state systems, all or most of the school teaching staff consists of state-certified staff teachers. In prisons for older inmates, however, funds for education rarely permit operation of the school program without inmates as instructors. Frequently the best educated inmate available as a teacher has no more than a high-school education, and many do not even have that. But deficiencies in the teacher's educational qualifications are the least of the problems arising when inmates are used as teachers.

Evidence of the conflict inherent in the role of inmate teacher was a by-product of many of the interviews with prisoners conducted by our project staff. Men who had been assigned to school teaching in the penitentiaries told of the pressure from inmates to give good grades, to allow cheating on assignments or tests, and to let class discussions wander for indefinite periods to sports, crime, or other topics irrelevant to the assigned study topic. The inmate teachers who balked at this were subject to reprisal from other inmates, while the inmate teachers who complied might expect reciprocal favors, and had a "soft job" in which they were considered "right guys."

The role of teacher requires a certain amount of authority. In schools outside of prison, much authority is granted by students automatically when they recognize a person in the status of teacher in a classroom situation. Where the person in the teacher's position is identified as a fellow-inmate, and he seeks to regulate the behavior of his students, he is likely not to elicit the compliance that a regular teacher can expect. The inmate teacher's difficulties are particularly great with those students who are not attending the prison school because of an interest in learning, but only because they cannot get a preferred assignment unless they raise their grade level or because they have been advised that the parole board will be favorably impressed if they raise their grade level.

During the course of our project several measures to cope with the above problems were taken in the two federal penitentiaries where our research was conducted. At Leavenworth an effort was made to enhance the status and qualification of inmate teachers by various types of special recognition and training. Notable here were college-level education courses, for inmate teachers only, taught by a professor of education from a nearby college.

At Terre Haute, while the school program was being expanded in 1960-62, the number of inmate teachers was markedly reduced. The inmate teachers remaining generally worked in a class where a staff member also was present, such as a room where inmates practiced art work and lettering. Also these were inmates who commanded unusual respect because of their professional attainments outside of prison in the field that they taught—for example, one was a professional artist. These inmate teachers also were involved in teaching elective topics and hobby activities, rather than education credit courses. Stretching the budget to replace inmates by first quality civilian teachers was achieved mainly by employing on a part-time basis teachers from adjacent schools and colleges. Usually they simply repeated at the prison, in the late afternoon or evening, an hour or two of the teaching which they were doing at the same time outside the prison.

Correspondence Courses in Prison

Special problems arise in the prisons in the administration of correspondence courses. When our researchers questioned inmates and parolees whose record indicated the completion of many correspondence courses in prison, admissions often were received of three types of collusion among inmates which lead to a distorted picture of accomplishment in these courses. One was the accumulation of copies of completed lessons in the inmate quarters. Frequently this was accomplished by making copies of someone's lessons before they were sent to the school; sometimes carbon copies of completed lessons were peddled in the prison. Of course, this practice is found also in some of the most respected college fraternities, but the correspondence course and the inmate's situation seem to make it especially frequent in the prison.

A second method of collusion was collaboration of inmates in completing the lessons, especially when a more educated inmate not taking the course did the lessons for a less educated inmate in exchange for commissary goods or other favors. The third method was simply that of getting correspondence school records falsified by the inmate clerks who worked in the school.

Scattered accounts of the above types of incident were supplemented by our project in 1959 with a statistical analysis of correspondence-school records in the five federal prisons where project staff were stationed. In two of the prisons, phenomenal rates of completion of the courses were demonstrated for an appreciable number of inmates.

During the period May 5th through June 22nd, 1959, in one prison, one third of 220 correspondence courses completed were finished in one week. These were courses which take most of a year for persons enrolled outside of prison and usually take several months for completion in the greater leisure of prison life. A few inmates completing many courses rapidly account for much of this picture, rather than one-quarter or one-third of the students. Also, it appears that some students may have been allowed to do much work on a course before formally registering in it, to reduce the dropout rate from students deciding that they did not want to finish, once they had started a course. However, there were numerous independent reports by inmates and parolees to confirm the impression that these statistics reflect much collusion by inmate students and inmate clerks in the prison school to exaggerate prison correspondence course attainments.

The above situation, of course, was corrected. Similar conditions in correspondence-school administration are reported to have been exposed some years earlier in another prison, and that exposure led to prompt corrective measures. The point in reporting on these past events here is not to record them as a matter of history, but to indicate pitfalls inherent in the social structure of educational administration in prisons. These pitfalls must be continually guarded against if prison educational programs are to be most effective in raising the educational attainment of prisoners and if the prison education record is to supply reliable information for classification and parole decisions.

A major corrective for the problems involved in the use of inmates as teachers and in prison correspondence-school administration is exclusively staff control of the conduct of final examinations and of the records of inmate educational attainment. Inmates can be used to teach where necessary, to mark papers, and to keep records of performance on separate quizzes and assignments, but information on critical examination performance and course completion should be consigned to those records which every prison must reserve for control by persons other than inmates. Stimulated in part by our research, the federal prisons have moved rapidly in this direction.

UTILIZATION OF PRISON EDUCATION IN POSTRELEASE EMPLOYMENT

In the fourth interview of our Postrelease Panel Study, in conjunction with inquiries on the use of prison work experience in postrelease employment (described in chapter 11), questions also were asked about the use of prison education. Our interviewers prepared from prison classification reports a "List of Learning Activities in Prison Other Than Work Assignments," and this section of the interview began by checking the list with the subject for completeness and accuracy, thereby also refreshing his memory. The designation "learning activities" is somewhat ambiguous; the activities covered were primarily in prison school programs, but they also included some hobby and sports program, such as music and umpiring.

As noted in chapter 5, 140 releasees received this fourth postrelease interview, generally about four months after their release. However, at the time of this interview, 24 of these men had not yet found any employment lasting a week or more. Of the remaining 116, only 95 had been involved in some sort of educational activity in prison, and these 95 releasees had a total of 156 postrelease jobs lasting one week or longer. After reviewing the list of learning activities with them, our interviewer asked about each of their postrelease jobs, "Has the work you did (or 'are doing') on this job in any way been helped by any of the things that we went over on this list?" Affirmative responses on this question were given by only 26 of the 95 releasees, and with respect to 32 of their 156 jobs. In other words, *those prison education programs not part of the work assignments in prison were reported to be helpful in postrelease employment for a little more than a quarter of the inmates who both had such programs in prison and had postrelease employment; the prison education was useful in about one fifth of the jobs that these inmates held in their first four months out of prison.*

For these thirty-two jobs in which benefits were claimed from prison education, we inquired as to which particular learning activity was beneficial. In nine of the jobs, or 28 per cent, elementary-school education in prison was credited, and in three of the jobs, or 9 per cent, credit was given to high-school academic courses. Such a low level of education may seem

unimpressive to people with college degrees, but it can be an immense contribution to the job prospects and performance of those who enter prison
with a low educational attainment. For example, "Alex," Case R-023,
procured postrelease employment as an electroplater. This required complex micrometer measurement, time recording, and calculation, in order to
plate parts of precise machinery exactly as specified. He could not begin
to hold this job if he had not acquired both an elementary and a high-school
diploma during his eight and one-half years of federal imprisonment.
"Jackson," Case R-703, found employment managing a small neighborhood
grocery store; he could not do this had he not learned to read in a federal
correctional institution. "John," Case R-230, completed fourteen courses
in prison, most of them on an elementary-school level. While he only loads
trucks now, he states that before he went to prison he would have been
incapable of the writing and arithmetic necessary for the preparation and
checking of his tally sheets.

In another nine jobs, or 28 per cent, credit was given to a "white collar"
type of prison training course, such as typing, bookkeeping, salesmanship,
and business law. Selling is a competitive type of employment. Talented
releasees sometimes find it to be the field where they can most quickly
achieve an income and status to make up for the time lost in prison; this
is in sharp contrast to jobs where rewards more closely reflect seniority or
experience. "Walter," Case R-242, worked in the plumbing shop in prison
and completed a vocational training course on plumbing. He also completed
high school in prison and took courses in salesmanship and in business law.
After release he was a "natural" for employment in a plumbing supply
store. As he says, proudly: "They look on you better when you have a
high-school diploma. And you have to know a little about contracts so you
know how to tell people what they're signing." Similarly, "Fred," Case
R-239, who completed bookkeeping and business law courses in prison and
then became a salesman, says of these courses: "They helped me understand the other man's business viewpoint. I'm selling only to businessmen,
and it helped me tremendously on my vocabulary."

In five jobs, or 15 per cent, prison personality improvement courses,
including the Dale Carnegie course, were credited with being helpful.
These included three hospital jobs, one job as an office filing clerk and one
job as a restaurant manager.

In only five jobs, or 15 per cent, were mechanical trade courses in prison
reported to be helpful. A drafting course led to employment as a draftsman
for one releasee and was credited with being useful by two men on carpentry
jobs. An electronics course with International Correspondence Schools
made possible one releasee's employment with a major television manu-
facturer. In the fifth case, knowledge acquired in an industrial safety
course at Leavenworth was credited by a releasee with protecting him from
injury on several occasions.

We also asked in what ways the prison education had been helpful for each of these thirty-two jobs. In nineteen, or 59 per cent, of these jobs, the releasee claimed that he learned specific techniques or methods in the prison course that he was using in his postrelease job. In thirteen, or 41 per cent, they credited the prison program merely with giving them some general skills, or the ability to get along with others, which would be useful on any job.

In the foregoing survey, the relatively small size of our sample and the need to rely on the releasee's judgment make the percentages presented as conclusions useful only as rough estimates. However, they illustrate some of the kinds of information procurable from postrelease surveys. With larger samples and more detailed and better validated information, one could more adequately appraise the utility of specific programs of study in the prisons. As suggested in discussing the postrelease utilization of prison work programs, this type of feedback information for prison school programs can be most adequately procured in any integrated correctional system through the regular parole supervision officers. *Ideally the parole supervision officer can be the prison's main source of intelligence on the effectiveness of prison programs, augmented in the federal system by the staff of prerelease centers.*

Procurement of this intelligence service for prison programs will require the development of efficient forms for recording and transmitting, in a standardized fashion, the information on the postrelease usefulness of prison training which the field correctional employees are in a unique position to collect. Indeed, much of this needed data consists of information on postrelease employment which these officers now routinely acquire, but which at present they do not record and transmit in a manner sufficiently standardized to permit statistical generalization.

PRISON EDUCATION AND RECIDIVISM

One of the earliest studies of the relationship of prison education to post-release behavior was conducted at the Joliet-Stateville Penitentiary in Illinois in 1940 by the Head Instructor of the Stateville Correspondence School, the highly publicized prisoner Nathan Leopold. In this period, in addition to being employed in the school, Leopold worked at criminological research with the sociologist-actuary. He contributed, under a pseudonym, an important publication in the development of parole prediction research.[5] The care and competence of his work have been vouchsafed by a number of prominent sociologists with whom he collaborated in other early parole prediction studies at Joliet.

Of 4517 inmates paroled from Joliet-Stateville to residence in the United

[5] William F. Lanne, "Parole Prediction as Science." *J. Crim. Law, Criminology and Police Science*, 26 (Sept. 1935), 377-400.

States during the period 1933-39, 187 had been enrolled in the Stateville Correspondence School. The parole violation rate, on what was then a three-year parole period for almost everyone, was 31 per cent for the nonstudents and 16 per cent for the students. Students differed from nonstudents in being more intelligent, younger, more likely to be guilty of robbery, and more likely to be first offenders. In being more often first offenders, of course, the students were less likely to violate than the nonstudents, regardless of the influence of education. Therefore, Leopold matched every student with the nonstudent case which corresponded to it most closely, successively matching by previous criminal record, intelligence, type of offense, and age. The 187 students had a violation rate of 16 per cent and the 187 matched nonstudents had a violation rate of 20 per cent, a difference which in this small a sample could occur by chance about once in seven times. The analysis of these cases also demonstrated that the students included significantly fewer inmates receiving three or more prison punishment citations than did the nonstudents. This suggests that prison education programs, by offering challenging preoccupations to inmates, have an important function in promoting adjustment to the institution.[6]

One of the most thorough studies of the relationship between prison education and recidivism was an evaluation of the University of Wisconsin Extension Division's day school at the Wisconsin State Prison. The results, reported by Alfred C. Schnur, were based on a sample of 1762 men paroled from this prison in 1936-41. Recidivism rates were found to be lower for men who were enrolled in the prison day school than for men not enrolled, especially for the men enrolled for six months or more. Actually the differences were not great in magnitude, the nonenrollees having a recidivism rate of 18 per cent and those enrolled six months or more a recidivism rate of 14 per cent. However, these differences are reported as statistically significant, in not readily occurring by chance in this size sample, even after controlling separately on ten different characteristics on which the students and nonstudents differed.[7]

---

[6] Head Instructor, *Education in Prison and Success on Parole,* Stateville Correspondence School Monograph Series No. 1, 1941. When Leopold matched students and nonstudents less closely, by dichotomizing the four variables indicated to create sixteen trait combinations, then randomly selecting from nonstudents with each combination a number of cases equal to the students with that combination, he found a violation rate of 22 for the nonstudents, as compared with the 16 per cent violation rate of the students. A difference of this size could occur by chance in two samples of 187 cases only about once in twenty-five times. However, this system of matching is not as rigorous as that cited in the text, in which 20 per cent violation was found for nonstudents matched most closely with the students by criminal record, intelligence, type of offense, and age.

[7] Alfred C. Schnur, "The Educational Treatment of Prisoners and Recidivism," *Am. J. Sociology, 54,* no. 2 (Sept. 1948), 142-47.

In 1962 S. J. Saden reported a comparison of students with nonstudents in a follow-up of 1000 men paroled between December 1945 and December 1949 from the Michigan State Prison at Jackson. Success on parole occurred for 74 per cent of the students and 64 per cent of the nonstudents. Among those parolees with previous criminal records, considered separately, 66 per cent of the students and 55 per cent of the nonstudents were successful on parole. Both of these differences were statistically significant, in that differences as large as these would occur by chance alone, in samples of this size, much less than once in one hundred times.[8]

Findings for Federal Releasees of 1956

Our investigation of the relationship between education and recidivism of federal prisoners did not yield evidence to suggest a clear crime reduction effect from education in prison. On the contrary, as Table 12.1 indicates, inmates enrolled in academic education in prison had higher failure rates than those who were not enrolled. Table 12.1 so strangely contradicts expectations as to provide a strong challenge for further research.

I suspect that we found higher failure rates for inmates in prison education programs than for those out of these programs not because the educational programs were harmful but because of the operation of several other factors. First, one should note that officials make especially great efforts to place those inmates in school who are academically retarded below their presumed mental capacity, especially those with normal intelligence who have not gone through the eighth grade. These inmates may be particularly poor risks as far as prospects for postrelease success are concerned. They may benefit somewhat from prison education, but in spite of this, especially in a short prison term, they are likely to have low prospects for economic self-sufficiency at legitimate employment on the outside. Secondly, sometimes education competes with other activities which may be more rehabilitative than school for some inmates. Perhaps many prisoners in school would have particularly benefited from assignment to prison industries, which generally are not assigned simultaneously with prison education, although they can be simultaneous. Thirdly, if prison education frequently is seen by inmates as a program to be pursued mainly for the purpose of favorably impressing the parole board, those who enroll may include many inmates who are insincere in self-improvement interest and relatively poor parole risks. Fourthly, it is very possible that "a little learning is a dangerous thing" in prison, as prison education may markedly raise an inmate's vocational aspirations without, in most cases, appreciably increasing his capacity to satisfy these aspirations upon release. This seems to apply

[8] S. J. Saden, "Correctional Research at Jackson Prison," *J. Correctional Education, 15,* no. 4 (Oct. 1962), 22-26.

TABLE 12.1   Postrelease Failure Rates and Enrollment in Prison Academic Education Programs, as Related to Education at Release, Prior Criminality, and Age, for 1956 Federal Releasees

(Number of cases given in parentheses below percentages)

	Enrolled in prison academic education	Never enrolled
All cases	39%	33%
	(361)	(654)
Highest grade completed at release		
6th grade or less	32%	32%
	(108)	(188)
7th or 8th grade	40%	30%
	(110)	(190)
9th grade or higher	43%[a]	35%[a]
	(143)	(276)
Prior felony commitments		
None	27%	25%
	(153)	(269)
One	37%	28%
	(110)	(143)
Two or more	59%[a]	45%[a]
	(98)	(242)
Age at release		
25 or under	47%	40%
	(142)	(179)
26 to 30	42%	34%
	(84)	(172)
31 to 40	28%	30%
	(94)	(162)
41 or over	29%	26%
	(41)	(141)

[a] Differences this large or larger could occur by chance alone, in samples of this size, less than once in twenty times.

especially to most inmates educated beyond the ninth-grade level in prison.

More adequate records on prison education and inmate background than we had available, on many more cases and for different prisons, would be necessary to check the foregoing interpretations by intricate cross-tabulation with postrelease data. The ideal check would be by controlled experiments in which groups of prisoners were randomly divided into subgroups, with some subgroups receiving prison education programs and some not, and the postrelease records of the subgroups compared.

Table 12.2 suggests that academic education in prison becomes useful only with long confinement, as though prison education has to be appreciable in scope to affect significantly the prospects of crime avoidance. Unfortunately, information on duration of enrollment and progress in schoolwork was not uniformly available in the classification records retained by the prisons for these past releasees. Possibly the association

TABLE 12.2 Postrelease Failure Rates and Enrollment in Prison Academic Education Programs, as Related to Time Confined and Institution from Which Released, for 1956 Federal Releasees
(Number of cases given in parentheses below percentages)

	Enrolled in prison academic education	Never enrolled
Time confined		
One year or less	33%	24%
	(73)	(202)
13 to 18 months	42%	31%
	(86)	(172)
19 to 24 months	42%	32%
	(65)	(117)
2 to 3 years	44%	44%
	(81)	(98)
3 years or more	30%[a]	48%[a]
	(56)	(65)
Institution from which released		
Maximum-security penitentiary (Atlanta or Leavenworth)	43%	40%
	(82)	(110)
Medium-security penitentiary (Lewisburg, Terre Haute, or McNeil Island)	21%[a]	38%[a]
	(52)	(105)
Youth Institutions (Chillicothe, El Reno, Petersburg, Englewood, or Ashland)	46%	37%
	(133)	(120)
Prison camps	20%	31%
	(20)	(72)
Correctional institutions	38%[a]	25%[a]
	(66)	(185)
Prison hospitals and detention center	50%	31%
	(8)	(62)

[a] Differences this large or larger could occur by chance alone, in samples of this size, less than once in twenty times.

of lower failure rates with prison education in medium-security penitentiaries reflects the fact that those both long-confined and relatively unadvanced in criminality are most likely to be in this type of institution. Prison education was associated with higher failure rates in the correctional institutions, where the average confinement is briefest, but this seems to reflect the mixture of petty thieves and drug addicts with white collar offenders at these institutions; education there is not provided extensively for the latter category, which has low failure rates. The prison camp population is also diverse, some camps specializing in liquor law violators, some in immigration violations (at the Mexican border), and some in inmates transferred from medium-security penitentiaries. Perhaps the latter group, which includes many long-termers, account mainly for the predominant association of education with postrelease success at these camps.

Data for Youth Correction Act Offenders

Support for the judgment that prison education must be extensive if it is to be associated with lower recidivism rates is provided also by data on another type of federal prisoner. For the Youth Correction Act offenders committed in fiscal year 1954-55, the U. S. Board of Parole, in consultation with the U. S. Bureau of Prisons, developed record forms much superior in many respects to those normally maintained. These forms were used for certain hand tabulations, to summarize in the Board's Annual Reports their initial experience with the Federal Youth Correction Act. Our project, in consultation with Mr. James C. Neagles, Staff Director of the Board, developed forms for coding these special records to permit us to analyze their data by machine tabulation.

TABLE 12.3   Per Cent Violating First Parole, as Related to Prison School Attendance and Time Confined, for Federal Youth Correction Act Offenders Committed in Fiscal Year 1954–55.

(Number of cases given in parentheses below percentages)

Duration of prison school attendance (day or evening)	TIME CONFINED			Total cases[a]
	12 months or less	13–18 months	19 or more months	
None	67%	60%	76%	69%
	(15)	(30)	(46)	(91)
Under 6 months	43%	55%	71%	59%
	(35)	(42)	(56)	(133)
7 months or more	55%	55%	61%	58%
	(11)	(33)	(54)	(98)
Total	51%	55%	69%	61%
	(61)	(105)	(156)	(322)

[a] Chi Square 3.52, 2 df, .05 <p <.10 (marginally significant).

Table 12.3 presents the relationship between the violation rates of these offenders on their first parole and the duration of their prison school attendance prior to their first parole. It will be noted that on the first parole of this initial group of youth offenders, the revocation rates were unusually high. Parole revocation was more frequent for those confined long than for those confined briefly, and, of course, those confined long had more opportunity to attend school. Despite this fact conducive to greater violation rates for school enrollees, fewer Youth Correction Act offenders enrolled in prison schools violated parole than those who were not enrolled. Violation rates somewhat lower for those in school than for those not in school were consistently found among inmates confined for similar durations of time, particularly for those both long confined and long in school. A relevant factor in this association of postrelease success with schooling may also have been the fact that most of these offenders were in the Federal Youth Correctional Institution at Ashland, Kentucky, where an especially intensive educational program was organized.

The Parole Board's special records on these Youth Correction Act cases also provided information on change in educational attainment during imprisonment. This was determined by periodically testing the prisoners, usually with the Stanford Achievement Test. As indicated in Table 12.4,

TABLE 12.4 Per Cent Violating First Parole, as Related to Time Confined and to Increase in Academic Attainment Level (by Test) During Confinement, for Federal Youth Correction Act Offenders Committed in Fiscal Year 1954–55
(Number of cases in parentheses)

Change in academic attainment level during confinement	TIME CONFINED			Total cases[a]
	12 months or less	13–18 months	19 or more months	
No change (or slight decrease)	60%	61%	74%	67%
	(35)	(49)	(72)	(156)
Increase	38%	52%	65%	57%
	(26)	(56)	(84)	(166)
Total cases	51%	56%	69%	61%
	(61)	(105)	(156)	(322)

[a] Chi square 3.42, 1 df, .05 < p < .10 (marginally significant).

the inmates whose educational attainment improved during confinement had definitely lower failure rates than those who did not improve, regardless of time confined, but rates were lowest for those who were confined most briefly. The small range of educational progress during most imprisonment and the relatively low level of the average initial education of prison inmates may account for our failure to find dramatic relationships between prison schooling and recidivism. If prison education were sufficiently intensive and extended to make a major difference in a person's educational level, one would expect it to affect greatly his employment prospects in the free community. The basis for this conclusion is summarized in Table 12.5, which indicates the relationship of high-school graduation to unemployment rates and to type of occupation. These data are for males in the United States, sixteen to twenty-four years of age, not enrolled in school, which is the major problem group among released prisoners. The table indicates that the types of jobs which these youth procure are very limited in quality, especially for nonwhites. For both racial groups, however, education through high school or beyond markedly improves job prospects.

It should be stressed that employment opportunities promoted by education do not come exclusively from vocational training. Linguistic and mathematical facility from more purely academic education may also enhance a man's performance at many jobs, and a diploma is a formal requirement for much employment. In addition, education may conceivably affect an inmate's identification of himself with the more conventional segments of society and his acceptance of traditional values.

TABLE 12.5 Employment Status and Occupation of U.S. Males, Age 16-24,
Not Enrolled in Regular or Special School, by Education and Race, October 1959

Race and educational attainment	Per cent unemployed	Per cent not in labor force[a]	PER CENT OF TOTAL EMPLOYED, IN MAJOR OCCUPATIONAL GROUPS							
			Laborers, non-farm	Farm laborers	Service workers	Operatives, etc.	Craftsmen, foremen, etc.	Sales	Clerical, etc.	Professionals, Managers, owners, etc.
Whites:										
Not high-school graduates	12.0	7.4	19.5	11.0	6.6	38.0	13.7	3.1	3.3	4.9
High-school graduates or beyond	6.2	2.1	10.1	4.3	3.3	25.7	15.9	7.8	14.1	18.8
Total whites	8.8	4.6	14.1	7.2	4.7	30.9	15.0	5.8	9.5	12.8
Nonwhites:										
Not high-school graduates	17.8	4.5	35.8	21.6	11.7	19.4	5.5	0.5	3.0	2.5
High-school graduates or beyond	9.9	5.4	26.0	4.6	18.5	24.3	11.6	2.3	10.4	2.3
Total nonwhites	15.6	4.8	32.9	16.5	13.7	20.9	7.3	1.0	5.2	2.4

[a] Not seeking work, e.g., unable to work, seasonal workers laid off at time of census survey, etc.

Based on U. S. Bureau of Census and U. S. D. A., "Educational Status, College Plans, and Occupational Status of Farm and Non Farm Youths: October 1959," *Farm Population* (Aug. 1961), Series Census-ERS (p-27), No. 30, p. 29, Table 19.

Social Education and Recidivism

Special courses frequently are conducted in prison to deal exclusively with questions of values and with adjustment in interpersonal relationships, marriage, alcoholism, and other personal behavior matters not bearing directly on any vocation. These courses often are designated "social education," although they have many names. Such programs usually involve the chaplains, psychologists, and other prison staff, in addition to teachers from the prison school. Frequently the social education courses are conducted in conjunction with group and individual counseling programs. In the U. S. Parole Board's special study of the first 322 inmates committed under the Federal Youth Correction Act, fifty-four inmates reported to have been enrolled in a social education course had a 50 per cent violation rate on first parole, as compared with 64 per cent violation for those not enrolled. A more optimum evaluation, of course, would involve matching those taking the course with a control group not able to receive it.

Late in 1961 the U. S. Bureau of Prisons initiated an experimental intensive social education program in the federal reformatory at Englewood, Colorado. The staff for this program included two Ph.D.'s in psychology and three special teachers, as well as consultants from universities in Colorado. The program was administered to three classes of ten students, meeting five days a week, one and a half hours per day, for a total of 105 sessions. Another thirty inmates, matched in important respects with these students, did not attend the special classes, and thus formed a control group. The special education program included use of extensive visual aids and group discussion on a variety of attitudinal and moral problems which were expected to affect the self-concept of the students and the way in which they subsequently related themselves to conventional and noncriminal members of society. The initial evaluation of this Englewood program has been in terms of change in inmate responses to psychological tests, and by prison disciplinary records. The first comparisons were not favorable to the experimental group, but the experiment is continuing with some modification in program.

Social education classes in other federal prisons are being evaluated by administering psychological adjustment tests before and after enrollment in the classes. A problem with evaluation of social education programs by such devices is the likelihood that these courses teach the inmates what might be called a "vocabulary of adjustment." This permits them to respond to questions in a manner indicating adjustment, regardless of whether or not they are changed profoundly and permanently enough to alter their actual behavior when confronted with the realities in their postrelease situation. While it is doubtless well that inmates are exposed to discussion and lectures on the nature of conventional postrelease adjustment, the hard test of the imprint from this exposure will consist in following the treated and the control-group inmates for several years in the free community, to see if there is a difference in their postrelease recidivism rates.

Achievements and Needs of Prison Education

The impact of the prison school also is affected by the prison's total work and self-improvement incentive program and its "social climate." Professor Reinhardt, of the University of Nebraska, has made some trenchant comments on these aspects of education in prison:

One of the most depressing sights that one can see in a prison schoolroom is a teacher "doing time" right along with his students. The teacher doesn't have to be "serving" time to be "doing" it either. . . .

No place on earth, perhaps, is so thoroughly stocked with men who have poor work habits, and poor work experiences as is a prison. . . .

The education program should employ means for giving the inmate a sense of independent effort. Prison training that has no purpose and no meaning serves only to fortify the sense of utter failure that most all prisoners have experienced or feel. Education for the inmate is achievement or it is nothing, and at least for a prisoner few things can so profoundly affect the personality as a sense of worthless effort. Something learned in a prison classroom . . . becomes alive when associated with a wider range of values that have personal and social significance. . . . Success in a schoolroom . . . must give the individual a sense of dignity and obligation in the performance of daily tasks.[9]

In chapter 4 a number of cases were briefly described to illustrate instances of "clear reformation." In many of these, use of prison work and education in successful postrelease employment was cited. Many more such cases could have been presented. Indeed, the clearest illustrations of the prison's contribution to rehabilitation are provided by the numerous individuals with no skilled or steady employment before prison who after release used prison training to achieve secure careers as skilled tradesmen, foremen, salesmen, or businessmen, or in other vocations.

Our data on prison education at present suggest only the following tentative and highly qualified conclusions:

J1. For most inmates, prison education is statistically associated with above average postrelease success only when the education is extensive and occurs in the course of prolonged confinement.

J2. For most prisoners, especially for those with extensive prior felony records, the usual duration and type of involvement in prison education is associated with higher than average postrelease failure rates; while

[9] James M. Reinhardt, "Prison Education," *J. Correctional Research,* University of Alabama (Oct. 1956).

J3. A small amount of education in prison frequently impairs postrelease prospects of inmates indirectly, by inspiring them with unrealistic aspirations, or by the education's being pursued instead of alternative prison programs which could provide more useful preparation for postrelease life.

Many individual cases of reformation encountered by us, in which prison training and education were clearly major assets in a new way of life for the released offender, demonstrate a great prison education potential. However, our statistics measure the extent to which the prison achieves this potential when its inmates present many other reformation problems and postprison handicaps, for which correctional resources are limited. The statistics presented in this chapter, and in the preceding chapter, indicate that the gap between inmate vocational needs and achievement remains large.

RECREATION AND RELIGION AS MAJOR FIELDS OF PRISON EDUCATION

Frequently no sharp line can be drawn between education and recreation in prison. Inmates diligently pursue hobbies, games, art, athletics, bodybuilding, creative writing, and other diversions, studies and avocations, both in and outside of the prison school program. These activities occur in classes, clubs, teams, informal groups, and privately. All such activity enriches the prisoner's enjoyment of life, enhances his conception of his own worth, and makes his institutional stay more bearable. Frequently the new interest, whether it be music, public speaking, chess or bridge, opens the door for the offender to new noncriminal social relationships on the outside. Indeed, these contacts may begin in prison, through affiliation of prison hobby or game clubs with national or local organizations on the outside.

All the foregoing virtues could be ascribed, much more emphatically, to religion in prison. Prison chaplains and voluntary religious workers from both prison staff and outside organizations are a major educational force in prison and a leading source of noncriminal ties between the prisoner and the outside world. Inmates have the time, and frequently are in a mood, which makes them unusually amenable to conversion to a new conception of the spiritual meaning of their lives and of their relationship to mankind and to their God. The religious staff, in addition to conducting services, teach classes on religious subjects, sponsor inmate clubs and societies, and have an active casework and counseling function. We have already shown, by the testimonials in chapter 6, how much greater is the rehabilitative impact of prison chaplains than that of most other staff, despite the relatively small number of chaplains compared with holders of other staff positions. Members of many church-affiliated lay organizations and interdenominational quasi-religious organizations, such as Alcoholics Anonymous and Narcotics Anonymous, routinely visit members in prison, meet them on release, and assist them in settling into a noncriminal life on the outside. These activities will be discussed further in chapter 15, on the ex-prisoner's social world. A majority of the private welfare organizations servicing prisoners and newly released ex-prisoners also are church-affiliated.

Prison religious activities, recreation, medical services, and some other prison functions should be evaluated by specialists in these fields. However, the effectiveness of a prison program, from the point of view of this book, is the program's effect on the inmate's life after he leaves the prison. For this reason even technically specialized prison operations, such as industry and education, can usefully be studied by persons who are specialists only in criminological research, although a large-scale study ideally might employ an interdisciplinary research team. Any such studies will be incomplete unless they gather systematic observations of postprison experience. That is the concern of Part III of this report.

Part III
THE POSTRELEASE EXPERIENCE

★ ★ ★

CHAPTER 13

The Decision to Imprison and The Decision to Release

In a society that values freedom, the decision to imprison a man is one of the heaviest responsibilities anyone can assume. Perhaps that is why those concerned with the administration of criminal law have repeatedly shifted parts of this burden. An examination of these decision processes in the past, the present, and the foreseeable future may guide one to the integration and coordination of the many official decisions which direct the fate of a convicted criminal.

THE DISTRIBUTION OF JUDICIAL AND CORRECTIONAL DECISIONS

The first attempts to reduce the human strain in making sentencing decisions were efforts to establish impersonal principles and procedures by which correct penalties might be determined. In ancient times this took the form of rituals to secure direction from the supernatural. When the democratic and scientific revolutions of the eighteenth century deified reason, criminal law reformers, such as Beccaria and Bentham, called for abstract principles or a calculus of pleasure and pain with which to prescribe a "correct" punishment for each type of crime. This classical tradition of "a rule of law, not men," still leads us to set limits to the penalties that judges can impose. However, in the nineteenth and twentieth centuries, concern with the type of offense was partially replaced by interest in the character of the offender. Relief from the personal responsibility of making decisions on the fate of criminals then was achieved by distributing the burden of assessing the offender among several persons, and over an extended period of time.

Once it has been determined that a man is guilty of a crime, three major decisions are involved in sentencing him. The first, of course, is whether or not he should go to prison. The judge seeks assistance in this decision by calling for presentence investigations and reports from his probation staff. By granting probation he can defer the decision on imprisonment.

When it is ruled that an offender should go to prison, two decisions remain: how long he should stay there, and to which prison he should go. With the development of parole, the judge retained only authority to set broad limits to the possible duration of confinement. Further decision on this is completely delegated to the parole board. The board, in turn, defers its decision to the date of first parole eligibility, and may defer again one or more times. In addition, it calls on prison officials and others for information and advice. With the development of prerelease guidance centers (described in chapter 16), the parole board can defer its final decision until the offender has been observed in a situation where part of the time he is in a prison-operated institution and part of the time he is free in the community.

The designation of the specific institution in which an offender should be confined was, in the first half of the twentieth century, almost everywhere shifted from the court to state or national prison administrators. They, in turn, draw upon their local prison staff for advice, and to some extent they defer this decision until the prisoner can be tested, interviewed, and observed in the reception unit of the first prison to which he is delivered. Assistance in this decision then is provided by a prison classification committee. (As indicated in chapter 9, our research and recent federal experiments suggest that the committee might well be replaced by a number of treatment teams.) The decision as to where to imprison becomes completely intertwined with a host of other classification decisions which these staff units must make in an effort to arrange the optimum program for promoting the prisoner's rehabilitation while maintaining him in state custody.

The developments in federal sentencing law since 1958 involve the prisons and the U. S. Board of Parole to a greater extent than ever in judicial sentencing decisions. Instead of the traditional federal practices of imposing a definite sentence, with the prisoner eligible for parole after serving one-third, the court may elect to fix any other date as the point of parole eligibility, or it may delegate to the parole board full responsibility for fixing this date. Furthermore, the court may defer the sentencing decision completely and commit a convicted offender to prison for study, with the request that the prison submit a diagnostic report and recommendations for sentencing within ninety days. The prison may also request an extension of this ninety-day period. As Bureau of Prisons Director Bennett aptly expressed it, the courts are going through a "countdown for judicial sentencing."[1] The courts increasingly share the sentencing function with nonjudicial agencies.

[1] James V. Bennett, "Countdown for Judicial Sentencing," *Federal Probation, 25,* no. 3 (Sept. 1961), 22-26. See also: Frank J. Remington and Donald J. Newman, "The Highland Park Institute on Sentence Disparity," *Federal Probation, 26,* no. 1 (March 1962), 3-9; George J. Reed, "Federal Parole and the Indeterminate Sentence," *Federal Probation, 23,* no. 4 (Dec. 1959), 12-15.

THE PREDICTION PROCESS IN JUDICIAL AND CORRECTIONAL DECISION MAKING

All this modern division and deferral of decisions on imprisonment is presumed to increase the knowledge of the offender available for guiding each decision from the court's first presentence investigation to the prison's last reclassification meeting and the parole board's final hearing. At each of these steps the officials must consider the offender's previous behavior and assess his potentialities as a means of predicting his probable future conduct in the situations into which alternative possible official actions would place him.

All these predictions are either inferences made from prior experience or blind guesses. If they are based on prior experience, this experience consists of more or less systematic knowledge about human beings generally and criminals particularly, as well as the separate experience reported or directly observed with each unique individual on whom decisions must be made. Parole boards face the problem of how to integrate intimate knowledge of characteristics of a particular prisoner with general knowledge about broad categories of offenders. This is one of the most persistently perplexing difficulties of judicial and correctional decision making. It has come to be known as the problem of "statistical versus clinical prediction," or as "actuarial versus case-study prediction."

When the heat of controversy and commitment to a polemical position are removed from consideration of this problem, it becomes apparent that the alternatives posed by many formulators of this problem are not real. Actuarial and case-study predictions need not be in opposition; they depend upon each other, are always applied together, and can assist in each other's improvement. This is because both types of prediction, as applied to an individual offender, require that one determine what type of case is involved and what the past experience has been with such cases. However, in clinical or case-study prediction, one also attempts to identify unique characteristics of an individual, especially complex constellations of interpersonal relationships and processes of change.

The end product of a thorough case study is a diagnostic report which presents a composite portrayal of an individual offender as exemplifying one or more categories of offenders and also as having some unique personal traits and social relationships. These impressions are integrated in the mind of the caseworker or other diagnostician to yield prognostic statements predicting the probable future behavior of the offender under specific circumstances, such as a proposed probation, parole, or prison program.

In contrast, the end product of an actuarial prediction applied to an individual is a classification of that individual by a series of traits, known as "predictors." Usually a "prediction score" also is presented, which is determined by assigning weights to the predictors. The predictors vary greatly; they may consist of broad and impressionistic personality or offense categories, to which the offender is assigned on the basis of case studies, or they may consist of very specific and objective information, such as age at first penal commitment or score on a personality test. From a "prediction table" based on past research, the actuary asserts that the offender under consideration is in a class of offenders of which a particular percentage exhibited certain behavior in the past; it is implied that the probability of the individual under consideration exhibiting this behavior in the future is the same as its percentage for this class of offender in the past. In most actuarial studies the behavior predicted—called the "criterion"—has been violation of probation or parole, but actuarial methods could be applied to any other behavior for which judicial or correctional decisions require predictions. This includes the prediction of specific types of postrelease infraction.

THE INTEGRATION OF ACTUARIAL AND CASE-STUDY METHODS

The major argument for actuarial rather than case-study prediction is that systematic comparisons of actuarial and case-study predictions for large numbers of cases, in a variety of situations, have almost always found the actuarial predictions most accurate.[2] Other arguments include its economy and the relative objectivity and uniformity of the prediction, regardless of the person who applies the prediction table. In contrast, it can be shown that case-study predictions vary considerably, depending on the training, perspicacity, and personal idiosyncracies of the particular case analyst.[3]

The major argument for case-study prediction is the existence in each case of unique characteristics not taken into account by prediction tables. Faced with the statistics that for large cross-sections of cases actuarial tables predict more accurately than case-study prognoses, the case-study advocate can still argue that some diagnosticians are more accurate than the tables

[2] For summaries of this evidence and a more extensive discussion of the two types of predictions, see: Harrison G. Gough, "Clinical Versus Statistical Prediction in Psychology," chapter 9 in L. J. Postman, ed., *Psychology in the Making* (New York, Knopf, 1962); Paul E. Meehl, *Clinical Versus Statistical Prediction* (Minneapolis, University of Minnesota Press, 1954).

[3] See: Daniel Glaser, "The Efficacy of Alternative Approaches to Parole Prediction," *Am. Sociological Rev. 20,* no. 3 (June 1955), 283-87; Don M. Gottfredson, "Comparing and Combining Subjective and Objective Parole Predictions," California Department of Corrections *Research Newsletter* (Sept.–Dec. 1961), 11-17.

with respect to certain cases or under certain circumstances. It can be argued that ideal diagnosis and prognosis would involve a series of rules for the case analyst to employ in deciding when to rely on a table and when to use his personal judgment.[4]

Furthermore, regardless of their superiority to case studies, even the best prediction tables at present are not as accurate as one hopes they can become; there is no reason for complacent satisfaction with the capacity of any available procedure or resource for predicting the future behavior of offenders. In view of this situation, and as a result of the great personal responsibility assumed by an official in major decisions on the fate of another individual, it is unlikely that the case-study approach ever will be abandoned. What can happen instead, it seems to me, is that case-study and actuarial approaches can be used to complement each other.

Essentially, a prediction table consists of any compilation of statistics on the subsequent behavior of offenders who previously were differentiated into categories by some sort of measurement, judgment, observation, or record. In any judicial or correctional decision involving some sort of prognosis or prediction regarding offenders, it is possible to record those attributes of the offenders which are considered most useful in making these predictions. The separate prognoses of specific case analysts can also be recorded as additional predictors. When sufficient time elapses for the accuracy of the predictions to be known, tables can be constructed to show the relationship between these attributes or prognoses and that behavior which was predicted.

This compilation of the relationship between prediction and outcome is, essentially, what practitioners do when they appraise how good their judgment has been with different types of offender in different prison programs, on probation, or on parole. A prediction table provides only a more systematic application of this process than we can achieve in our heads. The tables can cover all cases in a representative sample; when we compile experience in our head we are likely to recall some cases more vividly than others and thus get a distorted and incomplete summary of actual experience. All that is needed for this kind of progressive improvement on prognostic knowledge is systematic record keeping, both on prior prognoses or observations and on subsequent outcome, together with periodic compilations of tables to show how the prior information and subsequent outcome were related.

Whenever prognoses of a particular case analyst are shown to be more accurate than prediction tables, for any or all types of cases, one can study

---

[4] See: Paul E. Meehl, "The Cognitive Activity of the Clinician," *Am. Psychologist, 15,* no. 1 (Jan. 1960), 19-27.

the considerations that lead to this more accurate prediction. This can suggest new types of information to include in future prediction tables. It also may suggest the types of case for which case-study prognoses may be most valuable, thus permitting the most efficient use of a limited diagnostic staff. Conversely, when the tables are more accurate, the case-study prognosticator can learn to take into consideration the factors stressed by the table, and possibly less effort need be spent on diagnostic services for these cases (if the table happens to be one which does not employ information derived from intensive case studies). More important, when the tables are shown to be more accurate than case-study prognoses, decision makers can learn to be particularly cautious about making decisions which seem to be contra-indicated by the tables. This does not mean that they should never make such decisions, but they should know from past experience when their judgment is going against the odds, and they should record their reasons for going against the odds as a basis for evaluating these judgments in the light of subsequent experience.

The decisions officials must make as to what risks of further crime they can properly take by releasing particular individuals are moral decisions. No tables can make these moral decisions on what risks to take; tables and case-study prognoses only indicate what the risks probably are. Case-study information will always be needed for these moral decisions. If these studies and prediction tables are both available, and if they are systematically checked against each other for the progressive improvement of both, officials can have the best guidance possible as to the most probable behavior of offenders under alternative possible conditions.

CONFIGURATION TABLES

It is apparent in reading reactions of judicial and correctional officials to prediction tables that many are resistant to the idea of relying upon a numerical prediction score for guidance in a highly responsible decision regarding another human being.[5] These scores were devised as a means of combining information from several different types of predictors into a single predictive statement. One system of scoring is to assign an offender one point for each trait that he has in a list of traits found to be above average in their association with the behavior to be predicted (the Burgess system). Another system assigns points for each trait equal to the percentage of cases with that trait which previously had the behavior to be predicted (the Glueck system). A mathematically more sophisticated

[5] See: Victor Evjen, "Current Thinking on Parole Prediction Tables," *Crime and Delinquency, 8,* no. 3 (July 1962), 215-38.

system assigns points that are a function both of prior statistical relationships between the predictors and their relationship to the behavior to be predicted (the discriminant function method of multiple linear regression analysis). Each of these scoring systems has been shown to yield predictions more accurate than could be procured from the traits on which they are based, taken separately.

From the standpoint of judicial or correctional officials, the numerical prediction score has the disadvantage that it seems impersonal. It is presented as the basis for a predictive probability statement, from the table, and one may then readily lose sight of the information which was combined to arrive at the score. It thus becomes difficult to assess the score from the standpoint of the accuracy of the information from which the score was derived for a particular case, or to relate the prediction table guidance to unique influences or trends which seem to be operating in this case.

In the course of our research project I applied to federal offenders a method of combining predictor information which does not involve employment of a prediction score. I have called the resulting prediction table a "configuration table." I believe it may yield prediction advantages over other types of table, but, more important, I believe that it will prove more readily usable by officials in conjunction with case-study material.[6]

The ideal prediction table would classify cases into those which succeed if a particular action is taken with them (such as granting them probation or parole, or placing them in a specific institutional program), and those which fail. Unfortunately, we have no tables nor any case-study procedures which are so ideal when applied to any large cross-section of offenders. However, the configuration table construction method which I have developed combines predictors according to the extent to which they permit one to approach this ideal. It is a procedure for searching for the predictive information which classifies the cases into categories having success or failure rates most deviant from that for all cases taken collectively. In other words, it is intended to discern extreme risk groups as large as possible, both the extremely unfavorable prospects and the extremely favorable ones. A few illustrations will make this evident.

Example One: A Configuration Table for Predicting Postrelease Success or Failure of All Adult Male Federal Prisoners

This table was developed for our 1015-man cross-section of all adult male federal prisoners released in 1956, described in chapter 2 and cited

---

[6] A fuller presentation of the material in this chapter will be found in Daniel Glaser, "Prediction Tables as Accounting Devices for Judges and Parole Boards," *Crime and Delinquency, 8,* no. 3 (July 1962), 239-58.

repeatedly in subsequent chapters. The criterion to be predicted was post-release success, defined as not being returned to prison or receiving any nonprison sentence for a felony-like offense by 1959. For the sample as a whole, 65 per cent were successful. The prediction problem, of potential value as guidance for parole decisions, was to determine how to utilize information available when these men were in prison to divide them into categories with success rates markedly above or below 65 per cent.

The potentially predictive information for these men consisted of all of the "Admission Summary" and "Progress" reports which had been prepared for their classification and parole consideration in the federal prisons. This information was classified into sixty-three predictors. These included twelve different classifications of information on the man's criminal record, eight classifications of information on his family and home background, and classifications of his work history and of reports on his alcoholism or narcotics usage, his marital experience, his education, and his military record. In addition, there were classifications of information on each man's prison behavior and experience, including the assignments he received, his work reports, disciplinary reports, self-improvement activities, communication with outsiders, and release plans and arrangements, as well as the psychological and psychiatric diagnoses and test results reported for him.

The differentiation of extreme risk groups requires the establishment of a series of arbitrary definitions of "extreme risk" for the particular sample. The boundaries of these groups are made as extreme as is possible while still differentiating enough cases with each predictor to minimize the likelihood that their extreme risk record is purely a matter of chance. For this sample, the "most favorable risk groups" were first designated as those with over 76.6 per cent success, which is above the 65 per cent success of the sample as a whole by one third of the difference between 65 and 100 per cent. The "most unfavorable risk groups" were designated as those with less than 43.3 per cent success, which is below the sample's 65 per cent figure by one third of the difference between 65 per cent and zero. I considered more extreme boundaries but found that few of our predictors, taken alone, differentiated a significant number of cases into more extreme risk groups.

The first step in developing the configuration table was to see which of our sixty-three predictors would place the largest percentage of the sample into a category or categories with success rates outside the 43.3 to 76.7 per cent range. The most differentiating of the predictors, from this standpoint, was Prior Penal Institution Commitments. One-third of the sample, who had no prior institutional commitments, had a 77 per cent success rate. The remaining two-thirds had a 59 per cent success rate. Some other predictors differentiated somewhat more extreme risk groups, but none classified as many as one-third of the cases outside the 43.3 to 76.7 per cent range. Therefore, Prior Institution Commitments provided the first step in our configuration table, which is presented as Table 13.1[7]

The second step in developing the configuration table was to classify each of the two groups differentiated in the first step by all of the other sixty-two predictors, trying to distinguish more extreme risk groups if possible or to place a larger percentage of the sample into the previous extreme risk range. For the most favorable of the two groups resulting from the first step, those with no prior institutional commitments, we defined a still more favorable risk group, those with more than 88.3 per cent success, which is at two-thirds of the difference between 65 and 100. We found that the predictor Age at Release distinguished the most cases into this more extremely favorable range, with 93 per cent success for the 7 per cent of these federal releasees who had both no prior institutional commitments and were thirty-six or older at release. Sixteen per cent of federal releasees, who had no prior institutional commitment and were twenty-four through thirty-six years of age, had a 78 per cent success rate. Classifying these by all remaining sixty-one pieces of information, we distinguished in this group 5 per cent of all the releasees, with an 85 per cent success rate, by selecting those with three or more years of employment at the longest job in the free community.

We could have distinguished, in this no-prior-incarceration group of age

[7] An abstract measure of the extent to which a classification of cases by prerelease information differentiates them into extreme risk groups has been developed by Richard John, who has been at times on the project staff. This statistic, which we shall call *J*, or the "Coefficient of Dichotomous Selectivity," is given by the formula:

$$J = \frac{\displaystyle\sum_{i=1}^{k} n_i |p_i - p_s|}{2\,N_s\,p_s\,q_s}$$

where:

n_i = the number of cases in the *i*th of *k* categories of a predictor;

p_i = the proportion of cases in this *category* which have a particular value (e.g., "success") of a dichotomous criterion;

p_s = the proportion of cases in the *sample* which have this value of the dichotomous criterion;

q_s = the number of cases in the sample which have the other value of this dichotomous criterion (e.g., "failure");

N_s = the number of cases in the sample.

This coefficient varies in magnitude from zero, where all of the categories have the same proportion of success or failure, to 1.0, where all of the categories have either nothing but successes or nothing but failures. The value of *J* for the configuration table presented as Table 13.1 is 0.26. See Richard John, "Prediction Improvement Using the Split-Sample Technique and Criterion-Scaled Independent Variables" (Master's thesis, University of Illinois, 1963). This thesis also introduces several other useful coefficients for measuring different prediction functions.

TABLE 13.1 Configuration Table for Systematic Sample of All Adult Male Federal Prisoners Released During 1956

A. No prior institutional commitment (33% of cases) 77% Success
- AA. 36 and older at release (7% of cases) 93% Success
- AB. 24 through 35 at release (16% of cases) 78% Success
  - ABA. Three or more years employment at longest job in free community (5% of cases) 85% Success
  - ABB. Less than three years at longest job in free community (11% of cases) 76% Success
- AC. 23 or younger at release (10% of cases) 64% Success

B. One or more prior institutional commitments (jail, training school, prison, etc.) (67% of cases) 59% Success
- BA. Satisfactory prison adjustment indicated in first classification progress report (52% of cases) 62% Success
  - BAA. Longest job four or more years (6% of cases) 79% Success
  - BAB. Longest job less than four years (46% of cases) 62% Success
    - BABA. Never violated a prior parole (from training school, reformatory or prison) (34% of cases) 66% Success
      - BABAA. 31 or older at release (16% of cases) 72% Success
        - BABAAA. Not more than one prior conviction for felony offenses (7% of cases) 78% Success
        - BABAAB. Two or more prior convictions for felony offenses (9% of cases) 67% Success
      - BABAB. 30 or younger at release (18% of cases) 60% Success
    - BABB. Violated one or more prior paroles (from training school, reformatory or prison) (12% of cases) 51% Success
      - BABBA. 19 or older at first arrest (5% of cases) 59% Success
      - BABBB. 18 or under at first arrest (7% of cases) 47% Success
- BB. Unsatisfactory prison adjustment indicated in first classification report (15% of cases) 42% Success
  - BBA. Employed more than 25% of time, or student or unemployable 75% of time or more, in last two years of civilian life (8% of cases) 50% Success
  - BBB. Employed less than 26% of time, and not student or unemployable 75% of time or more in last two years of civilian life (7% of cases) 34% Success

296

twenty-four through thirty-five, 3 per cent of our sample of federal releasees who had four or more years of employment at their longest job and a 94 per cent success rate. However, it is appropriate in this type of research to set a lower limit on the size of the group from which one is willing to generalize conclusions; for this sample our limit was 4.5 per cent of the 1015 cases. Information on an appreciable number of cases, which represent more experience, increases confidence that one's findings are not likely to be largely a matter of chance. Confidence also is enhanced when similar risk differentiations are found recurrently with random samples of releasees from different years.

Returning to Table 13.1, it may now be appropriate to discuss some of the differentiations on the right-hand side of the configuration. This starts with the "B" Group, the two-thirds of federal prison releasees who had one or more prior institutional commitments (to jail, prison, training school, or any other correctional institution). This group was classified on all remaining sixty-two items of information to see what would separate from it the most cases in an extreme poor risk category, with less than 43.3 per cent success. Here an unsatisfactory initial prison adjustment report was found most predictive, since it distinguished 15 per cent of all the releasees into a group with only 42 per cent success.

The above finding, the "BA" and "BB" distinction in Table 13.1, is interesting because many critics of parole prediction tables have complained that these tables seldom include prison behavior information. Generally such critics neglect to observe that prison behavior information is collected by those who develop prediction tables but that this information seldom proves nearly as predictive of postrelease behavior as information based on the offender's life before he gets to prison. What the configuration table technique brings out is some unique predictive relationships between prison behavior information and preprison information, relationships that would not be disclosed by other methods of combining prediction data.[8]

Unsatisfactory prison adjustment was not the best predictor of postrelease behavior when applied to all of this sample of federal releasees, for it had

[8] In terms of statistical analysis, the configuration technique may be said to reveal some of the variance of the criterion, postrelease behavior, which is a function of interaction between separate predictor variables, rather than merely the variance which is a function of the linear relationships between predictors and criterion.

For mathematically more sophisticated configuration table construction, see: Leslie T. Wilkins and P. McNaughton-Smith, "New Prediction and Classification Methods in Criminology," *J. Research in Crime and Delinquency, 1,* no. 1 (Jan. 1964), 19-32; Don M. Gottfredson, Kelley B. Ballard, and Leonard Lane, *Association Analysis in a Prison Sample and Prediction of Parole Performance,* Report no. 2 (Vacaville, Calif., Institute for the Study of Crime and Delinquency, Nov. 1963); Gottfredson and Ballard, *Predictive Attribute Analysis and Prediction of Parole Performance,* Report no. 3 (*idem.,* Dec. 1963).

relatively little significance for those prisoners who had not been in correctional institutions before. Furthermore, inmates with prior incarceration were poor risks only if they had poor adjustment records when first in prison; those for whom favorable prison adjustment was indicated on the first prison progress reports but who had institutional difficulties later were not distinctly unsuccessful after release. This is one of many illustrations of unanticipated discoveries emerging from configuration analysis; the cross-tabulation and search procedure in making configuration tables have what in academic jargon could be called a "heuristic" or "serendipity" function. They challenge us to revise theory and extend research by exposing anomalous and unanticipated relationships.

Our further differentiation of the releasees with prior institutionalization (the "B" groups) to find the most cases in categories with low success rates is indicated in Table 13.1. In subdividing these categories, the definition of "poor risk group" had to be repeatedly brought closer to the 65 per cent success rate for the sample as a whole, in order to discern types of information which would place over 4.5 per cent of our cases into poor risk categories.

The disappointment in all prediction work thus far, especially when one starts with a cross-section of all types of offenders, is that a large proportion of the cases remain in categories with success rates close to the rates of the average case for the population studied. However, a major motivation to pursue actuarial prediction work further is that other types of prediction place even larger proportions of offenders into the middle risk ranges only.[9] Progress to greater differentiation probably depends primarily upon procuring more precise and theoretically significant prerelease information on larger numbers of cases, particularly for cases within the middle risk categories.

Example Two: A Configuration Table for Predicting Outcome of First Parole for Federal Youth Correction Act Prisoners

As indicated in chapter 2, shortly after the Federal Youth Correction Act went into effect in 1954 the U. S. Board of Parole initiated a special follow-up of all cases imprisoned under this Act in the first year of the law's operation. For this study the Board, in consultation with the Bureau of Prisons, developed special forms to record systematically what were considered the most important aspects of each offender's prison treatment and behavior record. These were completed by prison caseworkers. Special preprison and postprison data collecting forms also were developed for this study and the postprison forms completed by U. S. Probation Officers.

---

[9] For comparison of case-study predictions by psychiatrists, case-study predictions by sociologists, and actuarial predictions, see the references cited in footnotes 3 and 6 of this chapter.

Although only 322 cases were involved in the Parole Board's Youth Study, the unusually detailed and standardized information on them and the fact that youthful offenders have been the least predictable of offenders made it seem particularly desirable to try to develop a configuration table for these cases. For this purpose we first had to develop coding forms to transfer the Parole Board Youth Study record information to punched cards for machine tabulation; lacking a research staff of its own, and initiating the project before the Bureau of Prisons had its own research branch, the Board had been forced to analyze its information at a slow pace, counting all items by hand, and without much cross-tabulation.

As indicated in chapter 2, these first Federal Youth Correction Act cases had only a 38.5 per cent success rate on their first parole. Later success by those returned to prison after the first parole, but reparoled following further confinement, brought the total of immediate and "deferred" success to 58 per cent. Since the information for the Parole Board's Youth Study was collected prior to the first parole, our analysis has been on the prediction of success for first paroles. Incidentally, about one-third of the returns to prison of these parolees did not involve their being accused of committing new offenses. Possibly because they were sentenced under a new and experimental law, they were given unusually close supervision and therefore were returned for rule violations more frequently than might otherwise have been the case. At any rate, the success rate for these offenders seems to have improved in recent years.

Table 13.2 presents the configuration which we developed for predicting first-parole success in these cases. We first set our boundaries of extreme risk at one-third of the intervals above and below 38.5 per cent, to see which category with less than 25.7 or more than 59 per cent success would have the most cases. This search indicated that those of age fifteen or less at first prior institutional commitment constituted 18 per cent of the sample with a 22 per cent success rate. We then subdivided this group by the remaining items of information to see which category, if any, would have an appreciable number of cases with less than 19.25 per cent success, or one-half of the total sample's success rate. The Youth Study form required prison staff to report the frequency of each subject's letters and visits from his family, arbitrarily defining one visit as equaling two letters and calling five or more letters per month "frequent." This item separated out 12 per cent of the cases with only 16 per cent success among those aged fifteen or less when first confined, but, to our surprise, the low success group here were those who received *frequent* communications.

For the total sample of 322 Youth Correction Act parolees, those with "frequent" communications from friends and relatives had 49 per cent success, and those with "infrequent" communications or none at all had 28 per cent success. The median Youth Correction Act offender is about nine-

TABLE 13.2 Configuration Table for Predicting Success on First Parole for Federal Youth Correction Act Offenders (Based on U.S. Board of Parole Youth Study data for all 322 federal prisoners received under the Youth Correction Act in fiscal year 1955)

A. 16 or older at first prior institutional commitment, or no prior commitment *(82% of cases)* — 42% Success

- **AA. On-the-job training in prison, but for not over five months** (14% of cases) — 61% Success
  - **AAA. Offense other than auto theft** — (5% of cases) — 88% Success
  - **AAB. Auto theft (Dyer act) offense** — (9% of cases) — 45% Success
- **AB. No on-the-job training in prison or more than 5 months of on-the-job training in prison** (67% of cases) — 38% Success
  - **ABA. Custody level reduced during imprisonment** (45% of cases) — 44% Success
    - **ABAA. Educational achievement test 6th grade or higher** (23% of cases) — 53% Success
      - **ABAAA. Parole adviser obtained before release** — (17% of cases) — 61% Success
      - **ABAAB. No parole adviser (except U. S. P. O.) obtained before release** — (6% of cases) — 28% Success
    - **ABAB. Educational achievement test 5th grade or lower** (22% of cases) — 35% Success
      - **ABABA. No prison punishment** — (13% of cases) — 41% Success
      - **ABABB. Some prison punishment** — (10% of cases) — 26% Success
  - **ABB. Custody level not reduced while in prison** (22% of cases) — 27% Success
    - **ABBA. Frequent letters and visits from family** — (8% of cases) — 42% Success
    - **ABBB. Moderately frequent, infrequent or no letters and visits from family** — (14% of cases) — 18% Success

B. 15 or less at first prior institutional commitment *(18% of cases)* — 22% Success

- **BA. Moderately frequent, infrequent, or no letters and visits from family** — (6% of cases) — 25% Success
- **BB. Frequent letters and visits from family members** — (12% of cases) — 16% Success

teen years of age when committed. For those with no prior penal commitment, or whose first penal incarceration was when they were sixteen years
old or older, the direct relationship between frequency of communication
from home and success on parole was even greater than for the sample as
a whole. Why should this relationship be reversed for those who were
under sixteen at their first incarceration? When a family does not stop
very active communication to a youth who is repeatedly incarcerated from
early adolescence, is such a youth slower to develop adult responsibility
than a youth similarly incarcerated early who loses family attention if again
incarcerated? This sample is too small for high confidence that we are not
dealing here with a chance deviation from uniform significance of family
communication for all offenders. However, the table's suggestion that there
is a contrast, for different types of youth, in the relationship of family
attention to parole success demonstrates again the function of configuration
analysis in bringing out interrelationships which pose important problems
for theory and further research.

Returning to the youth sixteen or older at first prior institutional commitment or never previously committed (the 82 per cent of the sample who
fall in the "A" categories of Table 13.2), it will be seen that a high success
component of this group was most distinguished by having had on-the-job
training in prison. However, the on-the-job training happened to be recorded in terms of months of such training, and the high relationship to
success for such assignments in these cases dropped off if this training was
for more than five months. There were too few cases in the five-months
group to explore fully all possible factors in this complexity, but it appears
that success was related to being paroled or progressing to other assignments
after a limited period of on-the-job training.

Additional relationships of diverse types of information in predicting
youth parole outcome are indicated in Table 13.2. The number of cases
in the sample is small, but they provide further evidence that the most
differentiating actuarial prognoses can reflect observations of prison behavior if these observations are more systematically made and recorded than
is customary. The type of record-keeping in prison arranged for the Parole
Board's Youth Study cases should be the beginning of routine maintenance
of better records for all prisoners, if more adequate knowledge is to be
available to guide prison and parole policies. Programs for expanding
casework functions in the prison, like the treatment teams described in
chapter 9, could also contribute to prediction research by making the recorded observations on inmate behavior in prison more valid and complete.

PREDICTING OPTIMUM TIME FOR RELEASE

For the judge or parole board, the risk of recidivism in releasing a man
is but one of many considerations to appraise in making decisions. Im-

portant among these other considerations is the question of whether the risk in release will lessen or increase if release is deferred. Since about 99 per cent of those who become inmates of our prisons ultimately are released, the judge or parole board must not so much decide *if* a man should be released as *when* a man should be released. (Of course, the law provides a range for their judgment in this matter by fixing the legal minimum and the legal maximum period of confinement for an offense.)

The only way in which officials can judge the prospective change of risk in releasing a man at various times is to evaluate this in the light of whatever principles or past experience seem to them to be relevant to this matter. The varied experience of success or failure with offenders of specific types, confined for various lengths of time, under different circumstances, is a complex matter which no one can know very precisely. We can gain precision in our knowledge of this experience, however, if we make systematic efforts to record and analyze what this experience has been.

Table 13.3 indicates how postrelease success rates differed for cases in various categories of the configuration in Table 13.1 according to the duration of confinement before release. In general, the figures show that the older inmates without previous incarceration (the AA and AB categories) were good risks regardless of how long they were confined, while those

TABLE 13.3　Per Cent Success with Different Periods of Time Served Before Release, for Some Configuration Categories of Table 13.1
(Number of cases in parentheses)

	MONTHS SERVED BEFORE RELEASE			
Configuration category *(from Table 13.1)*	*12 months* *or less*	*13 through* *24 months*	*25 through* *36 months*	*37 months* *or more*
A. No prior institutional commitments	79% (125)	75% (137)	72% (40)	84% (31)
Includes:				
AA. 36 and older at release	93% (29)	90% (29)	100% (7)	100% (7)
AB. 24 through 35 at release	75% (61)	80% (59)	79% (19)	84% (19)
AC. 23 or younger at release	74% (35)	61% (49)	50% (14)	75% (4)
B. Some prior institutional commitments	69% (150)	60% (303)	51% (139)	52% (90)
Includes:				
BA. Satisfactory prison adjustment at first report	71% (127)	64% (254)	57% (93)	59% (54)
BB. Unsatisfactory prison adjustment at first report	57% (23)	39% (49)	39% (46)	42% (36)
All cases	73% (275)	65% (440)	56% (179)	60% (121)

younger inmates without previous incarceration (the AC category) who were released late were worse risks than those released early. For inmates with prior institutional confinement, risk of postrelease failure also was greatest for those longest confined, especially those with unsatisfactory prison adjustment indicated in their first prison classification progress reports.

Differences in the postrelease record of men with different durations of confinement, such as those shown in Table 13.3, need not signify that a change in the postrelease success rate results from change in time confined. If sentencing and parole policies impose the longest confinement on the men who have the worst postrelease success prospects, this fact, rather than the effects of long confinement *per se,* could account for low success rates with long confinement. However, we can find differences in the relationship between length of confinement and success rate for different types of offender; some types are better risks when long confined, while other types are worse risks. This suggests that more than judicial and parole board perspicacity in fixing sentences probably determines relationships between time served and postrelease success. Clearly a complex interrelationship among many influences affects an ex-prisoner's behavior. Also, any effect of length of confinement presumably is a function of the nature of confinement conditions, communications, and activities.

This book provides voluminous evidence that the optimum conditions and length of confinement for each offender are not determined easily. It suggests that more precise evaluation of the significance of time served requires more adequate research. This can include extensive correlational studies (1) to identify instances where what appear to be similar groups of individuals are in a given correctional program for different lengths of time, and (2) to determine what consistent relationships prevail between their length of time in the program and their subsequent behavior. More rapid and conclusive knowledge would come from experimental use of purely random selection to divide offenders into groups receiving different periods of confinement and/or different programs. This would increase our certainty that groups compared, if large, probably were similar before selection for different treatment.

There are a few signs that we already are reaching this experimental stage in determining optimum sentencing policy. Perhaps most notable is the Community Treatment Project in Sacramento and Stockton, California. When offenders from these two cities are committed for the first time to the custody of the California Youth Authority, that agency selects the approximately 75 per cent of the boys and 95 per cent of the girls who are least emotionally disturbed or criminally notorious, then randomly divides these into experimental and control cases. The former are released for intensive treatment in their home community, while the latter receive the regular correctional institution program of the Authority.[10] Only by such experimentation with new treatments versus old remedies did medicine make rapid progress in establishing facts on the effectiveness of particular treatments for certain ailments. Within the limits of judicial discretion authorized by law, similar experimentation in judicial and parole practice is needed for rapid progress in the determination of optimum duration and character of treatment for particular categories of offender.

THE VALUE AND LIMITATIONS OF STATISTICAL GUIDANCE IN JUDICIAL AND CORRECTIONAL DECISIONS

I know of no instance where an established academic criminologist, judge, or correctional administrator has advocated the replacement of case studies and subjective evaluation by statistical tables for sentencing, parole, or other major decisions on the fate of an offender. The many reasons for insisting upon case data may be grouped into two major categories. First of all, these officials must make moral decisions for the state as a whole in determining what risks justify withholding from or granting freedom to a man. For these moral decisions they must try to know each man as a person and know his relationships to other persons who love or fear him. Secondly, there always is some information on a case too special to be readily taken into account by any conceivable table in estimating what risks are involved in a specific official action. Thirdly, there are many types of prediction besides the overall prospect of violation which judges and parole boards must consider. These include the type of violation and the consequences of certain types of violation for community treatment of other parolees.

Statistical prediction tables can only indicate the prognostic significance of that information which researchers have tabulated against the subsequent behavior of offenders. Usually many separate tabulations are investigated by researchers before they eventually formulate that multifactor table which makes the greatest discrimination that they can achieve between successes and failures. Thus, for the configuration presented as Table 13.1, we started with separate tabulations on sixty-three types of preprison and prison information on each man; to make the configuration in Table 13.2 we started with tabulations on twenty-one pieces of preprison information and twenty-eight items of prison information collected on each youth offender by the U. S. Board of Parole. From information not recorded systematically or never tabulated, there can be no statistical prediction.

[10] Herman G. Stark, "A Substitute for Institutionalization of Serious Delinquents: A California Youth Authority Experiment," *Crime and Delinquency, 9,* no. 3 (July 1963), 242-48; Marguerite Q. Grant and Martin Warren, "Alternates to Institutionalization," *Children, 10,* no. 4 (July-August 1963), 147-52; Marguerite Q. Warren *et al., Community Treatment Project,* Research Report no. 5 (Sacramento, Calif., Department of the Youth Authority, Division of Research, Feb. 1964).

Officials often wonder why most multifactor prediction tables, including our configuration tables, rely upon so few factors. This results simply from the fact that, while numerous features of a case may be related to post-release outcome, most of these features are interrelated with each other. For example, a man's work record, his arrest record, and his excessive use of alcohol are likely to be interrelated. Although information on any one of these features classifies cases into highly divergent risk groups, once one distinguishes a high or low risk group by one of these three types of information, the other two pieces of information may not differentiate this high or low risk group much further into categories with highly divergent risk rates. This is often an asset where information on an important factor, such as alcoholism, is vague and unreliable; more objective information, such as work or arrest record, may adequately reflect the predictive significance of alcoholism. In general, tables made with the few items of information which most differentiate cases into extreme risk groups have proved more accurate in their predictions over long periods of time than tables with these plus additional items of information. Each additional predictive factor seems generally to add a fairly constant amount of random sampling error to a prediction table and a decreasing amount of predictive discrimination, assuming one starts with the most predictive single item and constantly adds the most discriminating of remaining items.[11]

The major limitation of the prediction tables presented in this chapter are that they are based on too few cases and on releasees of too limited a period of time. With all prediction tables, the results from one sample of cases may be inflated by chance. This risk is somewhat reduced when the samples are large and when one excludes from the final prediction tables categories with very few cases. The ideal table is based only on findings found to be consistent in many samples of appreciable size, which cover several periods of time.

One major reason for tables serving only as an aid in estimation, rather than as a final determinant of postrelease failure risks, is that many cases will be characterized by some feature which impresses an official as of predictive significance but for which no tabulation of previous experience is available. From such cases, of course, officials may advise their researchers on items for which they desire a study of predictive significance in past experience; also, if the officials record their impressions of the predictive significance of this factor in particular cases, future research can compare such impressions with the actual postrelease behavior of these cases. Thus

[11] See: Louis Guttman, "An Outline of the Statistical Theory of Prediction," Part V in Paul Horst, ed., *The Prediction of Personal Adjustment,* Bulletin 48 (New York, Social Science Research Council, 1941), pp. 299-300; A. J. Reiss, Jr., "The Accuracy, Efficiency and Validity of a Prediction Instrument," *Am. J. Sociology, 56,* no. 6, (May 1951), 552-61.

the prediction research and the individual judgment of officials may cross-fertilize each other.

My view that prediction tables serve mainly as a source of caution for officials but not as a substitute for individual judgment is well stated by three former chairmen of parole boards who now are in academic life. Dean Joseph D. Lohman of the University of California's School of Criminology, referring to his tenure as Chairman of the Illinois Parole and Pardon Board, states:

. . . if the decision of the Board, either affirmative or negative, was at odds with the probable score as to success or failure, then the Board was prepared to specify more clearly particular grounds on which the parole was granted or denied. Under these conditions, such tables were in no sense a substitute for Board action; nevertheless, they afforded an important caution against irresponsible or subjective action by the Parole Board.[12]

Professor George G. Killinger of Florida State University, formerly Chairman of the U. S. Board of Parole, advises similarly:

Prediction scales should be administered as a routine preparole procedure. Their use is warranted if they do nothing more than make a board of parole look twice at their selection methods and parole decisions.[13]

Professor Paul Tappan of the University of California, also a former Chairman of the U. S. Board of Parole, notes:

. . . parole prediction research . . . is surely useful, both as a matter of evaluating the relationship of particular prediction criteria to success and also as a device to assist parole boards in making release decisions. . . . However, . . . prediction formula should not be used mechanically to determine eligibility for parole. This is so, in part, because a large proportion of cases lie in the middle range and the unfortunate tendency might be to exclude many cases that could do well on release.[14]

A more extreme caution regarding the use of prediction tables asserts that they may lead to only good risks being paroled and would thus eliminate professional challenge from parole supervision staff, who would no longer be confronted by the need to develop services adequate to prevent failure by poor release risks.[15] This seems most unlikely, for the trend is quite in the opposite direction. Those jurisdictions concerned with employing statistical research to improve knowledge of parole risk are also among those which release the largest proportion of prisoners by parole. A high evalua-

[12] Quoted in Victor Evjen, *op. cit.*

[13] *Ibid.*

[14] *Ibid.*

[15] Ralph W. England, Jr., "Some Dangers in Parole Prediction," *Crime and Delinquency, 8,* no. 3 (July 1962), 265-69.

tion of parole as a release method and a willingness to invest in parole prediction research seem to go together. Notable here is California, which since 1958, in both the Department of Corrections and the Youth Authority, has conducted the most extensive and sophisticated criminological prediction research of all times.[16] Following closely are Wisconsin and New York research projects, which, incidentally, sought the example and advice of our project and adopted configuration tables for combining different types of prediction information.[17] In these states, as well as in Washington and Ohio, officials seem to have desired statistical knowledge as a guide to optimum parole action but not as a deterrent to parole for anyone. Indeed, if the risk information is passed on, knowledge of which parolees are poor risks may challenge parole supervision staffs to maximize their efforts with these cases rather than eliminate challenge from their work; simultaneously, information as to which are the best risks may indicate which parolees require the least parole supervision investment.

"Prediction tables," defined as any compilation of statistics on the postrelease behavior of different types of offenders, can provide parole boards with statistics indicating the prognostic value, in past experience, of any type of prerelease behavior report, personal attribute, test result, background trait, or diagnosis, or combinations of these pieces of information, by which offenders may be differentiated. This knowledge is essential if parole selection is to be improved systematically. Experience thus far supports the conclusions:

K1. Because of the large number and variety of prerelease variables and postrelease circumstances affecting behavior after prison, any predictions of the postrelease behavior of prisoners are likely to be inaccurate in an appreciable proportion of cases, regardless of the persons or procedures employed for prediction.

K2. The most selective prediction tables are more consistently accurate than case-study prognoses in predicting parole outcome for large groups of offenders, but individual cases persistently are encountered which raise

[16] Robert F. Beverly, *A Method of Determination of Base Expectancies for Use in the Assessment of Effectiveness of Correctional Treatment,* Research Report No. 3 (Sacramento, Department of the Youth Authority, 1959): Don M. Gottfredson and Jack A. Bonds, *Systematic Study of Experience as an Aid to Decisions,* Research Report No. 2 (Sacramento, Department of Corrections, 1961).

[17] John W. Mannering and Dean Babst, *Wisconsin Base Expectancies for Adult Male Probationers,* Progress Report no. 1 (Madison, State Dept. of Public Welfare, 1962); *idem., Wisconsin Base Expectancies for Adult Male Parolees,* Progress Report no. 4 (Madison, State Dept. of Public Welfare, 1963); Mannering, "Current Plans for Use of Parole Experience Tables in Wisconsin," *Proceedings, American Correctional Association* (1962), pp. 83-89; State of New York, "Some Factors Associated with Delinquent Parolee Behavior," in *32nd Annual Report of the Division of Parole of the Executive Department,* Legislative Document no. 112 (Albany, 1962), pp. 65-93, esp. pp. 75-76.

prediction issues that do not appear to be taken into account in available statistical tabulations.

K3. Both prediction tables and case-study prognoses, and their application, can be improved continually if each is used routinely as a check on the other; for example, if case analyst or parole board member prognoses are recorded in a definite form, subsequent research can analyze their accuracy and can study those case prognoses which disagree with the predictions from statistical tables, to determine the circumstances under which one method of prognosis is more accurate than the other.

In California and Wisconsin, following earlier use by Wilkins in Britain, the prediction tables have been employed not only for prognoses on individual cases, but to differentiate the general prison population into better and worse risk groups, known as "base expectancy categories." This permits comparison of different correctional assignments, such as forestry camps or vocational training programs, in terms of the parole outcome not only for all those sent to these units, but also for specific risk groups sent there. Thus, if Program A receives predominantly good risk cases and Program B receives the worst risks, lower violation rates among those released from Program A than among those released from Program B might not reflect any advantage of one program over another, but simply the selection of different types of case for each program. Base expectancy analysis permits one to compare programs separately for each risk group, assuming that some cases in each category will be found to have received each program. One can then draw conclusions as to which program is best for each risk category, and one can estimate how the postrelease outcome rates from two programs would compare if they received the same proportions of cases from each risk category.

Experience with this type of analysis has been somewhat less conclusive than had been anticipated originally. At one time Wilkins reported that his analysis showed open Borstal institutions were ten per cent more rehabilitative than closed ones,[18] but in subsequent conversations he advised me and others that reanalysis indicated that most of the ten per cent difference could be accounted for by a "lad-on-lad" effect; good risks were better risks wherever concentrated with good risks, and bad risks were worse when concentrated with bad risks, regardless of what type of institution they were in. This suggests the overriding significance of interpersonal relationships, or "social climate," in correctional treatment, as compared with more formal or objective features of a program or a facility.

In the California Youth Authority there also has been a shift in the conclusions reached from base expectancy studies of the effectiveness of differ-

[18] Hermann Mannheim and Leslie T. Wilkins, *Prediction Methods in Relation to Borstal Training* (London: H. M. Stationery Office, 1955), pp. 108-13, 120-21, 212-14.

ent types of institution. Early analysis by Beverly suggested that keeping a youthful offender in a local jail made him a worse risk and sending him to a forestry camp made him a better risk, regardless of the risk category into which he would be classified by prediction tables for all persons committed to the Youth Authority.[19] A reanalysis by Beverly and Guttman, using better prediction tables and more sophisticated tests of statistical significance for a larger number of cases, again found that significantly lower violation rates consistently prevailed for all risk categories among youth released from the forestry camps, from a new Youth Training Center, and from Soledad Penitentiary, but previous findings on jails did not persist. However, they now speculate that selection factors not taken into account by their base expectancy tables, rather than the distinctive treatment at these installations, may account for the differences that they find. They propose controlled experiments as a more conclusive way of evaluating treatment facilities than base expectancy analysis. For example, they suggest that youthful offenders classified into good risks by the base expectancy tables should be randomly divided while still in the reception centers into a treatment and a control group, and the treatment group paroled immediately. They also suggest that, from the good risks remaining in the institutions, a randomly selected group should be sent to the forestry camps and a randomly selected control group should be retained in the other institutions. By starting the proposed selection from purely good risk cases, they reduce the risks which officials might fear in granting immediate parole or a low level of custodial security to mechanically selected individuals; by purely random methods of distinguishing treatment from control groups, they assure that any individual attribute affecting postrelease behavior is likely to be as frequently present in the control group as in the treatment group.[20]

As indicated in chapter 1 and repeatedly thereafter in this book, experimental research can make a contribution to the achievement of a science of correctional treatment comparable to its contribution to the science of medicine. In summary, regarding the application of prediction tables to the evaluation of alternative modes of judicial disposition or correctional treatment, we conclude:

K4. Prediction tables can be used to divide all cases in a correctional system into "base expectancy" categories of different parole violation or recidivism risk, so that the postrelease record of those receiving a specific treatment can thereby be evaluated in terms of its difference from the record of all

[19] R. F. Beverly, *An Analysis of Parole Performance by Institution of Release,* California Youth Authority Research Report No. 22 (Sacramento, 1961).

[20] R. F. Beverly and E. S. Guttman, *An Analysis of Parole Performance by Institution of Release, 1956-1960,* California Youth Authority Research Report No. 31 (Sacramento, 1962). The references in footnote 10 describe an implementation of these suggestions.

those in similar risk categories not receiving the specific treatment; however, because of continuous uncertainty as to whether or not all important prediction variables by which cases are selected for different types of treatment have been taken into account in these base expectancies, controlled experimentation with randomly selected treatment and control groups, wherever feasible, is the optimum method for evaluating a correctional treatment program.

It should again be observed, in conclusion, that public interest and moral responsibility, in addition to predictions of the behavior of prospective parolees, always enter into public decisions. The parole board member must estimate not merely the risk in releasing a man, but also what risks the public should take, what prospect there is of the risks changing, and what deprivation of the offender's liberty is morally justified by the risks in releasing him.

As our project ended, in 1963, we became increasingly involved in communication with members of parole boards, through the National Parole Institutes. These are a series of one-week meetings of groups of about twenty members of different parole boards. The programs of the institutes are designed to discuss, as objectively as possible, all aspects of the role of a parole board member. Psychiatrists, lawyers, psychologists, sociologists, social workers, and others share in this effort to formulate the relevant issues in a parole board member's decisions, the knowledge available which bears on these issues, and the knowledge needed. The concern here is not only with issues of parole selection, but also with the board member's responsibilities in parole supervision, administration, relationship to other government agencies, public relations, and other matters. It is anticipated that a Resource Book for Parole Board Operations will also be prepared. This program is financed by a grant to the National Council on Crime and Delinquency from the President's Committee on Youth Crime and Delinquency. It parallels, in many respects, a series of Sentencing Institutes for federal judges and the preparation of a "Desk Book for Sentencing," which were initiated under provisions of the Federal Judicial Sentencing Act of 1958.

CHAPTER 14

The Released Prisoner's Economic Resources and Opportunities

As was indicated in chapter 1, our project began with a study which provided substantial evidence of a close relationship, for adult males, between economic deprivation and the pursuit of crime. Therefore we were interested in knowing the financial resources and the jobs available to prisoners at release. In addition, one of the first research suggestions emerging from early discussions on our project was that we attempt to measure the extent to which prisoners develop exaggerated conceptions of their prospects for postrelease success in legitimate occupational pursuits. Implied here was the notion that excess of aspiration and expectation over actual prospects leads to postrelease disappointment and return to crime.

ECONOMIC EXPECTATIONS AND ASPIRATIONS

In an effort to estimate the extent of change during imprisonment in the inmate's perception of his future economic opportunities, we asked the following questions at every interview in our Prison Panel study: "What kind of job would you like to get when you get out? What kind of job do you expect you will be able to get? About what pay do you expect to get? What kind of job do you expect to have a year after you get out? About what pay do you expect to get? What kind of job do you expect to have five years after you get out? About what pay do you expect to get?" The inmates were urged to give details, and the answers were recorded verbatim. In the fourth interview of our Postrelease Panel Study we repeated the above questions with slight modifications to released prisoners; we asked what kind of job they would like "now," in "about six months," and in "four or five years." When the last two periods are added to 4.1 months, the median time since release from prison for these interviewees, it is apparent that these questions were focused on expectations for "about one year" and "about five years," after release, or approximately the same time as was specified in the questions addressed to the prison samples.

It was very difficult to classify into a limited number of categories the hundreds of types of employment which prisoners anticipate, and thereby to rank the jobs by their relative status or prestige. After studying the literature on the classification of occupations we ended up with five categories, based on the U. S. Census classification of occupations but adapted to the range of jobs expected by adult male prisoners. Many arbitrary decisions had to be made in the placement of certain types of employment within this scheme, and these decisions were incorporated into our classification instructions.

The final categories are indicated in Table 14.1, which summarizes the responses to our question on the kind of job wanted or expected. The

TABLE 14.1   Type of Employment Wanted and Expected at Various Intervals
(Prison Panel Study and Postrelease Panel Study)

Type of employment	Time of interview	Wanted at release (if in prison) or now (if 4 mos. out)	Expected at release	Expected about one year after release	Expected about five years after release
Professional, semiprofessional, business manager, or owner[a]	Prison entry	20%	10%	21%	42%
	Near release	16%	8%	20%	47%
	Four months out	15%	—	14%	54%
Craftsmen, foremen, skilled workers[b]	Prison entry	31%	23%	29%	26%
	Near release	26%	17%	25%	26%
	Four months out	19%	—	11%	14%
Service workers[c]	Prison entry	14%	14%	12%	8%
	Near release	11%	13%	10%	6%
	Four months out	18%	—	20%	14%
Operatives[d]	Prison entry	19%	27%	24%	15%
	Near release	31%	29%	30%	13%
	Four months out	30%	—	37%	10%
Unskilled heavy labor, farm labor or menial service work[e]	Prison entry	16%	26%	14%	9%
	Near release	16%	34%	16%	8%
	Four months out	18%	—	18%	7%
Total specific responses (base of above percentages)	Prison entry	263	249	237	228
	Near release	225	212	199	185
	Four months out	135	—	102	84
Nonspecific responses, "don't know," etc.	Prison entry	20 (7%)	34 (12%)	46 (16%)	55 (19%)
	Near release	23 (9%)	36 (15%)	49 (20%)	63 (26%)
	Four months out	5 (4%)	— —	38 (27%)	56 (40%)

Total responses: Prison entry, 283;   Near release, 248;   Four months out, 140.

Examples of types of employment:

[a] Manager or owner of business, including garage, restaurant, or farm; any work for which a college education or special vocational schooling beyond high school is required (stenographer, IBM clerk, bookkeeper, embalmer, medical technician, licensed barber, etc.).

[b] Carpenter, plumber, machinist, electrician, painter, crane or heavy-equipment operator, long-distance or heavy truck driver.

[c] Milkman, restaurant cook, waiter, salesman, gas-station attendant, cab driver.

[d] Semi- or unskilled factory machine-tender, shipping or stock clerk, unskilled office worker, packing-house laborer, local truck driver, etc.

[e] Dock worker, coal miner, railroad section hand, construction common labor, farm laborer or sharecropper owning neither land nor equipment, garbage collector, janitor, dishwasher.

"prison entry" figures are from interviews with men in their first week of imprisonment, while the "near release" responses are from prisoners who, in the median case, were only one month from release. Although one-tenth of the prison inmates *expected* to be in professional, semiprofessional or business-owner positions *at release,* a fifth *wanted* to enter one of these categories then and expected to achieve this goal within *one year,* and *almost half the prison inmates expected to have these professional or business positions by five years after release.* Some caution is suggested by the increasing proportion of nonspecific responses when the questions project more into the future, but it remains clear that the prisoners have unrealistic expectations of very rapid job improvement in their postrelease years. They were unrealistic from the standpoint of the probable career progress of persons with their limited employment experience and education, even ignoring the added handicap which they acquire in getting a prison record.

The men whom we interviewed when they were four months out of prison reported desires and expectations for the immediate future somewhat more moderate than those expressed by the prisoners. These men were more reluctant than those in prison to speculate as to the employment they could expect four or five years after release. Yet the men four months out of prison reported long-range expectations of professional or business careers even more frequently than did prison inmates.

Table 14.1 suggests that expectations of immediate occupational improvement on release characterize offenders before they get to the prison; they are not necessarily a product of the prison. However, their expectations on employment five years after release do increase during the course of imprisonment. There was little change in the responses of those in the prison entry group who were reinterviewed in their fourth and sixth month in prison (not included in Table 14.1). The main change indicated in prison was that near release the men lowered their standards regarding the type of job they wanted or expected immediately. This probably is a readjustment to reality from awareness of the results of actual efforts to arrange a postrelease job while in prison, but this readjustment is in their short-range anticipations rather than in their long-range expectations.

A complementary picture is provided by Table 14.2, which deals with the pay expected on the jobs anticipated at release, one year after release, and five years after release. We recorded the rate of pay exactly as given by the subject, then converted all hourly, daily, weekly, or annual rates of pay to a monthly rate so as to permit comparison. We arbitrarily assumed 170 hours, 23 days, or 4.3 weeks per month. Where men answered in terms of a range, such as "$100 to $125 a week," we used the midpoint of the range as their answer.

Table 14.2 indicates that inmate expectations regarding pay *at release* increase during the first six months of confinement, then decrease near

TABLE 14.2 Pay Expected at Various Intervals, by Time When Interviewed
(Prison Panel Study and Postrelease Panel Study)

Dollars per month	PAY EXPECTED AT RELEASE			PAY EXPECTED ABOUT ONE YEAR AFTER RELEASE				PAY EXPECTED ABOUT FIVE YEARS AFTER RELEASE			
	Interviewed in prison		Near release	Interviewed in prison		Near release	Four months out	Interviewed in prison		Near release	Four months out
	First week	Sixth month		First week	Sixth month			First week	Sixth month		
$100 or more	98%	100%	100%	99%	100%	100%	100%	100%	100%	100%	100%
$200 or more	83%	91%	88%	93%	96%	99%	95%	96%	99%	99%	88%
$300 or more	53%	63%	59%	72%	85%	89%	80%	88%	96%	98%	84%
$400 or more	32%	36%	32%	53%	53%	64%	52%	76%	88%	90%	76%
$500 or more	16%	21%	13%	30%	39%	35%	35%	58%	70%	72%	65%
Number of responses on which percentages are based	240	163	194	210	136	171	102	185	105	140	74
Nonspecific responses (as per cent of total responses)	43 (15%)	39 (19%)	54 (22%)	73 (26%)	66 (33%)	77 (31%)	38 (27%)	98 (35%)	97 (48%)	108 (44%)	66 (47%)

release. Again, this probably reflects the fact that near-release prisoners either have arranged a postrelease job on which they know the pay, or they have been disappointed in efforts to arrange such a job. As time in prison elapses, an increase does occur in inmate expectations regarding pay one year after release and, especially, five years after release. Unlike our type-of-occupation data, our reports on pay expectations five years after release show a clear increase when one compares the first-week with the sixth-week responses. However, there also is marked increase in the frequency of nonspecific responses with the later interviews, which, if interpreted as evidence of caution, largely offsets the overall picture of progressive idealization of the future while in prison.

In the foregoing evidence on the progressive exaggeration hypothesis, it is noteworthy that the biggest increase in inmate postrelease pay expectations occurs during the first six months in prison. Inmates acquire a more realistic perception of immediate pay prospects near release and immediately after release, and this seems also to reduce somewhat their expectations with regard to the distant future. In short, the inmate and releasee expectations on income do not seem as unrealistically high as their occupational expectations. When four months out of prison, many were reluctant to speculate regarding their future pay, and those who estimated were not quite as hopeful regarding pay five years after release as were the men near release who were still in prison.

Clemmer estimates from questionnaire responses that felons in District of Columbia prisons spend sixteen hours per week in reverie. He felt that this should cause them to develop imaginative expectations of the future. However, he was disappointed at the similarity of their descriptions of an ideal and of the actually expected situation or arrangement for themselves on release from prison. He reports:

By and large and with nine per cent exceptions, our inmates could not devise or imagine situations upon release even under ideal conditions much different in type or degree to their social conditioning; or, in other words, and in spite of optimistic reverie experiences for the future, the prisoners could not even under urging permit their conscious imaginations to project a remunerative or fashionable or successful future except for a negligible percentage. . . . For the most part our men wanted and expected to go back to the locale where they came from, to live with whom they formerly had lived, to be supervised as little as possible, to work steady at modest wages and to drift along in the leisure time patterns to which they were accustomed. . . .[1]

Our data seem consistent with those of Clemmer in terms of inmates having modest expectations regarding employment and pay *at* release. The evidence of possibly overactive imagination which we elicited was their

[1] Donald Clemmer, "The Prisoner's Pre-Release Expectations in the Free Community," *Proceedings, American Correctional Association* (1959), pp. 247-48.

anticipation of unusually rapid upward progress in job status during the years *following* release.

Our interviews with violators and with those members of our Postrelease Panel making a poor adjustment convey an impression that impatience with a modest rate of progress is a major factor in the ultimate violations of many parolees and mandatory releasees who seemed to be satisfied with their circumstances when first freed from prison. Prisoners apparently have an acute case of the short range in future outlook which studies find characterize the lower socioeconomic strata from which the majority of offenders come.[2] Staff engaged in prison counseling and in postrelease supervision would appear to be well advised to focus heavily on trying to extend the time perspective of their charges. One approach to this is by stressing techniques and incentives for long-range education, work, and budget planning. In this connection, one might note that the most clear-cut evidence of help from probation officer and parole adviser counseling which we have distinguished in our case interviews involves continuous aid in budgeting. This also is evident in case reports on men in the prerelease guidance centers described in chapter 16. Essentially, the counseling problem is to convert those reared in a lower-class delinquent youth culture which emphasizes immediate impulse gratification, to the so-called "middle-class" values and time prespectives necessary for stable lower-class existence or for upward mobility in the socioeconomic status system.

FINANCIAL RESOURCES AT THE PRISON GATE

The National Survey of Financial Assistance to Released Prisoners, which we administered with the John Howard Association, revealed large differences in the assistance provided by various correctional systems. The survey covered both cash gratuities and other types of economic assistance.[3]

[2] See, for example: Lawrence LeShan, "Time Orientation and Social Class," *J. Abnormal and Social Psychology, 47* (1952), 589-92; Louis Schneider and Sverre Lysgaard, "The Deferred Gratification Pattern: A Preliminary Study," *Am. Sociological Rev., 18,* no. 2 (April 1953), 142-49. A study finding deferred gratification habits more related to upward movement in social class than to any particular class position is reported in Murray A. Strauss, "Deferred Gratification, Social Class, and the Achievement Syndrome," *Am. Sociological Rev., 27,* no. 3 (June 1962), 326-35.

[3] The most detailed report on this survey is: Daniel Glaser, Eugene S. Zemans, and Charles W. Dean, *Money Against Crime: A Survey of Economic Assistance to Released Offenders* (Chicago, The John Howard Association, 1961). Single copies of this report are available from this Association, at 608 S. Dearborn Street, Chicago 5, Illinois. Incidentally, over 500 copies of this report have been distributed in response to requests from correctional officials and libraries all over the United States and in many foreign countries following stories and editorials on the report in *The New York Times* and in Chicago papers, as well as coverage by the news service agencies. Another summary of the findings, more detailed than that presented here, is: Daniel Glaser, "Research on Economic Assistance for Released Prisoners," *Proceedings, American Correctional Association* (1960), pp. 363-80.

Clothing, Transportation, and Cash

The most universal type of gratuity at release from American prison systems consists of free civilian clothing. Most prisons require inmates to ship home or sign over to a welfare agency the clothing which they wear when delivered to the prison. At release, the prisons replace with civilian clothing the conspicuously numbered denims of many state prisons or whatever uniform prisoners are required to wear while in custody. Jails, and a few prisons, sometimes save for short-term prisoners the clothing they wear on arrival or even permit them to wear their own clothing while confined. Also, many prisons allow inmates to receive civilian clothing from outside sources on the day of their release.

In our survey, which received responses from every American state prison system except that of Arkansas, the issuance of free clothing at release was reported by all prisons except Hawaii. Hawaiian officials observed that the warm climate and short travel distances make clothing issue less important there than elsewhere. Georgia reported that prisoners are issued a gratuity of $8 in cash if they have their own clothing, but are charged up to $8 if clothing is provided for them by the state. The question of how long prison-issued release clothing is utilized and, therefore, the extent to which it saves the inmate expenditures for clothing at release are discussed later in this chapter.

The next most frequently provided type of financial assistance at release consists of transportation expenses for the trip away from the area where the prison is located. The federal, the District of Columbia, and forty-one state prisons provide releasees with some assistance in meeting transportation costs. Texas provides transportation costs for parolees but not for dischargees, partly because their parolees receive smaller cash gratuities than dischargees. Maryland limits to $3 its payment for transportation and provides no cash gratuity. Massachusetts, Minnesota, Montana, Texas, and Oregon pay larger cash gratuities at release than most states but pay nothing toward transportation. In these states, quite clearly, the net funds available to a releasee for resuming economic self-sufficiency in the free community are very much a function of the distance of his postprison home from the prison.

Many states pay for travel of releasees only to an approved destination within the state or to the state border. In federal prisons every releasee receives transportation to the place of his approved postrelease residence, which can routinely be either the federal judicial district in which he was convicted or the district in which he had a bona fide residence prior to conviction. Transportation to an alternative destination may also be granted if there is evidence that this will provide the most preferred postrelease home or job opportunity for an individual.

Six states reported paying no cash gratuity to prisoners at release (Delaware, Hawaii, Maryland, North Dakota, South Carolina, and Virginia). As indicated, one should add Georgia to this group, since it pays some cash only if the prisoners provide their own clothing, while almost all other states provide free clothing. Michigan and Rhode Island issue gratuities only to dischargees and not to parolees. Six states reported usually paying less than $10 per releasee (Kentucky, New Jersey, Oklahoma, Pennsylvania, Tennessee, and West Virginia), while twelve paid between $10 and $20 and the remainder paid over $20. Texas reported paying $50 to dischargees, the highest routine gratuity reported, but only $5 to parolees.

Twenty-nine of the forty-two states that issue cash gratuities to releasees described their payment as a uniform sum to almost every prisoner, regardless of differences in need (this includes the three states with fixed sum payment to dischargees different from the payment to parolees). Eleven states reported some type of uniform formula for determining the amount of gratuity. In four of these states (Alabama, Louisiana, North Carolina, and Vermont) the formula makes the gratuity a function of time served, such as $1 per month in Vermont, or in Alabama, $10 for terms of up to five years plus $2 per year for every year served beyond five. In the seven remaining formula states (Kansas, Massachusetts, New Jersey, Pennsylvania, Rhode Island, Oregon, and Washington), the gratuity consists of the difference between some fixed sum ($10, $25, or $50) and the prisoner's savings (often compulsory) out of prison earnings. Only two states (California and Idaho) and the federal prisons reported highly variable gratuity payments which fluctuated on the basis of the prison's appraisal of an inmate's needs, rather than by a standard formula.

Money Earned in Prison

In all but six states, as well as in federal and District of Columbia prisons, inmates earn money while confined. In many states this is a more important source of cash at release than the gratuity. Many prison administrators consider earnings for work in prison preferable to gratuities as a way of providing financial assistance to prisoners at release, since the earnings provide an incentive to industrious behavior and give the inmate some pride in saving. In twenty-four states and in the federal and District of Columbia prisons a certain amount of saving from prison earnings is compulsory, to assure funds at release. The most frequent savings requirement is fifty per cent of earnings. These savings often are compulsory only until a particular balance is reached, ranging from $20 in Maryland to $100 in many federal prisons, although the latter make separate decisions on compulsory savings requirements in each case. A few states require a certain amount of savings per unit of time, ranging from 5 cents a day in Kentucky to $4 per month in Ohio. Wisconsin is unique in specifying only the maximum amount of prison earnings that can be spent per day, 25 cents, the remainder to be saved.

In only twenty states and the District of Columbia were ninety to one hundred per cent of the inmates reported to earn money in prison. In five states no more than ten per cent earn money. As observed in chapter 11, when only a fraction of the inmates can earn wages at their prison work, the jobs for which wages are paid are predominantly confined to those in prison industry because legislatures are more willing to grant funds for payment of such labor. Of course, the rates of inmate wage payment vary markedly, ranging from as little as 4 cents to over $1 per day. While even the latter seems ridiculously low by outside standards, the higher figure permits accumulation of several hundred dollars if half or more is saved over a period of a few years. Although North Dakota pays no release gratuity, 95 per cent of its prisoners earn money while in prison, and because they are required to save 90 per cent of their earnings until they accumulate $50, the *minimum* funds of North Dakota prisoners at release appear to be higher than those in any other state.

Average Resources at Release

When asked the average amount of cash from all sources issued to their inmates at release, twenty states reported that this figure was unavailable, but most of the remainder submitted rough estimations, and a few computed the exact average for a recent period. The highest average payment reported was $120, in Minnesota, but it should be recalled that prisoners in this state must pay their own transportation expenses from these funds. Massachusetts reported the next highest payment, of $80, but their prisoners also must pay for their own transportation. The lowest average amount reported was $6 in Tennessee and in Delaware, both of which provide transportation costs. Possibly several of the states not reporting an average figure issue less than $6. Georgia was the only state which reported that it neither permitted inmates to earn money while confined nor paid them a release gratuity (except for their issuance of up to $8 to those who provide their own release clothing).

All federal prisoners have some funds at release from prison. However, almost half of the cases in our Postrelease Panel sample had less than $50 available to them for immediate use upon release. Twenty-three per cent had between $50 and $100, 21 per cent had over a hundred dollars, and 9 per cent of the sample had five hundred dollars or more. The median amount of funds at release for all federal parolees and mandatory releasees in our sample was $56. Eighty-five per cent indicated that they had no savings anywhere outside the prison at the time of release. The fifteen per cent of the sample who reported such savings had a median amount of $433.

It is possible that some of these men reported savings from prison earnings which long-term prisoners are allowed to use for purchase of U. S. Savings Bonds for deposit in their name with civilian banks, or to send to relatives, who save it for them.

Stimulated by our early reports on economic problems of returned violators, one of the first projects of the U. S. Bureau of Prisons Research and Statistics Branch after its establishment in 1960 was a survey of the financial and employment resources of persons released from federal prisons. This showed that 94 per cent of federal prisoners received some money while confined and 70 per cent had some funds in their accounts at release, the median amount being $44. The maximum gratuity payment in federal prisons was $30, but funds were not available to give this to many. The Bureau of Prisons survey showed that 37 per cent of the federal prison releasees received no gratuity at all, 35 per cent received the then prevailing maximum of $30, and the average gratuity payment was $23. Those not receiving any gratuity presumably had adequate funds from saving prison earnings or from other sources. Of those who did receive a gratuity, 96 per cent had $50 or less in their personal account at the time of release and 48 per cent had no funds at all.[4]

Where an inmate's funds in the institution at release are in excess of one hundred dollars, the prison administration may elect to give him only part of the money at release. The balance is mailed to his probation officer, by a check which the releasee can pick up some weeks after he is in the free community. Seventy-seven per cent of those in our Postrelease Panel sample received the full amount of their prison funds at release. Ten per cent of the sample could look forward to checks of less than a hundred dollars, 8 per cent could expect between one hundred and three hundred dollars, and 5 per cent of the sample were sent amounts in excess of three hundred dollars. The median amount of these postrelease payments from prison savings was $135.

For the more than three-quarters of the sample who received all their money at release, the median payment was $47. Fifteen per cent received less than $30 at release, 49 per cent received between $30 and $60, and 32 per cent received between $60 and $100. Only 5 per cent received one hundred dollars or more in cash at the prison gate.

One aspect of these payments which may be of some interest is that funds issued at release from prison were almost identical for all racial groups. The median amount of total payments from all sources at release was $57 for whites and $55 for nonwhites.

---

[4] *The Financial and Employment Resources of Persons Released from Federal Institutions* (Washington, Research and Statistics Branch, U. S. Bureau of Prisons, January 1962).

JOB ARRANGEMENT BEFORE RELEASE

A traditional condition of parole is that the prisoner must have a bona fide job arranged before he is released from the prison. The parole board's release procedure generally is to issue an order authorizing the parole of an individual on a specific date if his parole plan is approved. The plan must state the residence and employment which the parolee will have, and in the federal system a parole adviser is also specified. Where possible, the prospective parole supervision office investigates the plan and reports on whether the proposed arrangements are approved. Usually the employer is required to sign a form agreeing to employ the prisoner on his release, but there is no way of enforcing this requirement.

In practice, it frequently is difficult for men still in prison to procure promises of satisfactory employment should they be released. As indicated in our chapter 11 on work in prison, inmates generally have little sustained work experience in the free community and few skills. They are predominantly from poor families and from broken homes, so that they are limited in the extent to which relatives can help to arrange jobs for them.

A consequence of this situation is that some men granted parole remain in prison long after their parole date, waiting to get a job. Alternatively, they procure promises of employment which are provided as a favor by their relatives or friends, who in fact are not in a position to employ them. Often the employers are small tradesmen who hire help only irregularly and cannot predict their employee requirements in advance for a period as long as the several weeks or months that often elapse between their promise and the prisoner's release on parole. Under these circumstances, when parolees come out of prison the promised jobs often are not available, are highly unsatisfactory in pay or other features, or are provided with the understanding that they are only temporary.

Outcome of Prerelease Jobs

Table 14.3 summarizes the outcome of prerelease arrangements for three samples of federal parolees whom we interviewed and for two samples of parolees studied by the Pennsylvania Board of Parole.[5] Only parolees are included in the federal tabulations here, to make them more comparable with the Pennsylvania sample. The differences between the Postrelease Panel figures and those for the other federal samples may reflect the fact that only the Panel was a purely urban sample. Also, the data on the Postrelease Panel cases were procured when the subjects were in their first month out of prison, while the postrelease circumstances of the returned violators and the successful releasees were recalled by the subjects when

[5] William L. Jacks, "Release on Parole with and without Employment," *Am. J. Correction*, 24, no. 6 (Nov.-Dec. 1962), 12-16.

TABLE 14.3 Outcome of Prerelease Arrangements for Postrelease Employment of Federal and Pennsylvania Parolees

| | PAROLEES | | | | |
| | FEDERAL | | | PENNSYLVANIA | |
Postrelease outcome of prerelease job arrangements	*Successful parolees*	*Returned parole violators*	*Postrelease Panel*	*1949 parole agent reports*	*1960 file data analysis*
Job secured	67%	60%	83%	70%	81%
Job lasted 90 days or more	49%	23%	34%	43%	56%
Job not available on releasee's arrival	23%	28%	12½%	19%	(not indicated)
Reason:					
"Job promise" only a favor to gain release	9%	8%	—	(reason not indicated)	—
Business conditions changed	14%	19%	11%		—
Other reason	—	1%	1½%		—
Job refused by releasee	10%	12%	4½%	11%	
Reason:					
Job or pay disliked	3%	1%	—	3%	3%a
Better job procured	4%	6%	3%	3%	20%a
Other reason	2%	3%	1½%	3%	22%a
No cause reported	1%	2%	—	3%	—
Total per cent not securing prearranged job	33%	40%	17%	30%	19%
Number of cases with prerelease job arrangements (base of above percentages)	142	144	71	427	354
Per cent of total parolees who had prerelease job arrangements	72%	75%	61%	not reported	83%

a Reason lasted less than 90 days.

they were interviewed one or more years after their release. It may be that in this longer retrospect, some short-lived jobs were regarded as not procured and some jobs that did not materialize were regarded as not arranged. A similar difference in perspective may explain the contrasts in findings of the two Pennsylvania studies. In their first survey, based on reports by parole agents, only 70 per cent were reported taking prearranged jobs, and only 43 per cent worked 90 days or more at the jobs; in their second study, based on parole supervision files, 81 per cent were reported as taking jobs, but only 56 per cent worked over 90 days. Presumably agents, looking back on case histories, might have reported some of those not working long at a job as not taking the job.

Dr. Nathan G. Mandel, Director of Research for the Minnesota Department of Corrections, made available to me a summary of findings by George Holland in an investigation of the initial placements of 200 state parolees released to the Minneapolis–St. Paul area between May 1959 and June 1960. Holland found that 17 per cent failed to show up at their prearranged job and 14 per cent were fired within a month due to their own negligence. He concludes, therefore, that 31 per cent of the placements were fruitless. However, 14 per cent were still employed at their prearranged job after one year. Of these 200 men, 32 were placed with the Salvation Army, in rest homes, or in other dependent situations, 107 were sent to unskilled jobs, 40 to semiskilled, and only 21 to skilled employment.

The most common cause of the failure of jobs to materialize was simply the employer's claim that conditions had changed between the time that he promised the job and the time when the releasee reported for the job. As Table 14.3 shows, an appreciable number of the successful releasees and returned violators actually admitted to us that their job arrangements were not bona fide, but were merely job offers procured through friends or relatives in order to promote an early parole. Possibly it was too soon after release for our Postrelease Panel cases to admit this. Table 14.3 covers only cases with prearranged jobs; 25 per cent of the returned parole violators, 28 per cent of the successful parolees, and 30 per cent of the Postrelease Panel parolees claimed they had no prearranged jobs.

Prerelease Job Arrangements and Recidivism

By January 1962, 21 per cent of the 193 released federal prisoners whom we interviewed at least once between November 1959 and June 1960 in our Postrelease Panel Study had been convicted of a felony, were reimprisoned, or were wanted for felonies or as parole or mandatory release violators. These 21 per cent we called "failures," in accordance with prior usage in this study. Table 14.4 indicates that whether or not these releasees arranged a job promise while they were in prison had no relationship to their failure rate. It is possible that release with a job is favorable, but that the parole board policy of releasing men without a job only when their prospects for postrelease assistance are outstanding equalizes the success prospects of those with and those without job arrangements at release.

The findings in Table 14.4 clearly suggest a lack of wisdom, from an individual case prediction standpoint, in traditional parole board practice or legislation which makes prerelease job arrangement a very rigid requirement for parole in all cases. Nevertheless, this leaves the parole board with difficult policy questions as to how freely they can issue waivers on the job arrangement requirement for parole without thereby discouraging prison inmates from making prerelease job procurement efforts. Indeed, the finding that lowest failure rates occur among those who seek a job while in prison but do not get it, if made the basis for parole selection, might encourage prisoners to fail deliberately in job search efforts. Unfortunately, we

TABLE 14.4 Prerelease Job Arrangements and Postrelease "Failure" of Federal Prison Releasees (Postrelease Panel Study)

Prerelease job arrangements or search, and postrelease job procurement	PAROLEES		MANDATORY RELEASEES	
	Per cent "failures"	No. of cases	Per cent "failures"	No. of cases
Job arranged and procured	22%	59	25%	4
Job "arranged" but not procured	17%	12	25%	4
Total job arranged cases	21%	71	25%	8
Job search, but no job arranged	14%	28	10%	20
No job search and no job arranged	29%	17	27%	49
Total no job arranged cases	20%	45	22%	69
Total cases	21%	116	22%	77

did not have information on the extent of job search efforts by those who succeeded in arranging a job while in prison. Table 14.4 prompts the hypothesis that those who get jobs by their own initiative are more successful than those for whom jobs are provided by friends or relatives, especially when these never were their former long-term employers.

Similar conclusions on the nonassociation of prerelease job procurement with postrelease success were reached in a Pennsylvania study of men "released to partial plans." The latter term is that state administration's designation for parole releases in which job, home, or other parole plan components are not all satisfactorily arranged in advance. The stumbling block in plan completion almost always is job procurement. A total of 238 parolees, who were a complete sample of Pennsylvania prisoners "paroled to partial plans" between December 1, 1959, and November, 1960, were followed up to May 31, 1961. At that time 84 per cent were in good standing and 16 per cent were delinquent, which were identical with the corresponding percentages for the state's entire parole system.[6] New York state had a similar experience with men given what that state calls a "reasonable assurance release," which is a parole without a job, granted when there is evidence that the man has a stable home or there is other indication that he can procure employment soon and not become a public charge.[7]

California's Special Intensive Parole Unit (SIPU) Experiment, described in chapter 17, has repeatedly compared parolees released without the prearranged job requirement to small parole-officer caseloads with parolees released with the usual job requirement, but to larger caseloads. The parolees released without the job requirement have regularly had as low or

[6] *Ibid.*

[7] Leonard R. Witt, "Parole Release Without Employment," *National Probation and Parole Assoc. J., 6,* no. 2 (April 1960), 170-74.

lower violation rates than those released with a job. In this case, of course, it is difficult to know whether or not the lack of job requirement had an unfavorable effect counteracted by a favorable effect of small caseloads.[8]

In data from the U. S. Board of Parole's study of the 322 persons committed to prison under the Federal Youth Correction Act during fiscal year 1954-55, we found that only 57 per cent had a job promise in their parole plan. However, of those who did not have a job promise, only 34 per cent succeeded on first parole, as compared with 43 per cent among those who had a job promise. This seems to suggest some special significance of prerelease job arrangements for youthful offenders. More adequate data on these cases, however, might reveal that this job arrangement is mainly an index of availability of family assistance for the youth, and is somewhat independent of actual employment on the postrelease job.

Jobs and "Overdue" Status on Parole

The requirement that a prisoner have a job before being released on parole often is a matter of law, although there usually is some provision for exceptions.[9] A consequence of this requirement is that inmates frequently are confined long after the date on which the parole board has declared them eligible for release by parole, if they have an approved parole plan. Without a job, these inmates have no approved plan, and become "overdue" parolees. Prisoners with few outside contacts and without highly marketable skills may linger for many months in prison after presumably "earning" their parole.

Parole authorities seem to relax the usual parole plan standards once men become "overdue" for parole, in an effort to get them out. This relaxation takes the form of waiving the job requirement, when this is legally permissible, or lowering the standards of acceptability for jobs. In the Pennsylvania study it was found that two-thirds of the men "released to partial plans" (without jobs) were held in prison past their parole date, over half of them more than twenty days.[10]

In 1959 one of our part-time staff members, Bruce K. Eckland, conducted a study of overdue parolees at the Federal Reformatory at Chillicothe, Ohio. He found that of 398 men paroled from that institution in the calendar year

[8] Ernest Reimer and Martin Warren, "Special Intensive Parole Unit," *National Probation and Parole Assoc. J., 3,* no. 3 (July 1952), 222-29; Joan Havel and Elaine Sulka, *Special Intensive Parole Unit Phase Three,* Research Report no. 3 (Sacramento, California Department of Corrections, 1962).

[9] For a summary of those laws see L. Stanley Clevenger and John M. Stanton, "Should an Inmate Have a Job Before Being Released on Parole," *National Probation and Parole Assoc. J, 6,* no. 2 (April 1960), 159-69.

[10] William L. Jacks, *Parolees Released to Partial Plans* (Harrisburg, Pa., Pennsylvania Parole Board [undated]), Table 3.

1958, 43 per cent were held one or more days beyond their effective date of parole. Twenty-two per cent of the men paroled from Chillicothe in 1958 were more than ten days overdue, and 14 per cent were more than twenty days overdue. In analyzing the principal contributing factors to the overdueness, he concluded that employment difficulties were involved in two-thirds of all overdue cases and in 91 per cent of those overdue for more than twenty days. Half of those held overdue because of no employment were finally released without employment arrangements, and many of the remaining half were released to clearly temporary and even questionable employment. This solution, of course, could just as well have been accepted at the time of parole eligibility. The following is one of many cases collected by Eckland which illustrates placement problems.[11]

The inmate, age 24, after a relatively delinquent career, received a 3 year sentence at a Federal reformatory for forging a thirty dollar check. He spent the greater portion of his incarceration assigned to the bakery vocational training program. In December of 1957, the institution wrote a letter to the inmate's married sister informing her that he would soon be appearing before the Parole Board and requested assistance in securing an offer of employment. There was no response to this letter.

Then, a few months later, in March, a letter was sent to the inmate's mother and step-father notifying them that he had been granted parole effective May 15 and requested their assistance in release plans. After a couple of weeks and no response, the matter was referred to the institution's Employment Placement Service. After another week had elapsed, the parents were again written inquiring whether any progress had been made.

In the meantime, the Placement Service, throughout the month of April, had been quite active in search for employment, with particular consideration to the inmate's training in the bakery. They sent out letters to various bakeries in his hometown, as well as to all the major industries there. After only a negligible response to these inquiries, letters were sent to several bakeries in another small city nearby.

Then on May 11 (four days before the effective release date) a reply was received from his mother stating that she had been unsuccessful. Five days later a letter was written to the mother requesting her to keep trying. On May 20 the placement service wrote the Mayor of the inmate's hometown soliciting his service in securing employment. Shortly after this, letters requesting employment were sent to five bakeries in a nearby metropolitan city.

Up to this time it had been assumed that the inmate would reside with his mother and step-father. However, on June 2nd a letter from the USPO was received which concluded that the parental home would not be conducive to a good parole adjustment, and suggested that the inmate's sister probably would provide his best opportunity. Thus, on the same day, the sister was written for the second time, requesting her assistance.

[11] Bruce K. Eckland, "Overdue Parolees in a Federal Reformatory," U. S. Bureau of Prisons *Progress Report, 8,* no. 1 (Jan.–March 1960), 5-14.

On June 5 the employment service wrote to a local restaurant union in the nearby metropolitan city seeking employment. On the following day, similar letters were sent to five hospitals in the same city.

Finally, on June 17, the institution received word from the sister stating that she and her husband would employ the inmate at interior decorating of their new home and provide him with a room, necessary transportation, and spending money until he could find a job on his own. The U. S. Probation Officer was informed immediately, and his approval of this plan was requested. This approval was received on June 25th, and the inmate was released on June 27th, 42 days overdue.

The foregoing case illustrates the large amount of effort expended by prison staff in often vain efforts to arrange a parole plan for a man still in prison. In addition to this cost of holding a man "overdue," there probably is a serious demoralization when every effort has been made to prepare a man for parole and he has eagerly anticipated freedom, only to linger day after day in uncertainty as to when he actually will be released. The last days of imprisonment are commonly known as the "longest" to the prisoner, when it is difficult for him to keep his mind on his prison work or training. Being "overdue" simply prolongs these longest of days.

INITIAL POSTRELEASE EMPLOYMENT

In our Postrelease Panel Study in 1959-60, our approximately monthly interviews with newly released federal parolees and mandatory releasees in four midwest cities revealed that almost a third were never employed in their first month out of prison. A sixth were never employed in their first three months out. These findings are summarized in Table 14.5.

The figures in Table 14.5, if they err, probably understate the amount of immediate postrelease unemployment of released offenders. For these figures, we defined as "employment" any job which the releasee believed to be "regular" when he was hired, even if he was fired at the end of the first day, and we also counted as "employment" any combination of odd jobs adding to fifteen hours or more or paying at least $25 in one week. Thus, some rather marginally employed men were counted as employed. Also, the sample from whom this job employment information was procured consisted of all those federal prisoners released for four or more months of supervision to Chicago, Detroit, St. Louis, and Cleveland in 1959-60, whom our staff was able to interview for three or more months.

The records indicated that those forty-eight releasees whom we were not able to interview for as much as three months after release, due to their absconding, being arrested, or missing interviews for other reasons, were more extensively unemployed than the 145 who reported for interviews regularly. (See Appendix C for details on the sample.) Therefore, the

TABLE 14.5   Rate of Employment of Federal Parolees and Mandatory Releasees During First Three Months out of Prison, and Relationship of Unemployment to Subsequent Success or Failure

Cases covered[a] and/or employment status	1st month after release[b]	2nd month after release[b]	3rd month after release[b]	First three months as a whole
Per cent of time employed during the period indicated (all cases):				
Never employed	31%	21%	25%	17%
1–19%	7%	3%	1%	4%
20–79%	35%	23%	10%	40%
80–100%	27%	52%	64%	39%
Per cent never employed among:				
Parolees (92)	22%	17%	23%	15%
Mandatory releasees (51)	47%	27%	29%	26%
Per cent never employed among:				
Subsequent successes (116)	27%	17%	20%	13%
Subsequent failures (29)	46%[c]	36%[c]	46%[d]	31%[c]

[a] Postrelease panel cases contacted for three months or more, of whom 29 were subsequent failures, i.e., returned to prison or wanted or convicted for felony without return to prison, within about two years after their release.

[b] Figures in this column are for two cases less than those in the "first three months as a whole" column, due to failure to record dates of employment in two cases, one a success case and one a failure case.

Differences as large as these would occur by chance, in samples of this size:

[c] less than once in ten times;

[d] less than once in one hundred times (by Chi Square test).

figures in Table 14.5 are a conservative estimate of unemployment in the first few months out of prison.

It will be seen from Table 14.5 that during the first month out of prison about one-third of the releasees had no employment, while barely a quarter were employed for 80 to 100 per cent of the time. During the second month out of prison over half the releasees worked 80 to 100 per cent of the time, and this proportion neared two-thirds in the third month out. However, many full-time jobs were temporary in nature, so that the number never employed did not decline from the second to the third month out, remaining above one-fifth of all the releasees in both these periods. Only two-fifths of the releasees were employed 80 to 100 per cent of their total first three months out of prison.

Mandatory releasees, in the federal system, are those denied parole, but released as though on parole for any prison-earned "good time" over 180 days. Unlike parolees, they do not require a prearranged job for release on their date of release eligibility. This probably accounts for their high rate of unemployment in the first month out, indicated in Table 14.5. Some convergence of parolee and mandatory release unemployment rates seems to occur after the first postrelease month.

Table 14.5 also indicates that the subsequent failures among the releasees whom we contacted were much more often unemployed in their first three months out of prison than were the subsequent successes. Indeed, after the first month out of prison the rates of unemployment were over twice as high for the failures as for those who were successful in avoiding further serious difficulties with the law. While this is not evidence that unemployment alone causes recidivism, it is one more piece of correlational data in our findings which suggest that unemployment may be among the principal causal factors involved in recidivism of adult male offenders. That this is not the only cause of failure is suggested by the fact that 44 per cent of the subsequent failures were employed full time in their third month out of prison. While this is less than the 68 per cent of the successes who were employed full time in this period, it also is noteworthy that 20 per cent of the subsequent successes were not employed in this third month out and 13 per cent were never employed in the first three months after their release.

Table 14.6 indicates the month after release from prison in which the releasees obtained their first job. While over ninety per cent had obtained

TABLE 14.6   Month Following Release in Which Federal Parolees and Mandatory
Releasees Acquired First Employment
(Postrelease Panel Study)

Month following release in which first job was found	No. of cases	No. and per cent of failures	No. and per cent of successes	Cumulative per cent with their first job, all cases
First month	99	15 (54%)	84 (73%)	69%
Second month	17	4 (14%)	13 (11%)	81%
Third month	3	—	3 (3%)	83%
Fourth month	9	4 (14%)	5 (4%)	89%
Fifth month or later	2	—	2 (2%)	91%
No job at last contact (median time out of prison 5.3 months)	13	5 (18%)	8 (8%)	
Total	143	28 (100%)	115 (100%)	100% (143)

a job at the time of our last contact with them, which in the median case was a 5.3-month postrelease check, the temporary nature of many of these jobs is indicated by the fact that the first job was not the only job obtained in this follow-up period for 52 per cent of those releasees who found some employment. The first job was the longest job in this period for only 18 per cent of those who found employment. However, of those employed in the first three months out, only 5 per cent averaged less than forty hours of work per week of employment, one-quarter averaged more than fifty hours of work per week, and almost one-fifth averaged over sixty hours of work in each week that they worked.

Although Table 14.6 reveals that failures experienced somewhat greater delay in procurement of the first job than successes, the major employment difference between these groups was that shown in Table 14.5. This consists of greater rates of unemployment for failures than for successes *after* the first employment, or specifically, progressively more frequent unemployment *after* the first month out of prison.

Type of Work Performed

The type of job procured by the newly released prisoners is, of course, a major factor in the steadiness of their employment. Our interviewers procured information on several aspects of each job lasting over a week held by the men in our Postrelease Panel Study. This covered a total of 251 separate jobs. Table 14.7 summarizes the nature of the work performed on these jobs, using a classification modeled on census categories.

TABLE 14.7   Type of Work Performed on Postrelease jobs
(Postrelease Panel Study)

Type of work[a]	First job	Jobs lasting over 2 months	All jobs
Professional, semiprofessional, manager or owner of business	8%	11%	6%
Craftsman or foreman	8%	5%	6%
Service worker	13%	15%	17%
Operative	39%	43%	41%
Unskilled heavy labor	16%	10%	16%
Menial or odd jobs	16%	17%	14%
Number of jobs covered in above analysis	129	103	251

[a] Examples of types of work included:
Professional, etc.: Manager or owner of business; any work requiring special education beyond high school.
Craftsman: Carpenter, machinist, electrician, painter, heavy construction equipment or heavy truck driver.
Service worker: Cook, waiter, salesman, gas-station attendant, cab driver, hospital attendant.
Operative: Semi- or unskilled factory machine tender, shipping or stock clerk, packing house labor, helper to skilled labor, light truck driver.
Unskilled heavy work: Dock worker, freight handler, construction laborer.
Menial or odd jobs: Dishwasher, janitor, car washer, pin setter, lawn work.

As might have been expected from the information presented in chapter 11 on prior work record of prisoners, the newly released men did not procure much skilled labor or white-collar employment. Their most frequent type of job was that of "operative," consisting predominantly of unskilled and semiskilled machine tending in factories, and various types of warehouse and storeroom work. Next in frequency were three other categories of employment—service workers, unskilled heavy labor, and menial or odd jobs—which were almost equally represented. These various types of unskilled and semiskilled jobs include the most unstable types of employment, and together they constituted five-sixths of the first jobs obtained by the releasees and seven-eighths of all jobs which they obtained in the first five or six months out of prison. Only the residual one-sixth of first jobs and of jobs lasting over two months were of a skilled or white-collar variety.

Table 14.8 compares the types of postrelease job procured by the successful releasees with the types procured by the returned violators. The

TABLE 14.8   Type of Work Performed on First, Longest, and Last Jobs by Successful Releasees and Returned Violators, and Interrelationship of These Jobs

	SUCCESSFUL RELEASEES			RETURNED VIOLATORS		
	First job	Longest job	Last job	First job	Longest job	Last job
Type of work performed						
Professional, semiprofessional, etc.	1%	3%	3%	1%	1%	1%
Sales or clerical	7%	8%	10%	9%	10%	9%
Skilled	23%	28%	26%	14%	16%	14%
Semiskilled (or helper to skilled) or light unskilled	48%	50%	48%	50%	50%	52%
Unskilled heavy labor	21%	12%	13%	27%	23%	23%

Median duration of longest postrelease job	13.4 months[a]	1.25 months[a]
Median postrelease period covered	20.2 months[b]	6.0 months[c]
Median number of jobs in this postrelease period	2.0[a]	1.1[a]
Overlap of first, longest, and last jobs:		
First job was only job	27%	48%
First job was longest of several jobs	15%	21%
Last job was longest of several jobs	39%	19%
Neither first nor last job was longest of several jobs	18%	12%
No. of cases covered in above analysis	238	244
Cases having no job lasting one week or more	12	64

[a] Does not count jobs of less than one week duration.
[b] From release date to date of our interview.
[c] From release date to date of violation.

major difference is that the successful releasees had skilled jobs almost twice as frequently as the returned violators. The successful releasees, of course, were in the free community longer, had more jobs, and therefore were able to move from unskilled heavy labor to other types of employment more frequently than could the returned violators.

It is difficult to say from the correlational data in Table 14.8 to what extent short employment was a cause of violation and to what extent it was a consequence of violation. This becomes clearly evident only when employment assistance is provided to releasees on an experimental basis, as in some of the remedies discussed in chapter 16.

Other Employment Surveys

The California Youth Authority made a special survey of every fifth male parolee under their supervision in May 1961, a total of 1432 youths. This group ranged in age from sixteen and one-half to twenty-four years. About half had been under parole supervision for over a year and the other half for less than a year. The following figures on employment apply only to the 71 per cent of their sample who were in the available labor force, in that they were not in school, in custody, hospitalized, under military supervision, or missing on parole. Of those 1020 young men who were presumed to be available for employment, 37 per cent were unemployed and 18 per cent had only part-time or intermittent employment, leaving only 45 per cent with full-time jobs. This figure is in contrast with concurrent U. S. Department of Labor estimates that 84 per cent of youth fourteen to twenty-four years of age in the nationwide labor force were employed. California labor force figures for this age group were believed comparable to the national figures.

The full-time employment rate of the California youthful parolees varied markedly with age, from 34 per cent for those in the labor force who were sixteen to seventeen years old, to 56 per cent for those twenty to twenty-four years old. There was also considerable variation by ethnic group; only 28 per cent of the Negro parolees were employed full time, another 21 per cent were employed part time, and 51 per cent were unemployed. This contrasted with 52 per cent employed full time and 17 per cent part time among the white parolees.[12] The relationship of employment to educational record for various age groups in the California sample were summarized in chapter 12.

I know of no comparable effort to tabulate systematically the employment record of adult parolees, although this information should be of crucial importance to any parole or probation supervision agency. Information on employment presumably is procured routinely by supervision officers, and it could be tabulated routinely with relatively simple reporting forms. Certainly if one-fourth to one-third of the men under correctional supervision in a community are unemployed, it is a major problem, and the heads of supervision agencies should watch closely to see if the figure can be reduced. It seems reasonable to infer from case data not only that employment affects a releasee's ability to support himself without recourse to crime but also that

[12] Joachim P. Seckel, *Employment and Employability Among California Youth Authority Wards: A Survey,* Research Report no. 30 (Sacramento, California, Department of the Youth Authority, August 31, 1962).

employment is a major influence on the nature of his associates, his use of leisure time, his conception of himself, and his expectations for the future.

In the Illinois Selective Service Felon Study, directed by Joseph D. Lohman, five hundred men paroled from prison to the U. S. Army during World War II were located and interviewed in 1951-53, and their military and current F.B.I. fingerprint records were procured. In a random sample of 176 cases from these 500, Dietrich C. Reitzes classified as "recidivists" the 26 per cent who subsequently received any conviction and sentence to jail or prison; he grouped as "borderline" the 15 per cent who had an arrest record but no jail or prison sentences; and the remaining 59 per cent he called "nonrecidivists." (Note: only that portion of the 26 per cent whose conviction was for a felony-like offense would fit the definition of postrelease "failure" employed in our study.) Reitzes found that only 14 per cent of the nonrecidivists had extended periods of unemployment, as compared with 62 per cent of the borderline cases and 41 per cent of the recidivists. Also, as might be expected, the nonrecidivists significantly more often than the recidivists progressed to more desirable types of employment, had successful marriages, maintained close relationships with their parental family, reported having friends, and belonged to organizations. Obviously the recidivism, and to some extent these other social conditions, may be causes of unemployment rather than consequences. However, it seems reasonable to infer that employment was usually a major factor making possible an integrated "style of life" which included nonrecidivism, successful marriage, and satisfaction in other social relationships.[13]

INITIAL POSTRELEASE INCOME

In trying to analyze the income of released prisoners, three distinctions are useful. The first is between cash income and intangibles, such as room and board. The latter will be considered later in this chapter in discussing the postrelease expenses of prisoners. The second major distinction is between earnings, that is, wages, salaries, or fees, and unearned income, such as gifts and loans. The third distinction is simply that of separating from the foregoing any residual or miscellaneous income, such as money from the collection of claims or from the sale of property. If these distinctions are kept in mind we can begin to make some order out of exceedingly complex data from our Postrelease Panel interviews.

Table 14.9 indicates the average cash income per month of the releasees in their first three months out of prison. It will be seen that the figures are exceedingly low during the first month out, with a median of only $80, but the median more than doubles in the second month out. Table 14.9's per-

[13] Dietrich C. Reitzes, "The Effect of Social Environment Upon Former Felons," *J. Crim. Law, Criminology and Police Science, 46,* no. 2 (July–August 1955), 226-31.

TABLE 14.9   Cash Earnings per Month of Federal Parolees and Mandatory Releasees
in First Three Months out of Prison, and Relationship to Subsequent
Success or Failure
(Postrelease Panel Study[a])

Sample and/or earnings	First month after release	Second month after release	Third month after release	Average monthly income in first 3 months
Total sample earnings:				
No earned income	30%	17%	24%	13%
$ 1–49	14%	10%	4%	10%
50–99	10%	8%	5%	10%
100–199	21%	20%	14%	27%
200–299	15%	22%	24%	23%
300–399	6%	14%	16%	10%
400–499	1%	4%	7%	3%
500 or more	2%	5%	6%	2%
Median monthly earnings:				
All cases	$80	$179	$204	$162
Parolees	$127	$200	$213	$179
Mandatory releasees[b]	$13	$145	$200	$129
Age 23 or younger	$75	$162	$158	$150
Age 24–35	$87	$164	$206	$154
Age 36 or older	$78	$215	$225	$183
Subsequent successes	$88	$188	$212	$175
Subsequent failures[b]	$42	$112	$38	$88

[a] This table is based on 135 cases of the "effective" sample (see Appendix C) for whom we had sufficient information to calculate average monthly cash earnings, out of 145 cases interviewed in their first three months or more out of prison. There were 27 failure cases and 108 successes for whom information on earnings was available.

[b] Differences as large as these would occur by chance in samples of this size less than once in 1000 times (by Chi Square test).

centages with no earned income are slightly lower than the percentages with no employment in Table 14.6, because of a few men who earned some money from odd jobs which were too meager to fit our definition of employment. It will be seen that the most frequent range of income for released prisoners was from $100 to $199 for the first month out of prison and from $200 to $299 in the subsequent months.

When comparing the median monthly earnings of parolees and mandatory releasees, one sees the same pattern that was apparent in comparing their rates of unemployment except that the earnings pattern is more pronounced. As Table 14.9 indicates, in the first month out of prison the median earnings of parolees were almost ten times those of mandatory releasees, but by the third month out their median earnings were almost identical.

The striking feature of Table 14.9 is the contrast between the income of successes and the income of failures. This difference in income was fore-shadowed, of course, by the data in Table 14.5, on the higher unemployment rates of the failures. Another striking feature of the failure cases is the sharp decline in their income from the second to the third month. We infer that this decline in income was a major factor in their subsequent return to crime. The validity of this influence can be tested well only by an experimental program, such as one in which a randomly selected group of releasees receive cash assistance, or possibly public employment, when unemployed, and the remainder act as a control group which receive no special assistance. A sharply lower failure rate in those receiving the special assistance would be expected on the basis of our inference from Table 14.9.

Gifts were reported as a source of cash income by 46 per cent of the men in our Postrelease Panel Study whom we contacted for three months or longer after they left prison, and loans were reported by 38 per cent of these men. The family was the source of about half of these gifts and loans. The median amount of cash income per month from these sources (for those receiving such income) was $12.80 for gifts and $13.10 for loans. We had the impression that some of the loans from family or close friends might more appropriately have been called gifts, as repayment of the exact amount by a particular date was not at all expected.

About a third of the releasees also reported miscellaneous cash income, such as proceeds from sale of possessions or collection of veteran's or welfare claims. Median income per month from all miscellaneous sources, for those with such income, was $37.

Totaling all types of income for each releasee, the median total cash income per month during the first three months out of prison was $195.65. Twenty-four per cent of the releasees averaged less than $100 per month cash income during this period, 28 per cent averaged between $100 and $199, 20 per cent averaged between $200 and $299, 15 per cent between $300 and $399, and 12 per cent averaged $400 or more. Of course, illicit income probably was not reported here. One parolee, who reported employment as a porter in a hotel and restaurant for $30 per week and meals, admitted at the terminal interview with us that he actually made additional money helping to run gambling operations at this establishment. However, it is unlikely that a major proportion of our subjects had such opportunities.

That the low income reported in Table 14.9 is mostly a consequence of unemployment is indicated by Table 14.10, on the actual rate of pay for those jobs of one week or more duration which these releasees were able to procure. It is difficult to state what constitutes an adequate rate of pay for a prison releasee, since needs vary with number of dependents, with the clothing and other economic resources available at release, and especially, with the releasee's standard of living.

Our returned violator cases indicate much variety in the significance of income for postrelease adjustment, even while employment is available. For example, a releasee whom we shall call "Henry" (V-106) had a wife

TABLE 14.10　Rate of Pay on Postrelease Job
(Postrelease Panel Study)

Pay per month[a]	First job	Jobs lasting over two months	All jobs
Under $100	2%	1%	2%
$100–199	24%	17%	21%
$200–299	43%	41%	39%
$300–399	17%	27%	18%
$400–499	7%	9%	11%
$500–599	4%	2%	5%
$600–699	2%	1%	2%
$700–799	1%	1%	1%
$800 or higher	1%	1%	(½%)
Median rate of pay	$258	$277	$268
Number of jobs covered in above analysis	122	94	234

[a] This is the beginning pay rate on the job; change in pay during the course of our contact was reported on 9 per cent of the jobs. In calculating rates of pay, nonmonthly pay rates were converted to monthly rates by counting 170 hours, 23 days or 4.3 weeks as equivalent to one month. Three per cent of the jobs covered above also provided meals, 2 per cent provided free residence, and 1 per cent provided room and board, none of which is covered in the above tabulations of monetary pay. Seventeen jobs with no pay rate information included some jobs with commission payment and some self-employment jobs, on which there was not yet enough experience to estimate income.

and four children to support, when they were denied further Aid to Dependent Children upon his return from prison. Henry was paroled with a gratuity of $28 and had a prearranged job driving a truck for his uncle at $1.65 per hour. Immediately he rented an apartment for his family, moving them out of the home of in-laws, and bought furniture for this on the installment plan. After several weeks he obtained a factory job as a spot-welder but was still able to drive the truck at night and on weekends. After three months he lost the welding job due to a lay-off and had only the truck-driving work. Meanwhile, his wife became pregnant again and then became ill, and he had to pay a neighbor to care for his children when he worked. His wife bore their fifth child, but remained ill. Between the medical bills, the installment payments, and the other extra expenses, he claimed he could not stretch his income to cover necessities. Henry was out for about a year before he returned to trafficking in narcotics, a quick-money temptation which he claimed he could not resist in his straitened circumstances.

Contrastingly, "Herbert" (V-073) had relatively liberal resources when he left Leavenworth by mandatory release after serving thirteen years on a twenty-year sentence for bank robbery. Prior to this he had been confined ten years for a similar crime. He had no dependents, and had a home at release with a married sister. His prison savings totaled almost nine hundred dollars, of which he used five hundred to pay a lawyer for successfully opposing the effort of another state to have him extradited on a warrant issued before his federal imprisonment. The remaining money was spent mostly on clothes. Soon after his release Herbert procured restaurant work at $1.25 per hour and rented a small apartment for himself. After about six months he was able to get building maintenance work at $2.50 per hour, was reported to be a flawless worker, and seemed to his supervision officer to be adjusting most successfully. However, Herbert said that as he looked around at how other men his age or younger owned their own homes, had new cars, and could live comfortably, he thought that he would feel "successful" only if he were able to own his own restaurant. A year after his release he contacted two men to help him rob a bank, but they were caught, he asserts, only because of the inexperience of his associates. From his past pattern, it seems likely that even if successful in this crime, he would have more readily been tempted back to another crime when he again craved more money, so that eventually this repeated risk-taking would have led to his capture.

One sees in Herbert's case a vicious cycle, described in chapter 18, in which impatience in "making up for lost time" in legitimate economic pursuits upon release ultimately motivates the releasee to return to crime. Each of the times that Herbert was apprehended for his return to crime he was given a longer prison sentence. He now will be a very old man if he lives long enough to be released again to try to "catch up" with those who have been free during his years of confinement. Fortunately, Herbert's pattern, return to crime even after clear success in legitimate employment, is relatively infrequent.

POSTRELEASE EXPENDITURES

Expectations of Expense

After ascertaining the job and pay expectations of our Prison Panel Study subjects, we asked: "In the situation that you expect to be in when you get out, what would be the smallest amount of money you'd need to have to get by for a month without a job right after you get out?" The responses which this elicited are summarized in Table 14.11.

As was expected, the older inmate populations, particularly Leavenworth, indicated a need for more money than the younger ones. This is consistent with youth's greater expectations of assistance from others, discussed in the next section of this chapter. The data in Table 14.9 suggest that actual income generally does not equal expected expenses in the first month out, except for the youth offenders, who expected little earned income and received little, but also anticipated few expenses.

During the course of imprisonment the sum which inmates thought they

TABLE 14.11   Median Sum of Money Which Inmates Say They Would Need as Minimum to "Get By" with for One Month in the Circumstances Which They Anticipate at Release, as Reported at Various Stages of Prison Term
(Prison Panel Study)

Prison	First week	Sixth month	Near release
Leavenworth	$127	$168	$124
	(60)*	(41[b])	(48[a])
Terre Haute	$ 96	$114	$ 24
	(49[a])	(35[a])	(36[b])
Milan	$ 98	$150	$140
	(60)	(36[e])	(44[f])
Chillicothe	$ 46	$ 78	$ 69
	(60)	(52)	(50)
Ashland	$ 47	$ 50	$ 16
	(53)	(28[f])	(50[a])

* Number in parentheses indicates number of subjects giving a definite response (basis for medians); letter indicates number of highly indefinite or "don't know" responses—e.g., a=1, b=2, etc.

needed to "get by with" for a month seemed to follow a U-shaped curve in all institutions; it increased in the first six months, then declined near release. The drop near release in the amount specified by Terre Haute inmates was especially large; most of them said they would need no more than $25 "to get by with" during their first month out of prison. This contrasts with medians of $124 and $140 near release at Leavenworth and Milan, and $69 at Chillicothe. Ashland inmates persistently and sharply dropped the amount of money they anticipated needing as their release date approached; of the near-release group, three-fourths specified less than $25.

We interpret the general pattern of near-release decline in perceived postprison financial need as a function of improved rapport between inmates and their parents or other kin, so that near release they expect more aid from these relatives than they did earlier in their prison term. Apparently the prisoners' conflicts with these relatives reach a climax with their arrest, conviction, and sentencing. This is consistent with findings presented in the next chapter regarding inmates' expectations from other persons. Of course, some decline in statement of needs may also reflect the inmates' more definite knowledge of postrelease jobs and homes. The latter is believed to be the major factor in the sharp drop in anticipated needs at Terre Haute, for, as indicated in Appendix B, Terre Haute inmates were seen at a date closer to their actual anticipated release date than any other institutional component of our near-release panel.

Spending for Pleasure

Our only other question on anticipated expenses dealt with the aspect opposite to that connoted by money needed "to get by"; it was concerned with the interests which might promote spending of money for pleasures rather than for necessities at release. This question was phrased: "What kind of enjoyment will you try to have as soon as you can when you get out?" The first responses to this inquiry are summarized in Table 14.12.

TABLE 14.12   Kind of Enjoyment to be Sought as Soon as Possible After Release (Prison Panel Study; 206 sixth-month and 248 near-release cases)

Kind of enjoyment	*Per cent*
Women, dates, dances, etc.	29
Drink, nightclubs, bars, etc.	13
Participation in sports or hobby	13
Movies, fairs, shows, etc.	12
Visiting with family or relatives	10
Special meals, eating out, etc.	5
Spectator at sports events	4
Watching television	2
Other kinds of enjoyment	4
None, won't have any, too busy, etc.	3
Don't know	4

The most frequent type of response at each of the five prisons, and the responses of a majority of the near-release inmates at the two youth institutions, indicated that the kind of enjoyment to be sought as soon as possible were activities with women. References to drinking and night club attendance, and to sports and hobbies, were rated second and third, and were almost equal in frequency. The hobby diversions ranged from working on their cars to fishing.

Women and wine pursuits, of course, can play havoc with the best-planned budgets. They serve ego needs in a manner which makes their fulfillment seem a matter of extreme urgency to these men, especially the youth. This pattern points up the particular importance of continuous post-release budget guidance, disbursing accumulated savings to parolees on a gradual basis, and friendly surveillance. Communication of adults with youth in an effort to lengthen the time perspective of youth, to set reasonable limits, and to assist in their social maturation seems imperative but is not easily accomplished in the time available to a supervision officer. Therefore, emphasis should be given to postrelease placement, preferably in a home, job, and community, which may facilitate a satisfying and orderly social life. The prerelease guidance centers described in chapter 16 permit officials to graduate carefully the youth's transition from the restrictions of confinement to the indulgences of freedom, to reduce the financial strain of this transition, and to provide continuous counseling in the course of this transition.

A kind of enjoyment mentioned with moderate frequency at the adult prisons was visiting with family or relatives, yet this was not mentioned at all in the near-release interviews at the youth institutions. This is interesting in the light of data to be presented in chapter 15, suggesting that as the prison term progresses the youthful inmate increasingly is reconciled with his close family and expects postrelease help from them. Perhaps the relatives are looked to by youth more exclusively as an economic resource, with social relationship satisfactions to be sought elsewhere, while older prisoners value relatives as a major source of social acceptance as well as for their economic assistance.

Many not easily explained differences between institutions were found in inmate reports on the enjoyment which they would seek as soon as possible after release. Chillicothe inmates stressed drinking and nightclubbing twice as frequently as inmates of any other institution. While all prison populations, particularly those of the youth prisons, made frequent reference to activities with women, this declined between the sixth-month and the near-release interviews at every prison except Ashland; at Ashland it more than doubled in this period. *Participation* in sports or hobbies was desired most at Leavenworth and at Ashland; but *observation* of sports events also was desired several times as often by Leavenworth inmates near release as by any other institution's inmates. Assertion that the first enjoyment they would have would consist of having good meals or eating in nice places, and other reference to food, increase between the sixth-month and the near-release interviews at Leavenworth, Terre Haute, and Chillicothe, but food was never mentioned at either interview in Milan or Ashland.

Room and Board Expenses

From the figures on postrelease cash earnings presented earlier in this chapter—such as a median earned income of $80 in the first month out of prison, and 30 per cent having no cash earned income in the first month out—it seems obvious that most releasees have some noncash resources when they leave prison. Without this, they could not even survive a month.

Our records indicate that half of the new releasees paid no rent at their first residence, generally because they were living with relatives. (Note that median time at this first residence, as indicated in chapter 15, was only slightly over two months.) Actually, a majority of these men indicated that they expected to pay rent at this first postrelease abode as soon as they had enough income, but 19 per cent indicated not even a future obligation to pay. The half who did not pay rent were included primarily in the 28 per cent who resided with one or both natural, step-, or foster-parents, the 23 per cent who lived with other relatives, and the 32 per cent who lived with their wives, with or without additional relatives or in-laws. For those who reported payment of cash for rent only, not for board, the median rate of payment was $15.77 per week at the first place of residence.

Thirty per cent of our reports on cash payments for rent, at our post-release interviews, were reports on lump-sum payments for room and board together. Furthermore, the releasees who received rent free usually acquired their food free also. We therefore combined food and rent figures for everyone in order to have a single tabulation of these expenses for all releasees. This is summarized in Table 14.13, which indicates the total amount spent by our sample for room and food during the period covered, which in the median case was the first 5.3 months after release from prison.

Table 14.13 indicates that in the first few months out of prison the median monthly expenditure for food and rent was $87. Twenty-nine per cent of these releasees paid less than $50 per month and a total of 58 per cent paid less than $100. The expenditures for rent and food increased with income, of course; the median cost of these items was only $64 for those with less than $150 of cash earnings per month but was $131 for those who earned $300 or more per month. The other major correlates of increased expenses were age and race, expenditures being higher for whites than for nonwhites and much less for youthful than for older releasees.

Prerelease Indebtedness

Three-eighths of our Postrelease Panel sample reported prerelease indebtedness which they expected to repay. The median indebtedness was $470, but the reported amounts ranged from $18 to $290,000. The description of releasees in terms of indebtedness suggested two clusterings: 20 per cent had debts of under $500 and 17 per cent had debts of $500 or more.

It is of interest to differentiate debts which are in one way or another the result of the offense from other types of preincarceration debts. Debts directly related to the offense include all money owed for restitution and fines and, where the offense involved the failure to pay a tax, debts for taxes. Indirectly related to the offense, but certainly a result of it, are debts for legal defense, for bail or bond, and some debts for family expenses incurred during the man's imprisonment. We designated all other debts as preincarceration debts.

Only about a third of the men in our postrelease sample who reported indebtedness cited debts directly related to their offense. A tenth reported debts indirectly related to the offense. However, of the men whose indebtedness amounted to five hundred dollars or more, five-eighths had debts di-

TABLE 14.13 The Cost of Necessities
Percentage distribution of average monthly expenditures of cash for housing and for food, combined, in the immediate postrelease period
(Postrelease Panel Study)

Average expenditures per month for housing and food combined	All cases	AVERAGE EARNED INCOME PER MONTH			WHITES				NONWHITES			
		Less than $150	$150–$299	$300 or more	Age 23 or younger	24–35	36 or older	Total whites	Age 23 or younger	24–35	36 or older	Total nonwhites
Less than $50	29%	42%	26%	11%	73%	16%	3%	27%	75%	36%	12%	31%
$50–99	29%	29%	29%	30%	14%	26%	31%	24%	25%	21%	52%	34%
$100–199	31%	27%	35%	30%	14%	39%	45%	34%	—	36%	24%	27%
$200 or more	11%	2%	10%	30%	—	19%	21%	15%	—	7%	12%	8%
Median average monthly expenditure	$87	$64	$92	$131	$34	$118	$144	$97	$33	$83	$86	$77
No. of cases on which above analysis is based (information deficient on others)	143	48	57	27	22	31	29	82	8	28	25	61

rectly from the offense and 15 per cent had debts indirectly from the offense. Nevertheless, most of these men also had debts dating from before their incarceration, and often from before their offense, which were in no way consequences of their offense. As might be expected, those with large debts were predominantly over thirty years of age, while those with debts of less than five hundred dollars were under thirty.

Clothing as a Postrelease Expenditure

As indicated earlier, almost every prison in the United States provides prisoners with some type of civilian apparel upon release, so that they may resume life in the free community not wearing a prison uniform. This also is presumed to reduce the immediate economic needs of the releasee and thus help him to become self-sufficient without recourse to crime.

The type of clothing provided at release varies considerably. In many state prisons the manufacture of clothing for inmates of state institutions is an important prison industry, and this manufacture frequently includes release clothing for prisoners. The main item of clothing issued often is a business suit, tailor-made at the institution, presumably to fit the releasee's measurements. A set of work clothes may also be provided, and a few changes in socks and underwear. Many institutions, however, realize that prisoners, particularly the younger ones, are not used to wearing business-type suits, so they provide slacks and jackets. In the winter months, in the colder areas of the country, overcoats and hats also are provided, and sometimes raincoats and water-repellent hats are provided in the summer.

The quality of this clothing varies greatly. Frequently the prison suits and coats are made from cheap cloth, which wrinkles easily. Much of it is ill-fitting, partly due to the incompetence of inmate tailors, sometimes due to the indifference of prison staff. It is common inmate talk, both in state and federal prisons, that payment of a few packs of cigarettes to inmates working in the release clothing unit is necessary to assure a first-class fit. While this may occur, it is probably not nearly as universal as inmate talk suggests. Because of the dangers that an inmate will use release apparel to escape from the prison by posing as an employee, the custody and distribution of this clothing is closely supervised by prison staff.

Regardless of the quality of prison clothing, inmates and released prisoners frequently complain that it makes them identifiable as ex-convicts. Sometimes they actually are identifiable by their manner, when still in the immediate vicinity of the prison or on the major route from it, and perhaps they ascribe to the clothes their self-consciousness and discomfiture. Releasees, however, also complain of the limited choice in style, cloth, and coloring in prison-issued clothing. To resolve these problems, the federal prisons have not attempted to manufacture all release clothing provided for prisoners, and they allow inmates a considerable choice of apparel. This usually takes the form of a "point system." For example, at Terre Haute an inmate could select clothing totaling 240 points, with a suit counting 150 points, sports coats and jackets from 35 to 105 points, trousers 23 to 50 points, shirts 11 to 20 points, shoes 36 to 50 points, underwear 5 points, and so forth. In this fashion, some inmates select primarily sports clothes, some stress work clothes, and others concentrate on more formal clothes. Some concentrate on quantity and some on quality of clothing selection. An overcoat is provided point free in winter months and one set of underwear is point free. The release clothing room has display cases where inmates may place their orders some weeks before their release. The available selection of clothing never approaches the variety found in a large commercial shopping area, since volume of business never suffices to warrant elaborate stocks, but anyone can be outfitted by the prison in what most objective persons would consider a reasonably adequate manner.

Of course, the releasees do not have to rely on prison-issued clothing exclusively, and may even reject it entirely. Prisoners may have civilian clothing sent them when they are nearly ready for release, and it is then issued to them just before they depart from the prison. Sometimes inmates are met at the institution by relatives or friends who bring the inmate a change of clothing to wear home. When confinement is not for a long period and the inmate does not change greatly in weight, his preprison wardrobe may still be usable if someone has taken care of it for him. At Terre Haute the inmates were charged points for clothing sent in for them, thus reducing the amount of prison-issued clothing they received, so that funds for release clothing could be extended to provide more liberally for those without such outside resources.

Since satisfaction with the release clothing is an aspect of the inmate's immediate economic resources on release, as well as a possible index of his attitude, we asked all releasees whom we interviewed how they utilized the clothing issued in prison. With the returned violators and successful releasees, the median time between release from prison and our interview was about two years. Their reports on their utilization of their release clothing are summarized in Table 14.14.

TABLE 14.14   Use of Prison-Issued Release Clothing by Returned Violators and Successful Releasees

Use of clothing	Returned violators	Successful releasees
Discarded as soon as possible	53%	34%
Retained and used	45%	58%
Retained but did not use	2%	8%
No. of cases covered	308	250

It will be seen from Table 14.14 that over half the returned violators discarded their release apparel as soon as possible. About a third of the successful releasees also discarded this clothing. The difference in these percentages suggests that the success of the latter group may have been, in part, a consequence of their more cautious husbanding of such economic resources. Nevertheless, the distinctive feature of these findings is that a large proportion of both groups failed to retain clothing which the institution made great effort to procure for them.

In our interviews it became apparent that there was considerable diversity of opinion on the prison-issued clothing in both the successful and the violating groups. Some releasees were quite satisfied with this clothing and used it until it wore out. At the time of our interviews several of the successful releasees were wearing the clothing that they received at the prison. Several who were interviewed at home brought the prison-issued clothing forth from their closets. In other cases releasees justified discarding the clothing on grounds that the clothes reminded them of prison. Men released from Leavenworth repeatedly told of a used-clothes dealer who met the bus bringing them to Kansas City, spotted the released prisoners readily, and talked them into trading in their prison clothing for other used clothing which he sold cheaply. There was some suspicion that he merely sewed commercial labels on prison-issued clothing which he purchased from other releasees.

We also asked about the prison-issued clothing in our first interview with each man in our Postrelease Panel Study. These interviews, in the median case, occurred when the men were only four days out of prison. Five per cent reported that they had already discarded the clothing, 9 per cent that they did not expect to use it any longer than necessary, and 4 per cent that they never accepted this clothing at the prison. However, four-fifths of the men at this time reported that they had worn the clothing and expected to continue wearing it.

One example of striking failure of the prison issue to satisfy a man was Postrelease Panel Case 090, whom we shall call "Alexander." When released from Leavenworth, he had $70. He expected to return to Chicago to live with his wife and two children in the home of his in-laws, but he expressed great concern with securing separate housing for his family as soon as possible. He was also anxious to save enough money to buy a small truck, in order to resume a trucking business. However, he had no funds other than $70, at release, and only a somewhat indefinite day labor job offer. Nevertheless, Alexander stopped at Kansas City and spent $60 on a suit, arriving in Chicago with only one dollar from the $70 with which he was released. He kept the prison-issued suit, but only to work in. For the "front" which he felt he needed when meeting his friends and family in Chicago, the prison suit was of no use.

Men in our Postrelease Panel sample did not keep detailed or precise records with which to answer our questions on their expenditures. Our interviews were approximately a month apart, which is a rather long period for remembering the details of one's utilization of money, except for major purchases. In addition to regular questions on room and board costs at each interview, we asked specifically about other "major purchases" at the first, second, third, fifth, and terminal interviews. The responses to these questions do not tell us reliably the exact totals spent by the releasees for clothing, but they indicate the relative frequency with which clothing was considered one of the major purchases. Clothing was mentioned in this connection more often than any other item—it was cited by 78 per cent of the interviewees, including over 90 per cent of the subjects who were 23 years of age or younger when released. Clothing obviously is a major postrelease expense on which many releasees could benefit from financial assistance. Yet assistance in the form of clothing issues at the prison proved a wasteful measure, since so many shun the apparel issued there.

Obviously, more efficient utilization of release assistance funds would be possible if one could minimize the amount expended for clothing destined to be discarded anyhow. Retired Assistant Director Loveland, in correspondence on this problem, comments:

A number of years ago we made a study of the problem since it appeared that releasees from some institutions were selling their clothing as soon as possible after discharge. The study included the probation officers and inmates in the institutions. It was following this study that clothing "stores" were placed in the institutions, that a committee was formed to improve the quality and increase and improve the cloth patterns, and institutions were permitted to purchase a number of articles of clothing from private sources. I believe that the number who retain their clothing can be increased by further efforts in this direction.

Possibly inmates with appreciable funds could be permitted to order some clothing from mail order catalogues before release, in lieu of, or in addition to, regular prison issue.

Automobiles as Postprison Necessities

As might be expected, a frequent item in the responses to our Postrelease Panel questions on major expenditures were reports of money paid for purchase or maintenance of automobiles. On the terminal interview with each of the releasees in this group, who in the median case were 5.3 months out of prison, we asked a number of specific questions regarding the automobiles purchased.

Table 14.15 shows the distribution of automobile ownership in the postrelease period for this sample. One striking feature is that the purchase of automobiles was very distinctly a characteristic of white rather than non-

white releasees. It was also somewhat more pronounced among the young
white than among the older white releasees.

TABLE 14.15   Federal Parolees and Mandatory Releasees Owning Automobiles in
First Five or Six Months out of Prison, by Age and Race
(Postrelease Panel Study)

	WHITES				NONWHITES				All cases
	23 or younger	*24–35*	*36 or older*	*Total*[a]	*23 or younger*	*24–35*	*36 or older*	*Total*[a]	*All cases*
Owns automobile	55%	54%	44%	51%	14%	4%	29%	15%	35%
Does not own automobile	45%	46%	56%	49%	86%	96%	71%	85%	65%
Number of cases	20	28	27	75	7	27	21	55	130[b]

[a] Differences as large as those between white and nonwhite rates of automobile ownership could occur by
chance, in samples of this size, less than once in a thousand times (by Chi Square test).

[b] Omits 14 cases not interviewed on the terminal interview form (which had questions on automobile ownership) because a further interview was expected, and one case in which the automobile section of the form was
left blank.

Whether an automobile is a necessity or a luxury could be debated. For
many individuals who lived in areas of poor public transportation or worked
at jobs not readily accessible by public transportation, the automobile was a
requirement for employment. Since nonwhites lived disproportionately in
the central sections of large cities, while whites lived in the more outlying
sections, nonwhites generally were closer to public transportation facilities
than whites. Of course, for the youthful whites particularly, and to some
extent for all releasees, the automobile served not just as a means of transportation but also as a means of expressing social status and independence.
It should be noted that 30 per cent of the whites in the sample, and 68 per
cent of the whites under 24 years of age, were sent to federal prison for
interstate transportation of a stolen auto. Only 10 per cent of the nonwhites were sentenced for this offense.

That the automobile is a major economic burden on the releasee becomes
apparent from the fact that half of those owning automobiles were making
payments on them at the time of the terminal interview. The median
monthly payment on the automobiles was $48. Eleven per cent of these
automobiles were the model of the current or preceding year, another 11 per
cent were three or four years old, and the remaining 78 per cent were
models of five or more years prior to the date of our interviews. Over 90
per cent of the releasees obviously exercised some caution in their purchase
in that they bought used automobiles rather than new ones. Nevertheless,
auto expense is a major concern for rehabilitation efforts with these prisoners, because of the financial strain caused by an automobile purchase,

particularly when postrelease employment is insecure for most of these releasees. Also of concern are difficulties with the law which automobiles may facilitate. A number of the youthful returned violators whom we studied were returned to prison, in part, for repeated vehicle offenses, including driving without a license, reckless driving, and drunken driving, for which they received fines and jail sentences.

Postprison Indebtedness

For information presented thus far on postrelease expenses, it becomes evident that economic strain from the cost of living in the first few months out of prison comes not so often from buying necessities of life as from paying large and burdensome expenses, such as clothing, preprison debts, or automobiles. The latter, as well as some clothing and furniture purchases, frequently led to postprison indebtedness, as the needy releasees are highly vulnerable to the appeals of installment selling. This mode of purchasing is especially dangerous for them because of the insecurity of their employment. Parole rules often forbid parolees to incur debts without the approval of their parole officer, but these rules are difficult to enforce.

In our interviews with successful releasees, some of the clearest illustrations of release benefit from parole supervision services involved assistance in budgeting and intervention with creditors. Several U. S. Probation Officers, notably Mrs. Sally Hanes in Springfield, Illinois, spent much time with each releasee working out a detailed budget and checked regularly on the success of budgeting efforts. Where releasees got themselves into severe financial difficulties, these officers intervened with creditors to prevent garnisheeing of wages that would jeopardize the parolee's job, or to prevent seizure of the purchased goods. In several cases the officers renegotiated installment purchase contracts for the parolees, procuring a reduction of excessive charges. In some instances, under these conditions, the parolee was required to report to the officer after each pay check and to make the budgeted payments on his debts at this time. Repeatedly this procedure led to solvency and self-sufficiency before the end of the parole period for men who had appeared earlier to be in desperate economic distress and, as a consequence, likely to violate their parole. Similarly, in the prerelease guidance centers described in chapter 16, much of the benefit apparent in the almost daily counseling sessions seems to come from the rationality in money management which the men develop in these sessions, at a time when they acquire their first postprison earnings.

POSTPRISON JOB PROCUREMENT

To conclude our discussion of the economic prospects of released prisoners, it may be appropriate to examine how they procure employment, the factors affecting their loss of employment, and their efforts to cope with unemployment.

Information on the sources of 238 jobs lasting one week or more was collected from the men in our Postrelease Panel Study. As indicated in Table 14.16, a majority of these jobs were procured through personal

TABLE 14.16   The Sources of Postrelease Jobs
(Postrelease Panel Study)

Source	First jobs	Jobs lasting over two months	All jobs
Personal relationship			
Referred by friend	16%	19%	21%
Rehired by former employer	19%	19%	16%
Referred by relative	20%	17%	15%
Referred by former employer	1%	3%	1%
Total	56%	58%	53%
Correctional or social-work agency			
Referred by private welfare or religious agency	7%	5%	5%
Prison employment placement office	2%	2%	1%
Referred by probation officer	4%	—	3%
Total	13%	7%	9%
Public employment procedures			
"Picked employer cold" and requested job	8%	8%	11%
Newspaper advertisement	7%	4%	8%
Private employment agency	5%	6%	5%
Public employment agency	5%	4%	4%
Total	25%	22%	28%
Other			
Self-employed	5%	9%	5%
Other	2%	3%	5%
Number of jobs covered in above analysis	120	99	238

relationships rather than by recourse to official agencies. Friends, relatives, and former employers were the major job sources. The interview accounts suggest that whenever these releasees needed employment, their procedure was to contact everyone who they knew was working, asking if his employer was looking for more men or if he knew of anyplace else that was hiring. Leads on possible job opportunities also were voluntarily conveyed to the unemployed releasees by their friends and relatives. Apparently, when these informal procedures failed to yield employment, the releasees were most likely simply to make the rounds of large firms or other possible employers on a "hunch" basis. This direct confrontation of a prospective employer was involved in more job placements than were any of the formal mediators between employee and employer, such as public or private employment agencies or correctional officials.

Reliance on personal relationships in job procurement appears to be a common characteristic of the poorer segments of our population, particularly those in unskilled or semiskilled employment. This pattern also has been found in the job search activities of manual workers who were not burdened by a criminal record.[14] Indeed, a significant contribution to the reduction of unemployment among released prisoners might result from programs promoting greater rapport and cooperation between them and the public employment agencies. In several large cities parole supervision officials have achieved this through coordinated efforts with the state employment service, which has assigned selected staff to specialize in aiding ex-convicts. In the prerelease guidance centers described in chapter 16, extensive personal assistance by each center's specialist in unemployment and counseling, facilitated by his small caseload, has made these youthful releasees strikingly successful in their job searches. By utilizing both public employment agencies and their personal contacts, the parolees released through these centers maximized their probabilities of encountering someone interested in hiring them.

DISCLOSURE OF CRIMINAL RECORD AND JOB SECURITY

A unique problem in the job search of a released prisoner is the burden of his criminal record. When asked for his employment history, how should he account for the time spent in prison? If asked point-blank whether or not he has a criminal record, should he lie, for fear that disclosure will result in his being denied the job, or should he tell the truth, for fear that revelation of his criminal record after he is employed will cause him to be discharged for lying about it? If he is not asked about prior criminality, should he voluntarily reveal it?

There seems to be little consensus as to the extent to which honesty about

14 A follow-up of employees discharged by the closing down of the Packard automobile plant in Detroit revealed that most of those who had found new employment procured their new jobs through personal contacts. See: Harold Sheppard and Louis Furman, *Too Old to Work, Too Young to Retire* (Detroit, Wayne State University Institute of Labor and Industrial Relations, 1962). (This is a reissue of a report of the U. S. Senate, Special Committee on Unemployment Problems, dated December 21, 1959, and printed in Washington by the Government Printing Office, 1960.) Indirect evidence of the emphasis on personal relationships in hiring also is provided by a study of employer hiring practice, which revealed that a majority of new personnel hired by industrial plants are procured by "direct gate hiring" and by recommendations of employees, friends of management personnel, and other employers, rather than through the use of employment services. See: Murray Edelman, *Channels of Employment* (Urbana, University of Illinois Institute of Labor and Industrial Relations, 1952).

the criminal record is the most rewarding policy for an ex-prisoner. When this issue is argued by correctional officials, some make moral assertions that officials should never advocate lying, but others argue that it is the parolee's affair, and even rationalize parolee deception in this matter. In one federal judicial district in which we interviewed, the Chief U. S. Probation Officer considered it a public obligation of his office to inform any employer when one of his employees was under supervision for a federal offense. In most other districts, care was taken to avoid making a parolee's record known to the employer, especially if the parolee cooperated in proving his regular employment to the U. S. Probation Officer by showing his pay-check stubs.

Most of the nonmoralistic argument on disclosure of criminal record consists of generalizations phrased in quantitative terms but based on illustrative cases rather than statistics. On this issue, however, one can find cases to illustrate every position. Some releasees have been denied employment because of their criminal record, but some have been hired by sympathetic employers because of their honesty in reporting criminal records. Some employers justify a policy of hiring ex-prisoners in terms of public responsibility, or cite cases where men aware of handicaps in getting a job showed exceptional loyalty to those who "took a chance" with them; other employers have tales of ex-convict employees who proved undependable. Many ex-prisoners, especially the returned violators, have tales of discharge from jobs when their criminal record was disclosed, and this has often been confirmed by supervision officers, but there also are numerous instances of men being employed despite their criminal record. Many tales suggest that the probability of getting a job is reduced if information on the criminal record is volunteered in applying for employment, but other accounts suggest that men generally will be retained in employment, despite company policy against hiring ex-convicts, if they establish a good work record before their criminal record is revealed.

Some releasees comment on the comfort of knowing they have nothing to hide, if they reveal their record when applying for work, but others complain of the discomfort of knowing that everyone at the job is aware of their record. Also, there are numerous tales of the ex-convict employees being unjustly blamed for every theft at their place of employment. As illustrated in the cases cited in chapter 4, many of the most successful releasees whom we encountered, with many years of distinguished performance in clearly legitimate employment, live in morbid fear that disclosure of their criminal record will destroy the good reputation which they have acquired.

Our interviews conveyed the impression, discussed in chapter 15, that the psychological burden of a criminal record was predominantly a function of the releasee's social relationships in his neighborhood and varied with his socioeconomic status. In the poorest and most disorganized slum neighborhoods, where criminality was widespread, a criminal record was not a major burden. However, the record was a source of shame if the releasee came from, or entered into, a more stable working-class or middle-class neighborhood. When the releasee was employed in the neighborhood of his residence, as in local restaurants, hotels, and service stations, or when he developed close personal relationships with his coworkers, his concern about the impact of the criminal record on the job was similar to his feelings about its impact on his residential neighborhood.

A survey of employer attitude toward hiring ex-convicts in the Greater Pittsburgh area in 1959 indicated that the greatest employment opportunities for ex-convicts were at skilled and semiskilled jobs and at typing. The white-collar job opportunities were primarily with the larger companies, employing from 1000 to 5000 men. When employers qualified their expression of willingness to hire ex-convicts by excluding certain offenses, they most commonly specified murder, sex offenses, narcotics offenses, and drunkenness, apparently unaware that murderers and rapists statistically are more likely to have a successful postrelease record than almost any other type of offender. Most employers stated that they would like to know of the criminal record on hiring a man and that the record would not prevent their employing a man but would prevent them from hiring him for certain responsible positions. However, they indicated a willingness to promote ex-convicts to more responsible positions on the basis of experience with them as employees.[15]

An optimum test of the consequences of criminal record disclosure in job procurement might result from an experiment in which several persons applied for employment with many employers, reporting a criminal record to a randomly selected half and not reporting it to the remainder. I have failed in several efforts to persuade agencies to arrange such an experiment, but some nonexperimental information on the extent to which criminal record is disclosed, and its consequences, was provided by our inquiries on this matter with the releasees in our Postrelease Panel sample.

Table 14.17 indicates that the criminal record was known at a majority of jobs of more than one week's duration held by these releasees in their first five or six months out of prison. Where the criminal record was known, it most often was known only to the employer or to certain executives,

---

[15] Gerald M. Farkas, "Industrial Employer Attitudes Toward Hiring Men with Criminal Records," *Personnel Administrator, 6,* no. 4 (July–August 1961), 6-7. A well-written impressionistic account of employment problems of men with prison records, by a former employment placement officer of the federal prison service, will be found in: Arthur F. Lykke, *Parolees and Payrolls* (Springfield, Ill., C. C. Thomas, 1957). For a British survey of employer attitudes, see: J. P. Martin. *Offenders as Employees* (London, Macmillan, 1960).

TABLE 14.17   Awareness of Releasee's Criminal Record at His Postrelease Job
(Postrelease Panel Study; all jobs of at least one week's duration)

Aspect of awareness	First jobs	Jobs lasting over two months	All jobs
Criminal record not known by anyone at the job	33%	35%	41%
Criminal record known only by relatives or old friends at the job[a]	9%	13%	12%
Only employer, manager, or other executives know of criminal record	34%	29%	27%
Only one or more coworkers know of criminal record	3%	1%	3%
Employer or executives *and* coworkers know of record	21%	22%	17%
Total jobs covered in above analysis (100%)	112	86	223

Source of knowledge of criminal record[b]

	First jobs	Jobs lasting over two months	All jobs
Informed by person or agency referring subject for the job	51%	44%	38%
Subject told them in applying for the job	18%	31%	31%
Subject worked there before prison	20%	11%	14%
Other sources of information[c]	11%	13%	15%
Number of jobs covered in above analysis (100%)	65	45	104

[a] Includes cases where relative or old friend is employer or manager.

[b] On jobs where it was known by person other than friends or relatives.

[c] Most often from subject being known in the neighborhood at the time of his prior arrest and trial; occasionally through accidental discovery by coworkers, as they gain familiarity with him.

rather than to the coworkers, and it was relatively rare for coworkers to know of the record without the employer or executives also knowing of it.

Naturally, knowledge of the criminal record was somewhat more frequent at first jobs than at subsequent jobs, and it was most often revealed by the referring agency at first jobs, since first jobs included those which the men procured while in prison. The fact that the criminal record was slightly more often known in jobs lasting over two months than in jobs of briefer duration suggests that knowledge of the criminal record was not a major barrier to job retention in this immediate postprison period. It is interesting that in about a quarter of all jobs on which the criminal record was known to others, the subject volunteered information on his criminal record in applying for the job.

That disclosure of the criminal record was not a handicap in job retention also is indicated by Table 14.18, on reasons for termination of employment during the period of our contact with these releasees. About half of these jobs were ended by the releasee quitting, instead of being discharged, and in a majority of the jobs where the releasees quit, they did not have another job arranged. When the men were discharged from their jobs, they rarely ascribed this to their criminal record; most discharges were explained simply as due to the completion of available work. This pattern of "laying off"

TABLE 14.18   Reason for Job Termination
(Postrelease Panel Study)

Reason for job termination	First jobs	Jobs lasting over two months	All jobs
Quit as pay too low[a]	9%	—	8%
Quit as work disliked[a]	11%	—	7%
Quit due to conflict with employer or other person at job[a]	7%	7%	5%
Quit as had better job arranged	21%	25%	17%
Quit for other reasons [a][b]	8%	18%	11%
Total quitting job	56%	50%	48%
Discharged when criminal record discovered	3%	—	4%
"Laid off"—discharged as no more work available	36%	43%	35%
Discharged for other reason[b]	5%	7%	13%
Total discharged from job	44%	50%	52%
Number of job terminations covered in above analysis	76	28	128[c]

[a] No other job arranged when quit.

[b] "Other" reasons were extremely diverse. Those given for quitting included dissatisfaction with idleness during a strike, rumors that they would soon be laid off anyway, and avoidance of paying a union initiation fee. Other reasons for discharge included illness, damaging property of the company, and violating nonsmoking rules.

[c] Covers all jobs reported as terminated during our interviewing except 12 for which reason for termination was unknown. On 111 jobs there was no termination—releasee was still working there at last report.

men between "batches" of work is especially common at unskilled and semi-skilled jobs, particularly for employees with low seniority, like our new releasees.

Table 14.18 indicates that quitting due to dissatisfaction with the pay or with the nature of the work was most common at the first postrelease jobs, and for this sample, it always occurred within the first two months of employment. This suggests a practice of taking clearly unsatisfactory jobs at first, probably with little intention of retaining them for long. Although half or more of those who quit had no other job arranged at the time, many had leads inspiring them with confidence that they could readily get another job. A study of a cross-section of workers in a midwest city found that only 26 per cent of those who quit a job for economic reasons had another job lined up at the time that they quit.[16]

Interpersonal conflict on the job was not a frequent source of job termination, as far as we could tell from our interviews with the releasees. This is consistent with our impressions that these men, most of whom had adjusted to prison discipline with little conflict, are usually quite capable of holding a job in which they are interested and for which they can qualify, despite their frequent earlier record of conflict with authorities. A large-scale

[16] R. C. Wilcock and I. Sobel, *Small City Job Markets* (Urbana, University of Illinois Institute of Labor and Industrial Relations, 1958), p. 63.

study of labor mobility ascribed only ten per cent of voluntary job shifts to interpersonal conflicts.[17]

While this suggests that the criminal record was not an important barrier to retaining a job, how did it affect the prospect of obtaining a job? Some suggestive evidence on this question was provided by our interviews with unemployed releasees.

JOB SEARCH EFFORTS BY UNEMPLOYED EX-PRISONERS

Whenever a man in our postrelease panel sample was unemployed at the time of our monthly interview with him or had been unemployed during the period since the preceding interview, our interviewers asked some questions about this period of unemployment. Our total tabulations are for 204 separate period-of-unemployment reports by 94 releasees, for a total of 117 different unemployment periods.

Table 14.19 indicates the relationship between the frequency with which the unemployed releasee applied for work and the duration of his unemploy-

TABLE 14.19   Number of Applications for Work by Unemployed Releasees in the Week Preceding Interview, by Duration of Unemployment
(Postrelease Panel Study)

| | DURATION OF UNEMPLOYMENT WHEN INTERVIEWED | | | |
Number of applications	*Less than one week*	*One week to two months*	*Over two months*	*All unemployment reports*
None	78%	22%	44%	43%
One	11%	13%	6%	10½%
2 or 3	2%	18%	15%	13%
4, 5, or 6	5%	26%	17%	18%
7, 8, or 9	—	5%	10%	5%
10 or more	4%	16%	8%	10½%
Number of unemployment interviews covered by above analysis	55	93	52	200

ment, as of the week preceding our last interview with him during a particular period of unemployment. It will be seen that most of those who were unemployed for less than a week had not yet looked for work at all, but most of these were unemployed less than three days. In general, our impression was that their search procedure was casually to "ask around" about job possibilities among their friends and relatives who were working, instead of going immediately to employment offices. Many also expressed the intention of resting, or of taking a little vacation before looking for work. How-

[17] Gladys L. Palmer, *Labor Mobility in Six Cities* (New York, Social Science Research Council, 1954), Table 27, p. 73.

ever, most of those unemployed for a week to two months were making several job applications per week, and 16 per cent claimed to have applied for work at more than ten places in the week preceding our interview. Nevertheless, 44 per cent of the group that had been unemployed for over two months at the time of the interview reported that they had not applied for a job in a week or more; these were the more chronically unemployed, including some who were ill.

The reasons given by those unemployed over a week for their failure to find employment, summarized in Table 14.20, may provide some explan-

TABLE 14.20   Unemployed Releasees' Explanations for Their Inability to Find Employment, by Duration of Unemployment
(Postrelease Panel Study)

| | DURATION OF UNEMPLOYMENT WHEN INTERVIEWED | | | |
Explanation	*Under one week*	*Over one week to two months*	*Over two months*	*All unemployment reports*
Hard times	22%	62%	61%	59%
Criminal record	22%	8%	8%	9%
Inexperience at work	11%	2%	8%	5%
Too old or in bad health	11%	2%	8%	5%
Lack tools, license, etc.	—	5%	2%	3%
Lack references or contacts	—	3%	—	2%
Have not tried hard enough	11%	8%	10%	9%
Other explanation	22%	9%	2%	8%
Number of unemployment interviews covered by above analysis	9	87	49	145
Have not yet looked at all	47	9	3	59

ation for their ostensibly passive effort at job-seeking. This tabulation does not include reasons given by men unemployed less than a week, because over three-quarters of these ascribed their unemployment simply to the fact that they had not yet started to look for work. It will be seen from Table 14.20 that most of those who were unsuccessful in job-search efforts ascribed their failure to hard times. Less than 10 per cent stated that their criminal record had something to do with their inability to find employment. Almost 10 per cent simply admitted that they had not tried hard enough to look for a job. These included a few whom we suspected were already involved in criminal employment, particularly in gambling operations on Chicago's South Side. It will be noted that when we checked on these men slightly over a year after their release, 20 per cent had either been returned to prison, were convicted of a felony offense without being returned to prison, or were wanted on felony charges.

Those unemployed releasees who reported that they had applied for work in the preceding week were asked by our staff what reasons for not hiring them had been given by the potential employers at the last place at which they had applied for work. The responses are summarized in Table 14.21.

TABLE 14.21   Reason Given for Not Hiring, in Week Preceding Our Interview, at Last Place Where Releasee Applied for Work and Was Not Hired (Postrelease Panel Study)

| | DURATION OF UNEMPLOYMENT WHEN INTERVIEWED | | | |
Reason given	Less than one week	One week to two months	Over two months	All unemployment reports
Not hiring now	47%	68%	74%	67%
Uncertain, but will call applicant if needed	13%	18%	15%	17%
Applicant lacks license, tools, etc.	—	6%	—	4%
Applicant lacks training, experience, etc.	7%	5%	3%	4%
Refused employment when applicant revealed prison record	13%	2%	6%	4%
Wanted more references	—	—	3%	1%
Other reason	20%	1%	—	3%
Number of instances of not hiring covered by above analysis	15	88	34	137

It will be seen that the most common explanation—"not hiring now"— largely accounts for the releasees' interpretation of their unemployment as due to "hard times." In five-sixths of the cases the employers either stated that they were not hiring now or gave an equivalent but less definite answer and took the applicant's name. Only one-sixth of the releasees reported receiving answers to their job applications which indicated that they were ineligible for the employment for which they had applied, and in only a minority of these cases was the criminal record cited as the reason for their ineligibility.

As might be expected, the longer the releasees were unemployed, the more pessimistic they became regarding their prospects of reemployment. Of those who would venture an estimate as to the probable time before they would again be employed, the median expected further duration of unemployment varied from a low of about a week, for those unemployed less than a week, to a high of about a month, for those unemployed for over two months. However, the number who would not venture a guess, claiming simply that they had no way of knowing how much longer they would be unemployed, increased from a third, for those unemployed less than a week, to over two-thirds for those unemployed over two months. The predominant pessimism and uncertainty of these releasees regarding their job prospects, combined with their reliance on personal contacts for most jobs, probably accounts for the apparent passivity of their job-search efforts when their unemployment became protracted.

SUMMARY

Our interviews with prisoners at various stages of their sentence, and shortly after release, predominantly supported the proposition:

L1. Prisoners have expectations of extremely rapid occupational advancement during the years immediately following their release, expectations which are unrealistic in the light of their limited work experience and lack of vocational skills.

It is probable that these extreme anticipations promote subsequent disappointment with conventional pursuits and reversion to crime.

Our survey of gratuities issued to prisoners at release indicated that these sums are minimal in most states, and not enough to support most releasees to their first pay checks. In some states assistance at release was scarcely enough to get the prisoner home. Generally the rate of payment is not a function of need but is a flat sum for every prisoner.

From the standpoint of the prison administration, the most effective arrangement for assisting inmates with cash appears to be that of paying them for work done while they are confined, since this can provide a major incentive to diligent work and to conformity to other behavior expectations of institution authorities. Compulsory saving of prison earnings and disbursement of large savings on a piecemeal rather than a lump-sum basis were devices used by some prison systems to maximize the contribution of an inmate's earnings to his postrelease needs. At most prisons the wages for work in prison were limited in their rehabilitative influence because they were available to inmates at only a portion of the jobs in the prison. The payment for wages for certain inmate jobs, such as any job in prison industry, and the denial of wages for most other tasks, such as numerous food-preparation and skilled maintenance jobs, are based not on the rehabilitative value of the tasks so much as on the convenience of government bookkeeping in allotting wages only from industry funds.

On the whole, our analysis of the findings from the survey of economic assistance at release suggests the hypothesis:

L2. Maximum rehabilitative influence of cash paid to inmates at release occurs with:
>   *a.* Payments issued to the inmates as wages for any work which they perform in prison, but at wage rates varied so as to reward diligence and improvement in skill;
>   *b.* Compulsory savings requirements, to assure availability of most earnings at release;

c. Issuance of large prison savings on a piecemeal basis following release, through checks disbursed by the parole supervision officer;

d. Release gratuity payments only to those who are unable to earn and save adequate funds in prison, such as those confined only briefly, those who are unemployable during confinement, and those who benefit most from schooling rather than work while confined.

Our research, and studies in Pennsylvania, suggest that postrelease jobs arranged while the offender is still in prison are not available for an appreciable portion of parolees, and when such jobs are available most of them are of brief duration. Our data and those of other studies also supported the proposition:

L3. Prerelease arrangement of a parole job is not associated with markedly greater rates of success on parole than release on parole without a prearranged job.

This finding appears to be a consequence of the high frequency of inadequate or totally spurious jobs arranged by prisoners in order to gain a parole, plus the fact that possession of a satisfactory job often reflects family assistance that can contribute as much or more to an inmate's parole success if it only means aid after his release while he seeks his own job. Several alternatives to the prearranged job requirement, as a method of meeting economic needs of prisoners at release, are discussed in chapter 16.

About one-third of the men whom we contacted in the immediate postrelease period were not employed in their first month out, and about one-sixth were never employed in their first three months out of prison. About 9 per cent still had no job at our last contact, which, in the median case, was 5.3 months after release. Meanwhile, the short-term character of much of the employment that was available resulted in 20 to 25 per cent of the releasees being unemployed during the second and third month out of prison. These are conservative estimates of unemployment rates which count much part-time or irregular work as employment. Five-sixths of the jobs which these releasees procured were unskilled or semiskilled in nature. In our long-term comparison of successful and returned violators, the successful cases were distinguished by their larger proportion of skilled postrelease jobs and particularly by the duration of their employment. Similarly, in our short-term follow-up, higher unemployment in the first three months out markedly differentiated those in subsequent difficulty with the law from those subsequently successful, supporting the basic assumption of this project:

L4. Recidivism of adult male offenders varies inversely with their postrelease employment.

Our study indicated that immediate postrelease income of prisoners is extremely low. The median earnings of our sample in the first month out was only $80; it was $179 in the second month out, and $207 in the third month out. These low earnings were due primarily to the frequency of unemployment; and low earnings due to unemployment, especially in the third month out, particularly characterized those who subsequently were in further difficulty with the law. The median rate of pay on the jobs which the men procured was $268 per month. The significance of a given income, of course, varied greatly, as a function of the releasee's sources of assistance and standard of living. The so-called "necessities of life," however, were not the major economic burdens indicated by our inquiries into the released inmate's cost of living.

When we asked prisoners, at various stages of their sentence, what expenses they expected at release, the younger prisoners indicated remarkably little money requirement at release. Most of what they did expect to spend was for indulgence in the pleasures they were denied in prison, a type of spending which is difficult to budget accurately in advance. The cash needs which the prisoners anticipated declined as their release approached, especially for the younger inmates. Our postrelease interviews indicated that the prisoners probably were realistic in expecting low expenses, for half of the postrelease interviewees paid no rent at their first residence, and most of these men also received meals free. The median expenditure for room and board was only $87 per month in the first few months out of prison, although the amount varied directly with income and with age, and it was higher for whites than for nonwhites.

About one-fifth of the inmates in our immediate postrelease sample had debts in excess of $500 at release, these debts generally being related to their offenses. About one-fifth had debts of under $500. Those without debts, or with small debts, were predominantly the younger inmates.

About one-fifth of the men interviewed during the first week out of prison reported that they had already discarded, or would not use, the clothing issued to them by the prison. In our interviews with successful releasees and returned violators, which in the median case occurred about two years after they left prison, one-third of the successes and one-half of the violators reported that they had discarded the prison-issued clothing as soon as possible. Nevertheless, when we asked releasees during their first five or six months out of prison what their major expenditures had been, the most commonly cited item was clothing.

Automobiles were a major postrelease expense for about half of the white releasees, but they were purchased by only 15 per cent of the nonwhites during the first five or six months out of prison. Half of those who had purchased autos were still making payments on them at the time of our last contact with them, the median payment being $48 per month. About 90 per cent purchased used autos. The automobile was frequently regarded as a necessity, especially by the white releasees who lived in areas or worked at locations where public transportation was not readily accessible, but it was apparent that the auto also served important status needs. It is evident that automobile costs may be a major factor to take into account in realistic budget planning with parolees. In general, our data on the immediate postrelease expenses of prisoners suggest that assistance in budgeting major expenses, particularly clothing and automobiles, and in the management of indebtedness, is among the most fruitful areas of counseling with most releasees in their first half-year out of prison.

Our interviews with those men who were employed during the first five or six months out of prison indicated that over half of their jobs were procured through someone with whom they had a prior personal relationship, such as a friend, a relative, or a former employer. Public employment agencies were used in getting only about ten per cent of these early postrelease jobs and correctional or social work agencies assisted in another ten per cent.

The men who were employed, in most cases, reported that their criminal record was known by others at the job. It was usually known by the employer, manager, or other executive, and it was rarely known by the coworkers without being also known by the senior officials. In about one-quarter of the postrelease jobs on which the releasee's criminal record was known, he had reported his criminal record in applying for the job. Only 4 per cent of the job terminations reported by the men in our postrelease sample were ascribed by them to their criminal record. Only in 9 per cent of their unemployment periods of more than one week's duration did these released offenders blame their criminal record for their inability to find employment. Indeed, for only 4 per cent of the last places where the unemployed releasees reported being refused a job did they state that they were refused employment when they revealed their prison record.

While experimental research alone can supply conclusive evidence on the extent to which the criminal record reduces employability, it appears that:

L5. The ex-prisoner's primary barrier to employment is not his criminal record so frequently as it is his lack of extensive or skilled work experience.

The ex-prisoners generally could obtain employment only as unskilled or semiskilled laborers, and appeared to be marginal and temporary employees, readily "laid off" when work declined. Their major requirement for secure employment appeared to be greater seniority, or the opportunity to develop and demonstrate skill at some vocation extensively in demand.

CHAPTER 15

The Ex-Prisoner's Social World

Man is a social animal. He evaluates himself from his perception of how others see him, and therefore his strongest motivations may come from his ties to other persons. Into what social relationships does the prisoner enter when he is released? How do they affect him?

EXPECTATIONS IN PRISON

Arguments and illustrations can be mustered to support each of two contradictory hypotheses regarding the effects of imprisonment on an offender's relationships with outside persons. The first is epitomized by the expression, "Out of sight, out of mind," implying that the interruption of communication with outsiders caused by imprisonment reduces the ties that the prisoner and the outsiders feel toward each other. The second hypothesis is epitomized by the expression, "Absence makes the heart grow fonder," implying that separation dims the memories of conflict and disappointment and brings basic sources of affection to the fore. Our data suggest that both these hypotheses are usually valid, but with respect to different relationships. *Friendship* ties generally are weakened by one party's imprisonment, but close *kinship* ties predominantly are stronger at the inmate's release than they were at the time of his offense and his initial confinement.

Visiting and Correspondence

The degree of isolation involved in imprisonment would seem to militate against any improvement in relationships with outside persons, including relatives. Sykes observes:

. . . imprisonment means that the inmate is cut off from family, relatives, and friends, not in the self-isolation of the hermit or the misanthrope, but in the involuntary seclusion of the outlaw. It is true that visiting and mailing privileges partially relieve the prisoner's isolation—if he can find someone to visit him or write to him and who will be approved as a visitor or correspondent by the prison officials. Many inmates, however, have found their links with persons in the free community weakening as the months and years pass by. This may explain in part the fact that an examination of the visiting records of a random sample of the inmate population, covering approximately a one-year period,

362

indicated that 41 per cent of the prisoners in the New Jersey State Prison had received no visits from the outside world.[1]

In federal prisons we generally found even less frequent visiting than that which Sykes reports, for the distance which friends and relatives must cover to reach a federal prison usually is much longer than the distances in New Jersey. (Most federal prisons draw their inmates from regions of the United States encompassing ten to thirty states.) However, while visits are seldom received by most prisoners, their correspondence with the outside world is often quite extensive.

Table 15.1 gives the frequency of correspondence and visiting reported by inmates of federal and state prisons in response to inquiries on our Prison Panel Supplement Study questionnaire. One question asked: "How often do you receive letters here from members of your family or others?" The inmates checked a five-point scale, from "Very Often" to "Never," as indicated on Table 15.1. In Leavenworth about one-fifth of the inmates checked "Never," but at Terre Haute and at the state penitentiaries the proportion checking "Never" was one-eighth or less, and at the reformatories it was negligible. The most frequent response, at most prisons, was "often" or "very often." This suggests that most inmates are relatively satisfied with the frequency of their correspondence, but because this evaluation is in subjective terms, we also asked how many letters they had received or sent in the last seven days.

In most prisons letters of inmates are censored, and the frequency and length of correspondence is limited by prison rule in order to reduce the work load of the censors. For example, letters sent out from the "Tight" Reformatory were limited to one per week, by regulation, and had to be on a standard one-page ruled letter form. Some prisons also restrict letters received, particularly by very new prisoners. Finally, the persons allowed to correspond with prison inmates generally are limited by prison regulation. In state prisons the number of correspondents usually is highly restricted, so that wives and close relatives become the only possible correspondents for most prisoners.

Despite these restrictions, the frequency of correspondence indicated in Table 15.1 is quite impressive, especially when one considers the relatively low level of literacy of most prisoners and of their relatives. The rate of correspondence also was fairly sustained, from the beginning to the end of the prison term. Two or more letters per week were sent and received by a majority of the prisoners in reformatories, prison camps, and the Terre Haute Medium Security Federal Penitentiary; between one and two letters per week were sent and received by most inmates at the other penitentiaries.

[1] Gresham M. Sykes, *The Society of Captives* (Princeton, Princeton University Press, 1958), p. 65.

TABLE 15.1   Inmate Reports on Their Communication with Outside Persons
(Prison Panel Supplement Study)

Prison	Stage of prison term[a]	DESCRIBES LETTER RECEIPT AS:					IN LAST SEVEN DAYS, MEDIAN:		Median visits in last 3 months	No. of cases[b]
		Very often	Often	Not very often	Almost never	Never	Letters received	Letters sent		
Federal Penitentiary:										
Leavenworth Maximum Security	Start	16%	25%	36%[c]	5%	18%	0-51%[d]	2.1	0-85%	78*
	End	17%	39%	22%	2%	20%	1.4	1.3	0-81%	83
Terre Haute Medium Security	Start	45%	25%	19%	3%	7%	3.3	3.3	0-60%	68
	End	25%	45%	20%	7%	1%	2.3	2.4	0-63%	83
State Penitentiary:										
"Busy"	Start	20%	28%	28%	14%	11%	1.5	1.6	0-77%	82*
	End	19%	58%	17%	2%	4%	1.9	1.7	0-67%	48
"Slow"	Start	15%	30%	37%	7%	11%	1.4	1.9	0-92%	27*
	End	25%	30%	25%	7%	13%	1.6	1.7	0-62%	71
"Full"	Start	11%	38%	36%	7%	8%	0-51%	1.1	0-80%	74*
Inside Group	End	28%	32%	28%	0	12%	1.4	1.7	0-84%	25
Outside Honor Group	End	31%	38%	29%	1%	0	1.8	2.1	1.0	69*

364

Federal or State Reformatories:

Chillicothe Federal	Start	34%	42%	18%	3%	3%	2.9	3.5	0-58%	65
	End	33%	28%	23%	12%	3%	3.0	3.0	0-57%	59
El Reno Federal	Start	21%	42%	31%	2%	5%	1.9	3.2	0-86%	64*
	End	17%	48%	26%	7%	3%	1.9	2.6	0-63%	90
"Slow" State	Start	37%	44%	17%	2%	0	3.0	1.9	1.5	44*
	End	40%	38%	21%	1%	0	2.4	2.4	1.7	74*
"Tight" State	Start	30%	48%	16%	5%	2%	3.1	1.0	1.5	64
	End	19%	38%	33%	10%	0	1.3	0.8	1.4	58

Prison Camps:

Allenwood Federal	Start	27%	55%	9%	9%	0	2.3	2.5	1.4	11
	End	44%	30%	17%	4%	6%	2.5	2.7	0-65%	55
McNeil Island Federal	Start	21%	21%	29%	7%	21%	1.5	2.7	0-57%	14
	End	26%	32%	19%	13%	10%	2.1	2.3	0-68%	32*
"Full" State	Start	40%	50%	10%	0	0	2.2	2.4	0-50%	20
	End	29%	52%	16%	3%	0	2.0	2.5	2.9	58*
Seagoville Federal Correctional Institution	Start	30%	28%	22%	7%	13%	2.3	2.7	0-65%	54
	End	40%	31%	17%	8%	4%	2.8	2.7	1.6	52

a "Start" is in first six months, "End" in last six months; for details see Appendix E.
b Number completing questionnaire satisfactorily is given. Asterisk after number indicates that one to three inmates in the group did not complete questionnaire satisfactorily.
c Italic indicates highest percentage in group.
d When median is zero, the percentage reporting zero follows the hyphen.

The time and cost of travel to visit a prisoner, the limited visiting time, and the unpleasant setting to which it often is restricted make visiting impractical for many parents or other relatives of prisoners. Often the inmates themselves discourage visiting. But letter-writing is maintained by kin.

Although the figures in Table 15.1 are derived from inmate reports, they correspond closely with statistics compiled from official records. Most prisons maintain records on the frequency of letters and visits, and on the outside persons involved (for custodial security, and as useful casework information). In our analysis of prison classification records on a 10 per cent sample of 1956 releasees from federal prisons, we categorized family interest on a scale derived from its description in the reports. The success rates varied directly with the degree of family interest indicated before release, from a high of 71 per cent success for those whom we classified as having "active" family interest (28 per cent of the sample), to a low of 50 per cent success for those whom the reports indicated received no communication from relatives (only 3 per cent of all the cases). In the U. S. Parole Board's study of 1954-55 Federal Youth Correction Act commitments, success rates on first parole ranged from a high of 49 per cent successful among the 48 per cent whom institution parole officers said had "frequent" letters and visits to a low of 28 per cent successful among the 26 per cent of the inmates classified as having "infrequent or no" letters and visits.

In Illinois parole prediction research a precise record of letters and visits to prisoners was kept, and family interest in the inmates was classified as follows: *very active*—receives five or more letters per month from relatives; *active*—receives two to five letters per month from relatives; *sustained*—receives fewer than two letters per month and more than one every three months; *passive*—receives some letters, but not more than one every three months; and *none*. In this tabulation, one visit was counted as two letters (probably too low a ratio, in terms of the time and cost of visiting). Even for the 1925-35 parolees from Joliet and Menard branches of the Illinois State Penitentiary, Ohlin found 5 per cent *very active,* 61 per cent *active,* and only 9 per cent *none,* with parole success rates declining from 75 per cent for the *very active* to 34 per cent for the *none.*[2] Using the same classification at the Pontiac Branch of the Illinois State Penitentiary, which has a reformatory-type population, I found among the 1940-49 parolees 50 per cent with *active* or *very active* family interest, and they had a 74 per cent parole success rate. Only 3 per cent had no family interest, and these had a 43 per cent success rate.[3]

[2] Lloyd E. Ohlin, *The Stability and Validity of Parole Experience Tables* (Ph.D. dissertation, University of Chicago, 1954), Table 42, Appendix B.

[3] Daniel Glaser, *A Reformulation and Testing of Parole Prediction Factors* (Ph.D. dissertation, University of Chicago, 1954), p. 231.

Expectations of Help

During each of our Prison Panel Study interviews in five federal prisons, we gave the prisoners a list of categories of relatives, friends, and other persons or agencies outside of prison, and referring to this sheet, we asked: "Which of these are you counting on most to help you on the outside? What kind of help do you expect them to give you? Which do you think are most likely to make it hard for you to go straight? How?"

As indicated at the bottom of Table 15.2, about one-eighth of our subjects stated that they did not expect anyone to help them, or that they

TABLE 15.2   Persons or Agencies Counted on Most for Postrelease Help, and Those Thought Most Likely to Make It Hard for Subject to "Go Straight"
(Prison Panel Study)

	First choices as persons or agencies counted on most	First choices as persons most likely to make it hard
Relatives:		
Close family: parents, brothers, sisters	54%	5%
Other blood relatives except children	4%	4%
Wife	16%	5%
Children	1%	—
In-laws	1%	5%
Total relatives	76%	19%
Nonrelatives:		
Girl-friend or fiancee	4%	1%
Probation officer	5%	7%
Parole adviser	2%	—
Church, welfare, and other agencies	4%	1%
Former or prospective employer	4%	2%
Law enforcement agencies	—	34%
Noncriminal friends	3%	3%
Criminal friends	1%	32%
Other	1%	1%
Total nonrelatives	24%	81%
No. responding: base of above percentages	998	684
No. responding "none, don't know," etc.	139	453
	(12%)	(40%)
Total cases	1137	1137

would not go to anyone for help. This proportion was only slightly higher at admission than when release was near. The proportion who denied that anyone would make it hard for them to go straight increased from three-eighths at the first week to half when near release.[4] In general, the trend was toward increasing optimism, but this is more a matter of less frequently expecting harm from others than of increasingly expecting help.

[4] Significant at the .01 level, comparing first-week with near-release frequencies.

Table 15.2 reveals that most inmates counted mainly on close family members for assistance at release, especially on parents, sisters, brothers, and other blood relatives. This dependence on blood relatives progressively increased from the beginning to the end of the prison term.[5] About half of this increase, however, seems merely to have been a replacement for declining expectations from wives.[6] About a third of our subjects were married when they entered prison, but about a third of these marriages appeared to be in process of rift at that time, and divorces presumably increased in the course of imprisonment. (The spouse's conviction for a felony constitutes adequate grounds for divorce in many states.) Some information regarding persons counted on most is provided in Table 15.3 for those never married

TABLE 15.3   Persons Counted on Most for Postrelease Assistance by Inmates Never Married and by Those Reported at Admission to be Married, with Children, and Maintaining Rapport with Their Wives
(Prison Panel Study)

Marital status (per admission summary report)	Stage of imprisonment at interview	Number of cases	Close blood relatives (parents, siblings, etc.) counted on most	Wives counted on most
Never married	First week	129	55%	—
	Near release	127	68%	—
Married, with children, and rapport indicated	First week	46	11%	52%
	Near release	49	35%	43%

and for those who at admission apparently were happily married and had children. The increased dependence on close relatives near release is especially pronounced for the latter group.[7]

Our Prison Panel Supplement Study questionnaires, administered to inmates at seven federal and six state prisons in the summer of 1962, included in a series of questions entitled "About Your Future" the queries: "Do you think that members of your family will do what they can to help you?" and "Do you think that your old friends will want to go around with you after you get out?" The prisoners would check one of four answers for each of these questions: "Yes, all of them; Yes, most of them; Yes, some of them; or No, none of them."

[5] Significant at the .01 level, comparing first-week with near-release frequencies.
[6] Significant at the .05 level, comparing first-week with near-release frequencies.
[7] Increase in per cent counting on blood relatives significant at .05 level for those never married and at .01 level for those married, with children, and rapport indicated, at admission. Fiedler and Bass, and Suttles, also found increasing favorableness of attitude toward relatives, during the course of confinement, among delinquents. F. E. Fiedler and A. R. Bass, *Delinquency, Confinement and Interpersonal Perception,* Technical Report no. 6 (Urbana, Ill., University of Illinois, 1959). Gerald Suttles, *Parson's Pattern Variables and Juvenile Delinquency* (M.A. thesis, University of Illinois, 1962).

To the question on whether members of their family would help, the most frequent response at every prison and for every sampling of the inmates was "Yes, all of them." The lowest percentages giving this response were 44 per cent among the most newly admitted inmates at "Busy" State Penitentiary and 50 per cent among the most newly admitted inmates at Leavenworth Federal Penitentiary. In all other inmate samplings at these two prisons, and in all samplings at the other eleven prisons, more than half the inmates checked this "all" response. The "No, none of them" response was checked by less than ten per cent at most institutions, the only exceptions being Leavenworth, "Busy" State, and the Federal Correctional Institution at Seagoville. These are all prisons with relatively high proportions of older inmates with long criminal records, and one would expect more complete alienation from relatives among them.

The most consistent difference between newly admitted and near-release inmates in answering the question on whether members of their family would help them was that those near release most often responded "Yes, some of them." Greater use of this response at the near-release than at the entrance stage of imprisonment occurred at twelve of the thirteen institutions. The only exception to this pattern was "Busy" State Penitentiary, where the "Yes, all of them" response increased (from 44 to 60 per cent) and the "No, none . . ." response decreased (from 15 to 4 per cent). It was clear at all the prisons surveyed that inmate expectations from relatives were increasingly positive. More than nine out of ten inmates expected assistance from some family members at release. Chapter 14's evidence that a majority of inmates do receive vital economic assistance from relatives when they are released shows that these positive anticipations during imprisonment are warranted.

On the question of whether old friends would want to go around with them after their release, the most common responses were "most of them" or "some of them." At all thirteen prisons except the two state reformatories, the beginning of sentence sample exceeded the near-release sample in selecting the "Yes, all of them" response; at the two reformatories there was a slight increase near release in this "all of them" response, but there was a sharp decrease in what had been the major response there at the beginning of sentence—"Yes, most of them." In short, most inmates at all institutions are aware of some loss of friends as a result of their imprisonment.

Determining what changes occur during imprisonment in the relationship of prisoners to their family members and to others on the outside is basic for the development of an adequate theory of rehabilitation in prison. In terms of physical contact, imprisonment obviously means that the offender is differentially associated with criminals and disassociated from outside persons who previously might have had an anticriminal influence upon him. However, in terms of identification and reference, it may very well be that the impact on an offender of parents, sisters, or other relatives, as well as teachers, clergy, and other anticriminal outsiders, increases after he is confined. We can arrive at this conclusion in a deductive fashion by the following series of fairly reasonable premises.

As a basic assumption, let us accept the approximate validity of the notion that a person's behavior is largely an outcome of competition in his lifetime between the influences of his many reference groups. In the light of this conception, recall our evidence in chapter 5 that the experiences of imprisonment are not uniformly or even predominantly conducive to increased cohesion among the prisoners, especially after they pass early youth. Furthermore, the experience of failure in crime and the effect of arrest in diminishing or eliminating communication of an offender with his partners in crime must often reduce the offender's identification with them (at least by comparison to the identification he is likely to have developed while successful in criminal forays). Thus, from one or both of these processes, alienation of an offender from criminals may often accompany imprisonment, despite increased physical contact with them. It follows from our basic assumption above that this alone would increase the relative impact of anticriminal influences, even if their absolute strength remained unchanged.

Independent of such diminution of criminal influences, in cases where prison separates an offender from relatives with whom he has been in conflict, it may facilitate the renewal and release of affection between them which was repressed during conflict. This principle, expressed in common speech as "absence makes the heart grow fonder," perhaps arises from the fact that separation permits memory to focus on a preconflict relationship. For offenders who had been out of contact with their family, imprisonment may actually mean a renewal of communication with the family.

Of course, there often also is a materialistic side to this, as blood relatives may be the only ones willing or allowed to send the inmate money for commissary expenditures. Finally, the inmate's dependence on assistance of relatives for the success of any realistic hopes he may have of achieving self-sufficiency after prison may directly enhance their influence as positive reference groups for him. Thus, confining an offender with criminals may actually increase his differential identification with anticriminal persons. This will happen especially where the prison staff can achieve a significant anticriminal influence.

As shown in Table 15.2, about one-third of the inmates designated the police, sheriff, or other law enforcement agency as their most likely sources of harm after release, and about one-third indicated that criminal friends were most likely to cause them trouble. As already noted, there was some decrease during imprisonment in the proportion of inmates who expected trouble from anyone. However, among those who feared trouble, fairly constant proportions were concerned with the police or with criminal friends. When we asked how these persons would harm them, the answers were as expected, and also constant from one stage of the prison term to the next. Those who feared the police indicated that they expected harassment by arrests and pickups, on the basis of their record and regardless of their post-release behavior. Many who feared trouble from criminal friends expressed recognition of their own tendencies to go along in illicit or disorderly activities when with friends. About one-sixth of the subjects who expected harm from anyone feared difficulty with a specific individual whom they claimed had a grudge against them. How much these fears were warranted cannot be determined.

At no time are probation officers seen by many inmates as a primary source of either aid or injury. However, although the frequencies are too low to provide confident conclusions, it may be of interest that inmate perception of probation officers seems to change during confinement. Immediately after their presentence contact with probation officers, at entrance to prison, offenders most often anticipated that probation officers would be a source of help; after a few months in prison, however, inmates more often designated probation officers as a source of postrelease harm. One might speculate that favorable impressions made by the probation officers in handling the offenders before prison are undone in prison by returned parole and mandatory release violators, who blame their reimprisonment on the federal probation officers who were their parole supervisors.

Our Prison Panel Supplement Study questionnaire included the inquiry: "Do you think that people in your neighborhood will try and make trouble for you when you get out, if you go back there?" The answers, from which one selection was to be checked, were similar to the choices cited previously, ranging from "Yes, all of them" to "No, none of them."

Fears of difficulty from neighbors were expressed by only a minority of the inmates in each of the thirteen prisons. Understandably, anticipations of such difficulty were most frequent in the reformatories, both state and federal, where over 40 per cent expressed some expectation of difficulty. The fear was predominantly from "some" neighbors, rather than from "most" or "all." Differences in these expressions of fear between the entrance and the near-release samples were not marked or in a consistent direction.

In our Prison Panel Study interviews, those indicating that they expected help from relatives were asked what kind of help this would be. As shown in Table 15.4, a marked increase was evident in the specificity of the type of assistance expected as the release date approached. Initially, the respondents seemed mainly to be indicating that they would value their most helpful relationships subjectively, as a source of friendship or guidance upon release. However, as time elapsed they increasingly emphasized a home as the

Table 15.4   Types of Assistance Anticipated from Persons or
Agencies Counted on Most
(Prison Panel Study)

Type of assistance	First-week interviews	Fourth-month interviews	Sixth-month interviews	Near-release interviews
Subjective (advice, friendship, etc.)	47%[a]	37%	29%	26%
Home	14%	26%	39%	48%
Employment (provide, or help to secure, a job)	22%	23%	19%	16%
Money or other material aid	13%	10%	10%	9%
Other or unspecific	4%	4%	3%	1%
Number responding definitely (base of above percentages)	244	103	186	220
Number responding "none," "don't know," etc., and their percentage of total responses	39 (14%)	16 (13%)	20 (10%)	28 (11%)

[a] Italic indicates highest percentage on a line.

assistance they were counting on most, often designating it simply as "a place to live."[8]   Only part of this change is accounted for by the decline in expectation of help from wives, or by the increase in dependence on close relatives (indicated for the total Prison Panel sample in Table 15.3), since these changes were much smaller than the change in type of assistance anticipated. Other specific forms of help, such as jobs or money, were not increasingly designated, but rather declined somewhat.

There were some institutional differences, especially near release, in the type of assistance expected from the person counted on most. The emphasis on provision of a home occurred mostly at Ashland, Chillicothe, and Terre Haute. Leavenworth and Milan inmates, who are the oldest, showed more concern than others with employment and financial assistance.[9]

Our data suggest that provision of a home and material assistance by close relatives is often a mixed blessing. On the one hand, conflict with relatives in the home frequently occurs, or conditions in the home and in its neighborhood may often have been conducive to crime. On the other hand, the data presented in chapter 14 suggest that destitution and return to crime in a month or two after release would characterize most federal parolees and mandatory releasees if room, board, and other types of economic assistance were not provided by relatives. The prerelease guidance centers described

[8] The decrease from first week to near release, in the proportion designating only subjective assistance, and the increase in proportion stressing home, were both significant at the .01 level. The first-week and near-release columns of Table 15.4, considered as a 2×5 contingency table, are significant at the .001 level (Chi Square 68.1, df 4).

[9] The contrasts between Leavenworth and Milan combined, and Ashland, Chillicothe, and Terre Haute combined, on expectation of home, employment, and money, are all significant at the .01 level.

in chapter 16 provide a means of assisting the releasee in procuring his economic needs *on his own,* and also permit him to explore prospective social relationships in the home before he is completely dependent on the home for survival without recourse to crime.

A frequent problem in attempting to assist a prisoner in making post-release plans is that certain persons or agencies appear willing to give him needed assistance, but he rejects the idea of going to these sources for help. In order to probe this aspect of the inmate's anticipations toward the future, while the Prison Panel interview subjects still held the sheet listing twenty categories of persons and agencies outside of prison, we asked them: "Is there anybody on the list that you would never go to for help even if you needed the kind of help they could offer?" If they designated someone, we asked "Why not?" The most definite trend manifested was that in the first week in prison 18 per cent said that there was no one to whom they would not go for help, but by the sixth month this proportion rose to 40 per cent, and it remained at this level thereafter.[10] About one-fifth regularly indicated one or more close relatives to whom they would never go for help. A similar proportion gave the "proper" answer that they would not seek help from criminal friends on the outside, while almost as many stated that they would never go to the police or other law enforcement agencies for assistance.

The reasons most often given for never asking for help from someone indicated the inmates' personal hostility rather than either humility or pride.[11] This was especially frequent when a wife or other relative was the person to whom they would not go. Concern with a "bad environment" was often cited at first, particularly with reference to not seeking help from criminal friends and friends made in prison, but was progressively less often mentioned as time in prison elapsed.

If we can come to any overall conclusion from this section, it is that the attitude of prisoners to outsiders, especially to close relatives, tends to improve with time in prison. The major exceptions to this, of course, are those marital relationships that deteriorate during imprisonment, but these are often replaced by closer relationships to blood relatives. Such improvement in relationships may be a major factor in the shift to a more stable and law-abiding life which seems evident in most of the ex-prisoners for whom one can compare postrelease with immediate preprison life. Of course, for some men, reunion with relatives may simply result in their returning, at release, to a conflict-generating home situation. Also, it should be noted that an improved relationship with relatives is largely a matter of

[10] Significant at .01 level, comparing first-week with either sixth-week or near-release responses.

[11] Significant at .01 level, comparing frequency of expressions of hostility with expressions of pride, for all stages of sentence groups combined (13% pride versus 26% hostility).

expediency; the major anticipation from the relationships, as the release date approaches, is the practical matter of room and board. As chapter 14 revealed, without recourse to free room and board most releasees would be hungry and shelterless before they procured their first legitimate income. What this trend in accepting relatives involves is the prisoner's reorientation to a dependent role again. Indeed, not just with relatives, but with all others, the prisoner becomes increasingly willing to become dependent on (accept help from) anyone as his release date approaches.

COMMUNITY OF FIRST POSTRELEASE RESIDENCE

Our Postrelease Panel Study was restricted to prisoners released on parole or mandatory release supervision in the metropolitan areas of Chicago, Cleveland, Detroit, or St. Louis, for it was in the U. S. Probation Office in each of these cities that we stationed a research employee for about a year.

Eighty-nine per cent of the men in this sample had a place to live arranged before they left prison. Ninety per cent of those with prearranged residence went to that residence on the day of their arrival in the city to which they were released. An additional 9 per cent went to the prearranged residence only on the second day or later. Most of those who delayed en route to their permanent residence indicated that they tarried in order to procure sexual satisfaction—to visit old girl friends or to seek prostitutes. One per cent, or two individuals, never went to their prearranged residence at all: one rejoined his wife when it was expected that he would go to a private welfare agency, while the other revealed later that he had made his first residence with a girl friend instead of residing with his parents as had been planned.

A requirement for federal parole, already indicated in chapter 14, is that employment and residence be arranged in advance, as the major components of a "parole plan." This plan must be investigated by the U. S. Probation Office for the area where the parolee is to be supervised, and the plan must then be approved by the U. S. Board of Parole before a prisoner can be released. Of course, any or all of these requirements may sometimes be waived by the Board. Unlike the parolees, mandatory releasees leave the prison automatically on the date of their eligibility, regardless of whether or not they have job or home arrangements. They are released when they have completed all of their sentence except for the various types of time off granted for good behavior or for farm or industry work in prison. The mandatory releasees are supervised "as though on parole" for all except the last 180 days of this "good time." This difference in prerelease requirements is reflected in the fact that only 5 per cent of the parolees in our sample, but 21 per cent of the mandatory releasees, had no prearranged residence.

Both parolees and mandatory releasees in the federal system normally designate as their residential area the U. S. Judicial District from which they were committed to prison or the judicial district in which they resided at the time of their commitment. If a man claims good job or home prospects in another district, the Chief U. S. Probation Officer in that district may be asked to accept him for supervision. Usually this probation officer's decision on acceptance is based on his evaluation of the quality of the home and job prospects of the individual in the district. Since the Chief U. S. Probation Officer is an appointee of a rather autonomous lifetime-appointed federal judge, these officers can be quite independent in deciding whether or not to accept the extra work load of supervising men not committed from or originally resident in their districts.

Considerable variation was observed by us in the acceptance policies of different federal judicial districts. Caseworkers at the federal prisons where we conducted research learned from experience to advise inmates that there was little prospect of their being accepted for supervision in certain districts if they had not previously resided or been committed from there, while in other districts their prospects were much better. In addition to this selection of the district for release, men already on federal parole or mandatory release can apply for transfer to another federal judicial district, but the Chief U. S. Probation Officer in that district must still accept this transfer. However, the releasees can also receive from their probation officer in the district where they already are under supervision a twenty-day permit to enter another district, to seek employment or for other reasons. This permit sometimes is renewed one or more times, but if a definite move is to be made by the releasee and a long period of supervision remains to be completed, he is not allowed to make this move unless accepted for supervision by the U. S. Probation Office in the district which he is entering.

In our second interview with the men in our Postrelease Panel "effective sample" (those seen for three months or more), we asked whether they previously resided in the same neighborhood as that in which they were then residing. We left the definition of "neighborhood" to their own interpretation. At the time of this inquiry these men had been out of prison, in the median case, for 1.7 months. Of 143 respondents from whom this information was procured, 45 per cent reported returning to the same neighborhood as that in which they resided when they were last committed to prison and 38 per cent to the same metropolitan area, but to another neighborhood. Altogether, 83 per cent of the released prisoners in this sample returned to the metropolis where they resided when they got into difficulty with the law. Another 9 per cent had also previously resided in the metropolitan area to which they were released but did not live there at the time of their last offense, and 8 per cent were released to a metropolitan area where they never previously resided.

Not only did the overwhelming majority of all releasees return to the metropolis in which they had resided before their last involvement in crime, but 71 per cent had lived in this metropolis for over ten years. As indicated in Table 15.5, a larger proportion of nonwhites than whites

TABLE. 15.5 Some Attributes Associated with Change or Stability in Place of Residence at Release, Compared to Residence at Last Commitment to Prison (Postrelease Panel Study, cases seen for three months or more)

| | RELATIONSHIP OF AREA OF RELEASE TO AREA OF RESIDENCE AT LAST COMMITMENT TO PRISON | | | | |
| | SAME METROPOLITAN AREA | | | | |
Attribute	Same neighborhood	Different neighborhood	Total, same met. area	Different metropolitan area	Total cases[a]
Race:					
White	43%	34%	77%	23%[b]	83 (100%)
Nonwhite	47%	45%	92%	8%[b]	60 (100%)
Age:					
23 or younger	69%	21%	90%	10%	29 (100%)
24 through 35	44%	34%	79%	21%	61 (100%)
36 or older	32%	53%	85%	15%	53 (100%)
Total cases[a]	45%	38%	83%	17%	143 (100%)
Criminal record in city to which released:					
None	16%	15%	15%	71%[c]	24%
Arrest or conviction only on last offense	28%	20%	24%	21%[c]	24%
Arrest or conviction on last and on prior offenses	56%	65%	61%	8%[c]	52%
Subsequent failures	17%	20%	18%	25%	20%
Subsequent successes	83%	80%	82%	75%	80%
Total cases[a]	64 (100%)	55 (100%)	119 (100%)	24 (100%)	143 (100%)

[a] Excludes two cases with insufficient information on prior residence.

Differences as large as those indicated here in comparison of same with different metropolitan areas would occur by change in samples of this size:

[b] Less than once in twenty times;

[c] Less than once in a thousand times (by Chi Square test).

returned to their preprison metropolitan area. The younger inmates exceeded the older ones in rate of return to what they considered their preprison neighborhood, but there was little relationship of age to the proportion returning to the same city. Parolees and mandatory releasees were similar in proportion released to the same and to different cities.

Federal prisoners frequently are arrested and sentenced in an area other than that in which they reside at the time of their offense, since their crimes often consist of interstate transportation of stolen goods. Therefore, although 83 per cent of our sample were released to the city where they claimed residence at the time of their last trial and commitment to prison, only 66 per cent were actually tried in this community on their last offense, and only 76 per cent had any criminal record in this community.

Whether or not these releasees in our Postrelease Panel Study went to the city of their immediate preprison residence proved to have no appreciable relationship to their rates of subsequent failure (further imprisonment or nonprison sentence for a felony-like offense). The figures in Table 15.5 apply only to failures subsequent to the first three months out of prison, since it was only for the releasees contacted this long or longer that we have data on change of neighborhood. However, the success rate findings are similar for the complete sample of all 193 men in our Postrelease Panel Study whom we interviewed one or more times in the 1959-60 period of our research. Of those with *no* prior arrest, trial, or confinement in the metropolitan area to which released, 79 per cent had no further imprisonment or nonprison sentence as of our January 1962 follow-up; but the success rate *also* was 79 per cent for those who did have prior arrest, trial, or confinement records in the metropolitan area to which they were released.

For a number of reasons, we were somewhat surprised at the finding of little difference in success rate with change in community of residence from before to after imprisonment. Even the differences shown in Table 15.5 are in the opposite direction from that which we anticipated. One reason for expecting those going to a different metropolitan area to be more successful was the evidence, shown in Table 15.5, that most of the men going to a new city would not be burdened by their criminal reputation there; 71 per cent of these men had no prior criminal record in the community to which they were released, whereas only 15 per cent of the men going to the metropolitan area of their preprison residence had never been arrested or convicted there. However, our expectation of a lower failure rate with change of community came mostly from impressions acquired in our interviews with 308 returned violators in the five federal prisons in which we had research staff during 1958-59.

A frequent contention of the returned violators was that they would have been successful on their previous release had they been allowed to go to a different community. Their complaints about the communities in which they violated parole or mandatory release were: (a) lack of employment opportunity; (b) conflict with their family, or with neighbors; (c) criminal or disorderly friends or relatives in the community whom they could not readily avoid, and with whom they engaged in the behavior which led to their violation; (d) police harassment, alleged prejudice against them by the U. S. Probation staff, or harassment by others in the area. But it appears that most of these excuses were rationalizations after the fact which did not adequately explain their violation, and many became adept at convincing others as well as themselves, unrealistically, that there are "greener pastures" elsewhere. When we compare the returned violators with the successful releasees, our records indicate that 28 per cent of the returned violators were released to a community where they had no previous arrest record, as against 18 per cent of the successful releasees. Furthermore, both the returned violators and the successful releasees had the same proportion—40 per cent—with a residence at release identical with residence at offense. For the releasees whom we studied, taken collectively, handicap by a criminal record in the community of release appears to have been more than compensated for by benefits from resources in the old community.

PERSONS WITH WHOM EX-PRISONERS LIVE

Information about the people with whom each releasee was living at his first residence was available for 140 of the 145 men in our "effective" Postrelease Panel sample. This information is summarized in Table 15.6.

TABLE 15.6 Person with Whom Releasee Lived at First Residence, as Related to Various Attributes of Releasees and Aspects of Their Residential Arrangement (Postrelease Panel Study, cases seen for three months or more)

	PERSON WITH WHOM RELEASEE LIVED AT HIS FIRST RESIDENCE						
Attribute of releasee or aspect of his residence	*Wife; wife and child*	*Relative and wife and/ or child*	*Parent*	*Other relative*	*Friends*	*Alone*	*Total cases*[a]
Age:							
23 or younger	—	—	68%	29%	4%	—	28 (100%)
24 through 35	27%	7%	25%	20%	2%	20%	60 (100%)
36 or older	44%	4%	12%	27%	4%	10%	52 (100%)
Community to which released, compared to residence at commitment:							
Same met. area and same neighborhood	38%	—	41%	14%	2%	5%	63 (100%)
Same met. area but different neighborhood	23%	6%	19%	34%	2%	17%	52 (100%)
Different met. area	9%	13%	13%	30%	9%	26%	23 (100%)
Race:							
White	26%	4%	31%	21%	3%	15%	80 (100%)
Nonwhite	30%	5%	25%	28%	3%	8%	60 (100%)
Per cent moving from first residence during our period of contact (5.3 months in median case)	40%	83%	30%	58%	50%	82%	49%
Subsequent failures	15%	17%	23%	24%	—	29%	21%
Subsequent successes	85%	83%	77%	76%	100%	71%	79%
Total cases[a]	39	6	40	34	4	17	140
Percentage distribution on total cases	28%	4%	29%	24%	3%	12%	100%

[a] Available information on person with whom releasee resided was adequate on only 140 of 145 cases, and prior neighborhood was not available on two of these 140.

Twenty-nine per cent of the releasees lived with their parents at their first residence, 32 per cent lived with their wives (and one or more children or other relatives), 24 per cent lived with other relatives only, 3 per cent lived with friends, and 12 per cent lived alone. Residence with wives or alone was most characteristic of older releasees. There was little difference between the racial groups in frequency of residence with various relatives. Those living alone or with a relative other than wives or parent were most likely to go to a community different from that in which they resided at their commitment. An analysis of detailed household composition, for seventy-five men in our sample from the Chicago area, indicated that of those living with parents, about 30 per cent live with both natural parents, about 30 per cent live with only one parent (usually the mother), and about 40 per cent live with a natural parent and one step-parent.[12]

Table 15.6 suggests that men whose first residence is with their wives have the fewest failures and those living alone have the most failures. These differences are too small for statistical significance in the sample on which Table 15.6 is based, but they are confirmed, for two larger samples, in Table 15.7. Those marriages that can survive the husband's imprisonment

TABLE 15.7   Postrelease Failure Rates of Federal Prison Releasees, by Expected Home at Release

	1956 FEDERAL PRISON RELEASEES		YOUTH CORRECTION ACT CASES COMMITTED 1953–58	
Expected home at release	Per cent failures	No. of cases	Per cent failures (on 1st parole)	No. of cases
Alone	49	121	64	28
With parents (or step-parents)	35[a]	359	55	174
With both natural parents	—	—	53	97
With one natural parent	—	—	57	77
With wife	25	248	62	24
With other relative	40	131	62	48
Other	28	29	77	22
No information	38	127	88	26
Total cases	35	1015	62	322

[a] Differences as large as that found between the failure rates alone and those with parents or step-parents, for 1956 releasees, would occur by chance less than once in a hundred times in samples of this size (by Chi Square test). The differences on Youth Correction Act cases are not beyond chance probability for samples of that size.

seem clearly to be a major asset. The higher than average failure rates for those living alone is a consistent finding of all tabulations and is not a function of age, since few of the youngest releasees live alone. However, the low failure rates of married releasees is largely accounted for by the fact that they are older than the average releasee, and, as we showed in chapter 3, failure rates decline with increasing age at release. In general, the only

12 Dale F. Lytton, *Family Relations and the Post-Release Behavior of Federal Prisoners* (M.A. thesis, University of Illinois, 1961), p. 33.

type of residential association consistently unfavorable in prognosis is living alone. Our impression from case studies is that residence alone is unfavorable largely through its requiring the releasee to find company away from his residence, and the tavern provided the most readily accessible "home away from home."

Table 15.8 shows dramatically the extent to which the released prisoners become involved in a network of kin relationships. Eighty-seven per cent of our sample had relatives in the metropolitan area to which they were released. If we count living with the wife as living with a relative, we find that 94 per cent of our sample had some type of relative in the metropolitan area. Still including wives with other relatives, we conclude that over 90

TABLE 15.8 Per Cent of Releasees Having Various Types of Relatives Available, by Aspect of Availability
(Postrelease Panel Study, effective sample)

Aspect of relative's availability	TYPE OF RELATIVE					
	Parents and step-parents	Siblings	Aunts, uncles, cousins, g-parents	Other relatives[a]	In-laws	All types of relative
Lives in metropolitan area[b]	59%	65%	36%	22%	14%	87%
At last report:						
Lives with releasee	30%	25%	7%	6%	4%	42%
Does not live with releasee	29%	52%	32%	16%	10%	74%
Frequency of releasee's contact with relatives in metropolitan area with whom he *does not* reside:[c]						
Once a week or more	83%	65%	39%	53%	71%	96%
Under once a week	8%	24%	33%	11%	21%	96%
Never	9%	11%	28%	37%	7%	4%
No. of cases on which contact frequency percentages are based	41	74	46	23	14	106
Received material assistance from relative[d]	78%	44%	38%	24%	55%	73%
Reports nonmaterial help only	9%	20%	10%	5%	10%	8%
Asserts relative of no help	13%	36%	52%	71%	35%	18%
No. of cases on which assistance percentages are based	82	64	50	21	20	120

[a] "Other relatives" include releasee's grown children with whom he is not living, nieces, nephews, grandchildren.

[b] Percentages in this top section (first three lines) are on a basis of 144, the number of releasees in the effective sample for whom adequate information on relatives was available. Second and third lines may cover more than one relative of one type, for a single releasee.

[c] Where there is more than one relative in a single category for a single case, the most frequently contacted one is tabulated. Based on 3rd interview, in median case 3.3 months after release. "All types of relative" entries here are based on every entry, on every category, so that they add to over 100 per cent.

[d] Relative counted as providing material assistance if this is reported or if subject lives in relatives' home; counted as nonmaterial if releasee says "he would help me if I wanted him to," "gave me advice," or any positive reference other than material aid. Based on 5th interview, in median case 5 months after release, for those with relatives in the metropolitan area.

per cent of the releasees have at least weekly contact with relatives. Also, almost three-quarters received some sort of material assistance from kin. This is especially impressive in view of the high frequency of broken and conflict-ridden homes in the family background of prisoners.

To summarize the data presented thus far in this chapter, we have seen a progressive increase during imprisonment in evidence of favorable relationships between prisoners and their kin, and we have found much dependence of newly released prisoners on relatives for material or social assistance. This is consistent with the findings of other research on modern urban life in the United States. Contrary to classical essays in sociological theory, which suggest that the large city emphasizes impersonal "secondary" relationships rather than kinship, separate studies in New York, Chicago, Los Angeles, St. Louis, Detroit, and Rochester all report "the extreme importance of kin relations to urban residents." Families have been found to provide the major source of companionship and assistance for most adult American city dwellers today, even when the families are scattered widely in a metropolitan area.[13]

Table 15.9 indicates again, as did Table 15.6, that subsequent success rate did not vary greatly in relationship to the person with whom a releasee lived. Table 15.9 differs from Table 15.6, however, in showing that subsequent success is very much a function of how the releasee interacted with these with whom he resided. At each interview, after asking the subjects where they were living, we inquired about how they were getting along there. We classified as "discord" any case in which, at any interview, the subject indicated some conflict with the relative with whom he was residing. The subsequent failure rate for those reporting discord was 38 per cent, over three times the 12 per cent failure rate of those never reporting any discord.

Unfortunately, with most of our subjects, we were not in a position to procure data for an intricate classification of their emotional relationship with the person with whom they resided. Nevertheless, our crude inquiry yielded consistent indication that discord in any type of residential association is correlated with postrelease failure, although the relationship was least pronounced in the case of residence with parents. The finding that accord in the home is more closely related to reformation than the category of relative present in the home is consistent with findings of other research; the work of the Gluecks and the McCords is outstanding for its evidence that conflict in the home is a much more important factor in delinquency than whether or not a home is broken by the absence of a parent.[14]

[13] Scott Greer, *The Emerging City* (Glencoe, Ill., Free Press, 1962), pp. 89-97; A. K. Cohen and H. M. Hodges, "Lower Blue Collar Class Characteristics," *Social Problems, 10*, no. 4 (Spring 1963), 303-34.

[14] Sheldon and Eleanor Glueck, *Unravelling Juvenile Delinquency* (New York, Commonwealth Fund, 1950), pp. 93-133; William and Joan McCord, *Origins of Crime* (New York, Columbia University Press, 1959), pp. 73-123.

TABLE 15.9 Success or Failure Rates of Releasees, by Relative with Whom Releasee Resided at Any Time, and by Report of Discord with These Relatives (Prison Panel Study, effective sample; median duration of contact 5.3 months after release from prison)

Residential arrangement and relationship	Per cent successes	Per cent failures	No. of cases
Lived *at some time* with:			
Wife	81	19	59
Parent	79	21	58
Other relatives only	77	23	22
Never lived with wife or any relative	82	18	17
Relationship between subject and predominant residential associate:			
Lived with parent:			
Discord reported	74	26	19
No discord reported	81	19	27
Lived with wife:[a]			
Discord reported	61	39	18
No discord reported	90	10	41
Lived with other relative only:[a]			
Discord reported	25	75	4
No discord reported	89	11	18
All who lived with relative or wife:[a]			
Discord reported	63	37	41
No discord reported	87	13	86
Total living with relative or wife	80	20	127
Total cases for which residential information is adequate	80	20	144

[a] Differences in success rate as great as these between releasees with discord reported and those with no discord reported would occur by chance alone, with samples of this size, less than once in a hundred times (by Chi Square test).

Some illustration of the nature of discord in the home life of members of our Postrelease Panel sample is provided by the following reports on Case 068: (from presentence report by U. S. Probation Officer)

. . . it is this officer's opinion that the father has rejected the boy over the years and it appears that the father does not really want the boy in the home. . . . The father and stepmother feel that they will not be able to come to the Court on the day of the defendant's disposition.

(postinstitutional material from interviews)

I stayed out real late one night drinking and didn't call home or anything and let them know where I was. I stayed at one of the guys' houses I was with. When I came home, my mother [stepmother] told me to pack my bags. So I did. Then my father came upstairs and beat me down to the floor and told me to stay.

. . . then they're always reminding me of what I've done. I haven't done nothing wrong yet [since release] and am not going to. But they sit me down and talk to me for two hours or so every day—reminding me of what I've done. I get tired of this. My mother says, "If it wasn't for you kids, I'd be in Milwaukee." My father is working on a job there now, and she's been up there for a while. Everything goes all right when she's gone. I wouldn't care if she'd go away and stay.

I wish they'd make up their minds if they want me there (at home) or not. I won't leave 'til they tell me to and I don't know where I'll go. But I won't stay if they don't want me.

The deep-seated nature of some conflicts of offenders with their parents is suggested by the following report by Case 033 which suggests the father's favorable motivation, yet total frustration due to incapacity in helping his son:

When I was younger, I used to go out quite a lot, and he [father] would always have something to say to me when I came back. He always accused me of something whether I was doing anything or not—for instance, I might be over in the park with the fellows and he would say when I got back—"Why are you taking out that damn whore, M.?" He knew everything, he thought—I don't know how he knew it but he did. I never did like to do the wrong thing, but then I started running around and getting into trouble.

Q. And your father didn't drink until you started running around like this and getting into trouble?

No, and while I was away, everything was all right at home. He stayed home and didn't drink. I knew it'd be like this when I got back. They [family] did all right when I was gone—my sister was working, and my father had a job. When I got back, and he left [father quit a "good job," started drinking again, and started living away from home], it made things a little rougher.

When he [father] comes over to the house, he will come in the door and *just look at me* [expressed very bitterly]. I will go in the bedroom or somewhere, and when I come out he will ask why I didn't speak to him—"After all, I am your father"—I will say that he didn't speak to me—why should I speak to him.

What seems to be illustrated in the foregoing cases of conflict between young adult offenders and their parents is a repetition, on each contact, of early struggles of the youth to achieve a sense of his own independence and competence. This is manifested in children and youth by what Plant has called "negativism"—an irritability at every instruction or suggestion from parents. It is particularly manifested when the parents are most oriented to being helpful; for example, the child stubbornly keeps his coat on or expresses hostility when his parent tells him to take it off as they come into an office, although the child had started to take his coat off on his own and would have done so peaceably had not the parent volunteered the instruction. As Plant puts it, children and youth are trying to achieve a conception of their own autonomy, of being independent persons, and to achieve this self-conception most youth put up a "thick and irritable wall" against bossy, nagging, or otherwise overdominating persons. This "wall" often makes for more pressure by the well-motivated but dominating parent, leading to increased resistance by the youth. Reduction of pressure is necessary to reduce such a youth's irritability, and to help him achieve a favorable self-conception by perceiving himself as having successfully performed desired behavior on his own initiative and direction.[15]

Predominant psychological and psychiatric theory indicates that personality traits developed by a child in his relationship to his parents tend to persist and are repeated in his subsequent relationships with other persons. Therefore it was not surprising that we frequently found evidence that a major determinant of the accord which a married releasee achieved when he resumed life with his wife was the extent to which her behavior failed to evoke his reaction to criticism. Here we did not have much detail on discord, but in the narratives recorded by one of our interviewers (Hutchinson) when subjects explained how their wives helped them adjust successfully, we repeatedly find phrases like:

By being encouraging and not nagging—not mentioning anything about it [record] and also not feeling sorry for me. (Case 063)

[She] don't say nothing about the past or nothing like that. [She] makes me feel like I've never been away from home. (Case 030)

Supported the good side of me without mentioning the bad. [He stated he probably could have not tolerated frequent references to the past. Wife has also accepted activities away from home without question—fishing trips with old friends, for example.] (Case 057)

Love, faith, by never nagging me—doesn't question where I'm going when I leave in the morning. (Case 060)

In interpreting the process by which an offender's discord with his parents or his wife leads to further crime, there often is divergence between psychologists or psychiatrists and sociologists. Psychological interpretations often view the crime as expressing an unconscious reaction to the discord, such as the offender returning to crime because of an unconscious desire to be punished, or to punish his parent or wife. Sociologists think of the offender's behavior as expressing competing social influences, so that they view conflict in the family as a factor in crime mainly because it reduces the capacity of the family to compete successfully with the influences on the offender of delinquent contacts outside the home. Our data on the extent of releasee dependence on relatives for material assistance would add a third interpretation, that discord in the home reduces the availability to the releasee of vital assistance during the immediate postprison months. It is

[15] James S. Plant, *Personality and the Cultural Pattern* (New York, Commonwealth Fund, 1937), pp. 121-25.

possible that all three of these interpretations are valid; the unconscious processes, the social competition, and the material resource effects of family discord each could be alone in primary significance in certain cases, and could operate together and reinforce each other in other cases. Further discussion of these theoretical implications will be deferred to chapter 18.

POSTRELEASE CHANGE OF RESIDENCE

As indicated in Table 15.6, only about half of the cases in our "effective sample" remained in their first postprison residence for the full period of our contact with them, which in the median case was 5.3 months. However, five out of six married men living with in-laws moved, as did five out of six of the men who lived alone at their first residence. The most common complaint about conditions in the first residence, however, were physical conditions of the housing, rather than characteristics of the people there. It appeared that the wives of married prisoners, having to subsist on a much lower income while their husbands were confined, often moved to much more crowded and inferior quarters in this period than those to which they were previously accustomed. These families procured better housing as soon as they could after the husband's release. The median duration of stay at the first postprison residence was only 2.1 months for husbands released to homes with both wives and other relatives, and 2.3 months for men who lived alone.

At the end of the first month following release, 83 per cent of the effective sample were still living in their first residence, 16 per cent were in their second residence, and 1 per cent had moved to a third residence. By the end of the third month, less than two-thirds of the sample were still living at the first residence, 26 per cent had moved to a second residence, 10 per cent were living in their third residence, and 1 per cent were in a fourth residence. At the end of the fifth month, 50 per cent of those still in the sample were still at their first postrelease residence, 33 per cent were at the second residence, 13 per cent had moved to a third residence, 3 per cent were living in their fourth residence, and 1 per cent had moved to a fifth residence.

As Table 15.10 indicates, the whites moved somewhat more frequently than did the nonwhites, perhaps reflecting the lesser housing choice for nonwhites. The youngest inmates moved least often, but no other relationship of age to mobility was clear. Three-quarters of those who went to a city different from that of their immediate preprison residence moved from their first postprison residence, but only one-third of those who returned to their preprison neighborhood moved. As might be expected, those who had no prearranged residence moved most frequently in the first postprison months, 70 per cent moving two or more times in our approximately half-year follow-up period. The releasees who moved only once had somewhat lower

TABLE 15.10　Characteristics of Movers and Nonmovers
(Postrelease Panel Study, cases seen for three months or more)

Characteristics	Never moved	Moved once only	Moved more than once	Total cases
Race:				
White	45%	33%	23%	83 (100%)
Nonwhite	57%	25%	18%	61 (100%)
Age:				
23 or younger	63%	27%	10%	30 (100%)
24 through 35	43%	32%	25%	60 (100%)
36 or older	50%	28%	22%	54 (100%)
Community to which released:[a]				
Same neighborhood	67%	28%	5%	64 (100%)
Different neighborhood	39%	31%	30%	54 (100%)
Different city	25%	29%	46%	24 (100%)
Prior criminal record in community to which released:				
None	47%	25%	28%	36 (100%)
Arrest or conviction on prior offense only	38%	38%	24%	34 (100%)
Arrest or conviction on last commitment	57%	27%	16%	74 (100%)
First residence was:[a]				
Prearranged	56%	31%	13%	124 (100%)
Not prearranged	15%	15%	70%	20 (100%)
Subsequent failures	19%	14%	30%	20%
Subsequent successes	81%	86%	70%	80%
Total cases	72 (50%)	42 (29%)	30 (21%)	144 (100%)

[a] Variations as large as these in the percentage distributions within different rows or columns under the characteristic indicated would occur by chance alone less than once in a thousand times (by Chi Square test).

failure rates than those who did not move, but the releasees who moved two or more times had over twice the failure rates of those who moved only once.

An analysis of 108 changes of residence by the men in our Postrelease Panel "effective sample" indicates that 43 per cent of the moves were away from the homes of parents or other relatives and 43 per cent were to live alone or with friends. Of the moves away from the homes of parents or relatives, however, 39 per cent were moves to other homes of the parents or relatives, 33 per cent were to live alone or with friends, and 28 per cent were to live with a wife or wife and offspring, with no other relatives. Of the moves away from residences where they lived alone or with friends, three-fourths were to other residences of the same type.

For persons moving but once in the course of our contact with them, the principal movement was to live with their wife or wife and offspring, and no other relatives. For those moving more than once, the principal move was to live alone. In all changes of residence the predominant orientation appears to be that of achieving independence from parents, by the releasee's living either alone or with a spouse. There was also a movement to better quarters and to more privacy, with a progressive increase on each move in the proportion having a room of their own or with spouse. This independence also is reflected among those who moved in the period of our contact with them, in an increase from half to five-sixths in the proportion who pay rent. Each successive move also was associated with an increase in the proportion expressing satisfaction with their current residence, and a decrease in the proportion who said that they expected to move in six months or less.

Table 15.11 deals separately with those changes of residence which separated releasees from the relatives who were their principal postrelease

TABLE 15.11   Success and Failure Rates Associated with Moves Away from Relatives According to Occurrence of Discord
(Postrelease Panel Study, effective sample, for our total period of contact with them, in median case 5.3 months)

	Per cent successes	Per cent failures	No. of cases
Discord reported:			
Moved so as to live no longer with relatives with whom discord occurred	44	56	9
Did not separate from persons with whom discord occurred	69	31	32
Total discord reported	63	37	41
No discord reported:			
Moved so as to live no longer with relative who was predominant postrelease residential associate	80	20	10
Did not separate from relative who was predominant postrelease residential associate	88	12	76
Total no discord reported	87	13	86
Total cases living with others:			
Moved from relative who was principal postrelease residential associate	63	37	19
Did not separate from principal postrelease residential associate	82	18	108

residential associates. It also separates cases where discord with a relative was reported from those in which no discord was mentioned. Since only nineteen of the releasees in our sample changed residence to alter their associates in this fashion, and discord occurred in only nine of those cases, one cannot make conclusive generalizations on such movement. Nevertheless, it is interesting that success was not associated with movement away from a discordant relationship; with or without discord, staying with relatives was associated with greater success than moving away from them.

While this is not conclusive enough evidence to suggest that any movement to escape discord is inadvisable, it suggests caution in such moves in the immediate postrelease months. Possibly the releasee is the main source of discord, and moving will not alter his pattern. Also, the economic hardship, psychological effects, and social influences in such moves may be criminogenic and may express a pattern of flight from, rather than solution to, problems. Yet, in other cases, departure may be the optimum solution. It would be interesting to reassess movement after experience with the prerelease centers described in chapter 16, in which the releasee usually is secure economically before he enters parole and has had time to test his relationships with those at his proposed home before he moves out of the center.

It should be noted that, as indicated in Table 15.11, a change in residence which does not change the relative who is a releasee's principal residential associate, such as movement *with* wife or parents, was not contraindicated. Such changes of residence were associated with success, perhaps because they were also associated with economic progress, for they seemed always to involve movement to better quarters.

The foregoing data on moving refer exclusively to movement within a federal judicial district. Moves from one district to another were recorded for the U. S. Parole Board's sample of all Federal Youth Correction Act commitments in fiscal year ending June 30, 1955. The 279 cases in this sample who were supervised in only one federal judicial district on their first parole had a 64 per cent failure rate, as compared with a 44 per cent failure rate for the thirty-four cases supervised in two or more districts. This would be a relatively simple problem to investigate further by compilation of statistics from parole board files, to see what attributes and circumstances are associated with successful and with unsuccessful moves.

OLD FRIENDS AND NEW

Association with Preprison Friends

At our second interview with our Postrelease Panel Study sample, in the median case 1.7 months after their release, we asked a series of questions about association with old friends. Ninety-eight per cent of 118 releasees who returned to the metropolitan area where they resided before imprisonment reported that they had friends or acquaintances in that area who would remember them from before their incarceration. Among twenty-four who were released to a city other than that of their preprison residence, only seven, or 29 per cent, reported having preprison friends there. At this second interview, 88 per cent of those who returned to the city of their former residence and only 21 per cent of those who returned to a different city reported that they had already seen preprison acquaintances.

Considering only those who had old acquaintances in the city of their release, 87 per cent had seen one or more of such acquaintances by the time of our second interview and only 6 per cent reported that they deliberately avoided encountering such persons. By the time of the second interview, 95 per cent of the nonwhites with former acquaintances in the city area already had seen one or more of these acquaintances, as against 84 per cent of the whites. The restricted section of the city in which nonwhites are forced to reside appears to have been a major factor in the greater frequency with which they renewed these prior contacts; the white population was more widely dispersed in the metropolitan area. The proportion who had seen old acquaintances was about the same for all age groups among the nonwhites, but it varied inversely with age for the whites, from 90 per cent for those twenty-three or younger to 74 per cent for those thirty-six or older.

Of the releasees who had some contact with preincarceration friends or acquaintances, 85 per cent indicated that at least half of these former acquaintances knew of their stay in prison. Ninety-five per cent of those who contacted friends who knew of their prison record said that this knowledge had no adverse effect on the response of their friends to them, but 24 per cent reported that they themselves were uncomfortable when associating with these preincarceration friends who knew of their record. Differences between these two groups were only slight with respect to extent of prior criminal record, age, and racial composition, and on the crucial test of subsequent failure, differences also were negligible.

Obviously, there can be much diversity in the criminality or conventionality of relationships with preprison friends. Our only clue to this arose from questions in the second interview, in which we asked the releasees to recapitulate their activities during three days of the preceding week: the last weekday, the last Saturday, and the last Sunday. They were also asked to indicate whether any of the persons with whom they associated on these days happened to be old friends, and if so, what they had done or how they had passed the time together. However, there was some resistance to this phase of the interview, especially when the subjects were pressed for time, and possibly some of our staffs' expectations that the subjects would resist this phase of the interviews was so reflected in their manner of administering it as to become a self-fulfilling prophecy. At any rate, this summary of three days' activities was procured from only three-fourths of our respondents. Of the 93 releasees who both had preprison friends in the metropolitan area where they resided and supplied us with a summary of three days' activities, 47 per cent reported association with such friends on these three days. Only 36 per cent described types of activities with these associates which could be presumed to be somewhat conducive to difficulty with the law for them, such as gambling, trying to pick up women, or visiting taverns.

Contact with Prison Acquaintances

In our fifth interview with our Postrelease Panel cases, which in the median case was 5 months after their departure from prison, we asked whether they encountered anyone since their release who had been in prison with them. Fifty-eight per cent reported that they had such contacts.

Seventy-five per cent of the nonwhite releasees, but only 49 per cent of the whites, reported encountering prison acquaintances after their release. There also was a racial difference in the number of prison contacts renewed: half of the nonwhites, but only 18 per cent of the whites, reported encountering three or more persons whom they had known in prison. This probably reflects the concentration of nonwhite releasees in limited areas of these cities, as a result of racial discrimination in housing.

Contact with three or more prison acquaintances was most frequent among the younger releasees, ranging from 38 per cent for those under twenty-four years old to 28 per cent for those twenty-four to thirty-five, and 24 per cent for those over thirty-five. This inverse relationship of age to renewal of prison contacts was especially pronounced among white releasees: one-third of the whites under twenty-four years old, but only one-ninth of whites twenty-four or older, met three or more of their prison acquaintances in approximately the first five months after their release. This, of course, is consistent with our prison data and other evidence that social cohesion is uniquely characteristic of youthful offenders.

Even among those men released to a city different from that in which they resided before prison, by the time of our fifth interview, 55 per cent had met some person whom they knew in prison, a proportion almost as high as the 61 per cent renewal of contacts by those releasees who returned to the city of their preprison residence. However, only 18 per cent of those released to a different city had met three or more of their prison acquaintances, as contrasted with 34 per cent among those returning to their city of prior residence.

Thirty-four per cent of those who encountered prison acquaintances after release stated that their first contact with those persons was at the U. S. Probation Office, where the men in this sample reported for parole or mandatory release supervision. The probation office was designated as the place of first contact by 49 per cent of the whites who encountered prison acquaintances, but by only 21 per cent of the nonwhites. This probably reflects the greater geographical dispersion of whites than nonwhites in the metropolitan areas where these probation offices were located, which made contact between white acquaintances outside the probation office less probable or easy than contact between nonwhites.

For the sample as a whole, the most frequently cited circumstances of contact with prison associates was by chance encounter on the street. Initial contacts under these circumstances were reported by about 60 per cent of those renewing prison acquantances: by 49 per cent of the white releasees and by 72 per cent of the nonwhites. Generally this contact was in the neighborhood of their residence, which may partially reflect the extent to which leisure time in slum areas is spent on the streets.

Perhaps most important is the fact that only 12 per cent of those who had seen prison acquaintances reported deliberate planning of this renewal of the prison association. Planned contacts with prison friends were reported by 16 per cent of nonwhites and 8 per cent of whites. Although 45 per cent of the nonwhites and 20 per cent of the whites who met prison acquaintances had their first encounter in their first month out of prison, at our fifth interviews (in the median case five months after the subject's release), 70 per cent of the whites and 40 per cent of the nonwhites reported only one encounter with these persons.

Only 11 per cent of either white or nonwhite releasees reporting encounters with prison acquaintances stated that they engaged in leisure-time activities with these persons. Although a majority of the released prisoners have some further contact with their prison associates, as far as we could learn very few attempt to renew or maintain prison friendships. Released prisoners apparently retain the cautious aloofness toward other prisoners which we found they developed in prison. The shared experience of imprisonment does not seem to inspire a corps of alumni proud of their past institutional identification with a prison alma mater and loyal to others who shared the same institutional involvement. Instead, our interviews suggest that most ex-prisoners strive to disassociate themselves from their former colleagues and to disengage themselves from prison ties.

Nevertheless, such contact as did occur with prison associates was the best predictor of subsequent criminality that we could find in our data on immediate postprison nonfamily social life. There were 134 men in our Postrelease Panel study with whom we had contact for three or more months in 1959-60 and from whom we collected responses to all of our inquiries on encounters with prison acquaintances (second and fifth interview). Of the fifty-four men who never saw any prison acquaintances, only 9 per cent were subsequent failures (returned to prison or given nonprison sentence for felony-like offense by January 1962). Of the forty-three men who saw prison acquaintances only once, 21 per cent were subsequent failures. Of the thirty-seven men who saw the prison acquaintances more than once, 32 per cent were subsequent failures.[16] Of course, many variables besides the influence of prison contacts are reflected here. For example, unemployed men were more likely than employed men to encounter prison acquaintances in the street and in their more frequent calls at the probation office.

New Friends

Although large cities have traditionally been portrayed as isolating their inhabitants from each other, it seems more accurate to say only that cities differ from rural areas in having lower rates of association and friendship between those who reside close to each other. People in the city's crowd are not necessarily lonely, but their friendships depend on only that small portion of their contacts with others in which they interact on a personal basis. The development of such personal interaction comes either from relationships of the past, such as those of kinship or of previous friendship, or from types of contact which break down the barriers to personal interaction that characterize most encounters between urbanites. This is evident in the processes by which the releasees whom we studied developed new friendships.

At our fifth interview with the Postrelease Panel sample (in the median case five months after release), 70 per cent of the men reported that they had made new friends since they left prison. New friendships were reported by only 66 per cent of those who were released to the city of their preprison residence, but by 86 per cent of those released to another city. To an open question on how they had met their new friends, some releasees responded in terms of the place and some in terms of the person through whom they made the new acquaintance, while some gave both the places and the persons involved. For white releasees, the place most frequently cited as the location where new friendships were formed was at work, but for nonwhites the most frequently cited places were commercial recreation establishments, such as taverns, restaurants, and pool halls. The neighborhood of residence was the second most frequently cited place for both racial groups, with work third for nonwhites and commercial recreational establishments third for whites. For all categories of releasees, old friends were cited in a majority of cases as the persons introducing new friends. Family members, including wife or in-laws, were second in frequency.

One might presume that new friends would be valued as a way of escaping from the stigma of a prison record. Indeed, fourteen of the nineteen men who were released to a city other than that of their preprison residence and reported having made new friends said that none of their new friends knew of their prison record, and four said that only a few friends

---

[16] Differences in success rates as great as these, for samples of this size, could occur by chance alone less than once in twenty times (by Chi Square test).

knew of it. On the other hand, 51 per cent of the seventy-three men who were released to the city of their preprison residence and reported new friends said that a majority of their new friends knew of their prison record. There was no appreciable racial difference in reported knowledge of prison record among new friends, but among whites this knowledge was especially often reported by the younger releasees. A widespread interest in hiding this record still is indicated by the fact that 39 per cent of all releasees with new friends said that none of these friends knew of their prison record, and 17 per cent said that only a small fraction knew.

Of the releasees who reported that some new friends knew of their prison record, 64 per cent stated that they themselves told them of this record. Contrary to what one might expect, old friends were not frequently believed by the releasees to have informed the new friends of their prison record. Next to the releasee himself, the most frequently cited source of information was simply the releasee's general reputation from the notoriety of his case, common gossip, or other general knowledge of this record in the neighborhood or in other social circles where he mingled. Those releasees who themselves reported their prison record to new friends seem to have been more criminalistic than the releasees whose new friends learned of their criminal record from some other source. The record-revealing inmates had more extensive prior arrest records and were three times as often arrested for their last offense in the city to which they were released as those not revealing their prison record themselves. Fifty-nine per cent of those who told their new friends of their record reported types of leisure activities with their new friends which could be considered conducive to a disorderly reputation, such as drinking and gambling, as against 24 per cent of those whose new friends learned of the criminal record from some other source.

There were 132 inmates whom we saw for three or more months after release and from whom we received a response to our inquiries on new friends. Somewhat surprisingly, of thirty-nine who reported *no* new friends, only 15 per cent were subsequent failures, compared to 23 per cent failures among ninety-three who reported new friends. There were 19 per cent failures among the thirty-six who said that none of their new friends knew of their prison record, compared to 23 per cent failures among the fifty-seven who said that some of their new friends knew of their record.

POLICE CONTACTS

A recurrent theme in the conversations of prison inmates is that, because of police harassment, an ex-convict does not have a chance in the free community. Numerous tales of being arrested when they are trying to "go straight" and being "shaken down" by police seeking bribes are recounted in prison conversations all over the country.

Whether or not the facts warrant a fear of police, such fears clearly exist. In 1952, for the Illinois Selective Service Felon Study, I interviewed a man in a suburb of Chicago who owned his own home, had a fine family, and for several years had held a good job in a suburban company. In his youth he lived in a Chicago stockyards area, from which he had been committed to the state training school twice and to the state prison once. He also had a brother with a similar record. This man was paroled from prison to the army in World War II, eight years before my interview with him. Yet he asserted that in his six years back in the Chicago area he never dared return near his old neighborhood and was even fearful of entering Chicago, because certain policemen had always picked him or his brother up when they recognized them. His relatives still lived in the old neighborhood, but he insisted on their coming to visit him rather than his going there.

One item in our Prison Panel Supplement Study questionnaire was: "What do you think the chances are that you will have trouble with the police harassing you or picking on you after you are arrested?" Answers to be checked were expressed in terms of probability: "absolutely no chance," "slight chance," "even chance," "better than even chance," and "almost certain."

At Leavenworth, and at all except "Busy" State Penitentiary among the six state prisons where this questionnaire was distributed, the most frequent answers to these questions were "even chance" and "slight chance." At "Busy" State, and at all of the seven federal prisons except Leavenworth, the predominant answers were "slight chance" and "absolutely no chance." The "almost certain" response to the question on expectation of harassment was checked by less than one-tenth of the inmates at prison camps and at "Busy" State Penitentiary, but by close to a fifth of the inmates at reformatories, the other state penitentiaries, and Leavenworth. Possibly the fact that both released federal offenders and released "Busy" State offenders are more widely dispersed than most released prisoners from other states makes them less vulnerable to police harassment. Also federal offenders deal with highly professionalized police agencies, who are less likely to indulge in harassment than some local police. However, many a federal prisoner, especially at Leavenworth, has a state felony record as well as his federal sentence and has created ample grounds for police suspicion that he will continue in criminality. No consistent pattern of change in these fears, from the beginning to the end of imprisonment, was evident.

Reports of police harassment were given to our interviewers by both returned violators and the successful releasees, but it is difficult to assess the validity of their complaints conclusively from the available file information and from their oral reports. An extreme illustration of the difficulties of interpreting ex-convict complaints regarding police harassment is provided by returned violator case V-035, whom we shall call John. John procured a job as a cook in a restaurant the day after his release from prison. He worked there for thirty-three days, then was arrested by the police on a robbery charge and was held in jail for a month. He was released with all charges dismissed and found a job with a construction company in about a day, where he worked for just over two weeks before he was again arrested by the police and held for eighteen days. This time, he says, he used all of his funds to get a lawyer who procured his release, so he was completely destitute at release, but found a job as a dishwasher within a day. John held this job for one and a half months, when he was again picked up by the police on a robbery charge and was released in less than three weeks without being convicted. He was then employed for five months at a packing house and for half a year operating his own truck. Finally, he was arrested and received a sentence for robbery for which he was confined in a state prison for four years, then returned to the federal prison as a conditional release violator.

John claims, of course, that he was innocent of all charges. He says his implication in the offense for which he got a state prison sentence occurred when he returned from hunting with a friend; the police were waiting to arrest his friend for a robbery in which another man was an accomplice, but John was accused. If one assumes that this is a cock-and-bull story and that John was properly convicted when sent to state prison, this leads one to suspect that the earlier arrests were based upon justifiable suspicion. Yet the fact that this subject was not convicted on his earlier arrests, and procured legitimate employment immediately after each release, suggests that his complaints of harassment on these occasions may have been bona fide.

It is well known that in some jurisdictions persons with a criminal record are subject to suspicion, and may be picked up by the police whenever crimes occur for which the police have no other leads. Yet it is notable that when men are picked up, it is often at a questionable place or hour, or with a questionable associate, so that the police suspicion is readily understood.

The following are some interesting reports and comments on police harassment from a letter to me by J. Glenn Hutchinson, in December 1959, when he was our researcher in the Chicago Federal Probation Office:

I held a second postrelease interview today with case #015, a young Spanish-American boy who had indicated in his first interview, that prior to his serving a Federal sentence, the police in the neighborhood where he lived were constantly throwing him in jail for "nothing at all." The respondent today told me that he had made one trip back to his old neighborhood to visit with some old pals of his (he lives about three miles away from this old neighborhood now). He states that he was eating in a restaurant and was about half through his meal when a policeman came in and recognized him as a person whom he had ar-

rested previously. He asked the respondent if his name wasn't _____
(giving his correct name), and the respondent replied "Yes." Whereupon the
police officer, according to respondent, told him to get out of his district and
stay out of it, and never let him catch him there again. This is essentially the
warning that was given to respondent #008 when he was taken to the 12th
Street Police Station (after being picked up in a Loop hotel, where he "crashed"
a large party). He claimed that the captain there had told him "to get the hell
out of his district and stay out of it," and not to let them catch him in the
district again. The respondent raised a quite pertinent question as to the logic
of such a warning, when this police district includes the Loop and the U. S.
Court House, where he must report for parole supervision.

This reaction on the part of police officers raises a couple of interesting problems. From the sociological angle, we are confronted here with the expression
of a sort of "occupational provincialism" in which the police officer (either
officer on the beat or captain at the station house) feels it incumbent upon himself in discharging his professional duties and protecting his own area or district,
to keep ex-cons physically out of the district. Logically, of course, this simply
means that if he keeps out of Officer A's district, he is *ipso facto* going to be in
Officer B's district, and Officer B will no doubt take the same provincial attitude. These incidents give evidence of the way in which police officers con-
ceptualize their professional duty in a very provincial manner. It should be
noted that they did not warn these respondents to stay out of "trouble" or to
stay away from illegal activity, but simply to stay out of the physical environs
over which these officers had responsibility. From the broad societal point of
view, it is obvious that such provincialism is completely meaningless since it is
immaterial to the society as a whole, whether suspicious character A is hanging
around the Palmer House or is hanging around the Edgewater Beach Hotel,
but the police captain in charge of security of the Loop hotels would apparently
be perfectly happy as long as A is out of the Loop.

My second comment on incidents such as this is from the social psychological
point of view. A major problem, of course, in rehabilitation of the offender is
the fact that authoritative agents of society continue to confront the ex-offender
with a self-image as an undesirable person, who ought literally to be physically
removed from areas such as police districts or barred from more sociological
"areas" such as employment or marriage.

Shortly after this letter was written, the Chicago police burglary scandal
broke, and that city's police force was drastically reorganized. We presume
Chicago police now are less "provincial." However, the policy of harassing
known offenders when there is inadequate grounds for conviction is well
established in police practice, particularly as a means of keeping prostitutes,
pickpockets, and confidence men out of the most "respectable" business
areas. When there is no intention to charge or even to arrest, there is less
concern with the legality of what might otherwise be an arrest procedure.[17]

[17] Wayne R. LaFave, "The Police and Non-Enforcement of the Law," *Wisconsin
Law Review,* no. 1 (Jan. 1962), 104-37, and no. 2 (March 1962), 172-239.

In our second interview with the "effective" Postrelease Panel sample, which in the median case was 1.7 months after their release, we asked those who had been released to a city where they previously resided whether they knew any of the police in their old neighborhood. Only 47 per cent of these men replied in the affirmative. Of those who knew police in their neighborhood, slightly over half had seen these police, but only a third said that they had both seen the police and the police had recognized them. This residual amounts to only seventeen cases of the 145 in the total sample, or 12 per cent.

With this same sample, from our second through our sixth interviews, we always asked each releasee whether any police officers had talked to him since the last time we had seen him. When they answered in the affirmative, we probed for the details of this experience. We also regularly checked the parole supervision file and frequently discussed each case with the supervision officers, so that we probably knew of all police contacts reported to the office. Forty per cent of the 145 men in our effective sample had some type of personal interaction with the police during the first half-year or so after their release, when they were in our study. For 17 per cent, this was a matter of being questioned, warned, or possibly searched by the police, but not arrested (although occasionally driven for a few blocks in a police car). For 11 per cent, the contact with police was for a traffic infraction only. For 9 per cent, the contact consisted only of casual or sociable conversation, with no hostility, although it sometimes included inquiry about the activities of their friends. Six per cent of the men were arrested on suspicion of having committed a felony, and 3 per cent on nontraffic misdemeanors. One releasee dealt with the police only when he called them to investigate a burglary of his apartment, in which some of his wife's valuables were taken; his own criminal record was not revealed in this. These contacts add to more than 40 per cent because some releasees had several of the above types of contact. Three of the men reported four different contacts with the police, two reported three contacts, and ten reported two contacts (not necessarily different types of contact).

The extent of the ex-prisoners' contact with police during the immediate postrelease period of our research seemed to be a good index of their subsequent "failure" (return to prison or a nonprison sentence for a felony-like offense in approximately the first two years out of prison) only when the police contact involved arrest on a felony charge. Five of the nine cases in our effective sample arrested on felony grounds were subsequent failures, as against only 18 per cent failures in the remainder of the effective sample, who had no felony arrests. Of the twenty-five men whose contact involved being questioned, searched, or warned, but not arrested, 28 per cent (seven men) were subsequent failures. The failure rate of the few men with only traffic infractions, casual contacts, or misdemeanor arrests by the police were somewhat below the failure rates of the men for whom no police contact whatsoever was reported. In general, these statistics suggest that where the police were suspicious of felony behavior there was likely to be a basis for their suspicion, and other types of police action had no serious implications.

There were several instances in which both returned violators and successful releasees reported being picked up by the police one or more times, but said that their federal probation officer then talked to the police and got the men relieved of police interference. One of the items on our questionnaire completed by 96 per cent of U. S. Probation Officers read as follows: "What do you generally do when a parolee under your supervision comes to you and tells you that the police have been harassing him?" The alternative answers which the probation officers could check, and the proportion selecting each, were as follows:

Contact the police personally and request them to leave the parolee
    alone unless they have good reason to suspect him of a crime.   13%
Arrange for parolee to go in and talk to police and straighten out
    the problem.   21%
Advise parolee to avoid situations which increase the likelihood
    of his being stopped.   63%
Nothing. If police are harassing the parolee, there must be a good
    reason.   ½ of 1%

Two per cent wrote in other answers and ½ of 1 per cent left this item blank.

It is, of course, possible that this question suggested alternatives which were seen by some probation officers mainly as norms to which they would like to conform and that they do not pursue these practices as frequently as their responses might suggest.

Despite the dramatic accounts of a few instances of alleged extreme injustice, the total number of cases in which a serious police harassment problem was indicated by the subject's account or the probation office record amount to only 6 per cent of the successful releasees and 8 per cent of the returned violators. It is understandable that one of the consequences of committing a crime is vulnerability to suspicion of further crime, and it is regrettable when this leads to violation of legal rights. However, most ex-criminals apparently live down their past reputations. Similarly, professional police forces learn that the arrest of an innocent man, when it causes him to lose his job and his hope for success in legitimate work, may directly contribute to his return to crime.

It should be noted that the prisoners' expectations of police harassment were more frequent than the actual occurrence of clear harassment. The percentage of federal prisoners "absolutely certain" of police harassment exceeded the percentage of releasees who seemed to us to be seriously disturbed by police harassment. In addition to the prisoners "absolutely certain," many considered their chances of police harassment "more than even" or "even."

Apparently police harassment of ex-prisoners who are not involved in illegitimate activities does occur with sufficient frequency in some jurisdictions for it to be a matter of realistic concern to ex-prisoners. Nevertheless, there are several reasons why one would expect the prisoners to have exaggerated expectations regarding the prospects of police harassment. The ego of any man who has failed to stay out of prison is assuaged if he can blame someone else for his failure. The police, who apprehend the offender, are a convenient scapegoat. The degradation of arrest and conviction, and any guilt feelings the offender may have for his crime, are effectively neutralized by charging the representatives of the law with criminal behavior.

I have been impressed with how quickly and how universally prisoners tell me their allegations of police, judicial, and prison injustice. Others have similar experience. As Sykes and Matza have implied in discussing delinquents, the ascription of criminality to legitimate officials is one of the techniques by which offenders achieve an ethical "neutralization" of their crimes.[18] These allegations are a countermeasure against the degradation of status resulting from the prisoner's conviction and imprisonment. Accusing "respectable" persons of crime helps the prisoner to reconcile his own criminality with his continued favorable conception of himself from the standpoint of his noncriminal reference groups. That is why accusations of the "evil" in "good" people are especially savored in prison and repeated, and in the recounting they are embellished for maximum verbal impact. They become part of an ideology, and sometimes a mythology, in behalf of the "cause" of convicts against the rest of the world.

One device sometimes employed by prison administrations to counter this excessive fear of police harassment by prisoners is to invite representatives of law enforcement agencies to speak in prison prerelease orientation programs and at the federal prerelease guidance centers. An effective speaker sometimes can counter inmate stereotypes of the police, and perhaps so convey the police point of view as to make releasees aware of the times and circumstances where they are most likely to be questioned by the police. I once heard one remind the prisoners that there are bars where the police would never question them and bars where they were very likely to be picked up, and that the drinks cost the same in both. In addition, of course, participation in these programs may enhance the extent to which police share the correctional interest in helping any releasees who sincerely endeavor to achieve a noncriminal way of life.

[18] Gresham M. Sykes and David Matza, "Techniques of Neutralization: A Theory of Delinquency," *Am. Sociological Rev., 22,* no. 6 (Dec. 1957), 664-70.

SUMMARY

Our interviews and questionnaires, administered to prison inmates at various stages of their term of confinement, led to the conclusions:

M1. As the date of their release approaches, the relationship between inmates and their parents or other blood relatives tends to improve ("absence makes the heart grow fonder"); therefore, inmates increasingly expect postrelease assistance from some relatives.

M2. Imprisonment tends to weaken ties with spouses and with former friends ("out of sight, out of mind").

M3. Inmate hostility to persons in the free community diminishes as their release date approaches, at least as indicated by inmates less frequently expecting harm from specific persons, and more frequently expressing a willingness to accept help from anyone.

Our monthly interviews with ex-federal prisoners in their immediate postrelease period, and our comparison of the postrelease experience of federal returned violators and successful releasees, as well as tabulations of information from prison files on past releasees, revealed that:

M4. Over 90 per cent of the men released from prison return to communities in which they previously resided.

M5. This means that they generally return to an area where their criminal reputation is known, but it also generally means that they return to the area where they can receive assistance from kin.

This probably is related to the indications that:

M6. Somewhat higher than average postrelease failure rates are associated with release to a community other than that of prior residence.

M7. The most unfavorable postrelease residential arrangement, in terms of postrelease failure rates, is that in which the ex-prisoner lives alone.

Nevertheless, not all residence with relatives seems favorable to postrelease success. Our findings confirmed expectations that:

M8. Discord with relatives in the releasee's place of residence is highly associated with subsequent failure.

Despite the extreme dependence of most released prisoners on parents or other relatives for room, board, and other economic assistance, the Postrelease Panel Study suggests that:

M9. Released prisoners move rapidly toward independence, moving away from the parental home or increasingly paying a share of the rent at home.

Since most released prisoners return to the communities of their prior residence, it is understandable that we found:

M10. Prisoners generally encounter old friends soon after release, and their prison record is widely known in their postrelease social circles.

Our data also indicated that:

M11. Most ex-prisoners re-encounter some prison acquaintances within a few months after their release.

M12. Persistent renewal of prison contacts is highly associated with reimprisonment.

However, most releasees do not maintain contact with those prison acquaintances whom they re-encounter, but rather:

M13. Most prisoners acquire new friends in the first few months after release, but usually the new friends know of the prison record of the releasee, often through their being informed by the releasee.

Nevertheless, the evidence also suggested:

M14. Development of new friendships, in which the criminal record of the releasee is not known, is associated with postrelease success.

Extensive inquiries among prisoners and releasees regarding police harassment indicated that:

M15. Most prisoners have real fears of suffering police harassment in their postrelease life.

M16. Although such harassment does occur and is sometimes so unjust or corrupt as to be of legitimate public concern, both serious and undeserved police harassment probably is not suffered by more than a few per cent of ex-prisoners.

CHAPTER 16

Remedies for Postprison Problems

The preceding chapters indicated the major problems encountered by newly released prisoners. Both an economic and a social adjustment in their post-prison life seemed to be necessary if they were to maximize prospects of avoiding further crime. They had to attain economic self-sufficiency by procuring adequate legitimate income. They needed also to achieve satisfying social relationships with noncriminal persons and to break off contact with criminals.

These two types of postrelease adjustment appeared to be interdependent: those who worked regularly were likely to make new social ties and break off criminal contacts; those who renewed previous ties with criminals or disorderly persons were not likely to work regularly. There were some exceptions to these patterns among the violators in our samples, but the postrelease conditions most persistently and pronouncedly differentiating the failures from the successes were the economic deprivation of the failures and their lack of integration into noncriminal social groups. What major remedies are available to help solve these economic and social problems?

GROWTH AND FLEXIBILITY IN EXISTING PRISON PROGRAMS

Governmental Financial Assistance

Chapter 14 reported a national survey of economic assistance to newly released prisoners. The survey's outstanding conclusion was that this assistance, in the average case, is meager. Secondly, the variations in the distribution of this assistance to different inmates, or their nonvariation, often reflects a concern for administrative convenience rather than for the most efficient use of available funds for reduction of recidivism.

Most states were found to issue a fixed sum of "gate money" as a release gratuity to all prisoners, regardless of differences in their needs when they left the prison. If a releasee had no other resources, this gratuity was never sufficient for his support until he could earn a first pay check, unless postrelease employment proved immediately available and was paid on a daily basis. In some prison systems appreciable cash savings at release could be accumulated by inmates long assigned to paid jobs, and compulsory savings requirements often assured this accumulation. However, this meant that prisoners not confined more than a year or two were not likely to accumulate much money, though their need might be great. Also, when the prisoner is likely to be destitute at release, the availability of pay rather than the possibility of meeting his training needs often determines the prison employment which he seeks and is given.

Our postrelease interviews indicated that most releasees subsist only through the assistance of friends and relatives. The latter are especially needed in the provision of room and board. To those who lack such assistance, emergency food and shelter is available at welfare missions in the "skid row" areas of large cities, but this is a condition not conducive to a self-sufficient noncriminal life. Sometimes released prisoners go to the home of relatives only because of the availability of free subsistence there, when the neighborhood or family social relationships to which they return foster further criminality.

After spending, in the average case, at least $1500 per year for several years to keep a man confined in prison, it appears to be extremely poor economics to deny him a few hundred dollars in postrelease aid if this would be a major factor in preventing his return to prison. Indeed, the cost of apprehension and of the return-to-prison procedure might exceed that of the aid which would prevent his return. Of course, financial assistance is not the only solution to the prevention of reimprisonment in every case, and it is not even required for many cases. This is precisely why more flexibility in the distribution of funds available for gratuities, or as prison earnings, is desirable. Provision of the most assistance where the need is greatest would be prudent from an economic as well as from a rehabilitative interest. The federal prison system is distinguished by much more liberality and flexibility than most other systems in this regard. Some increase in their gratuity payments occurred during the course of our research, including a 1962 law which increased the maximum permissible gratuity from $30 to $100.

Where some inmates save large sums in prison, some correctional systems adopt the practice of issuing their funds piecemeal, by checks distributed to the releasee through the parole supervision office. This would seem to be another prudent device for assuring maximum contribution of each dollar to prevent the inmate's return to prison. It is consistent with the growing conception that the state's deprivation of a felon's liberty is not necessarily a period of complete deprivation, abruptly terminated when the crime is "paid for." Instead, it is a period of graded variation in liberty, so regulated as to maximize the prospect of terminating criminality after full freedom is restored.

Encouragement of Noncriminal Contacts

Many prison procedures, including most of those noted in various chapters of Part II of this book, are designed to foster social ties between prisoners and various noncriminal persons. These include all practices that reduce the social distance between inmates and staff. Notable here are measures such as the treatment teams, for greater utilization of prison work supervisors and line custodial staff to augment the services of caseworkers. Also discussed in Part II was the integration of counseling with discipline, so as to reduce or prevent alienation of inmates from staff as a consequence of rule enforcement.

In addition to the foregoing, a number of measures should be mentioned which maximize a prison inmate's contact with noncriminal persons outside of prison, especially with those who will be available in the postrelease situation and can serve as an anticriminal influence. These are measures to encourage and facilitate letters and visits from relatives and from other persons not believed to represent a criminal influence.

During the course of our project the federal prisons made rapid strides in reducing censorship of inmate correspondence. After successful trials at Chillicothe, Ashland, and Terre Haute in 1958-1961, all routine censorship and restriction in volume of correspondence was eliminated in federal prisons in 1962. There still is a check for contraband objects, and occasional spot censoring of some mail, as well as careful surveillance when there is special reason to be suspicious of the correspondence of a specific individual. In this, as in many other areas of prison management, time-consuming routines introduced as custodial security measures proved not to be needed for security. (Indeed, the enhancement of inmate morale by removal of these routines may increase custodial security.)

Federal prisons are also distinguished by much more liberal and comfortable arrangements for outsiders interested in visiting prisoners than prevail in most state prisons. At all less than maximum security institutions, the visiting facilities include comfortable lounges, or, in pleasant weather, outside picnic areas rather than the traditional separation of inmates from visitors by wide tables or glass walls. Restrictions in the amount of physical contact between prisoners and visitors vary, but the volume of visiting is kept close to the maximum for which outsiders are available, particularly when the outsiders must travel far. The state of Mississippi has pioneered by allowing ten-day home leaves to selected prisoners who have served at least three years in the penitentiary. In the first twelve years of operation of this program they released 3204, of whom only fifteen failed to return, and twelve of these were accounted for. Mississippi also has pioneered in providing conjugal visits of wives to prisoners. Both home leaves and conjugal visits are well established in several foreign countries.[1]

[1] Eugene Zemans and Ruth S. Cavan, "Marital Relationships of Prisoners," *J. Crim. Law, Criminology, and Police Science*, 49, no. 1 (May–June 1958), 50-57; *idem.*, "Marital Relationships of Prisoners in Twenty-Eight Countries," *ibid., 49*, no. 2 (July–August 1958), 133-39.

A large number of private organizations provide casework visits and visits merely for the sake of friendship to inmates who lack ties with persons outside the prison who might visit them. These prison-visiting agencies include various church groups and agencies, such as the "Home Mission" of the Episcopal Church and the Society of Friends. There also are prison-visiting organizations dealing with special needs, such as Alcoholics Anonymous, and functionally specialized associations of persons sharing avocational interests with prisoners, such as chess clubs, bridge clubs, public-speaking organizations (Toastmasters), personality development groups (Dale Carnegie) and local service clubs (Jaycees, Lions, Optimists).

The initiative of prison officials generally can do much to stimulate the interest of outside organizations and individuals in visiting prisoners. In several federal prisons the wardens have been active in speaking to organizations in nearby communities, inviting them to visit the prison and encouraging them to establish auxiliary organizations among the inmates. Other prison staff have been urged to do the same. At several federal prisons groups of outside visitors are divided into pairs or trios, each of which is given an inmate guide. They are encouraged to socialize freely with inmates and to have meals with their inmate guides (generally in the officers' dining room). For special events at the prison, such as the issuance of diplomas and certificates for completion of studies, inmates have been encouraged to invite their relatives, who join the staff and inmates in a banquet and ceremony. Prison chaplains also have organized inmate branches of national religious laymen's organizations, like Yokefellows, and have encouraged joint meetings with outside units of those organizations.

At the U. S. Penitentiary at McNeil Island, Washington, the Catholic chaplain, Father Frances B. Prange, developed a large inmate group known as SIG (for "Self-Improvement Group"). It is essentially a discussion club on problems of the prisoners in achieving a self-sufficient noncriminal life, emphasizing self-analysis, but featuring one or more outside speakers at most of its meetings. Speakers come mainly from service or professional organizations in the Seattle-Tacoma area and have included police officials as well as businessmen, clergymen, educators, and others. The organization has its own newspaper circulating both in the prison and to the outside cooperating organizations and individuals. At its fifth anniversary, in April 1962, 450 visitors toured the prison and ate with the inmates of the group; every four visitors were assigned to one inmate who acted as their guide and host. Director James V. Bennett commented: "Not a single incident occurred that was in the least bit embarrassing. Five years ago I would not have thought that such a meeting could even be considered, but now I am convinced that it is helpful in bringing the inmates into contact with worthwhile institutional opportunities and giving them a chance to see for themselves how men and women on the outside feel toward the institution and its inmates."[2] Similar programs are developing at other federal and state prisons.

It seems reasonable to infer that all these contacts of outsiders with men in prison increase the extent to which the prisoners feel at ease with conventional persons when they are released. Also, in some instances, introduction to future employers, membership in religious or hobby organizations of their release community, or even close friendships with noncriminals develop from these contacts in prison.

Prerelease Orientation Programs

Many prisons have some type of prerelease orientation program for prisoners who are about to be paroled or discharged. These vary tremendously in magnitude and in quality. Optimum programs include counseling sessions on problems that men in prison are likely to encounter in seeking employment, including practice in completing employment application forms and arrangements to procure a Social Security card if the prisoner does not have one. In some of the more effective prerelease programs personnel men from industry and officials of labor unions are invited to talk to inmates on how to apply for a job and how to hold it. This has a dual benefit in educating the releasees for situations they are likely to encounter and in creating potential employers for released prisoners. Sometimes arrangements for employment are made before an inmate's release through such visits at the prison.

A standard feature of a good prison prerelease program is a discussion of parole rules and problems. This is done most effectively by one or more visiting parole supervision officers rather than by prison staff. Such visits have the advantage of counteracting unrealistic images of the parole supervision officer which inmates are likely to acquire from the rationalizations of returned violators. Evidence that federal prisoners have exaggerated notions of their prospective difficulties under parole supervision will be presented in chapter 17. California has progressed furthest in alleviating inmate apprehensions regarding parole by not only bringing parole supervision officers to speak to prisoners who are near release, but also bringing successful parolees back to the prison to talk to prospective releasees.

In federal and state prisons I have repeatedly noted much more continuous concern with maintenance of high standards in the orientation classes for newly admitted prisoners than in the prerelease classes. The latter seem to operate in spurts, being elaborately developed for some periods and then diminishing or disappearing altogether. They often decline

[2] James V. Bennett, "The Director's Page," *Federal Prison Service Newsletter, 49* (June 1962), 2. See also: Francis B. Prange, S.J., "The Self-Improvement Group at McNeil Island Penitentiary," *Federal Probation, 27,* no. 1 (March 1963), 34-36.

when staff in charge of these sessions leave the institution or become involved in other programs. Usually no one strongly complains about the interruption of the prerelease programs, so they readily slow to a halt or near halt. While the admission orientation programs also vary in the extent of their development, they seem to include an appreciable number of organized sessions more consistently than do the prerelease programs.

Several reasons for this discrepancy between admission and prerelease orientation program development are readily apparent. One is the fragmented nature of correctional administration in the United States. Prison administrations reap immediate benefits from admission orientation programs, since they make prison inmates more aware of prison training programs and of staff expectations. However, the prerelease programs operated by a prison affect only the work of the parole supervision officials, who operate independently of the prisons. Also, good prerelease programs depend more on voluntary participation of outsiders than do the admission orientation program.

It follows from this that one method of assuring a more consistently high standard in prerelease programs would be to make their organization and presentation a more definite responsibility of the parole supervision staff. This would require them to maintain liaison with the prisons to arrange class schedules and to recruit and transport outside speakers for the prison. Prison and parole staffs might share responsibility for classes on subjects relevant to the needs of all releasees, whether released by parole or by expiration of sentence. However, the benefits from these programs are visible only to parole staff, so that they should be able to evaluate and improve such programs more adequately than prison personnel. Merely a regular scheduling of parole officer visits to prisons to talk to releasees, rather than haphazard or intermittent visits, would be a major improvement over much current practice.

During the course of our project, and especially after our April 1961 summary of the Prison Panel Study, which indicated apprehensions in inmates regarding parole, the federal prisons improved their prerelease programs. A notable feature was more regular scheduling of visits to the prisons by U. S. Probation Officers to participate in these classes, facilitated by greater travel allowances for this purpose from the Administrative Office of U. S. Courts. U. S. Probation Officers are much more scattered, and generally more distant from the prisons, than state parole agents, but by scheduling officers from different cities months ahead to visit prisons, the continuous availability of parole supervision speakers was guaranteed. The burden of travel to the prison was also divided among all federal probation officers in the region. These visits came to be appreciated by the probation officers as a means by which they could become more familiar with the kinds of prison life and training experienced by the men whom they would supervise. When these officers came to address a prerelease class, they also visited the entire prison, and they arranged special interviews with those men likely to be released to their supervision in the next several months. At the Federal Youth Institution in Englewood, Colorado, prerelease groups have been taken on tours to Denver factories for employment counseling there.

An interesting innovation, intended to increase communication of prisoners with the outside persons with whom they will have to work after release, is the requirement that every prospective parolee write to his future parole supervision officer. This was introduced at the Federal Youth Institution at Englewood in 1960. The inmates write a personal letter to the head of the U. S. Probation Office of the district to which they expect to be released, indicating their job placement interests, their abilities, and any problems they anticipate. This places more responsibility for prerelease planning and arrangement on the inmates rather than only on prison caseworkers, and it may reduce the extent to which prison caseworkers are scapegoated by inmates when their best-laid parole plans go awry. Subsequent correspondence between the inmates and their parole supervision officers helps inmates become more realistic in their perceptions of the supervision situation.

Thus far we have summarized ways in which existing prison programs and facilities can be developed to enhance the economic security of newly released prisoners and to improve their relationships with noncriminal persons outside the prison. In addition to these measures within traditional frameworks, a number of rather drastic innovations were investigated in the course of our project, and some relevant evidence or experience can be reported on these measures.

LOANS FOR RELEASED PRISONERS

A frequently proposed remedy for postrelease economic problems of men who have been confined in prison is to provide them with financial loans to meet their immediate needs, which they may repay when they are well established economically.

Somewhat accidentally, at a meeting of the Advisory Board for this project, I discovered that the Board's representatives of America's leading correctional systems were in complete disagreement with respect to the desirability of loan funds for released prisoners. One state official reported the operation of such funds for decades in his system and had nothing but praise for this practice. Another knew of its success in a state system where he formerly had worked. Yet other officials there knew only of failure with loan funds and were certain that such operations were impractical. Accordingly, in our National Survey of Financial Assistance for Released Prisoners, we included some questions regarding loan fund operations by government agencies. We also asked the correctional officials replying to our inquiries to advise us of any loan funds administered by private agencies specifically for distribution to released prisoners.

The survey revealed that in five states loans to released prisoners had been administered for ten or more years, in five others they had been initiated more recently, but in the remaining forty states such funds were nonexistent. We also learned of loan programs which had been terminated, generally after a relatively brief time, when the original appropriation was depleted and not renewed.

Some of the features of the firmly established loan funds may suggest the reasons for their long existence. In California, where loan funds had been administered to parolees for over forty years, the most common loan was in the form of meal tickets or room credit certificates. These are issued by the parole office, on the approval of a parole officer, to completely destitute men. This type of loan, rather than cash, reduces the problem of funds being dissipated by alcoholics or narcotics addicts. It also makes the administration of the loans relatively simple. However, loans of up to $75 can be arranged for other needs vital to a man's employability, such as credits for the purchase of tools.

All the California loans are interest free. No one expects the loans to be fully repaid in all cases, and replenishment of the loan fund is routinely accepted as an annual budget item, for only 45 per cent of the loans are repaid. Nevertheless, the loans are considered a useful supplement to the gratuities issued at release, because of their flexible availability to meet critical needs which arise only after release. Richard McGee, Administrator of California's Youth and Adult Correctional Agency, expressed in conversation the opinion that his state's small annual loan fund replenishment appropriation has more than paid for itself, since it probably prevents several violations by economically desperate parolees each year, and the cost of processing and reimprisoning only a few violators would exceed the annual depletion of the loan fund. The significance of such a program is even greater if reckoned not just in economic terms, but in the rebuilding of lives. In the 1961-62 fiscal year the California Department of Corrections loaned $27,000 in some 18,000 loans. These averaged $1.50 per loan, but varied from $1 to $75. During this period $13,000 was collected on loans previously made, or almost half of what was paid out.[3]

The Louisiana Penitentiary's "Inmate Lending Fund" is not really for released prisoners. It is a unique fund, from inmate contributions, which is employed to assist needy inmates in preparations for release, particularly for legal assistance to procure removal of detainers filed against their release. This fund is administered by inmate representatives elected from the prison's

[3] Per letter dated January 22, 1963, from Walter Dunbar, Director of Corrections, State of California.

population, but it is under the supervision of a member of the prison staff. Repayment seldom is expected except when appreciable prison earnings are accumulated between the time when the loan is made and the prisoner's release.

Rates of repayment reported for loan funds other than that in Louisiana varied from under 10 per cent for the Kansas Reformatory Inmate Welfare Fund to 80 per cent for a loan at the Texas Penitentiary, which is financed by the prison rodeo. Connecticut, which shares with California the distinction of over forty years of loan service for parolees, reported 50 per cent repayment by men and 10 per cent by women. Michigan, which makes ninety-day loans, generally of $10, reports 75 per cent collection. Wisconsin reports 60 per cent collection, with most of its loans $20 for sixty days. The last two states each have over two decades of experience with their loan programs. Finally Utah, the only other state operating a loan fund for over a decade, reports 50 per cent repayment, with most loans $10 for thirty days. New York and Rhode Island had new and experimental loan funds at the time of our survey. In 1961, after our survey, the state of Washington passed legislation creating a revolving fund for loans to parolees.

One presumes that the rate of payment of loans is an inverse function of the liberality with which loans are issued. Repayment is high if they are issued only to good risks, but poor if they are freely made. The objective of loan funds presumably is to provide emergency assistance to those men whose other credit resources are poorest. Consequently, some loss of the funds is to be expected. When parole is of short duration, it is difficult to exert pressure for repayment, and the parole supervision officer may resist assuming the function of a collection agent.

The Massachusetts Parole Board responded to our inquiry on loans by advising that it receives a small annual appropriation for aid to parolees which it prefers to use for outright grants to the most needy rather than for loans, because "accounting for loans is impracticable." Nevertheless, there may be a rehabilitative benefit from a releasee's paying back a loan when he is able to do this, and there may be less loss of pride if a parolee asks for a loan rather than a gift, even if he is unlikely to be able to repay it. Conversely, there may be antirehabilitative consequences if pressures to repay are extremely great at a time when the parolee has many urgent needs. Apparently the states where loan funds are firmly established have evolved a satisfactory balance of these various considerations in the administration of their loan funds.

Eugene Zemans, Executive Director of the John Howard Association, extended our survey by inquiring about loans issued by organizations belonging to the International Prisoners Aid Association, of which he then was president. This revealed eleven loan funds in eight states, and other funds in each of three different provinces in Canada. We also learned of the Inmate Welfare Club of the Atlanta Federal Penitentiary, which issues loans to federal prison releasees through the Chicago and Atlanta U. S. Probation Offices.

Most of the sixty-seven organizations listed in the *Directory of Prisoners' Aid Agencies in Canada and the United States* provide financial assistance, but this generally is in the form of outright grants rather than loans. Sometimes the distinction between loans and grants is difficult to make. On the one hand, the Jewish Family Service of New York reports that it makes grants, not loans, to needy released prisoners, but that 15 per cent of these grants are ultimately paid back by the recipients. Mr. Robert R. Hannum, of the Osborne Association of New York, reported $1 to $25 loans in cash, meal tickets, and lodging or tool credits by his organization, with only about 20 per cent repaid in thirty years' experience. He observed: ". . . our average man considers it more dignified to sign a note as though his intention were to make a repayment even though the actual facts show that he kicks back only between 20 and 25 per cent, on the average." Hannum remarks that it is "an unholy thing" to call financial assistance a "loan" in a prisoners' aid society, but that "most of our agencies have the very great pleasure of receiving financial contributions from former beneficiaries now and then."

Government officials, in responding to our inquiry as to whether they knew of loans issued to prisoners by private agencies, most often mentioned the Salvation Army and the Volunteers of America. Yet both these organizations advised us that their assistance is provided on a grant basis rather than as loans (although it sometimes is repaid by the recipients). Indiana correctional officials reported establishment of a loan fund at Gary by the Citizens' Parole Advisory Council. Similar funds might well be initiated by such councils elsewhere.

Rather interesting cooperation between government and private agencies in the administration of some loan funds were reported to us. In Milwaukee, where a parole officer can authorize a state loan to a parolee, several days are required before the money is received as a check from the state capitol at Madison. However, the parolee generally is in urgent need of financial assistance at these times, so the Wisconsin Service Association will give him the money immediately, at the parole officer's request. The Association is then repaid a few days later by the state check, but the parolee owes his loan to the state rather than to the Association. Also, private contributions provided all or part of the loan funds administered by government correctional agencies in Connecticut, Rhode Island, and Utah.

Inmate activities provided the loan funds in Texas and Kansas prisons, as well as the funds administered by Atlanta and Chicago U. S. Probation Offices. In Los Angeles the Volunteers of America, although not making loans with its own funds, acts as trustee for two privately endowed loan funds for released prisoners. One of these funds is only for loans authorized by federal probation officers, and the other is only for loans authorized by agents of the Parole Department of the California Department of Corrections.[4]

Loans are by no means needed for every releasee. However, they are a resource for postrelease assistance which can prove uniquely valuable in helping certain cases. When there is a reasonable prospect that a releasee will become self-sufficient although at the moment he is destitute, a loan may be particularly appropriate. It may also be preferable to outright grants in other cases so as to define the assistance as something other than charity, even where prospects of repayment are poor. It makes one more flexible resource available to parole and other community casework agencies concerned with the many problems that men may encounter in trying to achieve economic independence legitimately after imprisonment.

UNEMPLOYMENT INSURANCE FOR RELEASED PRISONERS

In Great Britain, when a man who has no employment and few resources is released from prison, he is given railroad fare to his place of destination and just enough funds to sustain him for the duration of his journey. However, he can bring a certificate of release to the local office of the National Assistance Agency, which then handles his case like that of any other destitute person in the area. The available British services include a long-standing system of unemployment insurance payment sufficient to meet the man's presumed minimum needs, but not nearly as much as he could be expected to earn were he employed. He normally receives unemployment insurance only if he proves willing to work when reasonable employment can be procured for him.

In the United States we have developed unemployment insurance under the Social Security Act, but its provision is not nearly as extensive as that in Britain in terms of the proportion of the labor force who are covered, the readiness with which funds are available, and the duration of the assistance. Unemployment insurance is regulated currently by both federal and state legislation, so that practices vary somewhat from one state to another. In general, eligibility for insurance is dependent on two requirements that released prisoners have difficulty in meeting.

First of all, to be eligible for unemployment insurance a released prisoner must have been previously employed at a firm covered by the unemployment

---

[4] For further details on these loan funds, see: Daniel Glaser, Eugene S. Zemans, and Charles W. Dean, *Money Against Crime* (Chicago, John Howard Association, 1961, pp. 14-20; or Daniel Glaser, "Research on Economic Assistance for Released Prisoners," *Proceedings, American Correctional Association* (1960), pp. 363-80.

insurance regulations, so that his employer made contributions to unemployment insurance funds. Secondly, in order to be eligible for insurance at a particular date, one must have earned at least a specific amount in a designated period of the preceding year. For example, in Illinois, earnings of at least $700 in the preceding year are required, including $150 in each of two different quarters of that year. The fact that in the year preceding their immediate postrelease unemployment the ex-prisoners were confined means that they could not possibly be eligible for unemployment compensation under this requirement.

Denial of unemployment compensation to those ex-prisoners whose prior work led to substantial contributions by their employers to unemployment insurance funds would appear to be an injustice. If so, it is an injustice which also occurs, perhaps more extensively, among persons who were long hospitalized or disabled in a year which precedes their unsuccessful efforts to find reemployment. For example, it is especially unjust to persons in state hospitals or veterans' hospitals who were once long employed and who again seek employment after a year or more of hospitalization. Regardless of the number of years when they were employed regularly and contributions were made to unemployment insurance funds on their behalf, they cannot claim insurance benefits unless they happened to be employed in the year preceding their claim.

Ever since the enactment of the Social Security Act, almost every session of Congress has added some extension to its benefits. A reasonable extension would provide that anyone who can demonstrate that he was involuntarily unemployable during the period when employment is required for current benefits would be permitted to claim the benefits on the basis of a prior employment record, before the period of unemployability. This would require specific legislation defining imprisonment as involuntary unemployability, because court decisions have held that a prison or jail inmate is not involuntarily unemployed if his confinement results from voluntary performance of a criminal act.

The foregoing proposals, if enacted, would not relieve distress of those relatively new to the labor force. Many of these have never had sufficient employment to qualify for unemployment compensation. Available statistics indicate that young workers are particularly subject to unemployment and also are more prone than older workers to engage in crime when blocked in efforts to procure a legitimate income (or when inordinately expensive in their tastes). This suggests that a more realistic program of economic assistance for young workers would involve relief payments on the basis of actual need, regardless of prior employment, but in conjunction with a counseling, training, placement, and supervision program. The recent practice of issuing welfare payments to unemployed workers only if they engage in training that increases their prospects of employment is a step in this direction. While there always is a possibility of such assistance being abused, this is unlikely if the assistance is less ample than normal earnings, if it is granted on the basis that the recipient accept suitable employment when available, and if the recipient is required to participate in vocational training programs or public works.

In a comprehensive program for assistance to releasees, including the several measures described in this chapter, the extension of unemployment insurance would be especially valuable in an intermediate period; it may best meet needs between the immediate postrelease period, when assistance provided through the prison is still effective, and the period when the inmate has been in the free community long enough to have achieved eligibility for unemployment insurance under existing regulations.

PUBLIC EMPLOYMENT

It is an anomalous situation that men are employed by the federal and state governments to devote a major portion of their time to persuading private employers to hire ex-prisoners, yet these governments themselves are extremely reluctant to hire men who have been in prison. Although government agencies frequently have taken the leadership in the employment of other types of handicapped persons, they lag behind private industry in employment of men who have a criminal record. This is especially surprising from the standpoint of the government's economic interest, since any rehabilitation of an ex-prisoner through employment saves the government the cost of apprehension, trial, and reimprisonment, in addition to its contribution to the ex-prisoner's character and to the protection of the public.

For federal jobs, the standard employment application (Form 57), requests that the applicant report his convictions for any misdemeanor or felony. A prior conviction is not a barrier to federal employment, but it makes the applicant subject to special restrictions. It is the policy of the U. S. Civil Service Commission to require that two years elapse after discharge from a felony sentence, and one year after discharge from a misdemeanor sentence, before an applicant will be considered for any position requiring a high degree of integrity. A somewhat distinctive feature of the federal procedure is that it does not require the applicant to report any convictions which occurred before his 16th birthday.[5]

Obviously the government, like any other employer, requires information on the past criminality of any person in whom it must place unusual trust. Probably government service includes a larger proportion of jobs requiring

[5] Walter B. Irons, Executive Director, U. S. Civil Service Commission, "Policies of the U. S. Civil Service Commission on the Employment of Former Offenders," Supplement to *Federal Probation Officers' Association Newsletter* (April 1, 1962).

such trust than exist in most types of private employment. Nevertheless, there is a large range of government employment which does not differ appreciably from jobs in private business—for example, jobs in government hospitals, road and building maintenance staffs, automotive maintenance, and food preparation, all of which are types of employment for which prison training can be particularly applicable.

It would seem appropriate for government agencies to exercise leadership in expanding opportunities for the entrance of ex-prisoners into legitimate employment, rather than maintaining their present negative practices. Indeed, a labor shortage exists in many state hospitals because of their isolated locations and because of prejudices against working with the mentally ill. They especially need attendants and service personnel. Many prisoners who receive training in institutional cooking, nursing, and medical technician work would welcome opportunities to pursue such employment as a career.

PRERELEASE PLACEMENT AND GUIDANCE CENTERS

The period in which our research program was conducted saw the beginning of what I believe will be the most important breakthrough in this century for increasing the rate of prisoner rehabilitation—that is, the establishment of prerelease guidance centers in the large urban areas from which most prisoners come, to provide an intermediate condition either between probation and prison or between prison and parole or expiration-of-sentence discharge.

The federal prerelease guidance centers, stimulated in part by early reports of our project on the postrelease problems of returned violators, were opened in Chicago and New York on September 11, 1961, and in Los Angeles on October 16th of that year. A center that opened in Detroit about a year later is operated jointly with the Michigan Department of Corrections and holds both state and federal youthful offenders. Because the prerelease guidance centers were innovations, each one was designed to have some unique features, so as to provide initial experience with a variety of organizational forms. The center in Chicago was located in a large YMCA hotel. It consisted of small single rooms for twenty inmates plus rooms for staff offices and meetings. The New York center was located in a smaller neighborhood YMCA. The center in Los Angeles was installed in a separate house, procured exclusively for its use.

The initial intake for the prerelease guidance centers in New York, Chicago, and Los Angeles consisted of males committed under the Federal Juvenile Delinquency Act and the Federal Youth Correction Act. Most of these prisoners are released by parole, but they were transferred to the centers three to four months before their scheduled date of parole. At first only the better risks were carefully selected for these centers, but after confidence was gleaned from experience and it became apparent that the centers would not be full unless more men were released to them, they were used for all youths with parole destinations in the metropolitan areas where the centers were located. In a few instances, youths scheduled not for parole but for expiration-of-sentence discharge also were transferred to the centers shortly before their date of release. Finally, some new offenders sentenced to prison were taken directly from the courts to the center. The centers thus became their place of imprisonment, where this was considered advantageous, with their parole being from the center to the free community.

When a youth arrives at one of these centers, he is restricted to it for about two days. His family may visit him there. He arrives at the center in civilian clothes, in most cases those issued by the federal prison from which he is transferred to the center. He may receive other civilian clothes from his family or purchase them if this seems desirable. In his first days at the center he is made familiar with what will be expected of him there, and he is introduced to the facilities of the buildings. Those centers in a YMCA hotel utilize the YMCA cafeteria, for which the inmates of the center are given meal tickets. They also use the recreational facilities of these establishments and participate in recreational programs and clubs with other YMCA patrons.

The centers have a high ratio of staff to inmates, approximately one employee to every three inmates. This includes a director of the center, who has considerable correctional casework experience, a caseworker, and three correctional counselors, including a specialist in employment counseling. Additional part-time employees have been recruited from among local graduate students in sociology, social work, and psychology. These men often work at night and on weekends, so that there is at least one staff person present at all times.

The intensive counseling program includes individual counseling for each inmate, employment counseling, evening programs of group counseling, lectures, and audiovisual programs. The latter, and the speakers recruited from the community to talk to the center inmates, deal with various problems that young men encounter in trying to establish economic self-sufficiency and a satisfying social life in the community. For example, a typical month's program includes films entitled "Meaning of Engagement," "Marriage is a Partnership," "Why Vandalism," "Understanding Others," and "An American Girl." Lectures by outside specialists are regularly devoted to such practical topics as "How to Buy a Used Car," social diseases, and budgeting.

Two or three days after the men arrive, they have a first opportunity to utilize their employment counseling by going out to seek a job. They are given job leads, when possible, by the employment counselor, or they are referred to someone in the state employment office with whom the counselor has maintained liaison. They may also follow up employment leads procured on their own. The employment counselors will travel with some of the more inadequate youths to introduce them to personnel at the employment service, or to potential employers, but they prefer to have a youth apply for and secure a job on his own if possible.

When a youth finds employment, he leaves the center each morning to go to work and returns to the center each night. One of the rules of the centers is that men always leave the centers alone, and they are not supposed to meet each other after they go out. This is to encourage self-reliance and the formation of new social contacts rather than dependence on fellow-inmates.

As the men start earning an income from their employment, they are gradually required to pay for some of their expenses, including their meals and laundry. When they pay for their own meals and are near release, they are permitted to eat away from the center if they choose. They also are required to open a savings account, which is a joint account with their counselor until their release date, so that both must sign for withdrawal of any money. Generally they are expected to save all earnings over $35 per week for their first eight weeks in the center, and everything over $45 thereafter. A major emphasis in the counseling, when the men have some earnings, is on budgeting. The bank account, often containing several hundred dollars by their parole date, is a new experience for most of these youths, and its size is a source of considerable prestige among them. In several cases this experience seems to have made them infatuated with saving, possibly because it symbolizes a security and independence that most of them have not known before.

Not long after the men arrive at the centers they are introduced to their future parole supervision officer from the local U. S. Probation Office. Gradually counseling responsibility is shifted from the center staff to the probation officer. The latter is consulted on a youth's plan or problems while he still is in the center, and especially on any major decisions that may involve a change in parole home or job plans. By the time a youth is ready to start his parole, his counseling supervision has been completely shifted to the probation officer, and he is not encouraged to return to the center. However, in the few instances when men have returned to talk about postrelease problems with members of the center staff, their problems are discussed with them, but their probation officer also is called into the conference if possible or is kept informed.

At the end of their first day's work, and regularly thereafter, the inmates discuss their experience on the job with the employment counselor, or with other members of the staff. They may also discuss these and any other experiences of interest in the group counseling sessions. The men are given passes to leave the centers in order to visit their families or for recreational purposes. These are issued sparingly at first, but are gradually increased as release approaches. Their social contacts in the YMCA and on their passes are discussed in individual and group counseling sessions, with staff trying to get the men to anticipate the dangers in delinquent contacts. Where it seems desirable, the staff introduces them to church groups, YMCA's, and other social organizations in the neighborhood of their prospective release.

As their parole date nears, the men often spend weekends at their future homes. These visits, in some cases, reveal the likelihood of future home difficulties and permit a change in parole residence plans to be worked out before the actual date of parole.

In several cases, youths in the centers have been encouraged to go to school instead of working full time, or to go to school on a part-time basis. In one instance an employer arranged a youth's working hours so as to facilitate this and volunteered to pay his tuition.

At the 11 P.M. curfew the youths are supposed to be back in the center, except when on a weekend pass to their families. Each youth signs out every time he leaves and signs in when he returns. When an inmate persistently violates curfew or other rules, this is discussed with him and some disciplinary action may be taken, most commonly restriction to the center. In a few cases, where potentially serious violations were indicated, the youths involved were temporarily placed in the federal detention unit of the local jail. In several instances the parole board was requested to defer the parole date for such youths. In some of these cases, therefore, the men remain at the center longer than originally planned, and in other cases they are transferred back to regular federal prisons as not yet ready for the centers.

Evaluation of Centers

During the first year of operation of the prerelease guidance centers, 174 youths were processed through them. Twenty were returned from the center to prison for failure to cooperate with the staff of the center and other evidence that they were not yet ready to succeed on parole. The latter group may reasonably be considered as not in violation of parole; in fact, they had not started their parole but were returned to prison and had their parole date deferred by action of the U. S. Board of Parole.

In a very real sense, men returned to prison directly from the centers as not yet ready for parole may be considered not as failures of these centers but, instead, as gains in diagnostic acuity made possible by the centers. The theory of parole emphasizes that the date of an offender's readiness for release cannot be discerned so well at the time of sentencing as after he has been observed in prison. The centers permit one to assess readiness for release on the basis of observations much more relevant than those possible in a regular prison. At the center the youths are aided and observed in re-entering the community on a part-time basis, rather than being counseled and assessed only in the artificial situation of a regular prison.

The prerelease centers are the logical extension of the historical trend, observed in chapter 13, of a progressive distribution and deferral of the decision as to how long a criminal should be confined. In addition, the centers have the major advantage of making counseling services much more immediate and practical than they can be in a prison situation. Finally, by permitting the youths to confront their problems gradually rather than all at once and abruptly on departure from a regular prison, the centers make it much easier for them to cope with these problems.

For evaluation of the impact of the first three centers, I most strongly urged the Bureau of Prisons to establish an experimental design by selecting twice as many youths for release to the centers as the centers could accommodate, then randomly sending half to the center and allowing the other half to serve as a control group. However, this was not possible because it soon became apparent that the centers would have to receive all eligible federal youthful releasees in the metropolitan areas where they were located and some whom it was first thought would be ineligible, if the centers were to be kept full. Accordingly, a hypothetical control group was formed by analysis of the records of youths released in the preceding year to the three cities where the centers were established, with an effort to match these men by type of sentence, age, race, and other variables with those released to the center.

Other Experimental Centers

Institutions like the prerelease guidance centers were independently invented in many correctional situations. Their antecedents include the practice in several European prisons located near large cities of having men find employment and start work before they are discharged from the prisons. There also have been some "half-way houses" sponsored by religious and other private philanthropic organizations to provide shelter for homeless and destitute men upon their release from jails and prisons.

The major recent American experiment similar to the prerelease guidance centers is the Provo Experiment in Delinquency Rehabilitation. In this project, at Provo, Utah, a center has been established to which youth placed on probation are required to report on an almost daily basis, during several of the daytime hours in which they are not in school or at work. The emphasis in the Provo Experiment is on group counseling. The inmate groups collectively advise on programs and on penalties for their members. It has been observed that the group counseling in this situation has many advantages over similar counseling programs in regular penal institutions.

For example, counseling in the center deals with real and immediate problems which the boys face at the time of the discussion, and all of them often know the situations in their community to which the counseling discussions refer. One striking feature of this project is the operation of a controlled experiment to evaluate its effectiveness, whereby a judge randomly selects from an envelope a slip of paper to determine whether a boy found guilty will go on probation to the community, or to the experimental center as a condition of his probation.[6]

Another notable experiment of this type is the Community Treatment Project of the California Youth Authority. This is operated in two centers, located in and serving the cities of Sacramento and Stockton, California. They receive wards of the Youth Authority who have homes in these communities. The wards have been committed to the Youth Authority and are first processed through that agency's Reception Center for Northern California. However, instead of being sent from the reception center to a confinement institution, as would normally be the case, these youths are sent to the community centers. This also is operated with random assignment of a treatment group to the centers and a control group to regular programs, to permit evaluation of the centers. The first two years' experience indicates that the community-treated offenders commit markedly fewer and less serious new offenses than those kept in institutions—in the average case, eight months—before release. Yet the cost per man-day of this most intensive of community treatment programs is only about half that of California's youth correction institutions.[7]

Another California "half-way house," specifically for adult drug addicts on parole, was established in Los Angeles in 1962. Its program and evaluation are directed by Professors Gilbert Geis and Sethard Fisher of Los Angeles State College, under a grant from the National Institute of Mental Health. Counseling and supervision staff are provided by the California Department of Corrections.

Under their Huber Act, Wisconsin jails have long allowed some inmates to go to jobs in the community during the day, returning to jail at night and on weekends. A similar arrangement, known as the "Work Release Program," was introduced in North Carolina prisons in 1961. As of October 31, 1962, 1160 inmates had participated in this program, earning $617,041, of which they paid $230,976 to the Prison Department for maintenance and transportation, sent $203,825 to their families, paid

---

[6] LaMar T. Empey and Jerome Rabow, "The Provo Experiment in Delinquency Rehabilitation," *Am. Sociological Rev., 26,* no. 5 (Oct. 1961), 679-95; a similar report, by the same authors and with the same title is in *Proceedings, American Correctional Association* (1960), pp. 304-16.

[7] Marguerite Q. Warren *et al., Community Treatment Project,* Research Report No. 5 (Sacramento, California Department of the Youth Authority, Feb. 1964).

$23,292 in jail fees, spent $76,187 on personal expenses, and had $82,760 saved or issued to them at release.[8]

The growth of correctional institutions in our cities to provide a transition for urban offenders between the prisons or training schools and parole, or as an initial stage of probation, appears to be the next major development in corrections. Establishments like the prerelease guidance centers, the Provo Experiment Center, and the California Community Treatment Centers are likely to make much current investment in traditional institutions and procedures obsolete.

SUMMARY

Our conclusions as to the primary available correctional remedies for postrelease problems of prisoners can be summarized by the following propositions:

N1. Major advances in the contribution of prisons to the solution of inmate postrelease problems, with a relatively small percentage increase in total prison costs, could be achieved merely by systematic extension of programs already successfully initiated. Notable among these expandable programs are:

a. compulsory inmate saving of some prison earnings to meet postrelease expenses, supplemented by gratuities or loans where necessary;

b. graduation of the disbursement of such funds, through parole supervision offices;

c. facilitation of inmate communication with law-abiding outside persons, through reduction of censorship of correspondence and of impediments to visiting;

d. involvement of outside organizations in inmate organizations, and vice versa, through service and hobby clubs, personal development and mutual therapy groups, churches, and other types of voluntary organizations;

e. communication of parole supervision staff with inmates prior to the inmate's release (in correspondence, in prerelease classes, and in initial parole interviews at the prisons);

f. operation of loan funds as a flexible financial aid effective for some releasees, administered through parole supervision agencies in a manner based on the experience of the states that have operated these funds for decades.

N2. Routinization of these programs, so they will be more consistently operated and developed, requires their administration by persons who continu-

[8] Per enclosure to letter dated November 30, 1962, from George W. Randall, Director, Prison Department, State of North Carolina. See also the description of the Delaware half-way house program in Maurice A. Breslin and Robert G. Crosswhite, "Residential Aftercare: An Intermediate Step in the Correctional Process," *Federal Probation, 27,* no. 1 (March 1963), 37-46.

ally receive feedback indicating the consequences of these programs; this means that their operation at the prisons should be, at least in part, a regular responsibility of parole supervision staff.

N3. Selective employment of parolees and of prison dischargees by government agencies, and augmentation of their eligibility for unemployment insurance, can reduce the net social and economic costs to the public from recidivism and reimprisonment.

N4. This half-century's most promising correctional development for alleviating postrelease problems of prisoners consists of the counseling centers in metropolitan areas to which prisoners scheduled for release are transferred some months before their release date, and from which they regularly go forth to enter the job market and to develop correctionally acceptable postprison social relationships, before they are released on a regular parole or on any other traditional types of release from prison.

Residential centers for the community guidance and graduated release of convicted persons are a logical extension of a changing conception of the state's responsibility in dealing with felons. This is a change from the classic objective of completely depriving a man of his freedom for a period which ends abruptly when he has "paid for his crime," to the objective of both removing and restoring freedom on a gradual basis, in a manner which will most facilitate the felon's achievement of a noncriminal life. Parole and probation were earlier steps in this direction, but they were handicapped through the inability of staff to be in contact with their clients' lives in the free community as much as occurs with the new types of institution. However, we have found that parole and probation vary tremendously in these and other respects, both in actual administration and in the standards that officials seek to attain.

CHAPTER 17

The Role of the Parole
Supervision Officer

As indicated in chapter 13, the history of judicial and correctional policy can be interpreted as a progressive deferral and sharing of decisions on the deprivation of an offender's freedom. The decision as to when a man should be released from confinement, formerly made when sentence was imposed, now is delegated to a parole board and is deferred to the parole hearing. Even a parole board's decision on a man's freedom is not final when parole is granted, for until the man is discharged from parole the board may order his return to prison. Indeed, by stipulating and interpreting the rules to which the parolee must conform, the parole board also determines the extent to which freedom is partial or complete during the parole period.

The principal functions of parole supervision have been: (1) procurement of information on the parolee's postprison conduct, to aid the parole board in deciding whether it should continue a man on parole or declare him a violator; and (2) facilitating and graduating the transition between imprisonment and complete freedom, by assistance and by rule enforcement. All of these functions presumably are oriented to the goals of protecting the public and rehabilitating the offender. The manner in which these functions have been carried out, however, has reflected tremendous differences in the philosophy and training of parole supervision personnel and in policies promulgated by parole boards.

As reported in chapter 1, our project was interested in identifying the ways in which federal parole supervision is conducted by the approximately five hundred U. S. Probation Officers. We also wished to identify possible causal factors in any variation that might be encountered in their parole supervision, and to consider other implications of diverse practice in the parole supervision role. Determination of the effects of alternative styles of parole supervision on recidivism was beyond the scope of our project, but some California research on this problem will be summarized.

THE PAROLEE'S EXPECTATIONS FROM PAROLE
SUPERVISION

One of the series of questions used in our Prison Panel Study interviews was: "Suppose you do not commit any offense when you get out, what would be your chance of getting sentenced by a 'bum rap'? Do you expect to get out by parole or mandatory release, or by expiration of sentence?" If parole or mandatory release: "What would be your chance of being returned as a technical violator?" (Mandatory release is served under parole supervision but is granted automatically, to those denied parole, for all "good time" earned by acceptable behavior in prison, in excess of 180 days.) The responses to these inquiries were distributed almost identically in the sixth-month and the near-release interviews. About three-quarters considered chances of return on a "bum rap" as slight or absolutely non-existent, with little variation among institutions. The proportion expecting parole or mandatory release varied from a low of 44 per cent at Milan to 100 per cent at Ashland. These were always higher figures than the facts warranted, but they were proportional to actual rates for such releases at the different prisons. Paroles were fewest at Milan and most frequent at Ashland, due to the types of sentence characteristic of the men at these institutions. The fraction indicating a "fair," "even," or "more than even" chance of return as technical violators varied from about one-tenth at Ashland and Terre Haute to one-third at Leavenworth. These perceptions of violation risk are unrealistically low at Ashland and unrealistically high elsewhere, especially at Leavenworth, in terms of actual rates of return for nonfelony violations at these institutions. The reason for this difference between institutions is of some penological interest.

At Leavenworth, departure from prison by mandatory release rather than by parole was the most common expectation. Because many Leavenworth inmates have prior experience in state prisons, and because some were in federal prisons before the introduction of this type of release in the 1930's, many there contend that the mandatory release (formerly called "conditional release") is unfair or illegal. They argue that they had served their sentence when released because they "earned" their "good time." This is an illustration of the principle that what a donor conceives as a reward and a privilege, if very freely given, will be conceived by the recipient as a right.

Those returned to Leavenworth for flagrant violation of mandatory release rules, many of whom we interviewed in our Returned Violator Study, seemed particularly vociferous in contending that such a release was unfair. Indeed, some would simultaneously assert that they never had any intention of abiding by the conditions of their release and that these conditions are unfairly or too severely enforced. At the time of our interviews (1958-59), only 10 per cent received parole at Leavenworth, but half received mandatory releases; and their lengthy sentences made the mandatory-release periods longer than at most other prisons, thus increasing the chances of violation. We assume that the concentration at Leavenworth of an unusually large proportion of such violators means that the violator's perception of parole and mandatory release supervision by federal probation officers is communicated to all inmates. This would account for the exaggerated view there of the risk of return for technical violation. Although one-third of the Leavenworth inmates saw an appreciable chance of return to prison without committing new offenses if they received parole or mandatory release, the actual technical violation rate for Leavenworth men is only about 5 per cent. However, an additional 20 per cent violate by conviction for new offenses.

This is another illustration of "pluralistic ignorance" among prisoners regarding their future prospects, such as that pointed out in chapter 15 in discussing police harassment fears. Because inmates see the returned violators back in prison but seldom see the successes again, and because the returned violators often are highly articulate in rationalizing their failure to stay out of prison by charging government authorities with illegal or inconsiderate practices, prisoners tend to acquire unrealistically pessimistic anticipations regarding their own future experience.[1] However, Ashland, the only institution where an overestimate of technical violation rates did *not* occur, is unique in that persons who violate parole from that institution are not returned there but are sent to other federal prisons. Though hardly a complete remedy, it might be of some benefit for inmates to be advised of the rates of return at their institutions, so that they are neither overly pessimistic nor unrealistically optimistic, and to encourage their comparing themselves with the successes as well as with the failures. In chapter 16 we cited the California practice of employing successful parolees to speak in prison prerelease programs as one step towards increasing the realism of inmate anticipations regarding parole.

In accepting parole, prisoners agree to conform to a number of rules; their return to prison as parole violators is justified legally by their violation of these conditions. As we shall show later in this chapter, the interpretation of these rules by parole supervision officers varies considerably. Our concern here, however, is with inmate anticipations of difficulty in conforming to these rules. In the sixth-month and near-release interviews of our Prison Panel Study, we asked inmates who said they expected to be released by parole or mandatory release: "If you get parole (or mandatory release, according to the expectation they had indicated), what parole (or mandatory release) rules will be hardest for you to keep?" The most common response was "none," which was reported near release by about half the inmates at Ashland, but by only 13 per cent at Chillicothe. For those

---

[1] A series of hypotheses on parole outcome as a complex function of expectations developed in prison, in relation to postrelease experience, has been set forth in Jerome H. Skolnick, "A Developmental Theory of Parole," *Am. Sociological Rev.*, 25, no. 4 (August 1960), 542-49. Testing these hypotheses optimally would require long-term contact with the same offenders in prison and on parole. We contemplated such contact, but could not achieve it for an appreciable number of cases due to our limited time and the wide geographical scattering of federal prisoners.

specifying rules as difficult, the most frequently cited rules were those re-stricting travel, imposing a curfew, and forbidding drinking and association with ex-convicts. However, the latter two actually are not formal rules in U. S. parole practice. In general, we had the impression that many inmates had little knowledge of the rules, and that variation in the "none" response was largely a function of variations in the persistence with which our inter-viewers pressed the inmates to specify one rule as more difficult than others.

To overcome this inter-interviewer variation, in our Prison Panel Sup-plement questionnaire we included the inquiry: "If you get a parole or a conditional release, what one rule will be the hardest for you to keep?" The subjects were to check one of the following: "Associating with ex-cons," "Drinking regulations," "Travel restrictions," "Working steadily," "None of the above, but" (followed by a line on which they were asked to write the rule they considered hardest to keep), and "No rule will be hard at all." Since all subjects received the same questionnaire, in similar class-room-type situations, variation in their responses should not be affected appreciably by variation in the presentation of the question.

No consistent pattern of change in concern with specific rules was evident for all institutions. The Leavenworth inmates showed the least change, from arrival to release, in their perception of parole rules. This would be expected from the fact that they probably have the most extensive prior prison and parole experience. The rule against association with ex-convicts was more a concern of the inmates of state prisons than of those in federal prisons, except for "Busy" State Prison, which follows the federal pattern. "Busy" is a state with a smaller proportion of inmates from a single large metropolis and a larger proportion of rural inmates than the other prisons, so their releasees probably have least prospect of encountering other ex-convicts. Drinking and travel regulations were the most frequent concerns of prisoners at almost every prison, even at federal prisons where, as we shall see, inmates postulate rules on drinking which do not officially exist.

Rules for federal parolees and mandatory releasees, summarized in Table 17.1, are identical. They are called "conditions of parole" (or mandatory release) and are printed on the back of the parole or mandatory release certificates issued to the men at their release from prison. These conditions are expressed in twelve sentences, but the Board of Parole sometimes adds an additional sentence or two or authorizes an exception to a standard rule as a special stipulation in a particular case. The inmate signs the certificate stating that he has read these rules or has had them read to him, that he understands them all, that he agrees to abide by them, and that he under-stands that failure to follow these rules may lead to his being recommitted to prison.

At our first-week interview with the Postrelease Panel sample, and again at our terminal interview with them (in the median case, 5.3 months after

TABLE 17.1 Recall of Parole and Mandatory Supervision Rules, and Designations of Rule Hardest to Keep
(Postrelease Panel effective sample, first and terminal interviews)

Rule (with its number, if actually part of the official rules, or "none" if not one of official rules)	PER CENT RECALLING		PER CENT DESIGNATING RULE HARDEST TO KEEP	
	First week	Sixth month[a]	First week	Sixth month
1. Proceed directly to destination	5	1	—	—
1. Report to probation officer in person	16	15	—	1
2. Obey all laws	27	32	1	1
3. Don't leave district without permission	58	60	9	8
4. Make monthly reports	42	47	3	6
5. Notify probation office if unemployed	5	5	1	—
5. Work if able	20	16	2	—
5. Support dependents	4	—	—	—
6. Go to approved job and home	3	3	—	—
6. Don't change jobs without permission	23	9[b]	1	—
7. Answer probation office letters promptly	1	—	—	—
7. Answer probation office inquiries truthfully	3	2	—	—
8. Notify probation office if arrested	30	23	—	—
9. If cannot reach probation office, notify parole board	2	2	—	—
10. Avoid narcotics, users, sellers	37	31	2	1
11. Avoid bad company, bad places	71	76	19	12
11. Live clean and temperate life	16	12	—	1
12. Have no weapons	24	26	—	—
None. Avoid drinking, taverns, bars	21	13	3	3
None. Curfew; be home on time at night	25	20	3	4
None. Don't change residence within the district, without permission	14	9	—	—
None. Don't marry without approval of probation officer or without notifying probation officer	5	5	3	—
None. Rule other than above	26	30	1	4
No rules remembered or none harder to keep than others	8	5	51	58
Number of cases	145	131	145	131

[a] Sixth month in median cases; for time distribution of terminal interview see Appendix C.

[b] Differences in proportion as great as these, in samples of this size, would occur by chance alone less than once in a hundred times.

their release from prison), we asked the releasees what rules they remembered and which rule was hardest to keep. Our interviewers were instructed not to give the releasees any hints as to what the rules were but to encourage their recalling as many as they could, and to record any alleged rules cited by these men but not found in the printed rules.

As Table 17.1 shows, the rule that most impressed the federal parolees and mandatory releasees was that they should avoid bad company or places of bad reputation, a rule cited by three-fourths of the men. Over half remembered the specific rule against leaving the judicial district without permission, and almost half recalled the monthly report requirement. The rule to "obey all laws," the rules against narcotics and weapons possession, and the rule on notifying the probation office of any arrests were recalled by a fourth to over one-third of the men. The percentage of recall for these rules did not change markedly from the first-week to the terminal interviews, although there was some decline in reference to the narcotics-avoidance and arrest-reporting rules. The greatest change was in recall of the rule against changing jobs without permission, a regulation cited by 23 per cent at the first interview and by only 9 per cent at the terminal interview.

Although only 5 per cent of our sample had added conditions of release on the parole or mandatory release certificate, applying specifically to them, it will be seen in Table 17.1 that several times this 5 per cent reported the existence of rules not appearing on the official list. A quarter of the subjects in their first week out of prison, and a fifth at the terminal interview, mentioned a requirement that they be at home after a certain hour in the evening. An appreciable proportion also made reference to rules against drinking, or against changing residence within the district without permission. None of these restrictions is explicitly set forth in the twelve official conditions of parole or mandatory release. They are understood as parole supervision expectations through oral communication which apparently starts among inmates in prison and continues after their release.

Table 17.2 provides some indication of the role of the parole supervision officers in promoting perceptions of parole requirements different from those

TABLE 17.2   U. S. Probation Officer Assessment of Frequency with Which They Convey Particular Expectation to Parolees

(486 officers, 96% of those in the service in 1962)

Officer's action	FREQUENCY STATEMENT CHECKED				
	Always (95 -100%)	Very frequently (70–95%)	Often (30–70%)	Occasionally (5–30%)	Never (0–5%)
Emphasize that parolees are required to stay out of bars and poolrooms	5%	8%	16%	58%	12%
Prohibit parolees from working in bars	15%	17%	13%	43%	12%
Threaten with a violation warrant for changing jobs without permission	—	1%	2%	24%	73%
Require parolees to bring in paycheck stubs	3%	14%	20%	51%	12%
Require that parolee submit itemized budget	1%	5%	14%	61%	19%
When parolee lives with woman out of wedlock, insist that this be terminated	27%	20%	21%	25%	7%
Require parolee to live with his parents, against his wishes	1%	2%	8%	58%	29%

in the written rules. This table summarizes responses by our 96 per cent sample of U. S. Probation Officers to a few of our questions on their parole-supervision practices. To answer questions on these activities, the officers checked one of five statements on frequency giving a descriptive word and the percentage range that the words were taken to represent, such as "always (95-100%)" or "often (30-70%)." It will be seen that many officers try to control the drinking, working, and residential associations of some federal parolees, although the frequency of these practices among federal officers varies considerably.

The picture of diversity in practice presented in Table 17.2 is extended later in this chapter by statistics on officers' responses to our questions on their surveillance of parolees and on the circumstances under which they request issuance of a violation warrant. Possibly such officer actions determine the effective rules which the parolee encounters, rather than the responses to our questions as listed in Table 17.2. Whether there should be explicit rules or merely informal expectations in parole supervision, and whether rules should be rigidly or flexibly enforced, involve basic issues in the role of the parole supervision officer. To delineate the basic variables in the performance of this role and to determine the correlates of these variables were the main purposes of our questionnaire inquiry.

MAJOR DIMENSIONS IN THE PAROLE SUPERVISION ROLE

When parole was introduced in the United States around 1870, it was an outgrowth of a number of earlier experiments in Britain, Ireland, the United States, and Australia. These involved diverse approaches to the problem of graduating the transition from complete restriction of imprisonment to complete freedom after release. One line of interest was in continuing the prison's restriction of the criminal's movement and maintaining a knowledge of his location. This is represented by the "ticket of leave" system whereby prisoners in England and Ireland were released on a conditional basis, required to follow certain broadly stated rules of conduct, and required to report at the local police office periodically, generally at least once a month.

In Dublin, where many ticket-of-leave releasees were concentrated, a special officer other than a policeman was appointed to supervise and to assist them. In England and Ireland after 1864, prisoners' aid societies were organized, with government financial assistance, to visit the released prisoners and to help them acquire legitimate employment and meet other postrelease needs. Thus two goals were apparent in the earliest forms of parole supervision: *control* and *assistance*.

These two interests are reflected in the background of persons recruited for parole supervision employment. Initially, many had prior experience in police work. The parole supervision officers carried badges and guns, and the surveillance aspect of their job was perhaps most emphasized. Gradually the social-work profession became a source of recruitment for parole officers. This trend has reflected increased conception of parole as assistance, guidance, counseling and, where warranted and feasible, psychiatric treatment.

The demands of the public for protection from released criminals, and major attacks on parole whenever serious felonies are committed by parolees, have necessitated continuous concern with surveillance and rule enforcement in parole supervision. On the other hand, an awareness that the public is most protected if the releasee can be helped to achieve a non-criminal life and humanitarian values has motivated interest in the assistance component of the supervision job. These two components have come into conflict when there has been doubt as to the effectiveness of counseling by persons who also perform surveillance and take actions resulting in the reimprisonment of rule violators. This diversity of viewpoint and of background in parole supervision suggests the possibility that distinctly different styles of performance may be discerned in the parole supervision job and may be made the subject of special study.

Ohlin, Piven, and Pappenfort, after interviews with all probation and parole officers in one state, formulated a distinction among three major types of probation and parole officers:

1. The "punitive officer" is the guardian of middle-class community morality; he attempts to coerce the offender into conforming by means of threats and punishment and his emphasis is on control, protecting the community against the offender, and systematic suspicion of those under supervision.
2. The "protective agent" . . . vacillates between protecting the offender and protecting the community. His tools are direct assistance, lecturing, and praise and blame. He is recognized by his ambivalent emotional involvement with the offender and others in the community as he shifts back and forth in taking sides with one against the other.
3. The "welfare worker" . . . [has as his] ultimate goal the improved welfare of the client, a condition achieved by helping him in his individual adjustment within limits imposed by the client's capacity. He feels that the only genuine guarantee of community protection lies in the client's personal adjustment since external conformity will be only temporary and in the long run may make a successful adjustment more difficult. Emotional neutrality permeates his relationships. The diagnostic categories and treatment skills which he employs stem from an objective and theoretically based assessment of the client's situation, needs, and capacities. . . .[2]

In trying to apply the above trichotomy impressionistically some years ago, in parole offices of a state not as professionalized in its corrections as that which Ohlin and his colleagues studied, it seemed to me to be appropriate to add a fourth type which I called the "political opportunists."

[2] Lloyd E. Ohlin, Herman Piven, and Donnell M. Pappenfort, "Major Dilemmas of the Social Worker in Probation and Parole," *National Probation and Parole Association J.*, 2, no. 3 (July 1956), 211-25. ·

These were individuals who seemed to see their jobs as rewards granted for services elsewhere—in this case, in the political organization. However, it may be noted that not all political appointees fit this description; perhaps because of their political talents and interests, many displayed aptitudes and dedication in working with and for other people which made them outstanding correctional employees when their political commitments did not interfere with their correctional work. However, both in state and in federal service, a few officers impressed us as treating their jobs as sinecures, requiring only a minimum effort. Such a man might be called a "passive officer."

What Ohlin and his associates called the "protective agent" in their three-type classification might also be referred to as the "paternal officer." The traits connoted by the latter label seem to characterize many persons in corrections whose abilities derive mainly from experience, dedication, and a warm personality, rather than from formal training. These paternalistic officers, however, may lack some of the objectivity and the understanding of deviant behavior which appropriate education could provide.

We have thus distinguished four types of parole supervision officer: the paternal, the punitive, the welfare worker, and the passive. In talking to federal and state probation and parole officers at training sessions, I have described all four of these types, related them to different backgrounds of the officers, and indicated differences in the ways in which men of these types perceive their clients and evaluate their own competence. These may be conceived of as "ideal" types, representing extremes of continuous dimensions on which officers might be scaled.

It was suggested by George Pownall of our staff that these four types of parole supervision officer could be conceived as the product of all possible combinations of the two basic variables of their job: assistance and control. As shown in Figure 17A, the combination of high assistance with high control interest characterizes the paternal officer. Low control and high assistance would be expected of the welfare worker. The passive type is low on both assistance and control, while the punitive type is high only on control.

FIGURE 17A   Types of Parole Supervision Officer

EMPHASIS ON ASSISTANCE	EMPHASIS ON CONTROL	
	Low	High
High	Welfare	Paternal
Low	Passive	Punitive

It may be that the optimum rehabilitative service is provided by some combination of these polar patterns, but this scheme seemed useful to differentiate officers along presumably strategic dimensions, as a basis for ultimate research on the relationship between type of supervision and extent of rehabilitation.

The primary research problem in our survey of the supervision practices of U. S. Probation Officers was to develop independent measures of the control and the assistance orientation which would operationally define these four types of parole supervisor. The second problem was to see what other differences distinguished the four types, such as their occupational experience and training, their community and professional relationships, their criteria for evaluating their competence, and the prevailing pattern of the office in which they worked. The latter theme was suggested in a study by Piven, which concluded that officers of any of the three types indicated in the Ohlin, Piven, and Pappenfort article had to conform to the predominant expectations of their agency, regardless of their initial orientation or training.[3]

In consultation with the project staff and with officers of the U. S. Probation Office for Northern Illinois, Pownall developed 175 questions to probe these matters, including seventy questions on control and assistance activity. From these seventy questions, two sets of five were found to form statistically acceptable ordinal (or "Guttman") scales, one on control and one on assistance. The statistical acceptability tests are designed to indicate the extent to which a set of questions seems to be measuring one dimension. When the questions that form such a unidimensional ordinal scale are arranged from lowest to highest on whatever they measure, a person's response to one question in the scale predicts that he will not give a less positive response to questions lower in the scale or a less negative response to items higher in the scale. The usual rule of statistical acceptability here is that such a prediction of responses to other questions from the response to one question should be at least 90 per cent accurate. (Ordinal scaling is again explained, with different illustrations, in Appendix E, on our Prison Panel Supplement Study.)

In formulating questions on control, we distinguished three major types of activity. They were:

a. *Surveillance,* defined as any act involving direct or indirect observation of the parolees' activities to ascertain that they conform to supervision rules;
b. *Restriction,* defined as any coercion (actual or threatened) of the parolee's behavior or mobility;
c. *Punishment,* defined as imposition of a parole violation warrant.

To measure the control orientation, a series of hypothetical parole supervision situations were formulated in which a hypothetical officer took a

[3] Herman Piven, *Professionalism and Organizational Structure: Training and Agency Variables in Relation to Practitioner Orientation and Practice* (Doctor of Social Work Dissertation, Columbia University, 1961).

specific surveillance, restriction, or punishment action. The federal probation officers were asked to indicate the extent to which they approved or
disapproved of the action in the hypothetical situation and then to estimate
the frequency with which they themselves actually carried out the kind of
practice illustrated in the hypothetical situation. Some of these inquiries on
frequency of control action were cited in Table 17.2, to illustrate variations
of rule interpretation.

Only general frequency questions, rather than hypothetical situation questions, formed our control scale. The items in this scale, arranged from
lowest to highest in the extent of control that they represent, and scored as
indicated, were as follows:[4]

a. *How often do you check on your parolees for drinking?* An officer was
   scored positively on control if he checked *Always* (95%-100%), *Very frequently* (70%-95%), or *Often* (30%-70%). He received no score on control
   from this item if he checked *Occasionally* (5%-30%) or *Never* (0%-5%).
b. *How often do you check on your parolees for possible association with other
   parolees?* Scored same as *a* above.
c. *How often do you request a violation warrant when a parolee leaves the district without permission and gives no satisfactory explanation, but does not
   violate otherwise?* An officer was scored positively on control if his answer
   was anything indicated under *a* above except *Never.*
d. *How often do you request a violation warrant when a parolee persists in
   living out of wedlock with a woman?* Scored same as *c* above.
e. *How often do you call upon law enforcement agencies to aid you in checking up on your parolees?* Scored same as *c* above.

There was a high rate of agreement between responses on these questions
regarding control *practices* and responses to the corresponding questions on
their *norms,* in which they were asked if they approved of an officer's action
in a hypothetical situation. For example, the normative question preceding
question *a* above was:

Probation officer Powell receives information that parolee Adams, a 28-year-old
on parole for a sentence of check forgery, has been drinking regularly in a
specific tavern. Since Adams is not due for an office visit for three weeks, he
decides to check immediately by driving out to the tavern. What do you think
of the probation officer's action? [Answers: Strongly approve; Approve; Disapprove; Strongly disapprove.]

That preceding question *c* was:

Parolee Jackson, a 22-year-old paroled on a Dyer Act sentence, has been out
of the district without permission. When confronted with this by his probation
officer, he can provide no satisfactory explanation, after first trying to deny it.

---

[4] Coefficient of reproducibility 0.92. Minimum coefficient of reproducibility 0.71,
per Allan L. Edwards, *Techniques of Attitude Scale Construction* (New York, Appleton-Century-Crofts, 1957), pp. 191-93.

His probation officer requests a violation warrant. What do you think of the probation officer's action? [Same answers as above.]

That preceding question *e* was:

Probation officer King suspects that parolee Johnson may be again involved in narcotics activities. He calls a narcotics agent whom he knows at the Bureau of Narcotics and asks him to check up on parolee Johnson for him. What do you think of the probation officer's action? [Same answers as above.]

There was a close correlation between answers to the narrative questions and answers to the questions on control practices, especially for those questions high on the control orientation scale, on surveillance.[5] This suggests that the officers have definite opinions on this issue and they "practice what they preach."

Assistance was also conceived by us as having several major components, as follows:

a. *Material aid,* defined as the officer's taking almost all the action necessary to procure employment, money, clothing, or other economic aid for a parolee;
b. *Referral,* defined as directing the releasee to other agencies that may assist him;
c. *Counseling,* consisting of helping the releasee and possibly his family or other associates in thinking through his problems;
d. *Mediation,* in which the parole officer communicates with persons or agencies with whom the parolee is having difficulty, attempting to reduce their differences with the parolee.

To measure assistance orientation, the officers were asked which of several possible types of assistance they generally gave in a variety of problem situations. Six federal probation officers in Chicago agreed over 95 per cent of the time when ranking these answers as representing degrees of assistance. Space was left for the officer to write in another response if none of the alternatives described his general practice, but in the questions retained for our scale this space was seldom used. The questions forming the assistance scale, arranged from lowest to highest in the extent of assistance that they represent, with the alternative answers scored as indicated, were as follows:[6]

a. *What do you generally do when a parolee under your supervision comes to you and tells you that the police have been harassing him?* An officer was

[5] When answers to the questions in the control scale and answers to the corresponding hypothetical situation questions were each divided into high and low categories at the point nearest the median and cross-tabulated, Yule's Q values for these relationships for the five items of the control scale were: *a.* 0.63; *b.* 0.51; *c.* 0.86; *d.* 0.81; *e.* 0.92.

[6] Coefficient of reproducibility 0.92. Minimum coefficient of reproducibility 0.70 (per Edwards, *loc. cit.*)

scored positively on assistance if he checked "Contact the police personally and request them to leave the parolee alone unless they have good reason to suspect him of a crime," or "Arrange for parolee to go in and talk to police and straighten out the problem." He received no score on assistance if he checked the responses: "Advise parolee to avoid situations which increase the likelihood of his being stopped" or "Nothing, if the police are harassing the parolee, there must be a good reason," or if he wrote, in the space provided for "other" responses, answers not approximating those scored positively.

b. *When one of your parolees comes to you to tell you that his employer has been harassing him and asks for your help, what do you generally do?* An officer was scored positively on assistance if he checked "Personally contact the employer and try to straighten out the difficulties." He received no score on assistance if he checked: "Arrange for the parolee to talk the problem over with the employer," "Advise the parolee to talk out the problem with the employer," "Nothing, it is the parolee's problem to work out," or if he wrote, in the space provided for "other" responses, an action which did not approximate the response scored positively.

c. *If a parolee under your supervision has difficulty in paying off a fine which was imposed on him at the time of sentence for the offense for which he is now paroled, which of the following describes best what you generally would do when he comes to you for help?* An officer was scored positively on assistance if he checked "Contact the government agency and try to arrange a settlement, or work out a lenient installment plan." He received no score on assistance if he checked: "Arrange for parolee to see the agency to work out a plan for payment," "Advise parolee to see the agency to work out a plan for payment," "Nothing, it is the parolee's problem to work out," or if he wrote, in the space provided for "other" responses, an answer not approximating that scored positively.

d. *When one of your parolees has a drinking problem, what do you generally do?* An officer was scored positively on assistance if he checked "Personally counsel the parolee concerning his problem." He received no score on assistance if he checked "Arrange for the parolee to see an appropriate organization," or "Advise the parolee where he might get help," or "Nothing, it is the parolee's problem to work out," or if he wrote, in the space provided for "other" responses, an answer not approximating those scored positively.

e. *When a parolee under your supervision is having a marital problem, what do you generally do?* An officer was scored positively on assistance if he checked "Counsel the parolee and parties involved personally," or "contact an appropriate agency (like family service) and make an appointment for the parolee and his family." He received no score on assistance if he checked "Tell the parolee where he may go to obtain help," or "Nothing, it is his problem to work out," or if he wrote, in the space provided for "other" responses, an answer not approximating those scored positively.

On each of the above scales we found that if we know that a U. S. Probation Officer checked a positively scored response to one of the questions, we can predict with 92 per cent accuracy his answers to the other questions. If he checked a positively scored response to one question, we can predict that he also checked a positive answer to each of the questions lower than that one in the scales presented above. Conversely, if, on any question, he checked a response not scored positively, we can predict that he did not check a positively scored response on any question higher in the scale.

As shown in Table 17.3, the responses of the U. S. Probation Officers to our two scales tended to cluster in a middle range. Exploratory tabulations indicated that a classification of the federal officers into the four types

TABLE 17.3   Distribution of U. S. Probation Officers' Responses
on Control and Assistance Scales
(486 officers, 96% of those in the service in 1962)

Scale categories	Number of questions answered positively	LOW CONTROL			HIGH CONTROL			OFFICERS	
		Number of questions answered positively							
		0	1	2	3	4	5	No.	%
High assistance	5	2	7	14	11	8	5	47	10
	4	4	14	24	28	10	15	95	20
	3	9	22	31	35	17	15	129	27
	2	11	32	24	38	18	7	130	27
		(Welfare type) (194; 40%)			(Paternal type) (207; 43%)				
Low assistance	1	9	10	10	19	5	6	59	12
	0	2	4	4	8	5	3	26	5
		(Passive type) (39; 8%)			(Punitive type) (46; 9%)				
No. of officers		37	89	107	139	63	51	486	100
Percentage distribution		8%	18%	22%	29%	13%	10%	100%	—

represented in Figure 17A would yield greatest contrasts on other attributes if a near even division of the officers into "high" and "low" was made on the control scale, but if only the lower 18 per cent on the assistance scale were called "low assistance."

It is believed that this classification of so few as providing "low assistance" is justifiable also on the grounds that, compared to other correctional supervision agencies, the federal probation service places exceptionally high emphasis on assistance. This reflects the leadership in policy formulation and training of officers provided to federal district courts by the Administrative Office of U. S. Courts. Yet federal probation officers are hired independently by each district court, they do not have civil service tenure, and the recommendations by the Administrative Office on qualifications for probation officers are not binding on these courts. Therefore, some probation officers are former political associates, secretaries, or friends of a judge, or former U. S. Marshals, of diverse background. This may partially explain those responses in Table 17.3 that deviate from the predominant patterns. However, the clustering of responses near the middle ranges on both scales is a noteworthy indication of much uniformity in federal parole supervision practice.

Hardly any correlation was found between responses on control and responses on assistance.[7] This independence of the two scales justifies our cross-tabulating them to distinguish the four styles of parole supervision.

Table 17.4 illuminates some of the differences that distinguished the styles of parole supervision of the four groups of officers classified by Figure 17A and Table 17.3. The questions in Table 17.4, all of which deal with the handling of problems connected with a parolee's employment, are not the same as those presented earlier, by which the officers were scaled on the control and assistance dimensions.

It will be seen that over 90 per cent of the passive and welfare officers reported that they practically never request a violation warrant when a parolee changes jobs without permission, whereas over 40 per cent of the paternal and punitive officers reported that they request a warrant occasionally or more often in such cases. With respect to a parolee refusing to get employment, almost half the passive and welfare officers said that they would never request a warrant, a response in which they were joined by only a fifth of the paternal officers and a tenth of the punitive officers. Ninety per cent of the passive and welfare officers said that they checked with the employer on the parolee's adjustment only occasionally or never at all, but this figure was barely over 60 per cent for the other two categories. Finally, regarding assistance to a parolee who cannot find employment, over a third of the welfare and paternal officers state that they would personally try to line up a job for the parolee, an assertion made by only 13 per cent of the punitive and passive officers. On the other hand, almost two-thirds of the passive and punitive officers checked responses indicating the lowest kind of assistance, merely telling the unemployed parolee where he can go to get help, as compared with one-third of the welfare and paternal officers.

The foregoing suggests the differences in predominant tendency, with respect to control and assistance, of the four types of officers. Note that the differences are not absolute on all items; they are differences in degree, and in relative frequency, of control and assistance action. As Table 17.3 indicated, on these attributes as on most others, most people are in a middle range. When "types" are distinguished in impressionistic essays or lectures about parole officers, prisoners, or other people, these descriptions tend toward atypical extremes. However, we see important dimensions by focusing on extremes. Dramatic case studies indicate significant dimensions by

---

[7] Goodman-Kruskall Gamma 0.079.

TABLE 17.4   Responses by Federal Probation Officers Which Illuminate Differences
Among Four Styles of Parole Supervision
(486 officers; 96% of those in the service in 1962)

| | LOW CONTROL | | HIGH CONTROL | | |
	Low assistance (passive)	*High assistance (welfare)*	*High assistance (paternal)*	*Low assistance (punitive)*	*All officers*
Questions and responses					
How often do you threaten a parolee with a violation warrant when he changes jobs without permission?					
Always (95–100%)	—	—	—	—	—
Very frequently (70–95%)	—	—	1%	7%	1%
Often (30–70%)	—	—	4%	7%	2%
Occasionally (5–30%)	5%	10%	38%	30%	24%
Never (0–5%)	95%	90%	57%	57%	73%
How often do you request a violation warrant when a parolee under your supervision refuses to get employment, but does not violate otherwise?					
Always (95–100%)	3%	2%	7%	9%	5%
Very frequently (70–95%)	—	4%	10%	7%	6%
Often (30–70%)	5%	5%	13%	13%	9%
Occasionally (5–30%)	46%	43%	49%	63%	48%
Never (0–5%)	46%	47%	20%	9%	32%
How often do you check a parolee's job adjustment directly with his employer?					
Always (95–100%)	—	—	1%	2%	1%
Very frequently (70-95%)	—	2%	9%	9%	5%
Often (30–70%)	5%	8%	29%	26%	19%
Occasionally (5–30%)	85%	80%	59%	63%	70%
Never (0–5%)	10%	9%	2%	—	5%
What do you do when one of your parolees cannot find employment?					
Personally try to line up a job for him	13%	37%	36%	13%	32%
Contact specific employment agencies and make appointments for him	28%	30%	26%	24%	27%
Tell the parolee where he can go to get help	59%	33%	38%	63%	41%
Number of officers	39	194	207	46	486
Per cent of total	8%	40%	43%	9%	100%

illustrating their opposite extremes; less dramatic statistical research then is needed to measure these dimensions more precisely and to reveal their distribution and correlates. Extending this research to state parole or probation officers might have revealed greater contrasts among these several officer types.

Table 17.5 adds to our picture of the predominant characteristics of the four types of officers by providing information on their personal backgrounds. It will be seen that the passive officers tend to be the oldest of the four types. They are slightly higher than the other categories in the proportion with education beyond the bachelor's degree, and they are highest in the extent to which their last college specialization was in social work. Yet this group has the smallest percentage of chief probation officers. It would appear that this category includes a high proportion of officers who have been disappointed, or have become lazy, with respect to achieving the rank for which their graduate education qualified them. Possibly this includes many officers who react to the conflict between the permissive and trusting approach prescribed by their social-work indoctrination and the surveillance and control demanded by the courts and the public by eschewing control functions and assistance activities as well. One might suspect that this category includes many who view their federal employment as a sinecure until retirement, but it is noteworthy that this group contains an appreciable number of officers less than forty years old. Of course, the small number of officers whom we classified as passive makes these conclusions highly tentative.

The welfare officers have the lowest in median age of the four types, but they are highest in the proportion with a graduate degree and have the highest proportion of chief probation officers. The paternal officers have the smallest proportion of social-work-trained members of any of the four categories. They have the highest median length of service in the federal probation staff, and are high in proportion of chief or deputy chief probation officers. This group is the most active in churches, service groups, and professional organizations of any of the four major categories distinguished. They seem to be persons with strong community ties. The punitive officers have the lowest proportion with a graduate degree in college, but are high in the proportion whose last college major was sociology, corrections, criminology, or public administration. They are intermediate among the several types in most other characteristics we have distinguished.

It is interesting to note the extent to which the three types other than the passive have the attributes that one would predict from the earlier description of these three types by Ohlin and his associates which we cited. Of course, most of the differences in Table 17.5 are small, but the extent to which they are in the expected direction is noteworthy. One presumes that much blurring of presumed differences is due to imprecision of the scales as devices for identifying these types as well as to the influence of officers of diverse background on each other when working in the same agency. Presumably, some of the differences in style of parole supervision are also a function of individual personality characteristics independent of education, age, and other variables covered in Table 17.5.

The officers were also asked to check one of three completions for the statement: "Of the following, I get most of my intellectual stimulation

TABLE 17.5   Personal Attributes of U. S. Probation Officers Reporting Different Styles of Parole Supervision

| | LOW CONTROL | | HIGH CONTROL | | |
| | Low assistance (passive) | High assistance (welfare) | High assistance (paternal) | Low assistance (punitive) | All officers |
Personal attribute					
Age:					
Median	45.0	41.0	43.0	42.8	42.4
Over 50	31%	24%	30%	22%	27%
Over 40–50	31%	28%	30%	39%	30%
Over 30–40	39%	45%	35%	30%	39%
Under 30	0%	3%	5%	9%	4%
Education:					
No college	3%	5%	3%	2%	4%
Some college, no degree	8%	7%	10%	4%	8%
Bachelor's degree only	18%	20%	20%	26%	21%
Graduate study, no degree	33%	28%	31%	37%	31%
Law degree	3%	6%	7%	9%	6%
Master's degree or more	36%	35%	29%	22%	31%
Last college major:					
Psychology	5%	9%	7%	9%	8%
Sociology	8%	14%	15%	20%	15%
Social work	36%	28%	16%	22%	23%
Corrections, criminology, or public administration	5%	8%	8%	11%	8%
Other social sciences	10%	9%	16%	9%	12%
Education	18%	11%	15%	11%	14%
Other	15%	11%	13%	13%	12%
None or no information	3%	9%	9%	6%	8%
Longest prior related employment:					
Law enforcement	8%	16%	17%	17%	12%
Prison casework	8%	7%	5%	7%	6%
Social welfare	18%	14%	14%	20%	14%
Juvenile casework	23%	13%	10%	15%	13%
State parole or probation	15%	21%	20%	22%	20%
Teaching or coaching	21%	11%	18%	9%	15%
Business	3%	5%	3%	4%	4%
Other	—	8%	8%	4%	11%
None	5%	4%	5%	2%	4%
Number of officers	39	194	207	46	486
Per cent of total	8%	40%	43%	9%	100%
Median years as U. S. probation officer	7.2	7.0	7.6	7.1	7.2
Rank in U. S. probation service:					
Chief	8%	19%	18%	15%	17%
Deputy chief	3%	—	2%	7%	1%
Supervisor	8%	2%	4%	2%	4%
Probation officer	82%	79%	77%	76%	78%
Attendance at church, synagogue or other religious organizations:					
More than once per week	28%	32%	36%	28%	33%
Once per week	21%	29%	28%	30%	28%
Once or twice per month	23%	17%	15%	26%	18%

440

TABLE 17.5   (continued)

| Personal attribute | LOW CONTROL | | HIGH CONTROL | | All officers |
	Low assistance (passive)	High assistance (welfare)	High assistance (paternal)	Low assistance (punitive)	
Less than monthly	18%	11%	9%	11%	11%
Never	10%	9%	8%	4%	8%
Not indicated	—	2%	4%	—	2%
Denomination:					
None	5%	9%	9%	4%	8%
Protestant	49%	44%	50%	52%	48%
Catholic	23%	21%	17%	9%	18%
Jewish	3%	1%	—	4%	1%
Not indicated	21%	25%	25%	30%	25%
Participation in service clubs (some)	13%	10%	20%	15%	26%
Participation in professional organizations (some)	77%	68%	74%	78%	71%
Attend once a month or more	21%	24%	26%	24%	21%
One or more publications in past 5 years	18%	12%	15%	9%	15%
Number of officers	39	194	207	46	486
Per cent of total	8%	40%	43%	9%	100%

from:" The answer "colleagues in this probation office" was checked by 50 per cent of the punitive officers, 46 per cent of the paternal officers, 31 per cent of the welfare officers, and only 28 per cent of the passive officers. This suggests that high emphasis on control is mostly promoted within the agency itself, rather than by professional organizations; it may be a mutual defense of the officers in the agency's dealings with other organizations and the public. On the other hand, 54 per cent of the passive officers checked the answer "periodicals, books, and other publications," as their major source of intellectual stimulation; this also was checked by 47 per cent of the welfare officers, 37 per cent of the punitive officers, and 33 per cent of the paternal. This supports our picture of the passive officer as learned, but not highly identified with his work. The only remaining answer which the officers could choose, and the one on which the four types differed least, was "other professional associates elsewhere." It was checked by 13 per cent of the punitive, 17 per cent of the passive, 21 per cent of the paternal, and 22 per cent of the welfare officers.

There were only small differences in the extent to which the types of officers were found in judicial districts of diverse size. The 88 judicial districts varied in size from a low of one probation officer to a high of twenty-seven.

In general, the high level of education indicated by Table 17.5 for all federal probation officers is most impressive. Also, about one out of five federal probation officers, of every type, had prior employment in nonfederal parole or probation service. Federal probation officers are distinguished by active participation in religious organizations, with a majority reporting such participation once or more per week. About a quarter also reported some participation in service clubs. Participation in professional organizations was also extensively reported, as well as a moderate amount of publication, by all categories in our typology.

DIAGNOSIS VERSUS TREATMENT: THE TIME AND ACTIVITY OF FEDERAL PROBATION OFFICERS

A time-activity study of the federal probation officer's job was sponsored by the Federal Probation Officers' Association in 1961 and administered by the U. S. Probation Office for the Northern District of California, with consultation and assistance by our project and by the Administrative Office of U. S. Courts. For this study, from October 23, 1961 through November 10, 1961, in fifteen federal judicial districts, thirty-one male U. S. Probation Officers kept a minute-by-minute log of all their activity. They were a fairly representative sample of the entire federal probation service, and they logged 3323.3 man hours of work during the study period.[8]

[8] To select the male officers for the project, one large and one small office were chosen by lot from each of the six regions into which the United States is divided, for administrative purposes, by the federal probation service. A large district was defined as one with ten or more officers, and the remainder were called small districts except in the Central States and Southeastern States regions, where a large district was defined as one with six or more officers. (These two regions had no offices with as many as ten officers.)

In each large office, three probation officers were selected by lot, one from those whose case loads were mostly urban, one from those with largely suburban case loads, and one from those whose case loads were mostly rural. In each small office one officer with predominantly urban and one with predominantly rural cases was chosen. In two districts where no officers had many suburban or rural cases, officers with such case loads were chosen from immediately adjacent judicial districts. In addition, two urban officers were chosen from another large district in the densely populated Northeastern region.

These were intended to be line officers rather than supervisors or chief probation officers, and the reports of one officer were deleted from the tabulations when it was learned he was a supervisor inadvertently included.

This selection procedure was developed in consultation with the Board of Directors of the Federal Probation Officers' Association. It was designed primarily to permit some analysis, in the pilot study, of every factor which members of the Board believed to be highly significant in giving certain probation officers unique tasks: the size of the office, the region, and whether the cases are urban, suburban, or rural.

Forms for recording details of the officer's activity were repeatedly tested in different federal probation offices before the tabulations reported here were initiated. The final version of this form had one line for logging each activity, with a separate line used also for each case, and most of the entries consisting only of checks in the appropriate squares. However, the time for each activity was recorded separately, in hours and tenths of an hour, that is, to the nearest multiple of six minutes. See: Albert Wahl and Daniel Glaser, "A Pilot Time Study of the Federal Probation Officer's Job," *Federal Probation, 27,* no. 3 (Sept. 1963), pp. 20-24.

The U. S. Probation Officer has a work load almost unique in the correctional field. While functioning as probation officer for a U. S. District Court, he also acts as a parole officer for the U. S. Board of Parole and Bureau of Prisons, and for the Departments of the Army and Air Force. Eighty-two per cent of the time logged by the officers was ascribed by them to services for a specific case. As Table 17.6 shows, 41.3 per cent of this

TABLE 17.6   Allocation of U. S. Probation Officer's Time to All Types of Case
(Per cent of total time from time-activity sample of 31 officers
logging 3323 hours in 15 days, Oct.–Nov. 1961)

Type of case	Per cent of total time	Per cent as hours in 168-hour work month	Average case load[a]	Average hours per case	Ratio of one presentence investigation time to time for other types of casework per month	Percentage distribution of time designated as for a specific case
Presentence	33.7	56.6	4	14.1	1.0	41.3
Probation*	29.4	49.4	53	1.1	12.8	36.0
Parole*	11.6	19.5	12	1.6	8.8	14.2
Prison inmate	3.4	5.7	1	5.7[b]	2.5	4.1
Mandatory releasee*	2.3	3.9	4	1.0	14.1	2.8
Postsentence	1.1	1.8	—	—	—	1.4
Military parole*	0.2	0.3	0.2	1.5	9.4	0.3
Work not designated as for a specific case	18.4	30.9	—	—	—	—
Totals	100.0	168 hrs.	a	a	a	100.0
All supervision cases (marked *)	43.5	73.1	69.2	1.1	12.8	53.3

[a] Presentence and prison figures refer to investigations completed per month, by the average U. S. Probation Officer, in fiscal year 1961. Other figures refer to men under supervision as of June 30, 1961. Hours therefore, are for *completion* of one presentence or prisoner (preparole) investigation, and for *one month's supervision service* for the other cases, so they cannot reasonably be added. Figures derived from *Annual Report of the Administrative Office of U. S. Courts* (1961), Tables 1 through 4, pp. 176–87.

[b] This probably is an overestimate because it applies the average number of preparole investigations per month per officer—one—to the estimated hours per month of service for prison inmates, but some service for prison inmates is performed in addition to preparole investigations.

time was designated for presentence work, 36 per cent was assigned to the supervision of probationers, and 1.4 per cent of the time was devoted to postsentence work, a special type of counseling and assistance for men awaiting transfer from jail to prison or held in jail pending payment of fines.

Altogether, 78.7 per cent, or not quite four-fifths, of the federal probation officer's time devoted to specific cases was for the foregoing tasks. These might be considered the components of his probation officer role, with only the remainder available for his parole services. There was little variation in this probation services proportion: it was 79 per cent for large offices and 75 per cent for small offices, 83 per cent for officers with primarily suburban caseloads, 79 per cent for officers with primarily rural caseloads, and 78 per cent for officers with primarily urban caseloads. Regional variations ranged from a low of 74 per cent in the Far West to a high of 81 per cent in the Great Lakes area, with most of the other regions close to the latter figure. The stability of this figure through all of these special categories of officers suggests that a conclusion that about four-fifths of the federal probation officer's work is devoted to probation tasks is a highly reliable estimate, despite the small sample used.

The approximately one-fifth of the time designated as for specific cases which was used for *parole services* was divided as follows: 66 per cent to parole supervision, 19 per cent to services for men in prison (parole plan investigation or assistance), 13 per cent to mandatory releasee supervision, and about 1 per cent to the supervision of military parolees.

According to the *Annual Report of the Administrative Office of U. S. Courts,* during 1961 the average U. S. probation officer completed forty-eight presentence investigations, or four per month.[9] Considering that there are twenty-one working days or 168 hours in an average month, if 33.7 per cent of the officer's total time is devoted to presentence work, as Table 17.6 indicates, this would be 56.6 hours per month, or approximately fourteen hours per presentence investigation.

The average U. S. probation officer also, during 1961, completed slightly more than one preparole investigation per month. Generalizing from our pilot study findings that 3.4 per cent of the total time of the officer was devoted to work for men in prison, we can assign, at most, 5.7 hours per month for this task. It would be less than this to the extent that casework for prisoners is not for preparole investigation only.

As of June 30, 1961, the average U. S. probation officer was assigned the supervision of fifty-three probationers, twelve parolees, and four mandatory releasees, or a total of sixty-eight cases, plus one military parolee for every five officers.[10] Table 17.6 indicates the average hours per month required for supervision of these various types of case, as estimated by dividing this average caseload for each type of case into the hours per month indicated by our time-activity study as devoted to services for that type of case. Considering a total of about seventy-three hours used in supervision work for sixty-eight cases, we have an average of about 1.1 hours per month per supervison case. Comparing this with fourteen hours per presentence investigation completed, we have 12.8 times as much time per month devoted to a presentence investigation as to supervision of one case for one month. It is notable that probationers, on the average, seem to receive somewhat less time per month for supervision than parolees, possibly because parolees usually have greater problems than probationers.

[9] Derived from the total of 24,357 presentence investigations completed in 1961 by 506 U. S. Probation Officers, according to *Annual Report to the Administrative Office of U. S. Courts (1961),* pp. 177-79, Tables 1 and 4.

[10] *Ibid.,* Tables 3 and 4.

In estimating an officer's normal caseload, it has been customary in the federal probation service to equate one presentence investigation per month with four supervision cases. The interest of the Federal Probation Officers' Association in a time-activity study arose from the opinion among the officers that this ratio underestimates the relative time required by a presentence investigation, as compared to a supervision case. Several Association officials had suggested that a ratio of one presentence case to seven supervision cases would be more appropriate than one to four. Our figures indicate that a ratio of one to twelve or thirteen would be even closer to the actual proportions of time devoted to these two types of work by the officers.

One of the items in our questionnaire completed by 96 per cent of U. S. Probation Officers was: "If you could specialize on your job, which one of the following duties would you prefer to specialize in?" The answers, and the percentages responding with each, were as follows: presentence investigation, 40 per cent; probation supervision, 39 per cent; parole supervision, 10 per cent; all other definite alternatives (military parole supervision, postsentence work, etc.), 2 per cent; blank or multiple responses, 2 per cent; written-in objection to the question on grounds that they do not choose to specialize, 7 per cent. Adding together the parole, probationer, and military categories, we conclude that a majority of the officers *prefer* some type of supervision work or counseling to presentence investigation.

Apparently the demands of the federal probation job relationships, rather than the officers' preferences, account for the time given presentence work. This was indicated by responses to our question: "If four different problems came up and needed immediate action, which one of the following would you be most likely to give first priority?" The four alternatives provided, and the percentage checking each, were: presentence investigation, 69 per cent; probation supervision, 11 per cent; parole supervision, 12 per cent; postsentence counseling, 4 per cent. Three per cent gave multiple, blank, or other responses. While the officers do not actually *prefer* presentence to supervision work, they feel obliged to give it higher priority.

The high ratio of presentence to supervision time in this correctional service, and the priority given to presentence work, seem to express a pervasive tendency in casework. It is a development often observed also in mental health clinics, mental hospitals, juvenile correctional institutions, and prisons. This is the tendency for diagnostic activities to expand in volume, in comparison with counseling or other treatment services. There are several apparent reasons for this. Most obvious, of course, is that diagnostic reports are required by a specific deadline. Secondly, diagnostic reports are provided for higher officials, while treatment services are generally for persons not in authority over the caseworker. Thirdly, and perhaps of most strategic importance, is the fact that diagnostic activity produces a tangible product in the form of a diagnostic report, while the results of treatment are not so readily observed. Partly because of this visibility of the diagnostic report, superiors can more readily evaluate staff on diagnosis than on treatment, and also superiors are likely to base their decisions on the diagnostic analysis that they receive from their casework staff. They cannot as readily see the personal relationship of officer to client in counseling, or its ultimate consequence in reform or recidivism, cure or relapse. Only by making the latter effects more visible, as consequences of treatment service, could one expect a change from this emphasis on diagnosis.

In the federal probation service, of course, the judges depend on the presentence reports of the line probation officers. It is reasonable to expect that an officer is more likely to be praised and promoted by these diagnostic communications to his superiors, on which the superiors depend for their decisions, than on his relationship to the men whom he supervises, a relationship not readily perceived or evaluated. In addition, a presentence report involves the officer in direct personal communication with his superior, who may question him on it, whereas supervision services do not place him "on the spot" in the same urgent fashion. Of course, it may frequently be the case that many of the hours invested in diagnosis, by helping a court achieve wise sentencing decisions, contribute more to crime reduction than would the same number of hours in added supervision services. This is difficult to evaluate in the absence of systematic experiments with different styles of probation officer work, checked by long-run recidivism rates. Our task in this chapter is to describe the way in which the probation officer's work is performed and to explain the various styles of work, without trying to evaluate them.

The type of activity which the officers pursued, classified by a gross description of actual behavior, was as follows:

Face-to-face contact	40%	Phone	6%
Paperwork	33%	Waiting	2%
Travel	16%	Other activity	3%

Of the time which the officers spent in communicating with anyone, whether orally or in writing, 48 per cent was in communication with their clients, and 13 per cent with relatives of the clients. Another 13 per cent of this time was used in communication with judges, 10 per cent with other probation staff, 9 per cent with law enforcement agencies, 3 per cent with employers, and 2 per cent each with institutions and with attorneys.

Still another perspective for the description of probation officer work is provided by Table 17.7. Here it will be seen that the major type of releasee supervision activity performed by U. S. Probation Officers is what they describe as "counseling." Report-writing, while predominant in presentence work, was involved in less than one-eighth of the total supervision

TABLE 17.7 Per Cent of U.S. Probation Officers' Time Spent at Various Types of Work, for Major Types of Cases
(From time-activity sample of 31 officers logging 3323 hours in 15 days, Oct.–Nov. 1961)

Type of work performed	TYPE OF CASE WORKED WITH				Total work time
	Presentence	Probation supervision	Parole, mandatory or military parole release supervision	All other work activity	
Counseling	3.0	4/.1	40.2	3.1	21.2
Administrative	4.2	3.5	2.3	55.7	15.5
Report writing	22.8	12.3	11.9	4.5	14.0
Giving information	12.3	10.2	15.0	7.0	10.9
Case review	12.8	6.6	4.8	3.5	7.7
Initial interview	15.0	2.2	5.9	1.5	6.9
Home investigation	4.0	5.8	6.2	4.4	4.9
Job investigation	3.6	4.0	6.0	2.4	3.8
Other	22.3	8.3	7.7	17.9	15.1
Total	100.0	100.0	100.0	100.0	100.0
Per cent of total time by type of case	33.7	29.4	14.1	22.8	100.0
No. of cases worked with in average month[a]	4	53	16	—	[a]

[a] This compares presentence investigations *completed* during an average month in 1961, with number of men under probation, parole, or mandatory release supervision as of a given date in 1961, per *Annual Report of the Administrative Office of U. S. Courts* (1961), Tables 1 through 4, pp. 176–87.

work time. Indeed, counseling was given over three and one-half times as much of the officer's supervision time as report-writing.

In summary, the U. S. Probation Officer emphasizes counseling in his supervision, but the time which these officers give to supervision work, in proportion to the time devoted to presentence work, is only about one-third as much as has been assumed in the official caseload statistics. The latter equate one presentence investigation with only four supervision cases per month, when the data on time assigned to these activities suggest a ratio of over twelve to one.

Our findings might be employed as a basis for opposing the combination of probation and parole administration in a single staff, for it can be argued that presentence work tends to be given priority and can interfere with the quality of parole supervision. Opposing this are three major arguments: (1) Travel time and costs are saved, especially with the geographically scattered federal caseloads, by having one officer handle both the probation and the parole cases in a given geographic area. (2) Since many parolees originally received a presentence investigation, and sometimes were under probation supervision by a probation officer of the court to which he is released on parole, the officer does not require as much time and effort to become familiar with the parolee and his background as he would if parole supervision provided his first contact with the man. (3) If the influence of counseling depends on the development of a close relationship between the supervisor and his client, the effectiveness of counseling is impaired by any change of officer involved in supervision.

Opposing the third argument is the notion that the parolee represents a failure of probation, or, if committed to prison without prior probation for his offense, he may blame the presentence investigator for his prison sentence. It might be contended that under these circumstances a new supervision officer on parole might be in a better position to develop a beneficial relationship with the releasee than his prior probation officer. Of course, postsentence work and sometimes the probation officer's services for men in prison may prevent a prisoner from ascribing his sentence to the probation officer.

In large cities parolees and mandatory releasees frequently are sufficiently concentrated geographically to render the travel savings from combining probation and parole services negligible. In these circumstances, it might be appropriate to experiment with a specialized caseload of parolees and mandatory releasees for a few officers, to see how the more extensive control or assistance services which this would permit might affect violation and recidivism rates. Some large federal offices seem to approach this by making certain officers specialists in particular types of presentence investigation for which they have special qualifications and giving others a large proportion of the parolees and mandatory releasees not previously investigated by any of the staff.

THE PAROLE ADVISER SYSTEM

A distinctive feature of federal parole administration is that the parolee must have some citizen serve voluntarily as his parole adviser. This requirement has been abolished in some states and frequently is waived by the U. S. Board of Parole when satisfactory advisers prove unavailable, but in most cases federal parolees procure an approved adviser. When waiver occurs, the U. S. Probation Officer may be named the adviser, in addition to serving as supervision officer.

The criteria for selecting an adviser and the services expected of him are well summarized in the following statement from the *U. S. Probation Officer's Manual:*

The Advisor. The parole advisor should be an interested, reliable and responsible person in the community in which the parolee intends to live. Unless there are unusual circumstances the Board of Parole feels that a law enforcement officer, attorney, relative, or public official should not be approved as an advisor. The advisor should be of the same sex as the prospective parolee, and if possible should have at least the same cultural and educational background. Common interests also serve to improve the relationship between the two persons.

The advisor is not asked to assume any legal or financial responsibility for the parolee, but he should assume the moral obligation to assist with advice and counsel whenever it is needed. He will be asked to aid the parolee in making regular written monthly reports to the probation office and to certify their accuracy and correctness. He will also be under obligation to bring to the attention of the probation officer any suspected violations of the conditions of parole or any other conditions which may be conducive to such a violation.

In making the investigation and report on the prospective advisor, the probation officer will want to support his approval or disapproval of the advisor with sufficient data. The report should show the personal and professional reputation of the advisor and his general standing in the community, the nature of his past and present relations with the inmate and his family, the amount of time and attention that the advisor may be able to give to the person under supervision, and estimates of the degree to which the advisor can be expected to cooperate with the probation officer.[11]

Of the parolees in our successful releasee sample, 82 per cent had advisers, as against 69 per cent in our returned violator sample. In the U. S. Parole Board's study of all persons committed under the Federal Youth Correction Act in the fiscal year ending June 30, 1955, reports from the prison caseworkers before each youth's release indicated that two-thirds of this group had advisers, one-fifth were to have their U. S. Probation Officer serve as adviser, one-tenth had no parole adviser arrangement before release, and there was no information on the remaining 4 per cent. Success rates on first parole were 43 per cent for those with an adviser, 30 per cent for those with the probation officer as adviser, and only 19 per cent for those with no adviser. In the reports submitted later on this sample by their U. S. Probation Officers, no information on adviser arrangements was given in 28 per cent of the cases, but, again, two-thirds of those for whom information was provided were reported to have a parole adviser. However, success rates on first parole were 62 per cent for those with an adviser, 29 per cent for those without one, and only 7 per cent for the cases on whom adviser information was not provided.

Regardless of what the precise rates would be if information on advisers were complete for all cases, it appears that those parolees with an adviser had higher success rates than those without one. The crucial question, however, is whether this success reflects the services contributed by the adviser or simply the fact that the ties of the parolee in the community were sufficient to procure an acceptable adviser. A definitive answer to this question would be most adequately acquired by experimental elimination of the adviser requirement in a random sample of parole cases or in intermittent

[11] Administrative Office of U. S. Courts, *United States Probation Officer's Manual,* Section 8, p. 19a.

periods. In the absence of such experimentation, however, some basis for evaluating the adviser system may be provided by our information on the background of the advisers and the services they performed. This may suggest conditions under which advisers are likely to be beneficial and conditions where their value may be questioned.

About two-thirds of the releasees interviewed (in the postrelease panel, successful releasee, and returned violator samples) who had parole advisers had their adviser procured for them by their family, and about 40 per cent did not know their adviser before they were released. Almost half of the advisers were clergymen. All three of these proportions were slightly lower for the successful releasees than for the returned violators. The median frequency of contact with the adviser was weekly for the successful releasees and twice a month for the returned violators. Forty-five per cent of the successful releasees and 38 per cent of the returned violators described their adviser as helpful. Such slight differences as these may simply reflect the prejudices of the returned violators; indeed, it is of interest that the successful and the unsuccessful had so much agreement in describing and evaluating their advisers. No marked relationships were evident when we cross-tabulated the foregoing data; for example, neither occupation of adviser and frequency of contact, nor occupation and evaluation as helpful, were related.

The complaints about advisers which our interviewers received from parolees or returned violators were generally not of harm done but of lack of help. This is indicated by remarks like "He couldn't talk on my level or understand my problems," "Just asked how I was getting along," and "What could he help me with; only thing he did was sign my papers." Some complained of the religious fervor of clergymen advisers, as illustrated by the following remarks of returned violators:

I would get in the bathtub when he came to see me. He threatened me with hell and fire for my sinful ways.

He wanted me in church four times a week, but I went once a week. He acted like he didn't care about me.

He tried to convert me to the Baptist Church when I was a Catholic.

It always ended up in a lecture and telling me that if I'm not attending church, I must be getting into trouble.

Despite such complaints, when even two out of five returned violators and a somewhat higher ratio of successful releasees say the adviser was helpful, it would appear that the adviser system should not be abolished. Our successful releasee cases S-901 and S-902, whom we shall call "Walt" and "Will," and who were codefendants, illustrate the benefits that a good adviser may provide, and also show the part the probation officer can play in selecting the adviser and working with him.[12]

Walt returned from prison to his childhood home, a town of 6000 population. During Walt's childhood his father worked on farms as a day laborer, and the family was in a low socioeconomic bracket. Due to dire economic conditions, Walt dropped out of school while in the sixth grade. His brother served five years for check forgery, and other family members had felony arrests. Walt's parents were divorced when his mother had an affair with her oldest daughter's husband.

Prior to the current offense, Walt made a low-average income but drank excessively. After his debts became unmanageable, he and his codefendant, Will, while intoxicated, robbed a bank.

After Walt's parole was approved, the probation officer made a trip to Walt's home town, where the pastor of a large church was persuaded to act as parole adviser. The denomination was one commonly associated with the middle class. The pastor openly approached the young adult group in his church with Walt's release problems. Through the adviser's efforts, the congregation accepted Walt and his family. Walt procured employment as a cement finisher and within four months was general manager of the small company for which he worked. He went into business for himself two years later, and now his income is well into the five-figure range. Two years after his release he was elected a trustee in his church, he and his wife were active in the church choir and the young adult group, and he helped her in her work as a Girl Scout troop leader. The parole adviser was active in the case all the while. He advised Walt on budget and business matters, but stayed behind the scene. The adviser both encouraged Walt's participation in the social life of the church and promoted the congregation's acceptance of Walt and his family. It was through the adviser's encouragement that Walt went into business for himself, where even he has been surprised by his success.

While Walt's success came fast, it did not come without effort. His long working hours and the corresponding pressures caused marital strain, which soon exploded into a separation, with a divorce pending. The wife accused Walt of infidelity, but in the opinion of the parole adviser and probation officer, both of whom spent many hours with her, she seemed to be developing delusions on this. Walt moved into a hotel room, and she started spending her time with her sisters. A delegation of women from the parole adviser's church came to urge that he ask the Parole Board to declare Walt a parole violator. He suggested that if they or anyone else actually knew anything about Walt's infidelity, he would call the probation officer, and they could tell what they knew. They admitted that all they had was hearsay evidence.

The parole adviser performed several valuable functions in this case. The

[12] The remainder of this section relies primarily on the work of one of our staff, Charles W. Dean, who became particularly interested in the parole adviser role. See: Charles W. Dean, *Some Factors in Federal Penitentiary Parole Violation* (Master of Arts thesis, University of Illinois, 1961), ch. 6.

probation office was fifty miles from the subject's residence, and the parole adviser kept the probation officer informed of the developments in the case and of the community attitudes. Especially important, he was able to correct, verify, or investigate stories the probation officer heard from Walt and his wife during the period of marital strife. The parole adviser was able to perform his role in such a way that, even if the probation office had been in the same town instead of fifty miles away, his service would have been complementary and valuable. In this case, we can see the adviser, through his church, providing the parolee with a new social situation, offering advice in budget matters and encouragement in business, and acting as mediator in a marital dispute. However, he finally advised the subject to get a good lawyer and withdrew from the marital problem. In addition, he provided the probation officer with information and corrected false information from biased sources.

Will, our Case S-902, was Walt's codefendant. They were reared in the same small town, under similar circumstances, but since their release they have avoided one another, and each blamed the other for their trouble with the law. The probation officer procured a minister of one of the other large churches as Will's parole adviser. The job in the parole plan was not available after Will was released, so he was unemployed for several weeks. The adviser wrote the probation officer that both he and Will were doing all they could to find him employment, but work was scarce, as the local industry was temporarily out of operation. Will went to a nearby city to look for work, but returned home because he could not read the street signs and never knew where he was. During this period the adviser averaged two letters a month to the probation officer, as well as numerous others to various prospective employers. About nine months after release, the probation officer's log read:

> Rev. _____ has taken a great deal of time and trouble to try and do something for this subject, although he realizes as I do, that we do not have very encouraging material to work with. He can scarcely read or write, and is very weak. His wife is also very weak.

At the time of Will's release, his ex-wife was receiving welfare funds and Will still owed many debts. The probation officer and adviser agreed that he should have all his debts paid and a hundred dollars in the bank before they could re-marry. Will was driving a milk truck and his ex-wife was keeping his books for him, as he was incapable of the bookkeeping work. The adviser checked the books each week to see that there was no confusion, until it became apparent that the wife was capable of the work.

The month after he started the milk route, he wanted to buy a life insurance policy. The probation officer told him to talk it over with the adviser, and get the adviser's opinion on the reputation of the company.

About one month after this, Will wanted to buy a used furniture store. The adviser investigated and after learning that the former owner made a profit only because of shrewd trading, suggested to the probation officer that Will not be given permission to buy the business. The next month Will procured employment as a baker, a trade he had learned while incarcerated.

This probation officer required that a parolee have the adviser's permission before spending any large sums of money. Around three months after Will started work as a baker, he told his adviser he could trade cars for a hundred dollars plus his old car. The adviser approved this, but when the probation officer visited Will's home, both cars were there. The probation officer and adviser immediately went to see Will, and he told them that the dealer just hadn't come after the old car at that time. They checked on this story, and found it to be true.

Three months after this, Will wanted to buy a house, and talked it over with his adviser. After they wrote it all out on paper, it was evident that the payments, taxes, and insurance would cost much more than Will could afford.

At this time Will's parole period was over, but a three-year probation period had to be served. The probation officer requested the adviser to continue, and he agreed to do so.

After our interview with Will, subsequent discussions with the probation officer revealed that Will has purchased a home and now is owner of the bakery where he used to work. The adviser thoroughly investigated both transactions and gave his approval. After the purchase of the bakery, the adviser wrote the probation officer a letter. Following are the three central paragraphs.

Dear _____:

Among all the monthly reports which we have been sending you during the past years, this one, no doubt, will be the most outstanding. As one later reviews this case, the finger might well point to this particular month [February 1961] as the climax of this entire probation, as the attainment of the goal, as the reaching of the peak after a most strenuous climb.

As I understand the matter of probation, the purpose is not merely to watch over someone's conduct and actions (any policeman can do that), but the primary purpose is to give guidance to the individual, in order that he may be readjusted and rehabilitated to life in society, and, even more, that he may become an honorable citizen who will live a life which will be useful and beneficial to his fellow men.

As I look back (and you surely can also clearly call back across the stage of memory the situation and scenes of not too many years ago), and see _____ in his wrongs, his insufficiencies, his unreliability, his unstableness, and behold the broken home, the wife, _____, as she divorced _____ while in prison, the three small children with their dark and uncertain future; and then the long and hard climb, the inability to secure a job, the back-log of debts and the parade of bill-collectors; and the gradual progress, the re-marriage of _____ and _____, the family slowly becoming a unity again, the organizing of the home into a respectable and orderly household; your patience and kindness and tact at work—your suggestions for proper preparation of balanced meals, your guidance for buying food and clothing, and economizing, your help in enabling them to set up a budget and a simple accounting system of the family's income and expenditures, and the formation of savings account; the advancing from one job to another, slow steps, indeed, at times, but always some degree toward improvement, as I recall all of this, and then today, with this month's report can inform you that _____ has become one of the businessmen of this city, having purchased the _____ Bakery, of which he is sole owner and operator. It certainly is cause for tremendous rejoicing, for here has been attained the goal of "probation" in its real and fullest sense; the development of a man, once confined behind bars, like a vicious lion in a cage, unable to live with his fellow men, into an upright citizen living a life of honor and of beneficial service to his fellow men.

This same probation officer had another case where the parole adviser was equally important. In this case the adviser was an insurance salesman who also became involved in the family and financial problems of the parolee and made numerous calls to the probation officer when trouble arose.

In each instance, no effort was made to conceal the fact that the adviser and probation officer were working together. They discussed problems and presented a unified front when confronting the parolee.

The adviser was given authority not specifically described in the *Probation Officer's Manual*. Yet all roles were clearly defined through informal communication. In all three cases, the adviser was an assistant to the probation officer. It was made clear that, while the probation officer was responsible, and made the final decisions, the parolee had a responsibility to the adviser.

During the course of the interviews, all three parolees expressed gratitude for the work of their advisers and probation officers. Such supervision techniques could not have been used successfully unless the supervisee was convinced that the officer and adviser were sincerely interested in him as a person.

Another judicial district which has had profitable experiences with parole advisers has a somewhat different approach. For a parolee who lived some distance away from the probation officer, a police officer was asked to be the parole adviser. While, at a glance, this may appear dubious, it proved to be successful for S-664, whom we shall call Walker.

Walker's parole adviser, selected by the probation officer, was the captain of detectives in the city police department of a city of 40,000 population. Two months after Walker's release, the police department received three complaints against him. The adviser, upon investigation, learned that Walker had been dating a girl who was pregnant by another man and that this other man was the one who was telephoning the complaints, which proved to be false.

Three months after this, Walker discussed a residence change with his adviser. At first he was paying room and board to his parents, but his sister was destitute, so shortly after release he moved in with her. The sister's husband refused to work, but frequently reported to the adviser how Walker spent his money and made anonymous phone calls informing on Walker. It was learned that this brother-in-law was dishonest in giving this information and was exploiting

Walker, so that the adviser recommended that Walker move to a hotel room. While living in a downtown hotel, he saw his adviser almost daily for several months. Nine months after Walker's release, the adviser wrote the probation officer that he was keeping in very close contact with Walker, who seemed to be adjusting satisfactorily, and he would continue to make a special effort in the case. Three months later the adviser wrote that Walker frequently went out of his way to visit him informally. Our researcher questioned Walker closely regarding his parole adviser, since the *Probation Officer's Manual* states that "Unless there are unusual circumstances, the Board of Parole feels that law enforcement officials, lawyers, etc., should not be approved as an advisor." Walker seemed to have the greatest respect for his adviser and to consider him as a personal friend.

Walker's case makes an interesting comparison with the cases of Walt and Will. The advisers for both of the latter were ministers, who usually perform a nonauthoritarian advisory function but in this case assumed a more authoritarian role by controlling expenditure of funds and credit. However, in Walker's case a law-enforcement official, who is by definition authoritarian, assumed a counselor-adviser role. In all cases, both the parolees and probation officers considered the parole advisers to be excellent. These examples call into question a rigid rule against particular occupations in selecting parole advisers.

In another case, that of Wesley, in the same district as Walker, the adviser was an uncle with whom the parolee lived. The probation officer procured employment for Wesley, and he proved to be an excellent worker. The employer developed such a paternal interest in Wesley that he discharged one other employee who, he feared, would influence Wesley in the wrong direction. The employer worked closely with the probation officer, and was, in effect, a second parole adviser.

Wesley had been reared in an unstable home and was a constant disciplinary problem. His only sister was sentenced to a girls' school and has not been heard from since her release. This young man was incarcerated for the first time when sixteen years of age. He ran away from the minimum security youth institution four times. Three months after release he stole a car and was sentenced to a state boys' reform school. Ten months after his release, he was arrested and sentenced under the Youth Corrections Act for a Dyer Act violation. Since Wesley's family was obviously ineffectual in its efforts to control him, the probation officer and Wesley's mother agreed that Wesley would profit by a different residential situation. He had an uncle and aunt who agreed to accept him and, since he had no parole adviser, the uncle agreed to act in that capacity also.

In the state to which this man was released, state laws require that anyone on parole or probation must have his probation officer's permission to obtain a driver's license. Subject was given permission to buy a car and to apply for his driver's license.

Shortly after Wesley purchased his car, the probation officer was informed during a routine home visit to the adviser's home that Wesley had been running around in his car every day, whereas formerly he had stayed close to home. Also, he had established contact with a young man he had met in prison. Wesley told his aunt and uncle that this young man was just out of the army, and they offered to let him live with them until he found a place of his own, although he did not accept the invitation. The probation officer informed the aunt that the young man was on parole and had been in a reformatory, not the army. The aunt and uncle were disappointed that Wesley had been dishonest, but this precipitated a closer working relationship between the adviser, his wife, and the probation officer.

The next day a call to the employer revealed that Wesley had been missing work, and was not in town that day. When he did report to work, he informed his employer he had "been out, playing around." The probation officer firmly reprimanded the parolee for his general misbehavior, withdrew his permission for a driver's license for several months, and instructed him to report weekly. The aunt agreed to inform the probation officer about the subject's associates. About six months later another federal parolee visited the subject, and they spent a Sunday afternoon together. After learning this, the probation officer requested the adviser to call him at his office or home immediately after any new acquaintances appeared at their home.

A short time later this parolee tried to help his brother purchase a car, and the finance company called his uncle. The uncle informed the probation officer of this matter, and the transaction was canceled.

This was the last problem which presented itself in this case. The subject was eventually laid off along with most of his co-workers, and while waiting to be called back to work, found a better job. On this new job he has made an entire new circle of conventional friends. At the time of the interview he was engaged to a girl from an excellent home, and was due to be released from parole within six months, due to his fine adjustment.

The fact that these cases all come from two offices warrants a closer look at the supervision techniques common to both offices. Both offices are characterized by an intensive surveillance effort. Both are firm in their exercise of control. Neither office attempts to avoid situations where they must assume an authoritative role or, as they say, "lay the cards on the table." Still, they maintain a congenial relationship with the men under their supervision and not one criticism was received from the twenty-five successful releasees interviewed in the two offices. Both offices, whenever possible, try to procure a parole adviser for the men with whom the probation officer can work closely, and they give the adviser enough authority and responsibility to prevent his feeling that his is a perfunctory role.

It should be stressed that the advisers are especially useful at locations too distant from the parole supervision office for the officer to maintain close contact with the parolee. In other locations the advantage of an adviser may not offset the time required for the officer to recruit or investigate advisers so as to be confident that they will be satisfactory.

CALIFORNIA RESEARCH ON THE EFFECTIVENESS OF PAROLE SUPERVISION ALTERNATIVES

Probably the most extensive controlled experiment in American correctional history, and perhaps in world history, is California's "Special Intensive Parole Unit," abbreviated "SIPU." In its first phase, begun in 1953, a randomly selected experimental group of parolees was released three months before their scheduled release dates and placed for three months in parole-agent caseloads of only fifteen men. When this group was compared with a control group released at the regular dates to the then standard ninety-man caseloads, differences in postrelease infractions were found to be negligible, but the saving in confinement costs from early release more than compensated for the extra cost of fifteen-man caseloads. There was some suggestion that certain offenders had higher violation rates under the experimental conditions because the smaller caseload permitted parole agents to become aware of more minor infractions, while, conversely, parolees needing assistance in procuring jobs at release had lower violation rates because they got more help when in the small caseloads. Neither of these aspects was systematically explored.

The second phase of SIPU involved reaction to the findings of Phase I by changing the supervision of the experimental group to thirty-man caseloads for six months. Comparison with a control group yielded results very similar to those of Phase I. It should be stressed that Phase I and Phase II findings were extremely valuable in that they may well have saved millions of dollars by effectively countering those who contended that merely increasing the number of parole agents so as to reduce caseloads would greatly reduce the violation rates of parolees.

In SIPU Phase III the parole agents of the experimental caseloads maintained supervision of all cases in thirty-five-man caseloads until supervision was terminated. This eliminated possible negative effects in Phases I and II from transfer of parolees to other parole agents, with regular caseloads, three months or six months after release. A control group of 2806 cases were in the regular seventy-two-man caseloads.

Before Phase III was completed the Research Division had been established in the Department of Corrections. It had already been able to apply parole prediction analysis to representative samples of all California adult offender records, using multiple correlations of factors most related to postrelease outcome to classify men into risk groups (called "base expectancy categories"). Analysis by those risk categories revealed that the lower-middle risk cases in the SIPU groups had distinctly fewer infractions on parole than those in the same risk category in the control groups, and there were also slight differences between the experimental and the control group cases who were in highly favorable or highly unfavorable risk categories. For example, at twenty-four months after release on parole, the per cent returned to prison, by risk category, for SIPU and control cases were: poor risks, SIPU 50 per cent, control 52 per cent; medium-poor risks, SIPU 35 per cent, control 45 per cent; medium-good risks, SIPU 40 per cent, control 42 per cent; good risks, SIPU 22 per cent, control 25 per cent. In other words, for those who would probably succeed anyhow, or for those for whom prior experience had never indicated much success, the small caseloads did not greatly affect outcome, but small caseloads were somewhat effective for cases intermediate between these extremes.[13]

Phase IV of SIPU, initiated before the results of Phase III were known, involves an attempt to classify parole agents according to their stress on giving parolees counseling ("internal" assistance), or on helping the parolees to get better homes, jobs, associates, or other environmental assets ("external" assistance). It also involves classification of parolees on a scale of interpersonal maturity (I-level) developed by Department of Corrections Research Director J. Douglas Grant and his associates during prior research in a Navy correctional installation.[14] Finally, caseloads are more varied, including fifteen-, thirty-, and seventy-man sizes.

In Phase V of SIPU, begun while Phase IV was still in progress, parole agents begin to work with their cases while the latter are still in prison. This includes not only individual prerelease planning conferences but also participation of the agents in the inmate group meetings at the prison (described in chapter 8). It also will attempt the classification of inmates and agents initiated in Phase IV.

Research on parole administration for cases under supervision of the California Youth Authority is distinguished by being concentrated in highly limited areas. This makes travel a less severe problem and permits more intensive study than would be possible with more geographically widespread undertakings. The most advanced project was started in 1959 in Oakland and covers all of Alameda County. Additional parole agents were placed in that county to establish ten experimental caseloads of thirty-six parolees each and five geographically matched caseloads of seventy-two parolees each. Extensive interviews, time studies, tests, and systematic observations have been conducted with agents and parolees in both the experi-

[13] See: Joan Havel and Elaine Sulka, *Special Intensive Parole Unit, Phase Three,* Research Report no. 3 (California Department of Corrections, Sacramento, March 1962).

[14] See: J. D. and M. Q. Grant, "A Group Dynamics Approach to the Treatment of Nonconformists in the Navy," *Annals of the American Academy of Political and Social Science, 322* (1959), 126-35.

mental and the control groups in an effort to identify qualitative factors in success and failure on parole.

Initial findings from the Alameda County study reveal only that in the first six months the small caseload parolees had only 8 per cent revocations, compared to 23 per cent for those in the large caseloads. However, a time factor seems to have been operating here, as there was little difference in rate of revocation at the end of two years of supervision. A time-activity study indicated that many agents with small caseloads retained the same supervision habits that they had with large caseloads. A separate analysis tabulated the frequency of parole agent contacts with the ward, or on behalf of the ward with parents, teachers, employers, or others. Those cases in which these contacts were most frequent (averaging five per month) had a violation rate of 11 per cent in ten months on parole, while those in which contacts were least frequent (averaging one per month) had a violation rate of 50 per cent. Further analysis also indicated that youth previously on parole had higher rates of revocation in the small caseloads than in the large, but those with no prior commitments did markedly better in small caseloads.

Periodic investigations of parolee experience and parole supervision practice were conducted with ninety-seven randomly selected parolees from the reduced and regular-sized caseloads described above. To each of these parolees an environment-rating schedule was applied which classified their family, peers, employment, school, police contacts, organized recreation, and other current experiences as supportive, irrelevant, stressful, or unpredictable. The parole success rates were 67 per cent for those with most supportive environments, 31 per cent for those with most stressful environments, and 54 per cent for a middle group. Parole supervision also was classified into a favorable category (from "above minimal" to "superior") and an unfavorable category ("minimal," "below minimal," "inappropriate," or "misdirected"). Success rates were 73 per cent with favorable supervision and 32 per cent with unfavorable. Favorable supervision was significantly associated with higher success rates on both the most supportive and the most stressful environment cases. Although there is the possibility that these findings reflect rater bias in evaluating quality of supervision and nature of the environment, the results are so promising as to indicate that further investigation of these two variables in relation to parole outcome is highly desirable.[15] Experimentation differentiating parole supervision prac-

[15] See: Bertram M. Johnson, *Parole Performance of the First Year's Releases, Parole Research Project: Evaluation of Reduced Caseloads,* Research Report no. 27 (Sacramento, California Department of the Youth Authority, January 1962); Johnson, *An Analysis of Predictions of Parole Performance and Judgments of Supervision in the Parole Research Project,* Research Report no. 32 (Sacramento, California Department of the Youth Authority, December 1962); Keith S. Griffith, *Current Status Report of Research Activities,* Third Annual Report (Sacramento, California Department of the Youth Authority, October 1962), pp. 19-21.

tice in terms of the assistance and control dimensions distinguished in this chapter, and analyzing outcome separately for different types of parolee, would greatly strengthen the scientific foundation for parole supervision policy decisions.

SUMMARY

Our study of prisoner expectations regarding parole supervision supported previous indications that inmates develop in prison an unduly pessimistic view of their future relationships with government officials. It was inferred that this is largely a result of the inmates' disproportionate contact in prison with returned violators rather than with successful releasees. This interpretation was supported by our finding a somewhat overoptimistic pattern of postrelease expectations only at Ashland, the one prison we studied that received no parole violators. In short, our tentative conclusion is:

O1. Unless prisoners are isolated from returned violators, they generally develop unrealistic overestimates of their prospects of being reimprisoned as technical violators of parole.

Responses of prison inmates to our questions about the parole rules they expected would be most difficult to follow and similar responses of parolees and mandatory releasees already out indicated that the written rules have only a limited relationship to the releasees' subjective perception of the rules. Some items of the questionnaire completed for us by U. S. Probation Officers suggested that the releasees may acquire their misconception of the formal rules not just from other offenders, but also through orders and warnings that their parole supervision officers issue on topics other than those covered in the rules. In general, our data suggested:

O2. The parole rules about which both prisoners expecting parole and men already on parole will be most apprehensive are rules against associating with other ex-criminals, drinking, travel, and being out of their homes late at night.

O3. Concern with these parole rules will prevail regardless of whether or not such rules actually exist among the written conditions of parole to which the men officially are subjected.

O4. Inmate and parolee anticipations of difficulty in conforming with rules regulating their employment decline markedly in the first few months after men are released from prison.

Our questionnaire on policies and practices of federal parole supervision demonstrated that:

O5. The performance of the parole supervision role can be scaled along two major dimensions, assistance and control, which differentiate four polar styles of role performance:

a. *paternal*—high control, high assistance;
b. *punitive*—high control, low assistance;
c. *welfare*—low control, high assistance;
d. *passive*—low control, low assistance.

Some suggestive data was reported on various correlates of these four styles.

Our time-activity study of actual work logs by a sample of U. S. Probation Officers, and the responses of officers to questions on their work preferences and priorities, indicated that they place more emphasis on their presentence work than on other aspects of their job and that the presentence work takes more of their time than had previously been assumed. This was interpreted by us as an instance of a more general strain towards diagnosis in casework, which can be summarized as:

O6. When a caseworker has both diagnosis and treatment responsibilities in dealing with offenders, the time devoted to diagnostic investigation and to the preparation of diagnostic reports tends to receive first priority, at the expense of time devoted to other functions, including treatment; this time devoted to diagnostic functions becomes more extensive than generally is assumed in official workload budgets which emphasize treatment.

Although the parole adviser system frequently is criticized, our interviews indicated that two out of five releasees found their advisers helpful. Case data describe some advisers as extremely important in assisting parolees to achieve self-sufficiency in a conventional way of life and suggest that:

O7. The parole adviser system can greatly enhance the extent to which a parole supervision officer achieves his counseling and his surveillance objectives in some cases if the officer can exercise considerable choice in recruiting or accepting the adviser, can maintain active communication with him, and is not rigidly required to have an adviser in all cases.

The greatest promise for determining the exact contribution of alternative types of parole supervision services for different types of offenders was seen in experimental research, in which California has led the way.

Part IV
IMPLICATIONS

★   ★   ★

CHAPTER 18

The Crime and Noncrime Career Cycle

The function of theory in science is to account for a large number or variety of observations by a relatively concise verbal or mathematical formulation. By interrelating prior observations, theories lead to new observations. Thus, the theory of universal gravitation dramatically interconnected accumulating evidence that the earth was a sphere (from which people did not fall off!) and that the earth and other planets revolved around the sun. The theory even led to accurate prediction that new planets would be found in the solar system. Similarly, the theory of evolution interrelated vast and intricate observations of plants and animals, observations previously lacking such unity. Also, the theory correctly anticipated that "missing links" in lines of descent would be found in the skeletons and fossils of plant and animal life from prior ages.

It is unlikely that any brief and unified theory will adequately interconnect and explain all the behavior which comes to be called "crime," for any survey of crime and criminals soon reveals an immense diversity. Nevertheless, several efforts have been made to summarize in a few generalizations the most important knowledge acquired on major aspects of criminality. Such theories become useful as they direct one's attention to facts that provide a basis for effective action in handling criminals. The concern of this chapter is with the implications of our study for improving the practical utility of theory in criminology.

STATIC AND DYNAMIC CONCEPTIONS OF THE CRIMINAL

The history of theory about criminals is one of change. Older writings conveyed a static conception of the criminal as a qualitatively different type of person from the noncriminal. Writings of the present century increasingly report the difference between criminal and noncriminal in terms of the quantity or degree of attributes which both share, and as something which can alter.

In the nineteenth century, when the effort to explain crime in scientific terms got its first clear start, the focus was on distinguishing biological indexes of an innately criminal type of human being. The implication of this approach to crime was that criminal tendencies were predominantly fixed by heredity. Theories first associated visible physical defects with criminal types, ascribing both crime and the defects to a primitive stage of human evolution. In the early twentieth century these theories were replaced by notions of inherited mental defects not indicated by external signs. However, the conception of a "born criminal" remained widespread until well into the second quarter of the twentieth century and has not yet completely disappeared.

It should be noted that theory gives us an image of the nature of the criminal which determines what we look for and what we overlook when studying criminals. If we think of criminality as inborn, we assume that there is little one can do to alter it. In the twentieth century, more and more stress has been placed on experience and environment rather than heredity as causes of crime. This has the implication that one can change the criminal's behavior by altering his learning experience, especially by changing the social influences that impinge upon him.

Despite this shift from hereditary to environmental interpretations of crime, there still is a tendency to think of the person whose experiences make him a criminal as distinctly different from the noncriminal. Theories for the explanation of criminality, from "multiple causation" to "differential association" to "containment," all seem to imply that when the totality of influences making for criminality exceed the totality of influences making for noncriminality, the individual becomes a criminal. As these theories usually are applied, they ascribe an individual's criminality to a long development of criminal influences or to the nondevelopment of controls over such influences. The implication is that once criminality results from this process, it usually is a fairly steady state, not readily or quickly reversed.

The main significance which our data have for criminological theory is their implication that at least 90 per cent of the felons who are imprisoned would be viewed more realistically if we thought of them as men who keep alternating from criminal to noncriminal means of pursuing economic or other objectives, rather than as persistently criminal. Most of these men shift from crime to noncrime to crime, and back again. Some terminate this cycle early, while some do not cease these fluctuations until late in life and a few never cease.

In general, success in crime seems to evoke persistence in it, but periodic failure is almost inevitable if the risk-taking involved in crime is sufficiently repeated. Those failures in crime which result in imprisonment seem generally to be followed by some effort to employ legitimate behavior, but subsequent failure to find satisfaction in legitimate pursuits often leads to further ventures in crime. This is the "zig-zag path" of the criminal's career to which reference was made at the close of chapter 4.

This view of criminality as generally an oscillating behavior pattern suggests that it may be more fruitful, for rehabilitation objectives, to shift the focus of criminological theories from search for the processes that make for persistence in crime to development and test of a theory on the conditions that promote change from crime to noncrime and back again. A review of the evidence that crime is an unsteady state in the criminals with whom prison and parole systems are most frequently confronted may provide a first step toward such a recasting of theory.

CRIME AS YOUTHFUL ERROR

In dealing with the men whom one encounters in prison, it is easy to forget the selective process that concentrates certain types of offenders there. One may thus get a distorted view of what the typical person convicted of a felony is like. This was noted in chapter 2, which pointed out the tendency to generalize about all men *sent* to prison during a given period on the basis of all men *in* prison at a given time.

Obviously, those in prison at a given time include a larger percentage of long-termers than are found among those sent to prison in any single period. Since the men who persist most in criminality tend to get the longest sentences and the fewest early paroles, a view of the prison population at any given moment yields an exaggerated picture of the extent to which prisoners are committed to felonies. Such a view also yields insufficient recognition of the least persistent criminals received in prison, for these generally are not kept there so long and are not so readily visible as the long-termers.

People who work in prisons also readily misperceive the effectiveness of probation as an alternative to imprisonment. Youth prisons, especially, have a large concentration of men below age twenty who have extensive prior delinquency or criminal records that did not lead to prison sentences. Many of these inmates received probation repeatedly or were only briefly confined in detention homes and training schools, despite the fact that their offenses were sufficiently serious to provide legal grounds for imprisonment. Such extensive prior criminal records in youthful prisoners reflect the tendency of some courts to view imprisonment as a last resort for young criminals more than for older offenders, even when the older offenders may be better probation risks. When confronted with a youth who repeatedly violated sentences of probation by committing new offenses, many prison staff ask why the youth was not sent to prison earlier. They contend that institutional employees might succeed more in influencing such youths as first offenders than when they finally reach prison. On the other hand, most prison staff also know many prisoners whom they believe would never have been in further difficulty if given probation instead of a prison sentence.

What prison staff forget sometimes, in viewing probation failures sent to prison, is that the men whom they receive in prison after probation trial are not the typical products of probation. This is evident from the fact that nine of eleven follow-up studies of persons placed on probation in various jurisdictions show an absence of further misdemeanor or felony record for 70 to 90 per cent of the cases, with follow-up periods of as much as five years. Obviously, if prison personnel only see that 10 to 20 per cent of probationers who fail most seriously, they may develop misconceptions of probation. As Ralph W. England concludes, after summarizing these findings:

Much recent research has indicated that most people commit one or two crimes in the course of their lives for which they are not caught, but that most of them refrain from making a habit of it. It seems quite possible that probation is tapping into this "self-correcting" segment of offenders, since probation deals mainly with first offenders and minor recidivists. For another group of "non-self-correcting offenders" who might otherwise persist in criminal behavior, the mere exposure to surveillance under suspended sentence may be sufficient (for reasons having perhaps nothing to do with the theoretical values of probation) to prevent further lawbreaking.[1]

Questionnaires administered to cross-sections of the United States population, including successful and widely respected persons as well as less successful individuals, indicate that most persons at one time or another commit offenses which could get them into serious difficulty with the law.[2] These deviancies most commonly occur in adolescence or early youth. Most people have this kind of experience in their past but were never caught or, if caught, were never prosecuted. Usually their crimes were brief episodes which did not seriously impair their achievement of legitimate careers.

Whenever an individual engages in crime, a number of social influences affect him. If his crime is committed when he is an adolescent, he will, in most cases, have committed it not alone, but in company with one or more other adolescents. The social support of his peers is likely to have been a major factor in his deviation from the norms demanded by adults. All youth, of course, go through some moments of rebellion at their subjugation to adults, but these moments rarely mean permanent alienation from the adult world, which they all ultimately expect to enter. Indeed, much youth crime, such as "joy-riding" in a "borrowed" automobile, may be pursued primarily as an exciting type of play at being an independent adult.

In committing such crimes, adolescents are aware that they run the risk of an unfavorable reaction from many adults and from anticriminal ado-

[1] Ralph W. England, Jr., "What Is Responsible for Satisfactory Probation and Post-Probation Outcome?", *J. Crim. Law, Criminology and Police Science, 47,* no. 6 (March-April 1957), 667-76.

[2] James S. Wallerstein and Clement J. Wyle, "Our Law-Abiding Law-Breakers," *Probation, 25* (April 1947), 107-12; A. L. Porterfield, "Delinquency and its Outcome in Court and College," *Am. J. Sociology, 49,* no. 3 (Nov. 1943), 199-208; John P. Clark and Eugene P. Wenninger, "Social-Economic Class and Area as Correlates of Illegal Behavior Among Juveniles," *Am. Sociological Rev., 27,* no. 6 (Dec. 1962), 826-34.

lescents. They may risk disgrace at school, shame at home, alienation from girls; and if they already are working, they risk their jobs. It is probable that the growing perception of these risks, as these youths mature, is a major basis for the "self-correcting" process in early crime to which England refers. It also accounts for the extent to which crime is a phenomenon of those who are very young, and especially, of those youths who are least successful in school, at work, or in their family relationships. These are the persons who, as Jackson Toby puts it, have least "stake in conformity," and hence risk least when engaging in crime.[3] That is why they are the ones who seem most persistent in taking such risks.

It is also noteworthy that a close relationship exists between the age at which specific types of felony are most often committed, and the age at which persons in our society first try to enter the legitimate pursuits for which these felonies substitute. This is shown in Table 18.1.

TABLE 18.1   Median Age of Persons Arrested in U. S. Cities,
by Major Felony Categories, 1962

Offense	Number of arrests	Median age
Property Felonies:		
Auto theft	67,419	16.9
Burglary	132,867	17.9
Larceny	255,170	17.5
Receiving stolen property	11,943	22.2
Robbery	35,384	21.9
Forgery	22,405	28.9
Embezzlement and fraud	35,991	32.8
Other felonies:		
Forcible rape	7,489	22.5
Narcotics	29,068	27.2
Aggravated assault	58,315	29.1
Murder	4,918	31.4

From: Federal Bureau of Investigation, *Uniform Crime Reports, 1962* (Washington, D. C., 1963), Table 20.

In the middle of their teen years, boys reach physical maturity, are permitted to leave school, and are likely to seek such sources of a sense of independence as automobiles and spending money. It is at this age, when they are least prepared to procure these items by legitimate means, that they most often engage in the simple felonies directly addressed to procuring money or to getting types of property which they most desire, notably automobiles. While auto theft, burglary, and larceny are committed by persons at later ages, their concentration in early youth is indicated in Table 18.1 by the median ages of seventeen to eighteen for arrestees charged with these

[3] Jackson Toby, "Social Disorganization and Stake in Conformity: Complementary Factors in the Predatory Behavior of Young Hoodlums," *J. Crim. Law, Criminology and Police Science, 48,* no. 1 (May–June 1957), 12-17.

offenses. This type of offense thus clearly is a phenomenon most characteristic of adolescence. The low median age suggests that most of those who enter into these offenses during adolescence cease such activity thereafter. It is especially notable also that these early-terminated types of crime are the most numerous of the felonies reported to police in the United States.

The median age for receiving stolen property, for robbery, and for rape, is about twenty-two. Doing business in stolen property presumably requires more sophistication than simple theft, which may explain why those arrested for it have a slightly older median age than larceny arrestees. Actually, highly professional dealers in stolen goods are likely to be older than twenty-two, but younger persons often are arrested on stolen property charges when suspected of larceny or burglary, if the evidence when they are arrested is only that they possess stolen goods. The fact that robbery is a more daring offense than theft, and usually is oriented towards procurement of larger sums, may explain its attraction to persons who have reached an age of somewhat more independence and economic need than characterizes early adolescence. The sexual pursuits for which rape is a criminal substitute also reach a peak, according to Kinsey, somewhat after adolescence.[4]

Each age in a person's life brings somewhat unique rights, as well as obligations. To be a child in our society implies both the right to have economic needs provided by adults and the obligation to obey certain adults, such as parents and teachers, who restrict the child's movement and pleasure pursuit. Conversely, adults in our society have the right to move about and to pursue their pleasures more freely than a child can, but they are obliged to procure their own economic needs. The problem reflected in crime at adolescence, the stage between childhood and adulthood, is the adolescent's wish for the *rights* of an adult when he is not prepared or allowed to assume adult *obligations*.[5] As Albert J. Reiss has pointed out, the adolescent is a marginal person in this sense. He adds:

. . . most of the norms governing adolescent behavior do not have adolescent behavior patterns as their reference point. . . . The exhortations of parents and other adults admonish the adolescent either to "behave like a grown-up" or to "quit behaving like a child." They rarely encourage him to "behave like an adolescent." There are, then, no highly institutionalized expectations of how one

[4] Alfred C. Kinsey, Wardell B. Pomeroy, and Clyde E. Martin, *Sexual Behavior in the Human Male* (Philadelphia, W. B. Saunders Company, 1949), chapter 7.

[5] Sociologists will recognize that I here am using "rights" as largely equivalent to "status," and "obligations" as largely equivalent to "role." This usage, with respect to institutionalized roles, is explicit in Harry M. Johnson, *Sociology: A Systematic Introduction* (New York, Harcourt, Brace, 1960), pp. 16-19. It is implicit in Talcott Parsons and Edward A. Shils, *Towards a General Theory of Action* (Cambridge, Harvard University Press, 1951), Part II, chapter 4.

is to behave like an adolescent, in the sense that achievement of these status expectations is a positive transitional link with the adult status.[6]

Actually, the quotation from Reiss somewhat overstates its case, since there are some roles prescribed for adolescents, such as that of student, and of apprentice or helper at skilled jobs, for which conceptions of proper behavior are widely shared. These exemplify institutionalized ways of "behaving like an adolescent" which facilitate the ex-child's eventual transition to a conventional adulthood. However, conflict with authorities, truancy, and retardation in school are among the closest correlates of early delinquency, and the criminality of the late teen years is concentrated in out-of-school and out-of-work youths. Crime is an alternative path to possible adult independence for these youths who have been unable to stay in the more legitimate paths of school and work.

A majority of all felony offenses known to the police are subsumed in the types of crime discussed thus far. That nonfelonious behavior eventually is learned by most persons committing these crimes is suggested by the low median age of these felony arrestees. The fact that so many felony arrests occur at an age when adult occupational and social roles are not long and firmly established suggests that, in most cases, these offenses actually are deviations from a course of life intended to have as its destination a secure adult independence. The crimes appear to be either momentary play at being independent, not regarded as a permanent way of life (such as riding in a stolen car), or attempted short-cuts to the destination of independent adulthood.

It seems reasonable to assume that almost all who take the short-cuts to economic independence represented by larceny, burglary, and robbery eventually end in the blind alley of conflict with the law. This follows from the laws of probability, which, as any gambler knows, prevent one from compounding risk-taking indefinitely without losing periodically. Even if some growth in criminal skills partially reduces the risks in such crime, they never eliminate the risk to the point of providing a long and steady career for many. The low median ages of arrest for larceny, burglary, and robbery suggest that most youths ultimately recognize this path of crime as a cul-de-sac and find another course to more secure adulthood.

Acquiring the ability to satisfy adult needs without serious conflict with the law, like other learning, may require learning from mistakes. In the process of achieving this adult ability, some people receive more guidance, experience, and encouragement than others, so that they progress more rapidly, with fewer serious mistakes. Their progress to adult roles is most likely if they succeed in adolescent roles, such as that of student. But if a person has major setbacks in his early learning years and develops habits

[6] Albert J. Reiss, "Sex Offenses: The Marginal Status of the Adolescent," *Law and Contemporary Problems, 25,* no. 2 (Spring 1960), 309-33.

conducive to frequent failure in conventional adolescent and adult roles, he may be long in correcting these habits, or he may never choose to alter them. Furthermore, some who have initial success still encounter difficulties later, and may only then explore criminal byways presumed to lead to adult security. What are the characteristics of these diverse persons who commit crimes when they have clearly passed their youth?

OFFENSES AT AN OLDER AGE

Forgery, fraud, and embezzlement, the only property felonies which have a median age at arrest beyond early youth, are crimes that usually require some prior experience in conventional adult occupational roles. These offenses generally must be committed by someone who has developed familiarity and ease with the procedures and equipment used in legitimate business. Most of these offenses are unique in representing not a failure at initial entry into adult occupations, but difficulties at a later age, often associated with alcoholism or other unusual personal problems.

Narcotics, assault, and murder, the remaining felonies listed in Table 18.1, all have a median age somewhat beyond early youth, and generally are expressive acts rather than alternatives to legitimate ways of procuring an income. Research indicates the origin of most narcotic offenses in the United States today in a "retreatist subculture" of persons frustrated alike in criminal and in conventional career pursuits; their involvement in ordinary property crimes usually precedes their use of narcotics, and narcotics use pressures them to further crime because of the high cost of their drugs.[7] Research also indicates that murder and assault occur most often in a "subculture of violence," a large part of whose adherents have a background of property offenses.[8] While the theory developed in this chapter is oriented primarily to understanding the reform or recidivism of property offenders, it may have some relevance also to coping with those felons whose narcotics usage or assaultive behavior grows out of their involvement in groups committing property crimes.

As indicated in chapter 3, larceny and burglary, in addition to occurring much more frequently than any other type of felony, are also among the most recidivistic of felonies. Therefore, although most arrests for these crimes occur during adolescence, they also are common grounds for the arrest of older persons. Indeed, in the United States, larceny is the most frequent felony charge against arrestees of any age. Burglary is second in frequency until age thirty, but for persons beyond that age it drops to fourth in rank among major categories of felony arrest. Embezzlement,

[7] Harold Finestone, "Narcotics and Criminality," *Law and Contemporary Problems, 22,* no. 1 (Winter 1957), 69-85.

[8] Marvin E. Wolfgang, *Patterns in Criminal Homicide* (Philadelphia, University of Pennsylvania Press, 1958).

fraud, and forgery, taken collectively, are second in frequency to larceny as grounds for felony arrest of persons of age thirty or over. Aggravated assault is third.

For persons age fifty and over, aggravated assault is second to larceny as a basis for felony arrests. Of course, arrests on felony assault charges frequently are not prosecuted or are prosecuted only as misdemeanors, such as simple assault, disorderly conduct, or drunkenness. The median age of arrest for drunkenness is forty-two. Older persons are not arrested for property felonies nearly as often as youth are, but older persons greatly exceed youth in frequency of arrest for misdemeanors such as disorderly conduct, drunkenness, and vagrancy, a type of problem that is beyond the scope of this study.[9]

At any age, an individual's involvement in crime may cause him to be rejected by conventional persons and integrated into a criminal social world. In addition, time spent in criminal pursuits retards development of non-criminal occupational skills and anticriminal social relationships. That is why indexes of the extent of prior involvement in crime, such as number of prior convictions or earliness of first arrest, are associated with high rates of return to crime. Nevertheless, the evidence suggests that even those long involved in crime eventually disengage themselves from it.

Table 18.2 shows that for prisoners with any particular number of felony convictions, the postrelease failure rate tends to decline as age at release increases. Similarly, for prisoners of any age at first arrest, failure rates generally decrease with increasing age at release, but this is not perfectly consistent for all ages of first arrest. The major exception in our tabulations is that persons first arrested when twenty-one or over had about the same failure rate for every category of age at release (rather than age at first arrest). Nevertheless, those who started crime earliest are, on the whole, the ones who are most likely to continue in crime.

The foregoing suggests that the earlier crime begins, the longer its span is likely to be. Such a conclusion is supported by data from a much different type of study, the McCords' 1955 follow-up of presumed predelinquent youth in the Cambridge-Somerville experiment in delinquency prevention. The youth in this sample were first selected for research in 1937, when their average age was nine, and their delinquency and crime records were compiled for the subsequent eighteen years, during which they reached an average age of twenty-seven.[10]

It would appear from Tables 18.1 and 18.2, and from our discussion

[9] Figures presented in the preceding two paragraphs are derived from Federal Bureau of Investigation, *Crime in the United States: Uniform Crime Reports, 1962* (Washington, D. C., 1963), Table 20. One of the best studies of older misdemeanants is: David J. Pittman and C. Wayne Gordon, *Revolving Door: A Study of the Chronic Police Case Inebriate* (Glencoe, Ill., Free Press, 1958).

[10] William and Joan McCord, *Origins of Crime* (New York, Columbia University Press, 1959), pp. 157-58.

TABLE 18.2   Per Cent of Postrelease Failures[a] Among 1956 Federal Releasees of Various Ages, by Prior Involvements in Crime

	AGE AT RELEASE FROM PRISON				
Prior involvement in crime	*18–21*	*22–25*	*26–35*	*36 and over*	*All cases*
No. of prior sentences for felony-like offenses:					
None	44% (78)[b]	31% (98)	21% (151)	11% (96)	25% (423)
One	52% (31)	46% (37)	34% (105)	25% (48)	37% (221)
Two	57% (23)	52% (27)	45% (64)	28% (40)	44% (154)
Three or more	45% (11)	63% (16)	48% (86)	42% (104)	46% (217)
Age at first arrest:					
16 and under	53% (94)	43% (68)	43% (106)	40% (36)	46% (304)
17–20	37% (49)	45% (73)	41% (116)	28% (78)	38% (316)
21 and over	—	24% (37)	24% (184)	24% (174)	24% (395)
Time confined:					
18 months or under	44% (78)	39% (96)	27% (202)	24% (157)	31% (533)
Over 18 months	52% (65)	41% (82)	41% (204)	31% (131)	40% (482)
All cases	48% (143)	40% (178)	34% (406)	27% (288)	35% (1015)

[a] "Failure" means return to prison for new offense or as parole violator, or any nonprison sentence for a felony-like offense.

[b] Number of cases in parentheses.

thus far, that most crimes resulting in imprisonment reflect either a brief "error," a longer "fixation," or a later "regression" in the process of development from the dependence of childhood to the independence connoted by adult status in our society. It should be clear that the development involved here is not biological development, but social and cultural transition from the status of child to the conventional status of adult in our society; the duration of this transition period varies greatly from one person to the next. It is largely independent of biological maturation, and for some the transition is never completed. Property offenders seek adult independence through criminal behavior, but the consequent imprisonment deprives them of independence. How does prison affect their subsequent career?

THE IMPACT OF PRISON

Chapter 2 presented our first evidence on fluctuation in criminality by demonstrating that not nearly so many released prisoners are reimprisoned as is generally assumed. Examining the basis for common assertions that about two-thirds of the men released from prison return there, we found that the available facts support an opposite assertion, that about two-thirds of the men released from prison do not return.

Somewhat more direct evidence on instability in crime is provided by our data on the immediate postprison activities of those released prisoners who violated parole or mandatory release. In our study of 308 returned federal parole and mandatory release violators, we found consensus of supervision reports and our interviews in indicating that only about 6 per cent reverted to the pursuit of crime almost immediately upon release from prison, and only 16 per cent, or about one-sixth, appeared to have resumed felonious activity within a month of their release (although many of them who had resumed were not caught that early). Five-sixths of these returned violators made some efforts to "go straight" for more than a month, and many continued this effort for several years. Violators amount to only about 24 per cent of federal parolees and mandatory releasees. If only one-sixth of the violators returned to crime within a month, it follows that only one-sixth of 24, or 4 per cent, of all federal parolees and mandatory releasees revert within a month of release to crimes which will send them back to prison.

The expiration-of-sentence releasees are not covered in the above tabulation. These cases include mostly those not paroled whose sentences were so short as to prevent their earning more than the minimum of 180 days of good time needed for eligibility for mandatory release. It also included a few whose misconduct in prison led to permanent revocation of what good time they had earned. In our three-year follow-up of a cohort of over a thousand 1956 releasees, expiration-of-sentence cases had a 34 per cent failure rate, which was higher than the 28 per cent failure rate for parolees and lower than the 44 per cent rate for mandatory releasees. It seems reasonable to assume, at least tentatively, that the expiration-of-sentence cases are also intermediate between parolees and mandatory releasees in their rate of recidivism during the first month out, as they are in overall recidivism rates. Likewise, from the similarity of state and federal prisoners in overall recidivism, according to the data presented in chapter 2, one can infer that the state prisoners probably are similar to federal prisoners in a low rate of return to crime during the first month out.

We can never really know precisely how many men return to crime, nor how soon, but it would seem to be a conservative inference to more than double the figure indicated by the foregoing data, and to conclude that:

P1. At least 90 per cent of American prison releasees seek legitimate careers for a month or more after they leave prison.

This figure also seems conservative in the light of our contacts with newly released prisoners in our Postrelease Panel study and of the data presented in chapter 2, which suggest that most persons released from prison avoid further imprisonment for many years or for life, although many of these do not avoid further arrest. The foregoing strongly suggests that if one places a felon in a prison, he is more likely than not to come out no longer a felon, and he is especially likely to come out not immediately a felon.

How does one account for this change from criminality just before imprisonment to noncriminality at release? What occurs in prison?

In chapter 5, particularly, and to some extent in several of the other chapters, evidence was presented which indicated that the prison experience is not one of progressively increasing criminalization for all or most of those involved. Consistent with separate studies by Wheeler and Garabedian in Washington prisons, we found some evidence of a U-shaped curve of attitudes during imprisonment. Toward the middle of the confinement period, inmate attitudes seemed to reflect most adaptation to confinement, or prisonization. The inmates changed to an orientation toward a conventional postrelease life near the end of their prison terms.

Our data seemed to support the view that prisonization and criminalization can vary independently. Men in prison seemed to develop social relationships and modes of thought to minimize the discomforts of their life there, just as they adjust to military life, to life as resident students at a college, or to life in other "total institutions." At the same time that they adjust to these life-encompassing organizations by acquiring an inmate subculture, they may also be oriented to avoid return to such an institution once they get out. This is a familiar experience to the many civilians who were in military service during national emergencies with no intention of entering the service as a career.

Life in prison, and in other total institutions, may be seen by inmates as a transition period. While seeking the most congenial company and the greatest self-esteem available as prisoners, they may have a different longrun perspective. Thus we found that many preserve or even augment ties with outside anticriminal associates, and plan a noncriminal postinstitution life. However, many others submerge long-range conventional orientations during confinement in preoccupation with the pursuit of immediate gratification in prison. Indeed, a lack of long-range focus on either criminal or conventional life after prison seems to distinguish the most highly prisonized or institutionalized individuals, who may therefore prove relatively inept at both criminal and noncriminal pursuits after release.

Our data on relationships among inmates in prison suggested considerable variation in their adjustment to a social world of other prisoners. Most of the younger inmates seemed oriented to making as many friends as they could with their fellow prisoners, but the older inmates were concerned with limiting their prison social relationships to only a few inmate friends or none at all. With age the prisoners more often perceived of their fellow inmates as sources of "trouble," and were consequently concerned with "doing their own time." A progression from dependence to independence is suggested here, and this may account for the declining postrelease failure rates with increasing age at release. More important than just increasing independence, however, may be a shift in reference groups, that is, a change in the type of person with whom the prisoners were interested in developing social relationships.

The adolescent and youthful prisoners have a background of life in the outside community's adolescent social worlds, where they have provided each other with acceptance, admiration, and other social support. The evidence that gang membership and alienation from parents and school most differentiate delinquents from nondelinquents suggests that this social support from peers is particularly attractive to those adolescents who are unsuccessful in procuring a gratifying relationship with adults.[11] It has been well established by experimental psychology that individuals will act and think in a deviant fashion much more readily when they have even one person supporting their deviance than they would alone.[12] It is notable that 80 to 90 per cent of juveniles found delinquent have committed their offenses with one or more associates. They seem to need such mutual support to define deviant behavior as acceptable. Perhaps they also need mutual support to bolster their courage in risking criminality, for partners in delinquency provide each other with an audience in front of whom they must perform well.

As suggested earlier, much delinquency is, indeed, a play at adult independence, and thus the terms "audience" and "performance" above are distinctly appropriate. If an adolescent seeks to assert his adulthood, the optimum person with whom to do this would be an older person. It is interesting that in prison we found inmates predominantly describing the inmate from whom they got their best advice as somewhat older than themselves. Also, predominantly older companions distinguished delinquents from nondelinquents in the Glueck study.[13] It would therefore ap-

[11] Gang membership and truancy from school were the first and second most differentiating items in the Gluecks' comparison of delinquents and nondelinquents, and their most discriminating combination of items has been their "Social Prediction Table," which is based on alienation of the youth from his parents. See: Sheldon and Eleanor Glueck, *Unravelling Juvenile Delinquency* (New York, Commonwealth Fund, 1950). Similar major differentiation by gang membership, and by items reflecting alienation from parents, were found by the McCords, in the work cited above.

[12] The classic work of Asch and Sherif are notable here, such as that reported in: S. E. Asch, *Social Psychology* (New York, Prentice-Hall, 1952), chapter 16; M. Sherif, *The Psychology of Social Norms* (New York, Harpers, 1936).

[13] Gluecks, *op. cit.,* p. 163.

pear that staff might be strategic influences for younger prisoners, but a variety of sources of alienation of staff from inmates create a gap between these two components of the prison community which is only partially and intermittently bridged.

Our study illuminated a number of deficiencies in prison casework, education, and work programs. It suggested a variety of innovations in practice to reduce isolation of prisoners from staff and to facilitate and motivate inmate preparation for postrelease economic self-sufficiency at legitimate occupations. But why, despite the deficiencies in existing programs, do we find both arrest rate and questionnaire evidence that a preponderance of prison inmates turn from crime during imprisonment?

Near the end of each of our Prison Panel Study interviews, we asked the inmates a series of very broad questions regarding their outlook for the future. These were, to some extent, "fishing expeditions," to seek an overall index of the impact of prison experience on the prisoner's attitude to correctional agencies and to help in bringing the interviews to a logical conclusion. Nevertheless, they are of some interest in considering the impact of prison experience.

One of these questions was: "Of the inmates here, about what per cent would you guess *want* to go straight when they get out?" This was presumed to be indicative of the subject's perception of the inclinations of other inmates, though perhaps in many cases it was a projection of his own inclinations. However, the main purpose of this question was to set the stage for a projective question oriented more specifically to obtaining their view of their own possibilities in achieving self-subsistence on a legitimate basis after release. This second question was: "How many of these will really make it going straight?" Interviewers were instructed to obtain the answer to this second question as a percentage of the answer given to the first question; for example, if the subject thought that of a hundred inmates, eighty would *wish* to go straight but only forty would *be able* to go straight, the answer to the first question would be "80 per cent" and the answer to the second question would be "50 per cent." Finally, a third question was asked: "Why won't the other _____ per cent make it?" (The interviewer was to inject in the blank the difference between 100 and the percentage given as response to the second question.)

Answers to the first two questions are summarized in Table 18.3. It will be seen that Ashland inmates, who were the youngest, were more optimistic than were inmates at the other prisons. However, Ashland inmates also changed during imprisonment, so that after reaching a peak where they thought that about three-quarters of the inmates would try to "go straight" and two-thirds of these would succeed, they grew more pessimistic; their views near release did not differ greatly from those of inmates of other prisons. The per cent of other inmates perceived as wanting to "go straight"

TABLE 18.3   Median Estimates of the Percentage of Other Inmates Who Want to "Go Straight" and Who Will Be Able to "Go Straight" (Prison Panel Study)

Institution	Stage of confinement at interview	Number interviewed	Per cent who want to "go straight"	Per cent of these who will be able to "go straight"
Leavenworth	First week	60	64% (58)[a]	49% (56)
Penitentiary	Fourth month	31	60% (31)	53% (29)
	Sixth month	43	40% (41)	51% (41)
	Near release	49	31% (44)	52% (44)
Terre Haute	First week	50	54% (46)	55% (43)
Penitentiary	Fourth month	17	57% (17)	57% (15)
	Sixth month	36	52% (34)	58% (33)
	Near release	48	54% (46)	58% (45)
Milan	First week	60	63% (42)	38% (39)
Correctional	Fourth month	24	55% (16)	54% (16)
Institution	Sixth month	41	56% (35)	60% (32)
	Near release	50	51% (42)	37% (37)
Chillicothe	First week	60	57% (59)	55% (59)
Reformatory	Fourth month	30	60% (29)	57% (28)
	Sixth month	52	59% (50)	57% (50)
	Near release	50	41% (50)	55% (50)
Ashland	First week	53	73% (53)	57% (53)
Youth	Fourth month	17	76% (17)	65% (17)
Correctional	Sixth month	34	76% (34)	66% (34)
Institution	Near release	51	56% (51)	58% (51)

[a] Numbers giving definite answer, on which medians are based, are given in parentheses.

declined most markedly during imprisonment at Leavenworth, and there was a decline at all of the other institutions except Terre Haute. I am uncertain as to the reason for the unique constancy of Terre Haute inmate perceptions of the per cent of other inmates who want to "go straight." I suspect that an actually greater decline at Milan than Table 18.3 indicates is masked by the prevalence of a pessimistic view among the many Milan inmates, predominantly Negroes, who did not give a definite answer.

On the whole, inmates seemed to think that about half of the prisoners in their institutions wanted to "go straight," but only about half of these would succeed in this effort. In other words, their prediction was that about three-quarters of the inmates would return to crime. In the absence of systematic tabulation of recidivism rates by the F.B.I. from its fingerprint report files, one cannot know exactly how many inmates are likely to return to crime; however, the best tabulations available, summarized in chapter 2, suggest that the figure for prison systems as a whole is closer to 35 than to 75 per cent. Therefore, the more pessimistic inmate prediction can be taken as further support for our conclusion in chapter 5 and for Cloward's "pluralistic ignorance" theme, both of which contend that inmates perceive other inmates as more criminalistic than they are in fact. This is because the criminal point of view is most freely expressed, and anticriminal views are less readily uttered in inmate social life.

After the inmates told us how many of those who want to "go straight" would succeed, we asked them why the others would not "make it," and we recorded their responses to this verbatim. These responses are classified and tabulated in Table 18.4.

TABLE 18.4   Inmate Perceptions of Reason for Failure of Those Who Want to "Go Straight" but Fail to Do So
(First responses of near-release panel)

Type of reason, with typical remarks	Leavenworth Penitentiary	Terre Haute Penitentiary	Milan Correctional Institution	Chillicothe Reformatory	Ashland Youth Institution
Weak will (can't resist temptation)	23%	16%	23%	29%[a]	27%
Impatient or lazy (only want fast buck, won't work)	30%	8%	3%	10%	6%
Emotional reaction (get upset and then don't care what they do)	5%	8%	—	—	14%
Not deterred (not afraid of prison any more, too used to prison life)	5%	3%	—	6%	2%
Total, various personal deficiencies	63%	35%	26%	45%	49%
Economic hardship (run out of money, and out of job)	23%	26%	49%	35%	20%
Influence of criminal friends	5%	13%	6%	8%	10%
Vices (drink, dope)	—	8%	9%	8%	12%
Lack "good" friends or family (nobody to hold them back)	10%	16%	6%	2%	4%
Total, various environmental deficiencies	38%	63%	69%	53%	46%
Other	—	3%	6%	2%	4%
Number of classifiable responses (base of above percentage)	40	38	35	49	49
Indefinite or "don't know" responses	9	10	15	1	2
	(18%)	(21%)	(30%)	(2%)	(4%)

[a] Italic indicates highest percentage on a line.

Institutional differences are interesting, despite the appreciable number of indefinite responses at the three adult prisons (particularly at Milan). Leavenworth inmates predominantly placed the cause for inability to "go straight" in personality deficiency, while Milan inmates were the most inclined to blame environmental conditions, especially economic difficulties. The probable higher concentration of highly recidivist or semiprofessional criminals at Leavenworth makes understandable their ascription of crime to impatience with legitimate work. In view of the extreme insecurity of

Negro employment, the predominance of Negroes in the Milan population must have much to do with their concern with economic difficulties.

One of two concluding questions directed at obtaining the inmate's evaluation of his correctional experience was: "What do you think there is about your life in prison so far that would help you most if you wanted to go straight?" The classification which we worked out for the responses to this question, and their distribution, are summarized in Table 18.5. Although

TABLE 18.5   Inmate Perceptions of Aspect of Federal Prison Experience Helping Them Most if They Wish to "Go Straight"
(Prison Panel Study, near-release sample only)

Aspect, with typical remarks	Leavenworth Penitentiary	Terre Haute Penitentiary	Milan Correctional Institution	Chillicothe Reformatory	Ashland Youth Institution
Nothing (prison doesn't help at all)	8%	17%	22%	4%	6%
Deterrent effect (thinking about being locked up)	37%	44%	54%	50%	31%
Assistance of staff, other than chaplain, and apart from program (personal influence)	2%	—	—	2%	4%
Education, academic	14%	2%	—	4%	6%
Trade education or experience in prison	14%	10%	2%	22%	35%
Religion, including any chaplain help	2%	4%	2%	—	2%
Conformity (learn to obey rules)	4%	6%	—	8%	8%
Appreciate family or friends more	2%	—	4%	6%	—
Personal growth (self-insight, learn to think, maturity)	14%	6%	8%	4%	8%
Other	2%	8%	6%	—	—
Don't know	—	2%	2%	—	—
Number of cases	49	48	50	50	51

the prison system does not officially assert that deterrence is one of its primary means of rehabilitating offenders, the aspect of prison most often mentioned by the inmates as of the greatest assistance in helping them "go straight" was the unpleasantness of the confinement experience. Of course, a large proportion of the prisoners, notably at Milan, insisted that prison was of no benefit in helping them to "go straight." The aspect of official prison programs most often credited with assistance was trade training, particularly at the youth prisons, with academic education cited as often as trade training only at Leavenworth, where long sentences permit more academic diploma completion and there is little vocational training. A variety of other positive features of prison experience were mentioned by a few inmates, but none by any large proportion of those at any single institution.

As noted at the beginning of chapter 5, of the 250 successful releasees whom we interviewed, 52 per cent said that it was during imprisonment that they changed most permanently from interest in crime. An additional 13 per cent claimed to have changed at the time of sentencing, or between sentencing and imprisonment—in short, when they first faced the prospect of a prison sentence. When we asked them how this change came about, 62 per cent made reference to their deterrence by the unpleasantness of imprisonment. This was the most frequently mentioned type of abstract influence in their reformation. In addition, 54 per cent referred to their maturation, and 30 per cent to their learning a trade or acquiring good work habits.

In 1948 Galway interviewed 275 inmates about to be released from Chillicothe, asking them if they had benefited from imprisonment. Of these, 72 per cent stated they had benefited. The most frequent alleged benefit was "maturing and settling down," the second most frequent alleged benefit was the deterrent effect, and the third in frequency was learning a trade.[14]

Offenders themselves may not be capable of identifying precisely the factors in their change. However, if they have changed, their judgment should be of some significance, in the absence of more adequate knowledge. In my opinion, the extent of deterrence by imprisonment has never been satisfactorily assessed in research. There is evidence that the extent of any deterrent effect does not increase at a uniform rate in proportion to increments in the severity of a sentence. However, this does not eliminate the possibility of major deterrence occurring from a certain minimum sentence, the most effective minimum probably being much less for first offenders than for advanced offenders. This is a matter on which the F.B.I. may throw some light from extensive statistics on recidivism rates for different lengths of confinement, for various types of offender. This could be derived by follow-up of criminals from fingerprint reports, discussed in chapter 2.

The number of inmate and releasee responses indicating fear of return to prison suggests that a counselor might effectively utilize this anxiety in motivating releasees to long-range planning and avoidance of excessive risks, but only if such fear is not reinstilled by threat or warning but is used to help the releasee perceive the sources of his prior difficulties and current risks. If the releasee's cooperation is to be maintained, the counselor must manage to convey the fact that he is a helpful person who can aid the offender in achieving safeguards against return, rather than as a hostile person who would hasten return to prison.

Our first effort to obtain the inmate's evaluation of his correctional experience was the question: "What do you think there is about life in prison so far that has done the most to make it hard for you to go straight?" There was little change in responses to this item during the course of imprison-

[14] Edward J. Galway, *A Measurement of the Effectiveness of a Reformatory Program* (Unpublished Ph.D. dissertation, Ohio State University, 1948).

ment, although inmates of the adult prisons became slightly more optimistic and inmates of the youth prisons became somewhat more pessimistic, as evidenced by shifts in the proportion answering "Nothing at all." Table 18.6 shows institutional differences in these responses on the Near-

TABLE 18.6   Inmates' Perception of Aspect of Federal Prison Life Making It Hard to "Go Straight"
(Prison Panel Study, near-release sample only)

Aspect, with typical remarks	Leavenworth Penitentiary	Terre Haute Penitentiary	Milan Correctional Institution	Chillicothe Reformatory	Ashland Youth Institution
Nothing (nothing here can keep me from going straight)	69%	67%	80%	32%	45%
Criminal record (being an ex-con, no jobs for ex-cons)	18%	17%	10%	26%	29%
Influence of other inmates (talk of crime, look you up on the outside)	4%	4%	4%	12%	10%
Embitterment (leave prison with chip on your shoulder)	4%	10%	—	12%	6%
Institutionalization (locked up too long, don't care if come back, too regulated)	2%	—	—	10%	2%
Other	2%	2%	4%	8%	6%
Don't know	—	—	2%	—	2%
Number of cases	49	48	50	50	51

release Panel. Inmates of all prisons, but especially those of the youth prisons, were the most concerned about the effects of their becoming "ex-cons"; probably the adult prison populations were less concerned because they included fewer to whom this was a new experience. For similar reasons, perhaps, the inmates of the youth prisons were more concerned than the others with the influence which their inmate associates might have on them.

We terminated the interviews with the broadest questions of the series. One of these was: "What difficulty do you think you will encounter when you get to your release destination?" The most frequent specific type of response, particularly at Milan, dealt with economic needs, but many responses were highly unspecific. Either the inmates insisted that they expected nothing which they would consider a problem or a difficulty, or they spoke in vague terms of the problems of getting used to being free and of walking the city streets again. The latter type of response, which we have labeled "general adjustment," increased progressively through our successive interviews from the first week to near the release date, and was especially frequent at Ashland. The next most often cited problem was that of coping with their criminal reputation or record. As indicated in Table

18.7, which covers the near-release interviews only, Ashland was the most deviant institution in the problems which inmates anticipated, since its youthful inmates were much less concerned with economic problems than were the inmates of the other institutions. This is consistent with the find-

TABLE 18.7 Inmates' Perception of the Biggest Problem They Will Encounter
After Release
(Prison Panel Study, near-release sample only)

Problem, with typical remarks	Leavenworth Penitentiary	Terre Haute Penitentiary	Milan Correctional Institution	Chillicothe Reformatory	Ashland Youth Institution
General adjustment (getting used to civilian life, getting started, etc.)	22%	17%	6%	16%	45%
Economic (getting job, money, place to stay, etc.)	41%	38%	46%	38%	18%
Family (getting along with wife, parents, etc.)	2%	13%	6%	6%	8%
Criminal reputation (facing non-criminal friends, gossip, living down reputation, etc.)	6%	6%	12%	18%	14%
Drinking	—	—	2%	6%	—
Avoiding criminal friends	—	2%	2%	—	4%
Parole regulations other than drinking or avoiding criminals	6%	2%	—	—	4%
Other problem	12%	4%	8%	10%	4%
No problems expected	10%	19%	18%	6%	4%
Number of cases	49	48	50	50	51

ings and interpretation of our collateral inquiry, early in this project, which found that a close relationship between crime rates and unemployment characterizes only adult offenders, and that there is a somewhat inverse relationship between unemployment and juvenile arrest rates.[15] It is also consistent with our findings in chapter 14 that most youth in prison have the economic necessities of their postrelease life—room and board—provided by their parents or other relatives.

  The final question was: "What do you think is going to help you most to keep out of further trouble with the law?" The responses to this are summarized in Table 18.8. Consistent with the findings of the preceding question, presented in Table 18.7, the most frequently cited specific feature of postrelease life was economic security. Again, however, Ashland inmates deviated by stressing economic factors less than did inmates of the other prisons; Leavenworth inmates also deviated somewhat in this, as in several previous questions, in their greater emphasis upon their personalities and their personal decisions as the key to their future relationship with

  [15] Daniel Glaser and Kent Rice, "Crime, Age and Employment," *Am. Sociological Rev., 24,* no. 5 (Oct. 1959), 679-86.

TABLE 18.8 Inmates' Perception of the Feature of Postrelease Life That Will Help
Most to Keep Them Out of Further Trouble with the Law
(Prison Panel Study, near-release sample only)

Feature, with typical remarks	Leavenworth Penitentiary	Terre Haute Penitentiary	Milan Correctional Institution	Chillicothe Reformatory	Ashland Youth Institution
Economic security (regular employ- ment)	27%	44%	44%	32%	26%
Time utilization (keeping busy, off the streets, etc.)	6%	2%	4%	6%	24%
Responsibility (to family or others)	10%	19%	4%	16%	26%
Deterrence (fear of return to prison)	8%	6%	2%	12%	16%
Avoiding criminals (no bad company)	14%	4%	14%	8%	—
Own will power (control vices)	29%	10%	10%	14%	2%
Religious convictions (church)	—	4%	6%	4%	2%
Help from others (nonchurch help)	—	4%	—	4%	2%
Other	6%	2%	10%	4%	—
Don't know	—	4%	6%	—	4%
Number of cases	49	48	50	50	51

law enforcement agencies. Especially characteristic of Ashland inmates
was concern with their family relationships and with having attractive
activity when released. This suggests the special significance of home placement arrangements and leisure-time associates for youthful releasees.

In summary, our broad questions regarding inmate evaluations of their
prison experience and perception of future problems have yielded a picture
of: (1) pessimism regarding the prospects of their fellows succeeding in
avoiding further difficulty with the law; (2) perception of the prison's influence in avoiding future crime as being primarily achieved by deterrence,
through instilling them with a fear of return to prison; (3) appreciation
of trade training more often than of any of the various other types of prison
rehabilitation effort (but this appreciation centered in the youth prisons);
(4) perception of future problems as primarily consisting of economic difficulties, especially at the adult institutions; (5) considerable concern in the
Ashland Youth Institution about postrelease social relationships and leisure-
time pursuits. Other data on the inmates' more specific expectations regarding jobs, income, associates, and further difficulties with the law were presented in earlier chapters.

Because most of the inquiries reported above employed broad questions,
with the answers recorded verbatim, they had the advantage of procuring a
relatively spontaneous and uninhibited picture of the immediate reactions
of the inmates. In contrast, questions that limit one to a forced choice
among proffered answers may suggest a response which the subject would
not have thought of spontaneously. On the other hand, our findings with
the broad questions may have suffered distortion from the necessity of the

interviewer's editing a voluminous response to record what seemed to be its essential point. Several other sources of distortion in our findings could be mentioned—for example, distortion from the variation of interviewers in the extent to which they probed by further questions when inmate responses were vague or indefinite. Most important, these verbal responses may not be reliable indicators of actual prison influence on inmates, and may not predict much postprison behavior; the inmates themselves can never know the prison's influence precisely. What their responses provide is a general picture of the mood of inmate reactions to imprisonment, which may help us to explain our more objective data on their actual postrelease criminal and noncriminal behavior.

If one theme is evident from all of these disparate snatches of verbalization, it is that inmates view each other as in a struggle to achieve a secure and satisfying noncriminal life, but without great confidence that most will win out in this struggle. This is understandable, since their presence in prison indicates that they have been defeated once before. Also, they see others go out of prison and return as failures. One should note again that prisoners see a disproportionate number of failures, since the successes do not get sent back to prison, and thus, prisoners are likely to have an unrealistically pessimistic view of their postrelease prospects. However, to most people in prison, including most of those there for the first time, failure has been a common feature of their own experience, both at legitimate and at criminal pursuits. As a consequence, it is understandable that caseworkers often note a defeatist attitude in the men who confront the problem of securing income and acceptance in a noncriminal way of life upon release from prison.

It is well established in psychology that punishment usually does not change behavior patterns as effectively as rewarding alternative behavior. It follows from psychological learning theory that if a pattern of response (crime) has been gratifying to a certain type of stimulus (need or desire), punishment may promote inhibition of this old response, but the old response will not be extinguished unless a new type of response proves more rewarding. Only after the new response (legitimate alternative behavior) is repeatedly rewarded (reinforced) will the old stimulus (need or desire) fail to renew the initial response (crime).[16]

Our data suggest that prison does deter men from crime, and in this sense it is a punishment. Our data also indicate that the men released from prison generally have had little reward for behavior that is an alternative to

[16] This synopsis of learning theory and research is elaborated in a variety of psychological literature, notably: B. F. Skinner, *Science and Human Behavior* (New York, Macmillan, 1953). Its principal adaptation to the interpretation of social phenomena is: George C. Homans, *Social Behavior: Its Elementary Forms* (New York, Harcourt, Brace and World, 1961).

crime. Consequently, from the learning theory frame of reference set forth above, one would not expect criminal response patterns to be extinguished unless some gratification in legitimate occupational and social pursuits is experienced in the postrelease world.

THE IMPACT OF POSTRELEASE EXPERIENCE

Our regular interviews with men newly released from federal prisons in Chicago, Detroit, Cleveland, and St. Louis in 1959-60 revealed that about a third found no employment during their first month out of prison. One-sixth of the men were continuously unemployed for their first three months of freedom. Many who had jobs at release or shortly thereafter found only temporary employment, so that even during the second and third month out of prison, 20 to 25 per cent of the prisoners were unemployed for a whole month. The median cash income for all federal releasees in these four cities was $80 in the first month out of prison, $179 in the second month out, and $207 in the third month. These are conservative estimates of the prevailing low rates of employment and low income just after imprisonment, since releasees in the above tabulation did not include those who absconded, were reimprisoned, or were transferred during their first three months out. Up to their loss from the sample the latter cases were more extensively unemployed than those with whom we were able to maintain contact for three months or more.

How do these men live when they have so little cash income? The federal prisons provide some inmates with an opportunity to earn and save a little money while confined, or give them a cash gratuity. Nevertheless, the median amount of money possessed at release by the men in our sample was only $56, and nearly half had less than $50, which is hardly sufficient to sustain one through a long siege of unemployment. Indeed, with first paychecks frequently not issued until one or more weeks after a man starts employment, some supplementary assistance often was necessary even if the releasee found employment immediately.

Our interviews indicated that half the federal prison releasees paid no rent at their first postprison residence, generally because they were living with relatives. Family assistance, especially in the form of room and board, seems to have been the major resource of released prisoners. However, the families providing assistance generally were poor, and prolonged dependence on them was usually not acceptable to them or to the releasee.

Over four-fifths of the federal releasees returned to the metropolitan area where they resided at the time of their last conviction, and almost half returned to the same neighborhood within that metropolis. Only 8 per cent were released to a metropolitan area where they never previously had lived. About 90 per cent had their residence arranged before they left prison, about a third living with their parents, a third with their spouses, and most of the remainder with other relatives.

Almost 90 per cent of those who returned to the areas of their prior residence contacted old friends within their first six or seven weeks out of prison. Eighty-five per cent of these said that half or more of their friends knew of their prison record.

When interviewed in their sixth or seventh week out of prison and asked briefly what they did and whom they were with on the last weekday, Saturday, and Sunday preceding the interview, about half had been with preprison friends. Thus the majority of prisoners apparently return to previous primary groups, of family and friends, and their criminal record is a piece of their reputation in these groups which they cannot hide. It is probable that these proportions are even higher for state than for federal prisoners, since federal offenders more often are arrested and tried far from their place of residence.

When interviewed about five months after they left prison, 58 per cent of the men released from federal prisons had encountered, on the outside, men with whom they had become acquainted in prison. Over half of these contacts were ascribed to chance encounters on the street or in public places, and about a third occurred in the parole supervision office. It appeared that not over an eighth of these renewals of prison acquaintanceships involved extensive subsequent contact. In short, integration into prison social groups during confinement, if it occurred, was usually a temporary adaptation rather than a permanent social relationship.

The releasee's prison record was known at his place of employment, in a majority of the cases, but usually it was known only by the employer or by a few senior officials, rather than by the majority of the releasee's coworkers. The prison record was cited as the reason for job termination, or for inability to procure employment, by less than 10 per cent of those releasees who lost jobs or were unemployed. It appears that it is not so much the criminal record in itself as the lack of a sustained or skilled prior work record which is the main barrier to employment for men newly out of prison.

At our interviews with men five months out of prison, 70 per cent reported that they had made new friends since they left prison. The place of contact was predominantly at work, for white releasees, but it was somewhat more frequently in the neighborhood, for nonwhites. About 40 per cent of those with new friends said that their new friends did not know of their prison record, and 17 per cent said that only a small fraction knew. The postrelease experience of prisoners in noncriminal pursuits is insecure even when gratifying, and frequently includes extreme deprivation and frustration.

Over 90 per cent of felony arrests reported in the United States as a whole, and an even higher per cent of recidivist felonies, involve the taking of someone else's money or other property. This, in conjunction with the considerable association between recidivism and unemployment, suggests that the criminal activity which sends men back to prison in the United States is undertaken primarily as an alternative to legitimate gainful employment. Of course, we encountered some recidivism among ostensibly well-employed releasees and some nonrecidivism among long destitute ex-prisoners. But those releasees who did not return to crime seemed generally to be distinguished by their achievement of economic self-sufficiency and satisfaction in primary group relationships not requiring or encouraging disorderly or criminal activity.

Data were presented earlier to support the estimates that over 90 per cent of men released from prison seek noncriminal careers for a month or more, and that about 65 per cent pursue such careers indefinitely. Our findings on what happens after the first month out of prison suggest some of the experiences that send the 35 per cent (approximately) back into the pursuit of crime again at various times in the first few postrelease years. However, both social and economic aspects of their experience seem relevant, and their significance includes psychological effects on self-conception. These components are all interwoven. Satisfaction with economic and social circumstances, and risk-taking in the pursuit of crime, seem to be complex functions of an ex-prisoner's aspirations, social relationships, and self-conceptions, in conventional and criminal activities. To what extent can these be interrelated in a single general formulation on the causes of change from crime to noncrime and back again, and of what use is such a formulation?

DIFFERENTIAL ANTICIPATION IN CRIME AND RECAPITULATION OF ADOLESCENCE IN RECIDIVISM

As a first stage in trying to develop a more dynamic theory of criminality, this chapter summarized evidence that the bulk of felony activity both begins and terminates during adolescence. In addition, the felonies committed after adolescence were seen as generally a "fixation" in, or a "regression" to, a characteristically adolescent behavior pattern. This pattern is one of deviant and risky experimentation when frustrated in aspirations for that sense of independence identified with adulthood. Such behavior, especially in youth, usually is carried on jointly by two or more associates who share common problems and have previously participated in delinquent groups. However, few if any persons can reach maturity without also developing ties with anticriminal persons and cultivating aspirations to noncriminal careers.

It was inferred from our data that over 90 per cent of the men released from prison initially seek legitimate employment and try to achieve self-sufficiency without engaging in crime. The material in this and in preceding chapters suggested that those who later revert to crime do so largely because they have difficulty in procuring adequate noncriminal employment, because they have inadequate economic resources at release, and because they continue social contacts with persons of criminal background. Furthermore, the releasees have limited confidence in their ability to achieve their economic goals legitimately. This lack of confidence is justified by their past failures and by their continuing difficulties, which reflect their lack of the skills and the experience required to attain legitimately the occupations and the standards of living to which they aspire. Nevertheless, it is evident that most ex-criminals eventually persist in a way of life in which they are not subject to arrest for felonies, for only this can account for the low median age of felony arrestees, and for the evidence that most men released from prison do not return there.

A theory to integrate these data into an image of criminal behavior which should aid the planning of more effective correctional programs can be set forth in a few propositions, beginning with the following:

P2. When there is the possibility of performing either a criminal or a non-criminal act as alternative means for achieving certain ends, or where the only possibilities are to employ a criminal means or to forsake the ends that crime might serve, people take that course of action from which they anticipate the most favorable conception of themselves.

This statement simply restates the classical perception of criminal acts as voluntary and rational. This is equivalent in modern social psychology to saying that crimes are self-conscious acts, rather than purely reflexive expressions of feeling.[17] Such a perception underlies the law's interpretation of most crime (the major exception being in laws on criminal negligence).

It is through conception of self that a person's anticipations are affected by his moral beliefs and feelings, heretofore neglected in our analysis. The fact that most adults do not steal in all or most circumstances where they might safely steal clearly reflects not just their appraisal of the objective risks involved but also their conception of stealing as right or wrong. The validity of this proposition is demonstrated by numerous examples of honesty "beyond the call of duty," such as a finder's zealous efforts to locate the loser of found money. Self-conscious, that is, deliberate or voluntary

[17] For an outstanding discussion of the nature of voluntary behavior see: Tamotsu Shibutani, *Society and Personality* (Englewood Cliffs, N. J., Prentice-Hall, 1961), chapters 6 through 9. The psychological learning theory for which the works of Skinner and Homans were cited, while conceivably applicable, has not been related to the complex self-conscious acts involved in most crime, including the reinforcement of initial impulse by rationalizaton and social support.

action, by definition, involves imagining the consequences of one's behavior and reacting to these expected consequences in determining whether or not to perform an act.

Although moral revulsion to some types of behavior is a familiar part of experience, individuals vary greatly in the criteria of morality which they apply to criminal activities. It has been shown, for example, that most people are much less disapproving of theft from a large business or from the government than of theft from a small business or from an individual.[18] A vast range of moral reactions has been ascribed by psychiatrists to different individuals, from alleged lack of conscience in psychopaths to excessive conscience in some compulsive neurotics; a pattern between these two extremes probably characterizes most men, both in and out of prison.

Thus a future conception of oneself as good or evil can be considered part of the anticipation involved in criminal decision-making, in addition to the more objective monetary or punitive consequences of crime. But further analysis of crime as a voluntary act would mainly be relevant to the legal interpretation of crime. For purposes of controlling crime one must shift to a frame of reference which relates criminal behavior to circumstances which might be altered. Such a shift may be expressed in highly generalized terms as:

P3. A person's self-conception in his pursuit of either criminal or noncriminal alternative actions is determined by both his prior experiences and his present circumstances.

Such a formulation departs from the free-will frame of reference of Proposition P2, essential if one is to *judge* behavior from a legal, theological, or moral standpoint, and shifts to a deterministic frame of reference, necessary if one tries to *explain* why a deliberate act occurs. *Both* free-will and deterministic points of view are unavoidable, even for those who argue the virtues of one against alleged vices of the other; the two points of view do not conflict, provided each is applied to its different task in the two types of interpretation of behavior needed by society—evaluative judgment and causal explanation.

The essence of traditional sociological explanations of crime is that the prior circumstances most influencing an individual's self-conceptions are those intimate primary social relationships with family and close friends in which a person incorporates into his own thinking the folkways and mores of the groups with which he identifies himself. This perspective is commonly illustrated by case histories of youths deeply involved in delinquent gangs, reared in neighborhoods and families where crime is frequent, progressing in a career of crime from one incarceration to the next, and receiv-

[18] Erwin O. Smigel, "Public Attitudes Toward Stealing as Related to the Size of the Victim Organization," *Am. Sociological Rev., 21,* no. 3 (June 1956), 320-27.

ing gratifying conceptions of themselves only with "underworld" rather than with "respectable" associates. Obviously, a person with this background probably would have anticipations of the consequences of crime different from those which would be expected by most persons from very law-abiding families or communities, who have had no appreciable conflict with their families or association with delinquents or criminals, and to whom crime would mean humiliation and disgrace. However, most people do not seem to fit either of these extremes, not even those in high delinquency areas or prisons. That is one reason why the postrelease behavior of prisoners is only imperfectly predicted or explained.

Certainly crime, like other behavior, not only reflects perceptions and values shared with identifiable groups but also expresses individual personality traits which are a product of past experiences. These traits normally include needs for recognition from others and for self-esteem, but may also include repressed hostility, unconscious sexual cravings, or other conditions, of which the offender is often unaware. Nevertheless, there is need to explain why such personality attributes are expressed in crime by one person, in business enterprise by another, and in an academic or artistic career by yet another. Our project has sought to describe and analyze in released offenders the stimulation and opportunities for conventional and for criminal expression of man's broader motivations, such as the desire to perceive oneself as a success, the interest in acquiring material wealth, and the need for acceptance by others.

It is evident that all offenders must have expressed their personalities in their noncriminal as well as their criminal pasts. Our data indicate that almost all preserve some ties with anticriminal as well as with criminal persons. This chapter pointed out the concentration of felony behavior in the adolescent years and suggested that crime represented to youth an effort to achieve adult independence. Evidence was cited that most persons in our society experiment with criminal short-cuts for traversing the difficult route from the dependence of childhood to the independence of adulthood, although only a relatively few suffer a prolonged detour through prison. Chapters 14 and 15 indicated that most prisoners renew, at release, their earlier dependence on parent figures for material assistance, as they cannot subsist without aid until they get their first postrelease income. The data also indicated that their prospects of further imprisonment are increased if they cannot achieve accord with the relatives with whom they must live, or if they live alone.

Case data suggest that a renewal of adolescent and childhood patterns of intrafamily conflict, after the prisoner is released to live with his kin, may be a major factor in the releasee's postprison discord at home. Thus, family relationships after release from prison, as in adolescence, may greatly determine what Reckless would call a man's "insulation" from the criminal influences he encounters. This is because family relationships greatly affect the ability of a releasee to achieve both economic security and satisfying social relationships in an anticriminal social world. The association of recidivism with persistent unemployment and with persistent renewal of prison acquantances parallels the association of adolescent delinquency with being out of school and out of work and having social prestige and a favorable self-conception only in delinquent peer groups. This suggests that there are extensive similarities between immediate postprison life and the period of adolescence, an analogy which can be summarized as:

P4. Immediately after each release from prison, most prisoners recapitulate their adolescent dependence on parent figures and their youthful struggles to achieve a sense of their own independence and adulthood.

P5. After each release from prison, most prisoners are reformed, or recidivate, according to whether or not adequate change develops from their prior patterns of coping with dependence on relatives and with the need to achieve social and economic independence.

However, conclusions reasonably abstracted from our postrelease data and from behaviorial science theory include:

P6. Persistence in a postprison change from prior adolescent delinquent patterns in dealing with parent figures and peers depends on whether or not new patterns are reinforced through greater gratification in legitimate than in illegitimate economic pursuits.

P7. Greater gratification in legitimate than in illegitimate economic pursuits requires not so much greater immediate rewards as more favorable *anticipations,* and this implies development of a longer time perspective than characterizes adolescent delinquent thinking.

The foregoing theory suggests that analysis of the complex social and psychological experiences of an offender's adolescence may be crucial not only for understanding his past criminality, but for suggesting how one can most effectively assist him in prison and after release. The problem is to try to alter his perspectives in the postrelease quasi-adolescence from those of his adolescence, especially his anticipations in regard to his relationships with parents, peers, and anticriminal persons. Economic self-sufficiency is a major foundation for a change in these relationships, and it may be reinforced by changed relationships which develop during imprisonment. As indicated in chapter 15, the period of imprisonment is one of some deterioration in the ties of most convicts with their friends on the outside, and at the same time the prisoner's relationships with parents may improve from their state at the time the offender was engaged in crime and was committed to prison. Our research suggests the simple rule for corrections that:

P8. The correctional treatments of maximum reformative effect are those that enhance a prisoner's opportunities in legitimate economic pursuits and those that improve his conception of himself when he identifies with anti-criminal persons.

Propositions P2 and P3 above summarize, on a very broad level of generality, the theory of crime that I have called "differential anticipation." They provide a frame of reference for Proposition P4, which might be called the "recapitulation of adolescence" model of postprison behavior. This model is suggested by the concentration of felony offenses in the adolescent years and by the return of most prisoners to adolescent-like dependence on kin at release. Proposition P5, a general rule for corrections, is a theorem deducible from the three preceding propositions and from sociological interpretations of crimes, plus an instrumental view of property crimes. This general rule for corrections also could be deduced by interpreting the findings of our study in terms of psychological learning theory: Conviction and sentencing by imprisonment are generally perceived by offenders as an unfavorable consequence (punishment) of their illegitimate behavior to gain economic goals; the correctional actions in carrying out the sentence will extinguish this illegitimate behavior pattern if it not only punishes it, but also rewards alternative behavior directly by economic rewards (primary reinforcement), and indirectly, by making the social consequences of legitimate behavior attractive (secondary reinforcement). This view is elaborated in Propositions P6 through P8.

"Differential anticipation" theory, like the more elaborate formulations of Cloward and Ohlin, views behavior as varying with legitimate and illegitimate opportunities, as well as with learning and social support. In my opinion, "differential anticipation" also is compatible with the Reckless "containment" theory, as limited by him to the representation of crimes which are in a middle range between deep-seated psychological compulsions and actions in conformity to a purely criminal enculturation.[19] All of these theories, like legal theory, share a conception of the criminal act as self-conscious behavior, and an image of the offender as inculcated with both conventional and criminal values.

In spite of the foregoing, it seems to me that the connotations of the terms in these alternative theories direct us to somewhat different aspects of crime. "Differential anticipation," as I have interpreted it, focuses our attention more than do other theories on the decision to commit a crime. In the perspective of differential anticipation, this decision is a dynamic emergent in the course of an offender's interaction with himself, and with real or

---

[19] See: Richard A. Cloward, "Illegitimate Means, Anomie, and Deviant Behavior," *Am. Sociological Rev., 24,* no. 2 (April 1959), 164-76; Cloward and Lloyd E. Ohlin, *Delinquency and Opportunity* (Glencoe, Illinois, The Free Press, 1961), chapter 6; Walter C. Reckless, *The Crime Problem,* 3rd ed. (New York, Appleton-Century-Crofts, 1961), pp. 335-59; Reckless, "A New Theory of Delinquency and Crime," *Federal Probation, 25,* no. 4 (Dec. 1961), 42-46.

imaginary other persons (his reference groups), in particular social and economic circumstances. Such a dynamic view of crime is most useful to corrections if, as our data suggest, offenders usually are oriented to avoidance of crime at release, but this orientation wavers if it is not reinforced by postrelease experiences which promote more favorable anticipations from legitimate activity than the offender is likely to have acquired in his prior efforts at legitimate occupations.

Our data have indicated that the careers of individual offenders oscillate between criminal and noncriminal pursuits, persisting in each alternative according to the gratifications that they come to anticipate there. This gives hope to corrections, and also a challenge: the challenge to frustrate the crime phase of this cycle as early and as permanently as possible, and to facilitate entry and stable gratification in the noncriminal phase.

Methods of meeting this challenge may be inferred from Proposition P6 above. An underlying criminological theory affects what administrators consider is the most effective allocation of funds and personnel for alternative types of rehabilitation service. It seems to me that the major new correctional measures favorably reported in this book, such as the treatment teams discussed in chapter 9 and the prerelease placement and guidance centers described in chapter 16, can be understood and directed more adequately when interpreted from the perspective of the differential anticipation theory and the recapitulation of adolescence model.

Every theory is a sort of shorthand, a concise code for summarizing in a few sentences or formulas the essential relationships with which one is concerned in an array of variegated observations. The utility of a theory is that it helps bring order out of disorder, simplicity out of complexity. But when a theory abstracts the uniformities from an apparent diversity, it necessarily neglects some of the unique features of each separate observation. As well stated by the physicist-philosopher Phillip Frank: "There is certainly no theory which is in complete agreement with all our observations. If we require such a complete agreement, we can certainly achieve it by merely recording the observations."[20] Also, he points out, "every acceptance of a debatable theory is due to a compromise between . . . agreement with facts and efficiency as a code."[21]

The process of relating research to theory makes the contributions of research cumulative, for that which is accumulated is a body of theory sufficiently tested to be accepted as knowledge. Such knowledge, in the form of theoretical principles, in turn directs one to new knowledge. For example, if the differential anticipation and recapitulation of adolescence theories are sound, in almost every correctional situation they will suggest some things

[20] Phillip Frank, *Philosophy of Science* (Englewood Cliffs, N. J., Prentice-Hall, 1957), p. 353.
[21] *Ibid.*, p. 341.

which correctional personnel might do to maximize the rehabilitative significance of their services. In addition, the numbered conclusions in earlier
chapters offer a series of specific suggestions supplementing the broad
theories set forth in this chapter. To maximize the utility of any of these
conclusions, they must repeatedly be tested by new correctional research,
preferably of an experimental design. On the basis of such research, our
conclusions may be modified or extended. This raises the practical problem of how correctional research and correctional administration can most
effectively be integrated, for maximum benefit to each. The experience
gained from our project may offer some suggestions for a solution to this
problem.

CHAPTER 19

The Practical Use of
Research in Corrections

In corrections, as in every other field, one can never afford to stop learning. Measures proven advantageous today may not be the best for all time. Each innovation, no matter how well it solves old problems, also creates some new problems for which adequate knowledge is lacking. Changes in the law, in police or court practice, in correctional success, and in the technology, economic conditions, or military status of our society change the proportions of various types of offenders whom a correctional agency must handle. They also alter the problems that released offenders encounter. All these changes pose new problems for correctional administrators, and new types of research may be needed to solve new problems.

The principle of *feedback* receives much emphasis in recent research and writing on ways to augment the effectiveness of industry, education, space exploration, and other fields of human endeavor. This principle means simply the guidance of current effort by information on the effects of past actions. Feedback is not a new idea, and, broadly speaking, it has always characterized learning from experience. This principle has now come to the fore because of demonstrated gains in efficiency from its more prompt, precise, and relevant use.

Correctional management surely has enough in common with these other kinds of management to have similar benefits from improved feedback. If so, research on the effectiveness of prison and parole practices, in terms of postrelease recidivism, is likely to become increasingly important. While periodic profit and loss analyses have not yet been demanded of correctional managers, these administrators continually encounter demands for information about the effectiveness of their operations. Increasingly, correctional officials must meet such demands with definite knowledge rather than with impressionistic opinions. They must have precise tabulations to support their requests for financial and legislative assistance, and to cope with the inquiries or accusations of various interest groups. Because of these continuing needs, the contribution of research to correctional administration is never finished.

The appendixes of this report, which discuss our research operations in somewhat more detail than does the text, indicate that much of our research could have been performed more efficiently by correctional administrations than by our project. Information on the behavior of inmates, prior to and during imprisonment and on parole, were collected by our staff through interviews in the prison and in parole supervision offices, and by analysis of records in these agencies. Large portions of this information, especially in the postrelease situation, dealt with matters about which the correctional staff also routinely inquire. For example, the officers now maintain a record of the parolee's employment and residence. Repeatedly we have pointed out how research by the state could be more fruitful if more of their record-keeping were performed in a standardized fashion, so that it could be statistically tabulated for the evaluation of correctional programs.

With a small investment in research staff, including a few superior clerical personnel responsible for seeing that records on the prison and postprison behavior of offenders are maintained in a precise and uniform manner, correctional systems could evaluate their prison and parole programs in the light of the behavior of the offenders after release. As indicated in chapter 11, for example, the value of work and education programs in prisons would grow tremendously if these programs were regularly guided by information collected through parole supervision agencies and prerelease guidance centers on the utilization of prison training in postrelease employment. In the course of our project's operations, correctional research programs within government agencies were highly developed in California and grew rapidly in Wisconsin, in several other states, and in the federal government. As indicated in chapter 1, our project has had a major interest in stimulating such programs within correctional agencies and has conducted much correspondence, publication, and participation in professional meetings for this purpose.

University-centered correctional research programs will always be justifiable for special purposes, especially for experimentation with new types of research. A university can contribute a certain amount of detachment, which may be more difficult for government researchers to achieve. Also, university researchers are free from the correctional administration's obligation to maintain routine programs, although other types of pressure may also restrict the research time that university personnel can provide. However, a university is expected to probe abstract matters relevant to theory, where the state is less committed to such basic research. Finally, the interests of the university, even on practical matters, can extend beyond those of any separate government agency.

In contrast to the foregoing, one would expect research conducted by a government agency to be more closely integrated with the administration of that agency than university research would be. Because the span of control between government policy-makers and their research staff is short and the control is complete, administrators should be able to procure information from their own staff more quickly than they could from a university. Also, information from government researchers presumably should be more clearly in the language of the administrator and addressed to his needs than information from university research. It has been my impression, however, that the new research agencies in correctional administrations have not yet developed these abilities adequately, especially when dealing with research that is different from traditional annual report statistics. Therefore, in concluding this report on our research, it is appropriate to summarize what lessons our project may offer for the improvement of correctional agency research programs.

FIVE PRACTICAL RESEARCH SUGGESTIONS FOR CORRECTIONAL ADMINISTRATORS

The conclusion of our project marked the seventeenth year of my moving back and forth between the world of the correctional administrator and the world of the research criminologist. One impression that stands out above all others from this experience is that there has not been adequate communication between these two worlds. The research criminologist has not sufficiently placed himself in the role of the correctional administrator and has not adjusted to the public expectations with which the administrator is confronted. The administrator has not addressed appropriate questions to the researchers in the universities, or even to those researchers employed on his staff.

My concern here is with suggesting ways in which the administrator of a correctional system, through research, may improve his communication to those segments of the general public and those legislative and executive agencies of government which are most significant to him. The designation "five practical suggestions" for these impressionistic conclusions from my personal experience is a very arbitrary enumeration. Possibly other suggestions are as important as those presented here, and these five suggestions could have been subdivided. At any rate, the first suggestion is simply:

Q1. Maximum determination and communication of correctional needs require compilation of the most complete postrelease information that any correctional agency now has within its own facilities, or can readily obtain, on the offenders recently released from its custody or still under its supervision.

Correctional administrators are habitually nonplused when confronted by inquisitive legislators or journalists who ask for proof that correctional measures prevent crime. Often a correctional administrator seems reluctant to gather any postrelease statistics when he cannot get perfect statistics. Alternatives sometimes relied upon are to present guesses as statistics or to cite individual cases with no way of knowing how representative they are.

If the administrator makes even a minimal tabulation, he can begin to show the difference in postrelease crime rates for prisoners in different pro-grams. Merely as a first step, a correctional administration, from its own records, can determine the number of individuals whom it released in past years who were again committed to the same correctional system. This is useful for any correctional administration, whether it be county, state, or national. While such information certainly does not provide all of the criminal record, it provides much more adequate knowledge than subjective impressions, whether for reporting trends in postrelease criminality, for comparing the postrelease criminal records of different types of offenders, or for comparing similar offenders subjected to different types of treatment.

All criminal record information is bound to be incomplete, for one never knows about the offenses for which a man is not caught. One assumes in all statistical comparisons that the degree of incompleteness is approximately evenly distributed over all categories of offenders who are compared. One can then make comparisons between relative postrelease criminality rates, showing which is more and which is less. This yields valuable knowledge even without having absolutely complete postrelease crime information. For example, if one can show that for a given type of offender with a given type of prior record, those receiving probation have less further criminality within the county, state, or nation ten years later than those sent to prison, one will have a strong foothold in evaluative knowledge.

This type of knowledge can be gradually enhanced by procuring more complete information, covering longer follow-up periods, larger numbers of cases, and ideally, a larger range of jurisdictions. The optimum follow-up statistics on postrelease felony convictions would be based on current F.B.I. fingerprint record sheets for offenders released in past years. This brings us to my second suggestion:

Q2. Evaluation of correctional program effectiveness can be most conclusive and persuasive if the presentation of postrelease data is focused on the responsibilities which the correctional agency must meet.

It is a great achievement if someone who is a felon can be converted to a saint, but the agencies for dealing with felons fulfill their primary responsi-bility if they reduce the recurrence of felonies among the persons whom they release. Even a change from felonious behavior to occasional misdemeanors represents partial success. One of the major sources of obfuscation in the parole and probation field is the counting of all types of postrelease offense or infraction under a single label, such as probation "violation."

As elaborated in chapter 2, a clear dichotomy should be made between violations that involve the commission of new felonies and violations that involve only failure to comply with supervision regulations. One may even count as felonies both cases leading to new convictions and cases of viola-tion for rule infractions in which there is strong suspicion of felony involvement but no prosecution because of the man's return to prison as a violator. However, it is appropriate to distinguish these from violations that involve only failure to cooperate with supervision, such as absconding, refusal to work, or having criminal companions. This dichotomy is crucial in communication to the public because it is appropriate to label these nonfelony violation actions as "felony prevention actions."

Although nonfelony violations may be disappointing from the standpoint of maximum hopes in granting parole or probation to an offender, such actions do not represent failure from the standpoint of protecting the public. An agency is damaging its public communications unnecessarily if it confounds felony and felony-prevention actions in a single violation figure.

Other types of focus also aid communication greatly in reporting post-release behavior of offenders. For example, the contrast between offenders given special services or assistance at release and a control group often is very great in terms of deferral of further violation, even when the difference between the two groups is relatively small in terms of an overall violation rate. Therefore, the contrast between a special treatment group and a control group may well be presented not just as a gross violation rate, but in terms of months of reconfinement in a given number of years after release. This has been most effectively demonstrated by Stuart Adams, in his report on the PICO Project.[1]

A further advantage of a time of reconfinement measure, of course, is that it can easily be expressed in terms of the cost of reconfinement. With the cost of prison treatment approximately ten times the cost of supervision in the community, a strong economic justification can be made for any special services which reduce the time of reconfinement for a given group of offenders. This is not to imply that economic savings is the major moral justification for a correctional program. However, it is a very crucial and persuasive consideration in government. This is relevant to a third suggestion:

Q3. Economic problems of releasees can be remedied if the economic problems are known and if their solution is given much higher priority in correctional operations than has been the practice heretofore.

It becomes relatively meaningless to argue on whether the economic factor in recidivism is more important than the psychological factor, or whether either is more important than social or cultural factors; all certainly are intertwined, and an adequate criminological theory would generalize on

---

[1] Stuart Adams, "Interaction Between Individual Interview Therapy and Treatment Amenability in Older Youth Authority Wards," California Board of Correction Monograph No. 2, *Inquiries Concerning Kinds of Treatment for Kinds of Delinquents* (Sacramento, 1961), pp. 27-44. Republished in Norman Johnston *et al., The Sociology of Punishment and Correction* (New York, Wiley, 1962), pp. 213-24.

the nature of their interrelationship. It is sufficient to note that we can demonstrate statistically a close relationship between economic hardship and crime, for certain types of offenders. The first study undertaken in our project involved interrelating unemployment and crime for different age groups. This demonstrated rather conclusively that unemployment is closely related to crime for adult offenders, although not for juveniles.[2] One might also note that over 90 per cent of felonies reported to the police involve the taking of someone's money or property. Furthermore, economic problems of ordinary people are a type of problem that almost everyone can understand, without special training.

It is surprising that current literature on parole and probation problems almost completely ignores the economic difficulties of men released from confinement. I suspect that this problem affects supervision outcome much more than the size of caseloads or the shortage of psychiatrists. A major portion of the adult releasees are impoverished before they get into difficulties with the law. As chapter 14 revealed, they are acutely in need at the time of their release. Of course, this does not apply to all releasees, but the dimensions of the economic problems are massive enough to warrant its being a vital consideration in any overall effort to make parole and probation more effective. Considering the relative lack of accumulated clothing and other possessions and the pent-up desires of most newly released prisoners, their income needs in many ways exceed those of men not previously confined. With their combination of large needs and low income, and considering the background of most of these men, it is in many ways remarkable that at least nine out of ten of the adult offenders seem to spend at least their first month out of prison trying to solve their problems by legitimate means, and a majority seem to persist at such pursuits indefinitely.

Data from early stages of our research, on the postrelease economic problems of men who had violated parole and mandatory release, were among the stimulants to several federal measures of economic assistance for released prisoners. These measures included increased funds for release gratuities and an increase in the number of placement officers, prison employees whose sole function is to seek jobs for releasees. But by far the most significant development, for economic and for other aid, were the prerelease guidance centers described in chapter 16. The latter have been remarkably effective at increasing the extent and quality of releasee employment.

The action of officials when clearly and persistently faced with the facts on economic aspects of the correctional situation suggests my fourth generalization:

Q4. Facts on failure of treatment must be flaunted, not hidden, if improvements are to be procured.

[2] Daniel Glaser and Kent Rice, "Crime, Age and Employment," *Am. Sociological Rev., 24,* no. 5 (Oct. 1959), 679-86.

This becomes apparent when one recalls from chapter 1 the reference to the existence and interrelationship of two stages in correctional research. The first stage, correlational research, studies correctional operations as they are currently functioning or have existed in the past. When such research makes evident the existence of clear deficiencies in current practice, a major effort still is necessary to plan and to gain approval for the second stage, which is experimental research. First evidence from correlational research must therefore be supplemented by new and independent data, and repeatedly reported, before support is likely to be adequate for major experiments. This is partly because most research findings on failure of current practice can suggest a variety of alternative remedies. Innovations that are stimulated by correlational research, therefore, reflect also many judgments by officials and researchers on the problems of implementing new measures. A purpose of experimental research is to test these judgments.

In chapter 10 we illustrated this complex interaction of research results and administrative judgment in correctional change by recounting the evolution of the federal prison treatment teams as replacement for traditional institution classification committees. This experience, and the rapid growth of the prerelease guidance centers, indicate the validity of the generalization:

Q5. Improvements in correctional operations suggested by research findings will be most readily supported if introduced as piecemeal innovations, and if an evaluation program is part of the innovation proposal.

This is the essence of experimental research. Without experiments it is difficult to have any argument on the effectiveness of a correctional program more conclusive than one man's impressions against another's. It is apparent that legislators and executives controlling government expenditures for coping with crime have not been convinced that any group of experts has a guaranteed solution for these problems. Repeatedly in recent years, in federal and state agencies, money for innovations has been granted only when the measures were proposed as small-scale experiments, with planned evaluation. Because progress through trial and error, by research, has been prominent in recent years in so many fields where problems are pronounced, legislators seem more readily sold on proposals formulated as tests of new methods than on proposals presented as panaceas to be dispensed immediately to everyone.

For those correctional administrators who think they know what they need to make their services more effective, a government attitude that vetoes proposals for new programs is frustrating. But by following the five suggestions set forth here, I believe administrators can soon find themselves in a position to procure necessary funds, for they will be able to justify the fund requests more adequately. However, this requires a growth in communication between administrators and researchers. Each should feel free to criticize and to offer suggestions to the other. Research and development go hand in hand in industry today, but only by communication of researchers with administrators can research lead to development in corrections.

THE CONCLUSIONS OF THIS PROJECT AS HYPOTHESES FOR NEW RESEARCH

The numbered conclusions set forth in each of our separate chapters provide a synopsis of the principal findings of this study. Some of these findings were supported by extensive data, often from several independent sources, while other conclusions were much more tentative. In science, all findings must be considered somewhat tentative, in that all are subject to further test and possible revision and qualification. However, in administrative practice, even untested assumptions or speculative hypotheses must be relied upon until more conclusively tested knowledge is procured, on problems for which decisions cannot be avoided or deferred.

The numbered statements that follow may be considered the principal conclusions from our research and may be of potential value in the guidance of prison and parole programs. These propositions were not necessarily first conceived in our project, but for most of them we have presented more conclusive evidence than has generally accompanied assertion of such ideas. Nevertheless, any of the statements may appropriately be considered as hypotheses for further research by correctional staff themselves. These conclusions are:

A1. In the first two to five years after their release, only about a third of all the men released from an entire prison system are returned to prison.
A2. The proportion of releasees returned to prison tends to be higher:
    a. where probation is used extensively, so that only the worst risks go to prison, although this use of probation may make the long-run recidivism of all felons lower;
    b. where parole is used extensively, so that many poor risk parolees are released on a trial basis;
    c. where a large proportion of parolees are returned to prison when they have violated parole regulations but have not been charged with or convicted of new felonies;
    d. where there is a high overall crime rate in the communities to which prisoners are released, so that there is high prospect of the releasee coming from and going to highly criminogenic circumstances.
B1. The older a man is when released from prison, the less likely he is to return to crime.
B2. The younger a prisoner was when first arrested, convicted, or confined for any crime, the more likely he is to continue in crime.
B3. The earlier an offender of any age left home, the more likely he is to continue in crime.

B4. Felony offenses fall into three broad rankings of recidivism, as follows:
   a. The most recidivistic category consists of economic offenses not involving violence (larceny, burglary, auto theft, and forgery), and the most recidivistic single type of felony is auto theft.
   b. Consistently intermediate in recidivism rate are several common but diverse types of crime, such as narcotics offenses, robbery, and kidnapping.
   c. The lowest recidivism occurs with those offenses most associated with unusual circumstances in the offender's life rather than with offenses pursued as vocations; notable here are murder, rape, and embezzlement.

B5. The extent of the offender's prior criminal record and the likelihood of his becoming a recidivist are directly correlated.

C1. Prisoners, as a whole, are more oriented to maintain voluntary isolation from other prisoners than to achieve solidarity with other prisoners.

C2. Voluntary isolation of prisoners from each other is correlated directly with age of the prisoners; at low ages, the inverse of Proposition C1 may occur.

C3. Voluntary isolation of prisoners from each other is correlated directly with the amount of prior correctional confinement that they have experienced.

C4. Voluntary isolation of prisoners from each other is correlated directly with the degree of heterogeneity of prisoners in an institution; this heterogeneity may be measured in terms of: (a) race, (b) length of sentence, (c) social class, or (d) prior correctional confinement.

C5. Voluntary isolation of prisoners from each other varies in a U-shaped curve, being high at the beginning of confinement, decreasing towards the middle, and increasing near release.
   a. The amplitude of this curve varies inversely with age or prior confinement of the prisoners.
   b. The shape of this curve will be modified somewhat by the linear relationships with age, heterogeneity, and other variables indicated in the previous propositions.

C6. The flow of inter-inmate advice is predominantly from older to younger inmates.

C7a. Inmates will get along best with other inmates at jobs where they find: (1) a small number of other inmates; (2) low contact with the rest of the inmate population; (3) a trade training program; (4) limited access to contraband services or supplies; (5) careful selection of assignees.

C7b. Inmates are most likely to have trouble with other inmates at jobs with: (1) a high concentration of men rejected for assignment elsewhere; (2) a large number of prisoners assigned; (3) much contact with the rest of the inmate population; (4) access to services or supplies highly valued by most prisoners.

C8. A predominant interest of prison inmates is to adjust to the expectations of their keepers in order to stay "out of trouble" while confined.

C9. Most prison inmates maintain strong noncriminal interests, including vocational aspirations of a legitimate nature.

C10. Prisoners perceive other prisoners as having less commitment to staff-supported values than is, in fact, the case.

D1. Inmate pressures on other inmates to avoid communication with officers varies directly with the extent to which there is an impersonal and authoritarian orientation of staff to inmates.

D2. The value in the inmate community of any inmate's presumed unusual access to staff, or to prison files and records, varies directly with restriction of personal communication or friendship between staff and inmates.

D3. Voluntary isolation of inmates from each other varies directly with their isolation from officers.

D4. Staff influence on inmates varies directly with staff manifestation to inmates of the same types of personal behavior that cause a man to be liked in nonprison relationships.

    a. Inmates are most influenced by staff who act toward them in a friendly and considerate—rather than hostile—tone and manner.

    b. Inmates are most influenced by staff who treat them with fairness and predictability.

D5a. The more comprehensive and nonritualized the duties of any employee become in dealing with inmates, the more he is inclined to treat them on the basis of their personal attributes as individuals rather than on the basis of attitudes towards inmates as a class or social status, and the more inmates are inclined to reciprocate this treatment.

D5b. The more ritualistic and routinized the duties of an employee become in dealing with inmates, the more he is inclined to become authoritarian and punitive toward them (regardless of official policies and directives), and the more he is inclined to rationalize punitiveness by stereotyped unfavorable conceptions of inmates, which they are inclined to reciprocate.

D6. The prison employee who has the greatest reformative influence on an offender is the one who is able to demonstrate sincere and sustained concern for and confidence in the offender's rehabilitation.

D7. The prison employee's concern is most effectively manifested by gestures of interest and acts of assistance for the offender which exceed the minimal requirements of the employee's job in the prison.

E1. Promoting the isolation of inmates from each other fosters rehabilitation where the techniques for promoting isolation consist of:

    a. Providing physical arrangements of inmate housing which facilitate an inmate's achievement of privacy when he desires it;

    b. Separating inmates considered criminogenic influences on each other;

    c. Encouraging staff-desired patterns of inmate discrimination in choice of prisoner associates.

E2. Promoting the isolation of inmates from each other impedes rehabilitation where the technique employed is to promote the "Do your own time" ideology of the prison subculture, which includes the subcultural theme of indifference to the welfare of other inmates.

E3. Custody grading systems foster rehabilitation by providing effective incentives to self-improvement activity, and to inmate discrimination in choice of associates, but they impede rehabilitation:

    a. if the rewards for conformity to prison regulations include such reduction of inmate-staff contacts in quarters as to facilitate domination by inmate elements there who seek hedonistic escape from the effort of rehabilitation;

b. if they provide freedom without effectively imposing responsibility;

c. if one of their consequences is such concentration of antirehabilitative inmates in certain units that they dominate other inmates there and seriously impede their reformation, particularly in a unit through which most inmates are expected to pass in their progression up a custody-graded hierarchy of units.

F1. Objectionable behavior by men in prison is so diverse that no set of rules will encompass it all without being so long and complex as to be difficult to apply, or so arbitrary as to arouse resentment by dealing similarly with highly diverse acts; therefore, strain in inmate-staff relationships is minimized by a policy of flexible rules interpreted to fit each case, taking into account primarily the probable effect of each penalty on the future behavior of the offender.

F2. The administration of disciplinary penalties is most effective if it simultaneously:

a. minimizes alienation of the rule-violating inmate from staff;

b. maximizes his alienation from inmate supporters of his infraction;

c. promotes in him a clear regret over having committed the infraction; but

d. provides him with a perception of clearly available opportunities to pursue a course of behavior which will restore him to good standing in the prison and give him a more favorable self-conception than he had as a rule violator.

G1. The advancement of treatment goals requires centralization of more *authority* in the officials who are spokesmen for treatment interests, but decentralization of treatment *activity,* so as to increase the extent to which all staff in contact with inmates have a strong interest in treatment.

H1. Judiciously employed rewards and penalties to inmate groups, for the performances of the individual members of these groups:

a. mobilize for rehabilitative purposes the peer-group support and pressure that normally is more likely to be criminogenic;

b. reduce the authoritarian role of staff;

c. provide prison management with a powerful means of motivating individual inmates.

H2. Intergroup competition for a limited number of rewards usually is a way of increasing the total motivation yielded by whatever supply of rewards to inmates the prison has available.

H3. The cooperation of inmates with staff and inmate identification of themselves with noncriminal persons are enhanced by treating inmates as though they were subordinate members of a single staff, sharing with employees the task of running the prison for the maximum long-run benefit of all. This means:

a. Giving responsible inmate committees such nonpersonal prison financial and administrative information as is relevant to their understanding of those prison management problems in which inmates have an interest and which inmate cooperation can help solve;

b. Charging the committees with conveying this information to other inmates, and facilitating this, in conjunction with

c. Holding inmate groups responsible for behavior contributing to the solution of specific prison-management problems, as a condition for improvements in pleasures or privileges for inmates, particularly benefits to inmates made possible primarily by their improved behavior.

I1. Regular work during imprisonment, for even as little as one year, would be the longest and most continuous employment experience that most prisoners, and especially the younger prisoners, have ever had.

I2. Regularity of prior employment is more closely related than type of work previously performed to the postrelease success of prisoners in avoiding further felonies.

I3. At present the postrelease employment of at least half the men released from prison does not involve a level of skill that requires an appreciable amount of prior training, but for the minority who gain skills in prison at which they can find a postrelease vocation, prison work experience and training is a major rehabilitative influence.

I4. Not training in vocational skills, but, rather, habituation of inmates to regularity in constructive and rewarding employment, and anti-criminal personal influences of work supervisors on inmates, are—at present—the major contributions of work in prison to inmate rehabilitation.

J1. For most inmates, prison education is statistically associated with above average postrelease success only when the education is extensive and occurs in the course of prolonged confinement.

J2. For most prisoners, especially for those with extensive prior felony records, the usual duration and type of involvement in prison education programs is associated with higher than average postrelease failure rates.

J3. A small amount of education in prison frequently impairs postrelease prospects of inmates indirectly, by inspiring them with unrealistic aspirations, or by the education's being pursued instead of alternative prison programs which could provide more useful preparation for postrelease life.

K1. Because of the large number and variety of prerelease variables and postrelease circumstances affecting behavior after prison, any predictions of the postrelease behavior of prisoners are likely to be inaccurate in an appreciable proportion of cases, regardless of the persons or procedures employed for prediction.

K2. The most selective prediction tables are more consistently accurate than case-study prognoses in predicting parole outcome for large groups of offenders, but individual cases persistently are encountered which raise prediction issues that do not appear to be taken into account in available statistical tabulations.

K3. Both prediction tables and case-study prognoses, and their application, can be improved continually if each is used routinely as a check on the other; for example, if case-analyst or parole-board-member prognoses are recorded in a definite form, subsequent research can analyze their accuracy, and can study those case prognoses which disagree with the predictions from statistical tables, to determine the circumstances under which one method of prognosis is more accurate than the other.

K4. Prediction tables can be used to divide all cases in a correctional system into "base expectancy" categories of different parole violation or recidivism risk, so that the postrelease record of those receiving a specific treatment can thereby be evaluated in terms of its difference from the record of all those in similar risk categories not receiving the specific treatment; however, because of continuous uncertainty as to whether or not all important prediction variables by which cases arc selected for different types of treatment have been taken into account in these base expectancies, controlled experimentation with randomly selected treatment and control groups, wherever feasible, is the optimum method for evaluating a correctional treatment program.

L1. Prisoners have expectations of extremely rapid occupational advancement during the years immediately following their release, expectations which are unrealistic in the light of their limited work experience and lack of vocational skills.

L2. Maximum rehabilitative influence of cash paid to inmates at release occurs with:
   a. Payments issued to the inmates as wages for any work which they perform in prison, but at wage rates varied so as to reward diligence and improvement in skill;
   b. Compulsory savings requirements, to assure availability of most earnings at release;
   c. Issuance of large prison savings on a piecemeal basis following release, through checks disbursed by the parole supervision officer;
   d. Release gratuity payments only to those who are unable to earn and save adequate funds in prison, such as those confined only briefly, those who are unemployable during confinement, and those who benefit most from schooling—rather than work—while confined.

L3. Prerelease arrangement of a parole job is not associated with markedly greater rates of success on parole than release on parole without a prearranged job.

L4. Recidivism of adult male offenders varies inversely with their postrelease employment.

L5. The ex-prisoner's primary barrier to employment is not so frequently his criminal record as it is his lack of extensive or skilled work experience.

M1. As the date of their release approaches, the relationship between inmates and their parents or other blood relatives tends to improve ("absence makes the heart grow fonder"); therefore inmates increasingly expect postrelease assistance from some relatives.

M2. Imprisonment tends to weaken ties with spouses and with former friends ("out of sight, out of mind").

M3. Inmate hostility to persons in the free community diminishes as their release date approaches, at least as indicated by inmates less frequently expecting harm from specific persons, and more frequently expressing a willingness to accept help from anyone.

M4. Over 90 per cent of the men released from prison return to communities in which they previously resided.

M5. This means that they generally return to an area where their criminal reputation is known, but it also generally means that they return to the area where they can receive assistance from kin.

M6. Somewhat higher than average postrelease failure rates are associated with release to a community other than that of prior residence.

M7. The most unfavorable postrelease residential arrangement, in terms of postrelease failure rates, is that in which the ex-prisoner lives alone.

M8. Discord with relatives in the releasee's place of residence is highly associated with subsequent failure.

M9. Released prisoners move rapidly toward independence, moving away from the parental home or increasingly paying a share of the rent at home.

M10. Prisoners generally encounter old friends soon after release, and their prison record is widely known in their postrelease social circles.

M11. Most ex-prisoners re-encounter some prison acquaintances within a few months after their release.

M12. Persistent renewal of prison contacts is highly associated with reimprisonment.

M13. Most prisoners acquire new friends in the first few months after their release, but usually the new friends know of the prison record of the releasee, often through their being informed by the releasee.

M14. Development of new friendships, in which the criminal record of the releasee is not known, is associated with postrelease success.

M15. Most prisoners have real fears of suffering police harassment in their postrelease life.

M16. Although such harassment does occur and is sometimes so unjust or corrupt as to be of legitimate public concern, both serious and undeserved police harassment probably is not suffered by more than a few per cent of ex-prisoners.

N1. Major advances in the contribution of prisons to the solution of inmate postrelease problems, with a relatively small percentage increase in total prison costs, could be achieved merely by systematic extension of programs already successfully initiated. Notable among these expandable programs are:

a. compulsory inmate saving of some prison earnings to meet postrelease expenses, supplemented by gratuities or loans where necessary;

b. graduation of the disbursement of such funds, through parole supervision offices;

c. facilitation of inmate communication with law-abiding outside persons, through reduction of censorship of correspondence and of impediments to visiting;

d. involvement of outside organizations in inmate organizations, and vice versa through service and hobby clubs, personal development and mutual therapy groups, churches, and other types of voluntary organizations;

    e. communication of parole supervision staff with inmates prior to the inmate's release (in correspondence, in prerelease classes, and in initial parole interviews at the prisons);

    f. operation of loan funds as a flexible financial aid effective for some releasees, administered through parole supervision agencies in a manner based on the experience of the states that have operated these funds for decades.

N2. Routinization of these programs, so they will be more consistently operated and developed, requires their administration by persons who continually receive feedback indicating the consequences of these programs; this means that their operation at the prisons should be, at least in part, a regular responsibility of parole supervision staff.

N3. Selective employment of parolees and of prison dischargees by government agencies, and augmentation of their eligibility for unemployment insurance, can reduce the net social and economic costs to the public from recidivism and reimprisonment.

N4. This half-century's most promising correctional development for alleviating postrelease problems of prisoners consists of the counseling centers in metropolitan areas to which prisoners scheduled for release are transferred some months before their release date, and from which they regularly go forth to enter the job market and to develop correctionally acceptable postprison social relationships, before they are released on a regular parole or on any other traditional types of release from prison.

O1. Unless prisoners are isolated from returned violators, they generally develop unrealistic overestimates of their prospects of being reimprisoned as technical violators of parole.

O2. The parole rules about which both prisoners expecting parole and men already on parole will be most apprehensive are rules against associating with other ex-criminals, drinking, travel, and being out of their homes late at night.

O3. Concern with these parole rules will prevail regardless of whether or not such rules actually exist among the written conditions of parole to which the men officially are subjected.

O4. Inmate and parolee anticipations of difficulty in conforming with rules regulating their employment decline markedly in the first few months after men are released from prison.

O5. The performance of the parole supervision role can be scaled along two major dimensions, assistance and control, which differentiate four polar styles of role performance:

    a. paternal—high control, high assistance;

    b. punitive—high control, low assistance;

    c. welfare—low control, high assistance;

    d. passive—low control, low assistance.

O6. When a caseworker has both diagnosis and treatment responsibilities in dealing with offenders, the time devoted to diagnostic investigation and to the preparation of diagnostic reports tends to receive first priority, at the expense of time devoted to other functions, including treatment; this time devoted to diagnostic functions becomes more extensive than generally is assumed in official workload budgets which emphasize treatment.

O7. The parole adviser system can greatly enhance the extent to which a parole supervision officer achieves his counseling and his surveillance objectives in some cases, if the officer can exercise considerable choice in recruiting or accepting the adviser, can maintain active communication with him, and is not rigidly required to have an adviser in all cases.

P1. At least 90 per cent of American prison releasees seek legitimate careers for a month or more after they leave prison.

P2. When there is the possibility of performing either a criminal or a noncriminal act as alternative means for achieving certain ends, or where the only possibilities are to employ a criminal means or to forsake the ends that crime might serve, people take that course of action from which they anticipate the most favorable conception of themselves.

P3. A person's self-conception in his pursuit of either criminal or noncriminal alternative actions is determined by both his prior experiences and his present circumstances.

P4. Immediately after each release from prison most prisoners recapitulate their adolescent dependence on parent figures and their youthful struggles to achieve a sense of their own independence and adulthood.

P5. After each release from prison, most prisoners are reformed, or recidivate, according to whether or not adequate change develops from their prior patterns of coping with dependence on relatives and with the need to achieve social and economic independence.

P6. Persistence in a postprison change from prior adolescent delinquent patterns in dealing with parent figures and peers depends on whether or not new patterns are reinforced through greater gratification in legitimate than in illegitimate economic pursuits.

P7. Greater gratification in legitimate than in illegitimate economic pursuits requires not so much greater immediate rewards as more favorable *anticipations,* and this implies development of a longer time perspective than characterizes adolescent delinquent thinking.

P8. The correctional treatments of maximum reformative effect are those that enhance a prisoner's opportunities in legitimate economic pursuits and those that improve his conception of himself when he identifies with anticriminal persons.

Q1. Maximum determination and communication of correctional needs require compilation of the most complete postrelease information that any correctional agency now has within its own facilities, or can readily obtain, on the offenders recently released from its custody or still under its supervision.

Q2. Evaluation of correctional program effectiveness can be most conclusive and persuasive if the presentation of postrelease data is focused on the responsibilities which the correctional agency must meet.

Q3. Economic problems of releasees can be remedied if the economic problems are known and if their solution is given much higher priority in correctional operations than has been the practice heretofore.

Q4. Facts on failure of treatment must be flaunted, not hidden, if improvements are to be procured.

Q5. Improvements in correctional operations suggested by research findings will be most readily supported if introduced as piecemeal innovations, and if an evaluation program is part of the innovation proposal.

Despite the foregoing array of conclusions, one must feel humbled by the limited certainty of much that constitutes the most adequate knowledge now possible. The inquiries that corrections require have hardly been begun, let alone been concluded. We cannot yet be satisfied with our answers to the questions ascribed by Mr. Justice Frankfurter to his distinguished predecessor in the U. S. Supreme Court, Mr. Justice Holmes:

What have we better than a blind guess to show that the criminal law in its present form does more good than harm? I do not stop to refer to the effect which it has had in degrading prisoners and in plunging them further into crime, or to the question whether the fine and imprisonment do not fall more heavily on a criminal's wife and children than on himself. I have in mind more far-reaching questions. Does the punishment deter? Do we deal with criminals on proper principles?[3]

The source of better answers to these questions which our project indicates was also pointed out some years ago by the sociologist Vold:

Serious research needs the support of regular budgets and a stable, skilled group of research workers. That seems to be the principal next requirement, and the response must come, first of all, from top-level responsible administrators. When basic research gets budgetary support, as well as lip service, from those in control of budgets, several new pages may be turned in the still-to-be-written chapter on how to increase the proportion of inmates rehabilitated, or reformed, as a result of prison experience.[4]

As indicated in chapter 1, the project reported in this volume has been both a part and a stimulant of a research movement in corrections. Our report offers some chapters on how to increase the reformation of felons. There are many more chapters which this research movement in corrections still must write.

---

[3] Quoted by Frankfurter in his foreword to Sheldon and Eleanor T. Glueck, *After-Conduct of Discharged Offenders* (London, Macmillan, 1945), pp. 7-8.

[4] George B. Vold, "Does the Prison Reform?", *Annals of the American Academy of Political and Social Science*, 293 (May 1954), 50.

APPENDIXES

APPENDIX A

Some General Observations on the Research
Methods Employed in This Project

In reporting and interpreting our research findings, this book discussed details of investigative procedure only to the extent necessary to make the findings understandable. For readers interested in extending our research, or in making a technical evaluation of it from a methodological standpoint, the notes and appendixes provide further details on research methods and on the samples used. The appendixes also include our evaluation of the methods we employed, and some suggestions for those who may wish to continue such research.

The first appendix deals with some general methodological policies guiding all or most of our efforts. Subsequent appendixes present details on separate components of the project research.

RANGE OF PROBLEMS STUDIED

In the history of our project (outlined in chapter 1), an early choice had to be made between limiting the research to a few problems studied very intensively or extending our inquiries to many aspects of prisons and parole. The latter choice was made, despite some concern that our efforts might thereby be spread too thinly. It was felt that in this relatively early stage of correctional research it was desirable to explore many problems, and to employ a variety of procedures, so as to secure evidence on the relative fruitfulness of each procedure, and to assess the prospects of useful knowledge from investigations of many problems.

This broad range in our inquiry comes from the fact that our project was proposed by the Bureau of Prisons rather than by a university. Normally a university staff member would not have the temerity to expect the freedom that we enjoyed in wandering through all corners of prisons and parole agencies, and taking almost as much of the time of staff and inmates as we desired. Our research goal was conceived by Mr. Bennett, Dr. Sayre, and Mr. Loveland essentially as that of getting as much knowledge that would be helpful for practitioners in prisons and parole as funds and time permitted. Our interest in stimulating experimental change in practice, rather than just describing and interpreting the *status quo,* also prompted much meandering into tangential inquiry. Such initial sponsorship and continuing orientation made the project develop into a continuing series of

517

probes. New explorations into the possibility of procuring more adequate knowledge than that now available for guiding some correctional policy decision or allocation of resources were repeatedly begun.

While the major components of the research were set forth in the original proposal, the size of our investment in each operation, and much of their specific direction, were modified as obstacles were encountered or when new opportunities seemed to be opening. Problems encountered in the separate major components of our research are detailed in the appendixes that follow, together with suggestions on how they may be resolved more easily by others, on the basis of our experience.

In spite of the foregoing remarks, our advice in retrospect is that applied researchers serving a correctional agency should guard closely against over-extension of research operations. The dedicated investigator, anxious to be of value to his clients, is continually tempted to probe into more and more areas. This occurs because he observes the many problems and issues on which administrators must act without strong evidence as to the results of their pursuing one alternative rather than another.

From their graduate theses on, researchers repeatedly must guard against confusing a research project with a career. It is easy to extend any project to the point where it cannot readily be terminated. This has repeatedly occurred in other correctional research projects, both in universities and in correctional agencies. We frequently drifted close to this condition. It is necessary to summarize periodically the conclusions warranted at a given point in time, and to report them to others, even though the researcher would prefer to gather more adequate evidence. Such desires on the part of the researcher can best be expressed by qualifying the presentation of results appropriately. Only a report of findings after a given investment of scarce resources can justify decision, by the original researcher or others, on further investment.

An additional problem in applied research is that of determining the extent to which the investigator should concentrate his attention on abstract or theoretical problems—so-called "basic" research and theory—and the extent to which he should try to gather evidence bearing only on specific practical decisions of administrators. In our project, we have ranged from fairly abstract criminological investigations—such as our study of crime, age, and employment—to very specific questions, such as the size of gratuity payments and the type of clothing issued to prisoners at release.

In criminology, as in the behavioral sciences generally, preoccupation with "grand theory" yields only verbal representations of the world, in which an almost infinite variation of metaphor is possible. Conversely, so-called "abstracted empiricism," concerned with isolated questions as to how many and how much in a given place (like the population counting to which "research" is confined in many correctional agencies), becomes sterile until it is addressed to broad policy issues or theoretical questions of importance in directing correctional activities. The growth of a science of corrections or of any other type of science requires that men move from one level of abstraction to another. We have tried to do that in this project, through integrating specific facts by inductions of abstract principle, and through testing general ideas by making more precise observations than those on which the ideas previously were based.

OPINIONS VERSUS OBSERVATIONS AS DATA FOR CORRECTIONAL RESEARCH

Since the basic problem of this project is to find out how various prison and parole operations affect the prospects of further criminality by felons, one might say that we are trying to penetrate the minds of the felons in order to learn how they react to their correctional experience. What goes on in the mind of an individual, however, is a purely private matter. It cannot be observed directly but can only be inferred from its outward manifestations as behavior.

If it were possible, we would prefer to have our data consist of systematic observations of behavior, such as a log of criminal activity, work patterns, and use of leisure time by offenders. An ideal set of observations also would include recordings of the conversations of offenders with each other and with noncriminal persons. But such observations rarely are feasible on a systematic basis, and even then are difficult to reduce to concise summaries. Therefore, one must be content with indexes of behavior one would prefer to observe directly. Criminal activity, for example, can only be known to the extent that it is described in the official record of convictions or by informal admission of offenders, both of which are necessarily incomplete. To some extent, absence of criminal activity can be inferred from presence of verified work or school record, and other indexes of legitimate activity, but even here we know only what is recorded in official records or what will be admitted in interviews or questionnaires. These are limitations not only of research but of official action by correctional agencies. They rely on the best evidence available in making decisions affecting the liberties of individuals, but the best, unfortunately, is never as good as might be desired.

The available records frequently are limited in value for research purposes by the fact that they were not designed for research. They do not always cover the same areas for each case, nor do they investigate all of the questions that arise when we try to interpret prison and parole experience. Therefore, our project has often had to supplement official records with direct inquiries of the offenders regarding their recollections of past experiences and their attitudes, opinions, and expectations.

Inmate and staff reports as sources of information obviously have many defects. People are inclined to tell a listener that which they believe he would like to hear. In a correctional situation, the offenders may be oriented to making a good impression, so as to improve their prospects for freedom. Our researchers sometimes were assumed to be correctional staff by the prisoners or parolees, and occasionally they were suspected of being F.B.I. men. However, it is believed that we usually were successful in making clear our detachment from any action agencies, our objectivity, and the confidentiality of any information given to us.

We have vigorously maintained concern for confidentiality, which is why all of our case material is identified only by pseudonyms or case numbers. Both in the prisons and in the probation offices, our researchers were successful in establishing that they merited trust by the prisoners, the releasees, and the staff. This was evident in the frequency with which our researchers were advised of contraband or somewhat illegal activity, or of dissension, discontent, or routine "gripes." Fortunately, we were not expected to be informers by top staff, for that would have destroyed our ability to provide reliable information. At the same time, we were able to interview staff, prisoners, or parolees freely, and were given access to official files and records.

In administering questionnaires for the Prison Panel Supplement Study, we deliberately specified that the subjects were not to give us their names or their prison registry numbers. We wanted their frank opinions, and did not want to have anything in our records which would identify them. This has advantages and disadvantages from a research standpoint, which are discussed in Appendix E, on the Prison Panel Supplement Study.

Despite all of the foregoing, there certainly is likely to be much misinformation in all of our data. Error is inevitable, due both to some deliberate misrepresentation by subjects and to limitations in their own knowledge of the most accurate answers to some of our questions, as well as to ambiguity in our questions.

All of these limitations can be offset, to a large extent, by two types of methodological strategy which we have continuously pursued. One is the strategy of *comparison,* and the other is the strategy of *redundancy*.

Our conclusions rarely are based on the responses of one group of research subjects. They depend, instead, on comparison of responses, elicited in the same way from different samples of subjects, or from the same subjects in different times or situations. Assuming that the verbal expressions of opinion or attitude might not be completely accurate representations of what goes on in the minds of the separate individuals studied, we sought comparisons of these expressions by persons in different correctional situations, at different times, or by men with different attributes, such as age or criminal record. Granting some error in each separate observation, comparisons still are meaningful if we can assume that the error is of similar proportion in each group. If this assumption is valid, comparisons of verbal expressions may still accurately indicate the relatively greater or lesser existence of a particular trait in one group compared to another.

The strategy of redundancy directed us to seek a number of independent indexes of the same phenomenon, such as data on the same issue from different component studies of the project and from studies reported in the research literature. Knowledge in the complex and elusive fields that must be comprehended to know the impact of correctional operations necessarily is imperfect. We have simply attempted to arrive at the most adequate knowledge possible for us at this time, by comparing imperfect knowledge of many types, to seek strains of consistency.

A final note should be made regarding the use of statistical and case-study data. People often feel that they can understand the effectiveness of a correctional experience adequately only by getting a feeling for the nature of its impact on a particular person. Certainly, a subjective picture of an individual's feelings can give us a more vivid and detailed picture of a correctional operation than numbers provide. More important, case data highlights the dramatic, and helps us conceive of new dimensions to a problem, and new hypotheses on it.

The difficulty with case data is that one can generalize from a single case to other cases only if one knows how representative one case is of the others. What one usually finds is that the diversity and complexity of individuals, and the imperfection of knowledge, are such that no clear consistency is found in even a few cases. The only reliable conclusions, therefore, are broad statistical generalizations on the distribution of phenomena in many cases, expressed in terms of greater or lesser frequency, increases or decreases, or correlations between phenomena. What we have sought, therefore, has been a mixture of cases which *illustrate* problems with which we have been concerned and statistics which more adequately *demonstrate* what general conclusions are justifiable.

TESTS OF SIGNIFICANCE AND GENERALIZATIONS FROM FINDINGS

The samples of prisoners, parolees, or correctional staff from which our data were collected certainly were not random samples of the entire American correctional population to whom we may wish to extend our generalizations. An effort was made to procure the most representative samples possible with the means available, but a variety of limitations impinged upon these efforts. These limitations are indicated in the following appendixes, which deal with the sampling in our major separate studies.

When a sample is not randomly selected from the universe to which conclusions are addressed, statistical tests of significance may not be valid bases for generalizing from the research results. Errors in generalization

also arise from the limited reliability and validity of our indexes of subjective feeling or thought, as already indicated. Our main solution for such
inevitable deficiencies is in redundancy. We have tried to procure a variety
of independent answers to the same questions from many samples and situations, and by different types of information. When several independent
measures consistently support a given conclusion, we generally have considered this to be stronger evidence of how dependable the conclusion may
be than any separate statistical tests of significance.

It should also be noted that for policy decisions in corrections, the degree
of a relationship may be much more important than its sampling significance.
A small difference which would be statistically significant in a large sample
may not be of appreciable importance from a policy standpoint. On the
other hand, a larger difference, though validated by only a small sample,
may be of much concern for policy.

In conclusion, our approach on statistical tests of sampling significance
has been that such tests should only be a minimum requirement before one
generalizes with confidence from any statistical findings. We have presented
statistical tests of significance and statistical measures of relationship wherever it appeared that they might be of interest to some readers. We generally
cite only those tests that indicate less than 5 per cent probability of chance
occurrence. Significance tests should not be stressed as the major source
of confidence in a conclusion from this study, because most of the tests of
sampling significance make assumptions that the samples are randomly
drawn from all cases to which the conclusions will be applied. Although
some of our samples are randomly drawn from their larger sources, such
as the 10 per cent sample of 1956 releasees, variation in availability of
different subjects greatly affected our selection of other samples, notably
in the Postrelease Panel Study. These sources of bias are indicated in the
remaining appendixes, and they should be taken into account in assessing
the conclusions. Indeed, these limitations generally have been pointed out
in the course of our presentation of findings.

Even those samples that were randomly procured from all cases of the
type being studied represent randomly only the federal offenders at a particular time. Therefore, conclusions drawn from them may not be completely
representative of federal offenders at other times, or of state offenders to
whom one may wish to extend our conclusions. As Table A.1 shows, federal offenders include a smaller proportion of homicide cases, sex offenders,
assault cases, and burglars than state prisoners. The federal prisons, however, have a much higher proportion of auto thieves and of "other" offense
cases than are listed for state prisons. The "other" crimes include many
distinctly federal offenses, such as violation of immigration restrictions and
illegal liquor dealing ("moonshine" cases). As is indicated in Tables B.1,
C.2, D.1, and E.1 of the subsequent appendixes, as well as Table 3.4 of

TABLE A.1 Offense and Average Time Served (in Months) of Federal and State Felony Prisoners Released During 1960 for the First Release on Their Sentence

Offense	FEDERAL PRISONERS			STATE PRISONERS		
	Number	Per cent of total	Average months served	Number	Per cent of total	Average months served
Murder	14	0.1	111.0	1,668	2.6	121.4
Manslaughter	11	0.1	30.8	1,839	2.8	37.4
Robbery	229	2.0	56.1	6,915	10.6	42.4
Aggravated assault	62	0.5	27.1	3,660	5.6	25.0
Burglary	192	1.7	26.2	17,569	26.9	24.6
Theft, except auto	1,213	10.6	16.2	9,352	14.3	19.8
Auto theft	2,847	25.0	20.6	3,115	4.8	21.3
Embezzlement and fraud	712	6.2	11.7	1,450	2.2	16.7
Forgery	1,737	15.2	16.9	8,022	12.3	20.3
Rape	28	0.2	63.6	1,881	2.9	44.8
Other sex offenses	176	1.5	20.5	1,627	2.5	35.5
Drug laws	909	8.0	38.3	2,760	4.2	31.3
Weapons	57	0.5	21.2	345	0.5	22.4
Escape	38	0.3	20.6	1,103	1.7	18.5
Other	3,182	27.9	11.0	3,896	6.0	18.1
All first releasees	11,407	100.0	18.8	65,202	100.0	28.4

SOURCE: National Prisoner Statistics, *Prisoners Released from State and Federal Institutions, 1960* (Washington, U. S. Bureau of Prisons, 1963), Table 3, pp. 15–18. Note: Federal figures are based only on prisoners sentenced by civil courts; they exclude 153 first releasees sentenced by military courts-martial. State figures exclude New Jersey and Alaska; they include the other 48 states and the District of Columbia.

chapter 3, our federal samples were somewhat more similar to state prison populations than the cross-section of federal releasees covered in Table A.1. This is primarily because our samples did not include many of the short-term Mexican border violators now concentrated in federal prisons of the Southwest.

It should also be noted that nonfederal prisoners differ considerably from one state to the next as a function of variations in law and in population characteristics of the states. For example, while the federal prisoners generally serve more briefly, on the average, than do state prisoners, inmates of seven states (Maine, Vermont, Wisconsin, South Dakota, Maryland, Montana, and Wyoming) serve more briefly than do federal prisoners. All major variations in inmate characteristics, prison conditions, and release circumstances may somewhat limit the extent to which one can generalize from our findings to any other specific system. The greatest source of confidence in generalization comes from consistent findings for many prison or parole populations. That is why this book has cited comparable data from studies at other times or with other samples, wherever possible.

What we have attempted to report throughout is the most adequate knowledge obtainable, at this time, on the problems with which we deal. An awareness of the limitations in this knowledge should stimulate and direct continuous efforts to make it more perfect.

The Prison Panel Study

In the first meeting of our Advisory Board, in December 1958, J. Douglas Grant, of the California Department of Corrections, likened research on the effectiveness of correctional operations to research on the effects of a mysterious machine in a large black box. There are several ways of going about such research, he suggested. One approach is to compare the things that go into the box with those that come out. This is represented in our project by the effort to statistically relate postrelease information on prisoners to data on their admission characteristics. Another approach is to crawl into the box to see what goes on there. This is represented by the Prison Panel Study.

PROCEDURES

Although inspired by the impressionistic essays of sociologists on the prison social world cited in chapters 5 and 6, our study sought somewhat more objective statistical data than prevailed at that time in sociological literature. For this purpose, we planned to conduct systematic interviews with inmates at various stages in their prison experience. Late in 1958 we sent one research employee into each of five federal prisons. Two were men who had just received the Ph.D. in sociology and three were advanced graduate students in sociology. Four of the five had previous experience working in prisons, ranging from a few months to over a year. All had completed some academic study in criminology and penology.

At the time this research staff was entering the prisons, we completed the first draft of a Guide for Prison Researchers, which included a set of interview forms and instructions for their use, to be tried out on "pretest" cases. The questions on the forms often called for a narrative response, with the interviewer reformulating or supplementing the questions whenever the response seemed unclear or incomplete. The findings were reported on ten pages of form, covering both the interview and a check through the institution files on the inmate. These ten pages were to be supplemented by narrative accounts dictated by the researcher from notes beyond those which he could record on the form. The form and the guide were repeatedly revised according to our analysis of the inmate response which they were eliciting, and on the basis of suggestions from many sources. After pretests with several draft forms, a standard interview form was adopted in

February 1959. This form included a combination of multiple choice questions and other questions answered by brief narrative remarks.

In July 1959, when we had developed classifications of the most frequent narrative responses, we introduced a new form for the two groups of interviews still to be conducted (sixth-month and near-release). In the new forms the most common narrative responses were summarized on the form for the interviewer to check, rather than write out verbatim. He still recorded fully any response not immediately falling into one of the standard categories. This saved writing, and it also forced all interviewers to probe for an answer of at least the level of specificity indicated by the cited responses, thus countering some tendency of interviewers to accept responses too vague to be meaningful. We also dropped a few questions at this time and added a few others, but most were unchanged.

In addition to the foregoing, for all interviews we had a precoded form for summarizing from the prison files on the inmate interviewed.

By a "panel" we refer to a group of prisoners at a given stage of their prison term whom we contacted one or more times to find out their current experiences and thoughts. We had three panels, which we labeled the Entrance, Midterm, and Near-Release Panels. All members of the entrance panel were to be interviewed during their first week in prison, and again at the end of six months. It was later decided to try to interview half of them also during their fourth month in prison. The midterm panel was defined as inmates with sentences of thirty months or longer with a year served and a year still to be served before the expected release date. The near-release panel was to consist of inmates with a date of expected release already determined and not more than three months hence. Midterm and near-release panels were to be interviewed only once.

Table B.1 indicates those attributes on which the panels differ most, together with differences between the original entrance panel and those of its members available for the reinterviews. Our original target was 250 cases in each panel, fifty from each of the five prisons. The decline in number of cases on the successive interviews with the entrance panel was due to several factors. As indicated, the fourth-month interview was intended to be for only half the sample, but we were getting behind schedule before all of these could be completed. The main reason for a quarter of those interviewed in their first week in prison not being reinterviewed in their sixth month was their transfer to other prisons in the federal system in this period, but a few were lost because of their receiving early paroles on short sentences, and four cases at two different institutions remained to be interviewed when our interviewers had terminated their period of employment.

The purpose of reinterviewing the entrance panel and of selecting the other two panels on the basis of the proportion of their prison term served

TABLE B.1   Attributes on Which the Prison Panels Differ Most

Attribute	ENTRANCE PANEL			MID-TERM PANEL	NEAR-RELEASE PANEL	ALL CASES
	First-week interview	Fourth-month interview	Sixth-month interview			
Number of cases	283	119	206	281	248	1137
Median time served when interviewed	5.1 days	3.8 mos.	6.3 mos.	19.9 mos.	16.5 mos.	7.0 mos.
Sentence:						
Two years or less	35%	37%	35%	0%	*40%*[a]	28%
Over 2 through 4 years	20%	19%	19%	4%	17%	15%
Over 4 through 7 years	12%	11%	12%	*31%*	9%	16%
Over 7 years	7%	8%	8%	*36%*	8%	15%
Youth corrections act (60 days to 6 years)	20%	22%	21%	27%	18%	22%
Until age 21 (Juv. Del. Act)	5%	3%	4%	2%	*7%*	4%
Primary offense:						
Vehicle theft	42%	*43%*	40%	31%	38%	38%
Narcotics offense	11%	11%	11%	*31%*	7%	15%
Burglary or larceny	9%	13%	9%	6%	*15%*	10%
Robbery or kidnapping	4%	3%	4%	*13%*	4%	6%
Liquor offense	*9%*	8%	*9%*	(½%)	6%	6%
Forgery, fraud, income tax, and counterfeiting	*15%*	13%	*15%*	6%	*15%*	13%
Other offenses	11%	9%	12%	13%	*15%*	12%
Most serious prior commitment:						
None, or arrests and fines	21%	20%	19%	22%	*24%*	21%
Jail and/or probation	35%	37%	36%	36%	*41%*	37%
Reformatory or training school	12%	12%	13%	*19%*	13%	14%
Penitentiary	*32%*	31%	31%	22%	22%	27%
Median duration of longest job	1.0 yr.	1.0 yr.	11.5 mos.	11.2 mos.	1.4 yrs.	1.1 yrs.
Per cent nonwhite	32%	35%	35%	*42%*	34%	35%
Per cent never married	46%	43%	45%	*57%*	51%	49%

[a] Italics indicate the highest percentage on a line.

was to permit inferences regarding change during the course of imprisonment. This is achieved by comparing responses at different stages of the prison experience. It is apparent from Table B.1 that the midterm panel is too different from the other panels to consider it as an intermediate stage between the entrance and the near-release panel, except for inmates with sentences of over four years. The median near-release panel case had served less time than the median midterm panel case, although the median time until release for the near-release panel was only 0.9 months.

It should be noted that in both the prison and the probation office operations of this project, greater sampling restrictions than those ultimately employed were originally planned, but were abandoned when they resulted in too few cases being available at certain times or locations to keep the researchers occupied and to assure an adequate number of cases being seen before the end of our field work time. The major problem was that the definition of a sample in terms of any inmate attributes for the entire panel study yielded cases at certain institutions more readily than at others, so that we reverted ultimately to procuring a cross-section of all inmates at each location at each specified stage of their prison term.

It is believed that all four of our panels are representative of that population of the five prisons which fit the specifications of our selection instructions. This is because the prisoners interviewed were either complete samples or were selected by shuffling index cards for all inmates who fitted our stage-of-imprisonment specifications. Only nine interview refusals were reported, in contrast with 1137 interviews completed. There are individual questions on which some inmates gave answers which might be considered as avoiding the question. This may sometimes be more of an index of the inadequacy of the question than of noncooperation in the respondents. At any rate, in such cases we report the number who respond in this fashion, and sometimes the distribution of such answers is of interest. The methodological problem in this research is to advance the scientific adequacy of our knowledge beyond that achieved by penological literature or by expert opinion which conveys the author's impressions from his own experience or from his conversations with those inmates who are more articulate than others (and for this reason, probably are atypical). Explicating procedures, applying them systematically, and reporting the responses fully are necessary for the growth of scientific knowledge, for only then can findings be evaluated in terms of the procedures by which they were procured, and only then can one systematically improve procedures.

Table B.1 indicates that in contrast to the deviation of the midterm panel, the three interview groups of the entrance panel and the inmates of the near-release panel are fairly similar. However, the near-release group includes a somewhat larger proportion of short-term offenders, with less serious prior commitments. This is because the federal prisons were in the process of an overall shift in inmate characteristics to longer-term and more serious offenders. For example, for all federal institutions during the fiscal year ending June 30, 1959, the average sentence of inmates released was 26 months, but the average sentence of inmates received was 30.6 months.[1] This trend, found also in state prisons, reflects a combination of increased use of probation rather than short prison sentences for lesser offenders, and an increased use of extremely long prison sentences for narcotics offenders.

Table B.2 summarizes attributes on which the panels were most similar. It will be seen that even here the midterm panel is the most deviant from the others in being younger at admission and at first arrest, consistent with their higher prior reformatory and training-school record shown in Table B.1. However, these age differences are not great, and with respect to prior

[1] U. S. Dept. of Justice, *Federal Prisons 1959*, pp. 56, 64.

TABLE B.2   Attributes on Which the Panels Are Most Similar

| Attribute | ENTRANCE PANEL | | | MID-TERM PANEL | NEAR-RELEASE PANEL | ALL CASES |
	First-week interview	Fourth-month interview	Sixth-month interview			
Median age at admission (in years)	26.6	26.9	26.5	24.0	26.0	25.9
Median age at first arrest (in years)	18.7	18.5	18.7	17.9	17.8	18.4
Per cent with no prior confinement	32.5	31.9	29.1	28.5	32.7	30.9
Per cent for whom last employment was unskilled	50.5	50.4	49.5	49.5	47.6	49.4
Per cent for whom drinking was reported as a problem	29.0	32.8	30.1	28.1	30.6	29.8

unskilled work record, drinking problems, or proportion of first confinement cases the panels are highly similar.

Our interviewers were stationed in the prisons for three to four months, interviewing returned violators and pretesting our early panel interview forms, before the modification of these forms was terminated. By this time our interviewers had been tested by the prisoners and found trustworthy and had in other respects acquired a good reputation among the inmates. It is believed that the level of rapport achieved in almost all of the subsequent interviews was high, and that frank responses were elicited. Evidence of this was the frequency with which our researchers were told about things done in and out of prison which, if related to authorities, would have gotten the respondents into difficulties. A partial check on reliability was provided by having each researcher make a brief trip to interview at prisons other than that in which he was stationed, so that sixty inmates of the midterm panel could be reinterviewed by another researcher approximately three months after their first interview. This provided evidence on consistency of response with different interviewers over a short period in the middle of long sentences, when response should be most stable. (These reinterviews and over eighty pretest interviews are not counted in our 1137 interviews.)

One of the problems that arose in planning to interview the entrance panel on three successive occasions was whether a "response set" would be created by each inquiry, whereby the respondent would feel committed to answer consistently if asked the same question later, even if his views had changed. It was even conceivable that each assertion to us would constitute a "treatment," which would reduce the inmate's possible change.

It was possible for us to test for the existence of a response set since of those who received the sixth-month reinterview only about half had received the fourth-month interview. One question, fairly reliable on midterm panel reinterviews, which provides a good test item is: "What do you now think about your sentence; do you think it is fair or unfair?" Of ninety-seven entrance panel inmates interviewed only in the first week and sixth month, 28 per cent gave a response at the sixth month different from that given in the first week. Of 109 inmates interviewed in the first week, fourth month, and sixth month, only 22 per cent gave a response at the sixth month different from that given in the first week. This difference is in the direction of a response set, but it is not large enough to be significant statistically or to warrant much concern when considering major differences between first and subsequent interviews with the same subjects. On questions for which the answers included more than two alternatives, the evidence of a response set was much less.

THE FIVE PRISONS STUDIED

For the benefit of readers of this report who are not familiar with the five federal prisons in which we did our research, the following is a brief description of each institution as of 1959, when our interviews were conducted:

LEAVENWORTH is a high-security penitentiary housing about 2500 inmates. Established in 1895, it has somewhat diverse buildings of various ages and a high masonry wall. Most of the inmate housing is of the inside cellblock variety connected together in a huge main building which forms part of the wall. The institution is used predominantly for advanced offenders believed to be tractable but requiring secure custody. Average sentence is over nine years and average age is thirty-nine, with a large range around these averages. With Atlanta, this represents the highest security level in the federal system apart from the small "super-security" institution at Alcatraz. Over a third of the inmates are employed in five large prison industry installations (shoes, brushes, furniture, clothing, and printing). These are very efficiently operated, on a production-line basis, as is indicated by their net profit of over a million dollars per year. It also has a large farm, and an inmate school provides many correspondence and evening courses.

TERRE HAUTE is a medium-security penitentiary completed in 1940 and generally housing somewhat over 1300 inmates. Its buildings, mostly two-story, are connected together in a symmetrical telephone-pole design. It has inside and outside cell structures with over 600 single cells, the rest of the population having dormitory housing. The entire plant, except for some farm and maintenance buildings, is surrounded by a high double security fence. Sentences are very diverse, with the average about five years. Over 300 men are employed in industry, notably a large textile mill and a furniture renovation shop, and it has varied other work and training programs, including a large farm.

MILAN is one of the small prisons which the federal system calls a "correctional institution." It consists primarily of a square two-story building so constructed as to enclose completely a square inside courtyard. A small two-story inside cellblock juts into the courtyard on one side, with the rest of the inmates housed in ten small dormitory rooms in the main structure. In these rooms, a wire mesh interior wall parallel with the outer wall of the building creates a corridor from which the interior of the rooms may be observed. The institution population generally is just under 700, and two-thirds Negro. A majority of the latter serve narcotics offense sentences which range from two to five years in length, and from which parole is prohibited. However, a fifth of the population has sentences of a year or less, and over a quarter have sentences of under two years. About 150 inmates are employed in industry, at metal work. It also has a farm and varied education and vocational training programs.

CHILLICOTHE, the federal response to the reformatory movement, was built in 1925, in the "bigger-the-better" era. It holds about 1300 inmates in somewhat diverse separate structures strung out in a line about a quarter-mile long. These are set in the middle of a rectangular compound of seventy-two acres, which provides extensive grounds for athletics within the surrounding security fence. A separately fenced adjoining compound holds industry, powerhouse, and vocational training buildings. The average sentence is about three and one-half years, but a third have Youth Correction Act sentences, which permit parole between sixty days and four years. The average age of the inmates is about twenty, with over 90 per cent under twenty-five. About two-thirds are committed for interstate transportation of stolen autos. Inmate housing is in four cellblocks and six dormitory structures, which provide five gradations of custody ranging from maximum security to an honor unit where officers usually are not present. About 300 men work in prison industry, which operates a large chair factory and a foundry. The prisoners also operate a large farm and there is an extensive academic and vocational school program, notably an airplane mechanics school from which some inmates leave as Civil Aeronautics Authority licensed mechanics.

ASHLAND is a correctional institution opened in 1940, but designated as a youth center in 1954, upon implementation of the Federal Youth Correction Act. It houses about 500 inmates in an approximately telephone-pole arrangement of one- and two-story buildings. Housing is mostly of two types: long dormitory buildings with no major interior walls, and outside cell houses in which the cells have been converted to rooms with solid doors, generally unlocked. All the main buildings are in one compound, enclosed in a double security fence. The average age of the inmates is about eighteen, with none over twenty-one and four-fifths under twenty. About three-fourths of the inmates have Youth Correction Act sentences, and most of the remainder have Federal Juvenile Delinquency Act sentences. The latter generally started their minority term in the National Training School. Parolees from Ashland who violate are rarely returned to Ashland. About three-quarters of the inmates were committed for interstate transportation of stolen automobiles. Ashland has the highest concentration of treatment staff in relation to population of any of the prisons studied, including a full-time psychiatrist, a full-time psychologist, and a large education staff for this number of inmates. A furniture factory provides industrial employment, and there is also a farm.

Table B.3 summarizes attributes on which our samples from the five prisons differed most. As expected, at Leavenworth the median age of in-

TABLE B.3   Attributes of Inmates on Which Institutional Differences Were Greatest

Attribute	Leavenworth	Terre Haute	Milan	Chillicothe	Ashland
Median age at admission	34.4	28.2	32.6	21.5	18.8
Sentence:					
Youth Correction Act	0	0	2 (1%)	94 (39%)	151 (73%)
Fed. Juv. Delinquency Act	0	0	0	7 (3%)	42 (20%)
One year or less	2 (1%)	0	65 (28%)	9 (4%)	2 (1%)
Over one year through 18 months	2 (1%)	40 (20%)	28 (12%)	36 (15%)	4 (2%)
Over 18 months through two years	41 (16%)	24 (12%)	22 (10%)	42 (17%)	2 (1%)
Over two years through four years	47 (19%)	51 (25%)	40 (17%)	29 (12%)	7 (3%)
Over four years through seven years	59 (24%)	29 (14%)	75 (32%)	18 (7%)	0
Over seven years	100 (40%)	60 (29%)	0	7 (3%)	0
Primary offense:					
Vehicle theft for transportation	64 (25%)	46 (23%)	17 (7%)	152 (63%)	156 (75%)
Narcotics offense	65 (26%)	18 (9%)	85 (37%)	4 (2%)	0 —
Burglary or larceny	29 (12%)	16 (8%)	44 (19%)	7 (3%)	14 (7%)
Fraud, forgery or counterfeiting	40 (16%)	30 (15%)	21 (9%)	46 (19%)	9 (4%)
Robbery or kidnapping	40 (16%)	34 (17%)	3 (1%)	5 (2%)	4 (2%)
"Moonshine" offense	4 (2%)	7 (3%)	40 (17%)	9 (4%)	8 (4%)
All other offenses	9 (4%)	53 (26%)	22 (10%)	19 (8%)	17 (8%)
Total number of interviews (includes entrance panel re-interviews)	251	204	232	242	208

mates interviewed was highest and the sentences were longest. Terre Haute (the medium-security penitentiary), the Chillicothe reformatory, and the Ashland "youth correction institution" form a descending scale from Leavenworth in age and length of sentence of inmates. The Milan correctional institution does not fit in this scale well because it has a fairly equal mixture of two rather distinct types of population: short-term inmates from the Detroit area, including many theft and moonshine offenses, and long-term narcotics offenders. Median age at Milan, however, is almost as high as at Leavenworth. While we have analyzed some data by comparing the responses to our questions by inmates of different age, sentence, race, prior record, and marital status, the largest differences generally occur between the responses of inmates of different institutions. Therefore, most of our presentation is in terms of institutional differences.

Table B.4 shows some rather marked differences between prisons in

TABLE B.4   Some Attributes on Which Institution Components of Panels Vary

Attributes	Leavenworth	Terre Haute	Milan	Chillicothe	Ashland	All five prisons
Number of interviews, and per cent of total: Entrance panel:						
1st-week interview	60 (21%)	50 (18%)	60 (21%)	60 (21%)	53 (19%)	283 (100%)
4th-month interview	31 (26%)	17 (14%)	24 (20%)	30 (25%)	17 (14%)	119 (100%)
6th-month interview	43 (21%)	36 (17%)	41 (20%)	52 (25%)	34 (17%)	206 (100%)
Midterm panel	69 (25%)	53 (19%)	56 (20%)	50 (18%)	53 (19%)	281 (100%)
Near-release panel	49 (20%)	48 (19%)	50 (20%)	50 (20%)	51 (21%)	248 (100%)
All panel interviews	252 (22%)	204 (18%)	231 (20%)	242 (21%)	208 (18%)	1137 (100%)
Median time served when interviewed: Entrance panel:						
1st-week interview	4.9 days	2.8 days	5.1 days	4.4 days	7.8 days	5.1 days
4th-month interview	3.4 mos.	4.0 mos.	3.8 mos.	3.4 mos.	4.7 mos.	3.8 mos.
6th-month interview	6.7 mos.	7.2 mos.	6.2 mos.	6.7 mos.	6.0 mos.	6.3 mos.
Midterm panel	41 mos.	37 mos.	16 mos.	28 mos.	9 mos.	20 mos.
Near-release panel	38 mos.	22 mos.	9 mos.	15 mos.	16 mos.	17 mos.
Median time between date of near-release panel interview and date of expected release	1.7 mos.	0.5 mos.	1.2 mos.	1.1 mos.	0.9 mos.	0.9 mos.

the availability of subjects for the several interviews with the Entrance Panel. These reflect differences in length of sentence and rate of transfer of inmates at the separate prisons, supplemented by variations in the availability and efficiency of research personnel at critical times in the interviewing. Part of the differences in "efficiency," conceived as rate of completing interviews, was, of course, offset by differences in quality of interviewing.

Some of the diversity in both rate and quality of interviewing was a function of characteristics of the institution population and of their programs. At any rate, the proportion of the total interviews done at each of the five prisons deviates somewhat from 20 per cent. This deviation is most marked in the fourth-month reinterview of the entrance panel.

Inter-institutional differences on time served by our subjects in different panels are shown in Table B.4. As this indicates, we lagged somewhat from the planned schedules, so that the sixth-month interviews were mostly conducted in the seventh month and some of the fourth-month interviews were conducted in the fifth month.

Differences among prisons in time served at a particular interview were greatest for the midterm panel interview. The variations here reflect both inter-institutional differences in population and the definition of the midterm panel. At Milan, all but one of the midterm panel cases was serving a narcotics offense sentence; there were few other prisoners there who fit the selection stipulation of at least one year served and one year still to serve. At Ashland there were no inmates to whom one could fit these specifications, so special instructions were issued to select two midterm panels of Youth Correction Act cases there, half to be interviewed between their seventh and tenth month when awaiting a decision on whether they would be paroled that year, and half to be interviewed when they had served over ten months and had been advised that they were denied parole. However, few of the latter were available, so for the Ashland midterm panel we pooled all cases who were beyond the sixth month in time served and did not have an expected release date within three months. This makes Ashland have the only component of our midterm panel in which the subjects, in time served, are between the sixth-month interview group and the near-release panel.

The foregoing details of variation in panel attributes and in populations of separate prisons, as well as differences among the three interview groups of the entrance panel, affect the types of comparison and interpretation which one can make with our findings. We have reminded the reader of these matters wherever they seemed relevant to our discussion of the interview results.

Some further limitations of the Prison Panel Study are indicated in Appendix E, which explains our interest in undertaking the Prison Panel Supplement Study.

The Postrelease Panel Study

The Postrelease Panel Study was designed to procure information on the experiences of men in their first half-year out of prison. On the assumption that what happens to a man in these initial months may greatly affect his ultimate postrelease behavior, and because a major proportion of failures occur in this period, our objective was to make highly specific inquiries at frequent intervals. This was to minimize the extent to which our information on this period would be limited by the subject's inability to recollect details accurately. This contrasts with our study of the returned violators and successful releasees, where we sought an overall view of the total postrelease experience of two groups of men, based primarily on one contact with them at the end of the period in which we were interested.

Federal parolees and mandatory releasees are required to report to their supervising U. S. Probation Officer on the first weekday after their arrival from prison to their release destination. After this first visit to the probation office they normally are required to report monthly, but they may sometimes be instructed to report more frequently, especially when they are just out of prison and unemployed. Alternatively, when they are employed or for other reasons a trip to the probation office seems a hardship, they may be excused from reporting in person. They then mail in reports, and perhaps telephone or see their probation officer when he visits them. However, being excused from reporting in person at least once a month is relatively infrequent during the first half-year out of prison if the releasee lives in the city where the probation office is located.

Our original plans were to procure a detailed picture of the initial experience which follows release from prison. This was to be done by interviewing men in their first week after release and monthly thereafter for six months. Our sample was to consist of at least 200 men who were to be: (a) released from the five federal prisons in which we conducted our 1958-59 field research; (b) scheduled for six months or more of supervision in five federal probation offices where we planned to have research staff in 1959-60. These plans were developed in consultation with the Chief U. S. Probation Officers of the cities involved, who met in October 1959 with our Advisory Board and reviewed our proposals in detail. Some misgivings were expressed regarding the extent to which the releasees would cooperate, and there also was evidence that a few of the line probation officers might not be highly cooperative, but the predominant opinion was that this undertaking could be conducted successfully, and that it should be undertaken.

Specifically, the proposed procedure was that the releasees would be told about the research, and would be introduced to our researcher by the first U. S. Probation Officer to whom they talked after their arrival from the prison. We could not compel these releasees to participate in our interviews, and both the probation officer and our researcher emphasized the independence of the research from the superivison authorities. We hoped to establish an atmosphere in which each releasee would wish to cooperate, and at the same time we wished neither to impair his relationship with his probation officer nor to have him identify our researcher with the probation office staff.

A number of problems developed in attempting to carry out our procedures as planned, and therefore modifications had to be made in our procedures. We were able to place staff in only four federal probation offices (Chicago, Detroit, Cleveland, and St. Louis), and it soon became apparent that we could approach our target of 200 cases only if we included all men released from any federal prison for six months or more of supervision by these offices. For a diversity of reasons, we were unable to achieve as regular a schedule of contact with the releasees as we desired, and also some releasees who fitted our sample specifications never were referred to our researchers. Sometimes the probation office staff simply forgot to refer the releasees to our researchers, and a few officers apparently were less persuasive than most in this referral, for refusals of releasees to cooperate were largely confined to men under supervision of these few officers. In addition, we lost contact with some releasees before we were finished with our series of interviews with them because they were excused by their officer from further monthly reporting (for sound supervision reasons, usually related to job conflicts or travel difficulties in their reporting to the probation office).

An appreciable number of the releasees themselves, even when they first expressed interest in the research interviews, ultimately neglected to see the researcher after seeing their probation officer. On the other hand, on many occasions a number of releasees reported to our researcher at once, and not all could wait to be interviewed. Also, men who had completed their reporting to the probation office to meet their parole supervision requirements often claimed they were too pressed for time to remain for the research interview, so we would try to arrange another time for them, not always succesfully. In an effort to maintain the projected schedule, field interviews were sometimes made by our staff, but their trips to see a releasee, generally in the evening, did not always result in their encountering the subjects and sometimes did not provide a satisfactory interview situation. Finally, we failed to maintain the planned schedule of interviews with some subjects because they were arrested, had absconded, were dead, or were incapacitated at the time they were supposed to report to the probation office. Because of all of these problems, a number of modifications had to be made in our sampling and interviewing plans after the study got under way.

After five months of work in Chicago (and one to three months less in the other three cities), the Postrelease Panel sample specifications were altered to include all releasees who reported to these offices to be under supervision for at least three months; and the number of interviews planned was reduced to six: one during the man's first week out of prison, and one every month thereafter, for five months. In addition, when a man missed a scheduled interview and was not contacted again until a month or more later, the forms for the interview which he missed were completed at this later contact by asking him retrospectively about his situation a month earlier; he also received the interview for which he was then due. We were able to fill in much information on events between interview sessions by consulting the releasee's supervision officer, and sometimes by talking to the releasee on the phone.

On each of our interview forms, special attention was given to a particular topic. For example: the form for the first interview inquired about initial job and residence arrangements; the forms for the second and fifth interviews asked about contacts with old and new friends since release; the fourth interview form asked about use of prison training in postrelease employment; the first and sixth interview forms asked about parole rule perceptions; and the fifth interview form probed extensively into family relationships. This variation was partly because some topics were more relevant at one time than at another, partly to keep the duration of the separate interviews within manageable limits, and partly to maintain interest in the interviews by varying them. Certain inquiries, especially those on attitudes, tend to elicit stereotyped responses if asked too often in the same way. However, questions about major expenditures and about changes in employment, income, and residence were asked at each interview. A terminal-interview form was devised for use normally at the sixth interview, but to be used also at the fourth or fifth interview if it appeared that we would not be able to contact the releasee again. This provided for the completion, at that time, of all of the special inquiries that we usually would make on each of the remaining interviews.

Because of the difficulties in interviewing releasees according to a planned schedule, but in a permissive relationship with them, what we call the "Effective" Postrelease Panel sample consists of only 145 men; it was limited to those with whom our interviews covered three or more months of immediate postprison experience. An additional forty-eight men, or 193 altogether, comprised our total Postrelease Panel Study sample; this includes every releasee whom we interviewed one or more times. A careful check of the records of the four probation offices where this study was conducted revealed that another forty-eight men fitted our sample specifications at the time they first reported for supervision but never got into our sample. Thus we gave a first interview to 193 of a possible 241, or 80 per cent of those eligible. We were able to interview only 145 men for three or more months after release; these comprise 75 per cent of those with whom we had at least one interview, but only 60 per cent of those eligible for our sample at the time they first reported to the probation office.

Of the forty-eight men who never got into our total sample, twenty-five were never referred to our research staff by their probation officers, eight clearly indicated that they did not wish to participate in any research interviews, eight reported only when our researcher was out of the office, three were not interviewed by one of our researchers because he anticipated that the expiration of their supervision period would be so soon after three months that they would not report for a postrelease span of three months or more, and for four cases we could not establish the reason for noninclusion in our sample.

Table C.1 provides a comparison of the interview record of those in the effective sample with the record of the remainder of the men in the total sample. These statistics reflect both our problems in contacting releasees and the measures we undertook to cope with these problems.

The largest loss of cases after the first interview, but before the three months needed for inclusion of a releasee in our effective sample, was from outright refusal of thirteen youths to come for further research interviews. Also, five youths apparently avoided further interviews (usually by persistent failure to keep appointments) without outright refusal. Another three, with short supervision periods, started to miss appointments when their date of discharge drew near, and six were not accessible for further interviews because their probation officer excused them from the regular obligation to report to him monthly at the office. These twenty-seven total over half of the forty-eight cases whom we discontinued interviewing before they were three months out of prison.

It is believed that the actual dynamics involved in cessation of participation in our interviews were similar in most of the cases described above. The primary strain on participation was their involvement in employment and leisure-time activities distant from the office. Under these circumstances, the visit to the office meant taking time off from work, and often getting a friend or relative to drive them down and wait until they were through reporting. Nonparticipation in further interviews thus stemmed more from increased involvement in noncriminal activities than from objection to the research interview in itself; those who were not pressed for time, particularly those who were less successfully integrated into new work and social life,

TABLE C.1 Interview Record of Those in "Effective" Postrelease Panel Study Sample, Compared with Record of the Remainder of the Total Sample

	Effective sample	Remainder of total sample
Number of cases	145	48
Terminal interview completed	88%	—
Reason for not completing terminal interview:		
Could not make last appointment but most information supplied	2%	—
Researcher erroneously administered five or six interviews in less than three months	—	8%
Transferred to another district not in research region	—	13%
Subject excused from further reporting to probation office	1%	13%
Subject clearly refused further cooperation	3%	27%
Subject apparently avoided further cooperation	1%	10%
Probation office supervision expired	3%	6%
Subject died	1%	2%
Subject arrested or absconded	1%	17%
Excused during psychiatric treatment	—	4%
Span of time from prison release to last interview:		
Only one interview	—	60%
Under three months	—	40%
Three months to under four months	17%	—
Four months to under five months	17%	—
Five months to under six months	33%	—
Six months to under seven months	15%	—
Seven months to under eight months	9%	—
Eight months to under nine months	7%	—
Nine months or more	2%	—
Median postrelease time to last interview	5.3 months	—
Number of interview forms completed in the interview:		
Six	88%	6%
Five	5%	2%
Four	3%	2%
Three	2%	17%
Two	2%	13%
One	—	60%
Average number of interview forms completed per case	5.7	1.9
Total number of interview forms completed	836	92
Number of separate interview sessions:		
Six	23%	—
Five	28%	2%
Four	20%	—
Three	20%	21%
Two	9%	15%
One	—	62%
Average number of separate interview sessions completed per case	4.4	1.6
Total number of interview sessions completed	636	79

seemed to enjoy the interviews and frequently volunteered extra time for them.

The remaining twenty-one of the forty-eight who failed to complete three postrelease months of interviewing after the first interview included the most immediately criminal or maladjusted cases. These were eight who were arrested or absconded, one whom it was considered psychiatrically inadvisable to involve further in our interviews when he was placed under treatment for paranoia, and one who voluntarily committed himself to the U. S. Public Health Service Hospital at Lexington, Kentucky—in consultation with his probation officer—when he felt overwhelmingly attracted back to narcotics. In addition, six men were allowed to transfer supervision to another judicial district, and one died, before we had three months of postrelease contact with them.

Normally, three postprison months in our sample meant completion of no more than four interview forms—one in the first week out of prison and one every month thereafter. However, a peculiar misunderstanding of the interview plan by one of our researchers led to his completing four to six of the interview forms in less than three months for four men. These men were required to report to the probation office once or twice a week as a special supervision requirement during their first few months out of prison, a common practice in all of the probation offices, especially when men are unemployed. There was a lag in sending the interview reports to Urbana, while items were checked by the researcher in the probation office, so that before we became aware of this misunderstanding, these cases became too confounded in timing to retain in the sample. The assorted difficulties discussed thus far account for the large variation indicated in Table C.1 in our contact with the Postrelease Panel subjects and in the number of interview forms we completed with them.

We repeated at each interview a systematic series of questions on each change in employment, income, and residence since the last interview, and recorded the date of each change. For example, we had a Job Acquisition Sheet for each new job, a Job Satisfaction Sheet for each job on which the releasee had been employed for over a week, a Job Termination Sheet for each job which the releasee left, and a Job Search Sheet for each period of unemployment. These sheets were each of a different color, and the interviewer at each session readily took as many of these sheets as he needed to cover every job or every period of unemployment that the releasee had since the preceding interview session.

This procedure and similar complete recording of residence changes make our economic and residence information fairly complete for the span of time from prison release to the last interview, regardless of the number of interview sessions held in this span. Dates of all changed circumstances with respect to job and home were recorded, so that we could tabulate the economic situation separately for each month after release, regardless of the dates of the interviews. Also, as previously mentioned, in cases where we thought it would be our last contact with a releasee, our researcher from the fourth interview on administered the questions not covering jobs, income, or residence, from all of the remaining interview forms. Sometimes, of course, we erred in assuming that there would be another interview session with a particular releasee before our researchers terminated their employment in the probation offices. Thus we completed the sixth or "terminal" interview form on only 88 per cent of our effective sample. However, we actually had six separate interview sessions with only 23 per cent of the sample.

Wherever responses to a particular question were not procured from all of the sample, this is indicated in a footnote to the table. Also, whenever we tabulate the responses to a question asked on only one interview form, we report the median time of the interview session at which the form was administered. This time is expressed in terms of months between the subject's release from prison and the interview.

Table C.2 provides a comparison, on several attributes, of the cases included in our effective sample, the remainder of the total sample, and the cases eligible for our sample at the time they reported to the probation office, but not included. On the whole, these three groups of releasees appear quite similar. The most marked differences are the higher proportion of auto thieves and of whites in the cases not included in our effective sample. The excluded cases also were somewhat younger than the included cases, and were more frequently on mandatory release rather than parole. Nevertheless, the differences do not appear to be sufficiently marked to suggest that major bias in our findings would result from them.

As indicated in chapter 19, much of the research which our project undertook could be performed more efficiently and adequately by correctional agencies. This is especially true of the Postrelease Panel Study. We pioneered in systematically tabulating the postrelease economic and residential experience of prisoners in detail that, as far as I have been able to determine, has never been attempted before. Because this effort probed the unknown, we persisted in it despite the difficulties which have been described in this appendix. It seemed better to gather this imperfect information than to leave conclusions in this area dependent on much more imperfect general impressions made without an effort at systematic tabulation. But these types of objective information on postrelease experiences of releasees could be gathered much more completely, and at less expense, by the supervising officers, if such data collection were directed and carefully supervised by their administrative superiors.

For a parole supervision staff to be concerned with promoting the employment of its parolees without knowing how many are employed is like a

TABLE C.2 Some Attributes of Our Effective Postrelease Panel Study Sample, of the Remainder of Our Total Sample, and of Those Eligibles Not in Our Total Sample

	Effective sample	Remainder of total sample	Eligibles not in total sample[a]
Number of cases	145	48	48
Median time served on sentence at release	24.8 mos.	31 mos.	—
Type of federal prison from which released:			
Youth institution	10%	6%	10%
Reformatory	12%	27%	24%
Correctional institutions and prison camps	26%	25%	10%
Medium-security penitentiary	21%	19%	16%
Maximum-security penitentiary	19%	13%	24%
Prison camp	3%	4%	—
Prison hospital	9%	6%	16%
Ethnic group:			
White	58%	65%	77%
Nonwhite	42%	35%	23%
Mode of release:			
Parole	64%	48%	58%
Mandatory release	36%	52%	42%
Most serious prior criminal record:			
None	12%	2%	—
Arrests or fines only	12%	17%	—
Probation only	11%	15%	—
Jail (or equivalent) and/or probation	23%	17%	—
Training school	12%	13%	—
Reformatory	5%	8%	—
Penitentiary	26%	29%	—
Primary offense:			
Auto theft	21%	46%	36%
Narcotics	18%	15%	18%
Burglary or larceny	17%	6%	15%
Robbery	10%	6%	21%
Forgery or fraud	19%	4%	6%
All other	16%	23%	3%
Median age at first arrest	18.9	16.9	
Median age at release	32.1	29.4	28.5
Per cent subsequent failure (new conviction for felony-like offense or parole violation warrant issued, as of January 1962).	20%	25%	—

[a] Information on the attributes of the cases eligible for our sample when first released, but not included in it, was derived from record books and cards in the probation offices. These did not have as much information on each case as that which we procured from the case files on the men in the total sample. The percentages in this column, therefore, are based only on the "Eligible but not included" cases for whom we had information on the attributes indicated, which on most items was for only thirty-eight of the forty-eight cases.

business operating without knowing the extent of its expenses or sales. Most officers actually log notes on the employment status and other objective conditions of the men whom they supervise. It would be a simple matter to develop standard forms for this, to permit routine statistical tabulation of the economic status of men under supervision in an office. This would be an invaluable barometer of problems to be anticipated because of economic difficulties, and long-term trends in the figures would indicate the extent of success or failure in meeting economic problems. To my knowledge, the California Youth Authority is the only correctional agency that has done this, and they have done it only recently.[1]

Much of the more subjective information which we gathered also is collected routinely by supervision officers, such as information on the relatives, new friends, and old friends with whom a releasee is in contact. Any information collected systematically can be tabulated periodically and can be related to subsequent behavior, so as to build a more scientific basis for correctional policies and programs. The supervising officers, because of their authoritative position, have the advantage of more regular contact with the releasees than our researchers could achieve. While their authoritative relationship impedes their procurement of some of the attitude responses which we collected, most of our inquiries covered items on which answers could have been gathered even more reliably by an appropriately trained and motivated supervising officer.

---

[1] See: Selden Menefee, *Employment Trends Among California Youth Authority Wards on Parole—1948-1962*, California Youth Authority Research Report No. 34 (Sacramento, January 16, 1963).

The Comparison of Returned Violators
with Successful Releasees

This study was modeled on the monumental work by Sheldon and Eleanor Glueck, *Unravelling Juvenile Delinquency.*[1] The Gluecks compared 500 institutionalized juvenile delinquents from Boston, Massachusetts, with 500 Boston youths with no known record of significant delinquency, who were matched with the delinquents by age, I.Q., national origin, and type of neighborhood. Our objective was to compare the prison and postrelease experiences of 300 federal offenders returned to prison for violation of the conditions of their release with 300 federal offenders who maintained satisfactory postrelease records. These two groups were to be matched, as closely as possible, by prerelease characteristics, in order to isolate prison and postrelease correlates of success and failure.

During 1958-59, when our staff were located in five federal prisons and conducted the Prison Panel Study described in Appendix B, they also interviewed and investigated returned violators. Anticipating future difficulties of travel to contact successful releasees matched with the violators by region, we included in the returned-violator sample only men who had been under supervision in the federal judicial districts of the midwest, immediately adjacent to the anticipated locations of our staff in federal probation offices. We also confined our sample of returned violators to men whose release had been from one of the five prisons in which we had staff located, for it was felt we could interpret their prison experience best in an institution which our staff would come to know well. Actually, men who violated parole from Ashland were not returned to that institution (most of them went to Chillicothe), so our 308 returned-violator interviews were *conducted* only in Chillicothe, Milan, Terre Haute, and Leavenworth. This violator sample comprised all prisoners fitting the foregoing selection requirements who were in these prisons during the period when our staff was there.

In 1959-60, when our researchers were in four federal probation offices (Chicago, St. Louis, Cleveland, and Detroit), we anticipated that they would interview successful releasees not only in these locations but also in the adjacent judicial districts, so as to cover the same areas as those from

[1] Sheldon and Eleanor Glueck, *Unravelling Juvenile Delinquency* (New York, Commonwealth Fund, 1950).

which the returned violators were drawn. For purposes of this study we defined "success" as not being returned to prison or convicted of a felony, for one of our interests, reported in chapter 4, was to explore the variation in behavior associated with such "success."

Our first task in the study of these success cases was to compile an inventory of all persons under supervision for over six months and with a total supervision period of a year or more from the five prisons and in the fifteen federal judicial districts from which our returned violators came. To match the successes with the returned violators, we classified all men in both groups by a five-digit code number indicating: (1) prison from which released; (2) age at release; (3) mode of release; (4) race; (5) prior penal commitment. There were five prisons, four categories of age and of prior commitment, and two categories of mode of release and of race. This made 320 combinations of the matching variables possible, but it was anticipated that fewer than this number of combinations would be found, due primarily to the homogeneity of inmates at each institution. For example, our 308 returned violators had only eighty-eight of these combinations of traits. We proposed to match the successful releasees with the returned violators by these trait combinations as closely as would prove feasible.

Before we had listed the successful releasees in all of the judicial districts, it became apparent that there would be problems in matching them with the returned violators as perfectly as we had hoped. The main difficulty was in finding enough successful releasees with as many prior penal commitments as the returned violators. Also, the preoccupation of our research personnel with the Postrelease Panel Study interviews at these probation offices limited their availability for the successful-releasee interviews. Therefore, early in 1960, when we had less than fifty successful-releasee interviews completed, we decided to accept into the successful-releasee sample any federal parolee or mandatory releasee under supervision for over a year who had been involved in a felony offense on at least one occasion prior to the offense for which he had last been imprisoned. It was anticipated that this would provide a sample in which the average successful releasee would have as extensive a prior criminal record as the average returned violator, so that as a minimum, their success could not be ascribed simply to less prior involvement in crime. In short, we hoped to bias the "success" sample against success when compared to the returned violators, and this precaution was about all of the matching effort in which we could indulge if we hoped to approximate 300 successful releasee interviews with the time and staff available, in the area to be covered.

The process of interviewing the successful releasees was extremely time-consuming. Our interviewers, first of all, had to go into the federal probation office to make lists of the men under supervision there who fit our sample specifications, and to abstract information on these men from the office files. They then had to arrange appointments for interviews with the releasees, generally through their supervising federal probation officer. Usually this was done by the officer's sending a letter to the releasee, sometimes a phone call was employed, and in many instances our staff went along on the officer's field trips, to be introduced to the releasee in this fashion. Often there was difficulty in arranging a time for the interview convenient for the releasee, and sometimes mutually agreed upon appointments were made which the releasee did not keep. Our staff were authorized to offer an interviewee two dollars for his time and expenses, or to buy him a meal, when this seemed appropriate. Actually, most of these successful releasees were extremely cooperative, but the fact that they could only be seen when they were not employed, and that many were in locations distant from our staff, made the rate at which we could complete these interviews slower than we originally had anticipated.

We averaged less than one successful releasee interview completed per man-day devoted to this enterprise, and we had to continue these interviews in 1960-61, when we no longer had staff outside of Urbana, Illinois. All of the interviews in Indiana, Kentucky, and Wisconsin, and most of those in Illinois, as well as a few in Missouri and Ohio, were completed by research assistants sent from Urbana. The fact that these men were graduate students also restricted our efforts, since it somewhat limited the days when they could be away from their campus classes. By spring of 1961 we had interviewed just about every federal releasee who fit our sample specifications in all of the federal judicial districts of Illinois, Indiana, and Kentucky, in the Eastern Wisconsin judicial district, in all of Ohio except the Cincinnati area, and in the St. Louis and Detroit metropolitan areas. This was a total of 250 releasees. At this point, time and staff limitations forced us to stop gathering further cases and to concentrate on the analysis of the material already collected.

As in all of our other work, our staff interviewing returned violators and successful releasees identified themselves with the University of Illinois, indicated that the project was financed by the Ford Foundation, explained that it was concerned with helping people to understand better the experiences of men who have come out of prison, and assured the subjects of confidentiality, particularly that their remarks to us would not be transmitted to prison or probation staff. In the prisons, where the returned-violator and prison panel studies were conducted, the inmates soon heard of our staff's trustworthiness and interest in them. By the time we interviewed the successful releasees in the free community, many of these men had been in the prisons when our interviewing was conducted there and knew of our favorable reputation; in addition, this group probably was more oriented to cooperation with authority than most. Most important, however, our interviewers became skilled listeners, and seemed to have no difficulty in gaining rapport and eliciting full and frank responses in almost all cases.

Table D.1 indicates the extent to which our successful-releasee and

TABLE D.1 Comparison of the Returned-Violator and Successful-Releasee Samples on Attributes Established Prior to Their Postrelease Experiences

Attribute	Returned violator	Successful releasee	Attribute	Returned violator	Successful releasee
Number of cases	308	250	Federal prison from which released:		
			Ashland Youth Inst.	22%	15%
Median age at first			Chillicothe Ref.	24%	20%
arrest (in years)	17.3	17.4	Milan Corr. Inst.	12%	4%
			Terre Haute Pen.	19%	15%
Most serious criminal record			Leavenworth Pen.	22%	24%
prior to last imprisonment:			Other fed. prison	—	22%
No prior record	7%	4%			
Arrest or fine only	14%	10%			
Probation	9%	10%	Type of federal prison		
Jail or training school, or both	23%	34%	from which released:		
Reformatory	15%	15%	Youth institution	22%	19%
Penitentiary	32%	28%	Reformatory	24%	22%
			Correctional inst.	12%	6%
Sentence on which released:			Medium-security pen.	19%	19%
Federal Youth Correction			Maximum-security pen.	22%	29%
Act (Duration 6 Years)	27%	27%	Prison hospital	—	4%
			Prison camp	—	1%
Median duration of non-YCA					
sentences (in months)	42	103	Judicial district to which released:		
Median number of months			Northern Illinois and		
served on sentence at release	25	33	Northern Indiana	17%	24%
			Eastern Illinois and		
Primary offense:			Southern Indiana	17%	10%
Auto theft	46%	27%	Southern Illinois and		
Narcotics	9%	12%	Eastern Missouri	6%	14%
Burglary	12%	12%	Eastern Michigan	15%	7%
Robbery	8%	22%	Western Michigan and		
Forgery or fraud	17%	10%	Eastern Wisconsin	7%	6%
All other offenses	9%	17%	Western Missouri and Kansas	11%	—
			Northern Ohio	9%	19%
Median age at release (in years)	26.4	29.8	Southern Ohio and Kentucky	19%	19%
Mode of release:			Marital status at release:		
Parole	63%	79%	Married	23%	26%
Mandatory release	37%	21%	Divorced	24%	24%
			Never married	53%	49%
			Per cent nonwhite	22%	26%

returned-violator samples were comparable, before they had their divergent postrelease experiences. It will be seen that prior to their last imprisonment, our two samples had relatively similar criminal records. However, on their last commitment, the successful cases more often had longer sentences than did the returned violators. This difference resulted from our selecting only successful releasees with one or more years of postrelease supervision, so that their "success" could become fairly well established, whereas we interviewed all returned violators, including some whose sentences would not have given them a full year of postrelease supervision. This selection process also is reflected in the somewhat different distribution of offenses in the two groups;

the successful-releasee group is especially high on robbery cases, which receive long sentences in the federal courts, while the returned violator group is especially high on auto-theft cases, which receive relatively shorter sentences in federal courts and have high violation rates. Nevertheless, the difference in months actually served in prison before release is not nearly as extreme as the difference in length of sentence; a larger proportion of the successful releasees than of the returned violators were seen as good risks at the prison and were released by parole (for which only one-third of the sentence need be served) before they became eligible for mandatory release. (In the federal system mandatory release, formerly called "conditional release," is release under the same conditions as parole, for all of the period of "good time" earned in prison, less 180 days.)

Our broadening of the successful-releasee sample in order to include everyone in the geographical areas that we could cover who would approximate the attributes of the returned violators made for some differences between these two groups in prison from which released and in the geographical region in which supervised. Nevertheless, the differences are not extreme. The larger proportion of successful releasees who were released from maximum-security penitentiaries is accounted for by their larger proportion of long sentences and slightly older median age. The two groups were quite similar also in racial composition and in marital status at release.

Since these were pioneering inquiries, particularly with the successful releasees, we felt it wise not to limit the interviews too greatly by highly specific questions formulated in advance. Although there were such questions, we also had broad inquiries, and we encouraged the subjects to give an account of their postrelease experiences in narrative form. This has furnished a wealth of fascinating case material, much of which is cited at scattered points in the text, particularly in chapter 4. The diversity of postrelease experience, and the retrospection over several years which the interviews covered, also militated against highly structured questions.

More studies of such ex-prisoners are desirable, for criminology has been too long biased by limiting its contact with criminals to the time when they are most accessible for research—when they are in prison. Future studies may find it expedient to focus their inquiries more sharply, and may be able to match success and failure cases more closely in preprison or prerelease attributes. Studies of this type, in a large state correctional system, would not have to cope with the wide geographical dispersion which characterizes any appreciable sample of federal offenders.

The Prison Panel Supplement Study

The Prison Panel Study, described in Appendix B, was extremely time-consuming. Counting the pretest interviews and reliability checks, well over 1200 separate interviews were conducted during 1958-59 by our men in five federal prisons. Some of our staff averaged about three hours per interview and others somewhat less than an hour, the difference being mainly in time spent putting the inmate at ease by casual conversation before, during, and after the interview. Regardless of the researcher's pace when actually talking to the respondents, the number of interviews which could be completed per day was limited by the need to minimize interference of the interviewing schedule with the orderly operation of the prison's routine activities. Allowance also had to be made for the time needed by each inmate to come from his place of assignment in the prison to the research office. Besides, our researchers required time to review their notes, to check prison files on the interviewees, and to write up the narrative sections of the interview reports. Accordingly, our staff generally could not finish more than three interviews per day, and they could not average even this many.

A second problem with the interviewing procedure was subjectivity. We could not be certain of the extent to which differences between our findings at various prisons were the result of differences between the inmates, and not of differences between the interviewers. This was more of a concern with the open-ended questions than with the structured questions. An advantage of using a questionnaire, rather than interviewing, is that all subjects answering a questionnaire have each question presented to them in the same form, and each alternative possible answer has the same probability of being recorded for each subject.

Despite the deficiencies of the interview technique from the standpoints of efficiency and objectivity, there are strong arguments for it from the standpoint of rapport, and hence, of validity. Our consultants in 1958 and early 1959, in planning the Prison Panel Study procedure, were Richard H. McCleery, Lloyd E. Ohlin, and Richard A. Cloward, all of whom were just completing their editing of the report on a joint seminar of seven social scientists concerned with the informal social organization of prisons.[1] They were especially sensitized to the barriers to communication between staff and inmates in prisons, and to the prospect that an outsider would not elicit

[1] Richard A. Cloward, et al., *Theoretical Studies in Social Organization of the Prison,* Pamphlet 15 (New York, Social Science Research Council, 1960).

frank responses from prisoners unless he first was able to "sell himself" to the inmate community through long and informal involvement with them. This intimate and informal interaction with the prisoners would also be necessary to sensitize researchers to subtleties in inmate expressions, relevant both to formulating questions and to interpreting responses. Of course, we were aware of this rapport problem, but the influence of the consultants was to bring this more sharply to our attention. Accordingly, we felt obliged to devote much of our brief period in each prison and probation office to the establishment of good relationships there, and to the development of familiarity with the "atmosphere" and organization of these settings for our research.

Nevertheless, each of our interviewing studies inspired a desire to develop more efficient and objective research procedures. As indicated in chapter 5, as our Prison Panel Study was nearing completion we became familiar with the questionnaire studies of inmate-inmate and inmate-staff relationships conducted in Washington prisons by Wheeler and Garabedian.[2] Also, we were motivated to try questionnaires by the fact that our advisers in the U. S. Bureau of Prisons always regretted that the Prison Panel Study was limited to only five federal prisons—particularly, that we included no federal prison camps nor the unique federal correctional institution at Seagoville, Texas. In addition, of course, there was a continuing desire to obtain some comparison of state and federal prison data. Accordingly, we made some effort to develop, in the time and budget already committed to other project undertakings, questionnaire procedures for studying social relationships in prisons, and to extend these procedures to more prisons than were included in the Prison Panel Study.

THE ASHLAND QUESTIONNAIRE STUDY

In 1961, while we were administering the successful-releasee interviews and analyzing data from other operations, we had one of our staff, John Stratton, develop a questionnaire to procure data comparable to that from our Prison Panel Study on the social-psychological impact of prison experience. This was tested at the Ashland Federal Youth Institution. It was presumed that change in convicted persons during imprisonment would be greatest in youthful prisoners like those at Ashland, who less frequently had prior prison experience than inmates of any of the other prisons with which we dealt.

At Ashland our questionnaires were administered to groups of about twenty inmates at a time from a list of 419 inmates comprising all persons

[2] Stanton H. Wheeler, *Social Organization in a Correctional Community* (unpublished Ph.D. dissertation, University of Washington, 1958); Peter G. Garabedian, *Western Penitentiary: A Study of Social Organization* (unpublished Ph.D. dissertation, University of Washington, 1959).

then confined at Ashland who: (1) were committed under the Federal Youth Corrections Act (Paragraph 5010B) or the Federal Juvenile Delinquency Act; (2) had a grade of 4.5 or higher on an educational achievement test; (3) understood English well (several Puerto Ricans were excluded); (4) were not parole violators nor transfers from another penal institution.

In order to encourage frank responses, the subjects not only were orally assured of the confidentiality of their responses, but also were not required to indicate their name on the questionnaire. As a check on the validity of the responses, Stratton would note from the prison records the age, offense, record of prior convictions, and other background attributes of each group of twenty inmates whom he called to fill out the questionnaires. On the form itself, the subjects were asked to indicate their age and these other attributes. The distribution of responses on these items in each group called out was almost exactly that which the prison files confirmed.

A total of 364 inmates completed the questionnaire schedules. The fifty-five absentees included seven who were hospitalized, five in disciplinary segregation, and seven who could not leave a culinary assignment; but the others apparently were either not excused from their assignment by their officer, or declined to take the questionnaire and were allowed by their officer to remain on the assignment. Those who did not show up when called out once to fill the questionnaire were called another time; if they did not come on this call they were not called again. We were not informed of outright refusals, but eleven questionnaires were not usable because of obviously dishonest, nonsensical, or profane answers, or because of incompleteness. One additional case was deleted because of uncertainty as to the inmate's stage of imprisonment. This meant a total of 352 usable questionnaires, or 84 per cent of the potential sample of 419.

With the highly indeterminate juvenile delinquency and Youth Correction Act sentences at Ashland, from which almost all release is by parole, there is so much uncertainty as to time of release that it is difficult to classify inmates as having completed a specific proportion of their prison term. Of two inmates who have been confined five months, one may be halfway through his imprisonment while the other may not have served a fourth of the time which will elapse before his parole; one cannot be distinguished from the other with much certainty at the time that both have been confined only five months, for the future decisions of the parole board cannot be known at that time.

In the original analysis conducted by Stratton after consulting with Bureau of Prisons officials and with a statistics professor, he divided the Ashland sample into eight subgroups on the basis of presumed stage of imprisonment. These were:

(1) *Admission Unit:* 28 men, median time served 1.4 months, still confined in the dormitory for the reception and orientation of newly admitted inmates.

(2) *Postadmission Unit:* 42 men, median time served 2.9 months, in the general prison population, but still in their first four months of imprisonment.

(3) *Middle Group–1:* 80 men, median time served 8.2 months, who had one parole hearing, but had not yet heard its results.

(4) *Middle Group–2:* 121 men, median time served 14.3 months, who had one or more parole hearings, but had been refused parole on all of them.

(5) *Terminal Group–1:* 29 men, median time served 12 months, who were scheduled for parole within four months, after only one or two parole hearings.

(6) *Terminal Group–2:* 52 men, median time served 19.1 months, who were scheduled for parole within four months, after three or more parole hearings.

(7) *Total Entrance Group:* The first two groups above. Admission Unit and Postadmission Unit combined, 70 men, median time served 2.3 months.

(8) *Total Terminal Group:* The above two terminal groups combined, 81 men, median time served 17.6 months.

It was presumed that the first three groups and the last two groups would be comparable cross-sections of the prison intake, at different stages of imprisonment. It was also expected that Middle Group–2 and Terminal Group–2 would be comparable samples of "long-termers"—men singled out by the parole board for long confinement. Terminal Group–1 was thus a residual category of near-release "short-termers."

When the men were classified by preprison attributes, similar proportions of each sentence, offense, and prior criminal record category were found for two sets of subsamples. These two sets were:

(a) The Admission Unit, the Postadmission Unit, their combination as Total Entrance Group, the Total Terminal Group;

(b) Middle Group–2 and Terminal Group–2.

Differences in age between the groups in each of the above sets were little more than the difference in the time they had been in prison. Contrary to our expectation that Middle Group–1 would be similar to the subsamples in set (a) above, this group was found to have a number of unique attributes, in terms of type of sentence and criminal record, reflecting policies in the scheduling of first hearings by the parole board which had not been taken into account in planning this sample scheme. When making stage-of-imprisonment comparisons of material from these Ashland questionnaires in this report, only data from the Total Entrance and Total Terminal Groups are included; more complex subsample analysis is developed by Stratton.[3]

In addition to asking the inmates for information on their personal background, the questionnaire used at Ashland asked inmates about:

[3] John Stratton, *The Measurement of Inmate Change During Imprisonment* (Ph.D. thesis, University of Illinois, 1963).

   a. Their communication with other inmates, with staff, and with persons outside the institution.

   b. Their attitudes on crime, and their identification with other criminals.

   c. Their perception of themselves, their closest inmate friend, inmates in general, their prison work supervisor, their prison caseworker, their prison quarters officer, their mother, their father, their wife or girl-friend, and ex-convicts in general—all measured by an adjectival checklist modeled on Osgood's "semantic differential."

   d. Their experience in the institution (assignments, disciplinary record, etc.)

   e. Their loyalty to other inmates.

   f. Their postrelease expectations.

Most of these questions overlapped the probings of our Prison Panel Study, but some of the inquiries were made in a radically different style, generally adapted from other types of research.

THE 1962 "SURVEY OF INMATE ATTITUDES AND OPINIONS" IN THIRTEEN PRISONS

In the summer of 1962, when the project was in its one-year extension and the first draft of this volume already was well advanced, we decided to employ the Ashland questionnaire for a quick survey of other prisons. On the basis of Stratton's analysis of the responses from Ashland, we deleted a number of attitude items which seemed to overlap other questions, and we also abbreviated the social perception measures, which inmates had found tedious. However, we added some questions on the activities of the inmates on the day preceding their completion of the questionnaire, and we also added some questions developed by Garabedian as indexes of the inmate social types distinguished by Schrag in Washington state prisons.[4]

We adopted a simple sampling procedure, modeled on that of the Wheeler study,[5] in hopes of maximizing prospects for stage-of-imprisonment comparability in samples of inmates from diverse and scattered prisons. Our schedule required that we try to have prison officials arrange our questionnaire administration before our arrival at the prison. We asked that our three subsamples be selected from the total prison population on the basis of the following instructions:

1. *The Entrance Sample* will consist of inmates newest to the prison, but none who has served more than six months on his sentence or is expecting release in less than six months. We would start with the newest inmate registry

---

[4] Garabediän, *op. cit.;* Clarence Schrag, "Some Foundations for a Theory of Correction," chapter 8 in Donald R. Cressey, *The Prison* (New York, Holt, Rinehart, and Winston, 1961).

[5] Wheeler, *op. cit.* See also his: "Socialization in Correctional Communities," *Am. Sociological Rev., 26,* no. 5 (Oct. 1961), 697-712.

number and work back at least 100 numbers, or to six months ago, which-ever comes first, skipping all who are illiterate (under 4.5 in G.E.D.) in English, all returned as violators on the sentence they now are serving, and any men sentenced to less than 18 months.

2. *The Middle Sample* will consist of inmates who have served over six months and are not expecting release in less than six months, who fit the same standards as the Entrance Sample with respect to literacy and sentence. We would try to get a random sample by estimating the number of inmates "M" at this institution who fit this specification, then select a combination of last digits of the registry numbers which would give a proportion somewhat above 100/M. For example, if a prison had 560 inmates fitting these specifications, our proportion probably would be one-fifth; therefore, we would randomly pick two digits, say "3" and "8," and call all literate inmates whose numbers end with these digits who have the characteristics specified above.

3. The *Terminal Sample* will consist of inmates with the least time yet to serve, but in no case more than six months. We would start by listing all literate inmates with sentences of eighteen months or more, not returned as vio-lators on the sentence they now are serving, who have parole dates, either final or pending approval of release plans. We would then take the release calendar on expirations and mandatory releases, and list all literate inmates with sentences of eighteen months or more scheduled for nonparole release as far ahead in the future as the parolees. In any case we would try to call 100 or more of all types of releasee, going no further ahead in expected date of release for one type of releasee than for another, and in no case further ahead than six months.

For the prison camps, which have relatively few inmates, we did not employ the above sampling instructions, but asked instead to give the questionnaires to all inmates. The questionnaire itself asked each inmate to indicate the date when he began serving his sentence, the date when he expected to be released, and the dates of any prior paroles on this sentence. This informa-tion permitted us to classify the prison camp inmates into our three sample categories, and it also provided a check on the sampling of inmates at the other institutions.

The questionnaires were first tested at the U. S. Penitentiary in Terre Haute, Indiana. On the basis of inmate reactions there, the social perception items were further abbreviated, to make them less tedious. The Terre Haute experience also indicated that the questionnaires could be adminis-tered almost as well to a classroom full of inmates—perhaps thirty to forty—as to a group of only twenty. In the interest of minimizing travel time to other institutions at this stage in the project, and generally at the urging of officials at the prisons, the questionnaires were given to rooms full of as many inmates as could be accommodated comfortably; usually these were classrooms, but on two occasions they were dining halls.

In the state prisons, and in the federal prisons where we had not pre-viously done research, it was appropriate that the director of the project go

to the prison to administer the questionnaires. One or two research assistants accompanied him, and sometimes one or two graduate students came
along to visit the prison and to aid in the questionnaire distribution. (The
McNeil Island trip was a detour, by the director alone, while attending a
correctional meeting in Seattle.) Time pressures and expense did not permit a long stay at any of the prisons, and most of this time was spent becoming familiar with the program and policies of prisons new to our study.
Indeed, interruption of the preparation of this volume by these visits to
diverse prisons doubtless enriched greatly the interpretation of findings from
other project studies. The limited time, however, restricted the size of the
sample that could be collected, and often made it most convenient for the
prison officials to have us administer the questionnaire to all or most of the
sample at once, in large rooms.

   In soliciting the cooperation of state prison administrators, we agreed
not to identify their institutions in reporting the findings. We have given
each of the state institutions a pseudonym which summarizes the most distinguishing feature in its total impression on us. "Busy" was notable for the
extent to which, in work, school, and supervised recreation, all inmates
were kept fully occupied. "Full" prison and camp were conspicuously
overcrowded, and a large fraction of the inmates there had no work assignment. Idleness also was extensive in the "Slow" prisons, which were also
slower than the prisons of the other states in the development of classification, casework, and education programs. "Tight" state prison was distinguished for the extent of concern for custodial security which its staff
exhibited in all movement of prisoners within the institution enclosure.

   Unfortunately, the instructions for selecting the Middle Sample (at all
institutions except prison camps), proved to be too complicated for the
officials at several institutions. At Full State Prison, for example, we were
advised that the official in charge of arranging the administration of our
questionnaires had simply asked the prison caseworkers to see if each of
them could recruit about ten inmates with over six months served and over
six months to serve "who would be interested in taking the test." At some
prisons, even where we were able to ascertain that our sampling instructions
were scrupulously met, the average time served (and especially, the sum of
the time served and time expected to serve) was greater for almost everyone in the Middle Sample than for anyone in either the Entrance or the
Terminal Samples. Inmates for our Entrance and Terminal Samples appeared to have been selected according to our instructions at all of the institutions. Accordingly, in instances when time and staff shortages prevented
our coding and tabulating responses from all samples, we deferred this task
for the Middle Sample (for Leavenworth, Chillicothe, McNeil Island Camp,
Tight State, and Full State Camp).

   The most serious sampling problem was a lack of knowledge of the completeness with which a sample fitting our specifications was selected. At most prisons it was evident that some inmates listed for inclusion in our sample never got there. This was especially conspicuous at Allenwood Camp where, as inmates came from work, they were assembled in one building to have the research program explained to them, and they were then to go to another building to fill out the questionnaires. One inmate loudly argued that he was due for parole and did not want to fill out anything which might jeopardize his release. Despite our assurances that their names were not requested on the questionnaires, and that all of the forms would be taken back to the University of Illinois and not given to officials, an appreciable number of inmates never completed the move to the building where they were to fill out the questionnaires.

In all other institutions where inmates were sent in to complete the questionnaire as they came in from work at the end of the day, even when they were brought in an hour earlier than their usual "quitting time," a large proportion of the questionnaires had an excessive number of entries blank. This occurred at McNeil Island Camp, Full State Camp, and in a large part of the Middle and Terminal Samples at the Slow State institutions. By contrast, there was outstanding cooperation by the inmates of the Entrance Sample of Slow State Penitentiary; for them, the movement to a classroom for our questionnaire administration was one of the few breaks experienced in a several-week admission processing period of solitary confinement and idleness.

We established a rule of deleting from the sample any case in which more than a third of the items were left blank, on the assumption that the remaining items were then irresponsibly completed. Similarly, we deleted any cases which showed evidence of mechanical response, as when the same space was checked for all questions on a sheet of multiple choice questions.

The sampling of inmates was most fully according to plan, and the questionnaires were most completely filled, at Terre Haute, Leavenworth, Busy State, El Reno, and Seagoville. At these institutions it is believed that our data approximate a 90 per cent collection of the responses of those inmates who fit our sample specifications. At the other institutions, unusually cooperative inmates are overrepresented in our sampling. Partly for this reason, but mainly because of the complexity and the preliminary stage of our analysis of many of the more subjective items in the questionnaire, we summarized in the main chapters of this report responses on only those items least likely to be distorted by selection in sampling and most relevant to our discussions. Other data from these questionnaires will be reported in this appendix.

With the tremendous diversity of inmate population indicated in Table E.1, plus the sample procurement problems already described, it is understandable that many of our inquiries in the Prison Panel Supplement study

Table E.1 (Part One) Attributes of the Prison Panel Supplement Subsamples

Institutions and subsamples	Number of cases	Median age	Median time served[a]	Median time to serve[a]	Median no. of prior convictions	Median total years of life in jail, prison
Penitentiaries:						
Leavenworth Federal						
Entrance	79	38	3	45	4	8
Terminal	83	38	42	3	3	8
Terre Haute Federal						
Entrance	68	32	3	31	1	0–54%[b]
Middle	88	34	12	17	2	2
Terminal	83	31	25	2	4	5
"Busy" State						
Entrance	84	37	2	44	3	6
Middle	90	35	30	29	3	8
Terminal	48	37	39	3	3	6
"Slow" State						
Entrance	29	20	2	24	2	5
Middle	75	29	17	18	2	4
Terminal	71	31	23	3	2	4
"Full" State						
Entrance	78	26	2	30	3	2
Middle	74	31	27	25	2	5
Terminal:						
Inside units	71	33	38	1	2	5
Outside camps	25	38	54	3	3	9
Seagoville Federal Correctional Inst.:						
Entrance	54	35	4	22	2	2
Middle	76	35	16	16	1	3
Terminal	52	34	22	4	1	3
Reformatories and Youth Institutions:						
Chillicothe Federal						
Entrance	65	23	5	18	1	1
Terminal	59	23	24	2	1	2
El Reno Federal						
Entrance	65	20	4	28	2	1
Middle	99	25	16	15	2	2
Terminal	90	22	22	3	1	2
Ashland Federal		(Under 18)				
Entrance	70	(67%)	2	c	0–53%	c
Middle	201	(54%)	12	c	1	c
Terminal	81	(24%)	18	c	0–56%	c
"Slow" State						
Entrance	47	20	4	20	0–54%	1
Middle	60	20	16	16	2	2
Terminal	76	20	20	3	1	2
"Tight" State						
Entrance	64	20	4	40	2	2
Terminal	58	23	34	3	2	2
Prison Camps:						
Allenwood Federal						
Entrance	11	39	4	20	0–55%	1
Middle	67	37	30	17	1	5
Terminal	55	39	23	3	1	4

TABLE E.1 Attributes of the Prison Panel Supplement Subsamples
(Part One continued)

Institutions and subsamples	Number of cases	Median age	Median time served	Median time to serve	Median no. of prior convictions	Median total years of life in jail, prison
McNeil Island Federal						
Entrance	14	45	5	19	1	1
Terminal	34	39	35	3	2	6
"Full" State						
Entrance	20	34	6	20	3	5
Terminal	59	31	22	3	2	4

a Period of time served and to serve is given in months.
b Where the median is zero, the percentage to whom zero applies follows.
c Not available.

TABLE E.1 (Part Two) Attributes of the Prison Panel Supplement Subsamples

Institutions and subsamples	PERCENTAGE DISTRIBUTION OF OFFENSES						
	Auto theft	Narcotics	Forgery	Robbery	Burglary	Larceny	Other
Penitentiaries:							
Leavenworth Federal							
Entrance	37	8	21	13	—	8	13
Terminal	34	14	16	7	4	12	14
Terre Haute Federal							
Entrance	19	12	17	4	2	23	23
Middle	16	1	24	14	1	18	24
Terminal	41	3	26	7	2	7	14
"Busy" State							
Entrance	4	—	29	7	10	7	43
Middle	7	—	18	14	17	11	33
Terminal	5	—	25	11	23	7	30
"Slow" State							
Entrance	15	—	7	19	41	—	19
Middle	4	3	7	32	31	6	17
Terminal	6	1	13	16	35	13	16
"Full" State							
Entrance	12	4	8	12	18	16	29
Middle	3	5	8	41	14	3	27
Terminal:							
Inside units	2	8	8	19	23	22	19
Outside camps	—	22	9	26	13	9	22
Seagoville Federal Correctional Institution:							
Entrance	30	8	14	4	2	4	38
Middle	23	25	12	3	—	4	33
Terminal	33	19	19	2	2	12	14
Reformatories and Youth Institutions:							
Chillicothe Federal							
Entrance	63	7	10	7	2	7	5
Terminal	69	4	10	6	—	—	10
El Reno Federal							
Entrance	47	18	2	5	2	13	13
Middle	72	10	6	3	1	2	5
Terminal	72	5	9	—	—	9	6

TABLE E.1   Attributes of the Prison Panel Supplement Subsamples
(Part Two continued)

Institutions and subsamples	PERCENTAGE DISTRIBUTION OF OFFENSES						
	Auto theft	Narcotics	Forgery	Robbery	Burglary	Larceny	Other
Reformatories and Youth Institutions—Cont.							
Ashland Federal							
Entrance	80	—	—	—	—	—	20[a]
Middle	76	—	—	—	—	—	24[a]
Terminal	79	—	—	—	—	—	21[a]
"Slow" State							
Entrance	15	—	5	13	51	8	8
Middle	7	5	4	26	30	7	21
Terminal	7	1	4	18	61	3	6
"Tight" State							
Entrance	6	3	2	43	24	—	22
Terminal	11	4	2	45	25	2	11
Prison Camps:							
Allenwood Federal							
Entrance	—	20	20	10	—	—	50
Middle	8	42	15	3	—	5	28
Terminal	9	9	11	9	—	19	43
McNeil Island Federal							
Entrance	17	8	8	—	—	8	58
Terminal	32	18	14	4	4	14	14
"Full" State							
Entrance	5	10	15	5	40	10	15
Terminal	—	4	22	11	18	18	27

[a] Includes all non-auto theft.

yielded no uniform or highly predominant responses for all institutions. Table E.1 provides a summary of characteristics of the samples in our total Prison Panel Supplement Study. They vary in median age from under twenty to over forty, and in median years of total imprisonment (in all penal institutions) from zero to nine years. With respect to offenses, the samples vary from 2 per cent to 80 per cent auto thieves, from 2 to 29 per cent forgers, from 2 to 45 per cent robbers, and from zero to over 40 per cent narcotics law offenders.

The development of questionnaires yielding sensitive indexes of prisoner attitude appears desirable, so that one may have an efficient way of measuring the impact of prison programs, procedures, and staffing on various types of inmate. The sections that follow indicate our experience with three types of questionnaire device: inmate attitude scales, social perception measures, and an inmate social role classification procedure. It is believed that all of these will be of penological interest at present, and that they eventually may be developed to yield more efficient and profound measurement of the impact of imprisonment than now is available.

INMATE ATTITUDE SCALES

One of our interests in questionnaires for prisoners was to develop separate sets of questions to measure correctionally important attitudes in prison. Our hope was to form a series of what is known as "ordinal scales." Such a scale consists of a set of questions arranged and scored so as to indicate degrees of intensity in a single attitude.

This unidimensional quality in a set of questions may be identified by what is known as the Guttman or Scalogram procedure of statistical analysis. In this procedure, a set of questions or their scoring is revised until it can be demonstrated that if the questions are placed in a sequence presumed to indicate increasing intensity of a single attitude, knowledge of a person's answer to one question in the sequence permits one to predict his answers to the questions representing a higher intensity of this same attitude, or his answers to the questions representing a lower intensity of this attitude, or both. When such predictive potential, known as "reproducibility," achieves an accuracy of about 90 per cent or higher for a set of questions applied to an appreciable sample of persons who respond diversely to the questions, the set of questions is said to form a "scale" measuring a single dimension of attitude.[6]

The name one gives to the attitude that a set of questions taps is arbitrary. The statistical scale analysis only determines that the questions measure a single attitude; it cannot identify this attitude. The name assigned by a researcher to a set of questions which the scale is presumed to represent is only the researcher's guess as to what attitude the questions measure.

Scale relationships are illustrated by the following five statements which Stratton called Criminal Association Preference:

1. When I get out I don't want to associate with the kind of people that are always getting into trouble.
2. I would rather associate with people who obey the law than with those who don't.
3. I don't care to associate with the kind of people that are in prison.
4. I want to keep in touch with inmates I met here after I get out.
5. The people that I usually prefer as friends have little respect for the law.

Inmates were asked to check "strongly agree," "agree," "disagree," or "strongly disagree" after each statement, but their responses were then regrouped by Stratton as "agree" or "disagree," for scaling purposes. The wording of the statement is such that for the first three questions, disagreement was scored as indicating Criminal Association Preference, while on the last two questions, agreement indicated this preference.

Stratton showed that the foregoing set of questions on Preference for

[6] Allen L. Edwards, *Techniques of Attitude Scale Construction* (New York, Appleton-Century-Crofts, 1957), chapter 7.

Criminal Associates form a scale by demonstrating that they have 90 per cent reproducibility. This means that he would have about 90 per cent accuracy in predicting, for example, that an inmate who agreed with the third question would also agree with the first two questions. Or again, if an inmate agreed with the fourth question, he would give the Preference for Criminal Associates response—disagree—to the first three questions.

It should be noted that the sets of questions presented in this chapter are arranged in the sequence with which they formed scales of 90 to 94 per cent reproducibility, but the questions were not presented to inmates in these sequences. In both the Ashland questionnaire and the questionnaire distributed at other prisons, questions from different scales were mixed together in a random sequence, so as to minimize the possible effect of sequence on the relations between response to one question and response to another.

The following four questions, adapted from Clemmer's pioneer study of *The Prison Community,* form a scale which Stratton called "Inmate Solidarity."

1. I would tell my personal business:
    _____only to my close friends in here.
    _____only to inmates that I know well.
    _____to any inmate.
    _____to no one.
2. I would let myself be punished by institutional officials for something I didn't do:
    _____only to protect a close friend.
    _____to protect inmates that I know well.
    _____to protect any inmate at all.
    _____never.
3. I would share my commissary:
    _____only with my close friends.
    _____only with inmates that I know well.
    _____with any inmate.
    _____with no one.
4. When I'm released I would be willing to invite into my home:
    _____only those inmates that are my close friends.
    _____only those inmates that I know well.
    _____any inmate.
    _____no one who has done time.[7]

For the scalogram analysis, inmates were scored positively on Inmate Solidarity only on those questions in the above set on which they checked the second or third response.

[7] See: Donald Clemmer, *The Prison Community,* rev. ed. (New York, Rinehart, 1958).

For the extension of this questionnaire to prisons other than Ashland, during the summer of 1962, we were interested in separating preference and loyalty in dealing with fellow inmates within the prison from such attitudes with respect to ex-criminals outside the prison. Accordingly, we dropped the Preference for Criminal Associates scale and added a number of items on inmate loyalty, based upon Wheeler's questionnaire. The four items that form our Inmate Loyalty scale for institutions other than Ashland include the first item from the Ashland Inmate Solidarity scale and three other questions, in the following sequence of increasing loyalty (with loyalty scored positively for all of the answers marked with plus signs):

1. If I'm on a prison work crew digging ditches and I enjoy working hard because I'm feeling pretty good, but the other inmates complain that I'm digging my part faster than anybody else, and that the officer will start rushing them to keep up with me, I would:

   + 1. Slow down so as not to get ahead of them.
   + 2. Slow down a little so as not to be too much ahead of them.
   0 3. Work as hard as before.
   0 4. Work harder than before.

2. I would let myself be punished by institution officials for something I didn't do:

   + 1. Only to protect a close friend.
   + 2. To protect inmates that I know well.
   + 3. To protect any inmate at all.
   0 4. Never.

3. If I had a good friend in here who told me he had a five-dollar bill smuggled to him during a visit, and he thought he was going to be frisked, so he wanted me to hold it for him, I would:

   + 1. Certainly hold it for him.
   + 2. Probably hold it for him.
   0 3. Probably refuse to hold it for him.
   0 4. Certainly refuse to hold it for him.

4. If two inmates with long sentences wanted to escape and could escape if I smuggled them something from my work assignment, but I'd lose at least a year of good time if I got caught helping them this way, I would:

   + 1. Help them even if I knew that after they escaped officials would be able to prove I helped them.
   + 2. Only help them if I thought I had a pretty good chance of getting away with it.
   0 3. Only help them if I were sure I could not possibly get caught for it.
   0 4. Not help them under any circumstances.

One general theory believed applicable to most felonies, which I published in 1956 as a reconceptualization of Sutherland's theory, suggested that a person pursues crime insofar as he identifies himself with real or imaginary persons from whose perspective his criminal behavior seems acceptable.[8] Accordingly, Stratton developed the following scale, in which agreement with any statement indicates perceived similarity to criminals, as a measure of Criminal Identification:

1. People who have been in trouble with the law have the same sort of ideas about life that I have.
2. I think more like other inmates than like people on the outside.
3. People who have been in trouble with the law are more like me than people who don't have trouble with the law.
4. I'm more like the people who can make a living outside the law than I am like those who only break the law occasionally.
5. I don't have much in common with people who never break the law.

In extending our questionnaire to all prisons we deliberately probed Criminal Identification with items referring only to criminals rather than to inmates, and we obtained a highly reproducible scale with the following three items arranged in sequence of increasing Criminal Identification:

1. People who have been in trouble with the law have the same sort of ideas about life that I have.
2. People who never break the law are a lot different from me.
3. People who have trouble with the law are more like me than people who don't have trouble with the law.

For purposes of gross classification, men were called "low" in Criminal Identification if they agreed with none or only with the first of these statements, and "high" if they agreed with any more than this.

Since it is speculated that such solidarity with other inmates is independent of criminalistic influences from other inmates, Stratton developed a separate scale on Orientation to Criminal Means, adapted from the Minnesota Law Scale:[9]

1. A man should always obey the law no matter how much it interferes with his personal ambition.
2. It's alright for a person to break the law if he doesn't get caught.
3. It's alright to evade the law if you don't actually violate it.
4. A hungry man has the right to steal.
5. A person should obey only those laws which seem reasonable.

[8] See: Daniel Glaser, "Criminality Theories and Behavioral Images," *Am. J. Sociology, 61,* no. 5 (March 1956), 433-44.

[9] Minnesota Law Scale in E. A. Rundquist and Raymond F. Sletto, *Personality in the Depression* (Minneapolis, University of Minnesota Press, 1936).

6. A man's a fool to work for a living if he can get by some easier way, even if it means violating the law.

Acceptance of law violation was indicated by agreement with statements 2 through 6 and by disagreement with statement 1.

We simplified the language in some of these statements very slightly before applying them to prisons other than Ashland. At these other prisons we obtained a Criminality Scale using the following four statements, which are arranged in a rank order of increasing criminality if measured positively by agreement with the first and fourth items and by disagreement with the middle two:

1. It's alright to "get around" the law if you do not actually break it.
2. It is difficult to break the law and keep one's self-respect.
3. A man should always obey the laws, no matter how much they stand in the way of his ambitions.
4. It's alright for a person to break the law if he doesn't get caught.

For gross classification, men were classified as "low" in Criminality if they agreed or disagreed with the first statement, but agreed with the middle two and disagreed with the last; they were classified as "medium" in Criminality if they agreed with the first and third and disagreed with the second and fourth statements; they were classified as "high" if they agreed with the first statement, disagreed with the middle two, and either agreed or disa-agreed with the last.

Table E.2 indicates that Inmate Loyalty is inversely related to age and that it increases during imprisonment for all inmates younger than thirty-

TABLE E.2 Attitude Scale Responses in Relation to Age and Stage
of Imprisonment
(Prison Panel Supplement samples, all institutions except Ashland)

| | | AGE GROUP AND STAGE OF PRISON TERM | | | | | |
| | | 20 AND UNDER | | 21–30 | | 31 AND OVER | |
Attitude scale	Scale score	Entrance	Terminal	Entrance	Terminal	Entrance	Terminal
Inmate Loyalty	Low	33%	26%	38%	32%	42%	42%
	Medium	14%	13%	15%	10%	21%	20%
	High	53%	62%	48%	58%	37%	38%
Criminality	Low	55%	54%	61%	47%	70%	67%
	Medium	20%	19%	17%	17%	14%	14%
	High	25%	27%	22%	36%	16%	19%
Criminal Identification	Low	61%	61%	72%	70%	67%	72%
	High	39%	39%	28%	30%	33%	28%
Number of cases[a]		154	101	229	424	246	281

[a] This is the number of men answering all the questions in one attitude scale, a figure slightly different for each of the three scales; since their range of variation was less than 3 per cent, we cite above only the number of respondents for that scale on which this number was highest.

one. This is consistent with the findings presented in chapter 5, that the youngest inmates move most towards grouping with other inmates in prison, while the older inmates persist most in isolating themselves from other prisoners.

Differences between age groups were less clear-cut in response to our Criminality and Criminal Identification scales than for our Inmate Loyalty scale. However, the oldest inmates were lowest on all three scales. The inmates aged twenty and under were clearly highest in Criminal Identification as measured by our three-question scale, and for all age groups the responses to these items were quite similar at the Entrance and Terminal stages of imprisonment. However, on our Criminality scale, the high criminality responses were more frequent in the Terminal than in the Entrance stage of imprisonment for all age groups, and this change was most marked for the twenty-one- to thirty-year-olds. This middle age group was clearly the most criminal of any age group in its responses to our questions at the near-release stage.

Responses to Stratton's four scales by the Ashland population showed little change with stage of imprisonment, and had little relationship to age or to other background variables. The most marked change was an increase in Preference for Criminal Associates with time in prison. It is noteworthy that the change evident in this Ashland group, and the changes during imprisonment indicated in Table E.2, were more consistent on prisonization scales (relationship to inmates), than on criminalization scales (attitudes toward law and identification with criminals). This suggests that prison experience has a clearer effect in promoting adaptation to life in a total institution than in promoting criminality, a thesis set forth by Cressey and Irwin, and suggested by our analysis in Chapter 18.[10]

Table E.3 confirms expectations in showing that, on the whole, there is a direct correlation between number of prior commitments to penal institutions and Inmate Loyalty, Criminality, and Criminal Identification, as measured by our scales. However, differences between the adjacent categories in number of prior commitments are not always consistent; the direct relationship of our attitude scale responses to number of prior commitments is most apparent if one compares any pair of prior commitment categories which are not adjacent, such as "None" with "two or three," and "One" with "four or more." Those with four or more prior commitments were especially distinctive in their frequency of high responses on all three scales.

In general, our questionnaire attitude scale data suggest that, if administered with care to large samples, such scales can serve as efficient indicators of variations in attitude during correctional treatment. The validity of responses to such scales are not readily evaluated unless correlated with

[10] Donald R. Cressey and John Irwin, "Thieves, Convicts and the Inmate Culture," *Social Problems, 10,* no. 2 (Fall 1962), 142-55.

TABLE E.3   Attitude Scale Responses in Relation to Number of Prior Commitments and Stage of Imprisonment
(Prison Panel Supplement samples, all institutions except Ashland)

Attitude scale	Scale score	NUMBER OF PRIOR COMMITMENTS AND STAGE OF PRISON TERM							
		NONE		ONE		TWO OR THREE		FOUR OR MORE	
		Entrance	Terminal	Entrance	Terminal	Entrance	Terminal	Entrance	Terminal
Inmate	Low	46%	41%	42%	41%	34%	32%	27%	23%
Loyalty	Medium	22%	15%	14%	13%	13%	15%	14%	12%
	High	32%	44%	44%	47%	53%	51%	59%	65%
Criminality	Low	70%	64%	69%	57%	65%	60%	54%	45%
	Medium	15%	19%	20%	18%	16%	14%	16%	23%
	High	15%	17%	11%	26%	20%	25%	30%	33%
Criminal	Low	74%	78%	80%	74%	63%	66%	57%	58%
Identification	High	26%	22%	20%	26%	37%	34%	43%	41%
Number of cases[a]		201	233	107	135	170	176	138	137

[a] This is the number of men answering all the questions in one attitude scale, a figure slightly different for each of the three scales; since their range of variation was less than 3 per cent, we cite above only the number of respondents for that scale on which this number was highest.

subsequent criminality in a long-run study. Nevertheless, contrasts between large groups could strongly indicate differential effects of alternative treatments for particular types of offender. One could, for this purpose, compare the responses of large groups of offenders of similar background after they are randomly assigned to different treatment programs, or one could compare the before and after responses of offenders of clearly contrasting background after all have been exposed to the same treatment experience.

SOCIAL PERCEPTION SCALES

A standard device for the psychological measurement of variations in perception of something is to have subjects check the relative position of that thing, as they see it, on a line between two opposite adjectives. For example, in various research undertakings people have beeen asked to evaluate such diverse things as the United Nations, the President of the United States, their foreman, and price controls, on forms which looked like this:[11]

strong_____:_____:_____:_____:_____:_____weak
ugly_____:_____:_____:_____:_____:_____beautiful
pleasant_____:_____:_____:_____:_____:_____unpleasant

Practical applications of this "semantic differential" technique include many studies of the effectiveness of groups in which the leader indicates on

[11] Charles E. Osgood, G. J. Suci, and P. H. Tannenbaum, *The Measurement of Meaning* (Urbana, University of Illinois Press, 1957).

such a device a large difference between his perception of his most effective coworker and his perception of his least effective coworker. This is compared with the effectiveness of groups in which the leader does not differentiate greatly between the coworkers whom he rates on such devices. Of these two types of groups, those with leaders that differentiate most, by this measure, have been demonstrated to be most effective in a large variety of fields, including pig-iron production, naval bombing, anti-aircraft gunnery, and winning basketball games. For some tasks, a combination of leaders of different abilities has been shown most effective; for example, the most profitable farm cooperatives had board chairmen who did not see large differences between people and managers who did.[12]

In applying these devices, the ratings generally are converted to a numerical score. For example, when there are six spaces between adjectives, a check in the space next to the most unfavorable adjective is scored "one," a check in the next space is scored "two" and so forth, so that a check in the space next to the most favorable adjective is scored "six." The scores on each separate pair of adjectives in a list generally are added together, and the total score is called an "esteem score." Thus with twenty pairs of adjective scores the esteem scores can range from a low of 20 to a high of 120. A person may be asked to rate himself on these scales, yielding a "self-esteem" score, or he may be asked to rate another specific person, a category of persons, or even an inanimate object or an abstract concept. Of course the adjectives may be altered to best fit the thing being rated, but it has been found that little variation in scores results from change in the pairs of adjectives used, as long as a dozen or more pairs are used.

In one correctional application of this device, Fiedler and Bass compared the self-esteem scores of military offenders confined in a disciplinary unit, of offenders not under confinement, and of nonoffenders. They also compared the self-esteem scores of juvenile delinquents in a correctional institution, of delinquents not confined, and of nondelinquents. In both sets of comparisons, the nonoffenders rated themselves more favorably than the offenders did, but the confined offenders rated themselves more favorably than the nonconfined ones. Two interpretations of the latter contrast are offered—a psychological explanation and a sociological or social-psychological explanation. The psychological explanation is that offenders who are punished by confinement are thereby relieved of guilt feelings, and hence view themselves more favorably. The alternative interpretation rests on the findings of a variety of other research to the effect that a person's rating of himself varies with changes in the persons to whom he compares himself (his reference groups). It is suggested that when offenders are confined with other criminals they cease to evaluate themselves so much by com-

[12] See: Fred E. Fiedler, *Leader Attitudes and Group Effectiveness* (Urbana, University of Illinois Press, 1958).

parison with persons not in difficulty with the law, and compare themselves instead with their fellow inmates. From this confinement perspective they are more satisfied with themselves than they were before confinement, but it should be noted that even before confinement their self-perceptions were not as favorable as those of nonoffenders.[13]

It occurred to me that such a device might be useful in assessing inmate-inmate and inmate-staff relationships in various types of correctional situations. Therefore, in our Prison Panel Supplement Study, inmates were asked to apply the list of fifteen pairs of adjectives in Figure E.1 to them-

FIGURE *E. 1*   *Social Perception Rating Sheet*

Describe *yourself* as *you* ordinarily think about yourself.

Friendly___:___:___:___:___:___Unfriendly
Confident___:___:___:___:___:___Unsure
Childish___:___:___:___:___:___Not childish
Fair___:___:___:___:___:___Unfair
Hardworking___:___:___:___:___:___Lazy
Kind___:___:___:___:___:___Cruel
Stupid___:___:___:___:___:___Smart
Truthful___:___:___:___:___:___Liar
Dependable___:___:___:___:___:___Undependable
Gloomy___:___:___:___:___:___Cheerful
Brave___:___:___:___:___:___Afraid
Gets things done___:___:___:___:___Doesn't get things done
Cares about others___:___:___:___:___Doesn't care about others
Doesn't anger easily___:___:___:___:___Gets angry easily
Good___:___:___:___:___:___Bad

selves, to their best friend in prison, to inmates in general, to various institution staff members, and to certain persons outside of the prison. This list was phrased to take into account the low literacy of many inmates, and to include adjectives salient to the prison situation and to the persons on whom the inmates were probed.

The inmates were given a series of these adjectival check sheets, each with a different heading. In addition to a sheet requesting a self-rating, illustrated in Figure E.1, there were sheets with the following captions:

Think of the *inmate* who is your *closest friend* here, then describe how you ordinarily think of him.

On this page describe what you believe *inmates, in general,* are like.

[13] Fred E. Fiedler and Alan R. Bass, *Delinquency, Confinement, and Inter-Personal Perception,* Technical Report No. 6 (Urbana, Group Effectiveness Research Laboratory, 1960).

Think of the person who *supervises* your work on your prison job. If several persons do this, think of the one whom you most often think of as your *"boss."* Describe below how he seems to you.

On this page describe your *parole officer.*[14]

On this page describe your *unit officer.* (That is the officer in your unit that you have the most contact with at the present time.)

The inmates were somewhat resistant to the use of these rating forms. They had little objection to using the forms to rate themselves, but a number claimed that they could not rate other inmates, or they were wary of rating staff, despite assurances of anonymity. Some of these pages in our questionnaires were left completely or partially blank, despite instructions that they should put a check on every line. On some forms the checks were deliberately placed on the middle point of the line, rather than in one of the spaces. None of these forms could be used. Because of this experience at Ashland, the form with fifteen pairs of adjectives illustrated in Figure E.1 represents a simplification; as used at Ashland it had twenty-two pairs of adjectives. In addition to the terms in Figure E.1, it had "Cooperative—Uncooperative," "Helpful—Harmful," "Calm—Upset," "Ungrateful—Grateful," "Unimportant—Important," "Strong—Weak," "Careful—Careless," and "Quits easily—Keeps trying"; it did not have "Fair—Unfair." The Ashland form also had sheets on "father," "mother," "wife or (if unmarried) girl friend" and "ex-cons in general."

Table E.4 summarizes the responses to these social perception scales by the Ashland population. With twenty-two pairs of adjectives, each scored from 1 to 6, the maximum possible esteem score was 132. The reluctance of the inmates to rate some persons is indicated by the discrepancies between the number of inmates asked to respond, in each subsample, and the number completing a sheet for each person to be rated. (This number is indicated in parentheses.) The newly admitted prisoners were particularly reluctant to rate "ex-cons in general," and some claimed they had not been in the prison long enough to rate a closest friend in prison or their caseworker.

Data on inmate perception of staff at Ashland, as indicated in Table E.4, are consistent with our interview findings, presented in chapter 6. The Ashland inmates show a sharp decline in their rating of caseworkers and a

[14] The "parole officer" in federal prisons is the caseworker for classification processing, counseling, and other individual assistance and treatment services, including correspondence with outside persons or agencies on the inmate's affairs. In state prisons, "counselor (or sociologist or social worker)" was used on this sheet instead of "parole officer," as these were the caseworker designations reported to us in the state prisons surveyed. The findings on this item are designated as perception of—or esteem for—"caseworker" in all of our tabulations.

TABLE E.4   Average Esteem Scores of Ashland Inmates for Various Specific Persons or Categories of Persons

Sample information, and person or persons rated	CROSS-SECTION OF PRISON POPULATION			"LONG-TERMERS"		RESIDUAL	
	Admission unit	Post-admission unit	Total terminal group	Middle group–2	Terminal group–2	Middle group–1	Terminal group–1
Median months served	1.4	2.9	17.6	14.3	19.1	8.2	12.0
Number of inmates asked to respond	28	42	81	121	52	80	29
Person's self	109 (27)[a]	103 (39)	105 (73)	103 (115)	105 (46)	102 (72)	105 (27)
Closest friend in prison	103 (22)	106 (36)	104 (73)	103 (114)	106 (48)	101 (71)	101 (28)
Inmates in general	91 (24)	84 (38)	81 (76)	82 (112)	84 (48)	80 (71)	76 (28)
Work supervisor	103 (25)	106 (38)	110 (76)	105 (116)	114 (48)	105 (70)	104 (28)
Caseworker	117 (21)	100 (36)	94 (74)	91 (112)	93 (46)	95 (69)	95 (28)
Unit officer	110 (22)	111 (36)	97 (76)	101 (112)	94 (48)	106 (70)	101 (27)
Mother	112 (27)	118 (36)	116 (77)	116 (113)	116 (49)	118 (73)	115 (28)
Father	113 (24)	114 (35)	111 (74)	111 (107)	109 (47)	108 (68)	116 (27)
Wife (or girl friend)	114 (20)	116 (36)	108 (62)	110 (98)	110 (40)	111 (67)	104 (22)
Ex-cons in general	84 (18)	80 (39)	88 (71)	83 (109)	91 (46)	81 (72)	84 (25)

The table is headed SAMPLES AND STAGE OF IMPRISONMENT.

[a] Figures in parentheses indicate number of inmates completing usable rating sheet on this category of person.

sharp increase in their esteem for work supervisors during the course of imprisonment. The increasingly favorable view of the work supervisors is especially notable for the long-termers. Ratings of unit officers are relatively high, but decline somewhat when release is near. The exalted ratings of parents, especially mother, are noteworthy; a psychologist might be interested mainly in the cases which deviate from the average in these ratings. The esteem for self, other inmates, and various relatives do not fluctuate in a clear pattern. However, while most inmates rate "inmates in general" less favorably as their confinement progresses, this is not done by the long-termers. It also is of interest that while "ex-cons in general" received a relatively low rating as a rule, their ratings were better when made by inmates in the Terminal samples, who were soon to become "ex-cons" themselves; they were rated especially high by the long-termers near release.

An inmate's relationship with his work supervisor is likely to be increasingly close and personal the longer the inmate is on an assignment, and the more he develops skills and is given responsibility. This relationship is cooperative—each helps the other in the common responsibility of getting the job done. In the youth institution the work supervisor, because of his age and his expertness, because he can bestow praise and other rewards, and because he assumes authority and punishes deviant behavior, often acquires a role like that of a good father. The relationship of the inmate to his work supervisor generally is more continuous, throughout each day as well as in terms of overall duration, than the inmate's relationship to other staff. These are a few of the many reasons why the work supervisor may be in a more strategic position to have a rehabilitative influence on offenders than any other members of a prison staff.

Table E.5 shows the relationships between esteem scores at Ashland and responses to several questions on inmate relationships with staff and with

TABLE E.5   Relationship Between Frequency of Inmate Interaction with Others in the Prison and Their Perception of Prison Staff and of Themselves (Ashland Federal Youth Correctional Institution)

	AVERAGE ESTEEM SCORES FOR:			
Contact with others	*Self*	*Work supervisor*	*Caseworker*	*Unit officer*
Talk with employees:				
Low	101	102	88	97
High	106[b]	110[c]	102[c]	108[c]
Number of "strong friendships" with other inmates since in institution:				
Two or fewer	101	107	95	103
Three or more	106[b]	105	95	102
Most common socialization with other inmates:				
Ungrouped	103	103	98	103
Grouped	104	109[b]	93[a]	102

[a] Differences as great as these would occur by chance alone, with samples of this size, less than once in twenty times.

[b] Differences as great as these would occur by chance alone, with samples of this size, less than once in a hundred times.

[c] Differences as great as these would occur by chance alone, with samples of this size .less than once in a thousand times.

other inmates. The questions employed for classifying the inmates in terms of their contacts with other inmates and with staff were derived from the Clemmer and Wheeler studies cited, and were as follows:

Think back over the time that you have spent in this institution. How would you say that you spent most of your free time?

_____mostly by myself   _____with 1 or 2 inmates
_____with several different inmates,   _____mostly with a group of inmates
　　　but not in any one group　　　　　who are together quite a lot

Have you developed any strong friendships with other inmates since you have been in the institution?

_____no   _____yes, a few (3 to 5)
_____yes, 1 or 2   _____yes, several (more than 5)

On our form the separate answers were listed one under another, but they have been rearranged above to indicate their grouping in some of our cross-tabulations, for which the answers on the left above have been combined as the "low" responses and those on the right above are combined as the "high" responses. The first statement above repeats Clemmer's inquiry, the responses on the left indicating what Clemmer called an "ungrouped" inmate and those on the right indicating what he called a "grouped" inmate.

For rating frequency of inmate contact with staff, one question simply asked: "How much time do you spend talking with institutional employees?" The inmates were to check either "a great deal," "a fair amount," "very little," or "none." Those checking either of the first two we rated "high" and those checking either of the last two we rated "low" on "talk with employees." Another questionnaire item read: "Would you say that you have more contact with custody staff people (custodial officers, lieutenants, captains, associate warden custody), than the average inmate has, or less?" Inmates could check "much more than the average inmate," "a little more than the average inmate," "a little less than the average inmate," or "much less than the average inmate." Those checking either of the first two we classified together as "above average" and those checking either of the last two we designated collectively as "below average." These four alternative responses, which we combined similarly as above or below average, also were presented to the inmates following the question: "Would you say that you have had more contacts with treatment staff people (parole officers, associate warden treatment, psychologists, chaplains, etc.) than the average inmate has, or less?"

Esteem scores were closely related to the amount of interaction which inmates reported having with staff. Infrequent talking with staff was especially associated with low esteem for the caseworker and for the housing unit officer. Low contact of inmates with other inmates, identified either by their reporting few strong friendships or by their saying that they did not spend much time socializing with a group of inmates, was not associated with low esteem for all staff. However, the more solitary inmates had less esteem for work supervisors and more esteem for caseworkers than did the friendlier or grouped inmates. This suggests that the grouped inmates are most likely to share that perception of staff which is predominant in the inmate community. This could reflect both their own experiences and their greater familiarity with the experiences of other inmates.

Rather striking relationships are indicated in Table E.6 between inmate perception of staff and various indexes of their prison adjustment. The

TABLE E.6   Relationships Between Prison Adjustment and Perception of Prison Staff (Ashland Federal Youth Correctional Institution)

	AVERAGE ESTEEM SCORES FOR:				No. of cases[a]
	Self	*Work supervisor*	*Caseworker*	*Unit officer*	
Type of custody:		[c]		[c]	
Close	104	99	92	111	40
Medium-in	102	103	91	100	58
Medium-out	103	106	95	105	163
Minimum	105	112	101	95	65
Number of disciplinary reports in last three months:	[b]	[d]	[b]		
None	104	108	97	101	230
One	106	109	94	109	42
Two or more	99	94	89	102	51
Inmate's evaluation of his sentence:		[d]	[c]	[d]	
Very fair	105	113	102	111	52
Fair	102	109	100	104	126
Unfair	105	107	92	103	75
Very unfair	103	95	85	93	71

[a] This is the highest number of cases for which we have both the information on prison adjustment and one or more of the esteem scores.

[b] Differences as great as those between the extreme categories here would occur by chance alone, with samples of this size, less than once in twenty times.

[c] Differences as great as those between the extreme categories here would occur by chance alone, with samples of this size, less than once in a hundred times.

[d] Differences as great as those between the extreme categories here would occur by chance alone, with samples of this size, less than once in a thousand times.

close-custody inmates are subjected to the most restriction and control, and their officer's duties are more confined to surveillance and regulation than are those of other staff. Nevertheless, the inmates in close custody exceeded all others in their esteem for their unit officer. In contrast, esteem for work supervisors was greatest among those inmates with the most freedom from custodial controls, a freedom which presumably placed the work supervisor in a less authoritarian and restrictive role. Both of these findings make sense as support for the general proposition that increase in personal contact usually promotes more favorable perceptions of other persons. The finding for the close-custody inmates, however, suggests that there is a minimum of hostility expressed in the officer's surveillance and restriction activities. This interpretation is further supported by the fact that the number of disciplinary reports which an inmate had received in the last three months was not closely related to his perceptions of staff, although those with the highest number of reports were the most unfavorable in their view of the work supervisors and the caseworkers.

The inmates also were asked to check whether they thought their prison sentence was "very fair," "fair," "unfair," or "very unfair." This proved to be highly related to their perception of prison staff; the "very fair" respondents indicated much more esteem for all three types of staff about whom inquiry was made than did any other inmates, and the "very unfair" respondents gave much lower evaluations of staff than did the other inmates. Possibly the fairness responses indicated assumption of personal responsibility, while the unfairness responses indicated a tendency to blame others for one's troubles, hence low esteem for others.

Table E.7 indicates that both inmate self-esteem and esteem for staff are inversely related to endorsement of procriminal orientations. However, no such close relationship was found between loyalty to other inmates and

TABLE E.7   Relationships Between Inmate Perceptions of Staff and Their Orientations to Crime and to Other Inmates (Ashland Federal Youth Correctional Institution)

Orientation		Self	AVERAGE ESTEEM SCORES FOR:			No. of cases[a]
			Work supervisor	Caseworker	Unit officer	
Loyalty to other inmates	High	100	103	86	102	40
	Medium	105	108	97	103	211
	Low	102	102	95	102	76
Preference for association with criminals		c	b	d	d	
	High	101	102	90	98	126
	Medium	103	107	98	104	128
	Low	107	112	101	109	71
Identification with criminals		b	b	c	b	
	High	100	103	88	97	74
	Medium	104	106	97	104	181
	Low	106	111	101	107	71
Acceptance of law violation		c	b			
	High	100	100	91	101	56
	Medium	103	106	96	101	202
	Low	108	112	98	110	67

[a] This is the highest number of cases for which we have both the orientation response and one or more of the esteem scores.

[b] Differences as great as those between the extreme categories here would occur by chance alone, with samples of this size, less than once in twenty times.

[c] Differences as great as those between the extreme categories here would occur by chance alone, with samples of this size, less than once in a hundred times.

[d] Differences as great as those between the extreme categories here would occur by chance alone, with samples of this size, less than once in a thousand times.

perception of staff, and the most favorable perceptions were indicated by those medium in loyalty to inmates. This again suggests the independence of criminalization from prisonization during confinement, and suggests that high esteem for staff is associated with rehabilitation.

In the institutions other than Ashland, where we used our sheet with fifteen adjectival pairs, the maximum possible esteem score was 90. There was no marked or consistent shift in these scores for different stages of imprisonment at the various institutions. A large proportion of the respondents did not rate their caseworker, especially at the state prisons and particularly in the Entrance sample, for they claimed to have had no contact with him, or too little contact to form any judgment. As Table E.8 shows,

TABLE E.8   Average Esteem Scores, All Institutions Except Ashland, for Entrance and Terminal Samples

Person rated	Sample	No. of cases	Avg. esteem score
Self	Entrance	631	73
	Terminal	787	74
Closest inmate friend	Entrance	619	72
	Terminal	784	73
Inmates in general	Entrance	628	52
	Terminal	796	50
Work supervisor	Entrance	610	71
	Terminal	799	69
Caseworker	Entrance	545	68
	Terminal	724	66
Unit officer	Entrance	612	67
	Terminal	768	66

the overall findings on esteem scores in the several prisons were consistent with those at Ashland, and with the Prison Panel Study conclusions, in showing the work supervisors to be the most favorably perceived staff members. However, the differences involved here were small. The mean esteem scores for each of the staff categories was slightly lower for the Terminal than for the Entrance samples.

In addition to the esteem scores, the inmates' choice of adjectives to describe various individuals is of some interest. On the Ashland list, the inmates described themselves as "friendly" and "not childish." Inmates at the other institutions, with the fifteen-word list, rated themselves as "fair" and "kind." The Entrance samples rated themselves most unfavorably on the "smart-stupid" scale, but the near-release Terminal samples no longer considered themselves so stupid, and their most frequent unfavorable self-designation was "gets angry easily."

Inmates everywhere rated their best friend among the other inmates most highly on the friendliness scale, and most unfavorably on the "gets angry easily" scale. "Inmates in general" were rated relatively low on most of the scales, but received their highest rating on the friendliness scale; their lowest ratings were on the "grateful-ungrateful" scale, used only at Ashland, and elsewhere, on the scale for ease of getting angry.

The highest ratings of the work supervisors were on "gets things done," and their lowest ratings were on the "brave-afraid" scale. The caseworkers received their most favorable ratings on the "not childish" scale and their lowest ratings on the "cheerful-gloomy" scale. Unit officers at Ashland were rated most highly as "not childish" and as "calm." At the other institutions they were rated most favorably on the dependability scale by inmates of the Entrance samples, but the Terminal samples rated their unit officers most highly on the friendliness scales.

"Ex-cons," who were rated only by the Ashland inmates, were most often described as "careful" and "not childish." Also rated only at Ashland were "mother," described as "kind" and "hardworking," and "father," most often described as "strong" and "hardworking." "Wife" or (if unmarried) "girl friend," of course, was most often described as "kind" and "good."

Our experience with these social perception measures suggests that their use for research in correctional institutions would be most fruitful under circumstances where: (1) the research staff has worked with the subjects long enough to establish high rapport; (2) the social perception measures are administered only to small groups of subjects at a time; and (3) these instruments are not so long that it is a tedious task to complete them. The adjectives employed should be within the vocabulary of inmate subjects and meaningful when applied to the categories of persons rated. The Ashland findings and Fiedler's research in industrial, military, and other organizations suggest that these instruments may provide sensitive indicators of variation and change in the offender's perception of the many persons involved in correctional endeavors. They would also be useful for studies of correctional staff.

INMATE SOCIAL TYPE CLASSIFICATIONS

An appreciable literature has developed on so-called "inmate social types." These are presumed to be standard roles to which certain inmates become habituated in the course of their adjustment to the expectations of others in the prison community.

Sociologists studying prisons have differed in their criteria for identifying inmate social types. Clemmer reported three types: the "Elite," the "Middle-class," and the "Hoosier." These clearly were strata in a social-status hierarchy rather than distinct roles. Indeed, he notes some roles within certain strata, such as the "Politicians" in the Elite.[15] Schrag identified inmate-recognized behavior patterns by terms which he found inmates employed to label prisoners who epitomized these patterns. His four types were the "Right Guy," the "Politician," the "Outlaw," and the "Square John," plus a mixed residual category called "Dings."[16] Morris Caldwell distinguished inmate types in terms of their leisure-time pursuits in prison. He labeled the muscle-building enthusiasts "Spartans," the Bible devotees "Religionists," those making and peddling fermented beverages in prison "Moonshiners," and the hobbycraft devotees "Leather workers."[17] Sykes, like Schrag, was concerned with identifying the social types noted in the prisoners' own conversations. His "argot roles" represent distinctions along several independent dimensions of behavior, such as "wolves," "fags," and "punks" in homosexuality, or "ball-busters," "hipsters," "toughs," and "gorillas" on various aggression dimensions.[18]

Elsewhere I have argued that most of these distinctions of social type which develop in popular speech, both in prison and out, identify only extreme and atypical individuals. This is because few persons are as consistent in their behavior as is implied by the descriptions of social types. Several writers have observed that social science theory on complex human relationships often begins by being formulated in terms of pure or "ideal" types, and I have suggested that popular analyses also proceed in this fashion. Both lay persons of all levels of education and social scientists, in trying to generalize about human behavior, seek examples which dramatize their points. These illustrative cases reveal dimensions of behavior by illustrating the extremes; often the intermediate ranges would not be discernible without the perspective gained by noting extreme patterns. It is probable that most conformity of behavior to patterns which sociologists and psychologists think of as roles, or as personality traits, is distributed—like most psychological and physical abilities—in approximately a bell-shaped curve. However, the inconsistencies in human actions may frequently make these separate dimensions of behavior variation visible only by our focus on those humans with the most extreme and consistent behavior.[19] Indeed, the contribution of the case study approach to research is its illumination of im-

[15] Clemmer, *op. cit.,* pp. 298ff.

[16] Clarence Schrag, *Social Types in a Prison Community* (Master's thesis, University of Washington, 1944).

[17] Morris G. Caldwell, "Group Dynamics in the Prison Community," *J. Crim. Law, Criminology, and Police Science, 46* (Jan.–Feb. 1956), 648-57.

[18] Gresham M. Sykes, *The Society of Captives* (Princeton, Princeton University Press, 1958), chapter 5; Sykes, "Men, Merchants, and Toughs: A Study of Reactions to Imprisonment," *Social Problems, 4* (Oct. 1956), 130-38.

[19] Daniel Glaser and John R. Stratton, "Measuring Inmate Change in Prison," chapter 10 in Donald R. Cressey, *The Prison* (New York, Holt, Rinehart, and Winston, 1961).

portant behavioral phenomena by the portrayal of their most clear and dramatic occurrences.

Schrag has gone further than any current writer in laying the foundation for a theory of corrections closely integrated with established behavioral science theory.[20] One part of this theory relates his four major inmate social types with four more general patterns of conformity to conventional norms. These patterns are: the "asocial," represented by the "outlaw," the "pro-social," represented by the "square John," the "antisocial," represented by the "right guy," the "pseudo-social," represented by the "politician."

A capsule description of the inter-inmate and inmate-staff behavior identified with these four social types was provided in Schrag's master's thesis in 1944, from which the following is quoted:

The "outlaw," a daring, ruthless, egocentric individual . . . has few loyalty attachments, shows little regard for the common social pressures, and acts mostly in terms of what is momentarily advantageous. It is dangerous for the well-intentioned inmate to associate with him. The "right guy" is less aggressive, more willing to take his punishment, and intensely loyal toward his own group. He usually refuses to cooperate in any manner with the penal administrators. The "politician" has no strong sense of loyalty, but attempts to use his knowledge of inmate activities in bargaining for the good will of the administration, and sometimes encounters the violent opposition of the previously mentioned types. The situational offender whose loyalty is directed toward the administration is known as the "square John." He is not considered a "squealer" or "stool pigeon" even though he cooperates openly with the administration.[21]

One of Schrag's students, Peter Garabedian, developed a series of questions with which to classify prisoners into Schrag's four major inmate social types.[22] We intermingled his questions with those of our scales in our questionnaire in an effort to explore the distribution of these types under diverse conditions of imprisonment. These questions, for each of the types, are as follows:

Politician items:

You've got to have confidence in yourself if you're going to be successful.

There's a little larceny in everybody, if you're really honest about it.

Who you know is more important than what you know, and brains are more important than brawn.

[20] Clarence Schrag, "Some Foundations for a Theory of Correction," chapter 8 in Cressey, *op. cit.*
[21] Schrag, *Social Types in a Prison Community,* p. 44.
[22] Garabedian, *op. cit.*

Right-guy items:

  The biggest criminals are protected by society and rarely get to prison.

  Inmates can trust me to be honest and loyal in my dealings with them.

  Police, judges, prosecutors, and politicians are just as crooked as most of the people they send to prison.

Outlaw items:

  "Might is right" and "every man for himself" are the main rules for living, regardless of what people say.

  You have to take care of yourself because nobody else is going to take care of you.

  It makes me sore to have people tell me what to do.

Square John items:

  I generally feel guilty whenever I do wrong.

  The only criminals I really know are the ones here in the institution.

  Most people try to be law-abiding and true.

On each statement, inmates were asked to check "strongly agree," "agree," "disagree" or "strongly disagree." These answers were weighted by Garabedian 2, 1, —1, and —2. With three statements for each social type, every inmate completing all three questions for each type received a score for that type which could range from a low of —6 to a high of 6. We retained this scoring system.

Table E.9 summarizes the distribution of scores on the Garabedian measures of Schrag's Inmate Social Types, for our Prison Panel Supplement samples. There was notably little variation in the median and mean scores for the different stages of sentence, and among the thirteen institutions. On the whole, the reformatory inmates, especially near release, expressed the Outlaw perspective more markedly than did other prisoners, but this is not a dramatic or uniform contrast. The fact that most of the inmates did not score at the extremes of the score ranges for each social type suggests either that the questions are only very rough indicators of these social types (so there is a large error component in the responses), or that the four social types represent dimensions of attitude that are distributed in approximately bell-shaped curves, or both.

To explore these social types further we selected for special analysis the cases representing what might be called the more "pure" types. As a first step towards such a delineation, we separated out those cases with scores on one or more social types in that range which cut off the highest scoring 25 per cent of all cases. The highest scores cutting off 25 per cent, which sometimes also cut off appreciably more than 25 per cent, are indicated by the lines in Table E.9's section on "Response Distribution by Score Range." These score-cutting points proved to be the same for the Entrance, Middle,

TABLE E.9 Scores on Garabedian Scales for Schrag's Inmate Social Types
(Prison Panel Supplement samples)

	SOCIAL TYPES AND SAMPLE							
Aspect of score and sample	SQUARE JOHN		OUTLAW		RIGHT GUY		POLITICIAN	
	Entrance	Terminal	Entrance	Terminal	Entrance	Terminal	Entrance	Terminal
All institutions:								
Median	1.7	1.6	0.4	1.1	2.4	2.4	3.8	3.9
No. of cases scored	623	683	616	681	608	662	617	663
Response distribution by score range:								
5 or 6	8%	8%	6%	7%	16%	17%	28% a	27%
4	8%	7%	2%	4%	12% a	12%	20%	20%
3	14% a	14%	8%	8%	16%	13%	18%	17%
2	12%	12%	11% a	14%	14%	12%	19%	19%
Zero or 1	34%	32%	27%	28%	22%	23%	13%	14%
—1 or —2	19%	19%	35%	31%	17%	19%	3%	2%
—3 through —6	6%	8%	11%	7%	3%	3%	—	—
Average scores at separate institutions:								
Penitentiaries:								
Leavenworth Fed.	1.2	1.1	0	0.3	2.0	2.2	3.7	3.5
Terre Haute Fed.	1.7	1.3	—0.2	0.6	1.6	2.2	3.4	3.5
"Busy" State	1.4	1.9	0.4	—0.2	2.1	1.1	3.0	2.9
"Slow" State	0.2	1.0	0.4	0.9	2.4	2.2	2.6	3.1
"Full" State[b]	1.2	1.5	0	0.3	1.6	1.4	2.8	3.3
		1.0		0.1		1.2		3.1
Reformatories:								
Chillicothe Fed.	1.6	1.0	0.3	1.0	2.2	1.6	3.3	3.1
El Reno Fed.	1.2	2.1	0.5	1.1	1.8	1.9	3.2	3.4
"Slow" State	0.8	0.2	0.8	1.7	2.1	2.5	3.4	3.2
"Tight" State	0.4	0.6	0.8	0.4	2.5	1.8	3.3	2.5
Camps:								
Allenwood Fed.	—0.1	1.5	—1.3	—0.6	2.1	1.5	1.9	2.9
McNeil Island Fed.	1.8	1.7	0.5	—0.2	3.5	2.3	3.1	3.7
"Full" State	1.1	1.8	—0.1	—0.1	0.5	0.6	3.3	2.9
Seagoville Fed. Corr. Institution	1.6	1.7	0	—0.1	1.9	2.8	3.2	3.9

[a] All cases with scores above this line were dealt with separately for the "pure" type analysis.

[b] On the Terminal Sample, the first line refers to an honor camp population outside the wall and the second line to a unit inside the wall.

and Terminal samples. Combining all three of these samples, we found that 87 per cent of the cases, or seven-eighths, scored above the cutting point on one or more of the social types. Indeed, one per cent of the cases were in this high range on all four social types, 13 per cent were in this range on three types, 39 per cent were in this range on two types, and 34 per cent were in this range on only one type.

It may be of interest that Square John, which was the most frequent unmixed type, was clearly least frequent among cases fitting two or more types. On the other hand, the Right Guy was the most frequent among mixed types, and the least frequent of the unmixed types, in both respects closely followed by the Politician. As measured by Garabedian's questions, the Right Guy constitutes mainly an adaptation to the status of prisoner. Two of the statements are rationalizations which neutralize the status degradation that imprisonment involves; they employ the "technique of neutralization" that Sykes and Matza call "condemning the condemners."[23] The third Right Guy statement asserts loyalty to other inmates. Two of the Politician statements also serve primarily to neutralize the ego strains of imprisonment status by ascribing crime to everyone. The most consistently rejected statements were those of the Outlaw position, perhaps because they imply undependability in dealings with everyone, an orientation that is maladaptive to both prison and nonprison, as well as to criminal and noncriminal, social relationships.

For a further exploration of the social type distinctions we separated out for special analysis that 34 per cent of the sample which scored in the high range on only one social type. These men we called the "pure" social type cases.

Table E.10, on the attributes of those "pure" type cases, largely supports the description of the four major inmate social types which Schrag conveys. The "pure" Square John cases were older, of higher status background, more educated, more in communication with persons outside the prison, less in communication with inmates, more in communication with staff, and had less prior confinement than the inmates of any other "pure" types. On most items, the Outlaw cases differed more from the Square John cases than did cases in any other "pure" type; they were distinctly the youngest, least often married, least in communication with persons outside the prison, youngest at first arrest, least in communication with staff, but most in communication with inmates of any of the "pure" social type cases. This confirms Schrag's portrayal of these "asocial" individuals as the product of early conflict with the family and with other authority figures, but his portrayal seems somewhat contradicted by the Outlaws' more frequent claim of extensive friendship and socialization with other inmates. It is possible that this claim would not be validated if we had actual behavior observation records or if we had the reports of other inmates regarding their interaction with the inmates whom we classify as Outlaws.

As Schrag's formulations predict, the Politicians combined many attributes of the Square Johns and the Right Guys. The Politicians are more schooled than the Right Guys, almost as much in communication with persons outside the prison as are the Square Johns, and intermediate be-

[23] Gresham M. Sykes and David Matza, "Techniques of Neutralization: A Theory of Delinquency," *Am. Sociological Rev.*, 22, no. 6 (Dec. 1957), 664-70.

TABLE E.10   Attributes of the "Pure" Social Type Cases
(Prison Panel Supplement samples, all institutions except Ashland)

Attribute	Square John	Outlaw	Right Guy	Politician
Number of cases	304	178	112	145
Median age	31	24	30	28
Median socioeconomic status of father, on 10-point scale[a]	2.8	2.1	1.9	1.7
Median years of schooling completed	10.7	9.6	9.6	10.4
Per cent married	37%	25%	39%	37%
Median letters received in past week	2.2	1.8	1.8	1.9
Median letters written in past week	2.4	1.8	2.0	2.1
Per cent receiving one or more visits in past three months	47%	33%	37%	46%
Average months confined on present sentence	20.5	20.5	21.1	17.5
Average months further confinement expected on present sentence	14.7	16.2	15.9	15.6
Median age at first arrest	20.1	16.0	17.6	17.6
Median no. of prior correctional institution commitments (Jail, training school, prison, etc.)	1.4	2.0	1.6	2.0
Median total years confinement in correctional institutions, including present commitment	2.3	3.7	3.5	3.6
Offense for which confined:[b]				
Auto theft	17%	27%	24%	27%
Narcotics	4%	8%	9%	8%
Forgery	14%	4%	18%	4%
Robbery	14%	17%	8%	17%
Burglary	11%	15%	16%	15%
Larceny (non-auto)	12%	10%	4%	10%
Other	28%	18%	20%	18%
Number of "strong" friendships with other inmates since at institution:				
None	42%	29%	39%	34%
One or two	35%	32%	33%	37%
A few (three to five)	13%	18%	18%	21%
Many (more than five)	11%	21%	9%	8%
Most common socialization with other inmates:				
Ungrouped	59%	46%	57%	59%
Grouped	41%	54%	42%	40%
Talk with employees:				
Low	58%	82%	82%	72%
High	41%	18%	18%	28%
Contact with custody staff:				
Less than average inmate	71%	88%	87%	78%
More than average inmate	29%	12%	13%	22%
Contact with treatment staff:				
Less than average inmate	76%	90%	87%	81%
More than average inmate	24%	10%	13%	19%

[a] Inmates were asked "What kind of work does your father do? If he has died or retired, what kind of work did he do? If you were raised by someone other than your father, what did he or she do for a living?" The occupations were then rated numerically by us, using the first digit of the Socioeconomic Index in Table B-1, Appendix B, of Albert J. Reiss, Jr., *Occupations and Social Status* (Glencoe, Free Press, 1961).

[b] All percentages and medians in this table were based only on the questionnaires which provided information on the attribute. The number of cases blank generally ranged from zero to three per cent of the bases, but on offense it was 7 per cent for the Square Johns, 10 per cent for the Right Guys, and 11 per cent for the Outlaws and Politicians.

tween Right Guys and Square Johns in communication with staff. On the
other hand, one might infer that the Politicians and Right Guys share a "do
your own time" norm, for they are similar in frequent denial of friendship
with other inmates.

Table E.11 indicates how the "pure" inmate social type cases differed in
their response to our attitude scale questions. As expected, the Square
Johns were distinctly lower than the other types in their Criminality and

TABLE E.11   Attitude Scale Responses of the "Pure" Social Type Cases
(Prison Panel Supplement samples, all institutions except Ashland)

Attitude scale	Scale score	Square John	Outlaw	Right Guy	Politician
Inmate loyalty	High	32.0	59.0	48.6	49.0
	Medium	22.6	9.8	21.0	15.4
	Low	45.5	31.2	30.5	35.7
Criminality	High	4.7	41.5	28.3	20.1
	Medium	10.1	16.4	18.9	20.1
	Low	85.2	42.1	52.8	59.7
Criminal identification	High	24.1	47.4	26.7	24.6
	Low	75.9	52.6	73.3	75.4

Inmate Loyalty responses, but they were surprisingly close to the Right
Guys and Politicians on the Criminal Identification scale. On all three scales,
the Outlaws had a larger proportion scoring high than did any of the other
social types, but there were also many low-scoring Outlaws on each attitude
scale. The Outlaws tended to give extreme responses; they were lowest in
middle range respondents on the Criminality and Inmate Loyalty scales.
The Right Guys and Politicians had similar response distributions on all
the scales, although the Right Guys were somewhat higher on Criminality
than the Politicians.

On the whole, the data in Tables E.10 and E.11 support Schrag's claims
regarding the combinations of attributes which tend to be found together in
the four inmate social types. The overall distribution of social type scores,
and the frequency with which inmates scored in the upper range on several
types rather than just one, suggest that these types describe dimensions of
behavior not completely independent, on which all inmates are distributed
in an approximately bell-shaped curve. However, considerable high scoring
on several types also might result from a response set, that is, a tendency
to agree with all items. Indeed, it may be surprising that so few persons
were high on all four types. The possible effect of response set could be
eliminated by an equal number of agree and disagree questions. The three

questions provided by Garabedian for the identification of each of these types measure only crudely and partially the attributes which Schrag ascribes to each type. More research seems desirable, both to develop instruments which identify the social type traits more precisely, and to investigate the distribution and correlates of these traits more thoroughly.

Reports of or on the University of Illinois–Ford Foundation Research in the Federal Correctional System

PUBLICATIONS ISSUED BY AGENCIES OTHER THAN THE PROJECT OFFICE

John P. Conrad, "Do You Agree With This Researcher?", California Department of Corrections *Correctional Review, 16,* no. 6, April-May 1962, pp. 15-17.

Bruce K. Eckland, "Overdue Parolees in a Federal Reformatory," U. S. Bureau of Prisons *Progress Report,* January-March 1960, pp. 5-14.

Daniel Glaser, "A Review of Current Research in Correctional Treatment" and "The Ford Foundation Research Project," in U. S. Bureau of Prisons, *Conference of Wardens, University of Notre Dame, 1958,* pp. 3-13.

————, "Needed Research in Crime Prevention," *Alabama Correctional Journal, 6,* no. 1, April 1959, pp. 77-84.

————, "University of Illinois Research in the Federal Correctional System," California Department of Corrections *Research Newsletter,* July 1959.

————, "Research in Probation and Parole," in *Proceedings, American Correctional Association, 1959,* pp. 231-243. (Reprinted in part in California Department of Corrections *Research Newsletter,* March 1960.)

————, "New Commerce Between Academicians and Correctional Administrators," *Prison Journal, 40,* no. 2, Autumn 1960, pp. 52-62.

————, "Research on Economic Assistance for Released Prisoners," in *Proceedings, American Correctional Association, 1960,* pp. 363-380.

————, "Parole Follow-Up Studies in the Federal Correctional System," in N. Y. School of Social Work, *Research and Potential Application of Research in Probation, Parole and Delinquency Prediction.* 1961.

————, "Scientific Evidence on the Prison Potential," in *Proceedings, American Correctional Association, 1961,* pp. 134-149.

————, "Prediction Tables as Accounting Devices for Judges and Parole Boards," *Crime and Delinquency, 8,* no. 3, July 1962, pp. 239-258.

————, "Research Findings on Problems of the Released Offender," U. S. Bureau of Prisons, *Conference of Wardens, University of Colorado, 1962.*

————, "Parole Prediction Tables Applied to Jefferson State Reformatory Cases," *National Parole Institutes,* Institute I Participant's Binder, February 1963.

————, "Some New Views on Prisoners," *Menard Time,* 1963.

Daniel Glaser and Kent Rice, "Crime, Age and Employment," *American Sociological Review, 24,* no. 5, October 1959, pp. 679-686. (Reprinted as No. 95 in *Bobbs-Merrill Reprint Series in the Social Sciences;* reprinted as chapter 22 in M. E. Wolfgang, L. Savitz, and N. Johnston, *The Sociology of Crime and Delinquency.* New York: Wiley, 1962.)

Daniel Glaser and John R. Stratton, "Measuring Inmate Change in Prison," chapter 10 in Donald R. Cressey, ed., *The Prison.* New York: Holt, Rinehart and Winston, 1961.

Daniel Glaser, Eugene S. Zemans, and Charles W. Dean, *Money Against Crime: A Survey of Economic Assistance to Released Prisoners.* Chicago: The John Howard Association, 1961.

"University of Illinois Research in Federal Probation Offices," *Federal Probation, 23,* no. 4, December 1959, pp. 53-54.

Albert Wagner, "Findings in Recent Study of Five Federal Institutions," *Bordentown Counselor, 9,* no. 1, January 1962, pp. 1-6.

Albert Wahl and Daniel Glaser, "Pilot Time Study of the Probation Officer's Job," *Federal Probation, 27,* no. 3, September 1963, pp. 20-24.

REPORTS ISSUED ONLY BY THE PROJECT OFFICE

Quarterly Activity Reports, 1958; Bimonthly Reports, 1959-60; Periodic Reports, 1961-63.

University of Illinois Research Project in Federal Correctional Agencies. (Speech at Ohio Valley Sociological Society Meeting, 1959)

Federal Parole and Mandatory Release Violators, A Preliminary Analysis. February 1960.

Factors in Prognosis of Post-Release Adjustment of Federal Penitentiary Inmates. April 1960.

Types of Research on the Probation and Parole Officer's Job and Their Possible Application to the Federal Probation Service. February 1961.

Measuring Inmate Experience in Prison: The Prison Panel Study. April 1961.

Prognosis of Post-Release Behavior With Federal Youth Correction Act Offenders. May 1961.

Some Appendices to Measuring Inmate Experience in Prison. November 1961.

Five Practical Research Suggestions for Correctional Administrators. (Speech at National Institute on Crime and Delinquency, Seattle, 1962)

UNIVERSITY OF ILLINOIS, DEPARTMENT OF SOCIOLOGY, GRADUATE THESES COMPLETED ON PROJECT OPERATIONS

Charles W. Dean, "Some Factors in Federal Penitentiary Parole Violation," M.A., 1961.

Bruce K. Eckland, "An Analysis of Federal Parole Functions, With Special Reference to Federal Youth Parole Violation," M.A., 1960.

Richard John, "Prediction Improvement Using the Split-Sample Technique and Criterion-Scaled Independent Variables," M.A., 1963.

Dale F. Lytton, "Family Relations and the Post-Release Behavior of Federal Prisoners," M.A., 1961.

George A. Pownall, "The Role of the Parole Supervision Officer," Ph.D., 1963.

John R. Stratton, "The Measurement of Inmate Change During Imprisonment," Ph.D., 1963.

David A. Ward, "Prison Rule Enforcement and Changing Organizational Goals," Ph.D., 1960.

SOME OTHER PUBLICATIONS AFFECTING OR REFLECTING PROJECT OPERATIONS

Daniel Glaser, "Released Offender Statistics: A Proposal for a National Program," *American Journal of Correction,* March-April 1957, pp. 15-17, 25.

———, "Criminal Career Statistics," *Proceedings, American Correctional Association, 1957,* pp. 103-106.

———, "Differential Association Theory and Criminological Prediction," *Social Problems, 8,* no. 1, Summer 1960, pp. 6-14.

———, "Criminology," *Encyclopaedia Britannica,* 1962.

———, "The Differential Association Theory of Crime," in Arnold Rose, ed., *Human Behavior and Social Processes.* Boston: Houghton-Mifflin, 1962.

———, "Social Disorganization and Delinquent Subcultures," Chapter for Herbert C. Quay, *Research and Theory in Juvenile Delinquency.* New York: Van Nostrand (1964 publication expected).

Index

VERMONT   COLLEGE
MONTPELIER, VT.

N

r